A HISTORY OF MODERN ISRAEL

Second Edition

Colin Shindler's remarkable history begins in 1948, as waves of immigrants arrived in Israel from war-torn Europe to establish new cities, new institutions and a new culture founded on the Hebrew language. Optimistic beginnings were soon replaced with the sobering reality of wars with Arab neighbours, internal ideological differences and an ongoing confrontation with the Palestinians. The author paints a broad canvas that affords unusual insights into Israel's multicultural society, forged from more than 100 different Jewish communities and united by a common history. In this updated edition, Shindler covers the significant developments of the last decade, including the rise of the Israeli far Right, Hamas's takeover and the political rivalry between Gaza and the West Bank, Israel's uneasy dealings with the new administration in the United States, political Islam, the expansion of the Jewish settlements on the West Bank and the potential impact of the Arab Spring on the region as a whole. This sympathetic yet candid portrayal asks how a nation that emerged out of the ashes of the Holocaust and was the admiration of the world is now perceived by many Western governments in a less than benevolent light.

COLIN SHINDLER is Emeritus Professor and Pears Senior Research Fellow at the School of Oriental and African Studies, University of London. He is also founding chairman of the European Association of Israel Studies.

In Memory of

Rachel Shindler (1905–96)
and
Goldie Pollock (1919–2003)

A HISTORY OF
MODERN ISRAEL

Second Edition

COLIN SHINDLER

School of Oriental and African Studies, University of London

CAMBRIDGE UNIVERSITY PRESS

Cambridge, New York, Melbourne, Madrid, Cape Town,
Singapore, São Paulo, Delhi, Mexico City

Cambridge University Press
32 Avenue of the Americas, New York, NY 10013-2473, USA

www.cambridge.org
Information on this title: www.cambridge.org/9781107671775

First edition published 2008
Second edition published 2013

A catalog record for this publication is available from the British Library.

Library of Congress Cataloging in Publication data

Shindler, Colin, 1946–
A history of modern Israel / Colin Shindler. – 2nd ed.
p. cm.
Includes bibliographical references and index.
ISBN 978-1-107-02862-3 (hardback) – ISBN 978-1-107-67177-5 (pbk.)
1. Israel – History.   I. Title.
DS126.5.S45194   2012
956.9405–dc23   2012021356

ISBN 978-1-107-02862-3 Hardback
ISBN 978-1-107-67177-5 Paperback

Contents

Contents

Illustrations

Maps

Acknowledgements

To write a history of Israel always poses the question of what to leave in and what to leave out. Telescoping momentous events is never straightforward, but I hope that by following a pathway based on the ideologies of the main actors in this drama, I have given a shape to this history.

Several libraries and archives assisted me in my deliberations. In particular, I should like to thank the staff of the Jabotinsky archives, the Beit Berl archives of the Labour movement, the Yad Tabenkin archives, the Central Zionist archives, the American Jewish Joint Distribution Committee archives (Jerusalem) and the Israeli State archives – all in Israel. In addition, the British Library and the British Newspaper Library in London and the Jewish Division of the New York Public Library were enormously helpful. I must also say a 'thank you' to Peter 'Shmuel' Salinger, the Hebraica librarian at SOAS, University of London, for his guidance and friendship over many years.

My friends Anthony Julius and Shalom Lappin read the draft manuscript and I am grateful to them for their comments and feedback. Reuven Koffler of the Central Zionist archives helped me to locate some different and unusual early photographs which illustrate this work. I am particularly grateful to Matanya Fishaimer for his assistance in deciphering some of the Hebrew documents. Dror Etkes of Setdement Watch explained the rationale for the growth of Jewish settlements on the West Bank. During my visits to Israel, Hillel and Pinchas Davis and Uriel Fishaimer also provided some considered observations.

I must thank Marigold Acland of Cambridge University Press for asking me to write this book in the first place and for her support throughout. In addition, Helen Waterhouse, Sarah Parker and Elizabeth Davey skilfully guided the project through all the stages. Both Marigold and her colleagues have been totally professional and a pleasure to work with.

My family bore the brunt of my anxiety and determination to meet the deadline so that the first edition of the book could appear in 2008, the

60th anniversary of the establishment of the state of Israel. It seems that I lived in my office for most of 2006. My wife, Jean, put up with my hermit-like existence and her perceptive nature gave me the time and space to complete this endeavour. Without her support and advice, this book, like all my other works, would not have been possible.

As in my previous books, I have used a normal transliteration system with notable exceptions where familiarity has superseded convention. Any errors of fact or interpretation are mine alone.

Glossaries

Achdut Ha'avodah	socialist Zionist party, founded in 1919, by Ben-Gurion and Tabenkin
Agudat Yisrael	ultra-orthodox party, founded in 1912 to oppose the Zionist movement
Alignment	established by Labour and Mapam in 1969
Balad	Israeli Arab nationalist party, advocating Israel as a state for all its citizens, founded by Azmi Bishara in 1995
Betar	nationalist Zionist youth group, founded by Jabotinsky in Riga in 1923
Biluim	the settlers of the first Zionist immigration to Palestine in 1882
Brit Shalom	early peace group in the 1920s
Degel Ha'Torah	established by Eliezer Schach through the split in Agudat Yisrael in 1988
Democratic Movement for Change	established in 1977 as a centre party by Yigal Yadin
Free Centre	established in 1967 through a split in Herut
Gahal	established through an alignment between Herut and the Liberals in 1965

Gahelet	religious youth group which propounded redemptionist Zionism
General Zionists	promoted the views of small businessmen and private enterprise, established 1929
Hadash	Jewish-Arab party, emerging from the pro-Moscow wing of the Israeli Communist party
Haganah	the defence arm of the Yishuv and forerunner of the Israel Defence Forces (IDF)
Hapoel Hamizrachi	labour wing of religious Zionism and builder of religious kibbutzim, established 1922
Hapoel Hatzair	non-Marxist, Tolstoyan pioneering party, established in 1906
Hashomer Hatzair	dovish pioneering Marxist Zionist group, established in 1913
Herut	the Irgun as a political movement, established by Begin in 1948
Histadrut	General Federation of Workers in the Land of Israel, established in 1920
Irgun Zvai Leumi	nationalist military group, led by Begin from 1943
Kach	far Right party led by Meir Kahane, banned from participating in elections in 1986
Kadima	centre-Right party established by Ariel Sharon in 2005 in a split from Likud
Labour	established in 1968 from Mapai, Achdut Ha'avodah and Rafi
Left Poale Zion	pro-Communist party, merged with Achdut Ha'avodah in 1946

Lehi	Fighters for the Freedom of Israel, established by Avraham Stern in 1940
Liberals	formerly the General Zionists, established in 1961
Likud	the main right-wing Israeli party, established by Sharon and Begin in 1973
Maki	Euro-Communist split from the main Communist party (CP) in 1965, led by Moshe Sneh
Mapai	leading labour Zionist party, 1930–1968, during the state-building years
Mapam	Marxist Zionist party, founded in 1948, second-largest party in first Knesset
Matzpen	anti-Zionist split from the Israeli Communist party, close to European New Left
Maximalists	radical right wing of the Revisionist party in the 1930s
Meretz	Left Zionist party established in 1992 by Ratz, Mapam and Shinui
Mizrachi	first religious Zionist party, established in 1902 to oppose secularized education
Moked	established in 1973 through the merger of Maki and the Blue–Red movement
Moledet	transfer party of the far Right, established by Rechavam Ze'evi in 1988
National Religious party	founded in 1956, the main party of religious Zionism
National Union	far Right party, based on a coalition of four parties, established in 1999
Palmach	elite fighting force, allied to Achdut Ha'avodah, led by Yigal Allon in the 1940s

Poalei Agudat Yisrael	pioneering ultra-orthodox party, established 1922
Poale Zion	early socialist Zionist party in Palestine, founded by Jewish workers in 1906
Progressives	founded in 1948 by German immigrants and liberal General Zionists
Ra'am	Israeli Arab party, established in 1996 by the Arab Democratic party and the southern wing of the Islamic Movement in Israel
Rafi	established in 1965 after split from Mapai, led by Ben-Gurion, Dayan and Peres
Rakach	pro-Soviet wing of the CP, after the split in 1965
Ratz	civil rights and peace party, led by Shulamit Aloni in the 1980s
Redemptionist Zionists	religious Zionist settlers, who followed Zvi Yehuda Kook
Revisionist party	founded by Jabotinsky in 1925 to return to Herzlian Zionism
Shas	Sephardi ultra-orthodox party established by Ovadia Yosef in 1984
Sheli	dovish party, established in 1977 from Moked
Siach	Israeli New Left, established after the 1967 war
State List	Rafi faction that did not join the Labour party in 1968, led by Ben-Gurion
Ta'al	Israeli Arab party, founded by Ahmad Tibi in the 1990s
Tami	Sephardi breakaway from the National Religious party (NRP), established in 1981

Techiyah	far Right party, established in 1979 in opposition to the Camp David agreement
Tsomet	far Right party with Labour roots, established in 1983 through a split in Techiyah
United Torah Judaism	main ultra-orthodox party, established in 1992
Yisrael B'Aliyah	Russian party, founded in 1996
Yisrael Beitanu	far Right and Russian party, founded in 1999

GENERAL GLOSSARY

aliyah	Jewish immigration to Israel from the Diaspora
Aliyah Bet	illegal immigration to Palestine (1934–1948) during the British Mandate
Al-Aqsa Martyrs' Brigade	military group often associated with Fatah
Ashkenazim	Jews generally originating from Eastern Europe
Balfour Declaration	British declaration promising a Jewish national home in Palestine
Bar Kochba rebellion	uprising in Judea against Roman rule, 132–135
Canaanism	supporting the idea of an evolving Hebrew nation rather than a Jewish one
Davar	the Histadrut's Hebrew daily newspaper
Fatah	leading Palestinian Arab nationalist organization, founded by Arafat
Fedayeen	Palestinian Arab fighters during the 1950s
Fellahin	Palestinian Arab peasants and farmers
Green Line	1949 armistice boundary between Israel and the West Bank

Gush Etzion	Jewish settlement bloc in the pre-state era, now in the West Bank
Halakhah	Jewish religious law
Hamas	leading Palestinian Islamist organization founded in 1988
Haskalah	Jewish Enlightenment
Havlagah	military self-restraint in responding to Arab attacks
Islamic Jihad	Palestinian Islamist organization, originally influenced by the Iranian Revolution
kibbutz galuyot	ingathering of the exiles
Maronites	Lebanese Christians who practice the Eastern Catholic rites
Muslim Brotherhood	leading Sunni Islamist organization founded by Hassan al-Banna
nigun	humming tune associated with the chassidim
Phalangists	members of the Lebanese nationalist party, the Phalange
Popular Resistance Committees	Radical Palestinian Islamist military grouping
Al-Qassam Brigades	Hamas's military wing
Al-Quds Brigades	Islamic Jihad's armed wing
Salafists	followers of a more literal interpretation of Islam, often associated with jihadism
Sephardim	Jews generally originating from Spain and north Africa
Shechinah	the Divine Presence
Shoah	the Nazi Holocaust, 1939–1945
Shulchan Aruch	the code of Jewish law by Joseph Caro
Talmud	a compendium of rabbinical and scholarly opinions and teachings
Tephilin	phylacteries
Wissenschaft des Judentums	the Science of Judaism
Yeshiva	men's religious seminary

NAME GLOSSARY

Mahmoud Abbas (1936–)	known as Abu Mazen, President of the Palestinian National Authority 2005–
Haidar Abd al-Shafi (1919–2007)	non-aligned Palestinian politician
Abba Achimeir (1898–1962)	intellectual mentor of the Zionist Maximalists
Jamal al-din al-Afghani (1838–1897)	intellectual mentor of nationalist pan-Islamism
Mahmoud Ahmadinejad (1956–)	President of Iran 2005–
Musa al-Alami (1897–1984)	Palestinian activist during the Mandate period
Yigal Allon (1918–1980)	founder and commander of the Palmach, Foreign Minister 1974–1977
Shulamit Aloni (1928–)	leader of Meretz and the peace camp, Minister of Education 1992–1993
Natan Alterman (1910–1970)	Hebrew poet and translator
Yehuda Amichai (1924–2000)	Hebrew poet
Yasser Arafat (1929–2004)	PLO chairman, President, Palestinian National Authority
Moshe Arens (1925–)	Likud leader, Foreign Minister, Defence Minister
Chaim Arlosoroff (1899–1933)	Hapoel Hatzair activist, Mapai leader
Hanan Ashrawi (1946–)	Palestinian political activist

Bashar al-Assad (1965–) President of Syria 2000–

Hafez al-Assad (1930–2000) President of Syria 1971–2000

Meir Bar-Ilan (1880–1949) leader of Mizrachi and the national religious camp

Menachem Begin (1913–1992) Prime Minister of Israel 1977–1983

Yossi Beilin (1948–) architect of the Oslo Accords 1993; leader of the Meretz party

David Ben-Gurion (1886–1973) founding father of Israel; first Prime Minister 1949

Yitzhak Ben-Zvi (1884–1963) Israel's second President

Chaim Nachman Bialik (1873–1934) Hebrew national poet
Nathan Birnbaum (1864–1937) originator of the term 'Zionism'

Dov Ber Borochov (1881–1917) founder and theorist of Marxism–Zionism

Yosef Chaim Brenner (1881–1921) Hebrew writer and novelist

Martin Buber (1878–1965) Jewish philosopher and founder of Brit Shalom

Yosef Burg (1909–1999) leader of the National Religious party; Minister 1951–1986

Moshe Carmel (1911–2003) commander of the northern front 1948, operation Hiram

Richard Crossman (1907–1974) British Minister 1964–1970; editor, *New Statesman*

Moshe Dayan (1915–1981) IDF Chief of Staff 1955–1958, follower of Ben-Gurion

Abba Eban (1915–2002)	liberal politician, Foreign Minister 1966–1974
Raful Eitan (1929–2004)	IDF Chief of Staff 1978–1983, founder of Tsomet party
Liova Eliav (1921–2010)	peace activist and Secretary-General of the Labour party under Golda Meir
Racep Tayyip Erdogan (1954–)	Prime Minister of Turkey 2003–
Levi Eshkol (1895–1969)	Prime Minister of Israel 1963–1969
Israel Galili (1911–1986)	Achdut Ha'avodah leader, head of Haganah 1946–1948
John Glubb (1897–1986)	British commander of Transjordan's Arab Legion 1939–1956
Nachum Goldmann (1895–1982)	Zionist diplomat, founder of the World Jewish Congress
A. D. Gordon (1856–1922)	Zionist pioneer, Tolstoyan mentor of Labour Zionism
Yehudah Leib Gordon (1831–1892)	Hebrew poet and writer
Shlomo Goren (1917–1994)	leader of religious Zionism, Israeli Chief Rabbi 1973–1983
Uri Zvi Greenberg (1894–1981)	Zionist Maximalist, Hebrew poet
Ahad Ha'am (1856–1927)	Zionist intellectual and writer
George Habash (1926–2008)	radical Palestinian activist, founder of the PFLP
Ismail Haniyeh (1963–)	Prime Minister of Gaza 2006–

Naif Hawatmeh (1935–)   radical Palestinian
                                    activist, founder of the
                                    DFLP

Theodor Herzl (1860–1904)   father of the modern
                                    Zionist movement

Chaim Herzog (1918–1997)   President of Israel
                                    1983–1993

Moses Hess (1812–1875)   socialist theoretician,
                                    early progenitor of
                                    Socialism Zionism

Faisal Husseini (1940–2001)   Palestinian politician,
                                    Fatah representative in
                                    East Jerusalem

Abu Iyad (1933–1991)   Palestinian leader,
                                    founder of Fatah

Vladimir Jabotinsky (1880–1940)   Liberal nationalist,
                                    Revisionist Zionist,
                                    head of Betar

Abu Jihad (1935–1988)   Palestinian leader,
                                    founder of Fatah

Zvi Hirsch Kalischer (1795–1874)   early progenitor of
                                    religious Zionism

Chaim Kalvarisky (1868–1947)   early peace campaigner
Shimon Bar Kokhba (?–135)   leader of the Jewish
                                    revolt against the
                                    Romans 132–135

Teddy Kollek (1911–2007)   Mayor of Jerusalem
                                    1965–1993

Avraham Yitzhak Kook (1864–1935)   first Ashkenazi Chief
                                    Rabbi of Palestine

Zvi Yehuda Kook (1891–1982)   spiritual leader of
                                    Gush Emunim

Yitzhak Lamdan (1899–1954)   Hebrew poet and
                                    editor

Ferdinand Lassalle (1825–1864)   founding father of
                                    German socialism

Yitzhak Meir Levin (1894–1971)   leader of Agudat
                                    Yisrael

David Levy (1937–)   Israeli politician and
                                    Sephardi leader

Moses Leib Lilienblum (1843–1910) — Hebrew writer, Zionist publicist and literary critic

Karl Lueger (1844–1910) — Viennese politician, leader of the Christian Social party

Judah Magnes (1877–1948) — founder and President of the Hebrew University, Jerusalem

Abraham Mapu (1808–1867) — early Hebrew writer

Golda Meir (1898–1978) — Prime Minister of Israel 1969–1974

Khalid Meshal (1956–) — Hamas leader and chairman of its political bureau

Leo Motzkin (1867–1933) — Zionist leader, colleague of Herzl and Weizmann

Imad Mughniyeh (1962–2008) — Hezbollah leader

Abbas Mussawi (1952–1992) — Secretary-General of Hezbollah 1991–1992

Benjamin Netanyahu (1949–) — Prime Minister of Israel 1996–1999, 2009–

Max Nordau (1849–1923) — founder, modern Zionist movement, writer and philosopher

Shimon Peres (1923–) — Nobel Prize winner and President of Israel since 2007

Leon Pinsker (1821–1891) — Zionist leader, writer and publicist

Yitzhak Rabin (1922–1995) — Prime Minister of Israel 1974–1977, 1992–1995

Solomon Rapoport (1790–1867) — Haskalah scholar, rabbi and writer

Walter Rathenau (1867–1922) — German Foreign Minister, industrialist and writer

Yonatan Ratosh (1908–1981)	Hebrew writer and thinker, founder, Canaanite movement
David Raziel (1910–1941)	leader of the Irgun
Yitzhak Reines (1839–1915)	founder of the religious Zionist movement, first leader of Mizrachi
Mohammad Rashid Rida (1865–1935)	progenitor of nationalist pan-Islamism
Edmond de Rothschild (1845–1934)	supporter of early Jewish settlements
Arthur Ruppin (1876–1943)	facilitator in acquiring land for Jewish settlement
Yitzhak Sadeh (1890–1952)	founder and first commander of the Palmach
Herbert Samuel (1870–1963)	first British High Commissioner of Palestine
Pinchas Sapir (1907–1975)	Labour politician and Israeli Minister of Finance
Yossi Sarid (1940–)	former leader of Meretz and leading peace campaigner
Eliezer Menachem Schach (1898?–2001)	Talmudic scholar and founder of Degel Ha'Torah
Menachem Mendel Schneersohn (1902–1994)	leader of the Lubavitcher chassidim
Mendele Mocher Sefarim (1835–1917)	Hebrew and Yiddish writer
Chaim Moshe Shapira (1902–1970)	Israeli politician and National Religious party (NRP) leader

Moshe Sharett (1894–1965)	Mapai politician, Prime Minister and Foreign Minister
Ariel Sharon (1925–)	Prime Minister of Israel 2001–2006
Menachem Sheinkin (1871–1924)	early Zionist leader
Avraham Shlonsky (1900–1973)	Hebrew poet, writer and translator
Peretz Smolenskin (1842–1885)	Haskalah publicist, advocate of cultural nationalism
Moshe Sneh (1909–1972)	Zionist activist and Israeli left-wing politician
Hatam Sofer (Moses Schreiber) (1762–1839)	leader of ultra-orthodoxy and scholar
Baruch Spinoza (1632–1677)	Dutch philosopher, rationalist and exponent of Biblical criticism
Avraham Stern (1907–1942)	poet, far Right ideologue and founder of Lehi
Nachman Syrkin (1868–1924)	early leader of Socialism Zionism and ideologue
Yitzhak Tabenkin (1887–1971)	founder, Labour Zionist and kibbutz movements
Saul Tchernikovsky (1875–1943)	Hebrew poet
Yosef Trumpeldor (1880–1920)	Zionist activist and founder of the Zion Mule Corps
Menachem Ussishkin (1863–1941)	Zionist activist and head of the Jewish National Fund
Zerach Warhaftig (1906–2002)	NRP leader and Israeli politician

Chaim Weizmann (1874–1952)	founding father and first President of Israel 1949–1952
Ezer Weizmann (1924–2005)	Israeli politician and President 1993–2000
Meir Ya'ari (1897–1987)	Marxist Zionist and Mapam leader
Yigal Yadin (1917–1984)	archaeologist, IDF Chief of Staff and Israeli politician
Ovadia Yosef (1920–)	Talmudic scholar and founder of Shas
Mahmoud Zahar (1945–)	Hamas founder and Foreign Minister in Gaza 2006–2007
Shneur Zalman of Lyady (1745–1813)	founder of the Lubavicher chassidim
Rechavam Ze'evi (1926–2001)	far Right politician and founder of Moledet

PRIME MINISTERS OF ISRAEL

David Ben-Gurion	1948–1953
Moshe Sharett	1953–1955
David Ben-Gurion	1955–1963
Levi Eshkol	1963–1969
Golda Meir	1969–1974
Yitzhak Rabin	1974–1977
Shimon Peres	1977
Menachem Begin	1977–1983
Yitzhak Shamir	1983–1984
Shimon Peres	1984–1986
Yitzhak Shamir	1986–1992
Yitzhak Rabin	1992–1995
Shimon Peres	1995–1996
Benjamin Netanyahu	1996–1999
Ehud Barak	1999–2001
Ariel Sharon	2001–2006
Ehud Olmert	2006–2009
Benjamin Netanyahu	2009–

Chronology

66–70	First Jewish war against the Romans
70	Fall of Jerusalem and destruction of the Temple
638	Arab conquest of Jerusalem
1099	Crusader massacre of the Jews of Jerusalem
1492	Expulsion of the Jews from Spain
1791	The Pale of Settlement established by Catherine the Great
1799	Napoleon invades Palestine from Egypt
1860	Theodor Herzl is born in Budapest
1862	*Rome and Jerusalem* by Moses Hess is published
1881	Pogroms in Russia following the assassination of the Tsar
1882	*Autoemancipation* by Leon Pinsker is published
1882	The emigration of the 'Biluim' from Russia to Palestine
1896	*The Jewish State* by Theodor Herzl is published
1897	First Zionist Congress takes place in Basel
1906	Ben-Gurion and Ben-Zvi establish Poale Zion in Palestine
1909	The first collective settlement established in Palestine
1917	The Balfour Declaration promises a national home for the Jews in Palestine
1919	The establishment of the Socialist Zionist party, Achdut Ha'avodah
1920	The Histadrut, the General Federation of Labour in Israel, is founded
1921	Transjordan, the eastern part of Mandatory Palestine, promised to Abdullah
1925	Jabotinsky establishes the Union of Revisionist Zionists
1929	The massacres of Jews in Hebron and Safed
1930	Mapai, the Labour Zionist party, formed
1936	The Arab Revolt breaks out in Palestine
1937	The Peel Commission visits Palestine

2002	Saudi peace initiative in Beirut
2002	Bush's Rose Garden speech
2003	The Quartet publicizes the Road Map
2003	Sharon advocates disengagement from part of the territories
2004	President Bush's letter recognizes Israel's right to annex some settlements
2004	Yasser Arafat, besieged and unrecognized by Israel and the United States, dies
2005	Abu Mazen elected President of the Palestinian Authority
2005	The Gaza settlements evacuated without violence
2005	Likud and Labour split and realign to form the Kadima party under Sharon
2006	Hamas defeats Fatah in elections for the Legislative Council
2006	Ehud Olmert, head of Kadima after Sharon's stroke, wins the election
2006	Hezbollah fights Israel in Lebanon in a thirty-four-day war
2007	Dan Halutz resigns as Chief of Staff and is succeeded by Gabi Ashkenazi
2007	Iron Dome anti-missile system given the go-ahead
2007	Conflict between Hamas and Fatah ends in the takeover of Gaza by Hamas
2008	Winograd report into the second Lebanon war released
2008	Imad Mughniyeh, veteran Hezbollah leader, killed by Damascus car bomb
2009	Israel initiates Operation Cast Lead against Gaza
2009	Benjamin Netanyahu becomes Prime Minister for the second time
2009	The Goldstone Report on Operation Cast Lead issued by the UN
2010	Stuxnet computer virus attacks centrifuges in an Iranian nuclear plant
2010	Gaza flotilla ends in the killing of several Turkish activists
2011	President Karlos Papoulias of Greece visits Israel
2011	Hamas and Fatah sign reconciliation agreement in the light of the Arab Spring
2011	First use of Iron Dome system in southern Israel
2011	Widespread social protest takes place in many Israeli cities
2011	The Muslim Brotherhood emerges victorious in Egyptian elections
2012	Magnetic car bomb kills senior official at Iranian nuclear plant

2012	Israel's population increases to 7,836,000 citizens
2012	Tsipi Livni resigns as leader of Kadima to be succeeded by Shaul Mofaz
2012	Kadima join Netanyahu's coalition government, representing ninety-four Knesset seats, and leaves two months later
2012	Mob attacks on African immigrants in south Tel Aviv
2012	Flame computer virus shuts down Iranian oil terminals
2012	Mohammed Morsi, candidate of the Muslim Brotherhood, elected President of Egypt

Preface to the second edition: Towards 2020

In 1948, the young Robert Kennedy, as yet unknown in public life, visited Palestine as a special correspondent for the *Boston Globe*. He wrote:

The Jewish people in Palestine who believe in and have been working toward this national state have become an immensely proud and determined people. It is already a truly great modern example of the birth of a nation with the primary ingredients of dignity and self-respect.[1]

Kennedy spoke of the 'undying spirit and unparalleled courage' of the Jews and compared their struggle to that of the Irish by quoting the speech from the dock of the Irish revolutionary Robert Emmet.[2]

In his articles, he captured the idealism and spirit of the times – themes which ran through his speeches in later life. Esther Cailingold, the same age as Kennedy but from England, died when the Jewish Quarter of the Old City of Jerusalem was overrun by numerically superior Arab forces. In her last letter to her family in London she wrote:

We have had a bitter fight: I have tasted of gehenom [hell]. – but it has been worthwhile because I am quite convinced that the end will see a Jewish state and the realisation of our longings.[3]

'Hebrew independence', the daily *Ha'aretz* commented, 'is not being renewed during an hour of mercy'. In 1948 Israel struggled to take its place at the table of nations.[4]

More than sixty years later, this sense of determination and self-sacrifice remained – if somewhat buffeted by the waves of political reality and rampant materialism. The founding fathers had passed into history. Politicians were no longer placed on pedestals. Poets were no longer adored

---

[1] *Boston Globe* 4 June 1948. See Lenny Ben-David jcpa.org/article/robert-kennedys-1948-reports-from-palestine/.

[2] *Boston Globe* 6 June 1948.

[3] Yehuda Avner, *The Prime Ministers: An Intimate Narrative of Israeli Leadership* (London 2010) p. 59.

[4] *Ha'aretz* 14 May 1948.

national figures. Instead presidents went to prison and failed politicians were resurrected within a couple of years of resigning. In a certain sense, 1948 had been a simpler time, when choices were straightforward. To fight or to die. To change the course of Jewish history. To build and be built. To create a perfect future.

Hindsight brings with it the revelation that the past was a complicated place. It is always accompanied by a revision of treasured memories by a succeeding generation. Yet the Israelis of the twenty-first century also remember the profound lessons that the past taught despite its myths. Sometimes this has proved to be an obstacle in achieving peace with their neighbours. In other instances, it has been an asset. While all carry this heavy burden, few dismiss its significance.

The rise of Palestinian Islamism in the twenty-first century led Israel to batten down the hatches and to hope that this period of religious intensity would be brief. It led to the ongoing construction of a separation barrier along and close to the Green Line. It stimulated wars of deterrence in Lebanon in 2006 and in Gaza in 2009. It persuaded the Israeli electorate to elect governments which increasingly leaned towards the Right as an instrument to protect the population. The Right in all its political manifestations was also ideologically committed to colonizing the West Bank and integrating it into Israel territorially and economically.

The advent of the Islamist suicide bomber in the spring of 1994 created a sense of indifference towards Palestinian aspirations. The peace camps in both Israel and Palestine were undermined in the process. Although opinion polls repeatedly indicated that a majority of Israelis were not in favour of the settlements, they came to be seen as a long-term buffer against irrational enemies – transient structures which could be negotiated away in better times.

During the first decade of the twenty-first century, the prospect of two territorially contiguous states began to disappear gradually as the West Bank fragmented into Palestinian enclaves through settler encroachment. One French illustrator, Julien Bousec, depicted the West Bank as an archipelago – an array of Palestinian islands surrounded by an Israeli sea and separated by a multitude of inlets, bearing names such as Baie de Shomron and Canal d'Ariel. Indeed some Palestinian commentators argued for a one-state solution – a state of all its citizens. Others suggested a variation on this theme, a return to UN Resolution 181 of November 1947 within an acceptance of partition into two states. The original resolution spoke of a customs and currency union and other instances of shared sovereignty. Palestinians recalled that Israel's war of independence had resulted in the conquest and integration of 21 per cent of the territory of the proposed Arab state.

Although the battle for Jerusalem took place in 1967, every inch of the holy city was still being contested nearly half a century later. Barak's offer to divide the city at the Camp David negotiations in 2000 seemed naive by 2012. The character of the city was changing – more religious and less secular. Israelis were also migrating to the suburbs or leaving to secure affordable housing and better employment opportunities. Scholarly predictions suggested a population of 60 per cent Jews and 40 per cent Arabs by 2020 and perhaps parity by 2035. Yet the borders of the city were not static as successive governments attempted to build a contiguous territorial presence over the Green Line to isolate Arab East Jerusalem.

Jerusalem ironically occupied a space whereby there was coalescence rather than fragmentation and polarization. On 1 December 2011, the first paying passengers stepped on board the Jerusalem Light Rail, which linked many areas of the city. Palestinian Arabs from East Jerusalem and haredim from ultra-orthodox enclaves in West Jerusalem and neighbourhoods over the Green Line such as Pisgat Ze'ev found common cause in the convenience and speed of the new railway. It gave an opportunity to view the other and to explore. Herzl had painted such an idyllic landscape in his utopian work *Altneuland* in 1902, depicting a future flawless society where the dignity of difference was exalted.

Although the service was three years behind schedule after four false starts, it was an important component in Israel's evolving transportation system, which would include a high-speed railway linking Jerusalem to Tel Aviv. Yet the reality of the political situation could not be held in abeyance, especially since Arab East Jerusalem, conquered in 1967, remained under Israeli rule. Therefore the participation in the railway consortium of two French companies, Veolia and Alstom, catalyzed legal action in France by the Palestine Liberation Organization (PLO) and divestment by an ethical Dutch bank and a Swedish pension fund. Saudi Arabia was requested to intervene because Alstom was part of a consortium to build the Mecca–Medina railway. The Gulf Cooperation Council was warned not to consider these two companies when offering a tender to build a railway linking six Gulf states.

Opinion polls of both Israelis and Palestinians often indicated a contrary view to the one voiced by politicians. In November 2010, the Palestinian Center for Public Opinion conducted a poll amongst the inhabitants of Arab East Jerusalem for Pechter Middle East Polls. It found that 35 per cent of its respondents would choose Israeli citizenship, compared to 30 per cent who would chose Palestinian citizenship. When asked what would happen if their neighbourhood in East Jerusalem became part of the new state of Palestine, nearly 40 per cent would prefer to move to another location within Israel. Their reasons were freedom of movement in Israel, a higher income, better employment opportunities and health insurance. Those who chose to remain stated that their patriotic inclinations came first.[5]

There seemed no indication that the security barrier around Jerusalem would be dismantled even though the age of the suicide bomber seemed to have passed for the time being. What was once deemed to be temporary was rapidly being seen as a permanent edifice of separation and an evolving border. Yet numerous Palestinian villages were either marooned or truncated. The village of Bil'in became a cause célèbre and was visited by the Elders group,which included Jimmy Carter and Desmond Tutu. Weekly demonstrations by Israeli leftists such as Anarchists against the Wall, characterized by often violent clashes with the Israel Defence Forces (IDF), drew international attention. In March 2010, the IDF declared it a closed military zone, thereby banning Israeli citizens and non-Israeli protesters from entering the area. In 2011, the military, acting on a Supreme Court judgement that the security argument was unconvincing, began instead to reroute the barrier.

Yet under the stewardship of Mahmoud Abbas (Abu Mazen) and Salam Fayyad, the standard of living of the West Bank Arabs increased by leaps and bounds. The struggle, however, between Palestinian nationalists and Islamists – between Fatah and Hamas – seemed insoluble despite the regular proclamations of brotherhood. The release of the Palestine Papers to *al-Jazeera* and the *Guardian* at the beginning of 2011 suggested that the Palestinian Authority (PA) was prepared in private to go some distance in striking a compromise with Israel. The right of return, however, continued to occupy an important place in Palestinian emotions. Yet the European Court of Human Rights had ruled in 2010 that Greeks who had fled or been expelled from northern Cyprus in 1974 as a result of the Turkish invasion did not have a right to return. Most Israelis considered the Palestinian return of millions a direct assault on their right to national self-determination. But how many would actually return if offered the opportunity? Khalil Shikaki's study in 2003 of more than 4,500 Palestinian respondents in the West Bank, Gaza, Lebanon and Jordan produced a scientific analysis for the first time. While virtually all demanded a recognition of a right of return,

---

[5] pechterpolls.com/wp-content/uploads/2011/01/Detailed-Survey-Results-on-E-Jerusalem-1–10-11–1034pm-Eastern.pdf.

Shikaki found that only 10 per cent demanded permanent residence in Israel – a percentage which fell away when respondents were informed that they would also have to accept Israeli citizenship.[6] Shikaki's research led him to the conclusion that initially the number of refugees who would wish to move from Lebanon and Jordan to any sovereign Palestinian state, alongside Israel, would be 784,049. The number who wished to exercise the same right to return to Israel was calculated at 373,673.[7] Hamas, however, believed in the absolute understanding of the right of return. Indeed Ismail Haniyeh, the Prime Minister in Gaza, commented in January 2011 that there was no alternative 'to a full return to lands that became Israeli in 1948'.[8]

After Hamas's takeover of Gaza in 2007, the break between Islamists and nationalists seemed final. Regular agreements in favour of reconciliation were abandoned with remarkable rapidity. The price for such a reconciliation and the inclusion of Hamas in a government of national unity under the stewardship of Mahmoud Abbas was the dismissal of Salam Fayyad, an independent who was a member of neither Fatah nor Hamas. Yet the United States regarded Fayyad as the practitioner of good governance and the architect of the West Bank's economic amelioration. Would the Palestinian Authority jeopardize the annual $600 million which the Americans provided? While the West Bank under the nationalists prospered, Gaza under the Islamists drifted into poverty under an Israeli state of siege. Would the West Bank and Gaza move further and further apart until they became two distinct entities, the East and West Pakistan template remodelled for a divided Palestine? Would Gaza eventually become a Palestinian Bangladesh?

The Oslo II agreement which was signed by Yitzhak Rabin just before his assassination had stipulated that there should be no change in the status of the West Bank before the completion of negotiations. This clause was buried by his successors. Was the prospect of a two-state solution now an impossibility under the weight of the settlement drive on the West Bank and the division within the Palestinians? While some Palestinians argued for a one-state solution of Israel and Palestine, other observers predicted that the Palestinian Authority would eventually be linked to Jordan in some fashion despite King Abdullah's wish to avoid this possibility. The prospect of the Islamists' governing in Egypt under Mohammed Morsi also raised

---

[6] *New York Times* 14 July 2003.
[7] Poll on Refugees' Preferences and Behaviour in a Palestinian–Israeli Permanent Refugee Agreement, Palestinian Center for Policy and Survey Research, 18 July 2003.
[8] *Ma'an News* 26 January 2011.

the question of what would be the relationship between a post-Mubarak regime in Cairo and a Gaza governed by Hamas. Would there similarly be some form of linkage here too? And what would this mean for Israel?

The potential fall of Assad in Syria posed a dilemma for Israel. On the one hand, the link to Iran would be broken. On the other, would Sunni Islamists replace an ostensibly secular regime? On both Naksa Day (the anniversary of the Six Day war) and Nakba Day (the anniversary of the founding of Israel) in 2011, Palestinians breached the Golan border, and there was a lethal response from the Israeli military. Many believed that the Assad regime had looked the other way in the hope that these incidents would divert international attention away from an incipient civil war.

The political stagnation continued. Sharon had always argued that there could be no negotiations if there was violence – whichever Palestinian faction was responsible for this. The President of the Palestinian Authority, Mahmoud Abbas, had similarly refused to conduct negotiations while settlement construction on the West Bank and in East Jerusalem was taking place. During the ten-month settlement freeze in 2010, construction had not ceased in East Jerusalem and its environs. Planning and all subsequent stages continued. There were even actual violations of the freeze by several West Bank settlements. While government construction certainly decreased, it was more than compensated for by a surge in private construction. At the beginning of 2011, the Netanyahu administration, unlike previous governments, proposed the legalization of outposts which were sited on state land while promising to continue to evacuate those built on private land.

Abbas questioned the real meaning of negotiations with Netanyahu, which in the absence of any political initiative seemed to go around in never-ending circles. Successive Israeli governments had continued the settlement drive through the expansion of already existing settlements. Peace Now's Settlement Watch discovered that whereas the areas of jurisdiction of cities and councils in Israel were placed in the public domain and therefore such knowledge was available to all, the same could not be said about the boundaries of West Bank settlements. A Freedom of Information request in January 2006 together with a later appeal to the Supreme Court coerced a reticent Civil Administration to release such information. Thus Mitzpeh Shalem, a settlement of about 200 souls, situated near the Dead Sea, was found to possess jurisdiction over 35,000 dunams of territory – the area of the city of Petah Tiqva.

The forward charge of Erdogan's neo-Ottomanist policies in Turkey, the uncertain end results of the Arab Spring and Ahmadinejad's ambiguous ambitions for a nuclearized Iran induced a sense of fear and isolation. While Iran had been a worry for many years, the intensified competition between Khamenei and Ahmadinejad transformed Israel into a political punch-bag between these rivals for absolute power. With new moves to outmanoeuvre the other, Israelis wondered how this power struggle would manifest itself in their region of the Middle East. This was compounded by cooler relations with Obama's White House and a divided and sometimes unfriendly Europe. Even the unilateral attempts by the Palestinian Authority to secure recognition within international bodies such as UNESCO and the WHO were seen in Israel as moves in the diplomatic chess game rather than positive initiatives in themselves. Debates about the ownership of contested religious and cultural sites such as Rachel's Tomb in Bethlehem/the Bilal bin Rabah Mosque became more intense and more convoluted.

There was a fatigue and disappointment in Israel which bred indifference to seeking a solution to the conflict. Between the signing of the Declaration of Principles in Oslo in 1993 and Sharon's walk on the Temple Mount, 256 Israelis had died, followed by another 1,097 during the subsequent years of Intifada.[9] Ismail Haniyeh, the Prime Minister in Gaza, had commented that suicide bombing was no more than a natural reaction to Zionist aggression.[10] The sense of fatalism was accompanied by a lack of confidence in the current generation of politicians. As the veteran left-wing commentator and politician Yossi Sarid commented:

The feeling that we are stuck with the same politicians: Governments come and go, but the same people remain. Soon there will be elections here, and the same bunch will sally forth from the ballot box, in slightly different dress. At most, after the elections, they will reshuffle the cabinet seats. One will be upgraded and another will barely find a seat. But the group picture will remain the same and with it the situation.[11]

Transparency International's findings in 2010 indicated that Israelis' lack of faith in their public bodies was amongst the highest in the world. With political parties and religious institutions deemed the most corrupt, some 82 per cent of the respondents thought that their government was worthy of this label.[12]

The era of optimism during Yitzhak Rabin's premiership was long gone, buried in the graveyard of good intentions. The idea that there was no one to

---

[9] Efraim Inbar, 'Israel's Palestinian Challenge', *Israel Affairs* vol.12 no.4 October 2006 pp. 823–842.
[10] *Ha'aretz* 2 April 2006.
[11] *Ha'aretz* 20 June 2008.
[12] *Ha'aretz* 10 December 2010.

speak to was promoted strongly during Sharon's tenure as Prime Minister. Sharon declared that 'Arafat is our Bin Laden'. The Saudi Initiative of March 2002 was glossed over, as was Arafat's call for a ceasefire in December 2001. Senior Palestinian figures such as Raed Karmi, who was obeying the ceasefire, were still assassinated. The weakening of the PA's infrastructure led to the resignation of the advisor on Palestinian affairs to the head of the Shin Bet and initiated a policy of solely relying on military deterrence for the next decade.[13]

The polarization of the situation had led the Israelis to elect Sharon to protect them. It had also persuaded the Palestinians to look to Hamas to protect them. The broadly based peace camps in Israel and Palestine had dwindled to the point of invisibility. Extra-parliamentary groups on the far Right such as Im Tirzu embarked on a campaign to attack liberal organizations such as the New Israel Fund, often merging them with genuinely far Left bodies with anti-Zionist inclinations. This attack on local dissent was partly funded by Kanit Azrieli, which owned the Azrieli Malls (30,000 shekels), and the Leo Schachter groups, a major exporter of processed diamonds (74,000 shekels). They were further supported by donations from US groups such as Christians United for Israel (748,000 shekels).

The once all-powerful Israeli Labour party, founder and mentor of the state, divided into two with single-seat representation in a Knesset of 120. In contrast, the rise of the far Right, exemplified by Avigdor Lieberman's Yisrael Beitanu, initiated a series of measures such as the expansion within West Bank settlements and an assault on civil liberties directed at both liberal Israelis and far Left activists. This ignited a growing disillusionment in the Jewish Diaspora, where even hitherto establishment figures were beginning to sound like enraged dissidents. Aliyah – emigration to Israel – had fallen from 77,000 in 1999 to 19,700 in 2007 to 16,600 in 2010. There was particular disgust felt at the incendiary remarks made by far Right members of the Knesset about black South Sudanese migrant workers, refugees and asylum seekers in south Tel Aviv in May 2012. Yet immigrants still arrived in Israel – and from unexpected quarters. In 2007, some 200 Jews were allowed to emigrate from Ahmadinejad's Iran. Diaspora Jews still turned their heads towards Israel, including ninety-two-year-old Mimi Reinhardt, who had been Oskar Schindler's secretary.

Although Israel was finally allowed to join the International Red Cross by using a red crystal as its emblem, the evolving diplomatic isolation of

---

[13] *Ha'aretz* 20 June 2008.

Israel continued. It was complemented by a drip-drip campaign of delegitimization in Europe by the far Left, which depicted Zionism as a poisonous weed planted by the forces of imperialism to maintain their control of the Middle East in post-colonialist times. This dovetailed with the opposition to the invasion of Iraq amongst social democrats and the liberal intelligentsia. It presented a focus of resentment to often perplexed mainstream Muslims in Europe, following the backlash after 9/11. In general, there was little space for alternative explanations of episodes in the tortuous Israel-Palestine conflict.

Ironically, it had only been through Soviet support in 1947 that a two-thirds majority in the United Nations in favour of creating a state with a majority of Jews had been attained. Indeed, if it had not been for Stalin, it can be argued that a state of Israel would not have gained international legitimacy and might not even have come into existence. Stalin probably wished to eliminate the British from Palestine and to stop the Americans from taking their place. The Zionist Left was strongly pro-Soviet and believed itself to be the USSR's true representative in Israel. Moreover, the Kremlin would have been extremely pleased to make use of Haifa as a deep warm water port. All this changed dramatically after Israel's declaration of independence. Some objectives had indeed been achieved, but the Arab masses were a much better prospect for Soviet national interests compared to the socialists of Israel.

The Old Left in Europe, which had fought with the Jews against local fascists, lived through the Shoah and borne witness to the establishment of Israel in 1948, was rapidly fading away by the twenty-first century. The successor generation of the 1960s was characterized by the epoch of decolonization, by the struggle of the Front de Libération Nationale (FLN) in Algeria against the French colons – and the Palestinians fitted much more easily into this imagery of many who were born after 1945. Social democrats and liberals were keenly aware of the abandonment of the Jews during World War II as well as, for example, the evils of apartheid. The conclusion was therefore to facilitate a space whereby Israelis and Palestinians could face each other within the framework of a two-state solution. For some on the far Left, however, revolutionary change preceded other considerations. A nation-state of the Jews was anathema.

'Zionist' became a pejorative term in the lexicon of political discourse and therefore could be separated from 'Jew'. Yet as Sartre pointed out in the 1960s, most Israelis just happened to be Jews. In intellectual circles, there was irritation that a majority of Jews were stubborn and refused to give up an identification with Israel despite having often profound reservations about successive Israeli governments. Even Richard Goldstone, whose inquiry into Operation Cast Lead led to harsh criticism in Israel, felt the need to denounce accusations that apartheid policies were being pursued.[14]

Such developments dovetailed with the growing acceptance in the Muslim world – in the absence of any political initiatives – that Israel was truly an illegitimate entity. The idea that the Jews were solely a religious community and not an ethnicity in their own right gathered momentum. Palestine between the river and the sea was an Islamic endowment whose land could not be bartered away for a peace agreement. On the other side of the coin was Netanyahu's insistence that Israel should now be recognized as a Jewish state.

Moreover, the ongoing plight of the Palestinians and the move to the far Right in Israel offered the far Left in Europe an opportunity for recruitment and expansion. This in turn fortified the far Right in Israel in enacting a campaign against liberal and left-wing dissenters in Israel itself. Many on the far Right in Israel believed that anti-Zionism was solely a cover for anti-Semitism. Many on the far Left in Europe believed that anti-Zionism could never be anti-Semitic. The reality was somewhere in between.

An inability to distance themselves from traditional anti-Jewish stereotypes affected the Palestinian Islamists far more than the Palestinian nationalists. A Hamas spokesman was therefore certain that 'the Jewish lobby' in the United States played a crucial role in fomenting the global economic crisis in 2008. The Iranian cleric, the Ayatollah Jannati, told worshippers that this was God's response to the misdeeds of both the Israelis and the Americans. Sometimes both messages were given. Hezbollah's Nasrallah told the Lebanese newspaper *al-Moharrer* that his organization's war was against Zionism and not Jews or Judaism.[15] A few weeks later at a Beirut rally, he told his followers that 'a few million vagabonds from all over the world, brought together by their Talmud and Jewish fanaticism, are celebrating their victory over the nation of 1.4 billion Muslims'.[16]

The underbelly of such political commentary was often far more insidious. In February 2011, the Obama White House accused the prestigious Lebanese Canadian Bank of laundering cocaine money on behalf of Hezbollah. A picture was painted of a network of connections between Colombian cartels and Mexican gangs, Lebanese Shi'ite businessmen and traders in conflict diamonds in Africa. Lebanon's chief drug enforcement

---

[14] *New York Times* 31 October 2011.
[15] *Al-Moharrer* 29 March 1998 in Nicholas Roe (ed.), *Voice of Hezbollah: The Statements of Sayed Hassan Nasrallah* (London 2007) p. 186.
[16] Ibid. p. 188.

officer said that one route into the country was 'a weekly Iranian-operated flight from Venezuela to Damascus'.[17]

Outside this ideological maelstrom, Israel continued to make its mark. In 2011 the Nobel Prize in chemistry was awarded to Dan Shechtman for his discovery of quasi-crystals, after analyzing electron diffraction patterns in the early 1980s. This was the fourth time in seven years that an Israeli scientist had won the Nobel Prize for chemistry, including the first Israeli woman, Ada Yonath, to do so. Israel had also pioneered the use of reverse osmosis to develop desalination of sea water to a high level. It was estimated that by 2050, some 41 per cent of Israel's drinking water would originate in the Mediterranean. The desalination plant on the seashore near Hadera serviced a million households with clean water each year. Since 2007 successive Israeli governments had invested heavily in the expansion of the Hadera, Ashkelon and Palmachim desalination plants. In August 2011, it was announced that a new plant would be constructed near Ashdod at a cost of $423 million and would begin desalination in 2013. Israel was also a world leader in the recycling of waste water. Some 70 per cent of the country's waste water was recycled compared to 12 per cent in Spain. Waste water was even seen as a means of energy production from the organic material found in it.

While such developments created a deep sense of pride in what had been achieved, the darker side of Israeli society was revealed when a bomb went off in the car of the Tel Aviv mobster Ya'akov Alperon – and killed him. This took place in broad daylight in a crowded Tel Aviv thoroughfare at the end of 2008. This was probably the eighth assassination attempt against Alperon, while his elder brother survived as many attempts against him as well. Other criminal fraternities, often centred around a family unit, were heavily involved in controlling the Tel Aviv drug trade or running a bottle recycling offshoot through offering restaurateurs protection in exchange for collecting empty bottles.

The power struggle between Ahmadinejad and Khameini unsettled many Israelis. How would the nuclear question be used in this contest? Given that Iran possessed a land mass eighty times that of Israel and nine times the population, it seemed unlikely that Israel would actually unleash a military attack on Iran despite a cacophony of bellicose noises emitted from Netanyahu and Barak. Significantly, both the present head of the Mossad, Tamir Pardo, and his predecessor publicly opposed any military assault on Iran. In 2012 the former head of the Shin Bet, Yuval Diskin,

---

[17] *New York Times* 13 December 2011.

similarly declared his opposition to military action. Although the United States sold the most advanced bunker buster bombs to Israel, any attack on the Bushehr reactor would release radioactive material, which would not only result in the deaths of large numbers of Iranians but also drift over Bahrain and Qatar. Moreover, any aircraft carrying out the 2,000-mile round trip would have to be supported by airborne refueling planes. It was believed that Israel lacked sufficient numbers of the latter to carry out a successful raid on Iran.

Israel's technological edge in cyber-weaponry was believed to be the crucial factor in inhibiting Iran from the immediate acquisition of nuclear weapons. The Stuxnet computer worm rather than airstrikes was thought by many commentators to be Israel's response. The worm seemed to have been activated only when a series of processes in a centrifuge plant were detected. The centrifuges then accelerated out of control while false signals were transmitted to the host system to assure it that everything was quite normal. Meir Dagan, the outgoing head of the Mossad, told a Knesset committee that Teheran had run into technological problems that would delay the manufacture of nuclear weapons until 2015. This seemed to be a reversal of the normal line that Iran was on the verge of success.

North Korean involvement in the Iranian nuclear project increased in 2011. There were reports that North Korea had supplied a computer programme that simulated neutron flow in reactors and that it had trained Iranians in its use.[18] The programme, MCNPX 2.6.0, had originally been developed at Los Alamos, and although it was subject to stringent US export controls, it had somehow found its way to Pyongyang. The sources argued that the calculation of neutron flow was a crucial component in building any nuclear weapon.

Following the success of Hezbollah's defensive warfare against the Israeli attacks in 2006, Iran concluded an agreement for 100 field operatives to undergo training in Pyongyang with the North Korean special forces – and particularly in the areas of counter-espionage and intelligence work. Under North Korean guidance, Hezbollah was believed to have expanded its bunker and tunnel system into the Beka'a Valley. In 2009, several consignments of weaponry in ships and planes for delivery in Iran en route to Hezbollah were uncovered. One chartered jet which was intercepted in Thailand in December 2009 was owned by a company in the United Arab Emirates, registered in Georgia, leased to a front company in New Zealand and then chartered to another front company in Hong Kong.

---

[18] *Sueddeutsche Zeitung* 24 August 2011.

A UN report in 2010 detailed Pyongyang's attempts to circumvent sanctions using multiple intermediaries, front companies and overseas criminal networks.[19]

In 2012, the prospects for Israel's economic development looked surprisingly good despite the problems in other parts of the world. In 2011 the Israeli economy grew by 4.8 per cent. Houston based Noble Energy Inc. declared that their off-shore explorations had concluded that Israel possessed twice as much natural gas as the United Kingdom. There was probably close to 30 trillion cubic feet of gas in the eastern Mediterranean. This opened up the potential for Israel to emerge as an exporter of gas to Asia and Europe as well as decreasing its own dependency on Egypt.

The idea of a socialist, egalitarian Israel was finally laid to rest in 1985 when the rotational government of Shimon Peres promoted deregulation and globalization to accompany the revolution in technology. A blueprint was formulated to transfer public control to private enterprise, to transform nationalized industries into private ones. In 2010, the annual Merrill Lynch–Capgemini World Wealth report commented that there were 10,153 millionaires in Israel with assets of $52 billion in liquid funds. This was an increase from $43 billion in 2009. The donation of $20 million by the Israeli shipping magnate Sami Ofer to the Tel Aviv Museum of Art, later retracted, was an indication of how far the society had changed from the time when a home-grown millionaire would have been an oddity and perhaps an outcast. Senior executives for companies that traded on the Tel Aviv Stock Exchange were reported to have doubled their monthly salaries from 378,000 shekels to 703,000 shekels between 1998 and 2007.[20]

The changed situation, however, raised the awkward question of why Diaspora donors should fund projects in Israel, as Israeli philanthropy stood at only 0.73 per cent of GDP compared to 2.1 per cent in the United States. While Israeli philanthropists were urged to follow in the path of Bill Gates, annual poverty reports issued by the National Insurance Institute continued to demonstrate little variation from the fifth of Israeli families living below the poverty line. In 2010, this comprised 1,733,400 people – of whom half were children.[21]

The growing disparity between the 'haves' and 'have-nots' in Israeli society erupted in 2011 through a proliferation of tent cities throughout the

---

[19] *Ha'aretz* 28 May 2010.
[20] *Jerusalem Post* 14 December 2008.
[21] *Ha'aretz* 17 November 2011.

country. Although the protesters were initially disparaged by the government as disaffected members of the Tel Aviv elite, Netanyahu recognized their legitimate concerns and established the Trajtenberg Commission, which recommended a 2 per cent wealth tax on incomes above one million shekels, a 5 per cent rise in the capital gains tax and an increase in the corporate rate tax to 25 per cent. Yet the Netanyahu government dallied on initiating relief. In July 2012 Moshe Silman, a fifty-seven-year-old son of Holocaust survivors, set fire to himself in Tel Aviv in protest about his situation. He died of his injuries a week later.

Poverty was particularly severe in the haredi sector of Israeli society. Towns such as Bnei Brak were amongst the poorest in the country. This was accentuated by the economic downturn outside Israel, which limited easy earning opportunities, and Diaspora donations began to dry up. Even so, a Freedom of Information request in 2012 revealed that Ateret Yerushalayim, a religious Zionist seminary and educational organization, had received donations of upwards of 1.5 million shekels from numerous anonymous donors. The Ministry of Justice's registrar of charities had unusually agreed to the non-publication of the donors' names. This provoked considerable controversy because a central task of Ateret Yerushalayim had been the settling of Jews in the Muslim Quarter of the Old City of Jerusalem.

Approximately 800,000 Jews – one in seven Israeli Jews – espoused an ultra-orthodox lifestyle. The average haredi father had six or seven mouths to feed – almost three times the non-haredi average. The population of the haredi community was expected to double by 2020.[22] Unlike their counterparts in the Diaspora, haredi schools did little to prepare their charges with relevant skills to enter the labour market.

In 2011, a quarter of those entering the first year of school were haredi children, compared to 7 per cent in 1960. This posed future problems for Israel's military forces. The head of the IDF Manpower Directorate predicted that by 2020 some 60 per cent of eligible Israelis would not be serving in the military forces.[23] The largest proportion of those conscripts exempted were those at yeshiva. David Ben-Gurion agreed with the sage the Hazon Ish to excuse several hundred students from military service, but since the early 1950s there had been an extrapolation from the brilliant and gifted downwards to include the mediocre and the indolent. The Tal Law, passed in 2002, permitted yeshiva students to work for a year in civilian service programmes without being conscripted. A choice would then have

---

[22] *Jerusalem Report* 1 February 2010.
[23] *Jerusalem Post* 20 November 2011.

to be made between a return to study or a shortened national service. In 2012 there were 4,000 haredim in such programs – three quarters of whom worked in welfare.

Yet there were haredi sections within the IDF such as the Netzah Yehuda battalion. Haredi men also trained as aircraft mechanics and technicians. The IDF also began to adapt to the religious sensitivities of those haredim who wished to serve in their country's armed forces. In March 2011, haredi men trained as social workers were attached as non-commissioned officers (NCOs) to haredi units. In conventional non-haredi units, such posts were usually filled by female workers – something which in the context of discussing personal matters would have been deemed unacceptable in the haredi world.

There were continuing clashes between the state, its laws and its under-standing of societal norms and the rabbis, their interpretation of halakhah (Jewish law) and communal standards. The Supreme Court twice ruled that barriers designed to separate men and women during the festival of Succot in the ultra-orthodox neighbourhood of Mea She'arim were illegal and should be removed. A protest march by the secularist 'Free Israel' movement, despite a heavy police protection, was eventually called off for fear of violence. This followed growing demands for segregation on buses which ran mainly between haredi areas and the removal of women from advertisements and billboards in Jerusalem. Such 'mehadrin lines' existed in Jerusalem, Safed, Ashdod and other areas to ferry the haredim between ultra-orthodox centres of population. Moreover, in May 2012, there was a vehement reaction from haredi political parties when the Supreme Court ruled that the salaries of several small community Reform and Conservative rabbis should be paid by the state. The ranking of nations, delineated by their gender gap, by the World Economic Forum indicated that Israel had fallen from 35th to 55th between 2006 and 2011 – behind Burundi, Sri Lanka and the Kyrgyz Republic. Yet such moves galvanized many Israeli women, both religious and non-religious, to protest, and they were supported by Hillary Clinton in December 2011.

This difference in the interpretation of Jewishness manifested itself in a clash between former chief rabbis of the armed forces and the defence establishment. The rabbis argued that if an officer gave an order which contradicted halakhah, it should first be referred to the Chief Rabbi of the IDF. If this was not done, then the individual had to consider whether refusing the order compromised security.

Moreover, there were some rabbis who believed that the evacuation of settlements on the West Bank contravened halakhah. And young soldiers often had much closer relationships with the rabbis who mentored them than the imposed rabbis of their military unit. Who had the loyalty of the recruit? The rabbis also demanded that the Har Bracha yeshiva should be reinstated in the hesder programme for religious recruits after its head had supported refusing any order to evacuate a settlement. In a survey by its Manpower Directorate, the IDF further discovered that the motivation to serve in combat units was highest amongst West Bank settlement youth.

Within the IDF's Personnel Directorate, there was a continuing struggle for authority between its component Education Corps and the Military Rabbinate – and especially over the status of female soldiers and officers. The growing tensions between the religious and the secular in the army were reflected in a letter to the Minister of Defence and the Chief of Staff by nineteen reserve Major Generals. It requested them not to alter the status quo in accommodating the demands of some religious leaders to end singing by women during public events.

All this conflict overflowed at the end of 2011 when radical haredim verbally abused religious primary schoolchildren on their way to school for being immodestly dressed.

Both Shas and National Religious rabbis opposed separation on buses and argued that there was no basis in Jewish law for this. Yet there was also a difference of view within the haredi community itself – and particularly between those born in the Diaspora and those who had grown up in Israel. Significantly, many haredi rabbis and the haredi media neither commented nor reported on what had been happening. Within the haredi community, there was a traditional reticence to step out of line, particularly since being labelled would produce a stigma – real or imagined – and this might well damage their children's chances of securing a suitable spouse. This opened the way for radical elements in the haredi community to set the agenda on the separation of the sexes.

However, the demonstrations against separation in Beit Shemesh by both secular and religious voiced the wider fear of the encroachment of the haredim upon the mainstream norms of Israeli society. This broadened out into a wider debate on their contribution – or lack of it – to society. All this was highly resented by the haredi community. Yet the fact of the rapid growth of the haredi community through its much higher birth rate was often raised. In Israel, 28 per cent of the population was younger than fourteen, whereas the figure for most western countries was 17 per cent. In 2012, haredi and Arab children accounted for half the entrants into primary school.

The release of Gilad Shalit in 2011 after more than five years' imprisonment by Hamas was an occasion for an outpouring of public emotion in Israel. Many Israelis could identify with the ordinariness of the sallow, pale recruit who emerged into the sunlight. The Shalit case typified an ongoing Israeli dogma – to recover its soldiers whether dead or alive from hostile territory. Since 1957 there had been eight prisoner exchanges. Some 12,482 Arab prisoners had been released to secure the return of 15 Israelis. In Shalit's case, 1,027 Palestinian prisoners were exchanged for one man. Some 41 prisoners were deported to Qatar, Turkey, Jordan and Syria – as Israel had originally refused to negotiate over their fate. The head of Hamas's military wing commented that the deportees had killed 569 Israelis.[24] Many of these were civilians killed in suicide bombings – and there was therefore strong opposition from the families of the victims. Others opposed the swap and argued that it would be a source of encouragement to repeat the exercise.

The heavy hand of the state bureaucracy continued to be placed on the shoulders of Israeli citizens. While special needs provision for children was far better than in numerous western European countries, the State Comptroller revealed in his report in 2011 that disputes between the Ministry of Health and the Ministry for Welfare Services had caused children who had special needs to miss school and not receive the medical supervision to which they were entitled. The State Comptroller listed a total of forty inter-Ministry disputes affecting fifteen ministries. Moreover, the desire for advisors and consultants now permeated Israeli governance. Imitating practice in countries such as Britain, the number of political aides in the Prime Minister's Office had increased sixfold since the death of Rabin in 1995. Yet there were often quiet examples whereby solutions to problems were swiftly located. After a complaint about the lack of parking places for disabled people in Bnei Brak, the municipality quickly installed them. In 2009, the Ministry of the Interior refused the applications for exit permits to visit the grave of the prophet Habil near Damascus by forty-three Israeli Druze women, while there were no such problems for their men. A complaint to the office of the State Comptroller reversed that decision.

As Israel approached the seventieth anniversary of its establishment, there were few who believed that it had reached its natural life span, that its vigour would dissipate, that it would become a passing episode in Jewish and world history. Yet the problems that beset the country remained, intensified and multiplied. Islamism with its absolutist approach towards Israel was clearly emerging as a dominant force within the Arab world. Would the Muslim Brotherhood and its Salafist allies tighten their hold on

[24] *Ha'aretz* 20 October 2011.

Egypt and restrict liberal and secular opinion? Would the Israel–Palestine conflict evolve into an existential one between Jews and Muslims?

Hamas too seemed to be changing and distancing itself from Assad's Syria in favour of the new Egypt. Teheran in turn reduced its funding to the organization. On 23 December 2011, Khalid Meshal instructed Hamas's armed wing, the Qassam Brigades, to desist from the military struggle against Israel. While some disaffected members of Hamas joined Islamic Jihad, Meshal was expounding his appreciation for the victorious Islamist Ennahda party in Tunisia. Was this the prelude to a unity government with Fatah and the eventual takeover of the PLO? Would the Islamicization of the Arab world produce a long-term ceasefire, but absolutely no recognition of Israel? As the developing world progressed and the first world seemingly declined, Israelis wondered what sorts of new alliances would need to be constructed and what kinds of political contortions they would now have to undergo.

Introduction

The state of Israel has been squandering, not only the lives of its sons, but also its miracle; that grand and rare opportunity that history bestowed upon it, the opportunity to establish here a state that is efficient, democratic, which abides by Jewish and universal values; a state that would be a national home and haven, also a place that would offer a new meaning to Jewish existence; a state that holds as an integral and essential part of its Jewish identity and its Jewish ethos, the observance of full equality and respect for its non-Jewish citizens.

Look at what has befallen us. Look what befell the young, bold, passionate country we had here, and how, as if it had undergone a quickened ageing process, Israel lurched from infancy and youth to a perpetual state of gripe, weakness and sourness.

How did this happen? When did we lose even the hope that we would eventually be able to live a different, better life? Moreover, how do we continue to watch from the side as though hypnotized by the insanity, rudeness, violence and racism that has overtaken our home?

And I ask you: How could it be that a people with such powers of creativity, renewal and vivacity as ours, a people that knew how to rise from the ashes time and again, finds itself today, despite its great military might, at such a state of laxity and inanity, a state where it is the victim once more, but this time its own victim, of its anxieties, its short-sightedness.

So spoke the Israeli writer David Grossman at a rally in November 2006 on the eleventh anniversary of the killing of Yitzhak Rabin.

Such hand-wringing is not uncommon in Israel. Despite all its achievements over sixty years, the harshest critics of Israel are often its own citizens. The dream of what could be, what should be, never departs. On this occasion, many Israeli commentators concurred, the glass was indeed half empty. Grossman's words were all the more poignant since he had lost his own son in the ill-fated conflict with Hezbollah a few months previously. And yet despite his personal anguish, Grossman's soul-searching was tempered by a profound belief that a way could be found to restore the ideals of the founding generation. Israel could yet be a light unto the nations.

Grossman's warning brought a rebuke from many who claimed that such noble sentiments did not reflect the current reality of living in the Middle East as a non-Arab, non-Muslim people. Moshe Dayan had famously commented that his generation had been condemned to live by the sword for the foreseeable future and many Israelis, decades later, felt that this was still the case. Indeed, between 1948 and 2006, 22,123 people had been killed in the defence of the state. The Peace Index for January 2007 indicated that nearly 60 per cent of Israelis believed that peace could not be obtained without evacuating the Palestinian territories, conquered during the Six Day war in 1967. Yet at the same time, nearly 70 per cent believed that the Palestinians would destroy the state of Israel, given the opportunity.

The founders of the state believed that they had changed the course of history and returned a marginalized and discriminated-against people to the centre. They had triumphed over their persecutors, from the Egyptian Pharaohs to the Spanish Inquisitors, from the Church Fathers to the Russian Tsars. In the words of the Soviet Yiddish poet Itzik Pfeffer, the Jews had survived to dance on Hitler's grave and to forge their own destiny. Israeli babies in the 1950s were named Atzmaut (independence), Medinah (state), Nitzhonah (her victory), Tikvah (hope) and Dror (freedom). The artist Aryeh Navon sketched a kibbutznik whose floppy hat bore the inscription 'Judea Libera' – a contemporary admonition of the Romans who had minted a coin bearing the inscription 'Judea Capta' following the destruction of the Temple and the sacking of Jerusalem in the year 70. In 1948, a majority of the world's Jews turned their faces towards Zion and identified with the new state of Israel which had seemingly risen from the ashes of the Holocaust. In the aftermath of destruction, Zionism was seen to be the successful ideological answer to the Jewish problem. For most Jews, Israel was at the forefront of Jewish history.

The reality of the tortuous Israel–Palestine conflict, however, challenged such dreams and dampened such deep emotions. The revelations of newly published archival material in the 1980s indicated that the official version of Israel's war of independence was far more complicated. The academics and writers known collectively as the 'new historians' punctured both the Israeli and Palestinian accounts of 1948 – and most human beings prefer an easy black and white version of history. Many Palestinian villages, emptied of their inhabitants by the violence of war, became the sites of new settlements for Jewish immigrants. Indeed, Ariel Sharon's farm was situated on the former Arab village of Hodj. The villagers had acted on behalf of the Haganah, the Zionist defence force, before 1948, but were expelled to Gaza despite promises of return. The mukhtar of the village was subsequendy executed by the Egyptians.[1]

For many Israelis, this heroic period of state-building has been replaced by an epoch of moral and political stagnation, punctuated by accusations of rape against a former President and corruption against a Prime Minister. In 1997, Israel was listed at tenth position in an 'honesty league' compiled by Transparency International, an anti-corruption group. By 2007, it had fallen to thirty-fourth place. The lack of leadership was felt most keenly in the inability to resolve the Palestinian question. The flaws in the Oslo Accords, the assassination of Rabin, the election of Netanyahu, the ineptitude of Arafat and the rise of Islamism all contributed to the stalling of the peace process in the 1990s and the outbreak of violence in 2000. The vehemence of the al-Aqsa Intifada, the Palestinian uprising, undermined Israeli public confidence in any Palestinian leadership. Instead, they placed greater trust in the Israeli military. Following the debacle of the conflict in Lebanon in 2006, the military budget was increased in 2007. The contest for the leadership of the Labour party in the summer of 2007 was between a general and an admiral.

For ten out of the fourteen years between 1992 and 2006, military men, Rabin, Barak and Sharon, were in power. In contrast, normative politicians such as Peres, Netanyahu and Olmert were seen as ineffectual leaders. In the same period – apart from Peres's short tenure in 1995–1996 and Peretz after 2006 – all the Ministers of Defence were army men. Yet Israel is no ordinary garrison state. Unlike other countries in which the military plays a central role, officers are forced to retire early. In spite of the perceived state of siege, there is no conventional loss of liberties, marked by a trend to authoritarianism.

In addition, since the Six Day war in 1967, seven out of the thirteen Chiefs of Staff went into politics – and the last two, Ya'alon and Halutz, have yet to make a decision. It is a long time since military leaders emulated the examples in the 1950s of Ya'akov Dori (Science Council) and Mordechai Maklef (Dead Sea Works).

Between 1998 and 2007, three military men with pronounced right-wing views, Mofaz, Ya'alon, Halutz, all served as Chief of Staff. Their period of office took place under Sharon's premiership during a period of suicide bombings and Palestinian violence. Rivals for the position such as Gabi

---

[1] *Yediot Aharanot* 6 January 2006.

Ashkenazi who openly feared for 'the loss of humanity because of the ongoing warfare' were seemingly passed over by Sharon. Ashkenazi's early retirement was short-lived following Halutz's resignation after the Lebanon war of 2006.[2]

Not all military leaders identified with the Right. Ya'akov Orr, the military coordinator in the West Bank and Gaza, condemned the Right's simplistic slogan 'let the IDF win' as a means of quelling the al-Aqsa Intifada:

> That is a statement without content or substance. There is no military answer to national popular confrontations... the army's task is to maintain security and ensure that our interests are not adversely affected. What does that have to do with the ability to win? Victory is a function of a political definition. I would assume that the definition says that ultimately peace has to come between the two entities.[3]

To some extent, this plea fell on deaf ears. Israelis were preoccupied with the deaths of 874 civilians in the Intifada, many as a result of suicide bombings. In 2006, the National Insurance Institute paid out almost $9 million to the victims of terror and their families. The prospect of a nuclear arms race in the Middle East is a growing possibility if Iran actually does develop nuclear weapons, but it could also mean closer Israeli contact with both Arab nationalists and Sunni Muslims who feel increasingly threatened by the repetitive certainty of President Ahmadinejad's pronouncements. Moreover, the advocates of Israeli nuclear deterrence point to the fact that Nasser in defeat in 1967 did not order the use of chemical weapons against Israel even though they had been used in the Yemen in 1962. Similarly Saddam Hussein did not implement the arming of the Scud missiles that hit Tel Aviv in 1991 with biological and chemical weapons, even though the Kurds of Halabja had suffered such a fate a few years earlier.[4]

The presence of an army in 1948 meant a break with Jewish history – a break with persecution and extermination. But it also meant a break with pre-state Zionism when Jews had purchased land. In the wars of 1948 and 1967, Jews had conquered land instead. Ben-Gurion promoted the army as the essence of 'Israeliness'. It was perceived as a melting pot for Ashkenazim and Sephardim, religious and secular, privileged and impoverished – a means of building an Israeli identity from over a hundred culturally disparate Jewish communities. The armed forces were increasingly venerated by a grateful public which could only see a continuing and sometimes

[2] *Ha'aretz* 23 January 2007.   [3] *Ha'aretz* 29 December 2000.
[4] Moshe Ya'alon, 'The IDF and the Israeli Spirit', *Azure* no.24 Spring 2006.

unremitting hostility towards the state of Israel from one quarter or another. By the twenty-first century, the IDF had evolved into an equal almost symbiotic partner with the political echelon in terms of policy making.

Given the place of the Israeli military in the governance of Israel, a growing view is that only military men rather than politicians can make peace with the Palestinians. Menachem Begin was able to agree on a bilateral agreement with Egypt in 1979, but he never accepted the PLO as a negotiating partner. It took a former Chief of Staff, Yitzhak Rabin, to do that.

On the other hand, Labour and the Israeli Left have no real answer to the rise of Islamism except the hope that it will die a quick death and negotiations will be resumed with rationalist Palestinian nationalists. Hamas does not wish to recognize Israel – and by extension does not wish to recognize or negotiate with the Israeli peace camp. Moreover, Islamism's suicide bombers have destroyed the political standing of advocates of a negotiated peace in the Israeli public arena. Yet Palestinian leaders including President Abu Mazen understand the crucial importance of an alliance with the Israeli peace camp in seeking a solution. Time, however, is running out for the rationalists. By 2010 there will be almost two million inhabitants of Gaza, which has the highest birth rate in the region. Half the population is under fifteen. The Jabalya refugee camp is three times as densely populated as Manhattan.[5]

In contrast, despite the Intifada, Israel's GDP grew by 4.4 per cent in 2004 over the previous year. Over half of Israel's exports are sophisticated products of advanced technology. Engineers make up the highest percentage of the workforce. Nearly a quarter of the Israeli workforce has university degrees – the third highest proportion in the industrialized world. In 2002, the national expenditure on research and development per capita was higher than in the United States, Japan and the United Kingdom. Manufacturing exports in high technology in that year were four times the figure for 1990. In 2008, Israel participated in the European Union's Galileo navigation satellite project – a network of thirty satellites designed to improve intelligence-gathering operations. However, the ongoing conflict has contributed to Israel's metamorphosis as a centre for arms manufacture. In 2003, it exported $2.8 billion of defence materiel – some 10 per cent of the world trade in that commodity.[6]

---

[5] Sara Roy, *London Review of Books* 3 November 2005.   [6] *Ha'aretz* 29 February 2004.

The involvement of a large proportion of the population in the technology sector has meant a widening of the gap between rich and poor – on a par with other developed countries. Poverty levels have been increasing steadily since the 1970s. A special Knesset committee compiled a report in 2002 based on figures and analyses from the Central Bureau of Statistics, the National Insurance Institute and academic specialists. It commented:

Israel is now rated second in the Western world, after the United States, in terms of social gaps in income, property, capital, education and spending, as well as in the extent of poverty. While many countries have suffered from a widening of social gaps, caused by the influence of globalization and the technological revolution over the past twenty years, this trend is more pronounced in Israel than elsewhere.[7]

Some 70 per cent of private capital is in the hands of the upper 10 per cent of the population. Indeed, Israel's move from old-time socialism to globalized capitalism manifested itself in the fact that it has the largest number of start-up companies proportionate to its population in the world. It is second in the world for venture capital funds. Outside of the United States and Canada, it has the largest number of NASDAQ listed companies. On a per capita basis, Israel has the largest number of bio-tech start-ups. Even so, the National Insurance Institute noted that 1.65 million people lived below the poverty line in 2006.

This transition was symbolized in the announcement in February 2007 that the very first kibbutz, Kibbutz Degania, had voted to reform its collective system in favour of limited individualism and amending the cooperative way of life. The dining room and the laundry service were privatized; individual cars and bank accounts were now permitted. Kibbutz members could now even invest in the stock market via the Internet.[8]

However, the collective ideal has not vanished. In 1998 a new kibbutz, Kibbutz Eshbal, was founded in the Western Galilee. The kibbutz members devote themselves to social work with underprivileged youth from the poorest sections of society and have established on its premises a boarding school mostly for Ethiopian young people. There are educational projects with a Bedouin tribe that lives in a recently recognized village near Kibbutz Eshbal. Yet this village does not receive even basic amenities from the state – running water, the provision of electricity, the disposal of sewerage. An estimated 75,000 Bedouin lived in unrecognized villages without public funding and services in 2007.

---

7 *Ha'aretz* 7 December 2002.   8 *Ha'aretz* 23 February 2007.

Several kibbutzim were established on the Golan Heights following the defeat of Syrian forces in 1967. They have developed the area as a prime grape-growing region which has elevated Israel's standing as an internationally recognized wine producer. The country's first organically grown Chardonnay was produced there in 2003. Yet the continuation of such enterprises is always precarious. Labour governments under Rabin and Barak have offered to return part of the Golan to the Syrians in exchange for peace and recognition. In May 2006, Arabs comprised 20 per cent of Israel's 7,026,000 citizens. The first Bedouin diplomat was appointed to San Francisco in 2006. In January 2007, the trade union leader Raleb Majadele became the first Arab minister to sit in an Israeli cabinet. Yet a survey of 10,000 Israelis in 2003–4 by the World Health Organization indicated differences in health care between Jews and Arabs. 23 per cent of Arab women underwent mammography compared with 48 per cent of Jewish women. 59 per cent of Jewish women were tested for cervical cancer, but only 13 per cent of Arab women. Access to medical facilities was more difficult for Arabs, often living in remoter areas and without knowledge of such testing techniques, but such issues were frequently raised in the context of Israeli Arabs as being less than full citizens of the state. Moreover, Sikkuy, the Association for the Advancement of Civic Equality in Israel, published data in March 2007 that asserted that the infant mortality for Arab babies under twelve months was double that of their Jewish counterparts.

In 1988, the Knesset decriminalized homosexuality and prevented discrimination on the shop floor. By 1997, such issues were permitted to be discussed on television and in 2000 the age of consent was lowered to sixteen. Both Islamist Arabs and ultra-orthodox Jews in Israel opposed activities such as the Gay Pride parade in Jerusalem. Israel was established as 'a community of communities' and the transition from dispersion to a nation state is still in progress. Nearly a million Russians arrived in Israel from the former Soviet Union in the 1990s and have successfully been absorbed. A vibrant sub-culture has developed through Russian language theatre, literature, music and the media. There are also close business ties with the old country. Their political parties, established in the 1990s, have now been devoured by both Likud and Labour. The Kishinev-born Avigdor Lieberman has emerged as a hate figure for Israeli Liberals. His party, Yisrael Beitanu (Israel Our Home), has transcended its definition as a purely Russian party and now attracts many other Israelis to the far Right.

The Sephardim or Mizrachim, mainly from Arab countries, may often be non-observant, yet they show a remarkable respect for tradition, religion and ethnicity by voting for the ultra-orthodox party, Shas. In the 2006 election, Shas secured twelve seats – as many as Netanyahu's Likud. Its political decisions are often made according to the judgement of its aged spiritual mentor, Ovadia Yosef, rather than through a democratic show of hands. Yet there are signs that it is beginning to move into the ground vacated by the national religious who are in ideological turmoil following the evacuation of the Gaza settlements in 2005 and who are now identified with the far Right in Israeli politics.

The Zionist national religious camp (mafdalim) have tended to become more religious while the non-Zionist ultra-orthodox (haredim) have become more nationalistic producing an emerging hybrid, appropriately termed the hardalim. Significantly, the number of pupils in ultra-orthodox primary schools is three times greater than a decade ago. There has been a steady stream of secular Jews leaving Jerusalem for other cities because of its accelerating religiosity. Moreover, 11 per cent of those who do not serve in the army receive exemptions for yeshiva study. This compares with only 2.4 per cent in 1974. Yet the Central Bureau of Statistics in Israel reported that secular Jews and those who define themselves as 'traditional, but not so religious' account for almost three quarters of all Israelis.

Secular Israeli identity is also fragmented. There are those in the national camp who believe that 'a Jewish state' and 'a Jewish majority in the state of Israel' are one and the same. Others see 'Israeliness' in a post-Zionist context, based on normalization, embourgeoisment and materialist individualism. In addition, those who relate to the Zionism of the founders of the state have been empowered in their convictions by the violence of recent years and the withering of the peace process. Ben-Gurion's vision of a homogeneous secular society has given way to a disparate multiculturalism.

Israel in its seventh decade is thus far removed from the state founded in 1948. The days when Israel abducted Adolf Eichmann, one of the facilitators of the Nazi extermination of the Jews, from Argentina and brought him to Israel to stand trial are now a distant memory. Though Israel is no longer admired by the international community, there is still, however, a sense of excitement in Israel at what has been achieved through its rebellion against the designated place of the Jews in history. Despite all the flaws and the foibles of its leaders, the clash between religious and secular, Ashkenazi and Sephardi, there is still a sense of a voyage of discovery – and that the present is far better than the passivity and persecution of the past. This understanding extends to identifying with the dismissed peoples of the world. An angry editorial in the daily *Ha'aretz* in February 2007 attacked the refusal to take in survivors of the massacres in Darfur.

The state of the Jews which was established as a land of refuge, does not have the moral right not to absorb refugees fleeing genocide . . . We have had enough of the excuses of ministers, judges, clerks and officers, the quotes from sections of the law against illegal entry that allow for the arrest or deportation of a Sudanese woman with a sick four year old boy who crossed the desert with nothing but the torn clothing on their backs, and were tossed back to Egypt or into jail despite their pleas.[9]

At the core of Israel's many problems remains the insolubility of the Palestinian question. If the Arab world had accepted UN Resolution 181 in November 1947, then a sovereign state of Palestine would also have been celebrating sixty years of progress and betterment for its people in 2008. The refugee camps remain islands of despair which Palestinians, from generation to generation, inhabit and regard almost as a substitute homeland. Guarding the past has become more important than building the future.

The saga of the conflict has produced thousands of books and remains a subject of incomprehensible fascination for outsiders. It occupies a disproportionate amount of space in the western media. Generations of politicians conjure up innovative plans to manage the conflict. Historians elegantly maul each other's version of events. Propagandists support their team in the megaphone war. Decent people from the four corners of the earth wade into the mire in the hope of ameliorating the suffering and bringing peace to the region.

The last sixty years have therefore induced strong emotions. Yet, within this scenario, a vibrant, dynamic state has been created which is recognized as a success – even within the Arab world. One hundred years ago, Tel Aviv did not exist and Jerusalem was an impoverished backwater. One of the founding fathers, Chaim Weizmann, commenting on the rise of Israel, famously noted that 'Difficult things take a long time, the impossible takes longer.' Yet even his lifespan of advocacy and activity has been exceeded by the duration of the intractability of the Israel–Palestine conflict. As Israel inexorably moves forward, Palestine tragically stands still.

The intention of this book is to explain the raison d'être for a state of the Jews and to elucidate the history of Israel using the yardstick of ideological debates and internal polemics. This book traces this remarkable odyssey and intends to illuminate the rationale for the path taken.

---

[9] *Ha'aretz* 4 February 2007.

CHAPTER I

Zionism and security

ZIONISM BEYOND DEMONIZATION

The course of Israel's history since the state's establishment in 1948 has been determined by two central factors, the guiding influence of a specific Zionist ideology and the need for security.

A central aim of Zionism was to safeguard the existence of the Jewish people from physical extinction and persecution on the one hand, and assimilation and disintegration on the other. The establishment of a state of Israel in the Land of Israel in 1948 was the most prominent realization of Zionism. A probable majority of the world's Jews identify with Israel as a spiritual centre – unlike any other diaspora and their mother country. Still others would argue that Zionism was more than the transient desire for a state; it was the ideal to build a perfect society.

Today, however, Zionism is often depicted in pejorative and satanic terms, as an appendage of imperialism and an offshoot of colonialism. Just as the Jews historically proved difficult to fit into political and theological theory, the uniqueness of Zionist ideology has meant that it is often easier to demonize it. The fog of the propaganda war surrounding the tortuous Israel–Palestine conflict has also aided in the intellectual burial of Zionism. Yet before 1948, it attracted the support, not only of large numbers of Jews, but also of the progressive intelligentsia. Bertrand Russell,[1] Jean-Paul Sartre and Aneurin Bevan[2] all embraced the Zionist cause, not simply as a haven for the persecuted, but because a state for the Jews offered the prospect of building a new society, free from Europe's flaws. Even Trotsky in Mexican exile expressed interest in the Yishuv, the Jewish settlements in Palestine.[3] His biographer Isaac Deutscher admitted his regret that he had not urged

---

[1] Bertrand Russell, *Zionism and the Peace Settlement in Palestine: A Jewish Commonwealth in Our Time* (Washington 1943) p. 18.
[2] Michael Foot, *Aneurin Bevan 1945–1960* (London 1975) p. 653.
[3] *Davar* 6 July 1956; Joseph Nedava *Trotsky and the Jews* (Philadelphia 1971) pp. 206–207.

Jews to leave for Palestine because 'I might have saved some of the lives that were later extinguished in Hitler's gas chambers'.[4] The Zeitgeist of post-war Europe led the international Left to strongly endorse the right of the Jews to national self-determination in Palestine. The establishment of the state of Israel in 1948 was partly understood as an act of affirmative action.[5]

Today Israel is often depicted as if it arose solely as a result of the Holocaust. Yet Zionism and the call for a state, of course, preceded the Holocaust. It was one of the many solutions proposed to ameliorate the sufferings of the Jews. Indeed, there had been a Protestant tradition which called for a return of the Jews to their ancient homeland since the Reformation. As early as 1621, Sir Henry Finch published his work *The World's Great Restauration or Calling of the Jews*. Both Napoleon and the second President of the United States, John Adams, favoured such a course.

By the late nineteenth century, Jews had begun to understand that the emancipation promised by the French Revolution had not lived up to its name. It was claimed that the case for the Jews had been argued according to logic, but not according to the reality in which the Jews found themselves. The emergence of the liberal nation state in Western Europe therefore was not always a bulwark against antisemitism, a guarantee against discrimination. By the late nineteenth century Jews were painfully realizing that whereas they truly believed that they were loyal and bone fide Frenchmen or Germans, many non-Jews did not view them in that way. Jews in public life, such as Ferdinand Lassalle, one of the founding fathers of German social democracy, often engaged in exercises of self-deprecation.

I do not like the Jews at all; indeed in general I abhor them. I see in them only degenerate sons of a great, but long past age. In the course of centuries of bondage those people acquired the characteristics of slaves, and this is why I am extremely unfavourable to them.[6]

Some, like the composer Gustav Mahler, converted and bored even deeper into the host society. Most Jews kept their heads below the parapets in an osmotic coexistence. A few, however, came to the conclusion that the answer was self-emancipation rather than emancipation by others. Following the pogroms of 1881 in Russia, Leon Pinsker wrote his book *Autoemancipation* in which he characterized the parlous situation of the Jewish Diaspora.

---

[4] Isaac Deutscher, *The Non-Jewish Jew and Other Essays* (Oxford 1968) p. 111.
[5] Arthur Hertzberg, speech to the Socialist Scholars Conference, 26 April 1992 in *Israel Horizons*, Summer/Autumn 1992.
[6] J. L. Talmon, *Israel Among the Nations* (London 1970) p. 96.

This ghostly apparition of a people without unity or organisation, without land or other bond of union, no longer alive, and yet moving among the living – this eerie form scarcely paralleled in history, unlike anything that preceded or followed it, could not fail to make a strange and peculiar impression upon the imagination of the nations. And if the fear of ghosts is something inborn, and has a certain justification in the psychic life of humanity, is it any wonder that it asserted itself so powerfully at the sight of this dead and yet living nation?[7]

Yet the possibilities for a solution to the Jewish problem were numerous – one estimate suggested that there were at least twenty-two competing ideologies.[8]

The upheavals of the nineteenth century fragmented and diversified Jewish identity. Some defined themselves by their universalism, others by their particularism. Indeed even escaping one's Jewish identity through acculturation, assimilation or conversion was so common that it too could be understood as a manifestation of Jewish identity. Some solutions posited a territorialist solution, a Zion in Palestine or a Zion in another land. One recent book carried the title *States for the Jews: Uganda, Birobidzhan and 34 Other Plans.*[9]

In 1891 the philanthropist Baron de Hirsch initiated a scheme to settle Jews in the province of Santa Fe in Argentina. In 1926, the Kremlin established the Jewish autonomous region of Birobidzhan on the border with China. In the 1930s, there was a proposal to settle Jews in Kimberley, Australia. As war approached, there were plans to save Jews from the Nazis by settling them in places as far apart as Alaska, Surinam and Tasmania. Most of these plans were stillborn, but all indicated the desire to find a territorial solution to the Jewish problem between the onset of pogroms in Russia in 1881 until the outbreak of world war in 1939.

Zionism regarded itself as the national liberation movement of the Jewish people and looked more to the French Revolution and the European Enlightenment than to the Bible. While the Zionist Left looked to the Jacobins, the Russian social revolutionaries and the Bolsheviks, the ideology of the Zionist Right was coloured by the Italian Risorgimento, Polish nationalism and Irish republicanism.

In one sense, Zionism was also a revolt against the rabbinical control of Jewish destiny. The early Zionists in Eastern Europe argued that Judaism did not have to be the sole determinant of Jewish identity, but that language,

---

7 Leon Pinsker, 'Auto-Emancipation: An Appeal to His People by a Russian Jew' in Arthur Hertzberg (ed.), *The Zionist Idea: A Historical Analysis and Reader* (Philadelphia 1997) p. 184.
8 Ezra Mendelsohn, *On Modern Jewish Politics* (Oxford 1993) p. 3.
9 Eliahu Benyamini, *States for the Jews: Uganda, Birobidzhan and 34 Other Plans* (Tel Aviv 1990).

history, literature, culture as well as religion all illustrated an unusual and rich Jewish civilization. Indeed, there was a profound difference between Jews in liberal Western Europe and those who lived under the Tsar's oppressive rule in the East. The advocate of a spiritual and cultural centre in Palestine, Ahad Ha'am, defined the acculturated existence of Jews in Western Europe as 'slavery in freedom', while those in Russia and Poland who adhered to their traditions and ideologies lived a life of 'freedom in slavery'.

The founder of the modern Zionist movement, Theodor Herzl, was an assimilated Viennese Jew, distant from his Jewishness and disdainful of the Jewish community. Yet the advent of modern antisemitism in Central Europe produced an intellectual turbulence within him which led him to the brink of converting to Christianity. Herzl reacted in particular to the antisemitism of Eugen Dühring's work *The Jewish Question as a Racial, Moral and Cultural Question*. Herzl even ominously predicted that antisemitism in Germany would be legalized.

That turbulence led him – while enjoying the musical strains of Wagner – to advance the idea that the Jews were not a marginalized, semi-tolerated, religious grouping, but a dispersed nation with a long history. The Jewish problem, he argued, could be solved for the benefit of Jews and non-Jews through the establishment of a state of the Jews.

Herzl was a strange combination of liberal pragmatist and otherworldly utopianist. Part of his revelatory tract *Der Judenstaat* ['The Jewish State'] was written during a manic flurry of scribblings, jottings and flights of fantasy – a period between 5 and 15 June 1895 when 'Herzl feared that he was losing his mind'.[10] He also dreamt of fighting a duel against Karl Lueger, the newly elected and reactionary mayor of Vienna. And if he was fortunate enough to kill his opponent, he would make a defiant speech in court condemning antisemitism in Austro-Hungary. Moreover, it was not even clear which country Herzl was specifying as the Jewish homeland. Yet this little book, 'The Jewish State', entranced the Jewish masses and gave them hope in dark times.

In Eastern Europe where the oppression of centuries had created an ethnic group which was more than the People of the Book, a small but flourishing Zionist movement looked upon Herzl's literary endeavour with astonishment and bemusement. He had never read the works of Moses Hess or Leon Pinsker or any of the progenitors of the Zionist

---

[10] Derek J. Penslar 'Herzl and the Palestinian Arabs: Myth and Counter-Myth', *Journal of Israeli History* vol.24 no.1 March 2005 pp. 65–77.

movement. Nathan Birnbaum, the coiner of the term 'Zionism', did not appear. Herzl did not speak or read Hebrew. He had no real knowledge of Judaism or Jewish history. There was no mention of Palestine and many of his views were either ill informed or absurd. Yet 'The Jewish State' lit a fire amongst the Jewish masses of Eastern Europe which the Zionist intellectuals and organizers had proved incapable of igniting despite decades of painstaking work.

Chaim Weizmann, later the first President of Israel, was originally a critic of Herzl. In his autobiography in 1949, he reflected the ambivalence of many East European activists towards Herzl.

As a personality, Herzl was both powerful and naïve. He was powerful in the belief that he had been called by destiny to this piece of work. He was naïve, as we already suspected from Der Judenstaat, and we definitely learned from our contact with his work, in his schematic approach to Zionism . . . Herzl was an organizer; he was also an inspiring personality; but he was not of the people, and did not grasp the nature of the forces which it harboured.[11]

Yet while Zionist leaders ridiculed him, Herzl's imagery moved multitudes. Without any real support behind him, he placed Zionism on the diplomatic map. He commented that his most closely kept secret was that he led 'an army of schnorrers (beggers) possessing a dream'. In 'The Jewish State', he wrote:

I would suggest a white flag with seven golden stars. The white field symbolizes our pure new life; the stars are the seven golden hours of our working day. For we shall march into the Promised Land carrying the badge of honour.[12]

For all the ridicule, Herzl changed the course of Jewish history. The historian Arthur Hertzberg noted that 'Herzl had thrown a large pebble into the pond of modern life, and the waves that he caused are still moving. In truth, he transformed the Jewish people.'[13] Herzl died in 1904 at the age of forty-four after eight years of frenetic activity. Many Jews in East European ghettoes sat 'shiva' – the traditional period of seven days of mourning – for him as if he was a member of their own family. Others were not so solemn. Many observant Jews regarded Zionism as a perverse carrier of secularism and the destroyer of religious harmony. Indeed, this fear had persuaded many famous rabbis such as Shneur Zalman of Lyady to favour the continued oppression of Tsar Alexander rather than support Napoleon's

---

[11] Chaim Weizmann, *Trial and Error* (London 1949) p. 44.

[12] Theodor Herzl, *The Jewish State: An Attempt at a Modern Solution of the Jewish Question* (London 1967) p. 72.

[13] Arthur Hertzberg, 'Theodor Herzl and Modern Zionism', *Judaism Today* no. 4 Spring 1996.

invasion in 1812. Herzl was viewed as yet another of the false messiahs that periodically peppered Jewish history. God's hand could not be forced through human intervention in returning the Jews to Zion. Ultra-orthodoxy argued that Jewish identity emanated from the Torah and the carrying out of its commandments and not from territory or language.

Many who embraced Zionism had come in from the cold of assimilation. Some had reacted against the revolutionary Left's inability to condemn popular antisemitism for fear of weakening its ties with 'the people'. The return, however, had been to a different type of Jewishness, to a secular and nationalist identity. Some rabbis were grateful that there had indeed been a return of the alienated; others such as the Lubavitcher Rebbe bitterly claimed that religion had been substituted for nationalism. The Zionists, he believed, had 'cast off the yoke of the Torah and mitzvot (commandments) and hold only to nationalism which will be their Judaism'.[14] While Herzl attempted to remain neutral towards religion and exuded respect, others such as Weizmann, versed in Jewish tradition, were determined that Zionist education should not be the domain of the orthodox and subservient to the rabbis.

Many Reform rabbis similarly wanted absolutely no truck with Jewish nationalism. The letter of the Protestrabbiner against the first Zionist Congress in 1897 protested their loyalty to Germany:

We, however, can say with complete conviction that we comprise a separate community solely with respect to religion. Regarding nationality, we feel totally at one with our fellow Germans and therefore strive towards the realization of the spiritual and moral goals of our dear fatherland with an enthusiasm equally theirs.[15]

The profound disagreement over the role of religion in the Zionist movement led to the first schisms. Weizmann formed the Democratic faction, the religious Zionists established Mizrachi and the anti-Zionist ultra-orthodox created Agudat Yisrael in 1912. Some, such as the first Chief Rabbi of Mandatory Palestine, Avraham Yitzhak Kook, disagreed with all these formulations and attempted to create a parallel religious rival. Known popularly as the rabbi of the Zionist pioneers, he was actually decidedly ambivalent towards Herzlian Zionism as he indicated in his memorial address on Herzl's death.[16] On this occasion, Kook was faced with a

[14] Ehud Luz, *Parallels Meet* (New York 1988) p. 213.
[15] Paul Mendes-Flohr and Jehuda Reinharz (eds.), *The Jew in the Modern World* (Oxford 1980) pp. 427–429.
[16] Avraham Yitzhak Kook, *When God Becomes History: Historical Essays of Rabbi Abraham Isaac Hakohen Kook*, tr. Bezalel Naor (New York 2003) pp. 3–30.

precarious balancing act. He had to appear as a Zionist to his flock, but he also had to appease the ultra-orthodox rabbis who were highly critical of Zionism and of the assimilated Herzl. Kook obliquely criticized Herzl by alluding to the late Zionist leader in his address as being 'in the footsteps of the messiah the son of Joseph'. The kabbalistic book the *Zohar* argued that the 'messiah son of Joseph' would not only be killed but would be 'desecrated and assimilated by the nations of the world'.[17] The real work of return would then be taken up by the 'messiah son of David'. Zion has the same gematria (based on numerical values given to letters of the Hebrew alphabet) as Joseph. Therefore Zionism would go the same way as 'Josephism' before being superseded by an authentic ideology.

In an open letter to the rabbis of his domain in 1912, which he never sent, Kook was scathing about modern Zionist literature:

The libraries established in our cities by the Zionist movement are mostly supplied with the new literature. A great portion of the books are written in a spirit pernicious to faith and holy sentiment. At risk are the morals of young readers who choose an extremely destructive path. The effect is insidious. In the opinion of the youth, these 'evil waters' flow from the source of Zionism, because they are imbibed in a house of culture established by the movement. Is it any wonder then that destruction of faith and religion proceed in step with the spread of Zionism?[18]

Yet Hebrew literature and the Hebrew language were the backbone of the cultural renaissance of the Jewish settlers of Palestine. A valiant and ultimately successful attempt was made to reclaim 'the holy language'. Throughout Jewish history, it had been regarded as the language of religious discourse and exposition. Jews were essentially a trilingual people. They spoke a lingua franca such as Greek or English, a language between themselves such as Aramaic or Yiddish – and Hebrew for holy matters. By 1910, according to one estimate, Palestine had less than a hundred families which spoke Hebrew.[19]

Cultural nationalism was a precursor of Zionism. The resurrection of the Hebrew language and its reclamation from being purely a language of religion was a building block of the Zionist movement. Although an early Hebrew novel was Abraham Mapu's *Ahavat Tsiyon* in 1853, Hebrew literature only began to acquire a nationalist colouring after the 1871 Odessa pogrom and most certainly after the wave of anti-Jewish violence

---

[17] Ibid. [18] Ibid.
[19] Zohar Shavit, 'Review of Nathan Efrati's *Milshon yehidim lilshon uma: hadibur ha'ivri be 'eretz Yisrael 1881–1992'* in *Ha'aretz* 19 November 2004.

in 1881–1882. Cultural nationalists such as Peretz Smolenskin, Yehuda Leib Gordon and Mendele Mocher Sefarim grew closer towards Zionism.

A transitional generation of young Hebrew writers and poets emerged from the yeshiva (religious seminary) and intentionally distanced themselves from the world of religious learning. On the other hand, they would not embrace an anti-religious secularism. Poetry became a vehicle for the transmission of their rage, directed towards the killings and expulsions of Jews – and their impotence to do anything about it. In 1899, Chaim Nachman Bialik wrote 'en kot ki rabot tzerartunu' (Nothing but Your Fierce Hounding).

> Nothing but your fierce hounding
> Has turned us into beasts of prey!
> With cruel fury
> We'll drink your blood.
> We'll have no pity
> When the whole nation rises, cries –
> 'Revenge!'[20]

Bialik's angry poems after the Kishinev pogrom in 1903 were read in Russian translation to mass audiences by young nationalists such as Vladimir Jabotinsky. Ya'akov Cahan similarly wrote a poem, 'Ha'Biryonim', after the Kishinev killings. 'In blood and fire, Judea fell, in blood and fire Judea will arise.' His words became the motto of Hashomer, the first Jewish self-defence group in Palestine, and were later taken up by Menachem Begin's Irgun.[21]

The first Jewish settlers, 'the Biluim',[22] arrived in Palestine in 1882 and established the settlement of Gedera on 3,300 dunams of land which had been purchased from the Arab village of Qatra. Only fifty-three 'Biluim' actually left Russia for Palestine.

However, the pattern of Baron de Rothschild's main settlements was on the model of European colonialist enterprises in Algeria. A fundamental break with this model came with the second wave of emigration in the wake of the Kishinev pogrom and the Russian revolution of 1905. Indeed, many of the new arrivals defined themselves as international socialists, the Zionist wing of the revolutionary movement. This was a period of mass migration

---

[20] David Aberbach, 'Hebrew Literature and Jewish Nationalism in the Tsarist Empire, 1881–1917', in Zvi Gitelman (ed.), *The Emergence of Modern Jewish Politics: Bundism and Zionism in Eastern Europe* (Pittsburgh 2003) pp. 132–150.

[21] Monty Noam Penkower, 'The Kishinev Pogrom of 1903: A Turning Point in Jewish history', *Modern Judaism* vol.24 no.3 October 2004, pp. 187–223.

[22] Biluim (Beit Yaakov Lekhu v'Nelkhah); 'House of Jacob, come and let us go' (Isaiah 2:5).

Fig. 1.1. A. Vilkovsky, a member of the Kharkov Biluim, 1885. Reproduced with kind permission from the Central Zionist archives.

of Jews, leaving behind the depressing drudgery of tsarist Russia. Over 1.2 million left for the United States. Some 30,000 left Odessa and Trieste before World War I to make a new life in Palestine. However, only one or two thousand were ideological Zionists. It was from the endeavours of this small number of activists and idealists that the state of Israel finally emerged in 1948.

Most of the immigrants were non-ideological and consisted mainly of families seeking a better life. Significantly, many were advised by Zionist organizers such as Arthur Ruppin and Menachem Sheinkin that Palestine was really no place for penniless families and that they would be better off in the USA. Although Jaffa provided a better standard of living than New York and food was cheaper, the dream of Zion was, in reality, a nightmare. The Hebrew newspaper *Hayom* reflected this reality in 1907.

Immigration to Eretz Israel, which stopped shortly before the holidays, is now returning to its previously chaotic state: People are arriving without money, without job qualifications, without preparation, without knowledge – and above all – without love for the country. Poor refugees wander through Jaffa like shadows. Roaming and cursing the day they were born, in the end opening little shops, nestled one beside the other, selling a few loaves of bread, a couple of bottles of wine, a few pounds of onions. Is it any wonder that this kind of immigration strikes no roots?

Prostitutes, pimps, swindlers and criminals frequented the points of disembarkation. The hard life eventually persuaded 75 per cent of all new arrivals to leave the country, including many of the ideological pioneers who became highly disillusioned.[23]

The few that remained were divided into two political groups, the Marxist Poale Zion and the non-Marxist Hapoel Hatzair. Poale Zion looked to Ber Borochov who attempted a synthesis between nationalism and Marxism whereas Hapoel Hatzair was influenced by Nachman Syrkin, the spokesman of socialist constructivism. He argued that Zionism, dressed in socialist garb, could belong to the entire Jewish nation. The pioneering youth of Hapoel Hatzair were also influenced by the middle-aged Tolstoyan A. D. Gordon, who was schooled in the approach that the right to the land could only be based on the labour exerted upon it. Land ownership was based on contact with the soil.

However, A. D. Gordon's criticism of Poale Zion was that socialism was simply a reflex action. The ideal of justice could not be realized through supporting the aspirations of one class but only through the embrace of the entire nation.

Socialism is so clear and smooth, so easily understood in all its phases, so very convenient for use in explaining everything in the life of man! This cannot be said of nationalism any more than it can be said of life itself. For this reason, socialism based the progress, the regeneration of human life upon the improvement of the social system, not upon the improvement and regeneration of the human spirit.[24]

Both groups set out to colonize the land rather than its Arab inhabitants. Unlike the first aliyah (period of immigration) which had based itself on the exploitation of Arab labour, the new immigrants did not wish to repeat the faults of a colonial experiment. The conquest of labour laid the basis for a separate Jewish society and economy in the hope that the Arabs would

---

[23] Zohar Shavit, 'Review of Gur Alroey's "Immigrantim"' in *Ha'aretz* 11 June 2004.
[24] A. D. Gordon, 'Nationalism and Socialism: Regarding the Clarification of Concepts', *A.D. Gordon: Selected Essays* (New York 1938).

Fig. 1.2. Kibbutz Merchavia, 1911. Reproduced with kind permission from the Central Zionist archives.

similarly construct a workers' society, free from exploitation by their notables. For the Jewish pioneers of the second aliyah, it also meant a break
with the economic structure of the past and their transformation into Jewish workers. The early townships of Zichron Ya'akov and Rishon L'Zion,
however, rebuffed such ideas. They had no desire to change their ways and
condemned the newcomers.

In June 1908, the new settlement of Kinneret was established in the
Galilee region. It immediately suffered financial problems and there were
also Bedouin attacks and outbreaks of malaria. After a year's difficulties,
the Kinneret leadership wanted to bring in cheap Arab labour to reduce
costs. There was a strike and a walkout by angry Jewish workers in October
1909. The issue was resolved solomonically. Kinneret was divided to try an
experiment in cooperative settlement. Funded by Ruppin's Palestine Land
Development Company, seven young pioneers brought into existence the
first kibbutz, Degania.

Poale Zion, however, had already begun a gradual movement away from
the European Marxism they had imbibed in Eastern Europe and adapted it

to a new geographical and political situation in the Middle East. The ditching of Borochovism in practice led to rifts. Some on the Zionist Left argued against the idea of Hebrew labour and instead for an immediate integration of Jewish and Arab workers rather than mere cooperation when workers' organizations were established. This issue became more pronounced after the October Revolution in 1917. Indeed Poale Zion split equally into pro-Communist and non-Communist camps in 1920.

In 1919, Berl Katznelson attempted to marginalize classification when he argued that 'we have no need to decide on any ideology – neither Zionist nor socialist – but only our existence as Jewish workers. That says everything'.[25] Ben-Gurion, on the other hand, while deeply impressed by Lenin and 'the moral strength inherent in communism' did not believe that the future of Zionism lay in subservience to the Soviet model. In 1924, he declared that socialist Zionists had come to Palestine not to realize Communism, but to develop the country in order to create a new nation.[26] Ben-Gurion followed a nationalist path in arguing for an 'am oved' (a working people) to be superseded by an 'am mamlachti' (a sovereign people). In this task, he called upon socialist Zionists to cooperate with whoever could help.

This was heresy to the ears of Yitzhak Tabenkin who remained a Marxist and condemned any social democratic tendencies which flirted with cooperation with capitalism. Tabenkin believed that a workers' society should be constructed to the exclusion of the bourgeoisie and the capitalists. He therefore opposed étatism and believed that the construction of the workers' society should come before any pretensions to a state. Tabenkin believed that the vehicle for constructing this new Jewish society was the kibbutz. For Ben-Gurion and Berl Katznelson, it was the Histadrut, the General Federation of Jewish Workers, and it was the workers' party, Mapai, that should be the leading force. Ben-Gurion defined the unique role of the Histadrut.

The Histadrut is not a trade union, not a political party, not a cooperative society, nor is it a mutual aid association, although it does engage in trade union activity, in politics, cooperative organisation and mutual aid. But it is much more than that. The Histadrut is a covenant of builders of a homeland, founders of a state, renewers of a nation, builders of an economy, creators of culture, reformers of

---

[25] Peretz Merchav, *The Israeli Left* (London 1980) p. 39.
[26] David Ben-Gurion, address to the conference of Achdut Ha'avodah, 1924, *Mi ma'amad le-am* (Tel Aviv 1955) p. 221.

society. And this covenant is based not on a membership card, not on legislation, but on a common fate and destiny – a commonality for life until death'.[27]

In the thirty years since Herzl's death, Zionist ideology had quickly renounced its monolithic character. At its inception, all were non-party Zionists. By the 1930s, clearly defined different interpretations of Zionist ideology had emerged. Even the non-party Zionists decided to form a party, the General Zionists. Yet each interpretation of Zionism and the path proposed for the development of the Yishuv (the Jewish settlements in Palestine) influenced the decisions taken in later years by the governing parties of the state.

David Ben-Gurion emerged as the strongman, guiding the Zionists towards their eventual goal of a state. His approach was shaped by a flexible and often ruthless pragmatism, according to the demands of a situation. In a speech at the Zionist Congress in Zurich in 1937 which addressed the question of partition into Jewish and Arab states, he said that:

The Zionist vision is rooted in the historical reality of the Jewish nation; but the external forces and circumstances condition the possibilities and methods of its realisation. These circumstances change from time to time. The changes are not produced by our lives and acts or dependent on our will – but we cannot ignore them when we are faced, from time to time, with decisions concerning our methods of action.[28]

This perhaps differentiated Ben-Gurion from the fatalism and romantic nationalism of Jabotinsky or the ideological straitjacket of Begin's military Zionism. When a Jewish state was officially discussed for the first time in 1937, there was no consensus. Even within his own party, Mapai, there was stringent opposition. From the Left, Yitzhak Tabenkin argued that the state should only be established after the conflict between the two national movements had been resolved. Establishing a state would mean prolonged conflict with the Arabs and thereby, he argued, the development of a militaristic society.

In hindsight, a state in 1937 may have saved thousands from the flames of the Holocaust, but Ben-Gurion, like many others, did not predict the unimaginable. Instead, he argued that partition advanced the cause of Zionism. Unlike Menachem Begin, but closer to Jabotinsky's thinking,

---

[27] David Ben-Gurion, 'In Anticipation of the Future, Address to the Histadrut's sixth conference January 1945' in *Mi ma'amad le-am* (Tel Aviv 1955) p. 520 quoted in Gideon Shimoni's *The Zionist Ideology* (Brandeis 1995) p. 201.

[28] David Ben-Gurion diary entry 20 July 1937; English translation in Eli Sha'altiel, 'David Ben-Gurion on Partition 1937', *Jerusalem Quarterly* no.10 Winter 1979 p. 42.

Ben-Gurion saw Zionism as an evolutionary movement based on gradualism rather than as a series of revolutionary acts.

THE NEED FOR SECURITY

If ideology divided the Zionists, the need for security derived from the Jews' unenviable journey through history, an experience common to all. Yet Zionism arose at approximately the same period in history as Arab nationalism. The need for security was therefore closely linked to Arab nationalism's acceptance or rejection of the Jews' right to be in Palestine and to fashion a national home.

Even before the Zionist influx, Jews did not fare well in the Holy Land. While Muslims had treated Jews far better than Christian Europe, they did not merit equal status. In contrast to Christianity, the Muslims did not accuse Jews of deicide. The Koran projected an ambivalent attitude towards Jews. On the one hand, they were the possessors of a holy book. On the other, they rebelled against Islam, claiming their right to religious independence. Jews were welcomed as guests in the Arab world and encouraged to practise their religion, but any assertiveness – especially national assertiveness – was frowned upon. For the mainly urban Christian Arabs, whether Greek Orthodox or Catholic, the centuries of anti-Judaism mingled with modern European antisemitism to produce a dislike of the Jews. By 1840, the blood libel had reached Damascus. In his writings on 'the eastern Question', Marx wrote in 1854:

Nothing equals the misery and suffering of the Jews at Jerusalem, inhabiting the filthiest quarter of the town, called haret-el-yahud, between Mount Zion and Mount Moriah, where their synagogues are situated – the constant objects of Mussulman oppression and intolerance, insulted by the Greeks, persecuted by the Latins and living only upon the scanty alms transmitted by their European brethren.[29]

In 1905, the Lebanese Arab nationalist Najib Azouri wrote *Le réveil de la nation arabe dans L'Asie turque*[30] in which he famously states that the Zionists and the Arab nationalists were destined to fight each other until one of them prevails. Although the conflict was probable, was it also inevitable?

---

[29] Karl Marx, *New York Daily Tribune* 15 April 1854 in Nathan Weinstock, 'Stories of Dogs', *Revue d'Histoire de la Shoah*, www.amitiesquebec-israel.org/textes/chiens.htm.
[30] Najib Azouri, *Le réveil de la nation arabe dans L'Asie turque* (Paris 1905) p. 5.

Arab nationalism had its origins in the nineteenth century, guided by the activities of figures such as Jamal al-din al-Afghani, but a national renaissance truly came about after the Young Turks revolt of 1908 and the policy of Turkification of the Arab world. Following the Young Turks revolution, there were Zionist initiatives to develop a benevolent policy based on Arab–Jewish cooperation. Yet pan-Arabism demanded a giving up of Jewish national aspirations. The Zionists regarded their nationhood, 'not as a reaction to external pressure, but as a function of vital forces within themselves. For them, it was not at bottom a question of self-defence; it was a question of self-expression.'[31]

Moreover, Palestine was also seen as the bridge between Arabia and Egypt and a Zionist presence geographically divided the Arab world. Attacks on Jews after 1908 became more decidedly nationalist in character. The separation based on labour, language, educational system and economy was viewed externally as a barrier to integration into the Arab world and its nationalist struggle.

Herzl's novel *Altneuland*, written in 1902, posits a utopian view of what the Zionists wished could have been. The novel's two central characters live for twenty years on a desert island and return only in 1923. They dock at Haifa and see a modern society. Astounded by the changes, they are told that this is due to the mass immigration of Jews. One of the new society's leaders is Rashid Bey from Haifa who waxes lyrical about the benefit of the arrival of the Jews during a tour of the Jezreel Valley. He is also proud about the tolerance shown by Muslims compared to antisemitic Christian Europe.

A nationalist rabbi, Dr Geyer, who wants to ban non-Jews from voting in the election, is depicted as the villain of the piece – and Herzl ensures in his novel that he is defeated in the election. In *Altneuland*, the Third Temple has been built and there is respect for religion on the Austro-Hungarian model. The new society has developed 'mutualism' – an ideology between capitalism and socialism. This meant the nationalization of banks, insurance companies and the stock exchange – an end to economic speculation. The state becomes secondary, almost invisible, and the development of a large cooperative society is emphasized. Even women get the vote in *Altneuland*.[32]

Herzl was inspired by other utopian writers such as Edward Bellamy and Etienne Cabet and in particular, Theodor Hertzka's *Freiland*.[33] Herzl also considered Moses Hess's Zionist work *Rome and Jerusalem* a utopian tract.

---

[31] Leonard Stein, *Zionism* (London 1925) p. 83.
[32] Uri Zilbersheid, 'The Utopia of Theodor Herzl', *Israel Studies* vol.9 no.3 2004.
[33] Zvi Shilony, *Ideology and Settlement: The Jewish National Fund 1897–1914* (Jerusalem 1998) p. 30.

As a close colleague of Marx at one period and the acknowledged father of socialist Zionism, Hess's writings were published both in Israel and East Germany in the 1950s. Herzl wrote in his diary in 1901, 'Since Spinoza, Judaism has brought forth no greater mind that this forgotten, blurred Moses Hess.'[34]

Herzl was also influenced in his vision by the Russian anarchist Prince Kropotkin and the Welsh social reformer Robert Owen. As a Zionist, Herzl did not renounce his liberal principles. He wrote:

Just to call to mind all those terrible episodes of the slave trade, of human beings who, merely because they were black, were stolen like cattle, taken prisoner, captured and sold...once I have witnessed the redemption of the Jews, my people, I wish also to assist in the redemption of the Africans.[35]

Despite this sentiment, Herzl hardly acknowledged the presence of the Arab inhabitants in the geographical area of Palestine in his writings. The writer Israel Zangwill's notion of 'a land without a nation for a nation without a land' was far more prevalent. In his letter to Yusuf al-Khalidi, a former mayor of Jerusalem, in 1899, Herzl assured him that the Zionists' intentions were benevolent and would benefit everyone.

Although Leo Motzkin had spoken about the Arabs of Palestine during the second Zionist Congress in 1898, Herzl's views, like many of the early Zionists', were anchored less in the political realities of the Middle East than specifically in the Jewish problem in Europe and the Tsarist Empire and the relationship with Palestine. As Derek Penslar has remarked, Herzl's schemes for social engineering involved Jews as well as Arabs. In 1901, he drew up a plan for a Land Company. Empowered by the Ottomans to buy land, it advocated the right to exchange economic enclaves, equal land for land in other parts of the empire, compensation for resettlement, loans for the construction of housing.[36] Although this plan never left the drawing-board, it contrasts both with Herzl's private advocacy of expropriation of Arab land in his diary entry in 1895 and his vision of a multicultural society in *Altneuland* in 1902. Even so, Rashid Bey is still the only Arab mentioned in Herzl's utopian depiction of the future. However, it indicated that a

---

[34] Theodor Herzl, *Diaries* 2 May 1901. See vol.3, ed. Alex Bein and others (Berlin 1983–1996) pp. 240–241.

[35] T. Herzl, *Altneuland* (New York 1960) p. 170.

[36] Derek J. Penslar, *Israel in History: The Jewish State in Comparative Perspective* (London 2007) pp. 51–61; Walid Khalidi, 'The Jewish-Ottoman Land Company: Herzl's Blueprint for the Colonization of Palestine', *Journal of Palestine Studies* vol.12 no.2 1993.

movement of populations and the separation of societies was a distinct possibility, however remote.[37]

Herzl's 'mutualism', taken from Proudhon's writings, provided a bridge to the socialism of the pioneers of the second aliyah.[38] Many of the early settlers exhibited a Eurocentric orientalism which Ahad Ha'am implicitly condemned in his controversial article 'Truth from the Land of Israel', following a visit to Palestine in 1891. Unlike Herzl, he recognized the Arabs as a collective rather than as individuals. Moreover, he believed that the Arabs of Palestine should be treated decently according to traditional Jewish imperatives, and condemned any approaches which would antagonize them. This initiated a different Zionist approach compared to the stand of Jabotinsky and later of Ben-Gurion. Ahad Ha'am was accused of 'batlanut', an ivory tower unworldliness.

The pioneers of the second aliyah opposed the use of violence in accordance with their socialist outlook. At the same time, they advocated separatism from the Arab sector in order that the way should not be open for mutual exploitation by plantation bosses and landowners. In addition, there was no great desire to integrate on both sides. While Islamic society did not charge Jews with deicide, there was a limit to the tolerance shown to Jews. This varied from location to location – and at different points in time. There were special taxes for Jews, they were unable to carry weapons for self-defence, synagogues often had to be smaller than mosques. This was topped by occasional massacres and incidences of forced conversions. In some Palestinian Arab towns, such as Nablus, Tulkarem and Kalkilya, no Jew had lived there for centuries. The *dhimmi* status of the Jews no doubt gave them a better quality of life compared to Christian Europe, but it did not give them equality.

Already at the 7th Zionist Congress in 1905, there were stirrings about the nature of Arab national awareness. The educator Yitzhak Epstein gave a lecture, 'A Hidden Question', in which he argued that the Zionists marginalized the question of the Arabs of Palestine. Yet he did not believe that there was an actual Arab national movement. In contrast, the proponent of 'muscular Judaism', Max Nordau, proposed an alliance with the Ottomans to outflank Arab nationalism.

[37] Derek J. Penslar, 'Herzl and the Palestinian Arabs: Myth and Counter-Myth', *Journal of Israeli History* vol.24 no.1 March 2005 pp. 65–77.

[38] Pierre Joseph Proudhon, *Système des Contradictions Economiques, ou Philosophie de La Misère* (Paris 1846); Proudhon, *De La Capacité Politique des Classes Ouvrières* (Paris 1865).

Between 1908 and 1914, both national movements began to educate themselves about the other. The journal *Falastin* published Menachem Ussishkin's *Our Programme*, while Nachum Sokolov headed a visiting delegation to Palestine to examine Arab–Zionist relations on the eve of World War I.

Poale Zion and other parts of the broad labour movement were divided on the question of cooperation with the fellahin who worked for lower wages. Following the withdrawal of Baron de Rothschild from Palestine, the parlous economic situation permitted employers to favour cheap Arab labour over unionized, organized Jewish workers. By organizing themselves as separate collectives on purchased land, the socialists believed that this would guarantee protection against land speculators and prevent Jewish and Arab capitalists from playing the fellahin off against the Jewish workers. They believed that this idea of 'Hebrew labour' would provide the basis for an independent Jewish workers' economy on nationalized land. Such collectives on contiguous land in areas of low Arab population would create the nucleus of a Jewish workers' homeland. When private enterprise failed to provide the funding for a capitalist economy, the Marxist Zionists resolved to circumvent the intermediate stage of capitalism and to construct instead one based on controlling the commanding heights of the economy. This desire was accentuated in the aftermath of the October Revolution in Russia where Bolshevik economic policy provided a template.

By excluding Arab labour from working in the Jewish sector, the early socialists believed that it would force the fellahin to work in the Arab sector and a class struggle against the Arab notables would ultimately take place. Together, the Jewish and Arab working classes would then cooperate in building a socialist society in Palestine. Ben-Gurion and others argued that the Zionists were not bringing colonialism to Palestine, but socialism. Moreover, the October Revolution would spread to and influence the Arab world. In his article 'Towards the Future', written at the beginning of World War I, Ben-Gurion argued that the Zionists neither wanted to dominate the Arabs nor to displace them – and that there was sufficient room in the country for both groups.

The socialists of Poale Zion wanted to prevent 'the combination of a national conflict with a class oriented one'.[39] The rise of Arab nationalism, opposed to a Zionist presence in Palestine, and the failure of a strong Arab

[39] Israel Kotlatt, 'The Zionist Movement and the Arabs' in Jehuda Reinharz and Anita Shapira (eds.), *Essential Papers on Zionism* (New York 1995) p. 620.

proletariat to emerge in Palestine doomed such early Zionist preconceptions. The failure of attempts to come to an agreement with the Arabs strengthened those in the Zionist movement who argued that it was in their interests to forge an alliance with the ruling power rather than with those who were opposed to it.

The defeat of the Turks, the British conquest of Palestine and the Balfour Declaration all heightened the nationalist sentiments of both Jews and Arabs. Although the Balfour Declaration had promised a national home rather than a state, there were real Arab fears about being excluded and dispossessed. The separatism of Hebrew labour, the growth of the Yishuv and the expected influx of Jewish immigrants unnerved the Arab population. There was often a contradictory approach by the Palestinian Arabs. On the one hand, the Arabs thought that they would be overwhelmed and displaced by the new arrivals. On the other, there was the belief that well-to-do Jews could improve their lives.

In Nablus, there was a deep fear that the Zionists would establish factories based on the local production of olive oil and compete for the production of soap and oil. Chaim Weizmann's professional prowess as a chemist was cited as proof of such intentions. Despite this rumour, Arab notables approached Weizmann to establish a bank in Nablus which would give long-term credit on mortgages.

Weizmann argued that Arab suspicions about Zionist intentions would not be dispelled through public relations, but 'only through the beginning of actual work in Palestine, and the association of the Arabs with that work'.[40] The British administration in Palestine fortified instead of dispelling Arab distrust of Zionist intentions. The Jewish problem and the question of Zionism were just too tangled and complicated. The Arabs, on the other hand, conformed much more to the British model of colonized natives. In a letter to his wife, Weizmann berated the archetypal British colonial bureaucrat in Palestine:

[He] naturally makes the best possible use of such a state of things in order to render the position of the Jewish intruder untenable, and make it so hot for him that he should be forced to resign. The life of the Jewish employees in the police, postal service, on the railways, customs house, and finally in the government offices on the Mount of Olives, is positively a martyrdom, and they have to work and live constantly in an atmosphere of tension and extreme provocation.[41]

---

40 Chaim Weizmann, letter to Lord Curzon 2 February 1920.
41 Chaim Weizmann, letter to Vera Weizmann 21 March 1920.

While liberals such as Weizmann and socialists such as Ben-Gurion believed that all was not lost, the opposing view was expounded by Vladimir Jabotinsky, the leader of the emerging nationalist camp. A romantic nationalist in the tradition of the early nineteenth century, he opposed both expulsion and ethnic cleansing. As a fatalist, he noted that in the past such situations would inevitably give rise to conflict between the two peoples. In two articles in 1923, 'The Iron Wall' and 'Beyond the Iron Wall', Jabotinsky argued that it was self-deluding to assume that the Palestinian Arabs would give 'voluntary consent' to the creation of a Jewish majority and that no compensation would therefore be adequate. Moreover, it did not matter how well the Zionists behaved; the local population would resist. Jabotinsky wrote:

We may tell them whatever we like about the innocence of our aims, watering them down and sweetening them with honeyed words to make them palatable, but they know what we want, as well as we know what they do not want. They feel at least the same instinctive jealous love of Palestine as the old Aztecs felt for ancient Mexico and the Sioux for their rolling prairies.[42]

Many on the Left vehemently disagreed with Jabotinsky's black and white attitude and believed that a modus vivendi with the Palestinian Arabs was still possible. They argued that there was a difference between colonialism and colonization, between expropriation and the purchase of land. The situation was complex not simple. Socialists and liberals recoiled at Jabotinsky's almost brutal commentary. Its bluntness destroyed dreams. They refused to consider such a bleak future of conflict concluding when the exhausted Arabs would agree to compromise. Violence was not inevitable, they reasoned, if Jewish–Arab relations were sensitively managed. The Left was still convinced that solidarity between the workers would win out in the end and triumph over naked nationalism. Others, however, welcomed this approach as unashamedly honest and a portent of things to come. Still others remained silent on the question of a local Arab nationalism emerging in Palestine.

Jabotinsky's arguments implied a national character of the resistance to Zionism, both on a local level and within Arab nationalism in general. The hostility of Arab nationalism, he argued, prevented Zionism from supporting the national aspirations of any Arab movement or even contemplating joining an Arab federation. Jewish settlement in Palestine would have to be

---

[42] Vladimir Jabotinsky, 'The Iron Wall', *Rassvet* 4 November 1923.

Fig. 1.3. The departure of the British High Commissioner, Sir John Chancellor, from Palestine, 2 September 1931. Reproduced with kind permission from the Central Zionist archives.

protected by a defence force – whether Jewish or British – an 'Iron Wall' which would repulse attempts to eradicate the Zionist project.

As long as the Arabs feel that there is the least hope of getting rid of us, they will refuse to give up this hope in return for kind words or for bread and butter, because they are not a rabble, but a living people. And when a living people yields in matters of such a vital character, it is only when there is no longer any hope of getting rid of us, because they can make no breach in the Iron Wall. Not till then will they drop their extremist leaders whose watchword is 'never'. And the leadership will pass to the moderate groups who will then approach us with a proposal that we should both agree to mutual concessions. Then we may expect them to discuss honestly practical questions such as a guarantee against displacement, equal rights for Arab citizens, Arab national integrity.[43]

JEWISH SOCIALISM AND ARAB NATIONALISM

In the inter-war years, the industrialization of Palestine and increased Jewish immigration under the British Mandate produced prosperity for both peoples. The Arab population in Palestine grew twice as swiftly as

[43] Ibid.

those of Syria and Lebanon. Tens of thousands of Arabs entered Palestine from surrounding countries increasing the Arab population by over 8 per cent. These dramatic changes disrupted feudal Palestinian Arab society and partially urbanized an essentially agricultural community. But when an Arab middle class emerged, it proved too weak to provide economic homes for the new Arab proletariat and those who had left – voluntarily or involuntarily – their rural villages. The disruption of their way of life with no suitable replacement, with accompanying impoverishment and dispossession, sowed the seeds of bitterness which grew into a radicalized Palestinian Arab nationalism. It not only provided the resentment needed to fuel the Arab national revolt of 1936, but also supplied support for the Islamist Izz al-din al Qassam. While violence cemented separation between the two communities, it also permitted the Zionists to deepen it. Thus, Jewish Tel Aviv was developed as a port when neighbouring Arab Jaffa was closed during the disturbances of 1936.

The policy of Hebrew labour thereby unintentionally grew into a national and cultural separation, a precursor for partition.

Complete integration of the two economies would have meant the reproduction of classical colonialism, but complete separation led to the strengthening of the anti-Zionist opposition to a far greater degree than the Zionist movement anticipated.[44]

A political philosophy which was supposed to prevent colonialism and exploitation instead produced a boycott of Arab labour – to the extent that the Histadrut initiated a campaign to remove Arab workers from the Jewish sector in the 1930s and exhorted Jews to volunteer for work in the fields. It was argued that if it was demonstrated that vacancies in the Jewish economy could be filled by Arab labour, then the British would utilize this to prevent Jewish immigration from Nazi Germany. While the Shaw Commission, the Hope-Simpson Report and the Passfield White Paper in 1930 had all criticized the principle of dual economies and the idea of an absorptive capacity in the Jewish sector, the threat still remained that such ideas would be implemented by the colonial power. The merger of Achdut Ha'avodah and Hapoel Hatzair to form Mapai in 1930 also decreased the ability of the Zionist Left to argue for Arab–Jewish solidarity. The mass killing of Jews in Hebron and Safed in 1929 further dampened any Zionist initiative. Ben-Gurion's private belief that an Arab national movement was probably emerging began to supplant his public proclamation of the traditional Achdut Ha'avodah approach of the class solution.

[44] Simcha Flapan, *Zionism and the Palestinian Arabs* (London 1979) p. 227.

The idea that there would be both a Jewish Histadrut and an Arab Histadrut began to fade in the face of the reality. Yet the Histadrut did help organize Arab workers in the national sector of the economy and supported them in industrial protests. Nationalism, however, proved more durable, a more potent force than class solidarity. In early 1935, the Histadrut offered funds to striking Arab workers in a conflict with the Iraq Petroleum Company, but the offer was rejected.[45]

Zionism originally did not envisage two totally different rates of development between the Jewish and Arab sectors. Such a disparity, however, proved too tempting for those who embraced an expansionist Zionism – and particularly in the face of Arab rejectionism.[46] While the Zionists had purchased less than 10 per cent of the often uncultivated land by the 1930s, over 250 Arab notable families controlled huge tracts of territory. The situation of the fellahin in Palestine was similar to that in other Arab countries where a third were landless or below the subsistence level. The landlords also controlled the crushing debt which weighed down on the shoulders of the fellahin. In 1930, the average debt was £27 per annum, 'a sum equal to his annual income and the debt charges amounted to one third of his income'.[47] Although Arab agricultural production had increased fivefold by the mid-1930s, it did not benefit the fellahin. Instead, land purchase from other Arabs by notables – including many involved in nationalist organizations such as the Supreme Muslim Council and the Muslim–Christian Associations – increased in the 1930s. Such territory was then sold on to the Zionists at much higher prices. During the period of the British Mandate, the Zionists paid some £10 million to Arab notables for land purchase, yet this served to enrich only the landlords and contradicted the idea that the Zionist experiment in Palestine would benefit all.[48]

Moreover, over half the land was bought from non-Palestinian Arabs, but only 9.4 per cent was purchased from the fellahin themselves.[49] The British, through the Johnson-Crosbie and the French reports, attempted to examine the state of Arab agriculture, the urbanization of the workers and landlessness in the early 1930s. A register of landless Arabs found that only 20 per cent of the 3,271 applications for resettlement were accepted by the

---

[45] Ibid. p. 208.

[46] Gershon Shafir, 'Israeli Decolonization and Critical Sociology', *Journal of Palestine Studies* vol.25 no.3 Spring 1996 p. 28.

[47] Ibid. p. 210.   [48] Ibid. p. 214.

[49] Yehoshua Porath, 'The Land Problem in Mandatory Palestine', *Jerusalem Quarterly* no.1 1976 pp. 18–27.

British Director of Development, Lewis French.[50] Despite all this, the Zionist movement never applied itself to examine and soften the blow that industrialization brought to the fellahin. In part, this was due to indifference caused by separation, but there was also a vested interest in ensuring that the fellahin moved to the cities, leaving the land free for purchase.

Ben-Gurion was evasive about the causes of the early Arab disturbances in 1920 and 1921. He also disagreed with Jabotinsky's 'Iron Wall' exposition. In 1924, he supported Tabenkin's position at the Ein Harod conference that there was no Arab national movement since it was devoid of progressive content. On one level, he differed from Tabenkin in wishing to have more cooperation rather than separation. On another, he pressed forward in creating a separate economy. The killings of 1929 propelled him towards a recognition of a national movement in Palestine – 'one droplet of the Arab people'.[51] He proposed an administrative parity between Jews and Arabs.

The massacres of 1929 and the outbreak of the Arab revolt in 1936 brought home the reality of two colliding national movements to both Ben-Gurion and Weizmann. The evolving Palestinian national movement was now very much in the hands of the Mufti of Jerusalem and his Husseini clan which projected a rejectionist and absolutist approach. During the 1920s, figures such as Chaim Kalvarisky attempted to build a dialogue with other Palestinian notables such as the Nashashibi family. There were ongoing discussions with Abdullah, the Emir of TransJordan. Ideas of a federation were mooted. And yet there was no real advance towards peace and reconciliation. It slowly began to dawn upon the Zionist leadership that the much hoped-for Arab democratization might not happen. There would be no strong Arab proletariat, free of the notables and the seduction of nationalism. Moreover, the old Arab leadership was dying out and being replaced by a new generation of radicalized nationalists which wished to fight both the Zionists and the British. As other nation states in the Arab world began to achieve their independence, they asked, why should Palestine be different?

The Arab middle class that had emerged was economically weak. While many Palestinian Arabs benefited from the growth in the Jewish economic sector, the industrialization of Palestine in the inter-war years disrupted the

---

[50] Yehoshua Porath argues that while French's definition of landless Arabs entitled to resettlement was restrictive, the register was compiled during the boom years in Palestine. Many displaced Palestinian Arabs had found jobs in other areas of the expanding economy. Although Porath believes that French's figure was low, he estimates the true figure as 'under four thousand'.

[51] Shabtai Teveth, *Ben-Gurion and the Palestinian Arabs* (Oxford 1985) pp. 93–94.

lifestyle of a hitherto agricultural community. Urbanization was a source of not only economic betterment, but also of profound embitterment. In this period, the very idea of cooperation, compromise and workers' solidarity was challenged by the growing tension of everyday life. The belief that two autonomous societies acting in harness could construct a magical new society seemed to be dramatically receding in the face of a dark reality. While this aspiration was not abandoned, the Zionists devoted more effort to their own agenda. Ben-Gurion and his party, Mapai, emphasized immigration, the construction of settlements and a Jewish economy while Jabotinsky's Revisionists preferred dramatic declarations for a Jewish majority on both sides of the river Jordan.

During the first half of the 1930s, the Jewish population of Palestine more than doubled due to an influx of immigrants from Nazi Germany and Poland. In addition, many on the Zionist Left now began to note the influence of authoritarian European regimes in the Arab world. It was not Mazzini who was the paradigm, but Mussolini. On one level, this was a reaction to British and French imperialism on the basis of 'the enemy of my enemy is my friend'. For the Zionists, however, Arab nationalism appeared to be embracing the dictatorial Right in Europe. If Zionism had emanated from a period when European nationalism was on the Left during the first half of the nineteenth century, it seemed that Arab nationalism now owed its allegiance to an epoch when nationalism had been embraced by reactionary and illiberal forces.

The Arab revolt was directed against the British because an end to the Mandate would also mean an end to the Zionist experiment. Palestinian Arab nationalism perceived Zionism to be solely an extension of British colonialism. The revolt symbolized the end of a common Arab–Jewish interest in a negotiated solution in a real sense; the future was now framed by the violence of armed conflict. The Zionists turned to building their national home and cooperating with the British. There was a resignation that the spirit of the times did not lend itself to compromise and moderation. The conflict became simplified, a question of them or us. When the Peel Commission visited Palestine in 1937 to investigate the Arab revolt, the Mufti was asked what would happen to the 400,000 Jews in the country in the event of an agreement between the Palestinian Arabs and the British. The Mufti responded that it would be 'a matter for the government that will be formed to deal with at the appropriate time. Its principle will be justice, and above all else it will concern itself with the interests and benefit of the country.' To another question, he replied that it was unlikely that the country could assimilate the Jews. The Peel Commission then asked what the logical outcome might therefore be.

Q. Some of them would have to be removed by a process kindly or painful as the case may be?

A. We must leave all this to the future.[52]

In response, the Peel Commission, in true British understatement, noted the tragic fate of the Assyrians in Iraq in 1933 despite treaty provisions and explicit assurances.

Nazi agents worked with leading notables in Palestine in the late 1930s and they exhibited 'great sympathy for the new Germany and its Fuhrer'. The German Consulate viewed a Jewish presence in Palestine as being an 'additional power base for international Jewry' and therefore it was in German national interests to 'strengthen the Arabs as a counter-weight'. Such cooperation unnerved the British authorities who cancelled a plan to bring 20,000 Jewish refugees from Nazi Germany to Palestine.[53]

Many leaders of the mainstream Palestinian national movement, including Fawzi al Qawuqji who commanded the Arab Liberation Army in Palestine in early 1948, spent the war years in Berlin. If Mussolini's armies in September 1940 had pressed on to Cairo, they would have been welcomed as liberators by the Egyptians. As Anwar Sadat commented, 'except for ill-luck, we would have joined forces with the Axis, struck a quick blow at the British, and perhaps won the war'.[54] The revolutionary underground in Egypt was in contact with German headquarters in Libya. Sadat himself was arrested by British counter-espionage at a meeting with two Nazi agents, seconded by the Afrika Corps in Cyrenaica. The Nazi connection further helped to cement negative stereotypes of conspiratorial Jews within pan-Arab nationalism – even Nasser was later to recommend the Protocols of the Elders of Zion.[55] Arab poetry in the Mandate period which featured the question of Palestine was often derogatory towards Jews per se and sometimes utilized unsavoury imagery of Jews in religious tradition.[56] Had it not been for the victory at El Alamein, SS Obersturmbannfuhrer Walter Rauff would have ordered his Einsatzkommando to liquidate the Jews of Palestine. The Nazis expected local participation in their actions.

The events of the 1930s moved Ben-Gurion and the Labour Zionist movement closer towards Jabotinsky's fatalism. There was a sense that Palestinian Arab rejectionism was all-pervading and regardless of any

[52] Zvi Elpeleg, *The Grand Mufti: Haj Amin al-Husseini: Founder of the Palestinian National Movement* (London 1993) pp. 45–46.

[53] Yaakov Lappin, *YNet News* 7 May 2006.   [54] Anwar Sadat, *Revolt on the Nile* (London 1957) p. 38.

[55] R.K. Karanjia, 'Interview with Nasser', *Blitz* 4 October 1958.

[56] S. Abraham, 'The Jew and the Israeli in Modern Arabic Literature', *Jerusalem Quarterly* no.2 Winter 1977 pp. 117–136.

moves that the Zionists made – generous or not – the die had already been cast. But despite all the passionate proclamations of Jabotinsky, it was Ben-Gurion and Mapai who had power in the Yishuv to make the decisions that would determine future history.

In the face of Arab attacks, Ben-Gurion's policy of havlagah – military self-restraint – was short-lived. The Haganah was unable to provide an adequate response to the killing of Jews and the burning of fields. While both Jabotinsky and Weizmann had reservations about retaliating, others took action. As early as March 1937, far Right radicals threw a bomb into an Arab coffee house outside Tel Aviv. On 'Black Sunday', 14 November 1937, the Irgun organized attacks on Arab buses and shops.[57] The slow demise of havlagah marked the end of the old Zionist dream. It was replaced by one coloured by the necessity and worship of military endeavour.

On the Right, Jabotinsky's emphasis on diplomacy and belief in England was pushed aside by Menachem Begin's doctrine of military Zionism. On the eve of World War II, the Polish military had already started to train members of the Irgun in camps in Poland. The Iron Wall was now interpreted differently by the radicalized Zionist Right:

We must create the bayonets – and many of them. We must prepare ourselves for a decisive struggle on a scale and with methods different from those that even we 'militarists' imagined. And therefore the formula from now on must not be 'defence training' but 'military training'.[58]

The Labour movement responded in kind in cooperating with the British through Orde Wingate's night squads and Yitzhak Sadeh's field battalions. Sadeh, a Red Army veteran, had argued the case in 1936 for 'breaking out of the perimeter' and the 'plugot ha'Sadeh' – mobile military units – were established in December 1937. The passage from the Book of Nechemiah, 'with one of his hands wrought in the work, and with the other hand held a weapon',[59] was elevated to the status of a motivating slogan. There were now reprisals by 'special operations' units against Arab villages which harboured assailants. Like the Zionist Right, the Left now moved from a purely defensive mode to Wingate's 'aggressive defensive' approach. Sadeh inculcated the idea of military prowess amongst the youth, typified by Moshe Dayan and Yigal Allon who would emerge as major military and political figures. It was on Sadeh's initiative that the Palmach was created in 1941 as an elite unit to repulse Arab attacks. Indeed

---

57 Colin Shindler, *The Triumph of Military Zionism: Nationalism and the Origins of the Israeli Right* (London 2006) pp. 194–196.
58 Yaakov Weinshal, *Hadam Asher Basaf* (Tel Aviv 1978) p. 115.   59 Nechemiah 4:11.

Dayan lost his eye in a British-backed advance into Vichy Syria. The British saw the Palmach as a potential guerrilla force if Rommel conquered Palestine and a bulwark against the pro-German Palestinian national movement. Over 25,000 Jews served in the British forces during the war despite the reluctance of Whitehall to accept them. The mainstream Palestinian Arab leadership spent the war years in Germany, hoping for a Nazi victory.

With the defeat of German forces at El Alamein, the British attempted to disband the Palmach since it no longer served their interests. There was a reversion to the proposals of the 1939 White Paper where the Jews were expected to remain a permanent minority in Palestine. Immigration would be dependent on Arab goodwill. At a time when Jews were desperately attempting to find ways out of Nazi-occupied Europe, this marked a turning point in Zionist relations with the British. Instead the Palmach disappeared into Achdut Ha'avodah's kibbutzim where Yitzhak Tabenkin structured a deal based on agricultural work and military training.

The period between 1936 and 1948 had dramatically weakened Palestinian Arab society and its ability to conduct military operations. By contrast, the Zionists gained experience, training and the military resolve to fight. The Palmach under Yigal Allon and Yitzhak Sadeh as the Chief of the General Staff of the Haganah not only laid the military foundations for the inevitable clash with both Palestinian and Arab nationalism in 1948, it also promoted the voice of the military in Israeli politics as more than a subservient advisor to the elected representatives of the people.

Ben-Gurion's lack of ideological rigidity allowed him to go along with this development even though he was concerned that his rival, Tabenkin, had effectively established a separate military force. The Biltmore agreement in New York in 1942 gave priority to a Jewish state over peace with the Arabs. The realization of the enormity of the Holocaust cemented that priority. The formation of the Arab League after the war reflected Arab determination to continue the struggle against the Zionists in Palestine. The probability of violence turned into the inevitability of conflict after UN Resolution 181 achieved a majority for a two-state solution on 29 November 1947. It was a struggle between two national movements, between a resurgent Israel and the Arab world. With the weight of history – and in particular recent history – on their shoulders, it was a struggle which the Jews understood they could not afford to lose.

CHAPTER 2

The Hebrew republic

THE END OF EMPIRE

The Declaration of Independence of the state of Israel on 14 May 1948 was one brief episode in an unravelling drama of survival for Palestine's Jews who were engaged in an increasingly bitter conflict with the Arab world. In his diary, Ben-Gurion wrote:

At eleven o'clock, Katriel [Katz] announced that Gush Etzion had fallen. The women were sent to Jerusalem and the men taken prisoner...At one o'clock, the People's Council approved the draft of the Declaration of Independence. At four o'clock, the [public] declaration.[1]

The ceremony at the Tel Aviv museum was hastily arranged. There was even indecision about the name of the new state, perhaps Judea, perhaps Ivriya.[2] Eventually, the designation of 'a state of Israel' in the Land of Israel was agreed.[3] The previous day Yigal Yadin, the head of operations for the Haganah, had told the National Administration that despite the arrival of Czech arms, in the absence of heavy weapons the prospects of the Jewish state surviving an invasion of Arab states were fifty-fifty.[4] Israel Galili, the head of the Haganah's territorial command, was similarly not optimistic about the future. Golda Meir had reported on her meeting with King Abdullah of Jordan and informed the National Administration that he now aligned himself with popular forces in the Arab world, calling for an invasion. As Mordechai Bentov later wrote in his memoirs: 'To most of us, it was not clear we would win, whereas if we were to fail – we, the members

---

[1] David Ben-Gurion, *Yoman ha-milhamah: milhemet ha-'atsmaut* (Tel Aviv 1982) 14 May 1948 p. 414.
[2] Interview with Arieh Handler 15 March 1998. The name 'Israel' had been chosen provisionally on 25 April.
[3] This had been proposed by Aharon Reuveni, the Hebrew writer and brother of Yitzhak Ben-Zvi, the second President of Israel, in an article in *Moznayim* 5 December 1947. *Ha'aretz* 1 May 2006.
[4] Provisional People's Executive 12 May 1948, *Protocols* 18 April–13 May 1948 (Jerusalem 1978).

of the government, would be the first the Arabs would hang in the middle of Allenby Square.'[5]

The US State Department was exerting pressure to delay statehood in favour of its own plan for a trusteeship. Its suspicion that any takeover by left-wing Zionists would provide a base for Soviet influence in the Middle East had been enhanced by the Czechoslovak coup d'état by local Communists. The long deliberations and reticence of the Zionists also reflected the psychological gap between their official ideology and their awe in taking a step into an uncertain future. It was a quantum leap in fundamentally changing the Jewish condition. After all, in their long history the Jews had spent more time dispersed in exile than concentrated in their own sovereign territory. Diaspora was a more natural condition than statehood. Indeed, Sir Herbert Samuel, a member of the British cabinet, argued in a private memorandum to his colleagues in government in January 1915:

To attempt to realize the aspiration of a Jewish state one century too soon might throw back its actual realization for many centuries more.[6]

Yet Samuel had neither predicted the swift rise and deep opposition of Arab nationalism nor foreseen the Holocaust. Times were profoundly different. Although no vote was taken, a decision was taken to issue a declaration of independence of a sovereign state of the Jews.

At four o'clock on that Friday afternoon, Ben-Gurion read out the Declaration of Independence to the invited audience. He recalled the tortuous odyssey of the Jews through history, from the conquests of King David to the mass extermination at the hands of the Nazis. The emergence of Zionism was recast as taking place at the end of millennia of degradation and suffering. Under Herzl's portrait, Ben-Gurion proclaimed the establishment of 'the Jewish State in Palestine' to applause from the audience and from the crowds outside the museum. It had taken all of thirty-two minutes to establish the third Jewish Commonwealth.[7]

Ben-Gurion's almost matter-of-fact statement on the establishment of a Hebrew republic after almost two millennia was symptomatic of a wider preoccupation by Israelis with basic survival. The previous day, the isolated four settlements in the Gush Etzion bloc – Massuot Yitzhak, Ein Zurim, Revadim and Kfar Etzion – were ordered to surrender by the Haganah.[8]

---

[5] Mordechai Bentov in Mordechai Naor, 'Those Heady Days in May', *Ha'aretz* 2 May 2006.

[6] Herbert Samuel, 'The Future of Palestine', memorandum to the British cabinet, January 1915. Samuel Archives, St Anthony's College, Oxford.

[7] Ze'ev Sharef, *Three Days* (London 1962) pp. 281–289.

[8] Benny Morris, *The Road to Jerusalem: Glubb Pasha, Palestine and the Jews* (London 2003) pp. 137–140.

The defenders of Kfar Etzion, ninety-seven men and twenty-seven women, were then killed by local Arab irregular forces on 13 May and their homes looted.[9] It made no difference that the Transjordanian Arab Legion which was responsible for the safety of the prisoners was nominally under British command. Sir John Glubb – Glubb Pasha – the commander of the Arab Legion later claimed that 'not a single Jew was killed at Kfar Etzion'.[10]

The sense of trepidation and fatigue overcame any jubilation at independence. Yitzhak Rabin remembered the exhausted members of his unit simply switching off the radio broadcast of Ben-Gurion's proclamation. The very idea of another four or five fronts opening up through the invasion of the Arab states filled most Israelis with fear and dread.

We were frail corks, being used to stop up hundreds of holes in a leaky dam, that a flood of our enemies might be expected at any time to overwhelm and drown us. There were never enough of us, and so many had already been killed. As fast as we stopped one leak, we would be withdrawn and rushed somewhere else to plug another.[11]

Ben-Gurion ended his diary entry with the observation that he had refrained from rejoicing – as he had done when the United Nations voted for a two-state solution. Dancing in the streets of Tel Aviv was accompanied by the sound of Egyptian bombers dropping their payload on the celebrants.

For the British, the exit from Palestine was a mixture of relief and remorse. The departing High Commissioner, Sir Alan Cunningham, believed that they had tried their best in impossible circumstances. He had proposed allowing displaced persons (DPs) into Palestine if they could show that they had relatives in Palestine, but this was rejected by the British government. Throughout 1948, the British had gradually diminished their presence in the Holy Land and withdrawn their forces piecemeal towards the port of Haifa. The Municipality had even laid on a farewell reception at the Zion Hotel. However, when General MacMillan was informed about the disappearance of three Cromwell tanks from the local airport, he blamed the Israelis and refused to come to the lunch. The Mayor of Haifa, Shabtai Levy, instead dined with the general on board a British cruiser in Haifa Bay. Such pleasantries masked a mutual animosity. There was a widespread suspicion that the British were intent on remaining in the

9 Kfar Etzion, Massuot Yitzhak and Ein Zurim were settlements established by the labour wing of the religious Zionists, Hapoel Hamizrachi. Revadim was a kibbutz established by the Marxist–Zionist Hashomer Hatzair.
10 *Times* 2 July 1968.   11 Lynne Reid Banks, *Torn Country* (New York 1982) p. 142.

Middle East by manipulating the Jordanian monarch and controlling the Arab Legion – now only tens of kilometres outside Tel Aviv. Indeed, they had prevented Jewish men of fighting age from leaving Aden for Palestine.[12] In a speech to the Provisional State Council, Ben-Gurion condemned British covert assistance to the invading states. He told his audience that according to captured documents, Haifa was to have fallen on 20 May, Tel Aviv and Jerusalem five days later. Abdullah would enter Jerusalem and be crowned king of a Greater Jordan.[13]

In the twilight of empire, British attitudes towards the Jews were mixed. Some saw the Jews as conspiratorial parasites in the tradition of the medieval usurer. Others perceived them as dangerous subversives who looked to Moscow. Yet still others were sympathetic to Zionist aspirations as a reaction to the revelations of the Shoah (Holocaust). Regardless of personal feelings, successive British administrations in Palestine had demonstrated their belief that economic interests pushed them inexorably towards the Arab world. Many believed that the window of opportunity for the Zionists, briefly opened by Lloyd-George and Balfour, was a mistake of monumental proportions and muddied the waters between Britain and the Arab world.

While the Zionists acknowledged that the British had watched over the construction of the Jewish settlement in Palestine and generously permitted the immigration of hundreds of thousands of Jews in the inter-war period, their sense of abandonment by Britain in their time of need was all-pervasive. After 1945, the reinforcement of the terms of the pre-war White Paper diminished any lingering respect for Weizmann's anglophilic diplomacy. In contrast, the Irgun's Menachem Begin found a ready audience for his nationalist castigation of the British.

For hundreds of years, you have been whipping 'natives' in your colonies – without retaliation. In your foolish pride you regard the Jews in the Land of Israel as natives too. You are mistaken. Zion is not exile. You will not whip Jews in their homeland. And if the British Authorities whip them – British officers will be whipped publicly in return.[14]

Ben-Gurion had alluded to the same point in a speech in May 1942: '[British officials] feel themselves much more at ease in dealing with Arabs

---

[12] Tudor Parfitt, *The Road to Redemption: The Jews of the Yemen 1900–1950* (Leiden 1996) p. 186.
[13] David Ben-Gurion, speech to the third session of the Provisional State Council, 3 June 1948 in David Ben-Gurion, *Rebirth and Destiny of Israel* (London 1959) p. 241.
[14] Menachem Begin, *The Revolt* (London 1979) p. 311.

1. United Nations Partition Plan, 29 November 1947.

and administering to their needs, where they could indulge their colonial habits of maintaining the status quo.'[15]

The withdrawal from India and Palestine initiated a new, but very different role in the world. The transition from empire to commonwealth was not easy – and Jews in Britain became victims of a rising anger, resulting from the military attacks of the Irgun. In an editorial in January 1947, the *Sunday Times* criticized British Jews for 'not performing their civic duty and moral obligation'[16] despite widespread Jewish opposition to the Irgun's campaign. Following the hanging of Sergeants Martin and Paice by the Irgun, there had been rioting in several major British cities in August 1947. Five days of attacks in Liverpool had damaged 300 Jewish properties and in West Derby a synagogue had been burned down.[17] Whereas the United States had taken eleven minutes after the end of the Mandate to accord de facto recognition, Britain took over eight months. Indeed, the Board of Deputies of British Jews repeatedly called upon the Atlee government to recognise the state of Israel and condemned government policy for funding and arming the invading Arab armies.[18]

DEFEAT AND VICTORY IN 1948

In 1920, Ben-Gurion had written about Jewish and Arab workers living 'a life of harmony and friendship'.[19] In 1931, he argued that Zionists had not come to Palestine to dispossess its inhabitants, but that they were an organic, inseparable part of the country. By 1947, Ben-Gurion was bemoaning the absolute nature of Arab opposition and its Islamist colouring – 'they want to treat us as they do the Jews of Baghdad, Cairo and Damascus'.[20] The 1930s perhaps saw the last possibility of a rapprochement between Zionist Jews and Palestinian Arabs slip away. The deepening national conflict persuaded both sides to harden their hearts and decide that there could be only one winner in this contest. Ideas for limiting Jewish sovereignty such as Martin Buber and Judah Magnes's proposals for a bi-national state or Hashomer Hatzair's proposition of communal federalism fell on stony ground in the post-war period. Moreover, there was little Arab response. As Sharett pointed out, 'for such a solution to be

[15] David Ben-Gurion, 'Palestine in the Post-war World', speech to an extraordinary Zionist Conference, New York, 9 May 1942 (London 1942).
[16] *Sunday Times* 5 January 1947. [17] *Jewish Chronicle* 8 August 1947.
[18] Shneur Levenberg, *The Board and Zion* (Hull 1985) pp. 151–152.
[19] David Ben-Gurion, 'Al Ha'falakh ve'admato' (1920) in *Anakhnu veshkheneynu* (Tel Aviv 1931) p. 56.
[20] David Ben-Gurion, statement to the Elected Assembly of Palestine Jewry 2 October 1947.

operative, presupposes two collective wills acting, by and large, in unison'.[21]
Those Arabs who did express support for the Jewish Left such as Fawzi
Darwish al-Husseini and Fahmi Taha were killed by the Mufti's agents.

This sentiment of a zero-sum conflict was transformed into all-out war
by United Nations Resolution 181 which partitioned Palestine into two
states. This was immediately rejected by the Palestinian Arabs and six
out of seven members of the Arab League. Only Abdullah's TransJordan
abstained.

Up until the declaration of independence of the state of Israel, a bitter
civil war between Zionist Jews and Palestinian Arabs took place in the first
half of 1948 where both sides evacuated villages at strategic points. Until
May 1948, the Arabs probably exercised 'an overall edge in men-under-
arms – 15,000–30,000' compared to 15,000-25,000 mobilized by the
Zionists.[22] In the war between Israel and the Arab states which followed
in May 1948, the Arabs initially exhibited an overwhelming superiority in
aircraft and heavy weaponry.

The Israelis had two tanks, one of them without a gun; and one, then two, batteries of light pre-World War I vintage 65 mm Mountain artillery; and makeshift
armoured cars, civilian trucks patched up with steel plates in Tel Aviv workshops.[23]

At the beginning of 1948, 75,000 Arabs took flight and this was followed
in April and May by the fall of major towns such as Tiberias, Haifa,
Safed and Acre. This included the Palestinian Arab leadership – only two
members of the Arab Higher Committee remained in Palestine for the
duration of the conflict.[24] Opinion was divided as to whether to leave.
The local leadership wanted to continue the resistance to the Zionists,
but the Mufti may have believed that this was now futile and rationalized
that a build-up of refugees on the borders of neighbouring states would
create a pressure on those states to invade on the declaration of a Jewish
state.[25] In addition, in April 1948, under the impact of the deteriorating
situation of Jewish Jerusalem, a policy was instigated 'to clear out and
destroy the clusters of hostile or potentially hostile villages dominating vital
axes'.[26]

---

[21] Moshe Sharett, oral testimony to the UN Special Committee on Palestine, 17 July 1947 in Paul
Mendes-Flohr and Jeliuda Reinharz (eds.), *The Jew in the Modern World: A Documentary History*
(Oxford 1980) pp. 475–476.
[22] Benny Morris, 'The Ignorance at the Heart of an Innuendo', *New Republic* 28 April 2006.
[23] Ibid.
[24] David Gilmour, *Dispossessed: The Ordeal of the Palestinians 1917–1980* (London 1980) p. 63.
[25] Benny Morris, *The Birth of the Palestinian Refugee Problem Revisited* (Cambridge 2004) p. 178.
[26] Benny Morris, *The Birth of the Palestinian Refugee Problem* (Cambridge 1988) p. 166.

But it was the brutal killings at Deir Yassin by the ill-disciplined Irgun and Lehi[27] and the use of this event as a tool in the megaphone war by the Arab media that acted as the catalyst for 'the psychosis of flight'. This initially came as a revelation to the Zionist leadership which then decided to exploit this development.

In the period between April and June 1948, the military campaign of the Zionists created the flight of 200,000–300,000 Palestinian Arabs. The proposed Jewish state of 538,000 Jews and 397,000 Arabs was in effect a bi-national state. An Arab majority would be attained within decades. The Provisional government of Israel rationalized that a return of refugees would act as a fifth column, given the past history of the Palestinian leadership. Their return, it was argued, presented a future of instability and violence. At an Israeli cabinet meeting on 16 June 1948, a decision was taken to bar the return of the Palestinian Arabs – at least for the duration of hostilities. While this qualification was designed to placate the leftist Mapam which supported a return of all 'peace-minded' refugees at the end of the war, Ben-Gurion appeared to rule this out. He envisaged an agreement with the Arab states, similar to that between Greece and Turkey in the 1920s. Sharett was similarly astounded by the exodus and argued against an immediate return. He cited the example of the expulsion of Germans from Czechoslovakia after the Nazi defeat. A Haganah document of June 1948 estimated that 391,000 Arabs had fled including 152,000 from the proposed Palestinian state.[28] It also noted that 14 out of 250 villages had been evacuated on express orders of the Haganah – some 20,000 people in total.

Ben-Gurion believed that the Haganah would have easily vanquished the forces of the Palestinian Arabs, had it not been for the British. The real fear was the possibility of invasion by the Arab states. At the beginning of 1948, he believed that Syria and Iraq were implacably 'hostile and belligerent', Egypt 'unrestrained enough to declare war' and TransJordan 'a paradox'.[29] The Iraqi massacre of 3,000 non-Arab Christian Assyrians in Simele in August 1933 had not been forgotten. Even if Arab leaders were reticent about military action, the Arab street resented the presence of Jews in the Arab heartland. Jews were both aliens and Crusaders, capitalists and Communists.

[27] Benny Morris, 'The Historiography of Deir Yassin', *Journal of Israeli History* vol.24 no.1 March 2005 pp. 79–107.

[28] Benny Morris, 'The Causes and Character of the Arab Exodus from Palestine: The Israel Defence Forces Intelligence Branch Analysis of June 1948', *Middle Eastern Studies* no.22 1986 pp. 182–183.

[29] David Ben-Gurion, address to the Mapai Central Committee, 8 January 1948 in Mordechai Nurock (ed.), *Rebirth and Destiny of Israel* (London 1959) p. 230.

The Jews therefore feared that they faced annihilation if they failed. After all the Secretary-General of the Arab League, Azzam Pasha, had declared on the eve of the Arab invasion that 'this will be a war of extermination and a momentous massacre which will be spoken of like the Mongolian massacre and the Crusades'.[30] Whether such threats were real or merely designed for domestic consumption, the lesson from history was extreme vigilance. Moshe Sharett later declared that his calmness on signing the Declaration of Independence on 14 May 1948 was a clever deception. He felt 'as though he were standing on a cliff with a gale blowing up all around him and nothing to hold onto except his determination not to be blown over into the raging sea below'.[31] A few hours later, with the British departed, the Arab states predictably invaded. Within a few weeks, the Egyptians had advanced to within twelve kilometres of Rechovot, the Syrians had established themselves in the Upper Galilee and the Jordanians were stationed between Ramle and Lydda – thirty minutes' drive from Tel Aviv. Israeli attacks around Latrun and Jenin had been repulsed by the Arab Legion. Significantly, the Jordanians rarely occupied the area designated in November 1947 for the Jewish state.[32] The invading forces totalled 22,000-28,000 troops, accompanied by several thousand irregulars. In addition to the main forces of the Egyptians, Jordanians and Syrians, Iraq, Lebanon, Saudi Arabia and Yemen all contributed troops. The IDF now fielded 27,000–30,000 troops plus an aging Home Guard of 6,000 and 2,000–3,000 Irgun members.[33] A month-long ceasefire commenced on 11 June 1948. Yigal Allon commented on the possible consequences if the Arab advance was not halted.

Because the enemy was so strong and so close to the most heavily populated Jewish areas, the Israelis dared not adopt a purely defensive strategy. It was clear that if the invading armies were allowed to enjoy the advantage of offensive action, they might break Israel's sparse line, crush its forces and gain possession of all Jewish-held territory, which because it lacked the dimension of depth was all too easy to subdue.[34]

Fighting resumed on 8 July with a ten-day Israeli offensive in which Lydda, Ramle and Nazareth fell. The next ceasefire lasted until 15 October 1948 which allowed the Israelis to rearm, reorganize their forces and train new immigrants. By the end of 1948, Israel was able to field 100,000 troops.

---

[30] Moshe Dayan , 'Israel's Border and Security Problems', *Foreign Affairs* January 1955.
[31] Golda Meir, *My Life* (London 1975) pp. 74–75.   [32] Morris, *The Road to Jerusalem* p. 241.
[33] Benny Morris, review of John J. Mearsheimer and Stephen M. Walt's 'The Israel Lobby and US Foreign Policy', *New Republic* 5 August 2006.
[34] Yigal Allon, 'Israel's War of Independence', *Revue Internationale d'Histoire Militaire* no.42 1979.

It is ironic that most of the weapons that saved the IDF from almost certain defeat came from Communist Czechoslovakia under an agreement signed in January 1948 when official sources in the United States and Europe were not permitted to enter into transactions with the Zionists. The Czechs supplied 50,000 rifles, 6,000 machine guns and 90 million bullets.[35] In addition, they supplied Messerschmitts and Israeli pilots and technicians were trained to use them in Czechoslovakia. This proved to be a potent counterbalance to the Egyptian Spitfires which the British had supplied. Most of the equipment had been manufactured by the Nazis in Czechoslovakia including even the uniforms which the Israelis wore.

During the inter-state war between Israel and the Arab world which followed, another 300,000 Palestinian Arabs left – some, this time, were expelled in considerable numbers by Israeli commanders at the local level. There was no doubt resentment at the unwillingness of the Arab world to contemplate negotiations and compromise; instead they waged a bitterly contested war in which they had calculated that they would emerge victorious. There was resentment at the high level of casualties that Israel was incurring. There was resentment that so soon after the Holocaust another attempt was being made to decimate the Jews. All this accentuated the desire to maximize the exodus which had commenced before the establishment of the state and to reduce the Arab population of Israel to a politically and militarily impotent minimum. There was also a probable, albeit silent, approval from many politicians.

Mapam, the main left-wing opposition to Ben-Gurion, consisted of two parties, Achdut Ha'avodah and Hashomer Hatzair. Achdut Ha'avodah was guided by Yitzhak Tabenkin whose Marxist Zionist teachings were translated into maximalist borders and a struggle against Arab reactionaries. Hashomer Hatzair, however, was much more conciliatory towards the prospect of a return and a renewed Jewish–Arab solidarity. Members of Achdut Ha'avodah were prominent in the Israeli forces. Israel Galili as head of the Haganah supervised the military preparations before the outbreak of war and became deputy Defence Minister in the Provisional government. Achdut Ha'avodah's Moshe Carmel and Yigal Allon commanded the northern and southern fronts respectively in military operations at the end of 1948 when many Palestinian villages were cleared of inhabitants. The expulsion of the inhabitants of Lydda and Ramie was authorized by Allon and Yitzhak Rabin – Ben-Gurion had characterized the towns as 'two thorns' at the cabinet meeting when a refugee return was blocked.

[35] *Ha'aretz* 9 May 2006.

The strong support of the towns' inhabitants for the Arab Legion, it was argued, posed an ongoing strategic threat to nearby Tel Aviv if Abdullah's forces mounted a counter-attack. There was, however, opposition from Hashomer Hatzair to Allon's use of refugee columns to hinder the advance of Abdullah's troops. Hashomer Hatzair campaigned to prevent the demolition of Arab villages and exerted political pressure to set aside land for the possible return of the refugees.[36] Yet ideology was not the only criterion and even Hashomer Hatzair was willing to establish new settlements outside the 1947 partition borders on 'surplus lands'. The prevailing wisdom was that the remaining land would be safeguarded for the returning fellahin and compensation paid to those whose land had been taken.[37] While there were ongoing protests from sections of the Israeli Left, many military commanders clearly felt that this was a war of survival for the Jews, a question of kill or be killed. A defeat for the Arabs would not signal the destruction of Arab civilization. Ezra Danin, who advised on Arab affairs for several Zionist and Israeli bodies, responded to one angry letter from a kibbutznik:

War is complicated and lacking in sentimentality. If the commanders believe that by destruction, murder and human suffering they will reach their goal more quickly – I would not stand in their way. If we do not hurry up and do [such things] – our enemies will do such things to us.[38]

The war transformed the illusion of 'a land without people for a people without land' into a distinct reality, from wishful thinking into a cruel opportunity. In the maelstrom of a deteriorating situation, the Peel Commission proposals in 1937 had encouraged the Zionists to consider transfer seriously while the Mufti's radicalism had initiated the aspiration of 'pushing the Jews into the sea'. The Palestinian Arabs came to believe that expulsion had always been a facet of Zionist ideology. The Jews came to believe the Arabs would never accept them and wished to finish Hitler's work. The culmination of this vicious conflict was the exodus of 600,000–760,000 Palestinian Arabs, the refusal of the Israelis to allow them to return and the inability and unwillingness of the Arab states apart from TransJordan to absorb them. Yet as Benny Morris commented, the

---

[36] To what extent ideology guided local commanders to expel Palestinian Arabs against a military necessity in time of war is a moot point. Perhaps the former reinforced the latter in some cases. Members of Hashomer Hatzair as opposed to Achdut Ha'avodah rarely occupied top positions in the military. Shimon Avidan commanded the Givati Brigade, but was also involved in evacuations when deemed militarily necessary.

[37] Morris, *The Birth of the Palestinian Refugee Problem Revisited* pp. 374–378.

[38] Ibid. p. 356.

Palestinian refugee problem was 'born of war, not by design, Jew or Arab'.[39] Al-Nakba was truly a catastrophe for the Palestinians, but this and past defeats forged a new identity, distinct from other Arab nation states'.

EXILE AND RETURN

In meetings with UN mediators Count Bernadotte and Ralph Bunche in June 1948, Sharett stated that there were probably three main causes for the intervention of the Arab states. Firstly, there was an objection to 'a foreign body' in the Middle East. Secondly, the rise of a Jewish state challenged the hegemony of the Sunnis and would encourage Shi'ites, Kurds and other religious and ethnic minorities to assert their independence. Finally, there was the fear that a progressive state would bring about change in neighbouring countries where conservative elites ruled.[40] In another meeting with Sharett, Bernadotte raised the question of 300,000 refugees as a humanitarian question that required a solution. Sharett argued that the return of the refugees could not be sanctioned while the conflict continued, but intimated that the Israelis would raise the question of the treatment of Jews in Arab countries and the large-scale confiscation of their property when peace finally did break out. Bernadotte continued to raise the question of the refugees with the Israelis, requesting that a limited number return to Jaffa and Haifa.[41] Sharett's response stated that there could be no readmission for reasons of security with the outcome of the war still in abeyance. He wrote to Bernadotte:

The Palestinian Arab exodus of 1948 is one of those cataclysmic phenomena which, according to the experience of other countries, changed the course of history. It is too early to say exactly how and in what measure the exodus will affect the future of Israel and of the neighbouring countries.[42]

At a subsequent meeting, Bernadotte raised the question of the return of citrus farmers, but again Sharett rejected the suggestion.[43] The Israeli attitude was clearly that it would be suicidal to readmit the refugees even after the war. What had been hard won on the battlefield, it was reasoned, would be lost through UN and western pressure and the continuing

---

[39] Morris, *The Birth of the Palestinian Refugee Problem* p. 286.
[40] Walter Eytan's notes of talks between Moshe Sharett and Count Bernadotte, 17 and 18 June 1948.
[41] Count Bernadotte, note on the subject of the Arab refugees 28 July 1948 Israel State archives.
[42] Moshe Sharett, letter to Count Bernadotte 1 August 1948 Israel State archives.
[43] Notes of a meeting between Moshe Sharett and Count Bernadotte 5 August 1948 Israel State archives.

hostility of the Arab world. In a report to Weizmann in August 1948, Sharett was clear about the Israeli stand:

With regard to the refugees, we are determined to be adamant while the war lasts. Once the return tide starts, it will be impossible to stem it, and it will prove our undoing. As for the future, we are equally determined – without, for the time being, formally closing the door to any eventuality – to explore all possibilities of getting rid, once and for all, of the huge Arab minority which originally threatened us. What can be achieved in this period of storm and stress will be quite unattainable once conditions get stabilized. A group of people from among our senior officials has already started working on the study of resettlement possibilities in other lands and of the finances necessary.[44]

In his desire to keep the gates shut, Sharett was aided by the Mufti who declared that no refugee should return while Israel existed. Yet he was well aware of the diplomatic problems that would arise if a fair solution was not found to the refugee question.[45]

UN mediators by September 1948 believed that for the most part the refugees would not wish to return to live in a Jewish state. The urban middle class would not wish to come to terms with Jewish nationalism while the fellahin would 'drift off' when they realized that their lands had been confiscated and their villages destroyed by the Israelis.[46] Some such as Musa al-Alami believed that Israel would expand into neighbouring states to fulfil the Biblical delineation of a state from 'the Nile to the Euphrates'. He argued that there had been an opportunity 'to finish with Zionism', but it was not taken. He explained:

The Jews proceeded along the lines of total war; we worked on a local basis, without unity, without totality, with a general command, our defence disjointed and our affairs disordered, every town fighting on its own and only those in areas adjacent to the Jews entering the battle at all, while the Jews conducted the war with a unified organization, a unified command and total conscription.[47]

In December 1948, the General Assembly of the United Nations established a conciliation committee under Resolution 194 (iii). Clause 11 stated that:

The refugees wishing to return to their homes and live at peace with their neighbours should be permitted to do so at the earliest practicable date, and

---

44 Moshe Sharett, letter to Chaim Weizmann 22 August 1948 Israel State archives.
45 Moshe Sharett, address to the Mapai Central Committee 24 July 1948 Central Zionist archives A245/391.
46 Notes of a meeting between Michael Comay and UN representatives Bunche, Reedman and Mohn 27 September 1948.
47 Musa al-Alami, 'The Lesson of Palestine', *The Middle East Journal* vol.3 no.4 October 1949.

Fig. 2.1. Moshe Dayan and Abdullah al Tal discuss the framework for a ceasefire, Jerusalem, 1948. Reproduced with kind permission from the Central Zionist archives.

that compensation should be paid for the property of those choosing not to return.

The failure to achieve peace with the Arab world in 1949 left the refugees in a limbo between an Israel which did not want to readmit them and Arab states which did not wish to absorb them. Either choice presented Israel with a dilemma. To allow entry offered the possibility of instability and the implosion of the state.[48] Yet to prevent entry projected indifference in the face of a humanitarian disaster. The latter was something which the West would not ignore. In March 1949, the Arab League interpreted UN Resolution 194 as a right to return, but refused to recognize Israel and a

---

[48] Gamal Abdul Nasser, *Zurcher Woche* 1 September 1961.

two-state solution according to UN Resolution 181. The United States pressed Israel to readmit 250,000 refugees, and at the Lausanne talks an unofficial meeting between a Palestinian refugee delegation and the Israelis produced a demand for 400,000 to return. The Israeli cabinet – against Sharett's wishes – suggested the annexation of Gaza. This would increase the Arab population of Israel to approximately the same level as the partition borders. Egypt, which now ruled Gaza, was decidedly unenthusiastic about handing over territory to Israel following its defeat. Israel's ultimate offer to take in 100,000 in August 1949 was harshly condemned by all the political parties in Israel and rejected by the Arab states two weeks later.

The stalemate left the refugees in an unenviable, parlous situation. Neither Israel nor the Arab states recognized the Palestinians as a national entity. The parts of the Palestinian state left unconquered by Israel were now under the rule of TransJordan and Egypt. Israel's stand – and hope – was that the Arab states would absorb the refugees. Sharett implied a quid pro quo in that Israel had absorbed 750,000 destitute new immigrants. The Israeli Foreign Ministry continuously pointed out previous examples of the integration of refugees – the divisions of Korea and Vietnam, Hindus and Sikhs fleeing from Pakistan, Muslims fleeing from India, Chinese arriving in Hong Kong, Germans expelled from Czechoslovakia, Turks from Bulgaria, Finns separated from their homeland by border changes.[49] A plan by oil interests in the United States to resettle the refugees in Libya as a means of placating pan-Arabism was mooted.[50] The refugees were marooned in a political no-man's land defined by the seemingly insurmountable hostility between Israel and the Arab states. In addition, the Palestinian Arabs believed that history could be reversed. The UNWRA report for 1956 commented:

Today [November 1956], the strongest feeling, vocally and bitterly expressed by the great mass of refugees, is the demand to return to their old homes . . . they have remained opposed to the development of large scale projects for self-support, which they erroneously link with permanent resettlement and the abandonment of hope for repatriation.[51]

A comprehensive classified analysis by Israeli Military Intelligence in August 1957 estimated that there were 809,000 refugees. 55 per cent were in TransJordan, 25 per cent in Gaza and the remainder in Syria and Lebanon. A majority of refugees from Jaffa, Lydda, Ramie, Jerusalem, Haifa,

---

49 Abba Eban, speech to the United Nations 17 November 1958 Israel State archives.
50 Ira Hirschmann, letter to Golda Meir 4 November 1958 Israel State archives.
51 *UNRWA Report for 1956*, supplement no.14 p. 13.

Tulkarem and Hebron had fled to TransJordan. Half the refugees from Beer Sheva had gone to Gaza. Most of the refugees from Acre and its environs ended up in Lebanon while many from Tiberias, Safed and Nazareth had gone to Syria.[52] In this political stand-off where neither return nor integration was offered, the Palestinians began to define themselves as a nation and not merely as part of a wider Arab world. By 1957, the United Nations had spent $244 million on the refugees, of which the United States had contributed $166 million.[53]

[52] 'The Arab Refugees', Research Division, Israeli Military Intelligence 25 August 1957 Israel State archives.
[53] *New York Times* 14 November 1957.

CHAPTER 3

New immigrants and first elections

THE SURVIVORS

Following the collapse of the Nazi regime, several hundred thousand displaced Jews inhabited Europe's DP camps. Prime Minister Atlee had rejected President Truman's request to allow 100,000 to immigrate in the autumn of 1945. Their experience in occupied Europe, however, defined and accentuated their Jewishness. One survivor, Samuel Gringauz, wrote in 1947:

The DPs are the surviving remnant of those Jews who, regardless of origin, culture, social position, ideology, class, yes even religion, were condemned to death only because they were Jewish. American and Swiss citizens, heroes of the First World War, the most respected representatives of European culture, manual labourers and bankers, Zionists and Socialists, Orthodox Jews and Catholics, all were collectively stripped of every attribute and, nameless and non-descript, were tortured and killed – as 'Jew X'. A Jewish tailor from Rhodes who could find no one in the camp to understand him and a Hungarian druggist baptised thirty years before, lay in the same wooden bunk with me, and died because they were Jewish. This is why the surviving remnant feels itself to be the embodiment of the unity of the Jewish experience. This is why they feel themselves prophets of a national rebirth, charged with the task of symbolising this unity and this rebirth, and of being the backbone of its realization. The belief in these extraordinary tasks intensifies the group consciousness of the surviving remnant and makes it see itself as a 'chosen group' within the 'chosen people'.[1]

Diaspora Jews united around this surviving remnant. Even those who had escaped through the good fortune of distance understood that now all Jews were survivors. Jacob Trobe, the first Jewish Joint Distribution Committee representative to arrive in Bergen-Belsen, estimated that

---

[1] Samuel Gringauz, 'Jewish Destiny as the DPs See It: The Ideology of the Surviving Remnant', *Commentary* 4 1947.

80 per cent of the camp's Jews wished to leave for Palestine.[2] Ben-Gurion had been the first Zionist leader to visit the DP camps in October 1945. He recorded in his diary that since the liberation of Bergen-Belsen, two thirds of the camp Jews, over 30,000, had died of typhus and tuberculosis. He naturally encouraged Jews to emigrate to Palestine and painted Zionism as the very antithesis to Diaspora subservience. Addressing 800 Jews in a converted monastery, he said:

Hitler was not far from Palestine. There could have been terrible destruction there, but what happened in Poland could not happen in Palestine. They would not have slaughtered us in synagogues. Every boy and every girl would have shot at every German soldier.[3]

Of 104,000 Jews who enlisted during the war of Israel's independence, nearly half were newcomers who had fled Europe during World War II or had arrived in 1948. Of 5,682 Jews who were killed in that war, 35 per cent had arrived since 1939. Many of the newcomers who had come from Europe to die in the war for Israel were Shoah (Holocaust) survivors.[4]

The desire of Jews to leave Europe for the shelter of Palestine was intense, instinctive and determined. Indeed, Ben-Gurion's visit to the camps had coincided with the fulfilment of the quota under the terms of the 1939 White Paper – 10,000 per annum for five years plus 25,000 refugees. If the Jews of the DP camps wished to enter Palestine, it would have to be carried out in defiance of British desires. The Jews, in British eyes, were not a special case. Most of the ships that attempted to run the British blockade of Palestine between April 1945 and January 1948 were intercepted. A default survivalist 'Zionism' emerged – a haven for the persecuted and downtrodden – which was distinct from classical interpretations of Zionist ideology, directed towards the goal of building a new Jewish society. In contrast, the British imperative was to prevent any large-scale influx of Jewish survivors.

When the news first emerged in 1942 that the Nazis had embarked on the systematic extermination of European Jewry, the British were concerned that there would be an 'unlimited demand' for accommodation by fleeing refugees. Yet while there was a genuine desire to save Jews from extermination, their emigration to both Britain and Palestine had to be

---

[2] Jacob Trobe, 5 July 1945, 6 July 1945; in Eric Nooter, 'The American Jewish Joint Distribution Committee and Bergen-Belsen' (unpublished article in the American Jewish Joint Distribution Committee archives, Jerusalem, 2000).
[3] Shabtai Teveth, *Ben-Gurion: The Burning Ground 1886–1948* (Boston 1987) p. 827.
[4] These figures are based on the research of Emanuel Sivan. *Ha'aretz* 25 April 2001.

prevented. Holding such refugees in neutral countries for the duration of the war was proposed as the answer before repatriating them to their countries of origin at the conclusion of hostilities. British intelligence had reported the existence of Auschwitz in early 1942. Amongst a minority in Britain, however, there was a growing realization that something unthinkable was taking place. It was followed by a sense that British plans were merely a fig leaf of a solution which had not even begun to address the Jewish tragedy. Indeed, by March 1943, there were already public estimates that two million Jews had been killed.[5] A former League of Nations High Commissioner for Refugees who advocated the entry of Jews into Palestine wrote that

no niggling approach to their problems will suffice. These are beyond the vision of old-time diplomacy with its dilatory commissions, White Papers, endless discussions and committees and unwillingness to face the pre-emptory need for bold planning and prompt action.[6]

Moreover, British officials had been at pains not to highlight specifically Jewish suffering, but to emphasize the general barbarity of the Nazi regime. This often extended to the press as well. The diplomatic correspondent of the *Times* later reflected:

There was not a special policy to promote any single aspect. News was news – that was the guiding principle... [Running the series of reports on the extermination of the Jews in December 1942] was a news decision essentially, based on the sure belief that news about German atrocities was an asset, a weapon in the allied war effort.[7]

This was cemented by a certain de-Judaising of Nazi bestialities. Even after the first revelations of the camps liberated by the British and the Americans in April 1945, there was hardly a mention that the inmates were by and large Jews. Visiting delegations and press coverage stressed the inhumanity of the Nazis and the tragedy of the human wreckage left behind. Journalists wrote powerful and moving accounts of Nordhausen and Buchenwald, but the antisemitic nature of the extermination process was often missing. In one sense, this underlined the classic European understanding of the Jewish problem that the solution was assimilation and acculturation – and not Jewish particularism and separation. When inmates from Buchenwald testified to their ordeal, a British journalist

5　Ernest S. Pisko, *Christian Science Monitor* March 1943.
6　James G. McDonald, *The Time for Discussion Is Past in Palestine: A Jewish Commonwealth in Our Time* (Zionist Organisation of America, Washington 1943) p. 12.
7　Iverach McDonald, letter to the author, 12 July 1995.

wrote – in all innocence – that 'with their hair cropped and their deep sunken eyes seeing far-off unspeakable things, they had a look of early Christian martyrs'.[8]

Most people in Britain were unable to imagine the unimaginable. Ordinary citizens in Britain and the United States were shocked beyond belief when the first press reports and photographs were published after the liberation of Buchenwald and Belsen in mid-April 1945. When film of the camps reached London cinema screens, all box office records were broken. Queues stretched from Charing Cross Road to Trafalgar Square and they were still there late at night.[9] Moreover, these were not extermination camps such as Auschwitz, but the receptacles of the death marches from the East. As the Nazi empire began to shrink, new inhabitants were added and Bergen-Belsen's population doubled between February and April 1945. Yet these powerful images of Nazi victims were universalist, stripped of their Jewishness. In contrast, German Jews were sometimes seen as Germans. A few days after the photographs of Belsen had been published, there were vehement protests in Birmingham that 'German workers' – in reality, refugee Jewish employees – had been taken on in the city.[10]

Amidst all this British confusion, the Zionists' demand for a state in Palestine began to gain sympathy amongst a few who had begun to comprehend the enormity of the Jewish catastrophe. Whilst there was an anti-aliens sentiment in 1945, there had also been a lot of contact with Jewish refugees who were domiciled in Britain. The left-liberal *Guardian* demanded 'a far more generous immigration policy' and endorsed the call for a Jewish state in Palestine.[11] There was a sense that the Jews had been abandoned through the collective will of governments, but that individuals acting in the name of moral conviction could now in some way make amends. Remarkably, the national executive of the British Labour party argued in 1944 for a transfer of the Arabs out of Palestine.

Let the Arabs be encouraged to move out as the Jews move in. Let them be compensated handsomely for their land and let their settlement elsewhere be carefully organized and generously financed. The Arabs have many wide territories of their own; they must not claim to exclude the Jews from this small area of Palestine less than the size of Wales.[12]

---

[8] *Daily Telegraph* 24 April 1945.   [9] *Daily Telegraph* 1 May 1945.
[10] *Times* 27 April 1945.   [11] *Guardian* 26 April 1945.
[12] Joseph Gorney, *The British Labour Movement and Zionism* (London 1983) pp. 178–179.

Even Vladimir Jabotinsky, the Revisionist Zionist leader and opponent of Ben-Gurion, had vehemently opposed the transfer of the Palestinian Arabs.[13]

Following the Labour victory in 1945, Atlee adopted a diametrically opposite policy which attempted a reversion to a pre-war situation as if the situation of the Jews had not changed. The realization of the enormity of the Shoah, however, manifested itself in the opposition of the Labour Left to the Atlee government's policies in Palestine.

The possibility of a Jewish socialist state in Palestine arising from the ashes of the Shoah was enticing and messianic in its imagery. The Labour party counted large numbers of Jews in its ranks – and together they had opposed local fascists in the 1930s. At the 1944 Labour party conference, when the first news of the mass extermination of Jews in Eastern Europe began to reach British ears, there had been emotive calls for a Jewish state. Moreover, as the Soviet Union, Britain's wartime ally, was warmly endorsing the Zionist cause, many in the Communist and Labour parties came to see the growing Jewish community in Palestine with its established institutions and grounded infrastructure as the belated answer to the Jewish problem and a practical solution to the problem of the Jewish DPs.

But the re-imposition of the 1939 White Paper which made Jewish immigration dependent on Arab agreement suggested that the new Labour government was simply not aware of the changes in Jewish national consciousness which the war had brought about. Ernest Bevin, the Foreign Secretary, and Clement Atlee, the Prime Minister, did not see the Jews in Palestine as an emerging nation, but only as a displaced religious group. Their scant understanding of Jews was based on their knowledge of London's East End. On a visit to Washington in November 1945, Bevin told President Truman that he hoped that Jews would play their part in the reconstruction of Europe and not 'over-emphasise their separateness from other peoples'.[14]

Yet there had always been a certain antipathy towards the Jews and their nationalist aspirations within some parts of the British Labour movement. In 1930, Sidney Webb, the Fabian intellectual and then Colonial Secretary, viewed the Jews as over-articulate and over-represented. Atlee and Bevin reflected this attitude after 1945 and according to one parliamentary colleague, they believed that 'it was the duty of an impartial British

---

[13] Vladimir Jabotinsky, 'Points from V. Jabotinsky's address', Dublin 12 January 1938, Jabotinsky archives.

[14] *Times* 14 November 1945.

statesman to treat everything they (the Zionists) said with the gravest suspicion, while putting the most favourable interpretation on the Arab case'.[15]

Bevin's impatience with the Jews and his frustration with the situation in Palestine pushed him into open dislike for Jews per se. For the right-wing Bevin, there was also the Communist threat. Indeed, he readily confided his bizarre belief that the Soviets had amassed a Jewish army in Odessa ready to invade.[16] In an era of decolonization, some viewed the Zionist pioneers as akin to the white settlers in Kenya. Others understood the Zionist struggle against the British during the 1940s as anti-colonialist. Still others such as Aneurin Bevan, the leader of the Labour Left, refused to equate Arab nationalism with progressive causes. Following Nasser's ascendancy to power, he later wrote:

If a social movement elects to take the path of revolution, it must pursue it to the end and the end is a complete transformation of society accompanied by transference of power from the old to the new social forces. Judged by this criterion, the movement first led by General Neguib and then by Nasser has not as yet added up to a social revolution or anything like it.[17]

Indeed, Bevan had earlier threatened to resign from the Atlee government because of Bevin's Palestine policy.[18] Several thousand volunteers, mainly Jews, fought in the 1948 war. In the aftermath of the Shoah, many saw the Arab invasion as an extension of the genocidal campaign against the Jews. Indeed, there were several left-wing non-Jews who fought – and died fighting – for Israel.[19]

There was little left-wing affection for the Palestinian Arab cause. Few Palestinian Arabs had enlisted to aid in the war effort against the Nazis. Instead, Arab nationalists had endorsed the approach that 'the enemy of my enemy is my friend' in a forlorn attempt to rid themselves of British colonialism.

British progressives were rationally anti-antisemitic in 1939 as part of the opposition to fascism, but were they 'emotionally pro-Jew'?[20] This fine, but profound distinction played itself out in the tensions between Britons and Diaspora Jews over Palestine between 1945 and 1947.

---

[15] Richard Crossman, *A Nation Reborn* (London 1960) p. 67.   [16] Ibid. p. 70.

[17] Aneurin Bevan, *Tribune* 3 August 1956.

[18] Hugh Dalton, *High Tide and After: Memoirs 1945–1960* (London 1962) p. 199.

[19] William Edmondson, an American of Irish immigrant parents, assisted the illegal emigration and was killed on the road to Jerusalem in July 1948. See A. Joseph Heckelman, *American Volunteers and Israel's War of Independence* (New York 1974) p. 57.

[20] Richard Crossman, *Palestine Mission: A Personal Record* (London 1947) p. 19.

All these conflicting arguments divided the Labour party such that there was no agreed solution which could accommodate the competing claims of the two national movements. Richard Crossman, a leading Labour academic whom Atlee had appointed to the Anglo–American Commission of Inquiry, outlined his political dilemma.

What stuck in my gullet was the idea that British troops should be used to hold the Arabs down while the Jews were given time to create an artificial Jewish majority. Sure enough, I did at last come to the conclusion that the injustice done to the Arabs by dividing the country and permitting the Jews to achieve a majority in their portion would be less than the injustice done to the Jews by implementing the 1939 White Paper. But this was a complicated, terribly difficult decision to reach.[21]

The Mandate had become unworkable because British obligations to both sides in the conflict were essentially unbridgeable. Many who were not previously sympathetic or interested in Zionism began to see the establishment of a Jewish state in Palestine as affirmative action on behalf of the Jews, a measure of positive discrimination following the Shoah. Bertrand Russell wrote:

For a long time I was doubtful as to the importance of a Jewish national home in Palestine as an element in such reparation, but I have gradually come to see that, in a dangerous and largely hostile world, it is essential to Jews to have some country which is theirs, some region where they are not suspected aliens, some state which embodies what is distinctive in their culture.[22]

Many Jews, however, preferred not to wait for the vagaries of British decision-making to reach a conclusion. Jewish survivors took part in the *Brichah* – the clandestine flight of Jews from post-war Poland to the British and American zones in Germany en route to Palestine. Both in the DP camps and in towns where Jewish survivors were attempting to rebuild their shattered lives, Zionist emissaries were active. As early as December 1944, the Labour Zionists in Palestine addressed 'a message to the survivors of our movement' in Europe.[23] Many survivors attempted to reach Palestine as part of *Aliyah Bet* – the illegal immigration into Palestine.

---

[21] Crossman, *A Nation Reborn* p. 54.
[22] Bertrand Russell, *Zionism and the Peace Settlement in Palestine* (Zionist Organization of America) July 1943.
[23] 'A Message to the Survivors of Our Movement', World Union Poale-Zion (ZS) – Hitachdut Tel Aviv March 1945.

Fig. 3.1. Jewish refugees from the Holocaust, with the Yellow Star of David on their backs, 1945. Reproduced with kind permission from the Central Zionist archives.

In 1947 we went as illegal immigrants on forged papers, saying we were demobilized Czech soldiers. We had fake names and we were attached to 'parents' – adults travelling on forged papers like us.[24]

Many boats carrying immigrants were intercepted by the British. The *Exodus 1947* reached the coast of Palestine and was apprehended. The British decision to return the boat and its human cargo of 4,500 to – of all places – Germany, was widely publicized and further increased public support for the Zionists.

[24] Aviva Liebeskind (Rakovsky), in Moshe Davis and Meir Hovav (eds.), *The Living Testify* (Jerusalem 1994) p. 47.

JEWISH IMMIGRATION INTO PALESTINE

Ben-Gurion termed immigration into Israel, 'the highest mission of the state'. The composition of the Israel Defence Forces was unprecedented in its international character. In addition to Israeli citizens, it consisted of volunteers from twenty-one European states, fourteen from the Americas, ten African countries, five from Asia and two from Australasia.[25] The UN partition of Palestine in November 1947 offered a state whose composition would be approximately 55 per cent Jews and 45 per cent Arab – almost a bi-national state. The outcome of the war of 1948 drastically changed that demography in the Jews' favour. Even so, Ben-Gurion believed that unless the Jewish majority was substantially increased, the state would be inherently unstable, given the higher birth rate of the Arabs and the unremitting hostility of its neighbours. In 2005, some 38 per cent of the world's Jews lived in Israel; in 1948, it was only 6 per cent – some 650,000 Jews. Within three years, this figure had virtually doubled.

Yet the Zionist imperative to facilitate 'the ingathering of the exiles' was rebuffed by the Soviet Union which refused to allow any of its two million Jews to leave. Paradoxically, there was external Soviet support for Israel amidst the internal repression of Zionists. The last years of Stalin's life bore witness to a reign of terror against Jews of all political beliefs and of none. Jewish intellectuals, writers and poets such as Peretz Markish and David Bergelson perished alongside diehard Jewish Communists – all tarred as 'Zionists'. Stalin's demise at the height of the anti-Jewish paranoia, generated by the mythical Doctors' plot to poison the leaders of the Kremlin, probably avoided the mass deportation of Soviet Jewry to Central Asia. Even so, the USSR did permit the return of 150,000 Polish Jews to Poland after the war – and from there many emigrated to Israel. Although emigration from the Soviet Union itself was barred, and Zionist activity subject to imprisonment in strict regime labour camps, 300,000 East European Jews reached Israel during the first four years of statehood.[26] Many came out of fear that the borders would soon be closed by the new Communist states, others out of profound insecurity in the aftermath of the Shoah. Yet there was no free emigration. Negotiations were conducted by the Mossad (General Security Service) with Communist regimes to 'buy' Jewish immigrants. The Hungarians initially wanted $80 a Jew before dramatically raising the

[25] David Ben-Gurion, 'Mission and Dedication', *State of Israel Government Yearbook 5711* (Tel Aviv 1950) p. 33.
[26] Dalia Ofer, 'Emigration and Aliyah: A Reassessment of Israeli and Jewish Policies' in Robert S. Wistrich (ed.), *Terms of Survival: The Jewish World since 1945* (London 1995) p. 67.

price, the Rumanians asked for $100 and the Bulgarians demanded $300 for Zionist prisoners.[27] In the end, mainly through funds raised by American Jews, some $5 million was paid to Romania and Bulgaria to permit the emigration of 160,000 Jews.

By the beginning of 1952, nearly a third of all East European Jews had left for Israel. In contrast, the countries of Western Europe, Latin America, Australasia and South Africa provided less than 40,000, just over 2 per cent of their combined Jewish populations.

The establishment of Israel provoked some surprising political reactions. Not only did Stalin's Russia embrace Zionist aims, but so did Afrikaner nationalism. Although Jabotinsky's visits in the late 1930s had established a firm base of nationalist activity, the response of the South African Jewish community to the rise of Israel was overshadowed by the unexpected election of the government of Daniel Malan. His Herenigde National party was a Christian party which barred Jews from membership. The sudden empowerment of the Afrikaner nationalists who were known for their pre-war antisemitism and opposition to immigration from Nazi Germany profoundly unnerved liberal South African Jews. The emergence of an Afrikaner nationalist government at the same point in time as the establishment of a state of the Jews was deeply ironic. Following the Jewish struggle against the British in Palestine, the hitherto Judeophobic Afrikaner press became much more interested in Zionism. The Jews were suddenly seen as brothers to the Afrikaners in their suffering – 'a chosen people' fighting the same enemy. The attraction of Israel brought the added bonus that fewer refugee Jews would wish to come to South Africa. All this initiated a complete about-turn in Afrikaner attitudes towards Jews. Moreover, much to Jewish bemusement, the Afrikaners also saw Judaism and Israel as the very embodiment of the apartheid system. Despite continued Jewish opposition to apartheid, this vision of Israel persisted. Indeed when Israel later voted against apartheid at the United Nations, the Afrikaners accused the Jewish state of not being true to itself.[28]

In Arab countries, the defeat of the Arab armies and the exodus of the Palestinian Arabs exacerbated an already difficult situation. In December 1947, a pogrom and the destruction of synagogues in Aleppo persuaded half the city's Jewish population to leave. In Egypt, arrests, killings and confiscations catalyzed the flight of nearly 40 per cent of the Jewish

---

[27] Tom Segev, *The First Israelis* (London 1986) pp. 95–116.
[28] Gideon Shimoni, *Jews and Zionism: The South African Experience 1910–1967* (Cape Town 1980) p. 219.

community by 1950. In Kuwait, the minuscule number of Jews were expelled. In Iraq, the Criminal Code was amended in July 1948 such that Zionists were lumped together with Anarchists and Communists. The death penalty could be meted out to adherents or they could be sentenced to many years' imprisonment.[29] Enforced emigration to Israel became the officially permitted route out of Iraq for an increasingly oppressed Jewish community. Israel ironically became the unlikely destination for many Jewish Communists despite their opposition to Zionism. In Libya, Algeria and Morocco, there were periodic outbreaks of anti-Jewish violence. Over 37 per cent of Jews in Islamic countries – the Arab world, Turkey, Iran and Afghanistan – left for Israel between May 1948 and the beginning of 1952. This amounted to 56 per cent of the total immigration.

While over half a million Jews left Eastern Europe and the Islamic countries for Israel, only 1,682 left North America whose Jewish population was 5,201,000. Clearly, Jews in the more affluent countries did not wish to leave their place of residence for the uncertainty of the Middle East. However, they were willing instead to identify through paying for the enormous costs of the absorption and rehabilitation of those who had suffered persecution and discrimination. After 1945, the great centres of Zionist endeavour in Eastern Europe no longer existed and the victory of Stalinism left those surviving Jews in a state of penury. In addition, the reaction of Arab nationalism to the establishment of Israel disenfranchised and impoverished Jews in the Arab world. The centres of immigration in the Diaspora now no longer coincided with the centre of capital. Many appeals to the Jewish community in the USA were answered extremely generously, but this was not exactly the fulfilment of Zionist ideology. Although they were necessary in the circumstances, Ben-Gurion was both adulatory and scathing in his comments about the fundraisers and the philanthropists:

The leaders of Zionism in tsarist Russia, some of them men of great means, did not stir from their hearths or bring their great wealth to the Land. And the Jews of America are no better than they.[30]

Ben-Gurion further compared American Jews to the majority of Babylonian Jews who refused to join the prophets Nechemiah and Ezra

---

[29] Moshe Gat, 'Israel and the Iraqi Jewish Community in the Political Crisis of 1949' in Eliezer Don-Yehiya (ed.), *Israel and Diaspora Jewry: Ideological and Political Perspectives* (Jerusalem 1991) pp. 161–182.

[30] David Ben-Gurion, 'Israel among the Nations', *Israel Government Yearbook 1952* (Jerusalem 1952) p. 16.

in returning to the Promised Land. Yet American Jews did not regard themselves as being in exile, but rather as being at home – as founders and builders of the United States. Some even came to extol the virtues of the Diaspora.

> [The Jews] have probably spent far more years of our historical lifetime in the Diaspora than in our own country and it makes no sense to characterize as abnormal a way of life that accounts for more than half of a people's historical existence. Diaspora is simply a characteristic condition of our history; paradoxically it might even be said to be more characteristic than statehood which we share with hundreds of other peoples.[31]

THE FIRST ELECTIONS

The price of war had been high. Some 6,000 Jews had been killed – an equivalent of two million US fatalities in the Vietnam war – and 12,000 wounded. Palestinian Arab losses were estimated at 8,000 dead and another 4,000 lost by the Arab armies.[32] The elections for the first Knesset in January 1949 therefore symbolized closure of the war with the Arabs and the normalization of the Jews as a nation in their sovereign state. It came at a time when a large number of its citizens were still on active service.

Questions such as the size of representation in the Knesset and whether Jews outside Israel also had a right to vote had to be resolved. The Jews of Israel realised the historic significance of the occasion – and they came out to vote in droves. Indeed, when the polling booths opened in Netanya, the queuing voters started to sing the national anthem, 'Hatikvah'. In an election-eve broadcast, Ben-Gurion declared that 'the revolutionary act of 14 May [the declaration of the self-legitimization of the Provisional Council of State] had had no formal authority and lacked a democratic basis'. The election, he argued, would be 'the legal ratification and the legal basis' for the new state.[33]

This election built on the experience of four previous elections for the *Asefat Hanivcharim* (Elected Assembly) in the pre-state era. The Transition Law of 1949 helped to define the electoral system in that people voted for the party and not the candidate, using the system of proportional

---

[31] Nachum Goldman, *Memories* (London 1970) p. 313.
[32] Benny Morris, review of John J. Mearsheimer and Stephen M. Walt's 'The Israel Lobby and US Foreign Policy', *New Republic* 5 August 2006.
[33] *Palestine Post* 25 January 1949.

Fig. 3.2. Voting in Nazareth in the first Israeli elections, January 1949. Reproduced with kind permission from the Central Zionist archives.

representation. The largest party would therefore be called upon to form a government. Ben-Gurion utilized this law to ensure that the President would not be elected by the voters and that it would be a purely symbolic position. Real power would reside with the Prime Minister. Ben-Gurion thus engineered the marginalization of Chaim Weizmann, the first President of Israel.

Some 21 parties struggled to overcome the 1 per cent barrier to qualify for representation, but only 12 actually succeeded. In previous elections, the social democratic Mapai (the Workers' party of the Land of Israel) or its predecessors had been the leading party. Moreover, its percentage of the vote had increased from 35 per cent in 1920 to nearly 53 per cent by 1944.[34] This proved to be the pattern for the future up until 1969; only after did the combined Labour vote dip below 50 per cent. In 1949, some 440,095 people cast their vote – nearly 87 per cent of the voting public. The oldest candidate was a seventy-nine-year-old landlord standing for the Progressive party while two twenty-one-year-old students were candidates for the Communists. One woman attempted to stand twice, as a journalist for the General

34 David M. *Zohar, Political Parties in Israel: The Evolution of Israeli Democracy* (New York 1974) p. 14.

Zionists and as a housewife for WIZO. The Central Elections Committee struck her off both lists. Some 200 polling stations were set up in army camps. The first returns came from Kfar Hittin, a cooperative settlement in the Lower Galilee which showed a predictable gain for the combined Labour movement. 10 per cent of those elected were women. One sixth were farmers – and excluded those who listed their profession as cabinet minister, trade union officer or kibbutz secretary. 3 Arabs were elected. There were also 7 lawyers, 5 rabbis, 3 bank managers, 2 teachers and a university professor. Of the 35 Cohens who stood, 3 were returned.

Only 10 per cent of those elected had been born in Israel. 86 out of the 120-member parliament had been born in Eastern Europe or Russia. Only 2 had been born in Islamic countries.[35] This reflected the composition of the pre-state leadership of the Zionist movement. Mapai, with Mapam to its left, had garnered 65 seats – enough for a blocking majority. Yet Ben-Gurion did not form a narrow socialist coalition, but opted for a broader coalition which included the Religious and the Progressives.

While there was a profound appreciation of the USSR, following the Red Army's struggle against Nazism and the delivery of Czech arms to Israel,[36] Ben-Gurion was wary about Mapam's pro-Soviet orientation. He retained his early admiration for Lenin's ruthless expediency, but this did not extend to the Soviet regime per se. The suppression of Zionism, underpinned by traditional Marxist-Leninist thinking on Jewish nationalism, remained official Soviet policy despite the Kremlin's support for Israel in 1948. Unlike Mapam, Ben-Gurion was not blinded by the continual good news issuing from Moscow. Moreover, Ben-Gurion was uncertain as to how the cold war would develop and who would eventually be the victor. Both superpowers had sizeable Jewish communities and as the Mapai election manifesto pointed out, it would be sheer folly to alienate one side. Moreover, the USA had sought to bolster Mapai and to counteract Mapam's influence by announcing a loan guarantee of $100 million to Israel on the eve of the election.

Mapam had been formed from three parties, Left Poale Zion, Achdut Ha'avodah and Hashomer Hatzair. The combined parties accounted for 25 per cent of the vote in the previous Zionist Congress, compared to Mapai's 35 per cent. In the Histadrut, it accumulated 43 per cent compared to

---

[35] Benjamin Akzin, 'The Knesset', *International Social Science Journal* vol.13 no.4 1961 p. 571.
[36] In fact, the arms deal had been agreed to by Jan Masaryk before the Communist takeover of Czechoslovakia. It continued even after the Soviet Union had started to distance itself from Israel. For example, a Czechoslovak–Israeli trade agreement was signed in March 1950.

Mapai's 50 per cent. Many of Israel's military leaders – Yigal Allon, Yitzhak Sadeh and Moshe Sneh – were party members. It therefore posed a considerable political threat to Ben-Gurion and the Mapai leadership. Hashomer's members constituted half the party and they had been waiting a long time for the Soviet Union to open its ideological eyes and to recognize their long-time loyal brothers within the Zionist fold. Hashomer blamed the Comintern for Soviet attitudes towards Zionism and rejoiced when Stalin decided to disband it in 1943. Indeed, it would have recommended to their members to accept Comintern discipline if the USSR's position on Zionism had been different. By 1948, Hashomer felt that its moment had come and its unrequited love had finally produced a response in Soviet support for Israel. At its founding conference, Mapam pledged itself to establish 'a workers' regime... a classless socialist society and a world of international fraternity'. The party programme spoke of the 'firm alliance between the workers of the world and the Soviet Union, the first workers' state... and fulfilling the historic mission of the October Revolution'.[37] Mapam expected a socialist Israel to be welcomed into the Soviet family of nations. It called in its manifesto for a united front of workers' parties:

Only the victory of the revolutionary party of the working class will safeguard the real progressive democratic nature of the coalition and the socialist hegemony in the Government and will prevent surrender to reaction and clericalism and thereby make possible the uprooting of fascism.[38]

Mapam raised the question of Arab rights in Israel in discussions with Ben-Gurion. It also spoke about the return of 'peace-loving Arab refugees... an economic union between the state of Israel and an independent democratic state in the other part of Palestine' and 'strengthening the progressive forces' in the Arab world – at a time when Ben-Gurion was resisting the return of any Palestinian Arabs. Moreover, Hashomer had called for a bi-national state right up to the outbreak of war. It argued for a joint sovereignty and a federation of two organized national communities. The central government, it postulated, would run along national and not geographical lines. Hashomer called for a Special Development Authority which would promote the settlement of two to three million Jews in Palestine over a twenty-year period, to raise the level of the Palestinian Arabs to the same living standards as the Jews and to merge the two

[37] 'The Unity Programme of Mapam' in Peretz Merchav, *The Israeli Left* (London 1980) p. 115.
[38] *Palestine Post* 10 December 1948.

separate economies. This bold plan, however, did not match the reality in the country. This alternative to partition collapsed through the lack of an Arab partner and through Soviet endorsement of the UNSCOP majority report in October 1947. Its junior partner in Mapam, Yitzhak Tabenkin's Achdut Ha'avodah, was far more hawkish. It did not want Arabs to join the Histadrut and actually rejected the idea of a bi-national state. While proclaiming solidarity with Arab workers, it expressed hostility towards Arab notables. Achdut Ha'avodah advocated an expanded Israel, based on the establishment of new kibbutzim on any land available.

Mapam was distinctly unhappy about Ben-Gurion's pledge of friendship to both superpowers. In particular, Mapam wanted to know how Mapai would act if Marshall aid was offered by the USA. Mapam was also keen to exclude any British bases – there would be no hint of an imperial presence in any part of historic Palestine. While the party would accept a peace accord with the Hashemites regarding Jordan, it rejected any agreement recognizing Jordanian authority over the West Bank which King Abdullah's forces had conquered and annexed. In the international sphere, Mapam demanded that Israel support a Big Five pact, armament reduction and the UN's efforts to outlaw nuclear weapons. There were also differences in perceptions of the Israeli armed forces. Mapam wanted a 'People's Army' whereas Mapai suggested that the Military Service Act should colour the 'pioneering character' of the state's armed forces. Mapam also favoured controls to promote a planned economy and regarded Mapai's approach as too ideologically lax. It also wanted the nationalization of natural resources, higher direct taxes and lower indirect ones.

Ben-Gurion had attempted to dilute left-wing leverage by dismissing Mapam's Israel Galili as head of the Haganah in May 1948. In November the Palmach, regarded as Achdut Ha'avodah's fighting arm, was disbanded on the basis that such separatist functions now had to be absorbed into the instruments of the state – a state now run by members of Mapai. It was not an argument that could easily be disputed since the Left had justified the sinking of the Irgun's arms ship, the *Altalena*, on similar grounds.

With nineteen seats, Mapam now expected to play a major role in government. Although it had only held two ministries in the Provisional Government, the party now demanded the Ministry of Defence and representation in the Foreign Ministry as well as participation in any economic body established. Mapam also suggested the partial politicization of the civil service.[39] Further negotiations led nowhere and on 2 March

---

[39] David Ben-Gurion, *Israel: A Personal History* (London 1971) pp. 340–347.

1949 Mapam decided against joining the government due to the Hashomer Hatzair faction outvoting Achdut Ha'avodah.[40] The following day the decision was conveyed to Ben-Gurion.[41] Mapam expected to be in opposition for a short period and believed that Ben-Gurion could not form a stable administration with the other parties.

THE DOMINANCE OF MAPAI

Ben-Gurion was renowned in the Yishuv (the Jewish settlement in Palestine) for his fierce anti-Communism.[42] Mapam, in his eyes, was little more than a fifth column and he saw little difference between them and the official Communist party. This suspicion of Mapam also extended to Moshe Sharett, the Foreign Minister, who galvanized moderate support within both the government and Mapai to endorse Ben-Gurion's more belligerent approach. Yet in July 1948, Aharon Tzisling, Mapam's Minister of Agriculture in the Provisional Government, attempted to persuade Sharett to lead a cabinet revolt with the aim of displacing Ben-Gurion. Although tempted, Sharett's loyalty to Mapai and opposition to Mapam's pro-Soviet dogmatism convinced him to reject the offer.[43] In the prelude to the Korean war, a Mapam platform had advocated 'the promotion of friendly relations – in times of peace as well as war – with the Soviet Union and the Peoples' Democracies'.[44]

Ben-Gurion's dislike of Jewish Communists and fellow travellers stretched all the way back to the split in Poale Zion, the predecessor of Mapai, in 1920 into pro-Soviet and Palestine-centred wings. Then, he had argued against those who preferred class solidarity between Jewish and Arab workers over the establishment of 'a centre of Jewish labour in Palestine'. In 1923, he travelled to the young Soviet state to oversee a Palestine stand at an agricultural fair in Moscow. Ben-Gurion noted that a rival stand had been erected by the Yevsektsia, the Jewish sections of the Communist party, in order to promote a different view of the Jewish future. Jewish Communists, he believed, exerted a pernicious influence within the walls of the Kremlin in influencing Soviet policy to condemn Zionism per se and to minimize the achievements of the Yishuv.[45]

[40] David Ben-Gurion, *Medinat Yisrael Ha-mechudeshet* (Tel Aviv 1969) p. 369.
[41] Ben-Gurion, *Israel: A Personal History* pp. 340–347.
[42] Shmuel Sandier, 'Ben-Gurion's Attitude towards the Soviet Union', *Jewish Journal of Sociology* no. 21 1979 pp. 145–160.
[43] Gabriel Sheffer, *Moshe Sharett* (London 1996) p. 372.   [44] *Jerusalem Post* 6 February 1951.
[45] Teveth, *Ben-Gurion: The Burning Ground* (Boston 1987) pp. 166–169.

On 21 July 1919, the Sovnarkom (the Soviet cabinet) had actually published a document which stated that 'the Zionist party had never been defined as counter-revolutionary' and no obstacles should be placed in its path. The Yevsektsia – many of its members were former Zionists – was able to block this decree.[46] Ironically, there were many Jewish Communists, albeit distant from their ethnic origins, such as Kamenev, as well as many non-Jewish Communists who were not hostile towards Zionism. For example, Anatoly Lunarcharski, the Commissar for Popular Enlightenment (Minister for Education and the Arts) was scheduled to speak at the farewell party held in honour of the Hebrew national poet, Chaim Nachman Bialik. The Yevsektsia attempted to revoke Bialik's exit visa and therefore the banquet was cancelled in case the celebration jeopardized his departure.[47] Ben-Gurion viewed Hashomer Hatzair's utopianism and general pro-Soviet attitude as little more than a repetition of his experiences in the 1920s.

By 1949, Communist parties under Soviet hegemony had destroyed the democratic Left in Eastern Europe. Ben-Gurion feared the same could happen in Israel. In a meeting with Mapai members of the Knesset in July 1949, he derided the zealotry of Mapam and raised the possibility of a military coup by the Left.[48] Such comments were made in the context of Ben-Gurion's worry about the disproportionate representation of Mapam in the Israeli army. Since 1948, he had been conducting an effective purge of Mapam sympathizers in the army and their replacement by Mapai adherents. Neither was Ben-Gurion pleased with Mapam's approach towards the Palestinian Arabs since his aim was to achieve security through settlement based on expanded Israeli borders. Mapam's expression of Jewish–Arab workers' solidarity extended to suggesting that Israel should conquer the West Bank from the Jordanians in order to establish a state there for the Palestinian Arabs.[49] There was also anger that Ben-Gurion had agreed to Farouk's Egypt controlling Gaza. In Ben-Gurion's eyes, it was not Israel's task to become involved in internecine Arab struggles.

The other faction of Mapam, Achdut Ha'avodah, was also pro-Soviet and had once been part of Mapai. The maximalist Achdut Ha'avodah, led by Yitzhak Tabenkin, believed that Labour Zionism should adhere to its founding principles of socialism, settlement and an undivided homeland.

[46] Arieh Raphaeli-Tsentiper, *B'ma'avak l'geulah* (Tel Aviv 1956) pp. 33–34.
[47] The testimony of Saadia Goldberg in Benjamin West, *Struggles of a Generation: The Jews under Soviet Rule* (Tel Aviv 1959) p. 141.
[48] Segev, *The First Israelis* p. 268. [49] Ibid. p. 20. *Al Hamishmar* 14 January 1949.

Moreover, the founding of a Jewish state was a secondary matter and should be left to future generations. Tabenkin thereby opposed Ben-Gurion's acceptance of the Peel Commission's recommendations in 1937 to partition Palestine into two states despite Ben-Gurion's comment that the borders of the state were not set in stone for all time. He also opposed the Biltmore Programme in 1942 which for the first time spoke of 'a Jewish Commonwealth'. The split within Mapai finally took place in August 1944 with Tabenkin leading his faction out of the party and eventually agreeing with Hashomer Hatzair to form Mapam. Ben-Gurion was also worried that both groups were influencing the youth of Mapai. Yet he had calculated correctly that Mapai would emerge strengthened and the largest party if supported by Mizrachi, the religious Zionists and the General Zionists.

Ben-Gurion's suspicion of the Left persuaded him in 1949 to form a coalition with the third largest party, the United Religious Front, establishing a government which included the religious, the progressive liberals and the Sephardim. In discussions, Mapam's representatives had told Ben-Gurion that it was willing to participate in a government together with the religious bloc, preferring them to the exclusion of the General Zionists.[50] Mapai, however, projected itself more broadly to appear both as state-builders to attract non-socialists and as the authentic voice of social democracy to seduce the Left.[51] Ben-Gurion had originally resolved to exclude only Begin's Herut and the Communists; but now instead of a broadly based administration, he also excluded Mapam from the Left and the General Zionists from the Right. The latter, which represented the liberal middle class, was also involved in pioneering activities and had established eight kibbutzim, including Mivtachim in the Negev desert. Yet the General Zionists, the party of private enterprise, was similarly regarded as outside the ideological pale and unsuitable as a governing partner.[52]

The United Religious Front consisted of four parties – two Zionist and two non-Zionist. One party, Agudat Yisrael, had in fact been formed in 1912 as an ultra-orthodox answer to Zionism. Those who opposed Zionism on theological grounds argued that human intervention in creating a Jewish state and ingathering the exiles amounted to forcing God's hand.[53] Moreover, such unwarranted action, they believed, brought in its wake the seeds of secularism. Before 1939, there had been great bitterness in

---

[50] Ben-Gurion, *Medinat Yisrael Ha-mechudeshet* p. 368.
[51] Moshe Sharett, Analysis of the Election Results, meeting of the Mapai Central Committee, 27 January 1949, Labour party archives, 2/23/1949/51.
[52] Israel Goldstein, *General Zionist Program*, ZOA pamphlet series 2 (New York 1947).
[53] Aviezer Ravitsky, *Messianism, Zionism, and Jewish Religious Radicalism* (Chicago 1996) pp. 10–39.

the ultra-orthodox community against the Zionists. Families were divided and dissidents expelled.

Even during the war, such feelings persisted. For a year, Lithuania was sandwiched in between the two revolutionary goliaths of Nazi Germany and Soviet Russia, yet the majority of the heads of the great learning academies, the *yeshivot*, advocated staying put rather than attempting to leave for Palestine. Instead they and their followers marched into the gas chambers singing *nigunim* (a repetitive humming). The Shoah destroyed the community of the faithful in Eastern Europe and the ultra-orthodox perished in vast numbers.[54]

Such a tragedy softened the position of the survivors towards Zionism. It moved many from an anti-Zionist position to a non-Zionist one. Indeed, it was remarkable that the two ultra-orthodox parties, Agudat Yisrael, and a labouring sister party, Poalei Agudat Yisrael, would even contemplate joining two religious Zionist parties, Mizrachi and Hapoel Hamizrachi, in forming an electoral bloc. The ultra-orthodox fear was that by remaining outside the governing institutions of the state, they would be unable to influence the direction of the government's religious policies. In particular, they wished to ensure that issues such as women's rights in questions of inheritance, marriage and divorce all remained within the jurisdiction of the rabbinical courts. The formation of a religious bloc to safeguard 'Torah and Tradition' therefore offered a fig leaf to gloss over its past virulent condemnations of Zionism.[55]

In contrast, there was a considerable number of religious Zionists who argued that the common basis of religious observance was insufficient to establish a common front. In particular, the Lamifneh faction of Hapoel Hamizrachi which included the religious kibbutzim strongly opposed a pact with the ultra-orthodox. They felt that the formation of a religious bloc would actually widen the split between secular and religious in Israel in that it would be viewed as solely concerned with religious issues and nothing else. Moreover, Agudat Yisrael opposed the desire of Hapoel Hamizrachi to include women in the list of candidates. With the endorsement of the revered sage Avraham Karelitz, known as the Chazon Ish, all objections were marginalized and the four parties agreed to a manifesto in November 1948 that spoke about bestowing upon the state 'its pristine

---

[54] Zorach Warhaftig, *Refugee and Survivor* (Jerusalem 1988) pp. 132–143.
[55] Yosef Fund, *Perud o hishtatfut: Agudat Yisrael mul ha 'Tsiyonut u Medinat Yisrael* (Jerusalem 1999) pp. 219–227.

Jewish character, for our nation is a nation by virtue of its Torah only'.[56]
The common platform of the religious bloc dwelt upon the observance
of the Sabbath and festivals, religious education and adherence to the
dietary laws in all government institutions. Moreover, the state should be
guided on matters of personal status such as marriage and divorce 'only
according to Jewish law'. In addition, Hapoel Hamizrachi published its
own programme which went far beyond religious concerns and included
immigration, absorption, the economy, and employment as well as proclaiming Jerusalem as the capital of Israel. On election day, sixteen seats
were secured for the bloc – ten for the religious Zionists and six for the
non-Zionist ultra-orthodox.

On 8 March 1949, Ben-Gurion announced the basic principles of the
government programme and its composition to the Constituent Assembly
in Tel Aviv. He reminded his parliamentary colleagues that if the state had
arisen in 1937, controlling immigration and defence, then 'European Jewry
might have been saved from destruction'. Nearly 200,000 immigrants had
streamed into Israel since the declaration of independence. Self-reliance
in all endeavours had proved itself in the past, he argued, and this would
continue. Ben-Gurion saw the Jews as renewing themselves as a people,
in a period of national genesis: 'a wasteland (that) must be made fertile'.[57]
A twenty-one-point development plan was announced which detailed 'the
rapid and balanced settlement of the under populated areas of the country . . . and establishing a network of villages in the vicinity (of Jerusalem)
and in the areas connecting it with the coastal plain'. Private capital was to
be encouraged in developing the country's economic potentiality. Irriga-
tion projects would be implemented in the Negev, all water sources would
be nationalized and neglected land would be compulsorily developed. The
programme resolved 'to eradicate ignorance, overcrowding and disease in
slum areas' and endeavoured 'to increase the birth rate through grants
and special allowances for large families'. There would be equal rights
for Arab workers and an amelioration of their situation; maternity leave
would be granted, mothers would be barred from night work and women
would secure equal pay with men; the employment of children would be
prohibited and the work condition of minors under eighteen would be
monitored.[58]

56 Moshe Unna, *Separate Ways: In the Religious Parties' Confrontation of Renascent Israel* (Jerusalem
    1987) p. 124.
57 Ben-Gurion, 'Mission and Dedication', p. 29.
58 David Ben-Gurion, 'Speech to the Constituent Assembly', 8 March 1949 Israel Office of Information,
    New York 1949.

Ben-Gurion further announced that he could not come to terms with the pro-Soviet Mapam on the Left or with the General Zionists on the Right who wanted a clause in the government programme which rejected the implementation of socialism. Ben-Gurion rejected the idea of a Mapai–Mapam bloc which would be the nucleus of a wider coalition. Instead Mapai opted to form a coalition with the Religious bloc, the Sephardim and the Progressives. Mapai would retain seven ministerial portfolios, the rest five.

Mapam's Meir Ya'ari responded that Israel had lost an opportunity to influence the future development of the state:

One [choice] was that the State should be led by the two large working class parties in cooperation with other constructive forces, who would mobilise all the moral and material resources of the people to transform the new immigrants into a nation of workers. The alternative was that there should be a coalition of reformists and clericals amenable to the pressure of internal reaction and the economic political dictation of external influences.[59]

Ya'ari accused Ben-Gurion of abandoning 'an original and unique Jewish socialism'. He stated that Ben-Gurion had told them in discussions that the construction of a socialist Israel would depend solely on his own party. There was no need for an agreed programme on social matters as this was already enshrined in Mapai's programme. Ya'ari protested that huge profits had been made during the war and that there was 'a constant retreat before the pressure of capitalists'. For the Zionist Left, this realization was a breach of faith by its natural partner. Ya'ari perceptively warned that an alliance with the religious – as happened in France and Italy – would lead to a more natural partnership with the nationalist Right. He accurately predicted a future alliance between Menachem Begin's Herut movement and the General Zionists which would come to rely on the religious members of the government to expound their views.

Ben-Gurion responded by berating Mapam for its support for a bi-national state, an international trusteeship and the desire to establish an Arab state alongside Israel. The nationalist Right, the religious and the ethnic parties – the Sephardim and the Yemenites – accounted for forty-three mandates, eighteen short of a blocking majority. Even at this early stage of Israel's political development, Ben-Gurion may have been determined to prevent such a coalescence by taking some of these parties into government while leaving others outside.

---

[59] Meir Ya'ari, 'Speech to the Constituent Assembly', 8 March 1949 in *'Mapai* Broke Faith: Why *Mapam* Is Not in the Government of Israel', United Workers Party *Mapam* pamphlet no. 3 April 1949.

In the guidelines for the government programme, Ben-Gurion had described Zionism as 'a magnificent, messianic enterprise', but Zerach Warhaftig who responded on behalf of the religious bloc pointedly ignored this, but asked him about questions of personal status. Ben-Gurion replied that any changes would create 'a deep chasm in the House of Israel' and that there were more pressing issues. Moreover, he stated that he was speaking not in the name of the government, but only on behalf of Mapai. By commenting that his government would not introduce non-religious marriage and divorce, Ben-Gurion implicitly accepted that such events would be based on halachah, Jewish religious law. This went beyond anything stated in the government's official guidelines.

Leading figures in Mapai such as Golda Myerson (Meir) were decidedly nervous about ceding the Ministry of Education to the religious Zionists of Mizrachi, given the profound difference in the interpretation of 'Jewish education' between secular and religious Zionists. Moshe Sharett noted that giving the education portfolio to another party was 'a bone stuck in his throat'.[60]

Yet Warhaftig significantly pledged the religious bloc's support for 'the socialist objectives' outlined in the programme because they regarded Israel as a labour state. Although the religious Zionists adopted a fairly pragmatic attitude, the ultra-orthodox trod the fine line between expediency and principle. They viewed a reborn Israel as not truly a Jewish state – this would only come to pass when the messiah finally arrived – but a state like any other except that the government and its functionaries happened to be Jews. But the ultra-orthodox also had their vested interests – and these would be safeguarded through participation where necessary.

In his pre-election broadcast, Ben-Gurion had stressed the need for full civil equality for women and the removal of discriminatory laws, the legacy of the Turkish and Mandatory systems. Indeed, a women's list, WIZO (Women's International Zionist Organization), had won representation 'to prevent the clerical parties from incorporating into the state code archaic religious laws which would prejudice the legal and social position of women'.[61] Yet Avraham Goldrat of Poalei Agudat Yisrael said that his party objected to the principle of equality of women and to the inclusion of Golda Meir in the cabinet. Others in the Zionist wing of the religious bloc – Mizrachi and Hapoel Hamizrachi – recalled that although the

---

[60] Moshe Sharett, discussion on the formation of the government, meeting of Mapai Central Committee, 21 February 1949, Labour party archives, 2/25/1949/12.

[61] Zohar, *Political Parties in Israel* p. 69.

begrudging injunction of the Prophet Samuel proclaimed that 'thou shall set him as king over you',[62] the medieval commentator Maimonides had pointed out that nowhere did it mention queens or that women should not rule over Israel. The principle of gender equality was later enacted by the Women's Equal Rights Law in 1951.

The composition of Ben-Gurion's first administration set the pattern for future governments. He had abandoned a core coalition of Mapai and Mapam which would forge a socialist future for the new state. Instead a working relationship with small parties and an agreement with the religious on the basis of no change and no interference in religious affairs became the foundation for the moulding of the new society. Ben-Gurion believed that his coalition partners would be happy in their subservience in this situation. The religious Zionists proved to be Mapai's long-term coalition partner, balanced by the secular Progressives. With troublesome, larger ideological parties excluded from government, Mapai, the dominant party, would now carry out its programme of state building. Moreover, it always held the crucial ministries – Foreign Affairs, Defence and Finance. Ben-Gurion waited until the Zionist Left had splintered before co-opting Achdut Ha'avodah in 1956.

Not only were ideological rivals outside both Mapai and the government, but prominent ideologues within Mapai such as Berl Katznelson and Dov Hoz were long dead. Alone and at the head of government, Ben-Gurion basked in the glow of the achievement of the state without the danger of anyone of standing presenting a challenge to his views.

---

[62] Samuel I 8:4–22.

CHAPTER 4

The politics of piety

THE BALANCING ACT

Shortly before he died in 1973, Ben-Gurion confided that he had been wrong to grant religious courts the right to make decisions in matters of personal status.[1] This and other issues relating to Jewish identity appeared with increasing frequency during the first decade of Israel's existence. Ongoing crises, resignations, the reshaping of coalitions and the downfall of governments came to characterize Israeli politics. The fragmentation of Jewish identity in the nineteenth century – an attempt to come to terms with post-Enlightenment modernity – had produced a plethora of variations. The Shoah and the establishment of the state, however, had caused the demise of numerous ideologies such as Bundism, yet other rivalries continued to thrive in Israel. Thus the devout secularists of Mapam and Mapai were as determined as the Council of Sages of Agudat Yisrael to stamp the future direction of the state with their imprimatur. The former believed that Zionism had revolutionized Jewish life and normalized the Jews. The latter wished to continue the tradition of eons and rebuild the spiritual walls of the past.

Although Ben-Gurion's aversion to Mapam created an alliance between Mapai and the non-Zionist and often anti-Zionist religious parties, there was a deep-seated desire to avoid a kulturkampf during the early years of state-building. In forming a government, Ben-Gurion's choice of coalition partners was between adherents of a political ideology and the worshippers of a faith. No doubt Ben-Gurion based his decision on the political realities of the time, but this alliance set the pattern for future coalitions. Mapam eventually drifted away from its infatuation with Stalin, split into two and dwindled in political influence, but the religious parties kept their faith and

---

[1] M. Shesher, *Chaim Cohn: Chief Justice* (Jerusalem 1989) p. 222 in Daphna Sharfman, *Living without a Constitution: Civil Rights in Israel* (New York 1993) pp. 90–91.

bolstered their political authority. Ben-Gurion well understood the dilemma that he was faced with. He was a member of that transitional generation that was moving from religion to secularism. Indeed, he preferred Rabbi Akiva who supported the Bar-Kochba revolt against the Romans over Yochanan Ben-Zakkai who was allowed to establish the yeshiva of Yavneh after the destruction of Jerusalem.[2] He was therefore not unaware of the potential dangers which the religious bloc posed to stable government, particularly as it changed its stance of safeguarding the interests of the religious community to one of minimum levels of observance for the whole country. The opening of restaurants, cinemas and theatres on the Jewish Sabbath reflected the desires of the non-observant majority, but it also outraged the ultra-orthodox who viewed such desecration as intolerable and an official encroachment into their way of life. Yet the vote of the religious Zionists and the ultra-orthodox only increased minimally – from 12 to 15 per cent – in elections between 1949 and 1969.

Both Agudat Yisrael and Poale Agudat Yisrael signed the Declaration of Independence which spoke of 'liberty of faith and conscience'. Despite this, there was determined ultra-orthodox opposition. Echoing a widely held view that orthodoxy was unable to recognise a 'live and let live' philosophy, Ben-Gurion commented:

The implementation of the fundamental principle of liberty of conscience, with which no religious individual openly disagrees, meets in practice with a covert and deep opposition implicit in the aspirations and purposes of the religious parties. The fact that a religious party exists, gives it, consciously or unconsciously, the desire to impose religious laws and the authority of rabbinical institutions on the state. The liberty of faith and conscience which the religious party demands for itself, it is not prepared to grant, or is not capable of granting to others as well.[3]

Ben-Gurion was careful not to attack religion per se and made a distinction between religious parties and religious people. He pointed out that most religious Jews did not belong to religious parties and despite the influx of the traditionally minded Sephardim, the vote for the religious parties in the 1951 election actually went down. There was, he contended, opposition both from secular freethinkers and from those who observed the prescriptions of the *shulchan aruch* (sixteenth-century compendium of Jewish law and practice). They considered that 'there is moral damage to the state and a falsification of the spirit of Judaism in the transformation of religion into a political instrument and the attempt to impose religious

---

[2] Ben-Gurion, 'Israel among the Nations', p. 41.
[3] David Ben-Gurion, 'Jewish Survival', *Israel Government Yearbook 1953/4* (Tel Aviv 1954) p. 19.

practices by the use of state sanctions. 'This does considerable harm to the respect felt by people for religion.'[4]

In targeting the political power of their rabbinical mentors, he argued that members of the religious parties did not accept the historical assessment of the Bible and the Talmud.

In their eyes there is neither early nor late Torah, so that the words of the latest rabbinical luminary and the commentaries of contemporary rabbis are coexistent with and equal to the very Law of Moses received on Sinai.[5]

Ben-Gurion made a clear distinction between rabbis as men of great religious learning and rabbis as men of good political judgement.

Although the draft constitution had been framed in accordance with the Declaration of Independence, both Mizrachi and the ultra-orthodox had long opposed any document not based on the Law of the Torah.[6] The United Religious Front thus objected to any constitution which was neither based on the Torah nor made any mention of it. Yet both Mizrachi and the ultra-orthodox had not envisaged a theocratic state before Israel's establishment. The designated disappearance of the constitution was opposed by both the Left and the Right, but supported by Mapai who feared the schism that would be caused in voting against the religious viewpoint. The historian Benzion Dinur argued that there was evidence in the Book of Exodus to justify a constitution and that the Torah had been given scroll by scroll.[7] This formed the basis of the Harari bill which proposed passing a series of basic laws over time which would then comprise a constitution. In the debate, Ben-Gurion attacked the belief that only the rabbis of Agudat Yisrael could exercise the sovereign authority to legislate and execute laws in the state.[8]

There was also profound reluctance by ultra-orthodox rabbis to allow their young men to serve in the army and in general to permit their communities to interact with secular Israeli institutions. Although, in March 1948, the army conscripted hundreds of yeshiva students in a non-combatant context, Ben-Gurion entered into an informal agreement that yeshiva students could defer their conscription while they remained in full-time study. This, in turn, provoked 'shabbat raids' into ultra-orthodox neighbourhoods by secular activists.

---

4 Ibid. p. 20.   5 Ibid. p. 21.   6 Unna, *Separate Ways* pp. 68–76.
7 David Ben-Gurion, 'Law or a Constitution?', Knesset speech 20 February 1950 in *Rebirth and Destiny of Israel* (London 1959) pp. 378–379.
8 Daphna Sharfman, *Living without a Constitution: Civil Rights in Israel* (New York 1993) pp. 38–45.

During the war, 800 Jewish children who had escaped the Shoah by travelling across the USSR sojourned in Teheran and finally entered Palestine. Their parents had met their fate at the hands of the Nazis. The Israeli political parties then squabbled over what sort of education the children should have before resolving the issue in accordance with the children's background and wishes. By early 1950, the new influx of immigrants had magnified this problem. The religious bloc accused Mapai of bringing economic pressure to induce immigrant children to go to a Labour movement school rather than to a Mizrachi or Agudat Yisrael one. This had been resolved by an agreement that all newly arrived Yemenite children in reception camps would have religious schooling while others could choose a religious or general educational framework. The fierce rivalry between the political parties to gain the adherence of the immigrants was also an ingredient in the melée. The Yemenites had aligned themselves with Mapai rather than Mizrachi. Most of the immigrants were then transferred to ma'abarot (transitional work camps) where they began to earn their own living. An amendment to the Compulsory Education Act stipulated that the agreement with the religious bloc did not apply to the ma'abarot since this came under 'permanent or temporary housing' and not 'immigrant camps'. This was supported on legal grounds by the Attorney-General. As a result thousands of children were transferred from religious to other networks. The religious ministers naturally argued that the agreement should also have applied to work camps. The Histadrut established the Oved hadati (religious part of the Histadrut) which led to accusations that this was simply Mapai in religious clothing. The religious bloc argued that teaching Bible courses in such schools did not amount to a religious education and that they were attempting to 'capture the children for their party'. One demonstration in Jerusalem against government policy paraded the slogan 'Save our children from conversion'.[9] Eventually a State Education Act was passed in 1953 which established two new streams of education, state and state religious. The Agudat Yisrael educational framework opted out.

Ben-Gurion proposed an amendment to the Compulsory Military Service Act which allowed ultra-orthodox young women to serve in ma'abarot or in religious settlements instead of the army. The amendment allowed the Minister of Defence to decide which were religious settlements. On his discretion, religious young women could be required to work in the military or in government offices. This led to threats of mass defiance from the

---

[9] *Jerusalem Post* 8 January 1951.

Fig. 4.1. David Ben-Gurion speaks at a Mapai election rally, Jerusalem, January 1949.
Reproduced with kind permission from the Central Zionist archives.

ultra-orthodox sector. Since there had already been a campaign directed
against symbols of secular hegemony such as theatres, cinemas, cafés and
restaurants and football stadia which wished to remain open during the
Jewish Sabbath, the amendment was quickly shelved – amidst the arrest of
radical ultra-orthodox Jews from the Hamachaneh group who discussed
blowing up the Knesset.[10] All this led the ultra-orthodox to conclude that
secularists in government were intent on waging an ideological war against
them and utilizing their political power to educate their children by non-
religious standards. They compared the activists of Mapai to the Hellenized
Jews of antiquity. In particular, they resented the Left's admiration for the
Soviet Union during a period of official antisemitism and mass arrests of
Jews.

By 1952, both ultra-orthodox parties had parted company with the
two religious Zionist parties, left the coalition and gone into opposition. Agudat Yisrael remained in opposition until 1977 when Menachem
Begin's Likud gained power. In the interim, the kulturkampf continued.
In 1954, a club was opened in Jerusalem for newly arrived Sephardi boys

[10] Ehud Sprinzak, *Brother against Brother: Violence and Extremism in Israeli Politics from the Altalena
to the Rabin Assassination* (New York 1999) pp. 60–67.

and girls whose activities involved mixed dancing and the singing of popular songs. The club which was situated opposite a shtiebel (small prayer house) of the Bratslaver Chassidim provoked clashes.

In August 1953, there was determined opposition to the passing of the bill to ensure compulsory conscription of women into Israeli auxiliary national service. This brought forth the condemnation of many renowned Torah scholars such as Yitzhak Ze'ev Soloveitchik, the Briisker Rav and Avraham Karelitz, the Chazon Ish. The refusal of the government to abort the bill indicated the political impotence of the rabbis amidst the astonishment of their followers that their opinion had not been heeded.

For the first time, probably, in our two thousand years of galut [exile], has a government so totally ignored the opinions, appeals and supplications of the spiritual heads of world Jewry. It must be made clear to Jewish public opinion that the measure taken by the bill has no other raison d'être than spite.[11]

This measure, too, remained on the statute books. The religious Zionists of Hapoel Hamizrachi took a totally opposite stand in embracing the prospect of military service for their young men and women, providing that all facilities were provided to allow them to continue an observant way of life. Secular pacifists who declared that war was against their principles wondered why they – unlike yeshiva students – were not granted exemption.

While there were different interpretations of 'Jewishness', Ben-Gurion accepted out of political necessity that Judaism could no longer remain privatized, a matter of private conscience, but had to be managed within the public domain. Quoting from the Book of Genesis, Jacob, he remarked, had changed his name to Israel.[12] In a Jewish rather than in a Judaic state, he opted for traditionalism rather than tradition per se. In Ben-Gurion's eyes, the coming of the state should have bestowed a sense of common responsibility on all citizens to participate in 'a framework of duty and compulsion'. The state had therefore given legal authority to the Chief Rabbinate. Many secularists objected to this because the Mandatory government had hitherto allowed citizens the possibility to withdraw from their authority. On the other hand, many religious Jews objected because they did not wish the decisions of the rabbis to be limited by the laws of the state. By 1955, in accordance with Mizrachi policy, the judges of rabbinical courts became state officials, As all sides in the debate pointed out, such integration would only work if the Rabbinate was subservient to the wishes of the state.

[11] 'World Jewry Protests against the Conscription! Do You Know the Facts?', Agudas Israel Organization of Great Britain (London 1953).
[12] Genesis 33:28.

This policy had emerged after the war as a result of the settlement of many ultra-orthodox Jews in Palestine. It offered the opportunity to live a traditional life and to rebuild the communities destroyed by the Nazis. They regarded Palestine as a haven for the persecuted rather than the location where the Jewish state would be built. While they still opposed Zionist ideology, they understood their journey to be to the 'Biblical' Eretz Israel (the Land of Israel) rather than to the modern Medinat Israel (the state of Israel). There, a spiritual centre would be established to await the arrival of the messiah, 'the only true redeemer of Israel and mankind'. Ultra-orthodox leaders such as Poalei Agudat Yisrael's Yitzhak Breuer argued that whereas the Haskalah and Reform Judaism had brought individual assimilation, Zionism brought national assimilation. Breuer was highly critical of the religious Zionists whom he accused of placing the nation rather than the Torah at the centre of their deliberations. They opposed the Biltmore Declaration for a Jewish state in 1942 and bemoaned the calls to resettle the DPs in Palestine after the war. As the President of Agudat Yisrael, who opposed the establishment of a state, commented in January 1947:

Jewish tradition knows how to differentiate between nations as metaphysical entities, as bearers of cultural missions in the course of history, and nation states as power centres, as the incarnation of sovereignty and self-idolatry.[13]

In 1947, Yitzhak Meir Levin of Agudat Yisrael, later the Minister of Welfare in the first government, asked Ben-Gurion for a ruling on where a future state would stand on issues such as Sabbath observance, kashrut (the dietary laws), the jurisdiction of halachah (Jewish law) on matters of personal status and whether parties such as Agudat Yisrael could maintain their autonomous system of schools and educational institutions. Levin's instrument of leverage was the arrival in Palestine of the UNSCOP Commission whose recommendations could affect the future course of events. Yitzhak Breuer had told the Anglo–American Commission in 1946: 'for us, the state is not a goal in itself'.[14] The Zionists were therefore adamant that a united front with complementing testimonies should be presented to the UNSCOP committee. Apart from the American chapter of Menachem Begin's Irgun, Agudat Yisrael was the only other group that insisted on its right to appear before UN committees. Levin received appropriate assurances to his questions in a letter signed by both Ben-Gurion and Rabbi Maimon, the religious Zionist leader. Levin thereby testified in a measured fashion, neither criticizing Zionism nor

[13] Jacob Rosenheim, 'Agudas Israel Faces the World Scene', lecture given to the Agudas Israel Youth Council 5 January 1947.
[14] Fund, *Perud o hishtatfut* pp. 210–211.

espousing it. The price of muting the ultra-orthodox who opposed the very idea of a Jewish state was the promise of fortifying religious traditions within its portals. The letter, however, was an expression of good will based on presumption rather than on commitment. The constructive ambiguity of the letter allowed a consensual approach to Judaism in a Jewish state to be ushered in.

If the ultra-orthodox wished to reconstruct the ghetto walls and to lead separatist lives, this was not the approach of Mizrachi and Hapoel Hamizrachi, the religious Zionists. The first Chief Rabbi of Mandatory Palestine, Avraham Yitzhak Kook, had viewed aetheistic kibbutzniks, who disdained organized religion, as God's chosen instrument in re-creating the Land of Israel. All Jews, he argued, contained *nitzotzot* – divine sparks – within them. After all, he pointed out, all Jews were permitted to participate in the rebuilding of the Temple. Religious Zionists who had discarded the black garb of the ultra-orthodox for modern dress viewed the establishment of the state as *atchalta d'geula*, the beginning of redemption, where Israel would be redeemed from its suffering and the arrival of the messiah would be expected. They pointed to the prophecies of the Hebrew prophets that the new era would herald an epoch of universal peace and quoted Isaiah and Micah about beating swords into ploughshares and spears into pruning hooks. The prophet Ezekiel in Babylonian exile, they recalled, stressed that redemption would be characterized by *kibbutz galuyot*, the ingathering of the exiles, and the establishment of a Jewish kingdom under the rule of a descendant of King David. For the religious Zionist, the state was regarded as a religious entity, but how quickly the various stages of redemption, such as the raising of the dead, would be enacted was a different matter. The ultra-orthodox, in contrast, ridiculed such spiritual fervour, preferring to recall that Jewish history had been peppered with false messiahs. No human intervention would force God's hand before the appointed time. They were therefore content to passively wait – and to engage with the so-called Jewish state's deliberations only when necessary. Israel, they argued, was not a Jewish state. It was no more than a state of Jews. Instead of non-Jews ruling them, it was now Jews who were ruling them.

WHO IS A JEW?

On 5 July 1950, the Knesset passed the Law of Return, which stated that 'Every Jew has the right to immigrate to the country' unless the Immigration Minister believed that immigrant was 'engaged in an activity directed against the Jewish people' or was likely 'to endanger public health' or pose a threat to the security of the state. The Provisional Government had abolished British regulations which limited Jewish emigration within days of Israel's establishment. Nearly 240,000 arrived in Israel in 1949. In Ben-Gurion's eyes, immigrants and the settlements that they created and populated stabilized the state and provided it with security. In 1949, 102 new settlements were founded; this increased to 127 the following year. The Law of Return, unlike matters of personal status, was not within the jurisdiction of the rabbinical courts, but was one of Israel's basic laws. The Minister of the Interior and his civil servants were not under any obligation to define any answer to the question 'Who is a Jew?' According to halachah, Jewish law, 'Jewishness' could only be preserved through the matrilineal line – a Jew was the offspring of a Jewish mother.

According to secular belief, 'Jewishness' could be defined much more widely. A Jew could be someone who believed himself to be a Jew or identified with the cause of the Jewish people. This different understanding of 'Jewishness' could be traced back to the advent of the *Wissenschaft des Judentums* movement in the afterglow of the Enlightenment. This suggested that 'Jewishness' could be defined in broad terms of Jewish civilization – language, culture, history, literature and religion. In contrast, pre-Enlightenment understanding viewed Judaism at being at the core, and governing every aspect, of Jewish life. In the new state of Israel, this led to an interchange between terms of definition – 'Jew', 'Israeli' and 'Hebrew'– which to some appeared synonymous and to others extremely different.

In 1955, the third Israeli elections produced a turn to the Left and Ben-Gurion appointed Achdut Ha'avodah's Israel Bar-Yehuda to the Ministry of the Interior. He quickly ruled that a person declaring himself in good faith to be a Jew by nationality should be included in the register and had a right to extend that status to his children. This provoked a cabinet crisis and the subsequent resignation of two ministers from the National Religious party. Ben-Gurion's solution was to set up a cabinet committee which then invited forty selected scholars to pronounce on the matter.[15] Many concurred that a Jew was someone born of a Jewish mother and Bar-Yehuda's directive was withdrawn. In the next Knesset, there was a swing away from the Left and the NRP was once more given control of the Ministry of the Interior. In 1960, the new appointee, Chaim Moshe Shapira, issued new regulations in accordance with the halachah.

---

[15] Baruch Litvin and Sidney B. Hoenig (eds.), *Jewish Identity: Modern Responsa and Opinions on the Recognition of Mixed Marriages* (New York 1965).

Benjamin Shalit had married a Scottish woman, brought her to Israel and later discovered that he could not register their two children as 'Jewish', only as 'Jewish father, non-Jewish mother'. Shalit further demanded that any affiliation should be registered as 'cultural' rather than as 'religious'. In 1970, the Israeli Supreme Court decided by five to four that the registration had to be carried out according to the wishes of the father rather than in obedience to the ministerial directive. The religious – both Zionist and the ultra-orthodox – naturally opposed this, but perhaps more importantly were supported by the nationalist Right as well as by members of the Labour party, both of whom competed to safeguard their influence with the religious. In 1963, the case of Brother Daniel (Ruffeisen) arose – he had been born a Jew, but converted to Catholicism. He proclaimed his Jewishness under the right of return. The religious Zionists further argued that the secular criteria were far too nebulous and could open up the path to anyone claiming Jewish nationality. The law was amended in 1970 to state:

For the purposes of this Law, 'Jew' means a person who was born of a Jewish mother or has become converted to Judaism and who is not a member of another religion.

The Labour government pertinently dropped the phrase 'according to the halachah' which Shapira had instituted in 1960. Any applicant would now be registered as a Jew according to this law. However, if that person wished to marry, it would be the rabbinical courts who would interpret the halachic status of the applicant. In essence, there would be two understandings of 'Who is a Jew?' Moreover, the law did not affect the authority of the rabbinical courts in matters of personal status which included conversion within Israel and recognition of conversion in the Diaspora. This effectively affirmed that non-orthodox conversions would not be recognized.

The four opposing judges in the Shalit case argued in the name of history and tradition that religion and nationality could not be separated. The argument went to the heart of defining Zionism. The secularists who had played the major role in creating the state worked to normalize the situation of the Jewish people in creating a nation state, fashioned on European nationalism with the Bible as a backdrop. Traditional Judaism, the religious Zionists pointed out, had preserved the Jewish people throughout the centuries of adversity. Judaism was a national religion and not the domain of the individual. They claimed that it was the sole source of unity. Secularists such as Vladimir Jabotinsky, the pre-state leader of the Revisionist Zionists, interpreted the role of Judaism differently:

If the people voluntarily encased their religious consciousness within an iron frame, dried it out to the point of fossilization, and turned a living religion into something like a mummified corpse of religion – it is clear that the holy treasure is not the religion, but something else, something for which this mummified corpse was supposed to serve as shell and protection.[16]

Ben-Gurion similarly spoke of a Jewish singularity 'garbed only in religious dress'.[17] Moreover, the Hebrew language, so cherished by the early Zionists, was perceived as a latent treasure hidden within the traditions of religion.

The Hebrew language, though not a vernacular, lived in the heart of the people, for it was the language of prayer and of the literature which was based on the Torah, developing steadily and serving as both the written language in the internal transaction of the communities and the 'international' means of communication between Jews of various countries. The religious festivals, steeped in national memories, were a kind of substitute for a common life in the Homeland.

Religious Zionists, however, contended that Israel was an eternal nation based on a covenant with God. It was not a new people that suddenly emerged in nineteenth-century Eastern Europe, but the rebirth of a national group with roots in antiquity. Its culture was not based on modern writers such as Bialik, Tchernikovsky and Brenner, but on the Torah. Shlomo Goren, Ashkenazi Chief Rabbi during the 1970s, commented:

The Torah preceded nationhood, both conceptually and in chronological order. For our nationhood was forged on the spiritual and ethical foundations of the Torah, and in the light of its goals and visions. Thus, any separation between religion and state detracts from the nation's completeness and oneness and deprives the state of its special meaning.

Other nations may be justified in separating religion from nationality since their nationhood is based on secular values – race, origin, language, character and territory. All these when joined together, blend individuals into a society that determines their national uniqueness, unconnected with religion or individual faith. Thus, their religion is common to members of various nations and cannot serve as a decisive factor in the consolidation of any one nation. This is patently not the case with regard to the Jewish people, scattered and dispersed among the nations of the world and speaking a babel of tongues.[18]

---

[16] Vladimir Jabotinsky, 'Zionism and the Land of Israel' (1905) in *Ketavim Tsiyoniyum Rishonim, Ketavim 8*, ed. Eri Jabotinsky (Jerusalem 1949) p. 118 quoted in Raphaella Bilski Ben-Hur, *Every Individual a King* (Washington 1993) pp. 123–124.

[17] Ben-Gurion, 'Jewish Survival', p. 4.

[18] Shlomo Goren, 'Problems of a Religious State', in Yosef Tirosh (ed.), *The Essence of Religious Zionism: An Anthology* (Jerusalem 1975) p. 184.

According to Goren, it was not the Land that had made the Jews into a nation. He cited the many nations throughout history that had disappeared once they had left their land. Judaism, after all, was a portable homeland. The Jews were a holy nation,[19] a people that dwelled alone and 'not to be reckoned amongst the nations'.[20]

The religious duty of observant Jews was to settle the Land. The re-establishment of the Jewish commonwealth, according to the medieval commentator Maimonides, would herald the coming of the messiah.[21] Moreover, the Talmud comments:

He who lives in the Land of Israel is judged as one who lives in the presence of God, whereas he who lives abroad is judged as one removed from the presence of God.[22]

Exile in the Diaspora was a form of punishment, not a location of opportunity. Only in the Land of Israel could observant Jews give full expression to embedded national characteristics. They thereby fought any dilution of 'Jewishness' in a religious and cultural sense and its displacement by the secularism of an all-embracing 'Israeliness'. Zerach Warhaftig, one of the leaders of religious Zionists, commented that any capitulation to civil marriage would undoubtedly lead to 'a democratic community, but hardly a Jewish state'.[23] The religious Zionists argued that there was a profound difference between identification with the Jewish people and Jewish identity. There was only one route to becoming a Jew – and that was through conversion to orthodox Judaism.

The stand of the religious Zionists was weakened through confrontation on two fronts: the secular majority who attacked them for their religious views and the ultra-orthodox minority who ridiculed them for their Zionism. Unlike the secular Zionists, they drew upon the writings of medieval commentators such as Nachmanides to support their views over human intervention in establishing the state.[24]

The conflict with the secularists went all the way back to the establishment of the modern Zionist movement. Herzl, at the first Zionist Congress, had stated that Zionism was a return to Judaism before it was a return to Zion and was at pains to avoid any schism over adherence to the faith. The official Zionist position was that faith was a purely private matter. The religious leadership had attempted to locate common ground through

---

[19] Exodus 19:6. [20] Numbers 23:9.
[21] Maimonides, Hilkhot Teshuva 9:2 Mishneh Torah. [22] Ketubot 110b.
[23] Zerach Warhaftig, 'The State of Israel: A Jewish State', in Yosef Tirosh (ed.), *The Essence of Religious Zionism: An Anthology* (Jerusalem 1975) p. 204.
[24] Nachmanides, Commentary on the Song of Songs 8:12.

Nachmanides's commandment to settle the land. Mordechai Eliasberg, one of the first religious proto-Zionists, had written:

This commandment has in it the power to bring together the distant ones and to knit together the torn portions in the house of Israel. The pious and the free-thinking can link arms together. There is no difference of opinion or difference of views to disturb this harmony.[25]

The Democratic Fraction, a short-lived group of mainly students and young people under the leadership of Chaim Weizmann and Leo Motzkin, demanded a democratization of the movement and implicitly criticized Herzl's autocratic methods. Their programmes advocated the promotion of the Hebrew language, Jewish art, a Hebrew university and Jewish museums. At the fifth Zionist Congress in 1901, Martin Buber proposed that 'The Congress declares the cultural improvement, that is, the education of the Jewish people in the national spirit, to be one of the essential elements of the Zionist programme and requires all its adherents to participate in it.'[26] The motion passed and led the estranged religious opposition to establish Mizrachi in Vilna in March 1902. They argued that faith and cultural nationalism were not one and the same. The Bible and the Talmud were not simply other examples of Jewish literature.

Yitzhak Yaakov Reines, in his opening speech to the first Mizrachi conference in Pressburg in August 1904, blamed the 'liberals' who had been rejected by the revolutionary movement and enlightened opinion 'and therefore hurried to find a refuge in Zion'.[27] According to the Mizrachi, 'nationalism separated from faith is like air, almost nothing, while faith without a drop of nationalism is but half a Judaism'.[28] The desire to envisage the rebuilding of a Jewish homeland was not the be-all and end-all of Mizrachi aspirations, but the aim of redemption was embellished in the Prophet Isaiah's maxim that 'out of Zion shall go forth Torah and the word of the Lord from Jerusalem'.[29] Mizrachi developed both within and outside the mainstream Zionist movement. Meir Bar-Ilan, Mizrachi's pre-eminent leader in the inter-war years, coined the phrase 'The Land of Israel for the People of Israel according to the Torah of Israel'. Shmuel Chaim Landau developed the idea of Torah v'Ha'avoda (Torah and Labour) which combined the idea of traditional learning of religious texts with working on the land. He synthesized the Chassidic traditions of the Kotsker rebbe and the Tolstoyan teachings of

---

[25] Mordechai Eliasberg, *Shevil Hazhav* (1897) in Judah L. Fishman, *The History of the Mizrachi Movement* (New York 1928) p. 24.
[26] Jehuda Reinharz.   [27] Ibid. p. 64.   [28] Ibid. p. 87.   [29] Book of Isaiah 2:3.

A. D. Gordon – this led to the first religious kibbutz. In education, Mizrachi established its own network of schools,[30] but the issue of education had given rise to factionalism within Zionism.

Mizrachi despaired of the refusal of both the Zionist Left and Right to incorporate religion as an integral part of the Zionist experiment. Meir Bar-Ilan had written in 1927 that 'the current notions and ideologies of the Zionist movement are but a feeble surrogate compared to the divinely given Torah and the faith of our forefathers and sages. It is our misfortune that this has not been understood by the present leadership.'[31]

THE ARRIVAL OF THE SEPHARDIM

Zionism attempted to create the new Jew by separating itself from Judaism. Many early Zionists initially concluded that assimilation into the host culture or transcending into an enveloping internationalism was the answer to the Jewish question. When they discovered that the world around them still considered them to be Jews, their embrace of Zionism was also a return to Jewishness. However, this was not the Jewishness of their origins, but one which integrated elements of European nationalism of their surroundings. The religious anti-Zionists viewed it as a form of collective assimilation. The ways of the Zionists, they argued, were not the ways of the Torah-true Jews. As Jabotinsky remarked:

The ghetto despised physical manhood, the principle of male power as understood and worshipped by all free peoples in history. Physical courage and physical force was of no use, prowess of the body rather an object of ridicule. The only true heroism of the Ghetto acknowledged was that of self-suppression and dogged obedience to the Will above.[32]

Like Jabotinsky, Ben-Gurion attempted to fashion the new Jew. However, Zionism required Jewish history and the Bible as an essential backdrop in order to create a different present. Zionism invoked both a connection and a disconnection with tradition.

Hebrew literature and poetry was attuned to exploring the idealism and complexities of the Zionist experiment. Yitzhak Lamdan's poem 'Masada' was emblematic of the pioneering Jew while Avraham

---

[30] Samuel Rosenblatt, *The History of the Mizrachi Movement* (New York 1951) pp. 20–24.
[31] Meir Bar-Ilan, 'Achievements and Aspirations', in Yosef Tirosh (ed.), *The Essence of Religious Zionism: An Anthology* (Jerusalem 1975) p. 103.
[32] Vladimir Jabotinsky, introduction to L.V. Snowman (ed.), *Chaim Nachman Bialik: Poems fom the Hebrew* (London 1924).

Shlonsky's early work bemoaned the loss of faith and the ongoing drudgery of contemporary life. Natan Alterman's 'The Silver Platter' – 'We are the silver platter upon which the Jewish State was served to you' – commemorated the self-sacrifice of young people to establish and preserve Israel's independence. In many works, the elimination of the Diaspora and Jewish history was a recurring theme. Moshe Shamir's recollections of his brother, killed in a convoy on the road to Jerusalem in January 1948, 'With His Own Hands', commences: 'Elik was born of the sea.' Canaanism, in the writings of Yonatan Ratosh, which distinguished between the Jew and the Hebrew and renounced any connection with the Diaspora, viewed Zionism as an unfinished ideological transformation, neither one thing nor the other.[33]

The problem of the secularization of Jewish tradition was that it was both liberating and incarcerating. Chaim Hazaz's short story 'The Sermon' depicts a populist, rambling speech by a hitherto silent kibbutznik, Yudka (little Jew):

> They invented a Messiah in heaven, but not as a legend out of the past, as a promise for their future. That's very important, terribly important – and they trust in him to come and bring their redemption, while they themselves are obliged to do nothing at all and there you have it . . . How can they believe in such a thing! And so to believe! To believe for two thousand years! Two thousand years![34]

Yudka labels the Talmud 'our Book of the Dead' and proclaims, 'we love suffering, for through suffering we are able to be Jews; it preserves us and maintains us, it proves we are bold and heroic, braver than any people in the whole world'. Through the incoherence of Yudka, Hazaz illustrated both the latent confusion of Israeli identity and their disdain for the certainty of religion. Yehuda Amichai alludes to this in his poem 'Jews in the Land of Israel' which commences: 'We forget where we came from. Our Jewish exile names expose us . . .'

With the birth of the state, Ben-Gurion realized that a sizeable proportion of Zionists remained loyal to tradition and – given the political constellation of the coalition – could not be ignored. A kulturkampf was an ideological luxury which could not be afforded at such an early stage in Israel's development. Moreover, the Biblical heritage, common to all Jews, could be utilized to cement unity and ultimately transformation.

Ben-Gurion attempted to bridge the gap between the observant and the secularist by often invoking the fact that messianic hope had sustained

---

[33] Boaz Evron, *Jewish State or Israeli Nation* (Indiana 1995) pp. 203–222.
[34] Chaim Hazaz, *The Sermon* in *First Fruits: A Harvest of 25 Years of Israeli Writing*, ed. James A. Michener (Philadelphia 1973) pp. 139–156.

the Jews throughout the centuries. The Talmud states that the day that the Temple was destroyed, the messiah was born. The religious thinker Shmuel Chaim Landau even argued that the content of the messianic idea was the same content offered by Zionism. Despite Ben-Gurion's invocations of common purpose and national determination, history's fragmentation of Jewish identity could neither be mended nor glossed over through the establishment of a state. Messianism, moreover, had profoundly different meanings for the socialist pioneer and for the devout religious Zionist. This became all the more apparent with the arrival of Jews from the Arab world and North Africa in the early 1950s.

In the wake of the defeat of the Arab armies in 1948, many Arab countries turned on their Jewish communities. At best they were made unwelcome, at worst they were the victims of a nationalist pogrom – and no distinction was made between Zionists and Jews per se. Both during times of religious intensity in the past and in the nationalist fervour during this period, violence, persecution and discrimination were visited upon Jewish communities in the Arab world. By the end of 1951, 93,000 Jews had left the Maghreb and Egypt; 180,000 had come from Iraq, Turkey and Iran; 48,000 departed Yemen and Aden.

Virtually the entire Yemenite Jewish community came to Israel through Operation Magic Carpet. Via Aden, DC-4 Skymasters, hired from Alaska Airways, flew around the clock. The British had to close the border with Yemen since the one holding camp was simply overcrowded. 10,000 Yemeni Jews thereby spent two months en route living in the desert, waiting to cross into Aden. The news of the establishment of Israel reached remote Jewish communities in countries such as Saudi Arabia and Eritrea. The Djiboutis and the Asmaras also made the trek to Aden. Egyptian Jews travelled to third countries and then on to Israel. In Iran, Jews from Kurdistan reached Teheran and were living in the Jewish cemetery, awaiting help from the Israelis.

The Israelis realized that they would have to prioritize emigration from specific countries. Iraq was soon added to this list. Next were the countries of the Maghreb which were French possessions or part of France itself. As Morocco and Tunisia prepared for independence, outbreaks of violence against local Jews took place with increasing frequency. This also reflected the realization that they did not have the facilities to cope with a simultaneous mass emigration.

The long history of Babylonian Jewry came to an end when 93 per cent of Iraq's Jews left. Unlike the departure from Yemen, this was a forced exodus. Following its independence from Britain in 1932, Iraq's governments discriminated against Zionists and Jewish Communists who were seen as two sides of the same coin. In 1941, the pro-German uprising of Rashid Ali against the British was accompanied by the Farhūd, the mass killing of Jews, the ransacking of synagogues and the looting of Jewish properties. In 1948, the Iraqi government practised systematic persecution of its Jewish citizens – mass arrests, expulsion from the professions and institutes of higher education, economic elimination of the business elite. Following the establishment of Israel, Jews could now be sentenced to seven years for 'Zionism'. Shafiq Addas was hanged in September 1948 – as both a Zionist and a Communist. A wave of arrests forced the clandestine flight of over 20,000 Jews to Iran who then emigrated to Israel.

On the inducement of payment from Israeli sources, the Iraqi government allowed Jews to leave legally. Having disposed of their properties at knockdown prices, Iraqi Jews were allowed to leave with meagre funds. The Denaturalization Act of 1950 permitted Jews to depart if they renounced their citizenship. In March 1951, all assets belonging to Jews were suddenly frozen and transferred to the Iraqi authorities who then proceeded to sell them.

In several Arab countries, this pattern was repeated as both the permanently poor and the newly impoverished fled from official fury. The emigration from Islamic countries, however, provided some dramatic contrasts. From Iraq, the professional and educated elite departed. From Kurdistan, virtually all the immigrants were illiterate. In Egypt, Jews considered themselves to be part of the 'European' community. They were both the mainstay of the business elite and the founders of the Communist party. In Yemen, they were artisans and peddlers who embraced Zion with a messianic expectation.

In 1948, Morocco was still a French Protectorate and not a member of the Arab League. In Casablanca, 20,000 Jews lived in the modern part of the city. They lived comfortable lives and showed little interest in Israel. The other 50,000 Jews lived in dire conditions behind the high walls of the *Melleh*, Casablanca's Jewish ghetto. A visitor at the time wrote:

There were narrow streets, heavily congested, tumble-down houses and shacks, no sanitation or sewers, poverty and filth wherever one walks. Sometimes as many as twelve to fourteen persons live in one room not much larger than nine feet square. Little wonder that most of the community suffer from some sort of sickness, the most prevailing being trachoma and ringworm of the scalp for most of the children and there are many cases of syphilis.[35]

It was the pious poor who were most enthusiastic about emigration to Israel. They wished to leave behind their *dhimmi* status and to provide their

---

[35] *Jerusalem Post* 10 January 1951.

children with a better opportunity in life. Although there were no diplomatic relations with Israel, emissaries operated quietly and there was even a transit camp. The emigrants left by ship for Marseilles and then travelled to Israel. The voyages to Israel also showed up the very different evolutions of Jewish communities and were a portent of future problems. On the transit ship the *Pam Crescent*, Hungarian girls took to sunbathing in their bikinis. This shocked and scandalized Moroccan men who had very different ideas as to how Jewish women should dress.[36]

The Jews who were termed under the misnomer 'Sephardim' came from a plethora of different backgrounds. In Libya, they spoke mainly Italian while the Jews of the Atlas mountains spoke Berber. But more important, these new immigrants had come from countries where the historical experiences were fundamentally different from those of Jews in Europe.

The corruption, authoritarianism and inefficiency of the Ottoman regime had blotted out both the European Enlightenment and the Haskalah. There was no progressive tradition and no development of socialism. The era of national revolutions had, by and large, passed them by. There was therefore no common ideological language with the Ashkenazi Jews of Israel. In countries such as Egypt and Iraq, which were influenced by European ideological developments, both the Zionist movement and Communist parties began to flourish. The Jews in the Arab world were a product of the societies in which they lived – and discriminated-against and ghettoized, they often inhabited the lowest strata of such societies. The British and French Mandates in the Middle East had brought an end to the second-class status of Jews in Islamic countries, but the simultaneous rise of Arab nationalism produced an interest in Jewish nationalism. In the early 1950s, Ben-Gurion noted that Jews in Islamic countries had contributed minimally to the advance of the Zionist movement. The number of shekel holders from Islamic countries at the last pre-war Zionist Congress in August 1939 accounted for 0.38 per cent. This compared to Eastern Europe's 40.9 per cent, the Americas' and the British Commonwealth's 32.4 per cent and Western Europe's 10.1 per cent. About 800,000 Jews lived in Islamic countries at that time; only 4,018 were shekel holders.[37]

Before the Shoah, approximately 20 per cent of the world's Jews had been Sephardim. With the destruction of the Jewish masses of Eastern Europe, this fraction increased dramatically. Moreover, the flight from the Arab

---

[36] Ernest Stock, *Chosen Instrument: The Jewish Agency in the First Decade of the State of Israel* (New York 1988) pp. 105–106.

[37] Ben-Gurion, 'Jewish Survival' p. 37.

world was to Israel almost exclusively. Thus, the balance of Ashkenazim and Sephardim in Israel did not reflect the dominance of Ashkenazim in world Jewry per se. In 1948, Israel's Jews accounted for 5.7 per cent of world Jewry. By 1954, it had increased to 12.8 per cent.[38] By the 1960s, the percentage of Sephardim in Israel reached 50 per cent. The country which had been built in the image of the European Enlightenment and socialism was alien to the religious heritage and cultural norms of the Sephardim.

Before this huge immigration, the Sephardi community in Israel comprised approximately 15 per cent of the population. Sephardi and Yemenite lists won five seats in the first election. In his speech in the debate on the formation of the government, the sole Yemenite representative reflected the traditionalism of his community. He attacked the secularism of Mapai and Mapam:

they think they have a monopoly on progress, labour and political understanding... they label those who are faithful to Jewish law and tradition – who still constitute the majority of the Jewish people throughout the world – as 'reaction', adding the term 'clericalism' which has a derogatory connotation and frightens those who did receive a sound religious education. We must not forget that the term 'clericalism' is a double-edged sword, because by this trenchant opposition to the Jewish tradition, they are in danger of developing a 'secular clericalism'. If only because of this attitude, the coalition should exclude them. Nationalism and religion in Judaism are one and the same thing. The Jewish nation is the body which creates and builds, and the spirit that guides it is that of the prophets, the sages, the Law and tradition.[39]

A member of the Sephardi list, Eliahu Eliashar, complained that there was discrimination against the Sephardim in the civil service. This early Sephardi protest reflected a widespread Ashkenazi view that, in Ben-Gurion's words, 'in recent centuries these (Islamic) countries have only played a passive part in Jewish history'[40] and that 'the shechinah [God's presence as Jewish creative achievement] withdrew from the Oriental Jewish communities'.[41] The Jews, he argued, were unlike any other people. They were a collection of tribes, separated from each other not only by geography, but also by history of development.[42] In Ben-Gurion's view, they would be redeemed by Zionism and become builders of the new state.[43]

[38] Asher Arian, *The Second Republic: Politics in Israel* (Chatham 1998) p. 26.
[39] Netanel Lorch (ed.), *Major Knesset Debates*, vol.2 *The Constituent Assembly: First Knesset 1949–1951* (London 1993) pp. 418–419.
[40] Ben-Gurion, 'Jewish Survival' p. 10.   [41] Ibid. p. 15.
[42] Ben-Gurion, *Medinat Yisrael Ha-mechudeshet* p. 407.
[43] David Ben-Gurion, speech to American Zionists in Jerusalem, 3 September 1950 in *Rebirth and Destiny of Israel* (London 1959) p. 535.

The emigration of Jews from Islamic countries averaged at 80 per cent of the annual influx during the 1950s. Their arrival in such large numbers virtually overwhelmed the capabilities of the young republic. Loan guarantees from the United States and the generosity of Jewish communities abroad alleviated the financial burden, but did not eliminate it. Their places of domicile were tent cities and transit camps with few amenities and primitive conditions. Such basic constructions were susceptible to flash floods and the Mediterranean sun. Moreover, only a small fraction of the immigrants possessed any kind of training or marketable skills. An attempt was made to settle many Sephardim on the land on the private holdings of moshavim rather than the collectivity of kibbutzim. Many Yemenites became farmers and the population of towns such as Beit Shean expanded tenfold. It was also a determined exercise in decentralization and an attempt to settle the entire country.

From the outset, the Sephardim felt undervalued and suffered from Ashkenazi disdain for their way of life. There was little respect for their religion and ancient customs. European civilization was perceived as superior. Officials were overwhelmed by the enormity of the problems they were obliged to solve and life became a bureaucratic hell for the Sephardim – pawns moved into new positions by invisible hands. The difficulties of acculturation and the meeting with modernity had not produced the Zion of their dreams. Despite all the good intentions to integrate the Sephardim, the worsening economic situation was increasingly producing a generation of the disaffected. Most Sephardim fell to the bottom of the economic and productive ladder, many living in less than salubrious areas such as the Hatikvah Quarter of Tel Aviv and Wadi Salib in Haifa, and their children failing at school. If they were not unemployed, they became the human material for unskilled jobs and menial labour and often drifted into petty crime.

While the Sephardim felt robbed, cheated and frustrated, the Ashkenazim were fearful that their dream of a socialist utopia was being undermined by their less 'progressive' cousins from the East. Despite this, the Sephardim clung to their moorings through the vehicles of family, community and religion. This was reflected in emphasizing ethnicity and Diaspora in the schools of the 1950s. The Mimuna festival at the end of Passover was reclaimed by the Moroccans to define their difference. Such developments evolved into assertions of identity, ethnic protest movements and ultimately into political parties.

CHAPTER 5

Retaliation or self-restraint

Operation Kadesh – the Israeli attack on Egyptian forces in Sinai in October 1956 – was an ideological watershed in Israeli politics. It brought to a head the debate between the *bitchonistim* – the activists led by Ben-Gurion and Moshe Dayan who placed the military search for defensible borders as a primary goal – and those such as Foreign Minister Moshe Sharett who did not accept the inevitability of 'a second round',[1] and insisted instead on exploring all avenues of contact with the Arab states. Sharett's enforced resignation in the summer of 1956 brought to an end a long and distinguished political career, but it also symbolized the demise of pursuing peace through negotiations during the next two decades. While Ben-Gurion looked to the generals and Sharett to his diplomats, their differences were firmly rooted in their political backgrounds.

Sharett's father had been one of the Biluim,[2] the first Zionist pioneers to reach Palestine in 1882. The Sharetts were part of the Zionist intelligentsia and were more influenced by Herzl's General Zionism and European liberalism per se. They did not join any of the political parties – neither the Marxist Poale Zion nor the Tolstoyan Hapoel Hatzair. They were originally attracted to the principle of non-alignment, endorsed by figures such as Berl Katznelson. When Achdut Ha'avodah was established out of a desire to have a unified workers' party, Moshe Sharett joined even though he was far closer to the non-Marxist Hapoel Hatzair. His close friend and colleague in Mapai in the 1930s was the former leader of Hapoel Hatzair, Chaim Arlosoroff. Moreover, Sharett's period of study at the London School of Economics in the 1920s brought him into contact with

---

[1] The Foreign Ministry had, in fact, opened a file, 'The Renewal of War', in July 1949. ISA 2403/12 in Mordechai Bar-On, *The Gates of Gaza: Israel's Road to Suez and Back 1955–1957* (London 1994) p. 23.

[2] Biluim (Beit Yaakov Lekhu v'Nelkhah); 'House of Jacob, come and let us go' (Isaiah 2:5).

Anglo–Jewry's liberal elite and the President of the World Zionist Organization, Chaim Weizmann, who was himself a General Zionist.

Ben-Gurion, however, had come alone like other socialist revolutionaries in the wake of the 1905 revolution. He had been one of the founders of Poale Zion and soon began to emerge as a workers' leader. Although the October Revolution fascinated him, he always kept Bolshevism at arm's length. Lenin was admired only for his exemplar creation of a new state and society. Indeed, Achdut Ha'avodah held a closed session in memory of Lenin following his death in 1924. Yet Communism and Zionism were in competition for the loyalty of the Jews. After all, the October Revolution and the Balfour Declaration had occurred within days of each other – and both appealed to the Jewish psyche. The formal start of mass persecution of Soviet Jews with the mass arrests of Zionists in September 1924 cemented a life-long suspicion of the Left for Ben-Gurion.

Ben-Gurion's view of the Arabs was then predicated on a theoretical collaboration between the Jewish and Arab working classes. This tenet of faith in Marxist Zionism was still strongly clasped even though an Arab nationalist movement was evolving in Palestine. The riots of 1920 and 1921 were interpreted as being the work of the Arab elites for economic and religious reasons, mingled with a dash of British collusion. Few in the broad labour camp considered this to be a genuine national movement. Moshe Sharett was an exception. In a letter to Ben-Gurion, he argued that two national movements had arisen in Palestine and that there were no easy answers to this clash of nationalisms.[3]

Sharett's upbringing in Palestine – he lived for two years in an Arab village – and his knowledge of Arabic had led him to work for the Land Acquisition and Arab Affairs section of the Zionist Commission. Negotiations with Arabs formulated an understanding of this narrative of the situation in Palestine. This is what distinguished him from Ben-Gurion – recognizing the validity of the Arab case while disagreeing with it. He perceived the Arab violence of 1929 and the killings of Jews in Hebron and Safed as an expression of nationalist fervour and not simply the actions of a radicalized periphery. While exploring contacts with Arab leaders, he argued at the same time for increased Jewish immigration, more settlements and land purchase.[4] Indeed, he was responsible for organizing several of Ben-Gurion's meetings with Arab political leaders in the 1930s including the Mufti's aide, Musa al-Alami, and Riad al-Sulh of the Istiqlal.

[3] Moshe Sharett, letter to Ben-Gurion 24 September 1921 Labour archives 104/iv/Ben-Gurion/6/c.
[4] Ibid.

Significantly, in 1948 Sharett had also been willing to consider the establishment of a Palestinian state, side by side with Israel, as opposed to
Ben-Gurion's support for the Jordanian option where Mandatory Palestine
would be partitioned solely between the Hashemites and the Zionists.[5]

Ben-Gurion's outlook had been shaped by a less than cosmopolitan
view of the world. The milieu of Russian revolutionary politics placed
the Jewish world at the centre of his ideological cosmos. There was little
room for sentiment – Ben-Gurion was far more an adherent of Herzl's
political Zionism and Bolshevik determinism than Ahad Ha'am's intellectual liberalism. Such hardness extended to his rationale that few Jews
had fought back against the Nazis because the Diaspora, unlike Israel, was
naturally unaccustomed to military struggle. The new Jews of Israel, forged
in the social revolutionary image of the second aliyah, would not return
to the traditions of Jewish martyrdom.[6] Even though his own niece and
her children had perished in Europe, he argued that a Jewish army in the
Land of Israel differentiated the Israeli from the Diaspora Jew. The point
of contact for the new Jew was not the Diaspora, present or recent past,
but the fighters and prophets of ancient Israel. The first defence group,
Hashomer, in 1907 and its ultimate successor, the Israel Defence Forces,
were defined as the descendants of the Maccabees and Bar-Kochba, the
leader of the revolt against the Romans. While Sharett understood Ben-
Gurion's desire to cement a hundred communities of disparate tongues and
cultures into one nation, if no attempt was made to think more widely,
could the idea of negotiations and compromise with the Arab world ever be
contemplated?

Such differences in world outlook and the interpretation of Jewish history had been submerged by the practicalities of working towards the
goal of a Jewish state. Sharett had laid down the foundations of Zionist
diplomacy and guided its meanderings, but he always deferred to Ben-
Gurion's leadership. He was simultaneously awestruck and antagonized
by Ben-Gurion. It was only after the struggle for independence had been
won and the Arab armies defeated that the quarrel over the direction that
foreign policy should follow became paramount. Ben-Gurion's central ally
in believing that the state would not survive if the armistice borders of
1949 were allowed to stand was the Chief of Staff of the IDF in the 1950s,

---

[5] Ilan Pappe, 'Moshe Sharett, David Ben-Gurion and the "Palestinian Option", 1948–1956', *Studies in Zionism* vol. 7 no. 1 Spring 1986 pp. 77–96.
[6] David Ben-Gurion, letter to A. S. Stein, 17 August 1955, in Roni Shtauber, *Holocaust and Heroism in Israel's Public Discourse in the 1950s; Memory and Ideology* (London 2006).

Fig. 5.1. Moshe Sharett addresses a Mapai election meeting, Jerusalem, January 1949.
Reproduced with kind permission from the Central Zionist archives.

Moshe Dayan. Both he and Ben-Gurion believed that the war of 1948 was a stage in an ongoing struggle for survival and that Israel had not reached her natural borders. Together with Achdut Ha'avodah's Israel Galili and Yigal Allon, they all believed that the borders of the state were directly defined by the limits of military force rather than by negotiations with the Arabs.

Unlike Sharett, Dayan was born into the labouring Zionist movement. His father was originally a member of Hapoel Hatzair and epitomized the virtue of pioneering collective settlements. During the Arab revolt, the son had become involved in the activities of Yitzhak Sadeh, originally a battalion commander in the Red Army. Sadeh developed the idea of an assault company, which would attack Arab locations deemed responsible for attacking Jews. This idea was furthered refined by the night squads of Major Orde Wingate who came from a family of Plymouth Brethren and believed in a literal interpretation of the Bible.[7] In 1941, Sadeh established the Palmach with British support.

Its first two companies under the commands of Moshe Dayan and Yigal Allon participated in the campaign against the Vichy French in Lebanon

---

[7] *Spectator* 29 May 1959.

and Syria. The Palmach's task was to conduct military actions against the Germans and Italians in the event of an invasion of Palestine. But the Zionists well understood that it could be used against both British forces and Arab armies after the war as well as to retaliate against Arab groups who attacked Jews. Many of Israel's future military leaders subsequently came from the ranks of the Palmach,[8] but with the death of figures such as Eliahu Golomb, one of the founders of the Haganah, it moved swiftly to the Left, influenced by Yitzhak Tabenkin and newcomers such as Moshe Sneh.

Dayan, who did not belong to a kibbutz, instinctively opposed this leftward turn. Although he had been distinctly uninterested in Mapai activities and only joined its Young Guard in 1944, he adulated Ben-Gurion. Unlike Allon who balked at handing over members of the dissident groups, the Irgun and Lehi, to the British, Dayan obediently followed Ben-Gurion's orders.[9] In 1946, he went with a party delegation to the 22nd Zionist Congress in Basel. Here, he related to Ben-Gurion's activism over Weizmann's increasingly fruitless and expiring diplomacy. Dayan's decision was to reject both Menachem Begin's Irgun and Allon's Palmach – he wrote that he was 'completely at one in my thinking and my actions with the path marked out by Ben-Gurion'.[10] Significantly, Ben-Gurion refused to appoint the Palmach's Allon as Commander of the Jerusalem Brigade in June 1948 even though he was preferred by the Israeli General Staff. The relatively unknown Dayan was selected instead.

THE DEVELOPING SCHISM

The Palmach, which had endured a disproportionate number of casualties in the war, was disbanded in the autumn of 1948. Ben-Gurion's action was not simply a means of unifying all the military groups within the Israel Defence Forces, but also a method of excluding leftist – and pro-Soviet in particular – influence. Ben-Gurion regarded the Palmach as Mapam's military fiefdom and was determined to staff the IDF with loyal members of Mapai. Members of the Palmach were made to feel unwelcome in the new army and those who were not marginalized resigned. Yitzhak Rabin was dispatched to study at Oxford. Yigal Allon's exclusion left the way open for Dayan's eventual appointment as head of Southern Command.

---

[8] The Palmach produced amongst others Yigal Allon, Israel Galili, Moshe Carmel, Yitzhak Rabin, Rechavam Ze'evi, Chaim Bar-Lev, David Elazar and Uzi Narkis.

[9] Martin van Crefeld, *Moshe Dayan* (London 2004) p. 56.

[10] Moshe Dayan, *Story of My Life* (New York 1976) p. 78.

The Israeli cabinet meeting of 16 June 1948 resolved not to allow any Palestinian Arab refugees to return. Yet many had returned or attempted to return.[11] In the aftermath of the bitterness of war, there was a deep fear that a returning Arab population would evolve into a fifth column, which would ultimately nullify the attainment of independence and turn military victory into national defeat. Many Israelis believed that the Arab world simply did not wish Israel to exist and were waiting to massacre and expel its Jewish population. The war therefore was no conventional conflict where there was an acceptance of victory and defeat, but instead the conflict was understood as a zero-sum game. This mindset also facilitated the destruction of deserted Arab villages and their replacement with Jewish settlements to produce a territorial contiguity.

Dayan reflected this mindset in a fundamental fashion. He instigated a shoot-to-kill policy of infiltrators and a rounding up of 'illegals'. In 1950, 1,000 Bedouin were expelled from the northern Negev to the Hebron hills. A threat to expel Bedouin to Egypt brought a counter-threat to expel Egyptian Jews and to confiscate their property.[12] The first Israeli raid on Egyptian-occupied Gaza occurred in October 1950.

A report of the unceremonious dumping of Bedouin and the action of the IDF soldiers found its way into the Western media.[13] This ensured that it attracted the attention of the Israeli Foreign Ministry, since protests against Dayan's actions began to blunt their diplomatic initiatives. Sharett raised the issue in a joint meeting of the Mapai secretariat and members of the Knesset in July 1950. He condemned the use of disproportionate force against both infiltrators and Israeli Arabs, terming it both stupid and insensitive. Dayan responded to this charge by suggesting that the excesses had been committed by new immigrants from Morocco and Iraq, but the general approach of the IDF, given the chaotic situation along the borders, had been the correct one. He argued that 'the only method that has been shown to be efficient – even if unjustified or not moral – is that of collective punishment'.[14] Dayan went on to dispute Sharett's claim that Israeli Arabs were no longer a fifth column and expressed a hope that they would be expelled if an opportunity arose.

---

[11] Moshe Sharett, speech to the Mapai Central Committee 24 July 1948, Central Zionist archives A245/391.
[12] Benny Morris, *Israel's Border Wars 1949–1956* (Oxford 1997) pp. 167–169.
[13] *Observer* 19 June 1950.
[14] Protocols of the Mapai secretariat meeting 9 July 1950; Mapai archives 11/1/3 quoted in Gabriel Sheffer, *Moshe Sharett: Biography of a Moderate* (Oxford 1996) p. 544.

The clear difference of approach indicated the split in Mapai, but it also divided the army and the Defence establishment from the Foreign Ministry, western chancelleries and a probable majority of Diaspora Jewry. Sharett embodied the liberalism, imbibed during his student years at the London School of Economics, which many Jews treasured, but was this a sufficient basis to deal with the reality of porous borders? Sharett argued that robust IDF actions would actually widen the USSR's window of opportunity to gain influence in the region and this, in turn, would draw increasing condemnation of Israel from the United States. In May 1950, Sharett told a meeting of army officers that there would be no new offensives to conquer further territory and that Israel had to be satisfied with the borders that it had attained in the war. He also argued that the issues of immigration and absorption could not coexist with wars against Israel's neighbours.[15] Humiliating the enemy, Sharett observed, would not turn him into a partner for peace. Sharett's minimalist and anti-expansionist approach found very little support outside the Foreign Ministry, certain Mapai circles and parts of the Israeli Left. Any negotiations would not compromise the military status quo achieved by the IDF. In Dayan's view, the term 'frontier security' had little meaning in terms of Israel's geography where the border stretched for 400 miles. He commented that 'the entire country is a frontier and the rhythm of national life is affected by any hostile activities from the territory of neighbouring states'.[16] The Arab states, he noted, did not have this problem.

Dayan and Ben-Gurion also wanted to complete the expansion of Israel from the borders stipulated by the United Nations in 1947 to more defensible ones, possibly up to the River Jordan eastwards, the Litani to the North and possibly to Suez in the South. Peace was therefore not their first goal. Even an alliance with the Catholic Maronites of Lebanon was entertained. There had reportedly been a secret treaty between the Maronite Church and the Jewish Agency in 1946.[17] Jerusalem, moreover, was still divided and the Jews were denied access to their holy places in the old city by the Jordanians. Opportunities were therefore to be seized if they presented themselves.

At a conference of Israeli ambassadors in July 1950, Sharett once again argued against a policy of expansionism and adventurism. Newly

---

[15] Moshe Sharett 15 May 1950 ISA FM 2454/21/A.
[16] Moshe Dayan, 'Israel's Border and Security Problems', *Foreign Affairs* January 1955.
[17] Neil Caplan and Ian Black, 'Israel and Lebanon: Origins of a Relationship', *Jerusalem Quarterly* no.27 Spring 1983.

conquered territory brought with it an increased Arab population and given their higher birth rate would swiftly eliminate a Jewish majority in Israel. The demographic argument was discarded by Ben-Gurion who argued that it was the creation of facts on the ground, often determined by the use of military force, which was the crucial factor. Foreign policy, Ben-Gurion argued, was subordinate in an era of state-building. To fortify this view, Dayan believed that the solidification of Arab states into warring blocs could prove advantageous to Israel's drive to expand its borders.[18] Thus, in the wake of King Abdullah's assassination in 1951, Ben-Gurion contemplated the occupation of the West Bank if Iraq, the other Hashemite monarchy, invaded and occupied the East Bank – the state of Jordan. The virulence and growing intransigence of the surrounding Arab states seemed to suggest that they too wanted a second round, another attempt to eliminate Israel. Dayan's logic was therefore to launch a preemptive strike at a time of Israel's choosing. By embarking on a policy of retaliation for every act of terror, Dayan ensured that the rationale of tit-for-tat became a spiral of violence. This, in turn, moved the Israeli public, in a psychological state of siege, to strongly support the army's approach.

The moderate majority that had supported Sharett's views began to decrease. Following Weizmann's death in 1952, the activist Yitzhak Ben-Zvi secured election over Yosef Sprinzak, originally from Hapoel Hatzair. When cabinet supporters such as Eliezer Kaplan and David Remez died, they were replaced by activists such as Levi Eshkol. Sharett's allies in cabinet now tended to come from the General Zionists, the Progressives and the religious Zionist group Hapoel Hamizrachi rather than from Mapai itself. Marooned between the Israeli protagonists of a military solution and the intransigence of Arab nationalism, Sharett's voice became progressively a solitary one. Within Israel, he was depicted as 'weak' by the advocates of the inevitability of war.

Ben-Gurion viewed Sharett as a brilliant peacetime Foreign Minister, but not one suited to an epoch of war. Shimon Peres, a supporter of Ben-Gurion and opponent of Sharett, observed:

Ben-Gurion respected the personal qualities of Sharett, his precision and thoroughness; he thought of him as a brilliant technician; but he felt that Sharett lived in an artificial world where gestures, words, were given great importance.[19]

---

[18] Conference of Israeli Ambassadors, 17–23 July 1950; ISA FM 2458/4.
[19] Interview with Shimon Peres, June 1966 in Michael Brecher's *The Foreign Policy System of Israel* (New Haven 1972) p. 255.

Ben-Gurion believed that the state had been established solely through the military achievements of the IDF in 1948. Sharett argued that it was also due to the efficacy of Zionist diplomacy, heralding UN Resolution 181 of 29 November 1947 as its finest moment. For Ben-Gurion, it was unimportant – a case of 'Oom, Schmoom' (the UN in Hebrew, accompanied by a derogatory Yiddishism). Ben-Gurion propagated the elevation of the IDF in Israeli national consciousness. In a country of new immigrants, the citizens' army was promoted as a symbol of national unity, a fighting force which distinguished the new Israeli from the ghetto Jew. This moved him closer to the inter-war approach of his Revisionist rival, Vladimir Jabotinsky. But unlike Jabotinsky, Ben-Gurion agreed to partition and knew how to distinguish between pragmatic politics and ideology. His breaking with the principle of self-restraint in the 1950s imitated the Irgun's policy of retaliation in the 1930s and there were resonances of Menachem Begin's doctrine of military Zionism. Moreover, following the demobilization of 1949, the army needed to be rebuilt and reinvigorated. Unlike Ben-Gurion, Sharett was willing to call the IDF to account when it was economical with the truth. At the end of March 1951, he challenged the official account of an IDF raid on the Syrian border and actually supported the interpretation of the USA and the UN.[20]

In May 1953, Ben-Gurion decided to step down as Prime Minister, but this prospect simply heightened the differences between the activists and their opponents. The IDF viewed the role of the Foreign Ministry as simply preparing international opinion for large-scale retaliation and providing diplomatic explanations for their views. Sharett did not view the Foreign Ministry as merely a diplomatic appendage to the IDF. Ben-Gurion, however, espoused such an approach and on the day before his resignation informed Sharett that he proposed to appoint Dayan as Chief of Staff and Shimon Peres as Secretary-General of the Ministry of Defence. Clearly, Ben-Gurion regarded the appointment of two leading 'activists' as a means of continuing his policies in his absence. Sharett vehemently opposed the appointment, arguing that 'Dayan's capacity for intrigues would bring about an indefinite source of complications'.[21] It was also opposed in cabinet by Sharett's allies the General Zionists and the appointment was only secured by a narrow majority. Moreover Mapai's old guard feared that the appointment of a young man to such a senior position would eventually leave them out in the cold. Ben-Gurion's bequest also extended to supporting the activist Levi Eshkol as his natural successor

[20] Sheffer, *Moshe Sharett* pp. 582–583.   [21] Ibid. p. 682.

rather than Sharett. At a meeting of the Mapai political committee in November 1953, Eshkol pointedly declined the nomination.

Ben-Gurion and Sharett differed substantially on the need for reprisals and the extent of any retaliation. Between the end of the war for Israel's independence and the beginning of the Suez campaign in 1956, 200–300 Israelis were killed and 500–1,000 injured by Arab infiltrators. In all likelihood, 2,700–5,000 Arab infiltrators were killed, of whom the majority were probably unarmed.[22] Initially, many of the infiltrators returned for family or economic reasons, but this sometimes involved acts of terror, perpetrated against Israeli civilians. Dayan regarded these attacks as merely a continuation of the pre-state killings of Jews and decided to dispense with any notion of self-restraint and to embark upon collective punishment.

This policy reached its apogee when a raid was carried out on the village of Qibya in Jordan, following the killing of an Israeli mother and her two children. Under the command of Major Ariel Sharon, unit 101 demolished forty-five homes of Qibya's inhabitants, thereby accidentally killing sixty-nine men, women and children. An initial Arab Legion examination, confirmed by IDF reports, suggested that the inhabitants had actually been killed by small arms fire. Condemnations from the United States and Europe were fierce – the threat of sanctions against Israel was suggested – and for the first time, the protests were joined by angry Diaspora leaders. In a cabinet discussion, Sharett urged that a formal apology be given while Ben-Gurion opted for a cover-up and the displacement of blame onto vengeful settlers. In a radio broadcast, Ben-Gurion declaimed that the cabinet had made a full investigation and that 'not a single army unit was absent from its base when Qibya was attacked.'[23] Sharett instructed his Ministry spokesman not to repeat this false explanation.[24] It was further intimated that the 'settlers' responsible were Holocaust survivors and new immigrants from North Africa. In protest, the United States froze the first instalment of a $26 million grant. Sharett was both furious and depressed especially as he had initially opposed the operation to the point of threatening resignation. Yet the decision had been taken by Ben-Gurion over his objections. This became the pattern of Sharett's brief tenure in the premiership after Ben-Gurion's first resignation in December 1953.

Sharett's views were disregarded time and again by Dayan and Lavon, the new Minister of Defence. Reprisals took place either without his knowledge or through the provision of partial information. The 'Prime

---

[22] Morris, *Israel's Border Wars* pp. 431–432. [23] Ibid. pp. 269–272.
[24] Sheffer, *Moshe Sharett*, p. 686.

Minister', in their eyes, remained David Ben-Gurion, their patron and mentor in his retirement at Sde Boker in the Negev. Sharett's attempts to exercise self-restraint and thereby repair the damage done to Israel's relations with the West were additionally undermined by increased attacks by Arab infiltrators. Despite Dayan's disloyalty, Sharett initially could count on approximately two thirds of the cabinet to support his approach and even the activists Levi Eshkol and Golda Meir were beginning to move away from Ben-Gurion's line. Indeed, Sharett proposed cutting military expenditure and reforming Mapai. Yet his enunciation of a new direction in March 1954 was brought to an immediate halt by an attack on a bus filled with civilians, en route to Tel Aviv at Ma'ale Akrabim in the Negev. Although it was unclear who had actually instigated this attack, it sparked criticism of Sharett's approach from his opponents in cabinet, the press and in the IDF. It seems that this was also a breaking point for Ben-Gurion who proved unable to remain silent and uninvolved in retirement.

NASSER'S METAMORPHOSIS

The meaning of the Free Officers' Revolution in Egypt was a subject of considerable debate within the Foreign Ministry and the Defence establishment. Sharett had contacted its leader, Muhammad Neguib, in July 1952 only a few days after the coup with a statement that Israel wanted to negotiate a comprehensive peace agreement with Egypt. While Sharett was enthusiastic about exploring this further, Ben-Gurion was more circumspect about such new developments. The establishment of kibbutz Ketziot in the demilitarized zone between Israel and Egypt in September 1953 was indicative of his determination not to give diplomacy a primary role. He differentiated between securing the existence of Israel and achieving peace with the Arabs. While he predicted 'a protracted spell of peacelessness', he also wrote:

There is no valid reason either for Egypt to persist in its feud and involvement. Between our two countries extends the vast desert of Sinai, and there is no room for border clashes. Politically and economically the two countries are not at odds. The reverse is true.[25]

While Dayan preferred to widen any differences between Arab states, he also met the Syrians and there was renewed contact with the Jordanians. Initially, the Egyptians had taken action against Palestinian infiltrators, but

---

[25] Ben-Gurion, 'Israel among the Nations', p. 24.

this had lasted only three months. At the end of October 1952, the Free Officers regime hardened their approach by criticizing the Israeli reparations agreement with Germany and tightening the blockade of Israeli goods passing through the Suez Canal. A Norwegian vessel carrying meat from Ethiopia was seized by the Egyptians. The number and range of infiltrations also increased. In part, this arose from the new regime's need to placate its Islamist opponents and to shore up domestic support. Although there was no rush to arrange clandestine meetings, Gamal Abdul Nasser, one of the strongmen of the new regime, sent a positive message through its Paris Embassy to Israeli leaders in February 1953. He stated that Egypt had no territorial designs and wished to initiate a dialogue with Israel. In response to an Israeli reply,[26] Nasser promised to look at lifting the Egyptian blockade on Israeli navigation through the Suez Canal. At this time, Nasser's focus was on the parlous economic situation and he wanted Israeli assistance in purchasing Egyptian cotton as well as smoothing the path to the White House. Despite this, Ben-Gurion was sceptical and eventually concluded that any negotiations with the Egyptians would be a futile exercise.

He argued that ongoing contacts and new ideas for peace were secondary to the regime's sensitivity to its domestic constituency and to criticism from rivals in the Arab world. On the one hand, Nasser wished to cultivate the United States to secure economic aid and to influence the British to evacuate the Canal Zone – and to secure Israeli acquiescence in smoothing the path. On the other, he wished to secure his status as a post-colonial leader and to export the revolution to other parts of the Arab world. The latter aim, however, involved casting Israel in the role of an imperialist outpost. The cause of Palestine progressively became the litmus test for Arab nationalists. This coincided with Soviet aims in the Middle East.

STALIN'S EMBRACE

Relations with Soviet Communism had always been ideologically difficult for Mapai since they reflected the division between democratic socialism and one-dimensional Leninism. Both Ben-Gurion and Sharett were particularly opposed to Jewish Communists and their fellow travellers and there was a certain ambivalence towards the Soviet Union.[27] It was not

---

[26] Reuven Shiloah, letter to Moshe Sharett 13 May 1953, ISA FM 2453/20.
[27] Ben-Gurion often referred to Jewish fellow travellers as the Yevsektsia, the Jewish sections of the CPSU.

forgotten that the USSR had played a significant role in establishing the state and had supplied Israel with badly needed fuel in 1948. Yet Israel had formally adopted a policy of non-identification with East and West. At the UN, Israel was one of the first non-Communist countries to recognise *de jure* Mao's China and to argue against the lifting of the diplomatic isolation of Franco's Spain. Yet Israel tended to vote against Soviet policies more than against American ones.

Despite supporting Israel in 1948, Stalin refused to allow any Soviet Jews to emigrate to Israel. This contrasted with the desire of other Communist states in Eastern Europe to allow their Jews to leave – often at a financial price. Moreover, Israel feared that any continued advocacy of the emigration of Soviet Jews – whether by diplomatic means or through a campaign by Diaspora Jews – would force the Kremlin to halt the departure of Jews from other countries in Eastern Europe. Yet the desire of Soviet Jews to identify with Israel was manifested by unprecedented mass demonstrations outside the Moscow Central Synagogue when the Israeli Ambassador, Golda Meir, attended the New Year[28] and Yom Kippur services in the autumn of 1948. The Israeli Embassy and the Jewish Anti-Fascist Committee became the recipients of appeals from Soviet Jews wishing to rejoin family in Israel or volunteering to fight in the war.[29] Such enthusiasm was quickly stifled by Ilya Ehrenburg's infamous, cautionary article in *Pravda*.[30] The writers of such appeals were arrested, Yiddish publishing houses and publications closed down and leading Jewish intellectuals and writers imprisoned. This campaign against 'rootless cosmopolitans' reached its apogee in the summer of 1952 when the first show trial of the Jewish intelligentsia was staged. Its defendants were found guilty and shot. Similarly, the preponderance of Jewish Communists in the leadership of the Czechoslovak party led to their uncovering as 'Zionists' and they too were duly dispatched.[31] Their ashes were sprinkled on the icy roads of Prague.

Israel now openly protested about Soviet policy towards its Jews. Ben-Gurion utilized the opportunity to attack Mapam in a series of articles in *Davar*. Mapam had advocated non-alignment while still invoking Marxist phraseology and pro-Soviet sentiments. The revelations of the Doctors' plot in January 1953, when Jewish physicians had been accused of poisoning

---

[28] Mordechai Namir, *Shlichut b'Moskva* (Tel Aviv 1971) pp. 48–51.   [29] Ibid. pp. 333–354.
[30] Ilya Ehrenburg, 'About a Certain Letter', *Pravda* 21 September 1948.
[31] See Artur London, *On Trial* (London 1968); Eugene Loebl, *Sentenced and Tried: The Stalinist Purges in Czechoslovakia* (London 1969).

Kremlin leaders, created great consternation in Israel in view of Stalin's past record. When a bomb exploded near the Soviet Embassy in Tel Aviv in February, the USSR severed diplomatic relations with Israel.

Yet Israel had already been reconsidering its 'non-identification' policy. Sharett was always wary about alienating the Soviet Union and wanted to cement good relations with the developing world. At a meeting of Israeli ambassadors and diplomats in the summer of 1950, there was a split between those who wished to modify the policy in favour of closer ties with the United States and those who argued in favour of improved relations with the USSR. The turning point came, not through the lack of a Soviet response to Israeli initiatives, but due to Israel's support in the United Nations for the USA's stance on Korea. An initial Israeli silence brought the freezing of an American loan – and it was self-evident that there was a clear dependency on US imports and economic assistance. Sharett attempted to maintain a policy of non-alignment, even advocating granting Communist China a seat at the UN, but it was to no avail. At the end of July 1950, Ben-Gurion called in the US Ambassador to Israel and effectively committed Israel to the West and requested help 'to build an effective Israeli army of 250,000 men'.[32] The following year James Jesus Angleton, who was in charge of the CIA's Israel desk, secretly visited Tel Aviv and concluded an agreement to cooperate in sharing intelligence.[33]

However, the election of a Republican administration whose Middle East policy was guided by the new Secretary of State, John Foster Dulles, was unwelcome. Dulles was decidedly less sympathetic towards Israel than his Democrat predecessor. The Eisenhower government was keen to entice Arab regimes into its attempt to form an anti-Communist bloc which would encircle the USSR. Its coolness was demonstrated by repeated refusals to sell arms to Israel. Even after the announcement of the Egyptian-Czech arms deal in 1955, both Eisenhower and Dulles continued with this policy in the hope that Egypt could be persuaded to abort its growing closeness to the USSR. This situation was further complemented by the election of a Conservative government in Britain in 1951 whose Foreign Minister, Anthony Eden, was similarly less than well-disposed towards the Israelis. Yet Nasser's formal takeover in January 1954 coincided with Sharett's own ascendancy as Prime Minister, but even this limited possibility for a new understanding between Israel and Egypt mutated into

---

[32] Uri Bialer, *Between East and West: Israel's Foreign Policy Orientation 1948–1956* (Cambridge 1990) p. 225.
[33] Ibid. p. 251.

a downward spiral which ended in the Suez campaign. The catalyst for this was the Lavon affair.

THE RETURN OF BEN-GURION

Pinchas Lavon surprised Sharett in that, once in office, he transformed himself from an intellectual with almost pacifist views into a military adventurer as Ben-Gurion's replacement as Minister of Defence. In 1954, three cells of local Jews and an Israeli supervised sabotage group were activated in Cairo and Alexandria by Unit 131 of Israeli military intelligence in an attempt to thwart the evacuation of British troops from the Suez Canal. The British presence was viewed by the Israelis as a necessary buffer between the two sides. The network consisted of members of Zionist youth groups who although they had undergone some basic training in Israel were inexperienced. They were also highly influenced by their charismatic Israeli handler, Avri Elad. Their primitive firebombs in the American libraries in Cairo and Alexandria caused little damage and thirteen members of the network were soon arrested and then tortured by the Egyptians. Two prisoners including the Israeli agent, Max Bennet, committed suicide. Yet Sharett knew nothing about the operation and its outcome for several months and soon discovered that other operations were also planned to take place in other Arab capitals.

The major question that Sharett had to determine was who had given the order to start this ill-fated operation. Lavon and his head of military intelligence, Binyamin Givli, blamed each other. Sharett thereby established an inquiry by Supreme Court Judge Yitzhak Olshan and former Chief of Staff Ya'akov Dori, but it was unable to conclude who had actually activated the network. It did, however, reveal a deleterious state of affairs in the Defence establishment where backbiting and plotting was the order of the day. Sharett already knew of considerable opposition to Dayan's appointment within the Ministry of Defence and growing criticism of Lavon. Several Mapai leaders demanded the resignations of Lavon, Givli and Dayan.

Despite Sharett's pleas to Nasser, a trial ended in a guilty verdict. The executions of two of the trial defendants, Moshe Marzuk and Shmuel Azar, went ahead. Nasser offered the explanation that similar sentences had been passed on six members of the Muslim Brotherhood who had tried to assassinate him. Even so, he released the ship the *Bat Galim* and its crew which had been sent to the Canal by the activists to test the new regime's willingness to allow Israeli navigation. Although the Olshan–Dori report had exposed the unhappy situation in the Defence establishment which had been Ben-Gurion's domain as the relevant Minister, it also posed a crisis of confidence in the ability of Israel to defend itself. Moreover, the death sentences – the defendants had caused neither deaths nor injuries – shocked and hardened the public's attitude towards Nasser's regime. In addition, Nasser was not averse to describing Israel as an artificial state which should disappear.[34] Lavon and Givli both paid the price for the affair and resigned. Ironically, although Ben-Gurion had been effectively the Minister responsible for the deleterious state of affairs in the Defence Ministry, these additional factors caused a groundswell of support within Mapai for the return of Ben-Gurion. Attempts to replace Lavon with other figures such as Levi Eshkol and Shaul Avigur met with rejection.

Sharett had little to show for his efforts. There had been no real breakthrough with Egypt. The Suez blockade continued and the Israelis had no access to a source of arms amidst a rising Arab belligerency. Ben-Gurion brought certainty and decisiveness in the public mind and they believed that his vision would restore confidence. The battered Sharett concurred in the mistaken hope that Ben-Gurion would play the part of the loyal subordinate. Thus Ben-Gurion returned after just a year's absence from office and significantly met Dayan before even speaking to Sharett. Indeed, meetings with Dayan and Peres became a weekly feature of Ben-Gurion's schedule. A few weeks later, an Israeli was murdered by infiltrators and Ben-Gurion and Dayan demanded approval of Operation Black Arrow, an attack on the Egyptians in Gaza. After a year of attempted restraint under Sharett's premiership, there was a general public demand for retaliation and increasing support for it within Mapai – particularly before the forthcoming election.

After the Qibya debacle, Dayan had changed IDF policy towards attacking military targets. Sharett had been assured once more that there would be minimal casualties, yet eight Israelis and thirty-seven Egyptians were killed in the operation – the greatest outbreak of violence between the two countries since the 1949 armistice. The IDF further gave out the version that Israeli soldiers had been attacked on Israeli territory and that they had followed the assailants across the border into Gaza.

While there had been acts of terror and Israeli reprisals throughout Sharett's year of office, the effects of the Gaza raid rebounded on Ben-Gurion and his allies. This was compounded by the revenge killings of five Bedouin by Israeli paratroopers which included Meir Har-Zion, a leading

---

[34] *Kathimerini* 8 May 1954.

light in Sharon's unit. Har-Zion's sister and her boyfriend had been murdered by assailants on a trek. Bedouin had been deemed responsible, yet
without obvious evidence, but although this was not an officially sanctioned operation, its operatives had been armed by Sharon. When this
affair erupted, Ben-Gurion protected Har-Zion and the army stonewalled
and refused to cooperate with the police. The end result was freedom for
the four paratroopers without charges being pressed. This symbolized in
Sharett's mind the denigration of the spirit of the past. In his diary, he
bemoaned the present:

This issue of the paratroop brigade and its dominant mood will definitely be the
subject of serious discussion between Ben-Gurion and me. In the days of self-
restraint *(havlagah)* in the 1930s we reined in vengeful impulses and educated the
public in this country, including ordinary people, to regard pure vengeance as an
utterly unacceptable provocation. These days, in contrast, we justify the strategy
of reprisals as an end in itself, without God forbid, presenting the principle of pure
revenge as acceptable; but we have unintentionally released the emotional and
moral brakes from this impulse, which is embedded in the human soul, and we have
thus permitted and enabled the paratroop brigade to elevate revenge to the rank of
a moral principle. This concept is indeed traditional among large sections of the
general public, especially among young people, but it has been crystallized and even
sanctified in this brigade, which has become the state's collective tool for revenge.
The spirit and education of this brigade have themselves become a provocative and
intensifying factor in reprisals. In contrast, each time that a retaliatory campaign
has been shelved by the prime minister, a mood of depression and anger has
prevailed in the brigade, turning it into a seething cauldron of incitement and
slander against the civilian government. The unique role of the paratroop brigade
in carrying out reprisal operations turns retaliation into its permanent mission
and its only justification for existence. What is more, it demands employment –
'Gimme gimme' (allusion to Proverbs 30: 15). Who knows whether the brigade
may not turn into a sick, evil thing that can only be repaired by being disbanded,
just as the Palmach was disbanded in its day.[35]

Sharett's authority in limiting Israeli retaliation was progressively diluted
as it passed down the chain of command from Ben-Gurion to Dayan to
Sharon.

THE SEARCH FOR ARMS

The Gaza raid allowed the British and the Americans to put forward their
own plan, Project Alpha, which called upon Israel to cede territory and to
move towards a solution of the refugee problem. While Churchill believed

[35] Moshe Sharett, *Yoman Ishi* 13 March 1955 p. 840.

that the British Foreign Office was 'riddled with Bevinism'[36] and institutionally supportive of the Arab world, its mandarins proceeded from the principle that Israel was 'the greatest irritant of all'[37] in the Middle East chess game. There was frustration with Israeli stubbornness and its refusal to make 'substantial concessions'. It exuded a belief that 'the Jews were doomed if they didn't change their ways'.[38] Indeed, by 1954, Israel had been excluded from all the alliances in the Middle East which had been constructed by the West. Inevitably, the proposals contained within Project Alpha were rejected by both Israel and Egypt, but Nasser clearly embarked on a different direction after the Gaza raid. Whether this move had been premeditated or not, the Gaza raid symbolized the first steps towards open warfare. The question of freedom of navigation in the Straits of Tiran remained an open sore for the Israelis who began to develop Eilat as a port in early 1955. The Czech arms deal in May 1955 heralded Egypt's turning away from the West and towards the USSR. This was followed by a Soviet offer to fund the building of the Aswan dam the following year. Nasser commenced a drive to export Arab nationalism and to radicalize the rest of the Arab world. Feudal and monarchical regimes with strong ties to the West now became targets for revolutionary overthrow.

Ben-Gurion had noted in 1952 that the Arab world was 215 times the geographical size of Israel and its population 57 times as numerous.[39] Nasser increasingly viewed Egypt as playing a heroic role within three circles, the Arab world, the continent of Africa and the Islamic world.[40] Even Sharett came to view Nasser as 'a man suffering from delusions of grandeur'.[41] Nasser's approach towards Israel moved away from a pragmatic, if erratic, accommodation towards one of unremitting hostility. Nasser terminated even clandestine contacts with Israel. Moreover, the Gaza raid also came a few days after Iraq, Egypt's rival for hegemony in the Arab world, signed the Baghdad Pact, a strategic alliance with the Turks which also attracted the interest of Saudi Arabia, Yemen and Jordan. Palestinian Arab fedayeen attacks – as opposed to infiltrators – were coordinated by the Egyptians and unleashed on Israel from Gaza, Jordan and Syria. An attack on a wedding party in March 1955 persuaded Ben-Gurion to urge an invasion of Gaza and to expel the 1948 refugees – some 200,000 people – to Jordan. Sharett argued that such a move would initiate a European arms

---

[36] Evelyn Shuckburgh, *Descent to Suez: Diaries 1951–1956* (London 1986) p. 251. [37] Ibid. p. 210.
[38] Ibid. p. 259. [39] Ben-Gurion, 'Israel Among the Nations', p. 14.
[40] Gamal Abdul Nasser, *The Philosophy of the Revolution* (Washington 1955) pp. 87–88.
[41] Moshe Sharett, *Yoman Ishi* 30 October 1956 p. 1806 in Neil Caplan (ed.), 'The 1956 Sinai Campaign Viewed from Asia: Selections from Moshe Sharett's Diaries', *Israel Studies* vol.7 no.1 p. 89.

embargo and the abandonment of the United States. The Israeli cabinet voted down Ben-Gurion's proposal by nine to four.

Ben-Gurion was significantly more successful in cabinet in securing a tied vote on a proposal to scrap the armistice agreement with Egypt. Ben-Gurion was convinced that Israel had to strike before the Czech arms deal became fully operational. Dayan's desire for conflict was now matched by Nasser's – and Sharett's pleas for restraint and moderation fell on deaf ears. With deals concluded with the French, the arms race developed a life of its own. Ben-Gurion exploited the situation and starkly polarized the differences between himself and Sharett such that the cabinet backed a mass attack on Khan Yunis that resulted in the deaths of seventy-two Egyptians and Palestinian Arabs. Sharett therefore decided to resign shortly before the 1955 elections and not to hold office after it.

Although Dayan had continually preached the inevitability of a second round, Nasser's vigorous pursuit of arms for 'defensive purposes' was breathtaking. The United States had offered to sell arms to the Free Officers' regime as early as November 1952. This faltered as Egypt offered to pay in cotton rather than dollars. The new Republican administration in Washington was keen to facilitate a rapprochement with the Arab world and thereby stopped Israeli orders for spare parts. It also placed obstacles in the path of Canadian arms reaching Israel. In selling arms to Arab states, the United States, Britain and France dismissed the very idea of arms parity between Israel and its neighbours. Jordan, Iraq and Egypt all had treaties with Britain and the desire to maintain the military balance, pledged by the West in the Tripartite Declaration of May 1950, seemed to have become meaningless. Indeed, the British chiefs of staff formulated 'Operation Cordage' in January 1956 whereby forces from Cyprus would attack Israel's airfields, impose a naval blockade and seize Eilat.[42]

The State Department under Dulles drew up a draft treaty between Israel and Egypt which called for Israeli concessions and US aid to Egypt. Several other plans emerged from both the Americans and the British which called upon Israel to give up a large part of the Negev in order to facilitate Egyptian territorial contiguity with the rest of the Arab world. Up to 100,000 refugees would be repatriated and the rest compensated. The holy places in Jerusalem would be under international supervision. France, however, proved to be the exception and suddenly changed course. Shaken by its defeats in Indo-China, it decided to bolster its weakening position in the Middle East by concluding an arms deal with Israel in July 1954.

---

[42] Keith Kyle, *Guardian* 13 July 2006.

Nasser had threatened to seek arms from the USSR on more than one occasion as a means of imposing leverage on the Americans. Previously Stalin had always rejected Egyptian pleas, but his ultimate successors Krushchev and Bulganin were keen to influence the emerging non-aligned bloc of developing countries. A Czech team arrived in Cairo in February 1955. The Gaza raid a few days later allowed the Egyptians to feel vindicated in their decision to deal with the Kremlin which had instructed the Czechs to accept Egyptian cotton as payment. The first Soviet arms via Czechoslovakia arrived at the end of the year. By May 1956, $250 million worth of arms were being delivered. The accumulation of such a huge arsenal far outstripped Israeli arms. The delivery was scheduled to include 170 T-34 medium and 60 Stalin-3 heavy tanks, light and heavy anti-aircraft guns, 100 MIG-15 jet fighters, 48 Ilushin-28 bombers, 2 destroyers, 4 minesweepers, 12 torpedo boats and 6 submarines.[43] There were 45 Egyptian bombers for Israel's 2. There were 200 Egyptian jets for Israel's 114.[44]

Nasser probably wished to deter Israel rather than defeat her. Although it enhanced his position as a leader of the post-colonial world, it had the opposite effect in that it encouraged Israel to embark on a pre-emptive strike. It tipped the balance towards Ben-Gurion and Dayan and away from Sharett. Moreover, Egyptian military intelligence informed Nasser that Israel had no desire to confront them on the field of battle. The alarm felt in Israel on all sides of the political spectrum was mirrored in Ben-Gurion's comment that the Czech arms deal was 'tantamount to selling poison to a convicted murderer'. Ordinary citizens began to contribute to a Volunteer Defence Fund, such was the feeling that an Egyptian attack was imminent and that Israel was unable to defend itself. This, in turn, persuaded both Eden and Dulles to come up with further plans – enhanced versions of Project Alpha – to offset the Czech arms agreement. Operation Gamma, which was designed to eliminate the Middle East from the US election campaign of 1956, called for a meeting between Nasser and Ben-Gurion. Israel wanted a guarantee for her borders rather than a mutual defence pact, but even this Dulles was reluctant to concede.

The British evacuation of Suez gave Nasser access to airfields along the Canal Zone and to large amounts of equipment. Radar stations were now under Egyptian control which would allow them to monitor large areas of

[43] Mordechai Bar-On, *The Gates of Gaza: Israel's Road to Suez and Back 1955–1957* (London 1994) pp. 16–17.

[44] Michael B. Oren, *The Origins of the Second Arab–Israeli War: Egypt, Israel and the Great Powers 1952–56* (London 1992) pp. 91–93.

2. The boundaries of Israel between 1949 and 1967.

The borders of Israel as designated by UN resolution 181, 29 November 1947

The borders of Israel according to the armistice agreements of 1949

Territory conquered during the war of 1948

Israeli air space. Initially, Ben-Gurion as Defence Minister was relatively isolated in the Israeli cabinet, but Egypt's growing military advantage persuaded several of Sharett's supporters including diplomats such as Eban and Raphael to move towards Ben-Gurion's approach. The growing anxiety in Israel was reflected in the proliferation of plans to pre-empt Arab military superiority such as the proposal to establish a friendly Maronite state in Lebanon and the annexation of the southern part of the country.

THE ROAD TO SUEZ

Despite Mapai's attempts to project itself as the party of defence and security, it lost seats in the 1955 election and there was a swing towards Begin's Herut and Tabenkin's Achdut Ha'avoda – both of which advocated a tough approach to Nasser's drive. Sharett's allies such as the General Zionists lost ground and he became more and more isolated as the Egyptian arms build-up proceeded apace. In the weeks after the election, there was an increase in fedayeen attacks from Gaza. Ben-Gurion's speech to present his new government dwelled on the increasing attacks on Israeli civilians and the problems of the borders. He was clear about his priorities:

The mission of our generation is in security, settling the desert, absorbing and integrating immigrants, raising human standards in Israel and strengthening our economic and political independence.[45]

In a speech to the Histadrut, he told Israeli workers that the choice before them was between 'increased wages and a higher standard of living' and 'immigration and new settlement'.[46] By November, Dayan proposed a military operation to open the Straits of Tiran only for it to be voted down by the cabinet. Instead Operation Olive Leaves – a retaliatory attack on the Syrian army on the shores of the Galilee – took place. Although Sharett had reluctantly agreed to return to his old position of Foreign Minister, his continuing objections to Israeli policy, the emphasis on military rather than diplomatic resolution of issues, his belief that Dayan's approach was irresponsible and adventurist and his influence in Mapai all created a wider schism with Ben-Gurion than in the past. The growing bellicosity of Nasser and neighbouring states made Sharett's position untenable and

---

[45] David Ben-Gurion, speech to the Knesset 2 November 1955 in Netanel Lorch (ed.), *Major Knesset Debates* vol.3 (Maryland 1993) p. 858.

[46] David Ben-Gurion, speech to the Histadrut 5 January 1956 in Ben-Gurion, *Israel: A Personal History* p. 473.

Fig. 5.2. Moshe Dayan explains the Israeli military campaign in Sinai to journalists, November 1956. Reproduced with kind permission from the Central Zionist archives.

gave credibility to Ben-Gurion's arguments. There had been a growing isolation of Israel – the Kremlin, the developing world, Britain and America had all distanced themselves from previously held positions. In Ben-Gurion's eyes, Sharett's approach did not reflect the changing reality; he thereby determined to remove him and threatened his own resignation if Sharett did not leave. In the summer of 1956, Ben-Gurion replaced him with someone closer to his own views, Golda Meir. The party approved his resignation by thirty-five votes to seven, but seventy-four members of the central committee abstained.

In the absence of Sharett's restraining influence and Nasser's nationalization of the Canal, the way was clear to make common ground with both the British and the French who would effectively shield Israel from

Western sanctions for a pre-emptive strike. For Ben-Gurion, linkage between a war initiated by Israel and a protective foreign power was all-important. Bitter threats from the Arab media were freely quoted by Ben-Gurion to an Israeli public that believed that it was about to be attacked by mightier, aggressive neighbours. Nasser proclaimed a determination to regain the rights of the Palestinians by force while his Minister of Defence, Abdul Hakim Amer, stated that the Egyptian armed forces could now 'wipe Israel off the map'. The Syrian Prime Minister told his parliament that his government's foreign policy was based on 'a war against imperialism, Zionism and Israel'. The movement of the Iraqi army into Jordan and the establishment of a joint military command between Egypt, Jordan and Syria were further causes for concern. In the USSR, history was being rewritten. A revised entry in the *Soviet Encyclopaedia* now suggested that the war of 1948 'was caused by American imperialism'.[47]

The coming to power in France of Guy Mollet produced an agreement in June 1956 which facilitated the passage of arms to Israel – these were quietly transported the following month. Any mention of the shipments was excised from the Israeli press and Ben-Gurion elliptically informed the Knesset by reciting a poem by Natan Alterman which asked 'when, after 1948, did the Jews decide once again; to break the ring surrounding them?'[48] The French supplied 300 tanks which fundamentally changed Israel's infantry-based army.

The nationalization of the Canal had brought in the British as a third partner. The clandestine meeting with the British Foreign Secretary, Selwyn Lloyd, and the agreement at Sèvres in October 1956 called for an Israeli paratroop drop near the canal and an attack on Gaza and Tiran. Britain and France would then demand the withdrawal of Israeli troops from the perimeter of the Canal area. Nasser's rejection of this ultimatum would initiate Operation Musketeer – the Anglo–French invasion of Egypt. Despite Dayan's certainty, Ben-Gurion only overcame his hesitancy to implement an Israeli pre-emptive strike when Britain and France set the agenda and effectively determined the course of the war against Nasser. Ben-Gurion was persuaded that if the British and the French faltered in their commitments, the military action could be passed off as merely another retaliatory raid.

---

[47] David Ben-Gurion, speech to IDF officers 14 November 1956 in Ben Gurion, *Israel: A Personal History* p. 516.
[48] David Ben-Gurion, speech to the Knesset 15 October 1956 in Lorch (ed.), *Major Knesset Debates* vol.3 p. 941.

Within days, the Israelis were controlling an area three times that of the state of Israel itself. Although only about a half of the Egyptian army was engaged by the Israelis, a huge amount of materiel fell into Israeli hands as did 6,000 officers and men. In the midst of an election campaign, Eisenhower reacted furiously, resulting, not in the fall of Nasser, but of Eden instead. While the Israeli army demonstrated its military brilliance and infiltration into Israel decreased dramatically after 1957, the political fruits of the collusion with Britain and France were minimal. In diplomatic terms, Israel had alienated the USA, the USSR and the developing world. In a letter to Ben-Gurion, Bulganin commented:

The Government of Israel is criminally and irresponsibly playing with the fate of the world, with the fate of its own people. It is sowing hatred of the State of Israel among the Eastern peoples, such as cannot but leave its mark on the future of Israel and places in question the very existence of Israel as a state.[49]

A few days after Israel launched Operation Kadesh, Ben-Gurion told the Knesset that there would be a new kingdom of Israel stretching from 'Dan (near the Lebanese border) to Yotvat [island of Tiran]'. He also spoke about the return of Gaza 'to our borders'. A few months later, Ben-Gurion bowed to US pressure and withdrew Israeli forces from Gaza despite Dayan's opposition. Even so, apart from the USSR, the maritime powers recognized that the Straits of Tiran was an international waterway and that Israel had a right to freedom of navigation. This allowed Israel to import oil and discharge it through a pipeline to the Haifa refineries. Apart from Nasser's ousting, all of Israel's objectives were attained. Less than 200 Israelis had perished in the war.

Despite American opposition to Operation Kadesh and the involvement of Britain and France, the Sinai Campaign set Israel firmly within the camp of the United States rather than that of the USSR. The rise of nationalist regimes and the Jordanian crisis in 1958 cemented a special relationship between Israel and the United States – a formal about-turn from its previous policy. Ben-Gurion emerged as the statesman-founder, enhanced in status and basking in the afterglow of military victory. Dayan and Peres were also transformed in the public mind into saviours of the nation at a low point in the history of Israel and were duly elected for Mapai in the 1959 election. All this and the break between Sharett and Ben-Gurion, in particular, proved to be the ideological basis for the emergence of the Right after 1967.

---

49 Nikolai Bulganin, letter to David Ben-Gurion 5 November 1956 in 'Between Moscow and Jerusalem', Ministry of Foreign Affairs (Jerusalem 1957).

CHAPTER 6

The rise of the Right

THE SIX DAY WAR

The Six Day war in 1967 altered the political landscape of Israel. The distinct possibility of an attack by Israel's Arab neighbours catalyzed the formation of a national coalition. For the first time, Menachem Begin, the veteran standard bearer of the Israeli Right, sat in government as Minister without Portfolio.

Unlike 1956, there had been no fatalistic expectation of a third round. Even so, a general anxiety had been increasing in the region. Egypt had concluded a defence pact with the regime in Damascus. There had also been an increasing number of military exchanges across the border with Syria – in April 1967, Israel shot down six Syrian MIG fighters. Both Israeli and Syrian settlements close to the border had been shelled.

The Soviet Union then seemingly exacerbated the prevailing tension by insisting that there had been a build-up of Israeli forces near the Syrian border with the intention of capturing Damascus.[1] Nasser's successful demand for the withdrawal of the UN Emergency Force, separating the forces of Israel and Egypt, and his closing the Straits of Tiran to vessels flying the Israeli flag precipitated the crisis. Moreover, President Johnson refused to act on the pledge which the USA had given to Israel in February 1957 that 'no nation has the right to prevent free and innocent passage' in the Straits of Tiran.[2] Despite President Kennedy's provision of Hawk ground-to-air missiles to Israel in August 1962, the United States wanted a diplomatic solution. Indeed, Israeli military intelligence had not predicted a new war. There were no US arms for Israel.

---

[1] Shimon Shamir and Vitaly Naumkin in Richard B. Parker (ed.), *The Six Day War: A Retrospective* (Florida 1996) pp. 24–46.
[2] US aide mémoire from Dulles to Eban 11 February 1957 in Parker (ed.), *The Six Day War: A Retrospective* p. 122.

During the period leading up to the outbreak of hostilities, Eshkol's government avoided antagonizing Nasser in the hope that a diplomatic solution to the crisis could be found. In contrast, the military warned that any delay increased the possibility of an Arab victory. In mid-May, the Chief of Staff, Yitzhak Rabin, had called for a military operation to undermine the new Baathist regime in Syria – and was promptly condemned by Eshkol. Nasser's mobilization of Egyptian forces, the military pacts with Syria and Jordan and the bellicose rhetoric 'to liquidate the Zionist state' conjured up fears of another Holocaust in Israel and beyond.

Egyptians were told that the shame of 1956 had been overcome and that it was now time to erase the humiliation of 1948. Israeli parks were prepared for mass burials and the sense that the Jews had been abandoned once more was all pervasive. The public tension during this period led to repeated calls for action and Ben-Gurion's return to power. Ben-Gurion once again supported the military against the politicians. Within the government, there was also support for the campaign against inaction, but there was no replay of the events that led up to the Suez crisis. Menachem Begin told Eshkol that Ben-Gurion should head a government of national unity – a suggestion which brought the hitherto bitter enemies, Ben-Gurion and Begin, together on a personal level. While Ben-Gurion wanted his old nemesis, Eshkol, replaced, his disciples Peres and Dayan did not support such a move. Instead, a broad coalition under Eshkol was formed with Dayan as Minister of Defence. Even so, opinion on a pre-emptive strike was divided.

Eshkol only moved with the mobilization of military forces across the Arab world and especially the deployment of Iraqi troops in Jordan. New Israeli intelligence presented to the Americans on 26 May suggested that Egypt would attack within forty-eight hours. Swift US protests to the Soviets forced Nasser to cancel the imminent military operation upon receipt of a letter from Soviet Premier Kosygin. However, top-secret Soviet MIG 25 RB aircraft had penetrated Israeli air space to monitor the nuclear facility at Dimona. The revelation of Israel's vulnerability prompted a two-day surgical operation to eliminate the Egyptian air force and a ground operation to counteract the Egyptian defence lines in Sinai. This limited operation took on a life of its own with the intervention of the Jordanians.[3]

The two sides were evenly matched with 240,000–260,000 troops. Israel took the offensive and initiated Operation Moked which decimated the

---

3 Michael Oren, 'The Revelations of 1967: New Research on the Six Day War and Its Lessons for the Contemporary Middle East', *Israel Studies*, vol.10 no.2 Summer 2005 pp. 1–14.

unprotected Egyptian air force on their airfields. Over 300 aircraft were destroyed, followed by devastating attacks on the Jordanian and Syrian air forces. Israel quickly outmanoeuvred the 100,000-strong Egyptian force in Sinai, many of whom were veterans of the war in Yemen.

Despite Israeli warnings, the Jordanians entered the war in the fight for Jerusalem. The Israelis defeated the well-trained Jordanians in the battle of Ammunition Hill and conquered Arab East Jerusalem. The Western outer wall of the Temple complex – the Wailing Wall – and the Temple Mount were now in Jewish hands for the first time since the Romans had sacked the city in the year 70.

Dayan pressed home Israel's military advantage with an attack on the Syrians – without cabinet approval. The Golan Heights were scaled and captured from the Syrians. There were less than 800 Israeli casualties. The combined Arab losses exceeded 20,000 killed and the wholesale loss of a major part of their military equipment. Between 200,000 and 300,000 West Bank Arabs fled across the Jordan as did tens of thousands of Syrians from the Golan Heights. The crushing victory in six days over Egypt, Jordan and Syria suddenly expanded territory under Israel's control almost fourfold.

Abba Eban declared that the 'Auschwitz borders' now no longer existed. Even though this had ostensibly not been a war for territory – and Israel had no wish to fight Jordan – the acquisition of the West Bank, Gaza, the Golan Heights, the old city of Jerusalem and cities of Biblical resonance such as Hebron and Nablus resurrected old Zionist debates about the borders of the state. Some looked forward to building the Third Temple in Jerusalem. Religious Zionists, impassioned nationalists and security specialists now all argued for a Greater Israel. All of a sudden, a besieged state now experienced the freedom of space, but the price was a fragmentation of its unity. Holding the territories now became the status quo. A stunning military victory had laid the foundations for the advance of the Israeli Right after decades in the political wilderness.

DESTROYING MAPAI FROM WITHIN

The internal crisis within Israeli politics as to how to handle the threat of a seemingly imminent attack by the Arab states effectively created a coalition of Begin's Gahal, Ben-Gurion's Rafi and the National Religious Party against Eshkol's Mapai. This prepared the ideological ground for the emergence of a Likud government under Menachem Begin a decade in the future. After Israel's victory in the Six Day war, they all believed that

Israel should not return the captured territories, but for fundamentally different reasons – nationalist, religious and security.

Ben-Gurion's last years were not glorious ones. While his followers in Mapai held him in awe and the Israeli public looked up to him as the forger of the state, he proved unable to stand aside and allow others to govern if their views did not accord with his own. He had also antagonized many of his colleagues by promoting younger people such as Dayan, Peres and Eban in their stead.

In 1963, Ben-Gurion stepped down for the last time and was replaced by the plodding Levi Eshkol who proved willing to reverse past decisions. Eshkol had been influenced by Hapoel Hatzair in his youth and did not relate to the dogmatic passion of Ben-Gurion. Thus, Eshkol overturned Ben-Gurion's refusal to permit Jabotinsky's re-interment in Israel following his death in New York in 1940. He also vetoed a first meeting between Ben-Gurion and Germany's Chancellor Adenauer.[4] He was less hostile to the Soviet Union and warned against alienating a superpower. Eshkol was also interested in forming an alignment with Achdut Ha'avodah – the unification of the different socialist parties was yet another issue where Ben-Gurion and Sharett had differed.

Hovering above the increasingly fractious world of Mapai politics was the unresolved Lavon affair. Although captured Israeli soldiers were returned, Dayan significantly did not demand the exchange of the incarcerated Jewish youth, sentenced in the Lavon affair, for Egyptian prisoners of war following the Suez campaign. In 1960, the Israeli agent in Egypt Avri Elad, who had controlled the network of Jewish youth, was sentenced to twelve years' imprisonment for being in possession of classified documents. His trustworthiness both as an agent and as a patriot was questioned. An emboldened Lavon demanded exoneration. Instead, Ben-Gurion threatened to resign and despite promises to the contrary, the Mapai leadership agreed to the removal of Lavon as head of the Histadrut.

The labyrinthine Lavon affair became increasingly public and Ben-Gurion's public image became increasingly tarnished. New inquiries supported Lavon's version of events – only to be matched by Ben-Gurion's insistent call for a further investigation. It seemed that Ben-Gurion did not wish to lay the blame for the affair at the doorstep of the military which in his eyes symbolized the transformation of the Jews in their own state. He also believed that Lavon as the Minister in charge should take his share of the responsibility for the failure. Pleas from public figures such as the

---

[4] Zaki Shalom, *Ben-Gurion's Political Struggles 1963–1967: A Lion in Winter* (London 2006) p. 18.

philosopher Martin Buber seemed only to fortify Ben-Gurion's certitude. An outraged Lavon threatened to open an insider's Pandora's box of Mapai's internal machinations for public consumption. In addition, Eshkol had discovered that the original letter of the head of military intelligence, Binyamin Givli, to Dayan about the initiation of the operation had been doctored on the instruction of the head of Unit 131, the military intelligence section responsible for the network. The crucial phrase 'in accordance with Lavon's order' had been added by Givli's secretary.

In October 1964, three Israeli lawyers examined the Lavon affair and yet again concluded that the cabinet committee had erred in denying the need for a judicial inquiry. This led to a renewed call by Ben-Gurion for a judicial inquiry in December 1964. Although this was supported by both the Attorney-General and the Minister of Justice, Eshkol refused to accept a reopening of the affair and instead abruptly submitted his own resignation. A meeting of the Mapai Central Committee, originally called to resolve the dispute over the Lavon affair, found itself instead having to decide whether Eshkol should continue in office or not. The Central Committee, tired of the issue and of Ben-Gurion's obsessive approach, voted strongly to support Eshkol. The subsequent party conference in February 1965 became the venue for the public and bitter confrontation between the different camps within Mapai. The Defence establishment faced their critics, the activists confronted their opponents, the young guard argued with the veterans – and Ben-Gurion's followers, Eshkol and Golda Meir, who had deferred to him throughout their careers, now openly defied him. Eshkol asked why Ben-Gurion had not reopened the Lavon affair when he had returned to power in 1955. He surmised that Ben-Gurion's real motive was to destabilize his government. The formal subjects of debate were the reopening of the Lavon affair and the proposed alignment with Achdut Ha'avodah which was believed to be sympathetic to Lavon's side of the argument. However, it was the speech of Moshe Sharett, suffering from cancer, who delivered from his wheelchair the most ringing denunciation of Ben-Gurion. Sharett accused Ben-Gurion of bringing the party to the abyss and tarnishing its public image.

The leader must not subjugate the movement, paralyse its mind, or impose his personal position on it by a show of his own authority. It is my hope that Mapai will now unite and rid itself of this nightmare, that it will free itself from this malaise so that it can breathe freely and attend to the problems of the future.[5]

[5] Central Zionist archives A245/139; Sheffer; *Moshe Sharett* pp. 1017–1018.

Some 10 per cent of those present chose not to support either camp, but 54 per cent supported the inarticulate, uncharismatic Eshkol over the founder of the state. A bigger majority supported the alignment with Achdut Ha'avodah. The spell of Ben-Gurion's authority was irrevocably broken.

Abba Eban who actually agreed that a judicial committee of inquiry was vital later wrote that Ben-Gurion's human failings – 'he was lonely, introspective, uninterested in outward forms, impatient of small talk' – eventually led to a path where 'none but the most uncritical of his devotees were willing to follow him'.[6]

At the age of eighty, Ben-Gurion was driven to widen the schism and encouraged his supporters to accompany him out of Mapai into a new party, Rafi. They included Peres and Dayan, but also Teddy Kollek, Chaim Herzog and Yosef Almogi as well as the first IDF Chief of Staff, Ya'akov Dori. Rafi projected itself as modern, dynamic, non-ideological and prag-matic, yet it failed dismally at the polls, collecting only ten seats in the 1965 election instead of the twenty-five which it expected. In contrast, the Mapai–Achdut Ha'avodah alignment secured forty-five seats. Ben-Gurion's obsession with the Lavon affair and his enmity towards the Mapai leader-ship had in effect exiled some of the party's most ambitious and talented young leaders. The realization that they had made a serious miscalcula-tion was quick in coming after Rafi's electoral defeat. Despite the fact that Ben-Gurion told Israeli workers that 'Rafi is the real Mapai'[7], the Rafi lead-ership soon began to explore the possibility of joining the Mapai–Achdut Ha'avodah alignment.

Ben-Gurion, however, sharpened his criticisms about the Mapai lead-ership. Eshkol had become 'a moral danger to the state'. Eban, who had implicitly condemned the 'adventurist policies' of the 1950s[8] and further argued that they had coloured Rafi's policies, became in Ben-Gurion's eyes 'a marionette of Eshkol'. But more important, Ben-Gurion stated that there could be a number of issues where there could be cooperation between Rafi and Menachem Begin's Gahal.[9]

One such area of cooperation was a change in the electoral system. The Rafi manifesto for the 1965 election had called for a change to the British system of constituencies. The Liberals within Gahal agreed with this, per-haps as a means of distancing themselves from their Herut partners after a

[6] Abba Eban, *Abba Eban: An Autobiography* (New York 1977) p. 294.
[7] Ben-Gurion's radio address before the Histadrut elections in 1965, Mapai archives, Beit Berl.
[8] *Mabat Hadash* 1 April 1966.   [9] *Yediot Aharanot* 25 February 1966.

disappointing election result and the pressure for unity. Half of Rafi's members were under the age of forty, yet apart from the policy of no criticism of Ben-Gurion, it had no clear identity. Although Peres had been energetic in building a party from scratch, its future direction was unmapped.[10] The emphasis on pragmatism and demoting ideology in political thinking characterized Peres's criticism of Mapai's economic policies. He argued that Israel should encourage private enterprise and widen the contribution of capitalism.[11] He also openly advocated the development of Israel's nuclear deterrent.[12]

On 13 September 1967, Peres formulated Rafi's programme in cooperation with Ben-Gurion. It argued that an 'urgent and energetic effort' should be made to establish a Jewish presence in East Jerusalem – 'in the north, south and east of Jerusalem without displacing its non-Jewish inhabitants'. Settlements should be established on the Golan Heights, along the River Jordan and in the Nablus and Hebron hills. Settlements that Jews had been forced to abandon in the past would be renewed including Hebron (1929) and Gush Etzion (1948). Ben-Gurion also advocated settlement activity around El Arish near Gaza and along the gulf of the Red Sea.[13]

Shortly afterwards, the Rafi Central Committee met to consider a merger with Mapai and Achdut Ha'avodah, following an invitation from Golda Meir. While Peres was a keen advocate of unification, Ben-Gurion once more resurrected the Lavon affair and spoke about 'the moral decay' in the leadership of Mapai and its flagship daily, *Davar*. Ben-Gurion argued that the supreme consideration of the state was 'national security and the integrity of its leaders' and announced that he was therefore unable to return under its current leadership. Dayan was less enthusiastic about the merger, but said that he would return to Mapai to oust both Eshkol and the Minister of Finance, Pinchas Sapir, as well as arguing for a reform of the Histadrut.[14] In addition, Dayan suggested that any merger with the Right seemed to be unlikely, following his unsuccessful attempts to persuade Menachem Begin that the electoral system needed to be changed. In the vote in December 1967, 58 per cent voted in favour of Rafi joining a united Labour party and the three-way merger duly came into existence on 21 January 1968. Nine out of the ten Rafi Knesset members joined the Israeli Labour party; only Ben-Gurion remained outside. The Rafi remnant stood

[10] *Hayom* 24 July 1966. [11] *Ma'ariv* 22 August 1966. [12] *Ha'aretz* 21 January 1966.
[13] Yossi Beilin, *Mechirav shel Ichud: Mifleget Ha'avodah ud milchemet yom kippur* (Tel Aviv 1985) p. 43.
[14] *Davar* 14 December 1967.

as the State List in the 1969 elections. Yet Ben-Gurion still argued against full-scale settlement on the West Bank. In November 1970, he advocated an evacuation of all territories conquered in 1967 with the exception of Jerusalem and the Golan Heights, stating that there was sufficient room within the pre-war borders for future immigrants.[15]

Ben-Gurion finally retired from political life in 1970.

OUT OF THE UNDERGROUND

The winner in Mapai's self-destruction was Menachem Begin. Like Ben-Gurion, for security reasons, Begin, for ideological ones, had long opposed accepting limitations on the borders of Israel. In 1948, he rejected the prospect of an agreement with Abdullah. 'He must be beaten instead of being treated as a partner for negotiations.'[16] Begin continuously pointed out that 'the partitioned state is not the Land of Israel, it is not our motherland . . . not a strip of land along the coast'.[17] Moreover, the need for a Greater Israel was more than ideological.

There can be no freedom without a motherland. The tiny partitioned area cannot secure freedom even for the few who inhabit it, let alone for the millions who must remain outside. If we do not expand we shall surely be thrown into the sea – not at once, of course, but in a little while, or with the next international upheaval.[18]

In the summer of 1948, Begin had turned the Irgun into the Herut movement upon emerging from the underground. Despite his desire to be the first amongst equals when it came to claiming Jabotinsky as a teacher and mentor, Begin, in fact, supported the views of the Maximalists in the Revisionist movement. As far back as April 1933, he had advocated 'a closing of the English chapter' – an implicit criticism of Jabotinsky's continued belief in England and diplomacy.[19] While Begin genuinely idolized Jabotinsky as an inspiring teacher, his different approach had been influenced by leaders of the Maximalists in Palestine such as Abba Achimeir and Yehoshua Heschel Yeivin who were admirers of Mussolini. Jabotinsky spent the last years of his life in an attempt to control the deepening radicalism of his acolytes in the Betar youth movement. While he urged his supporters to 'learn to shoot' to defend themselves, Begin called for a revision of Revisionism and advocated the doctrine of military

---

[15] *Jerusalem Post* 16 November 1970.
[16] Menachem Begin, speech in Petach Tikvah 29 August 1948, Jabotinsky archives.
[17] 'Motherland and Freedom', Herut movement, June 1948, Jabotinsky archives.
[18] Ibid.   [19] *Hazit Ha'am* 7 April 1933.

Fig. 6.1. Vladimir Jabotinsky opens the third World Conference of Betar in the Teatr Nowosci, Warsaw, September 1938. Reproduced with kind permission from the Jabotinsky archives.

Zionism to confront the British and the Palestinian Arabs. Jabotinsky urged youth to utilize their militancy constructively – 'when to press the accelerator, when to use the brake'.[20] Jabotinsky's sophisticated arguments were not always understood by the members of Betar who interpreted them as solely a call to arms.

Jabotinsky was no admirer of fascism. As early as 1926, Jabotinsky derided Mussolini when he wrote that 'buffaloes follow a leader, civilized men have no "leaders"'.[21] In July 1932, he wrote:

Adventurism? There are moments when it might bring benefits. An underground? Yes, too. But Betar is not and cannot be part of adventurism or of an underground; yet not anti-adventurism and not anti-underground. Betar, as I conceived it, is a school . . . where youth will learn to control their fists, their batons and all means of defence; to be able to stand to attention and to march well; to work; to foster beauty of form and ceremony; to scorn all forms of negligence . . . this is the type of school that Betar has to be. Yes, a school like that, for if not, better that Betar not exist at all.[22]

[20] Vladimir Jabotinsky, 'On Adventurism', *Haynt* 26 February 1932.
[21] *The Zionist* 25 June 1926.   [22] *Hazit Ha'am* 5 August 1932.

Twenty years later, as the leader of Herut, Begin ideologically cherry-picked Jabotinsky's writings and such inconvenient commentaries were glossed over.

The 'prime task' in Herut's stated foreign policy aims was 'to bring about the unification of all parts of our partitioned homeland under Hebrew rule'. Only secondly did Herut commit Israel to 'a policy of peace'. Herut's social policies were broad and undefined, but generally liberal. Herut promised to fight 'trusts and monopolies' which exploited the working man and argued that 'all public utility works and basic industries must be nationalized'. Herut advocated a progressive tax system and declared that private ownership of land would be limited. Jewish children would be taught Arabic as well as Hebrew. It proposed that the legislative branch of government would be composed of a lower body, an upper chamber and a Supreme Supervisory Board which would monitor all monetary and economic acts as well as transactions of state institutions.

In the 1955 election, Herut demanded that the Histadrut separate its dual functions of employer and trade union. The party manifesto proposed a bill that would make it unlawful for a trade union or a political body to own a business. All cartels, both private and cooperative, would be dissolved to ensure 'fair competition, greater productivity and lower prices'. Private enterprise was to be encouraged and capital investment made attractive. Party control over agricultural settlements would be abolished and foreign currency controls would be lifted. The aspiration of a Herut government was to reduce income tax by 25 per cent.[23] The sections in the manifesto dealing with economic policy and taxation far outstripped other areas in length and detail. By the next election in 1959, Herut was arguing that in breaking up the Histadrut economy:

Herut would change the illusionary 'workers' economy' in which the position of the worker is worse than his position in a private enterprise – into many workers' enterprises, cooperatives and associations. The lot of the worker and his shares in such an economy will not be fiction but real property.[24]

In 1965, Herut and the Liberals formed a parliamentary bloc, Gahal, in the hope of establishing 'a National–Liberal regime in Israel'.[25] The agreement between the two parties clearly laid out an agreed economic and

---

[23] Programme for a National Liberal government headed by Tenuat Ha'Herut: Election Manifesto for the 4th Knesset, 1959, Jabotinsky archives.

[24] Economic Programme of the Herut Movement: Guide for Lecturers and Canvassers in the Electoral Campaign for the 5th Knesset, Jabotinsky archives.

[25] Agreement for the Establishment of a Herut–Liberal bloc, Jabotinsky archives.

3. The territorial conquests of the Six Day war, 1967.

tax policy. It argued the case for individualism that 'Man was not created for the State. The State was created for Man.' In contrast to the previously held Herut position, the agreement proclaimed that 'the right to strike was a fundamental right of the worker in a free society'. It was, however, only Herut that maintained its right 'to continue to bear aloft...the principle of the integrity of the Homeland'. Although certainly less specific than previous Herut pronouncements, it was the only statement in the agreement which indicated a profound difference between the two parties that made up Gahal. Although there was opposition to cooperating with overt nationalists, the task to forge the agreement was made easier due to the secession of the liberal wing of the Liberals to form the Independent Liberal party. Begin had made considerable attempts to play down his image as a radical firebrand. The desire to annex the East Bank of the Jordan was quietly buried. The Liberals were hungry for power and any lingering reservations were dispelled by Begin's offer to give them disproportionately favourable positions on a joint list for the 1965 Knesset election.[26] The conquests of the Six Day war allowed Begin to advocate Jewish settlement in the West Bank and Gaza and to take a lead in promoting a Greater Israel.

THE IDEOLOGY OF OCCUPATION

The great enthusiasm for territory was reinforced by the Arab states' rejectionism. At Khartoum in August 1967, they publicly proclaimed 'no recognition, no negotiations, no peace'. Privately at Khartoum, however, King Hussein was supported in initiating diplomatic contacts with Israel. The Israelis, however, were not quick to respond to Hussein. Instead of the Foreign Minister, Abba Eban, the head of the Prime Minister's Office, Ya'akov Herzog, was sent to talk to Hussein in London.[27] Nasser, on the other hand, was once more talking about liberating the conquered territories by force only months after the Egyptian defeat.

Ben-Gurion argued that it was only Israeli force of arms that determined the borders, but qualified this with the rider that throughout history Jews had settled for the reality of what was achievable. Eilat, he noted, was outside the biblical borders, 'from Dan to Beer Sheba'.[28] He pointed out that God did not specify borders when he had instructed Abraham to go

---

[26] Colin Shindler, *Israel, Likud and the Zionist Dream: Power, Politics and Ideology from Begin to Netanyahu* (London 1995) pp. 57–61.

[27] Amos Elon, review of Tom Segev's *Veha'aretz she'enta etpanehah, Ha'aretz* 22 July 2005.

[28] Judges 20:1.

from Ur of the Chaldees to the land of Canaan. Moreover, Joshua had not conquered all the Land. In the Declaration of Independence, significantly there had been no mention of borders.[29] While such flexibility differentiated him from Herut's ideology and from the redemptionist Zionism of Zvi Yehuda Kook, the spiritual mentor of the 'young guard' of the religious Zionists, Ben-Gurion still advocated the establishment of some new settlements in areas conquered by Israel in 1967.

In addition, the Achdut Ha'avodah component of the Labour Alignment had a long history of maximalist positions when it came to defining the borders of the state. Its mentor, Yitzhak Tabenkin, argued that the conflict had emerged because the Arabs had not undergone the transformation that the Jews had undergone under the influence of the European Enlightenment and the French Revolution. There would be ongoing conflict as long as the Arabs were not free of their feudal social system. He had originally argued that the Arabs would eventually develop a working class and therefore a state should only be established when the conflict had been resolved between the parties. In 1947, he decried the second partition of Palestine and advocated a trusteeship rather than a state. Israel's war of independence, he believed, would not determine Israel's ultimate borders.[30] Wars were opportunities for Israel to expand and to plant settlements.

Tabenkin's profound belief in socialism led him to comment that 'a Palestine which would be built by private capital, will not be Jewish'.[31] Tabenkin deplored Ben-Gurion's drift towards étatism – 'from a class to a nation'. The Achdut Ha'avodah platform of 1924 at Ein Harod refused to recognize the development of a Palestinian Arab national movement, but gave rights to the Arabs as individuals. Hence there was no requirement to partition the land between two national movements. In 1967, Tabenkin still adhered to this.[32]

The establishment of the Labour party in 1968, comprising Mapai, Achdut Ha'avodah and the leadership of Rafi apart from Ben-Gurion, automatically created an ideological division between those who saw the danger of retaining the territories and those who did not. The stopgap, hawkish Golda Meir, became Prime Minister on Eshkol's death although this was partially offset by the establishment of a wider alignment between

---

[29] *Mabat Hadash* no. 85.
[30] Yitzhak Tabenkin, 'B'Or Medinat Yisrael', June 1948, *Naumim* vol.4 1943–1949 (Tel Aviv 1976) pp. 210–211.
[31] Yitzhak Tabenkin, 'On the Political and Economic Situation in Palestine', *Naumim* vol.1 p. 28.
[32] *Lamerchav* 14 October 1966.

Fig. 6.2. Yitzhak Tabenkin, c. 1960s. Reproduced with
kind permission from the Central Zionist archives.

the dovish Mapam and Labour in 1969. The Six Day war and its aftermath
therefore brought bitter internal conflict to this alliance of the four parties
of the ostensible Left. It created a paralysis of political action on the essential
question of the territories and the growing number of Jewish settlements.
Golda Meir's mandate, in part, was to ensure that Labour did not fragment
with the right wing under Dayan joining Menachem Begin. Moshe Dayan
was an iconic figure for many Israelis. In the 1969 election, his former Rafi
colleagues, now in the State List, collected over 100,000 signatures for their
'Dayan for Prime Minister' campaign.[33]

Israel's victory had expanded its own territory 3.3 times, although nearly
90 per cent of this expansion was due to the acquisition of the Sinai desert.
The immediate reaction of the Israeli government was to state that it would
return some land for peace. On 19 June 1967, by the narrow majority of

[33] Efraim Torgovnik, 'Party Factions and Election Issues' in Alan Arian (ed.), *The Elections in Israel:
1969* (Jerusalem 1972) p. 31.

eleven to ten, the Israeli cabinet offered to return Sinai to Egypt and the Golan Heights to Syria. There would be a special arrangement for Sharm el-Sheikh. Gaza was viewed as a security asset in order to prevent an Egyptian advance while the future of the West Bank was left in abeyance. Dayan opposed this initiative.

Eshkol also challenged Allon's proposal to immediately start a settlement programme in the territories.[34] Yet within a few weeks, Achdut Ha'avodah's Yigal Allon put forward his own plan. This advocated an effective partition of the West Bank between Israel and Jordan. Part of the West Bank, the Jordan Valley and the Judean Desert, along the Jordan River and the Dead Sea, would be controlled by Israel as its defence border. It would annex areas in the Jerusalem corridor. Jordan would control the major Palestinian population centres in two enclaves which would be connected to Jordan through a land corridor via Jericho. The proposed Israeli and Palestinian areas bisected each other, thereby requiring link roads to connect them. Such arrangements, Allon postulated, would meet Israel's security needs as well as Palestinian Arab national aspirations. The Allon Plan, unlike the earlier Israeli government position, advocated the expansion of Israel through the acquisition of territory. The ideological activism to retain the territories and the sense of public grievance at having to fight an unwanted war were reinforced by the rejectionism of the Arab states at the Khartoum Summit in August 1967 – neither to negotiate with Israel nor to recognize her. This undermined the position of the leading doves in the cabinet, Abba Eban and Pinchas Sapir. The Allon Plan, originally seen as hawkish, was now hailed as dovish. Even so, King Hussein in secret talks with the Israelis rejected it in September 1968.

Despite this, by November 1967, Israel and the Arab states could agree on UN Resolution 242 which called for the withdrawal of Israeli armed forces from territories occupied in the recent conflict and the termination of all claims or states of belligerency. It also called for the recognition of all established states by the belligerent parties and the establishment of secure and recognized boundaries for all parties. The English version of the resolution referred to 'territories' whereas the French version spoke of 'the territories'. All signed up to UN Resolution 242 because of the ambiguity of wording, but Israel and the Arab states interpreted it differendy – not least because of the absence of the definite article in its wording – and the PLO simply rejected it because of the omission of any mention of the Palestinians. The Arab states understood it as withdrawal from all the

---

[34] *Ha'aretz* 3 May 2002.

land conquered during the Six Day war while Israel viewed it as departing from only some of the territories.

Yigal Allon was a devoted follower of Tabenkin and epitomized Achdut Ha'avodah's desire to create a powerful defence force. In 1948, as the driving force behind Operations Yiftah, Dani and Yoav, Allon proved to be a brilliant military commander, yet in all the areas where his forces passed virtually all Arabs were evicted from their towns and villages. His use of refugee columns to block Arab attacks prompted his party colleague, Meir Ya'ari, to complain that 'we are losing our human image'.[35] Allon believed that Israel had won the war in 1948, but had lost the peace by not conquering the West Bank. He similarly believed that Israel had missed an opportunity to expand during the Sinai campaign in 1956.[36]

Although Allon argued that Israel should have conquered more territory in 1967 such as the Druse mountains, his plan to partition the West Bank between Israel and Jordan on the basis of functional responsibility represented a compromise on previously held positions. The Allon Plan thereby created astonishment and disbelief within his own party. However, leading members of Achdut Ha'avodah in government and in the Histadrut argued that Israel should not control the lives of a million Arabs. Other party leaders accused Allon of siding with Ben-Gurion, the historic enemy of Achdut Ha'avodah who similarly argued that Arab population centres should not be annexed. Tabenkin's response was that such niceties were irrelevant. He wanted to press ahead regardless with settlements since no peace plans would ever appease Arab hostility. Increased immigration was the answer to the demographic problem since the higher Arab birth rate would eventually create a Palestinian Arab majority in a Greater Israel.

This split between pragmatists and ideologues in Achdut Ha'avodah was reflected to a lesser extent in other components of the Labour Alignment. When the manifesto of the maximalist Land of Israel movement claimed that 'just as we are not allowed to give up the State of Israel, so we are ordered to keep what we have received there from the Land of Israel', nineteen out of the fifty-seven signatories were supporters of the Labour party.[37] When the formal advertisement, entitled 'For the Greater Land of Israel', appeared in the daily *Yediot Aharanot* on 22 September 1967, only weeks after the end of the war, the names of Israel's literary luminaries – Natan

---

[35] Morris, *The Birth of the Palestinian Refugee Problem Revisited* p. 434.

[36] Yigal Allon, *Masach shel Chol: Yisrael v'Aravim bein Milchama v'Shalom* (Tel Aviv 1959) quoted in Rael Jean Isaac, *Israel Divided: Ideological Politics in the Jewish State* (Baltimore 1976) p. 115.

[37] Manifesto of the Land of Israel movement, August 1967 in Rael Jean Isaac, *Israel Divided: Ideological Politics in the Jewish State* (Baltimore 1976) pp. 165–170.

Alterman, S. Y. Agnon, Uri Zvi Greenberg and many others – were appended. The leader of the Warsaw Ghetto Uprising, Yitzhak Zuckerman, better known by his nom de guerre 'Antek', and his wife also signed. It was a stunning array of signatories. Yet it also signified a generational difference of opinion. Younger writers such as Amos Oz and A. B. Yehoshua who were opposed to keeping the newly conquered territories were never approached to sign the advertisement.

While Achdut Ha'avodah embarked on settlement activity, particularly in the Jordan Valley whose inhabitants had fled to Jordan, Mapam refused to do so. When 'Swiss' tourists came to celebrate Passover in Hebron in 1968, stayed and instead created the first Jewish settlement on the West Bank, Yigal Allon became the first Israeli Minister to visit them.

While Allon and other members of Achdut Ha'avodah began to move away from their ideological moorings, Moshe Dayan, in contrast, moved towards the Right. Rafi had similarly downplayed the demographic argument by promoting the solution of increasing immigration. Dayan was pessimistic about the prospect of peace with Jordan and originally wanted to establish four new cities on the West Bank. He further argued for an economic linkage between Israel and the territories. Water, electricity and transportation would all be integrated into the Israeli system. Palestinian Arabs would not become Israeli citizens because of the demographic problem; instead they would have voting rights in Jordan. He believed that the Israeli government should pursue an activist policy in encouraging settlement and not restricting land purchase. At the Labour party conference in 1969, Dayan proposed changing the party's stand from 'secure and agreed borders' to 'secure strategic borders'. Eban responded by suggesting that the party might as well split since there was profound opposition to such a move.

The ideological differences within the parties and their competing plans not only polarized the Left, it also fragmented it. Those who wished to retain the territories gradually moved towards Begin and the Right. The movement in the opposite direction towards withdrawal was slower and more arduous. In 1970, Allon proposed the establishment of five settlement blocs in Gaza. Shimon Peres argued that there should not be so much concern about the demographic problem and commented that those who give up territory, even without peace, 'give up the future of the state'.[38] The Allon Plan became unofficial government policy by the early 1970s and was being implemented on the ground.

[38] Beilin, *Mechirav shel Ichud* pp. 73–74.

4. The Allon Plan, 1967.

JUDEA AND SAMARIA

Although Dayan was already signing Likud petitions by late 1974, he had opposed the first religious settlement in Hebron, which he described as 'a highjacking operation'. Dayan argued that its leader Moshe Levinger did not believe in coexistence with the Palestinians, but wished to transfer them instead. Allon, he argued, supported it because of the political rivalry between them – a harbinger of the situation between Peres and Rabin in the 1970s.[39] In 1968, Levinger had refused to obey Hebron's military governor and leave the city. Four weeks later, he and his followers moved into the headquarters of the military government and opened a religious seminary, a class for primary school children and a kindergarten. By 1970, the government authorized the construction of a Jewish quarter in Hebron and the urban settlement of Kiriat Arba on its outskirts. Although many Jews – mainly ultra-orthodox anti-Zionists – had been slaughtered there in 1929, the resettlement of Hebron was more than a nationalist goal. It symbolized the desire of religious Zionists to settle in Biblical Judea and Samaria. It marked the genesis of the religious settler movement and the colonization of the West Bank and Gaza. They embellished the zeal of the socialist Zionists of the past, but unlike the colonization of Israel, the settlement of the territories was coloured by all the trappings of a colonial enterprise.

Levinger had been influenced in the 1950s by the ideas espoused by Gahelet, a group of young people who belonged to the Bnei Akiva religious Zionist youth movement. Gahelet passionately espoused nationalism and Torah, but their activism and radicalism often led to accusations of undermining Bnei Akiva. Marooned between the ultra-orthodox and the secular leaders of Zionism, Gahelet members became more religious, looking to the discipline of the yeshiva rather than to the values of the religious kibbutz movement. Moreover, the ideal of 'Torah and labour' became secondary. Bnei Akiva had decided to allow its members to study for a year at yeshiva (religious seminary) before embarking on army service. This was followed by the establishment of high school yeshivot and the development of a scheme whereby students could combine religious learning with army service. This deepening of their religious consciousness created a new sense of self-esteem and confidence – 'religious pride'.[40] Even so, the Bnei Akiva

---

[39] *Yediot Aharanot* 27 April 1997.
[40] Gideon Aran, 'From Religious Zionism to Zionist Religion: The Roots of Gush Emunim' in Peter Y. Medding (ed.), *Studies in Contemporary Jewry* vol.2 (Indiana 1986) pp. 116–143.

leadership's counter-attack on Gahelet eventually led to a split in the group.
Many of those who left found a new home in Merkaz Harav, the yeshiva
of Zvi Yehuda Kook, the son of the revered first Chief Rabbi of Palestine,
Avraham Yitzhak Kook.

By 1963, adherents of Gahelet were criticizing the National Religious
Party's policies and together with the party's young guard were organizing
'the faction of the faithful'.

Gahelet approached Judaism and Zionism as a unity and embarked on a course
of dual radicalization: a more extreme orthodoxy together with a more extreme
nationalism . . . The solution offered by Gahelet embraced a nationalist–political
experience clothed in mystical–messianic terms; it was a deep and authentic religious revival that used Zionism as its medium . . . the beginnings of the change
from 'religious Zionism' to 'Zionist religion'.[41]

Redemptionist Zionism developed as a consequence of Gahelet's activities, but it had always existed since the establishment of the state. In 1949,
200 rabbis had signed a declaration that Israel was at the start of the redemp-
tive process. The elevation of spiritual ecstasy and divine imperative fuelled
the messianic colouring of Gahelet. Under the guidance of Kook's mystical
teachings, the victory of the Six Day war provided the spiritual atmosphere
and pioneering impetus to enact the settlement of the West Bank. The
conquest of Arab East Jerusalem led to the immediate construction of new
Jewish neighbourhoods such as Ramat Eshkol and French Hill. The NRP
had forged a good working relationship with Mapai after 1948 under the
leadership of Chaim Moshe Shapira who actually advocated not going
to war in 1967. The growing influence of Gahelet and the NRP's young
guard, however, produced a seismic change after the Six Day war in favour
of Kook's maximalist, messianic and redemptionist school of thought. The
victory in the Six Day war was perceived as divine revelation. The interpretation of the Yom Kippur war in 1973 was that the Jews should come
to terms with the fact that they were an abnormal people. Some religious
thinkers pointed out that there were numerous definitions of the borders in
Jewish texts. Some argued that it was not the place of the rabbinic authorities to tell the leaders of the state how to implement such policies. Yet it
was Kook's advocacy of active messianism that attracted the young.[42] He
told them that any decision by a Jewish political leader to return territory
will lack any legal force and will have contravened a dictate of the Torah.

---

[41] Ibid. pp. 138–139.
[42] Michael Rosenak, 'Religious Reactions: Testimony and Theology' in Stephen Roth (ed.), *The Impact
of the Six Day War* (Oxford 1987) pp. 220–226.

The NRP's Young Guard emerged as an important faction at the party's congress in October 1968 when they argued that the party should move beyond purely religious affairs. They quietly supported Dayan's attack on their own party leader, Chaim Moshe Shapira, who advocated dovish policies. Moreover, the NRP's stated acceptance of the official formula of 'agreed and secure borders' implied a willingness to give back territory. In contrast, the Young Guard opposed any 'land for peace' formula and the return of the newly conquered territory to 'foreign rule'. By the 1973 election, the influence of the Young Guard was even more marked. In its negotiations to join the government coalition, the NRP demanded the formation of a national coalition which would include the Likud and that there should be no government decision to withdraw from the West Bank.

When Yitzhak Rabin succeeded Golda Meir in 1974, the NRP refused to join the government without an agreement that had first been blessed by the hawkish Chief Rabbi Shlomo Goren and his colleagues. This reflected the growing influence of rabbinical figures in the party. The NRP was thus willing to block any negotiations with Jordan since it would ultimately involve surrendering Israeli sovereignty over parts of the West Bank and the probable evacuation of settlements. The NRP could and would bring down the Rabin government if necessary. By the 1977 election, the Young Guard managed to displace one of the party's veteran leaders, Yitzhak Raphael, from the number two position on the party list and to replace him with one of their own, Chaim Druckman. The religious kibbutzim refused to nominate a representative for the NRP's electoral list in 1977.

In 1974, Gush Emunim – the bloc of the Faithful – left the NRP and began a coordinated campaign of establishing housing in populated areas in the West Bank through Amana, its settlement arm. For the Israeli public, it provided a contemporary example of the pioneering spirit of the past. Indeed, on the eve of the Yom Kippur war, over 30 per cent of the Israeli public did not wish to return any land for peace; another 52.1 per cent only wanted to return 'a small part of the territories'.[43] For the Right, it provided a settlement movement which neither Herut nor the Liberals possessed. The Rabin government refused to support Gush Emunim because they insisted on settling in areas of high Arab population, but the combined pressure of large demonstrations, favourable public opinion and the internal rivalry within the leadership of the Labour party led to compromises and the establishment of new settlements.

---

[43] Efraim Torgovnik, 'The Election Campaign: Party Needs and Voter Concerns' in Asher Arian (ed.), *The Elections in Israel: 1973* (Jerusalem 1975) p. 77.

The national unity government of 1967–1970 contained Begin's Gahal, the changing NRP and Moshe Dayan – the first, albeit internal, governing alliance of the Right. Yet there had been an unwritten agreement between the leaders of Labour's factions, Meir, Galili and Dayan, on policy in the territories and the advancement of settlement. Dayan, in particular, was advocating the establishment of Yamit, south of Gaza, and the sale of land in the territories to individual Israelis. The Galili Plan of September 1973 placed the stamp of approval on the political status quo between the factions and pledged further security settlements in the Jordan Valley, Gaza and the Golan Heights. It also advocated stronger ties with the West Bank through the development of an economic infrastructure.

A month later, the Yom Kippur war and the deaths of 2,688 Israelis shattered such indolent thinking. Israeli intelligence had predicted that there would be no Egyptian attack until the delivery of Soviet bombers. Although there had been clear warnings in the run-up to the outbreak of war, Golda Meir decided against a pre-emptive strike which had been the Israeli action in 1967. On this occasion, the Egyptian forces were well protected by a Sam missile umbrella which prevented any attack by aircraft. Equipped with anti-tank weapons, they overwhelmed the fortified Bar–Lev line which was designed to deter any invading force. 2,225 Israelis were killed in the first week of the war alone. A military stand-off prevailed until Sadat unwisely ordered an advance beyond the missile umbrella. The Israelis counteracted, using makeshift bridges to cross the Suez Canal. The Egyptian Third Army was swiftly cut off and the Israelis threatened to advance on Cairo itself. On the Golan Heights, hugely outnumbered Israeli forces managed to hold off the Syrians and Iraqis before they entered Israel. The arrival of reservists pushed back the Arab armies to within forty kilometres of Damascus.

Unlike the Six Day war, these were heavy losses for a small country to bear. This time, there was no euphoria, only a sense that it had been a close-run thing. The Agranat Commission of Inquiry secured the resignations of the IDF Chief of Staff, the head of military intelligence and several leading officers. It spelled the political demise of the Labour old guard. Golda Meir and Moshe Dayan resigned within a year. The 1973 election came at the end of the war. Menachem Begin had the political fortune to have resigned from the cabinet in 1970. Therefore no political blame could be assigned to him over the debacle of the Yom Kippur war.

Moreover, earlier in 1973, the newly demobbed Ariel Sharon argued for the formation of an anti-Labour bloc of Begin's Gahal, the Free Centre of Ehud Olmert and the State List which Ben-Gurion had helped to establish.

Although this had been mooted privately in the hope of persuading Dayan and his supporters to defect from the Labour party,[44] Sharon acted as the midwife of this new alliance, the Likud.[45] Yet it did not fare well; the Histadrut elections of 1973 which took place before the war indicated that the Likud had achieved the same vote as the sum of its several components in 1969. The catastrophe of the Yom Kippur war which had cost so many lives was now laid at the door of the Labour government and the Labour Alignment paid heavily in the election.

The war had worked to the Likud's advantage. By default, Likud gained 30 per cent of the popular vote and together with the NRP accumulated forty-nine seats against Labour's fifty-one. Groups which had traditionally voted Labour now deserted the party in droves. The Likud now attracted the Sephardim, the religious and Israeli workers in great numbers. The Yom Kippur war had broken the logjam in the public's continuing adherence to Labour and forced the transfer of political allegiance. The Likud had also made a breakthrough on a municipal level. Young men such as Moshe Katzav were elected mayors of development towns while Shlomo Lahat had captured Tel Aviv for the Liberals.

Following Golda Meir's resignation, the rival candidates for the premiership – Rafi's Dayan and Achdut Ha'avodah's Allon – were passed over in favour of a less antagonistic figure. Untarred by past political intrigue, Yitzhak Rabin was elevated to the leadership on a mandate of reform of government and party. For the first time, Mapai did not hold any of the three leading positions in government. Rabin (Achdut Ha'avodah) was Prime Minister, Yigal Allon (Achdut Ha'avodah) became Foreign Minister and Shimon Peres (Rafi) held the post of Minister of Defence. This undoubtedly symbolized the changing of the guard and the end of the old political groupings.[46]

Rabin transformed Labour from a coalition of movements into a broader party where factions coalesced around ideological issues such as withdrawal from the territories. Yet old habits died hard and Rabin's attempt to cleanse the Augean stables in this transitional phase was marred by further revelations of corruption and financial mismanagement, characterized by trials and long sentences. In January 1977 Avraham Ofer, the Minister of Housing, shot himself in his car while under police

---

[44] Colin Shindler, *The Land beyond Promise: Israel, Likud and the Zionist Dream* (London 2002) p.72.
[45] *Jerusalem Post* 18 July 1973.
[46] Myron J. Aronoff, *Power and Ritual in the Israel Labour Party: A Study in Political Anthropology* (New York 1993) pp. 146–162.

investigation for apparent financial irregularities in a construction company with which he was associated.

Rabin, as virtually a non-factional figure, had narrowly beaten Shimon Peres for the Labour party leadership. Yet he had to contend with the machinations of his rivals, Peres, Yigal Allon and a brooding Moshe Dayan. This permitted the political opposition to capitalize on this situation and to play off one Labour actor against another. The hawkish Peres opposed interim agreements with both Egypt and Syria and supported settlement activity such as the establishment of Sebastia.

The growing coalescence of the Right was symbolized by a joint visit of Begin, Sharon and Zvi Yehuda Kook to the territories in 1974. The economic situation was dire. The cost-of-living index had tripled between 1969 and 1975. Defence expenditure had mushroomed while inflation hovered between 30 and 40 per cent during Rabin's tenure in office. The International Monetary Fund observed that Israel's export earnings had averaged 18 per cent between 1969 and 1974, but fell to 4 per cent in 1975. Rabin's misfortune had been to preside over a transition in Israeli society from a less complicated past, a time when accountability mattered less. Labour no longer embellished pioneering ideals and a socialist collective idealism. Ironically, even the hapless Rabin was forced to resign when he discovered that a joint foreign currency bank account that he held with his wife actually infringed Israeli law. Peres was left in charge of a sinking political ship on the eve of the 1977 election.

Rabin's inability to stem the tide persuaded many of Labour's natural supporters to seek new ways of expressing their disdain. Amnon Rubinstein's Shinui group and Yigal Yadin's Democratic movement combined with part of Shmuel Tamir's Free Centre to form the Democratic Movement for Change (DMC). Yadin, a leading military figure in 1948 and a renowned archaeologist, became the head of the new party and its stand was remarkably similar to Labour's on the question of the territories. The DMC scythed into Labour's majority, reducing it to thirty-two seats. Likud gained four more seats and was now the biggest party. Together with Sharon's Shlomzion party, the NRP and smaller religious parties, Likud now had a blocking majority of sixty-one and could form the next government. Menachem Begin, with considerable political astuteness, a fair amount of luck and the disintegration within Labour ranks became the first non-Labour movement Prime Minister at the age of sixty-four.

CHAPTER 7

The road to Beirut

MENACHEM BEGIN'S LEADERSHIP

Menachem Begin often wrestled with depression. His condition became worse once he had attained the premiership in 1977, when decision-making was sometimes defined by his highs and lows.[1] His autocratic nature led many opponents to either voluntarily leave his circle or be ousted. From the old Revisionists loyal to Jabotinsky's memory[2] (1951) to young upstarts such as Ehud Olmert (1966), to military men Ezer Weizmann (1972) and Moshe Dayan (1979), the pattern of eventual exit remained the same. Begin's need to be respected but unchallenged by his colleagues was reflected in the fact that he was probably the only democratic leader ever to have lost eight consecutive elections, but still continued in office. One former Israeli ambassador to Great Britain commented that while he swayed from 'elation to depression, from stagnation to hyperactivism, from chaotic disarray to monolithic uniformity', he was endowed with tremendous stamina and 'the patience of a hunter in ambush':

Begin's ability to deal with political adversaries – and competitors within his own camp – is unmatched. Weizmann, Dayan, Tamir, Hurwitz had to leave his government when they had reached the end of the rope so lavishly provided to them by Mr Begin. He did not drop them, he squeezed them out, one by one.[3]

Mapai, too, for its own political interests, had heaped a fair amount of opprobrium on Begin. Ben-Gurion wrote in his diary that the very existence of Herut was 'a black stain on Israeli democracy'.[4] Yet Begin was an astute practitioner of the black arts of Israeli politics. Until his election, Begin had repudiated most peace proposals and many conciliatory statements.

---

[1] Ofer Grosbard, *Menachem Begin: Portrait of a Leader* (Tel Aviv 2006); *Ha'aretz* 12 May 2006.
[2] The Lamerhav faction seceded from Herut at the beginning of 1951. Shmuel Tamir asked for Begin's resignation due to the stagnation of the party. See Yechiam Weitz, 'The Road to the "Upheaval": A Capsule History of the Herut Movement 1948–1977', *Israel Studies* vol.10 no.3 Indiana 2005 p. 58.
[3] Gideon Rafael, *Jerusalem Post* 20 December 1981.   [4] Ben-Gurion's diary 3 November 1959.

Replying to Begin's inaugural Knesset speech as Prime Minister, Shimon Peres, the leader of the opposition, reminded him that he had rejected the Armistice Agreements of 1949; the withdrawal from Gaza and Sinai in 1957; the ceasefire of August 1970; the Disengagement Agreements with Egypt in January 1974 and with Syria in May 1974; the Sinai Agreement of September 1975. Peres added pointedly that although such accords were less than peace, they rescued the region from additional wars.

After the Yom Kippur war, Begin reserved his wrath in particular for Anwar Sadat and opposed any talks with Egypt even though the Egyptian president had broken with the Kremlin and expelled 40,000 Soviet advisors. The Rabin government was harassed by Begin as if it was a reincarnation of the Sharett administration. Unilateral concessions were condemned, but mutual concessions, Begin argued, would take place within the context of peace negotiations following the cessation of hostilities.

Begin had won the election in 1977 through the implosion of Labour under Shimon Peres and through shrewd coalition building first with the Liberals, then with territorial maximalists from Labour and the Left. Begin had managed to construct a political umbrella under which all opponents of Labour could shelter and subscribe to a broad ideological programme.

The election victory, however, brought with it a national expectation to deal with the problems produced by the conquests of the Six Day war. For most Israelis, the occupation of the West Bank and Gaza in 1967 was seen to be an expansion of territory. Begin, however, took as his starting point a period much earlier in the history of the region. He considered the dimensions of post-1967 Israel as a contraction from the original borders of Mandatory Palestine. Yet despite Begin's projection of himself as a true believer who would never compromise, he had quietly shifted his ideological position in conformity with the reality of the times.[5]

In the war of 1948, he had spoken of 'our Amman' and dreamt of conquering the East Bank, thereby reversing the first partition of Mandatory Palestine[6]. By the mid-1950s, such claims gradually began to disappear from his rhetoric. Instead of talking about 'both banks of the Jordan', he now spoke more vaguely of the 'entire homeland'. Similarly the 'Western Land of Israel' became synonymous with 'the Land of Israel'. In part, this had been done to accommodate his political partners. However,

---

[5] Nadav G. Shalef, '"Both Banks of the Jordan" to the "Whole Land of Israel": Ideological Change in Revisionist Zionism', *Israel Studies* vol.9 no.1 Spring 2004 p. 139.

[6] Ibid. p. 130.

this shift had never been spelled out clearly to his party because Begin wished to maintain the loyalty of both his veteran supporters and the newcomers who now looked to him. While Begin never formally renounced the historical right to the East Bank, he remarked in the summer of 1982 that Israel now had neither the power nor the will to launch a war against Jordan to recover the territory.[7]

Unlike the cosmopolitan Jabotinsky who famously exhibited a practical disdain for religion,[8] Begin was a son of the Polish shtetl with an emotional attachment to Judaism. This coloured his political approach, a maximalist ideology with a theocratic infusion. Begin exhibited 'a super-temporal approach' to history, beginning with God's promise to Abraham and ending with the redemption of the Jewish people.[9] While he considered that this eternal right superseded any other right, Begin never accepted any of the numerous borders stated in the Bible. He never mentioned the delineation of the Promised Land in the Book of Genesis as stretching from the River of Egypt to the Euphrates in any of his speeches,[10] but adhered instead to the borders of the British Mandate. In one sense, he imitated Ben-Gurion who argued in 1957 that the source of the Jewish national renaissance and Zionist vision resided in 'the Book of Books, and not in the pamphlets that were written sixty years ago'.[11] In addition, like Ben-Gurion he believed that if an opportune moment arose, then it should be seized to expand the borders. On 19 June 1967, Begin voted for the return of Sinai to Egypt in exchange for peace, but opposed the return of the West Bank and Gaza. Sinai was outside the borders of Mandatory Palestine while the West Bank was Biblical Judea and Samaria.[12]

Similarly, both Dayan and Sharon felt that Sinai could be returned to forge a peace with Egypt while the West Bank should be retained for security rather than for ideological reasons. Both men had drifted from Mapai and now found themselves in agreement with the historic political enemy, Menachem Begin, who was only too happy to appoint the disciples of Ben-Gurion – Dayan, Sharon and Yadin – to his government. Dayan became Foreign Minister while Sharon accepted office as Minister of Agriculture. Yigal Yadin became deputy Prime Minister. Sharon also

[7] *Ma'ariv* 20 August 1982. See also Shalef, op. cit., reference 52.
[8] Shindler, *The Triumph of Military Zionism* pp. 63–65.
[9] Arye Naor, 'Hawks' Beaks, Doves' Feathers: Likud Prime Ministers between Ideology and Reality', *Israel Studies* vol.10 no.3 Winter 2005 p. 156.
[10] Ibid. p. 165.
[11] David Ben-Gurion, speech to the Jerusalem Ideological Conference, August 1957 in 'Zionism and Pseudo Zionism', *The Jerusalem Ideological Conference* (New York 1972) p. 154.
[12] *Yediot Aharanot* 8 November 1968.

became chairman of the ministerial cabinet committee which oversaw land and settlements both in Israel and in the territories. It was effectively a coalition of the political heirs of the Irgun and Ben-Gurion's generals.

The elements of a policy, forging a separate peace with Egypt while creating new settlements on the West Bank, were already in place during Begin's first meeting with Carter. The new Israeli Prime Minister privately promised Carter 'substantial withdrawals' from Sinai.[13]

As a hard ideological position became a wishful aspiration, the debate within the Israeli Right was transformed into a contest between the advocates of ideological purity and territorial gain and the pragmatists whose policies were based on securing the stability of the state. While trumpeting the former to his devoted supporters, Begin understood that practical politics dictated the latter. His worldview had evolved into 'a dialectic based on nullification of desires due to the recognition of the limits of strength'.[14] Such a bifurcated existence further awakened Begin's black dog of depression.

Unlike Dayan, Begin was a Diaspora Jew with little knowledge of Arabs. In his eyes, Arab nationalists wished to finish Hitler's work and the PLO was self-evidently a reincarnation of the Nazis. He was furthermore a believer in pan-Arabism whose legitimate domain, he argued, was outside the Land of Israel. Like Golda Meir, he regarded himself as 'a Palestinian' and was at pains not to acknowledge an emerging Palestinian nation. He therefore opposed the Jordanian option and unlike both Sharon and Shamir, Begin never accepted the notion that 'Jordan is Palestine'.

WHO ARE THE PALESTINIANS?

Begin came to power when many Israelis were beginning to recognize that another people, the Palestinians, had a claim to the Land. The issue of the Palestinians disappeared at the behest of Arab states. Israel, Egypt and Jordan had annexed the territory allocated by the UN to the Palestinian Arab state in 1947. Ironically, it was the rivalry of the Arab states – Egypt and Iraq – which reintroduced the Palestinian question in the early 1960s. It was Nasser who acted as the midwife to the birth of the PLO. Despite such opportunism, there were some Israelis who perceived – even before the conquest of the West Bank in the Six Day war – that perhaps at the core of the Israel–Arab conflict was actually the question of the Palestinian Arab refugees. In an atmosphere of mutual suspicion, even a return of some of

---

[13] Martin Gilbert, *Israel* (London 1998) p. 481. [14] Ibid. p. 163.

the refugees and compensation for those who did not wish to return resided within the context of a general solution to the conflict.[15] Those Israelis who opposed the occupation of the West Bank and Gaza in 1967 and the subsequent construction of settlements understood that an answer to the dilemma of seeking a fair solution to the question of the refugees while not denying the right of the Jews to national self-determination in Israel was the right of return to a Palestinian state alongside Israel. This return to the original idea of partition as envisaged in 1947 was strongly supported by an emerging peace camp, antagonized by a Labour government's inability and often unwillingness to stop settlement activity. As early as December 1967, the writer Amos Oz criticized the triumphalism and the lack of understanding about the Palestinians that permeated Israeli society:

The Arabs are here – because Palestine is the homeland of the Palestinians, just as Iraq is the homeland of the Iraqis and Holland the homeland of the Dutch. What cultural assets the Palestinians have created here, and to what extent they are already nationally conscious, is of no relevance to their right to their homeland. Needless to say, the Palestinian owes no deference to God's promise to Abraham, to the longings of Yehuda Halevi and Bialik, or to the declaration by that British peer, Lord Balfour.[16]

Before 1967, there was an inability to recognize that many of the old feudal regimes – Egypt, Syria, Iraq, Yemen – had been toppled by the forces of Arab nationalism. Following the Arab defeat, the displacement of the Mufti by Yasser Arafat and the emergence of a new generation of Palestinian Arabs who defined themselves as members of a Palestinian nation suggested to a growing number of Israelis that this was a clear development of a national consciousness. If previously the Palestinians had disappeared in the Israeli mindset due to Jordanian and Egyptian domination of the West Bank and Gaza, visits to those territories after 1967 indicated that the other people in Mandatory Palestine still existed. For the older generation of Israeli politicians, there was a determined effort not to recognize this. In this, they were aided by comparisons with the French colons in Algeria and the onset of acts of terror.

Abu Jihad (Khalil al-Wazir), Arafat's deputy, provided the revolution-ary image for Fatah and was influenced by the Maoist doctrine of a people's war. This was the era of the Algerian FLN, General Giap and the Vietnamese NLF, the epoch of Fanon and Guevara. Abu Jihad was

---

[15] Aharon Cohen, address to the Martin Buber Memorial Seminar for Jewish–Arab Understanding, *New Outlook* December 1966.
[16] Amos Oz, 'Meaning of Homeland', *New Outlook* no.93 December 1967.

regarded as the mastermind behind terror attacks on Israeli civilians such
as the assault on the Savoy Hotel in Tel Aviv in 1975 and the coastal road
killings in 1978. Abu Jihad believed that such attacks, their embellishment
and exaggeration allowed young Palestinians to reclaim their submerged
identity. There was a deep determination to show that despite their dispersion the Palestinian Arabs had not assimilated.

The sum total of people's war embodies the various facets and activities of the
Palestinian people as a whole, whether those facets and activities are political,
social, economic, military or cultural. This is how we understand the armed
struggle. This is also how we have proceeded to rebuild our people and reassert its
national identity in order to achieve the liberation of our land.[17]

At best, this was ignored as nihilist terrorism. Some 115 Israeli civilians
had been killed between 1967 and 1970. By 1982, that number had more
than trebled. At worst, Palestinian aspirations were marginalized by most
Israelis. The PLO itself reinforced the idea that there was no one to talk
to by its embrace of 'a democratic secular state' and the demands of its
national charter. The PLO, rooted in dispersion, was less realistic than
those who actually lived in the West Bank and Gaza. Yet they desired to
emerge as the symbol of a renascent forgotten people. Figures such as Aziz
Shehadeh and Mohammad al-Ja'bari, who shortly after the war in 1967
advocated a Palestinian state in the conquered territories, were vehemently
condemned by the PLO.[18]

In part, it was due to a historical legacy that led the Labour hierarchy
only to recognize pan-Arabism as the partner – hence the evolution of
'the Jordanian option', a federation with the Hashemites after 1967. Plans
by academics to create fifteen villages in the Jordan valley and to resettle
50,000 Gaza refugees in the El Arish area were quietly placed in abeyance
by government.[19] In part, it was also a desire not to return to the status
quo ante of November 1947 – a desire to maintain the partition of 'middle
Palestine' between Israel and Jordan and to control its people. The renaissance of Palestinian nationalism also resurrected the question of Palestinian
national rights. If the Arab states threatened Israel 'with what they might
do, militarily or otherwise', the Palestinians threatened Israel with what

---

[17] Abu Jihad, Filastiniyyah, 14 quoted in Yezid Sayigh, 'The Armed Struggle and Palestinian Nationalism', in Avraham Sela and Moshe Maoz (eds.), *The PLO and Israel: From Armed Struggle to Political
Solution 1964–1994* (London 1997) p. 27.
[18] Moshe Shemesh, 'The West Bank: Rise and Decline of Traditional Leadership June 1967–October
1973', *Middle Eastern Studies* vol.20 no.3 July 1984.
[19] *Al Hamishmar* 18 May 1972.

they are, rival claimants to the same land.'[20] Ignoring the Palestinians was also a means of not dealing with the festering sore of the refugee question. Hence Golda Meir's famous remark 'there is no such thing as a Palestinian people... they didn't exist'.[21] In one sense, this recognized the pan-Arabist approach. The Palestinian academic Walid Khalidi wrote in 1978:

From this [pan-Arab] perspective, the individual Arab states are deviant and transient entities: their frontiers illusory and permeable; their rulers interim caretakers, or obstacles to be removed... before such super-legitimacy, the legitimacy of the individual state shrinks into irrelevance.[22]

Many Israelis on the Left such as Moshe Sneh regarded Golda Meir's comment as 'nonsensical'.[23] Time had moved on from 1948 and the Palestinian Arabs had begun to see themselves as a nation. Indeed, the Israeli media soon began to use the term 'Palestinians'. Although such political usage did not mean the same as the right of the Palestinians to a state, more and more Israelis used the term 'Palestinians'. Even on the Israeli Left, figures such as Liova Eliav argued that any Palestinian state would not be viable – it would be a rump state led by irredentists.[24] Whereas most Palestinians did not initially accept Israel's right to exist, Israelis began to move slowly firstly towards a recognition of a Palestinian nation and then decades later to recognition of a two-state solution. There was also a transition in the Arab world from Nasser's pan-Arabism towards recognizing the PLO as the sole legitimate representative of the Palestinian people in Algiers in November 1973.

Some Labour politicians originally favoured a limited state under Israeli military jurisdiction, but this was superseded by espousing the Allon Plan. President Bourguiba of Tunisia had already argued in 1965 that there should be a return to UN Resolution 181 – a two-state solution. But Golda Meir ruled out withdrawal to the pre-1967 borders and pursued Allon's ideas.[25] Moshe Dayan opposed the right of Palestinian national self-determination especially if it meant that 'they should participate in drawing Israel's security frontiers in the South and East'.[26] The Labour party at first believed that it could continue its pre-1948 policy by purchasing land in the territories and establishing security settlements as envisaged

---

[20] Seth Tillman, 'Israeli and Palestinian Nationalism', *Journal of Palestine Studies* vol.9 no.1 Autumn 1979 pp. 46–47.
[21] *Sunday Times* 15 June 1969.   [22] Walid Khalidi, *Foreign Affairs* July 1978.
[23] Moshe Sneh, *Jewish Chronicle* 12 September 1969.   [24] Liova Eliav, *New Outlook* October 1972.
[25] Golda Meir, *Ma'ariv* 8 September 1972.
[26] Moshe Dayan, address to students in Beer Sheva 2 February 1970 in *New Outlook* November–December 1972.

by the Galili Plan of August 1973. Galili also proposed a four-year plan to rehabilitate the refugees in Gaza through the provision of housing, developing the economy, improving the health services and vocational training. International funding would be sought to finance the proposals.

The following year, the Israelis insisted that only the Jordanians could represent the Palestinians in negotiations after the Yom Kippur war. Although many Palestinians fled to Jordan in the aftermath of the Israeli conquest of the West Bank, others had moved to the East Bank because they were attracted by Hussein's economic policies. The population of Amman had increased from 35,000 in 1954 to 500,000 in 1973.

Yigal Allon, himself, argued that the idea of a Palestinian state had 'no deep roots even in the Arab world'.[27] There was no mention, he pointed out, of the status of the Palestinians in UN Resolutions 242 and 338 which the Arab states had agreed to support. They did not press for the Palestinians to be represented at the Geneva conference after the Yom Kippur war. The Arab consensus on the question of a Palestinian entity, he argued, only served to undermine the legitimacy of Israel. This mindset reflected the static thinking which permeated Israel after 1967. The absolutism of the emerging Palestinian national movement and its espousal of a democratic secular state only aided those Israelis who dismissed Palestinian aspirations out of hand. The PLO Charter of 1968 spoke of an Arab homeland where only those Jews who lived in Palestine before the 'Zionist invasion' would be considered Palestinians. It was unclear, therefore, what would happen to those who came after.

The disaster of the Yom Kippur war inspired new thinking about the Palestinians. Israeli theatre and literature also played a defining role in challenging Israeli perceptions of Palestinians. The playwright Hanoch Levin created great controversy after 1967 by challenging the older generation's ethos – most notably in *Queen of a Bathtub* during Golda Meir's premiership. In *Shitz*, Levin provocatively challenges the patronizing Israeli view in the aftermath of the Six Day war:

In my vision, people are working in the fields and the factory without hatred, without fear, working together, without any consideration of nationality, religion, race or sex, because they are all working for me. I'll put up factories for you. I'll give you machines and tools and you'll work for me. You'll work willingly with a song on your lips because you'll have something to work for – you'll have an aim, a vision – my vision.[28]

[27] Yigal Allon, 'Israel and the Palestinians', *Jerusalem Quarterly* no.6 Winter 1978 pp. 20–40.
[28] Gideon Ofrat, 'The Arab in Israeli Drama', *Jerusalem Quarterly* Spring 1979 p. 84.

In the same year, Yosef Mundi's play *The Governor of Jericho* featured a member of Fatah. The United States, too, was becoming aware of the Palestinians and even before his election as President, Jimmy Carter had spoken of 'a Palestinian homeland'. Although Sadat had expelled all his Soviet advisors in 1972, American minds were concentrated on the Palestinian question when the Gulf States proposed a 70 per cent increase in the price of oil during the Yom Kippur war. OPEC reduced its production and the Saudis put in place an embargo on oil export to the United States if Israel did not leave all the territories occupied in 1967. In contrast to the USA, the Europeans were far more vulnerable to the use of the oil weapon. Britain imported 60 per cent of her oil from the Arab world and was willing to refuse access to her bases to American aircraft en route to Israel. Unlike the Americans who increased aid to Israel to counterbalance increasing Soviet influence in the Middle East, the Europeans moved towards a more amenable position towards PLO demands such as the Venice Declaration of June 1980.

Between June 1967 and the end of 1969, Israel's casualties were estimated at 513 dead and 1959 wounded – proportionately higher than before the war.[29] The lack of security and a growing disillusionment with Labour led to the ascendancy of the Right. Menachem Begin had no desire to acknowledge the phrase 'the legitimate rights of the Palestinian people' in the English version of the Camp David 'Framework for Peace' in 1979. It had 'no meaning'.[30] The word 'Palestine' was 'jargon'.[31] Even translations of Jabotinsky's famous article 'The Iron Wall' were mistranslated from the Russian to avoid mention of 'Palestine' and 'Palestinian Arabs'.[32] Begin, of course, ideologically believed in a Greater Israel and was aided by the PLO's refusal to clearly state whether or not it accepted a two-state solution.

In Begin's eyes, through its armed struggle and acts of terror, the PLO became 'a Nazi organization' and its charter 'an Arabic Mein Kampf'. Begin opposed the very idea of a Palestinian state which he believed would be a fomenter of terrorism and a symbol of irredentism. Instead, he attempted to hold together the broad right-wing coalition that he had constructed and overseen since 1949 with exhortations to settle Judea, Samaria and Gaza. The five-year period of transition commenced with

---

[29] Yehoshua Raviv, *Ha'aretz* 5 February 1970.
[30] *Washington Post* 20 September 1978. [31] *Washington Post* 1 December 1977.
[32] Ian Lustick, 'To Build and to Be Built: Israel and the Hidden Logic of the Iron Wall', *Israel Studies* vol.1 no.1 1996.

Dayan's concept of 'functional compromise'. It ended with Begin's radical second government, immersed in the Lebanese quagmire amidst an expansion of settlement activity.

Despite Begin's rhetoric and his dual approach, it marked a movement of Israeli opinion away from pan-Arabism towards a Palestinian national entity. Begin's policies also catalyzed the growth of an extra-parliamentary peace movement whose representatives met PLO leaders outside of the Middle East. In 1982, the Israeli State archives were opened for the first time and researchers eagerly interpreted the new material. They were clustered under the public rubric of 'the new historians' even though there were considerable ideological differences between them. Although Arabic sources were hardly touched, books such as Benny Morris's comprehensive study on the birth of the refugee problem opened eyes and deepened public awareness about the national identity of the Palestinians. The new historians attempted to bridge the gap between the two narratives of 1948. As Noam Chomsky had declared in 1969: 'Each side sees itself as a genuine national liberation movement. Each is the authentic Vietcong.'[33] The Arab world had already declared their belief that the PLO rather than Jordan was the sole representative of the Palestinian people in November 1973.

THE REALITY OF NEGOTIATIONS

Begin's initial approach after his election was to press for a reconvening of the Geneva conference by October 1977. In this gathering chaired by the superpowers, Israel, Egypt, Syria and Lebanon would resolve their differences on the basis of UN Resolutions 242 and 338 – a basis which Begin had previously called 'marching backwards'. The Palestinians would be part of the Jordanian delegation. The PLO would be barred because they were 'the Jewish people's most implacable enemy since the Nazis'.[34] Moreover, Begin pointed out that the Knesset had passed a law in 1967 which further allowed the government to issue an ordinance extending the jurisdiction, law and administration of the state to every part of the Land of Israel.

In 1976, a new American President had come to power. Jimmy Carter combined a Biblical sympathy for Israel[35] with a deep belief in using

[33] Noam Chomsky 'Nationalism and Conflict in Palestine', *New Outlook* no.109 November–December 1969.

[34] Menachem Begin, speech to the Knesset 27 July 1977, Netanel Lorch (ed.), *Major Knesset Debates* vol.6 *1977–1981* (Maryland 1993) p. 2122.

[35] Jimmy Carter, *Keeping Faith* (London 1982) p. 274.

American power to further human rights. He was also the first American President to recognize that the Palestinians had legitimate rights that could not be airbrushed from the political canvas. He vehemently opposed the construction of new settlements and complained about Israeli incursions into Lebanon using military equipment which had been sold to them by the United States. Carter had spoken of the need for a 'Palestinian homeland' in March 1977, but clearly was unaware then of the complexities of the conflict. President Carter was therefore surprised when Begin told him that he passionately opposed the idea of 'a Palestinian entity' because it would inevitably lead to a state. Begin also refused to contemplate a freeze on settlements across the Green Line. When the US Secretary of State, Cyrus Vance, stated that the settlements violated international law, the Israeli government responded by authorizing Sharon's Ministerial Committee on Settlement Activity to establish new settlements.

Vance had initially proposed a UN Trusteeship over the West Bank which would be supervised by Israel and Jordan. In due course, there would be a referendum which would lead to national self-determination.[36] Begin rejected this and instead began to quietly prepare a modern-day autonomy plan for the Palestinians based on Jabotinsky's 1906 Helsingfors proposals[37] for Gegenwartsarbeit–Jewish national and political activities in the Diaspora.[38] Carter and the State Department returned to a resurrection of the Geneva conference. Sadat, however, began to look at the situation differently and concluded that all plans would come to nothing unless the psychological shackles separating Israel and Egypt were broken to facilitate a political breakthrough.

Sadat's visit to Jerusalem at the end of 1977 was certainly earth shattering and unimaginable even a few weeks before. Sadat told the Israeli Knesset that the Jews were conditionally welcome in the Middle East, 'with full security and safety'. He argued that the Yom Kippur war in 1973 was a turning point for Egypt and Israel and it should permit both nations to confront the situation honestly and outline the conditions for a full peace. In Sadat's opinion, these were the ending of the Israeli occupation of land conquered in 1967; accepting the right of national self-determination of the Palestinians including the right to establish a state; the right to live within secure and guaranteed boundaries; adherence to UN resolutions; ending the

---

[36] *Jerusalem Post* 6 July 1977.
[37] Vladimir Jabotinsky, *Neumim 1905–1926*, Ketavim 4 (Tel Aviv 1957/8) pp. 25–28.
[38] Joseph B. Schectman, *The Jabotinsky Story: Rebel and Statesman 1880–1923* (New York 1956) pp. 112–117.

state of belligerency in the region. Sadat qualified his statement by pointing out that he had not come to Jerusalem to sign a separate peace between Egypt and Israel and that there would not be a 'durable and just peace' in the region without a fair solution to the Palestinian problem.

Although he invited 'genuine spokesmen of the Palestinians of the Land of Israel' to come and hold talks, as well as telling Sadat publicly that 'everything should be open to negotiation', Begin's intention was directed towards securing a separate peace with Egypt while retaining the West Bank. Unlike Sadat, Begin looked to the past rather than to the present. He recapitulated Jewish history and the origins of the Zionist movement, paid tribute to the fighters of the Irgun and remembered the lessons of the Shoah, leaving it to the Communists, Tewfik Toubi and Meir Vilner, to ask why he had not addressed the centrality of the Palestinian question.

At the end of December 1977, Begin announced his autonomy plan. Whereas he had been elected on a platform of cultural autonomy for the Palestinian Arabs, he now proposed administrative autonomy through elections to an eleven-member council, sitting in Bethlehem. The military government in the territories would be abolished, but the Israelis would still retain responsibility for security and public order. The Palestinians would have functional responsibility for areas such as health, education, justice and tourism. In accordance with his non-recognition of a Palestinian people, Begin proposed that the inhabitants of the territories could accept either Israeli or Jordanian citizenship. Those who chose Israeli citizenship could acquire land and even settle in Israel. The settlement of Jews in the West Bank and Gaza was encouraged through permitting them to purchase land. The twenty-six-point programme finally proclaimed that 'for the sake of the agreement and peace', the question of sovereignty would be left open. All this indicated Dayan's imput. While it prevented both formal annexation to Israel and the emergence of a Greater Israel, it also punctured hopes for a Palestinian state next to Israel.

This had essentially been the price of Dayan's crossing the floor from Labour and his incorporation into the Likud coalition. Following Peres's takeover from Rabin, Dayan had not been rehabilitated politically and he still felt out of step with the more dovish aspirations of Allon and Eban. Together with Sharon and Weizmann, Dayan added to the military, national component of the government. Moreover, they had moved the political centre of gravity in Israel from the Left to the Right. Although Begin's tactics were ultimately designed to secure a peace with Egypt through separating the Palestinian question and leaving it in abeyance, the autonomy plan appeared to the far Right, gathered under the Likud umbrella, as highly dubious and potentially an ideological betrayal. Both within Herut and more broadly within the Likud, there were rumblings of discontent. This reflected a schism between centrist elements in the Likud and the far Right. During the next couple of years, far Right parties such as Techiya emerged which attracted both Achdut Ha'avodah maximalists and religious radicals. Those who sympathized such as Sharon and Shamir preferred to work within the Likud.

The marginalization of the Palestinian question confirmed Arab fears about Sadat who had already suffered multiple resignations from his government and an avalanche of bile from the Arab world. Indeed, West Bank leaders had been cautious enough not to attend the initial welcome for Sadat and only met him at the very end of his visit. The PLO's response – even before the publication of Begin's autonomy plan – was to speak of 'Sadat's treasonous visit to the Zionist entity', reject UN Resolutions 242 and 338 and condemn the prospect of a renewed conference in Geneva. The West Bank at this time was relatively free of Jewish settlements. Instead of exploiting this situation, the PLO aligned itself with the radical Arab states, Algeria, Syria, Iraq and Yemen, to proclaim 'a squandering of the rights of the Palestinians' by Egypt and a violation of the principles of the pan-Arab struggle. Diplomatic and financial relations with Egypt were severed and any Egyptian companies that traded with Israel were subject to a boycott. If any other nation or individual – meaning Jordan and King Hussein – followed Sadat's path, there would similarly be a day of reckoning. The PLO, in particular, feared that they would be displaced by a gradual inclusion of Jordan in the deliberations.[39]

Despite this, there appeared to be a sea-change in Egyptian public opinion – like the Israelis they welcomed the resolve of their politicians to seek a solution. Only the Islamists, Communists and Nasserists protested. Abba Eban commented that Sadat's achievement had been to make 'a simultaneous breach in the walls of Arab rejection and Israeli suspicion'.[40] It legitimized something deeper in the Jewish psyche.

The images that the Arabs deduce from their history do nothing to prepare them for the idea of a sovereign Jewish state in what they call 'the Arab region'. For them, the Middle East, in the political sense, is a monolith of a single Arab–Muslim colour; for us it is a tapestry of many colours of which the salient thread was woven by Jewish experience centuries ago. Jews do appear in the turbulent drama of Arab history, but always as subjects, members of a deviant

---

[39] Interview with Hani al-Hassan, *Merip Reports* no.72 November 1978.
[40] Abba Eban, 'Camp David: The Unfinished Business', *Foreign Affairs* Winter 1978–1979.

religious faith, merchants and craftsmen, scholars, doctors and advisors, sometimes as the objects of transient tolerance, more often as the victims of intolerance
and persecution, but never as the bearers of an autonomous political and territorial legacy. The Arab intellectual torment about the reality of modern Israel is
authentic and should not be taken lightly.[41]

In January 1978, Carter joined Sadat in the Aswan Declaration in arguing
that the Palestinians had 'legitimate rights' and that Israel should withdraw
to the 1967 borders. Begin's refusal to give way on the questions of both
Palestinian nationalism and the increasing number of Jewish settlements led
to a stalemate with Egypt and a virtual breakdown of the dialogue throughout 1978. The Americans were increasingly critical of new settlements by
stealth – official recognition for previously unauthorized ones; military
encampments turned over to civilian control; unauthorized outposts being
designated archaeological sites.[42] In early January 1978, the Israeli cabinet
resolved not to establish new settlements in Sinai, but instead to expand
existing ones.[43] Yet such actions created tensions within the Israeli cabinet with Weizmann threatening to resign. The Democratic Movement for
Change raised the possibility of early elections by threatening to leave the
coalition due to Begin's perceived inflexibility.

The PLO further undermined Sadat's position by instigating attacks
on Israel. In March 1978, a group belonging to Arafat's Fatah left Tyre in
Lebanon, landed on a deserted Israeli beach, killed an American wildlife
photographer, hijacked a Haifa-bound bus and redirected it towards Tel
Aviv. Aiming their fire at other motorists and buses, the 'coastal road
massacre' ended in a shoot-out in which thirty-six civilians were killed.
Dalal el Mughrabi, the female leader of the Fatah group, was subsequently
lionized in Palestinian folklore. Three days later, the Israeli Army marched
into Lebanon in 'Operation Litani' to confront PLO forces and eliminate
their bases. Over 300 PLO fighters were killed.

In September 1978, Carter attempted to break the stalemate by inviting
the Israelis and Egyptians to Camp David. Begin believed that it would
lead to protracted negotiations afterwards and therefore did not adequately
prepare beforehand. There was no background material, no counterpro-
posals. He had not set the boundaries of concessions and there were no
close ideological associates from his past who were present, ready to advise
him. Begin had been reluctant to attend, but agreed to attend the summit
due to the exhortations of Dayan and Weizmann. Moreover, there were no
agreed positions between members of the delegation beforehand.

---

[41] Ibid.   [42] *New York Times* 2 February 1978.   [43] *New York Times* 9 January 1978.

Sadat built on his counter-proposal to Begin's autonomy plan – a return to the 1967 borders and a turning over of the Palestinian problem to Egypt and the Arab world. Sadat further demanded the right of return of refugees and compensation for past wars. After such a maximalist proclamation, Sadat moved towards a more open position – free trade, recognition of the state, access to international waterways and an undivided Jerusalem – but Begin refused to concur. At first, Begin stonewalled, unaffected by the generous financial inducements which Carter had offered such as the construction of new airfields in the Negev. Carter even argued that now he rather than Begin represented Israeli public opinion. It was only when Sadat finally began to separate the issue of peace with Egypt from the autonomy issue that progress was made. Sharon telephoned Begin to assure him that the disassembling of the Jewish settlements in Sinai could be accomplished without any increased threat to the security of Israel. Despite the fact that God had given the Torah to the Jewish people at Sinai, in essence the Biblical cradle of Jewish civilization, Begin agreed to evacuate the settlements and the airfields in Sinai. The Egyptians agreed to effectively demilitarize Sinai apart from a thirty-mile swath of territory adjoining the Suez Canal. The question of the sovereignty of the West Bank and Gaza was effectively postponed.

There were therefore two agreements and two frameworks. One was a framework for peace in the Middle East which made the Palestinian question dependent on continuing negotiations. The other was a less precise framework for concluding a peace treaty between Israel and Egypt. Even so, the Egyptians categorically denied that they had agreed in effect to a separate peace.[44] Sadat could claim therefore that he had succeeded in moving Begin towards a position of full autonomy for the Palestinians as a self-governing authority, recognizing 'the legitimate rights of the Palestinian people' with a final status to be settled between Israel, Egypt, Jordan and Palestinian representatives. There was even a vague recommendation to resolve the refugee problem. Yet all this was in the future; the linkage between a peace with Egypt and a just solution for the Palestinians had been broken.

Begin steered a course where there was often space behind the written word for later interpretation. Sometimes different phrases were used in the Hebrew version compared to the Arabic or English texts. The Knesset voted on the Hebrew version, yet the English version was binding on all parties. Such ambiguity allowed each side to claim victory. As Carter later

---

44 Butrous Butrous Ghali, *Le Figaro* 6 October 1978.

claimed, 'Mr Begin's good words had multiple meanings which my advisors and I did not understand at the time.'[45] In the aftermath of Camp David, Carter believed that Begin had accepted a settlement freeze until the autonomy talks were concluded. Begin later – intentionally or unintentionally – offered a different explanation which permitted a short-term freeze and an expansion of existing settlements.[46] Begin, it appears, had conceded to his domestic opponents that existing settlements could be expanded despite the accord.[47] Dayan similarly evoked the right of Jews to settle in the West Bank and Gaza in an address to the UN General Assembly in October 1978. Sharon added to the friction by telling Carter that the West Bank was an inseparable part of Israel and would be home to a million Jews within twenty years.[48] Carter also attempted to link normalization of relations with Egypt with the institution of autonomy for the Palestinians, but Begin categorically refused. While Carter believed in reasoned arguments, there were no direct American interests involved in the question of the settlements. Begin's standpoint was undiluted 'hardball politics' where the central question, he argued, was national survival. Reasoning, in Begin's world, was insufficient, only actions counted.[49] He discounted any exchange of letters between Carter and Sadat over Jerusalem.

Jerusalem will remain the eternal united capital of Israel and that is that. What we declare on this issue is what will stick.[50]

On the other hand, the suspicious far Right were similarly mystified by Begin's use of language and feared the worst – moreover they acted upon their fears. Begin's explanation to his own party did not focus on his successful removal of the West Bank from the immediate agenda, but on the choice before them in Sinai – security or ideology. When the cabinet came to vote on the agreement, one faction of the Likud, the former State List of Ben-Gurion, voted against, Chaim Landau who had been Begin's number two in the Irgun abstained and the National Religious Party refused to take a stand. Moshe Arens, Yitzhak Shamir and Ehud Olmert all refrained from siding with Begin. Moshe Katzav favoured a referendum. Some of Begin's long-time supporters likened Camp David to the Munich

---

[45] Carter, *Keeping Faith* p. 300.
[46] Sasson Sofer, *Begin: An Anatomy of Leadership* (Oxford 1988) p. 196.
[47] William B. Quandt, *Camp David: Peacemaking and Politics* (Washington 1986) p. 277.
[48] William B. Quandt, *Peace Process* (New York 1993) p. 317.
[49] Tom Princen, 'Camp David: Problem-Solving or Power Politics as Usual', *Journal of Peace Research* vol.28 no.1 February 1991 p. 62.
[50] *Jewish Chronicle* 29 September 1978.

Fig. 7.1. Menachem Begin presents the Camp David agreement to the Knesset, 1978. A sceptical Yitzhak Shamir, the Knesset speaker, looks on. Reproduced with kind permission from the Israel Government Press Office.

Agreement of 1938[51] and he was greeted by protesters carrying Chamberlainesque black umbrellas.[52] Zvi Yehuda Kook, the mentor of Gush Emunim, denounced the accord while others recalled that Yitzhak Yaakov Reines, the founder of Mizrachi, the party of religious Zionism, had actually voted in 1903 for the Uganda Plan – a temporary Jewish stopover in East Africa rather than the Promised Land.[53]

Only two thirds of the parties belonging to the government coalition supported the Camp David Accord in the Knesset and only 57 per cent of Begin's own Herut party stood by him. Even the security conscious elite were split and there were still others who worried about the economic consequences of leaving Sinai. The Labour Alignment under Peres's leadership broadly supported the accord, but favoured the Jordanian option. Even so, there were profound differences in Labour's upper echelons. Yigal Allon, true to his Achdut Ha'avodah roots, opposed the evacuation of the Sinai settlements. Yitzhak Rabin wanted a transition period based on joint Jordanian–Israeli possibility for the territories rather than autonomy. Abba

[51] Shmuel Katz, *Jerusalem Post* 22 September 1978.   [52] *Ma'ariv* 23 September 1978.
[53] Pinchas Rozenblit, *Ha'aretz* 28 September 1978.

Fig. 7.2. Jewish settlers attempt to prevent Israeli soldiers from evacuating Yamit, 1982.
Reproduced with kind permission from the Israel Government Press Office.

Eban preferred a Benelux-style federation between Israel, the Palestinians and Jordan.[54] Yet 84 members of the 120-member Knesset voted for the accord and it permitted Begin to procrastinate over the Palestinian question once a bilateral agreement with Egypt had been obtained. On the day of the signing, the Palestinians in the territories declared a general strike.

---

[54] Abba Eban, 'The Palestinian Problem: A New Approach', *New Outlook* January–February 1980.

In the aftermath of Camp David, both Dayan and Weizmann began to feel the cold wind of change as Begin began to distance himself from negotiations on the future of the West Bank and the settlements. Both eventually resigned. Yosef Burg, the leader of the National Religious party, zealous advocate of colonizing all the conquered territories, was placed in charge to advance the autonomy talks. Stagnation was the inevitable result. Although Begin had been unable to avert a total split in the Right, the majority stayed with him. Within a short period of time, Carter had been defeated by the Republicans and the Iranian ayatollahs while Sadat was murdered by a jihadist. With both external and internal political constraints removed, Begin was ready to move to a more radical position following his victory in the 1981 Israeli election.

A MORE RADICAL HUE

Begin's commitment to the Camp David Accord meant the uprooting of the bloc of settlements in Sinai. Ironically, Labour ministers had initiated their construction as security settlements. Their inhabitants had come – not for theological or ideological reasons – but to develop the land agriculturally and were backed by generous government incentives. Yamit had been founded at Dayan's initiative in the early 1970s – despite the opposition of Labour's doves – as a deep-water port to be inhabited by potentially hundreds of thousands of citizens. Now mainly religious West Bank settlers campaigned to halt the withdrawal from Yamit. Both Begin and the cabinet initially hesitated in confronting the opposition from the far Right. In April 1982, the Israeli Army removed settlers and squatters and literally flattened the town of Yamit and other settlements. Egypt had offered to purchase them, but Begin refused for both psychological reasons and matters of security. The price of the Camp David agreement was the fragmentation of the grand coalition of the Right that Begin had been constructing since 1949.

On one side, those who had restrained Begin had left the political stage. Thus, Dayan had attracted former Ben-Gurion adherents in the Likud and established Telem[55] which advocated that Israel should bypass negotiations with the Egyptians and unilaterally implement self-government for the Palestinians.[56] Weizmann had been expelled from both Herut and the

---

[55] Yigal Hurwitz's resignation in 1981 also resulted in the pulling out of the State List and its realignment with Moshe Dayan rather than Menachem Begin. This resulted in the Telem party under Dayan's leadership in the 1981 election.

[56] *New Outlook* January–February 1980.

Likud after voting for a no-confidence motion. On the other side, part of the Right had seceded, voicing near certainty that Begin had betrayed them. They established a clearly defined far Right party, Techiya – this consisted of Herut and Achdut Ha'avodah loyalists and adherents of Gush Emunim. The Sephardim had also tired of Likud's promises to ameliorate their lot and established their own ethnic party, Tami.

While Begin was deemed to be the 'strong' leader who had made peace with Egypt, Likud's economic policies had badly affected its own supporters. Begin originally came to power with a mandate, stretching back to Jabotinsky's time, to espouse the cause of private enterprise, deregulation, entrepreneurship and privatization. Moreover, this coincided with the advent of Reaganomics and Thatcherism in the wider world. Amidst attacks on 'the kibbutz millionaires', the Liberals' Simcha Ehrlich followed his party's traditional path of supporting the middle class and the small businessman.[57] Israel, he argued, was too small and too poor to be a welfare state.[58] Government subsidies on basic goods were abolished and prices increased by 15 per cent. The cost of electricity and water provision went up by a quarter as did telephone charges. VAT increased by half. Although increases in welfare payments and child allowance compensated to some extent, Likud's working-class supporters were more than displeased by these initiatives.

Health care costs rose by 70 per cent and young couples found it nearly impossible to buy property. Even reasonably priced rental accommodation was hard to find. The business community, however, discovered that they could open accounts abroad, deposit limitless amounts of foreign currency in Israeli banks and trade more easily internationally due to lower customs duties. Ehrlich ended currency control and fixed exchange rates. Although Israel could now purchase Egyptian oil, by 1980, the inflation rate had reached 180 per cent. The State List's Yigal Hurwitz succeeded Ehrlich and proceeded to abolish even more subsidies while imposing a wage freeze on public sector workers. In tandem, the United States increased its package of military and economic assistance – between 1974 and 1981, it gave $18 billion to Israel.

By 1981, it appeared that a depressed, ailing and lethargic Begin could no longer steer the ship of state with a disintegrating government. Even a growing proportion of Likud voters did not look upon him favourably.[59]

[57] The Liberals and their predecessor, the General Zionists, had grown out of the aspirations of the Polish middle class of the fourth aliyah, 1924–1926. Jabotinsky had attempted to cultivate them with appropriate policies in the 1920s to join the Revisionist movement.

[58] *Jerusalem Post* 9 October 1977.

[59] Ilan Greilsammer, 'The Likud', in Howard R. Penniman and Daniel J. Elazar (eds.), *Israel at the Polls 1981* (Washington 1986) p. 73.

In January 1981, Hurwitz resigned over a proposed increase in teachers' salaries and took the State List out of the Likud.[60] At that point, opinion polls predicted twenty seats for the Likud in a general election. Yet Begin somehow summoned his inner resources and recovered psychologically and politically.

He initiated a consumerist policy under a new Finance Minister, Yoram Aridor. Restored subsidies on essential goods, tax reductions, compensation for three-figure inflation and a government imperative to spend, quickly restored Begin's standing in the polls. An energized Begin attacked Peres as untrustworthy and Labour as unpatriotic. Begin re-engaged with his populist constituency and courted the Sephardim who strongly identified with him as the perennial outsider in Israeli politics. Several Sephardi mayors of development towns, David Magen, Moshe Katzav, and Meir Shitreet, were already Likud members of Knesset. Five months after Hurwitz's resignation and despite much of the Arab vote swinging to Labour, Likud won the election with a record forty-eight seats. It soon transpired that Begin's radicalism was not merely a device to head off the far Right during the election campaign. Begin actually reflected the mood of the Israeli public's hawkishness – three quarters favoured continued settlement in the West Bank.[61]

His reversion from Jabotinskyian diplomacy to Betar activism was apparent in the new government's guidelines. The autonomy agreements at Camp David meant neither sovereignty nor self-determination and therefore 'under no conditions will a Palestinian state emerge in the territory of western Eretz Israel'. At the end of the five-year transitional period, Israel would 'act to realize its right of sovereignty' over the West Bank and Gaza. On settlements, it proclaimed:

The government will act to strengthen, expand and develop settlement. The government will honour the principle that Jewish settlement will not cause the eviction of any person from his land, his village or his city.

Israel would not 'descend from the Golan Heights' and even hinted that it would, in time, annex it through the extension of Israeli law. Jerusalem was 'indivisible' and would remain 'entirely' under Israeli sovereignty.

Begin appointed Yitzhak Shamir, the former head of operations for Lehi (Fighters for the Freedom of Israel) and opponent of Camp David, as

---

[60] Ben-Gurion's State List which contested the 1969 election later became a founding component of the Likud in 1973. Within the Likud, the State List joined with part of the Free Centre and Land of Israel movement adherents to establish the La'am faction. In 1978 Likud consisted of Herut (21), Liberals (15) and La'am (8).

[61] *Jerusalem Post* 6 May 1981.

Foreign Minister. Raful Eitan, known for his far Right views, remained Chief of Staff. It was Begin's appointment of Ariel Sharon, as Minister of Defence, in the face of opposition from the military establishment and former generals such as Dayan and Yadin that seemed to astound so many.

Sharon had been a controversial figure in the army, characterized by insubordination, recklessness, manipulation, deviousness and disobedience, yet he was a brilliant commander of men. Despite Dayan's explicit instructions not to enter the Mitla Pass during the Suez campaign, he had allowed his men to do so with the result that a quarter of all Israeli casualties were caused here. He was blamed for remaining outside the Pass while his men were trapped within and his career suffered for many years. On the eve of the Six Day war, when Eshkol decided to extend the diplomatic process in a forlorn attempt to avoid war, Sharon privately told a journalist that the Prime Minister should have been locked in his room and the generals would have made the right decision to go to war.[62] He seemingly told Rabin that the war could be started without the cabinet's approval and that such an action 'would be well received' by the public.[63]

An official account of the Yom Kippur war, published only in 2002 by the IDF's history department, pointed to Sharon's violation of orders as the commander of the 143rd division – to the point where discussions were held about removing him.[64] Known as 'the bulldozer', his ruthless determination to crush Palestinian insurgency had been demonstrated on many occasions. His ideological mentor was David Ben-Gurion rather than Jabotinsky and Begin. He therefore saw no rationale for retaining the West Bank and Gaza for theological reasons or ideological ones stemming from Revisionism. His support for the West Bank settlers was based primarily on security considerations in that they strengthened the state's ability to deter and repel invading armies. Israel, he argued, should not be merely a coastal strip of concrete construction on the Mediterranean coast. Three quarters of Israel's population lived in a ten-mile-wide band of territory. Sharon as a farmer also valued the Mapai doctrine of building settlements and reclaiming the Land of Israel in a physical sense. The settlement drive in the territories was therefore in his eyes a continuation of the pre-state era.

Sharon like Dayan had moved away from Labour's dovish policies after 1967. Begin had actually offered Sharon a place on the Gahal list for the 1969 election. Labour, however, ensured that Sharon remained in the army for fear that he would link up with Dayan and others on the Labour Right to form their own party. In 1973, Sharon finally left the army, having been

---

[62] *Ha'aretz* 19 November 2004.   [63] *Ha'aretz* 16 November 2004.   [64] *Ha'aretz* 15 September 2002.

passed over for Chief of Staff, and joined the Liberals. He then notably catalyzed the formation of the Likud before returning to military matters as Rabin's security advisor. Sharon's willingness to use military force to achieve political objectives was always present. Two weeks before the outbreak of the Yom Kippur war, he stated that there was no place between Baghdad and Khartoum, including Libya, that was beyond the capability of the Israeli army to strike.[65] While his prominence in military matters commended him to Begin, his return to the Likud was blocked by both the Liberals and the State List components of the party. Forming the Shlomzion party in order to get elected in 1977, Sharon dissolved it just as quickly and joined Herut within weeks of Begin's victory. Sharon had little regard for party politics, progressively moved towards the far Right and exhibited an individualistic style. His political contacts ranged from Robert Maxwell and Mobutu Sese Seko to the Serbian intelligence services.

Yet Begin was captivated by the imagery of Sharon, the Israeli warrior, which contrasted so starkly with the docile, persecuted, exterminated Polish Jews of his own background. Begin initially intended to appoint Sharon to head an office of internal security which unnerved many within the political establishment. Instead, Sharon's appointment as head of the ministerial committee on settlement effectively permitted him to develop and expand settlements on the West Bank and Gaza. In September 1977, he announced the Drobles Plan for expanding settlement and forging a central bloc from the Golan in the north to Sinai in the south. Unlike Labour's proposals in the past, it advocated settlements in densely populated Arab areas. Sharon predicted that two million Jews would populate such settlements over a period of twenty years. New towns would be built and settlements established on the West Bank and he ridiculed the demographic argument.

Increased settlement in strategic places was also designed to disrupt Palestinian territorial contiguity and thereby avert the emergence of a future Palestinian state. By 1981, the number of settlers on the West Bank had quadrupled since Likud had come to power. Yet the post which Sharon truly coveted was that of Defence Minister. By 1981, he finally secured it and in the absence of many of Begin's colleagues from the first Likud administration became a pivotal figure in shaping and initiating policies. His own radicalism encouraged Begin's and complemented it.

---

[65] *Ha'aretz* 20 September 1973.

Begin's election had been aided by his swift action against the military build-up of conventional PLO forces on the Lebanese border. Having been expelled from Jordan in 1970, the PLO had relocated to Lebanon and become part of an alliance of anti-Maronite forces. The relationship with the Lebanese Christians and an Israeli aspiration to rearrange Lebanon had been voiced by Ben-Gurion in the early 1950s. This continued with Camille Chamoun's clandestine meeting with Rabin on the outbreak of the Lebanese civil war in the 1970s. The subsequent Syrian takeover of Lebanon prompted quiet military assistance to the Maronites.

The existence of the Osirak nuclear reactor in Saddam's Iraq was a clear reminder that not all states in the Arab world wished to come to a political accommodation. Its destruction in June 1981 by Israeli F-16s was an indication of the extraordinary lengths that Israel would go to in order to secure its objectives.

Ben-Gurion had always wanted a nuclear umbrella to replace the protection of the colonial powers. Israel signed an agreement with France on the delivery of a small nuclear reactor in September 1956. By early 1958, Israel began to develop a site near Dimona. In February 1959, heavy water was purchased from Norway. The plutonium extraction unit was completed in 1964 and the element produced at the end of 1965.

While Ben-Gurion and Peres were enthusiastic about developing a nuclear deterrent, there were many others such as Golda Meir and Pinchas Sapir in Mapai who were far more sceptical. Both the doves of Mapam and the hawks of Achdut Ha'avodah argued against such a step. Leading physicists such as Amos de Shalit, IDF officers such as Yitzhak Rabin and religious intellectuals such as Yeshayahu Leibovitz all opposed Ben-Gurion. Significantly, Yigal Allon and Israel Galili of Achdut Ha'avodah argued that deterrence, based on mutually assured destruction, might work against the USSR, but the stability of a balance of terror in the Middle East was highly questionable. If Israel acquired nuclear weapons, it would initiate a nuclear arms race in the Arab world, placing Israel at even greater risk.

All this fell on deaf ears. Ben-Gurion assured President Kennedy in May 1961 that Israel's nuclear reactor would be used for peaceful purposes. Despite Ben-Gurion's explanation, President Kennedy pressured Israel to allow US representatives to regularly inspect the reactor. Kennedy, however, had broken with the previous Republican administration's policy of not selling arms to Israel. This was continued under Lyndon Johnson who authorized the delivery of Patton tanks and Skyhawk planes in July 1965. The Johnson White House further accepted a set of rather vague understandings in which Israel pledged not to be the first Middle Eastern state to introduce nuclear weapons. In effect, Eshkol persuaded the White House to lift its restraints on Israeli nuclear policy and prevented US monitoring of its facility at Dimona.[66]

The Iraqi reactor, however, had attracted the attention of successive Israeli governments since 1975. The Israelis suspected that the new Iraqi regime under Saddam Hussein wished to use the French-built reactor to manufacture weapons-grade plutonium. There had already been an attempt to destroy the reactor cores in Toulon in April 1979 and several Iraqi engineers connected with the project had died in mysterious circumstances. Israeli intelligence believed that the reactor would become active between July and September 1981.[67] Peres, however, regarded the Israeli military operation as merely a ploy to boost Likud's standing in the weeks before the 1981 election and vehemently opposed the attack on the reactor. Its destruction was also condemned by the United States and the United Nations.

In April 1981, the Syrians had installed Sam-6 missiles in the Bekaa Valley, following Israeli intervention in favour of the Maronite forces. Israeli support of the Maronites under Begin had become overt rather than covert and there had been frequent military exchanges across the Lebanese border with the PLO. This had led to PLO shelling of the coastal town of Nahariya and other border towns in Israel which forced the subsequent flight of many Israelis. For Begin, this was symbolic – a reversal of Zionist settlement on the northern borders. Israel responded by air attacks on the Fatah and Democratic Front headquarters in built-up West Beirut with attendant civilian casualties. In July 1981, a ceasefire, brokered by the Americans, temporarily safeguarded the peace.

While Fatah attempted to maintain the ceasefire, other Palestinian factions, both inside and outside the PLO, wished to breach it. Arafat's arguments that this would lead to an Israeli incursion were brushed aside – in particular by the Abu Nidal group. The disunity of the Palestinians and Arafat's inability and unwillingness to impose discipline was a weak link which the Israeli Right mercilessly exploited. By laying each and every misdemeanour and act of terror at the PLO's feet, the Likud could claim that there was no one to speak to. It also impeded the PLO's move from the armed struggle to diplomacy and the growing advocacy for a two-state solution.

---

[66] See Avner Cohen, *Israel and the Bomb* (New York 1998); Zaki Shalom, *Between Dimona and Washington: The Development of Israel's Nuclear Option 1960–1968* (Beer Sheva 2004).
[67] *Ha'aretz* 7 October 2003.

Abu Nidal had broken from Fatah in 1974 when the Palestine National Congress declared that 'an independent combatant national authority for the people [would be established] over every part of Palestinian territory that is liberated'. Abu Nidal surmised that this was the first step on the road to a two-state solution and eventual recognition of Israel.

Following Sadat's visit to Jerusalem, the Abu Nidal group killed PLO representatives in London, Brussels, Rome, Madrid and Kuwait in 1978 as well as *al-Ahram*'s editor-in-chief. In June 1982, the group attempted to kill the Israeli ambassador to Great Britain in central London. At the cabinet meeting the following day, Begin refused to differentiate between Abu Nidal and the PLO and rejected advice on this point from his advisor on terrorism. Although Iraqi intelligence and the Saddam Hussein regime were intimately involved in the attempted assassination, from a political perspective, Arafat and the PLO were the more important targets. Operation Peace for Galilee was therefore designed to clear PLO forces out of a forty-kilometre swathe of territory on the Lebanese side of Israel's northern border. Syrian forces, it was agreed, would not be attacked unless they initiated hostilities.

Sharon, however, had expressed serious doubt that the Syrians could be outflanked and that conflict could be avoided in his discussions with the army command. Sharon downplayed this point in cabinet, arguing that while there was no intention to confront the Syrians, there was no absolute guarantee that a clash would be averted. Unlike Begin's first cabinet where there were five generals, there was now only one, Mordechai Zippori. His questioning of Sharon's intentions was interpreted by other members of the cabinet as due to personal differences with Sharon. The cabinet, ill-equipped 'with organizational tools for policy analysis and for an examination of the significance and results which could be expected from such a military move', concurred with Sharon's grand plan.[68]

Although the forty-kilometre limit was discussed and essentially agreed in cabinet, it did not appear in the published cabinet decisions. The first Israeli landings on the Lebanese coast were therefore north of Sidon instead of south of the city as the cabinet had stipulated – this was beyond the authorized forty-kilometre limit. Moreover, Bashir Gemayel, the leader of the Christian Phalangists, had been asked to permit Israeli forces to land at Junieh, north of Beirut. All this suggested that Sharon had put into place his own plan, Operation Big Pines, which he had formulated on taking

---

[68] Arye Naor, 'The Israeli Cabinet in the Lebanon War (June 5–9 1982)', *Jerusalem Quarterly* no.39 1986.

office the previous year. The objective of this plan was to secure the northern border, destroy the Syrian military presence in Lebanon and reconstruct the country through an unspoken alliance with the Phalangists who would be installed as the major political force. The Phalangists were expected to liquidate the 15,000-strong PLO as a military force. This blow against Palestinian self-esteem, it was reasoned, would ensure quiet on the West Bank. Significantly, Begin issued an order which forbad the repair of the Palestinian refugee camps in Lebanon – an implicit instruction to depart.[69]

Israeli forces advanced along the Beirut–Damascus highway towards the Lebanese capital. The Syrians and their missiles were attacked in the Bekaa valley with a huge loss of Syrian aircraft. By 13 June, the Israelis had linked up with the Phalangists on the outskirts of Beirut. Sharon had ensured that only his own office would provide information to Begin rather than the Defence Ministry's intelligence service. Begin had acceded to Sharon's request that Mordechai Zippori, Minister of Communications and the second most senior military person in the cabinet, be excluded from the ministerial committee on defence matters.[70] The cabinet seemed to be totally unaware of the invasion's dimensions.

Begin, in turn, told both President Reagan and the Knesset that the forty-kilometre boundary had not been exceeded. He also said that there would be no military encounter with the Syrians despite the fact that he had asked for cabinet approval for an Israeli advance through the Shouf mountains towards the Beirut–Damascus highway.

Remarkably, Sharon had informed the Maronites of his plan in a clandestine meeting in February 1982. Such information then leaked out to both Lebanese and Syrian intelligence as well as to the PLO.[71] Begin had informed the US Secretary of State, Alexander Haig, of the plan at Sadat's funeral in October 1981[72] – and Haig had subsequently warned Sharon not to pursue it. Everyone, it seems, knew of Sharon's intentions except the Israeli cabinet.

Yet Sharon was able to dismiss any complaints about his conduct by pointing to the presence of Israeli troops in East Beirut, the rout of the PLO and the wholesale demolition of the Syrian air force and missile systems. The fait accompli of a brilliant unauthorized campaign trumped accusations of insubordination and subterfuge. In June 1982, opinion polls revealed that 93 per cent of Israelis backed the war.

[69] Ze'ev Schiff and Ehud Ya'ari, *Israel's Lebanon War* (New York 1984) p. 240.
[70] Ze'ev Schiff, review of Mordechai Zippori's *In a Straight Line*, *Ha'aretz* 17 December 1997.
[71] Ahron Bregman, *Israel's Wars 1947–1993* (London 2000) p. 106.   [72] *Ha'aretz* 10 June 1998.

Begin's populist rhetoric, honed over many decades, appealed to many Israelis who felt that they had been disenfranchised or marginalized by Mapai and its collectivism. This included the Sephardi underclass, anti-socialist entrepreneurs and small businessmen, the ultra-orthodox, the national religious and the settlers. Begin was happy to castigate the media and the intelligentsia for their views, real and imaginary, and their use of politically incorrect language. Israeli television was now instructed to use 'Judea and Samaria' for the administered territories, annexation became 'incorporation' and the Green Line suddenly disappeared from maps of Israel and the West Bank.

In response, a group of 170 workers in the media signed a letter which complained of 'the erosion in the democratic nature of the Israeli media'. While Begin continued to use Nazi epithets to describe the PLO, Sharon spoke about Israeli Arabs as 'zarim' – foreigners. All this projected a different self-imagery in Israel. It was a clash of values between the Israel of 1948 and the Israel of 1982. The invasion of Lebanon was conducted in this spirit – from Begin's emotional appeals to patriotism to Sharon's control of information to the public during the incursion. Many government supporters regarded the media as a fifth column and were vigilant to spot any dissent from the accepted wisdom.

Abba Eban, the former Labour Foreign Minister and an articulate practitioner of language, commented on the official commentary of the Lebanon war and in essence, the language of the new Israel:

> There is a new vocabulary with special verbs 'to pound', 'to crush', 'to liquidate', 'to eradicate all to the last man', 'to cleanse', 'to fumigate', 'to solve by other means', 'not to put up with', 'to mean business', 'to wipe out'. It is hard to say what the effects of this lexicon will be as it resounds in an endless and squalid rhythm from one day to the next. Not one word of humility, compassion or restraint has come from the Israeli government in many weeks, nothing but the rhetoric of self-assertion, the hubris that the Greeks saw as the gravest danger to a man's fate.[73]

It was not simply the war which divided Israel and broke the consensus, but the continual insult directed at the intellect through the manipulation of language and facts.

---

[73] Abba Eban, *Jerusalem Post* 8 August 1982.

CHAPTER 8

Dissent at home and abroad

THE END OF CONSENSUS

The Israeli invasion of Lebanon began to descend into internal acrimony and moral defeat the moment the Israeli army reached Beirut. Sharon's objective was to eliminate the PLO ensconced in West Beirut. On 1 July 1982, the Israeli army began to shell this section of the Lebanese capital which was inhabited by half a million people. A few days later, they cut off water and electricity. When this made little difference, Sharon began to adopt more extreme and desperate measures to put an end to the PLO presence.

Arafat, sensing the growing unease internationally, prevaricated and refused to move his forces out of Beirut. The destruction of housing blocks and the loss of civilian life provoked a plethora of protests. A massive bombardment on 11 and 12 August produced an angry response from Reagan. On 22 August, the PLO finally started to evacuate Beirut. On 1 September, the White House publicized the Reagan plan without any prior consultation with Begin. It argued that the West Bank settlements were an obstacle to peace and called for a freeze.

While it refused to recognize the PLO and the idea of a Palestinian state, the United States reintroduced linkage with Jordan. The Arabs of East Jerusalem, Reagan stipulated, should be permitted to vote in any Palestinian elections. All this, to Begin's astonishment, effectively questioned the Israeli raison d'être of the war. It did not permit Israel to exercise future control over the West Bank and Gaza as Begin and Sharon had expected. Instead, it clarified the anomalies of Camp David and continued Carter's quest for genuine self-government for the Palestinians. It also dissipated Begin's belief that despite all the setbacks and the welter of international criticism, the aims of the invasion had been achieved.

Reagan had previously opposed Begin's unilateral annexation of the Golan Heights and abrogated the USA's strategic understanding with Israel. Yet even before Reagan declared his political hand during the

Lebanon war, there was a growing awareness of unease within Israeli society. Sharon's tactics catalyzed a growing sense of revelation that they had been duped. Sharon, for example, had instructed Major-General Avigdor Ben-Gal to attack the First Syrian Division and then promised Begin on the telephone that he would move carefully so that the IDF 'would not provoke a clash with the Syrians'.[1] The war was neither over quickly nor was it 'clean'. Indeed, following the bombardment on 11 August, the cabinet stripped Sharon of his authority to initiate unilateral moves. While Israeli opinion polls still indicated broad support for the war, now over half of the respondents began to question the deviation from the operation's stated objectives.[2]

The explanations were no longer consistent. The operation had extended beyond the forty-kilometre boundary, Sharon argued, because the Israeli army had been provoked by the Syrians. On another occasion, he said that it was a pre-emptive strike to forestall a war with the PLO and Syria. Begin claimed that the PLO had sufficient war materiel to equip fifteen brigades only to be contradicted by the IDF which stated that it was actually five. The debate about the justification for the war began to rage within the army itself.

Debates took place between serving soldiers even as they were fighting. At the end of July, Colonel Eli Geva, a young brigade commander, asked to be relieved of his command because the actions of his tank column would cause civilian casualties. Eitan, Begin and Sharon all tried to persuade him not to leave. He rejected their admonitions and they in turn refused to allow him to stay with his men in Lebanon as he had desired. 'Soldiers against Silence' began its protests and demonstrators made a point of appearing in their army uniforms. Others started a campaign to refuse military decorations – 'No to the Ribbon'. Nearly a hundred reservists wrote to Sharon in July requesting his resignation. Begin biblically labelled them as 'rotten fruit' and compared such actions by men in uniform to Bolshevik agitators who undermined the Kerensky government in 1917.

The development of a protest movement in Israel also came about because it was the logical reaction of a free-thinking society. Information which was being passed back to family and friends by serving troops contradicted the official line. Military correspondents complained that there was excessive censorship while Sharon suggested that certain views

---

[1] Moshe Negbi, 'Review of Uzi Benziman's *Emet Dibarti: Sippur Mishpat Hadiba: Sharon neged Ha'aretz*', *Ha'aretz* 23 August 2002.
[2] Shindler, *Israel, Likud and the Zionist Dream*, pp. 133–134.

demoralized the troops.[3] Sharon was certainly no admirer of the media. He had referred to journalists as 'poisoners of wells' and believed that the media was no more than an appendage of the political Left. Indeed Begin had not met the editors' committee since 1978 and Sharon refused to convene it during the war. All information both to Begin and to the cabinet as well as the general public flowed through Sharon's office. There were suggestions from Likud stalwarts that the government should actually take over television at such times and that all demonstrations should be banned. Indeed, protest movements, it was alleged, were receiving Saudi funding. Soldiers' visits to Yad Vashem, the Holocaust memorial and institute, were banned by Eitan following contrary views on the war from some of its guides. Some members of staff on the army radio, Galei Zahal, were suspended when they literally aired their views.

The public perception was beginning to coalesce around the idea of a Sharon who was increasingly out of control and a Begin who was both out of his depth and did not know what was going on. Peace Now had been informed by its sympathizers within the government and the army that Sharon had formulated his 'Big Pines' scenario prior to the outbreak of war. Begin had mentioned it to Haig while Sharon had discussed it with Habib. On 16 May 1982, Peace Now demonstrated against the possibility of hostilities. Yet the first demonstrations against the war itself came from the Committee against the War in Lebanon – a single issue group which reflected the far Left on the political spectrum. It had emerged out of protests against the closure of Bir Zeit University on the West Bank by the Israelis. It attracted the Communists as well as Arab intellectuals such as Azmi Bishara, but distanced itself from Peace Now which was both too pro-establishment and too Zionist for its liking. Peace Now operated on the basis that tactically they had to bring the mainstream with them and not be confined to the political margins. Moreover, it had been the tradition not to break the national consensus while fighting was still taking place. Yet the Committee against the War in Lebanon now began to attract large numbers at their rallies and demonstrations. This persuaded Peace Now to organize its first demonstration at the beginning of July, which attracted 100,000 people.[4]

Begin's tactical response was to present the protests as merely a front for Labour party machinations[5] even though the latter was highly adept at not

[3] *Jerusalem Post* 28 June 1982.
[4] Mordechai Bar-On, *Shalom Achshav: Li-dioknah shel tenuah* (Tel Aviv 1986) pp. 103–105.
[5] *Ma'ariv* 17 July 1982.

committing itself. Labour, in reality, had been divided on the war. Its leader, Shimon Peres, was obfuscatory and ambiguous, Yossi Sarid and Yossi Beilin opposed the invasion while Chaim Herzog was strongly for it. The Likud, in turn, organized an even larger rally at which Begin attacked his opponents with relish and venom. Begin's mindset in travelling the path to war with Sharon was steeped in his own experience. At an address to a staff college in August 1982, he argued that the invasion of Lebanon was a war of choice and not one of last resort. The parallel that he drew was that of the inaction of the European powers when Nazi Germany occupied the Rhineland in March 1936. Begin's logic was that you have to make war in order to preserve the peace.[6] In addition, it was also an opportune time to carry out such an act.

Egypt was now out of the political equation. Iraq was engaged in a savage war with Khomeini's Iran. Begin was also keen to help the Maronites of Lebanon whom he saw as an endangered species in a Muslim Arab world. In part, Begin's thinking echoed the Revisionist Zionist attitude – and the Canaanite approach which sprang from it – of forging an alliance with non-Arab minorities.[7] Perhaps Israel's help to the Maronites, seemingly abandoned by the Christian world, projected a symbolism through his Polish Jewish eyes.

Begin never lost his desire to invoke Nazism to make a political point. The British had been Nazis as were the West Germans. In the 1950s, Mapai had been shown to be collaborating with the Nazis as evidenced by the proceedings of the Kastner affair. Following the Popular Front's attack on Kiriat Shemonah, he told the Knesset in April 1974 that the Palestinian assailants were 'two legged beasts, Arab Nazis'. After the Democratic Front's killing of schoolchildren at Ma'alot a few weeks later, Palestinian terror was described as 'renewed Nazism'. During the Lebanon war, Begin responded to criticism by the Knesset Foreign Affairs and Defence Committee about the shelling of West Beirut:

If in World War II, Adolf Hitler had taken shelter in some apartment along with a score of innocent civilians, nobody would have had any compunction about shelling the apartment even if it endangered the lives of the innocent as well.[8]

In a telegram to President Reagan, Begin spoke of his 'valiant army facing "Berlin" where amongst innocent civilians, Hitler and his henchmen hide in a bunker deep beneath the surface'.[9]

[6] Walter Laqueur and Barry Rubin (eds.), *The Israel–Arab Reader: A Documentary History of the Middle East Conflict* (London 1984) pp. 652–656.
[7] Evron, *Jewish State or Israeli Nation?* pp. 203–222.
[8] *Jerusalem Post* 15 June 1982.   [9] *Jerusalem Post* 3 August 1982.

There was considerable irritation within Israel at Begin's repeated mention of the Holocaust. The playwright Yehoshua Sobol accused Begin of using the Holocaust 'like a dishcloth with which to wipe one's dirty hands clean'.[10] A delegation of 'Mothers against Silence' was received by Begin:

[One of the mothers] came from the same village Begin came from in Poland . . . she showed him the [concentration camp] number on her arm. She was married and she had children but she lost them in the Holocaust – she was the only survivor. She came to Israel, she married again and she had two sons. She told Begin: 'Listen, I didn't go through all this in my life to now lose my two sons in Beirut. You'll never convince me that if I lose a son it was necessary'.[11]

Begin hoped to secure a peace treaty with the Maronites and effectively rearrange Lebanon's political map. It was, after all, the Lebanese civil war and the lack of a strong army that allowed the PLO to move their administrative and military infrastructure into southern Lebanon. The Maronites, however, proved less than willing to commit themselves openly to an alliance with Israel, let alone sign a peace treaty. On 14 September 1982, the newly elected Maronite President of Lebanon, Bashir Gemayel, was assassinated. A few hours later, Sharon moved his troops into West Beirut and permitted the Phalangists to enter the Palestinian refugee camps of Sabra and Shatilla. Sharon and Eitan knew at an early stage that a vicious bloodletting had commenced, but like the government and army, they were slow to move. The Red Cross estimated that 460 had been killed. IDF intelligence believed the figure was 600–800. The Palestinians claimed that the figure was actually 2,000. The killings were the final hammer blow at the consensus that had prevailed at the beginning of the war. There was outrage by senior army commanders and by ordinary members of the public. Yitzhak Berman, the Energy Minister, resigned from the cabinet. Amram Mitzna resigned as the head of the IDF College. The political commentator Ze'ev Schiff declared that 'a war crime had been committed' in *Ha'aretz*.[12] For many Israelis, the order to allow the Phalangists to enter the camp so soon after the slaying of their leader was 'a measure of moral obtuseness'.[13]

Begin's response that 'goyim (non-Jews) kill goyim and the whole world is trying to hang Jews for the crime' was perceived as distasteful and almost unworldly. Yet Arab claims that Israel rather than the Phalangists had

---

[10] *Al Hamishmar* 21 September 1982.

[11] 'A member of Mothers against Silence' quoted in David Hall-Cathala, *The Peace Movement in Israel 1967–1987* (London 1990) p. 169.

[12] *Ha'aretz* 20 September 1982. [13] Sofer, *Begin*, p. 213.

Fig. 8.1 Peace Now protest against Sharon during the Lebanon war, 1982. Reproduced with kind permission from the Israel Government Press Office.

actually carried out the massacre clearly evoked memories of pre-war Poland. The deep anger felt by large sections of the Israeli public and by all the intelligentsia at Begin and Sharon manifested itself in the largest demonstration in Israeli history. 400,000 protested in Tel Aviv in a demonstration organized by Peace Now which was attended by leading members of the Labour party. Yet even after Begin had grudgingly initiated an inquiry, he utilized false accusations from the Arab world that it was the Jews who had carried out the massacre to obscure Israeli moral responsibility for allowing the real killers, the Christian Phalangists, to enter the camps.[14]

In a sense, the Lebanon war brought Menachem Begin's long political odyssey to an unedifying close. The Kahan Commission in 1983 found that Sharon bore responsibility for what had taken place in Sabra and Shatilla and advised him to draw 'the appropriate personal conclusions'. It bluntly pointed out that Begin had the power to remove a minister from office if he so wished. Yet Sharon neither resigned nor did Begin dismiss him. Sharon was ultimately shunted aside and demoted to become a Minister without

[14] *New York Times* 2 October 1982.

Portfolio. All this, the death of his wife and the Kahan Commission's cold criticism of his conduct forced Menachem Begin back into a reclusive depression from which he never really emerged. Yet he left behind many broken families as a result of the Lebanon war.

Begin could no longer wrap himself in the flag and invoke the Holocaust in defence of his policies. A kibbutz member and former Warsaw Ghetto fighter who lost his only son in the war wrote to Begin:

Remember: The history of our ancient people will judge you with whips and scorpions and your deeds will be a warning and a verdict for generations to come. And if you have a spark of conscience and humanity within you, may my great pain – the suffering of a father in Israel whose entire world has been destroyed – pursue you forever, during your sleeping hours and when you are awake – may it be a mark of Cain upon you for all time.[15]

THE PEACE CAMP

The breakdown of the political consensus in 1982 was clearly defined by opposition to the Lebanon war and antagonism to Begin's ideology and style. Yet the Israeli peace camp had a longer history – an opposition both to Ben-Gurion and to Begin. It was situated within a wide range of parties including Labour – and within none. Even the label 'left-wing' did not really explain such a mood. In the pre-state period, there were proposals for a bi-national state which came from intellectuals such as Martin Buber and Judah Magnes as well as the Marxist Zionists of Hashomer Hatzair. The two-state partition proposals of 1947 effectively brought any consideration of bi-nationalism to an end. In 1948, the Hashomer Hatzair section of Mapam attempted to counteract any attempts at expulsion or transfer and was suspicious of Ben-Gurion's motives. Mapam's Arab department and kibbutzim such as Sha'ar Ha'amikim were instrumental in supporting the policies of Bechor Shitreet, the Minister for Minority Affairs, to allow friendly villages such as Jisr az Zarqa and Fureidis to remain, thereby counteracting the army's wishes.[16] Mapam's political committee – on the eve of the cabinet's decision not to permit the Palestinian Arabs to return – issued a statement that refugees should return to 'a life of peace, honour and productivity' at the end of hostilities.[17] Mapam and its ministers protested the destruction of Arab villages during five cabinet meetings during the second half of June 1948. While

---

[15] *Ha'aretz* 5 July 1982. [16] Morris, *The Birth of the Palestinian Refugee Problem Revisited* pp. 169–171.
[17] Ibid. pp. 320–321.

Ben-Gurion claimed ignorance, Mapam forced the establishment of a ministerial committee for abandoned property. In 1948, Israel expanded by 45 per cent in excess of the territory allocated by the decision of the United Nations. Confronted by the reality of the situation, Mapam agreed to establish settlements on lands which were beyond the original 1947 borders of the state. It assuaged its ideological predicament by accepting that surplus land would be set aside for any returning Palestinian Arabs.

Significantly, Hashomer Hatzair was at odds with the other faction of Mapam, Achdut Ha'avodah, and its military wing, the Palmach, which projected a predilection for expulsion and expansion. When atrocities were committed during Operation Hiram at the end of 1948 – a period when Israel's survival was not in question – there were profound differences between the two Mapam factions over the course of action to be taken. Indeed, when Ben-Gurion finally agreed to establish a ministerial committee of inquiry, the IDF refused to cooperate.[18]

In the aftermath of the war, the Communists, Mapam, and Achdut Ha'avodah worked together in the pro-Soviet Israel Peace Committee. The Israeli Communists had mindlessly repeated the Soviet accusations of the Doctors' plot in 1953 such that Ben-Gurion banned their organ, *Kol Ha'am*, from army bases.[19] However, with the revelations of Stalin's crimes in 1956 and the uprisings in East Germany and Hungary, the ideological differences within the Communist party of Israel became more pronounced.

In the 1960s, the Communist party itself underwent a series of fragmentations. In 1962, Matzpen split away. It saw itself as close to New Left currents in Europe, admirers of Mao, Trotsky and Gramsci and an advocate of a workers' state of Arabs and Jews. Matzpen further fragmented, spawning the Red Front whose leaders were tried and sentenced in 1973 for being in contact with Syrian agents. In 1965, the Communist party itself divided into pro-Moscow (Rakach) and 'Eurocommunist' (Maki) wings. The leader of Maki, Moshe Sneh, commented after the Six Day war that 'what united the 13 Arab states against us, irrespective of their regime, was not anti-imperialism, but pan-Arabism and anti-Jewish chauvinism'. He attacked Moscow for turning 'its back on the politics of the international Left'.[20] Maki later merged with Marxist Zionists to form parties such as Moked, Sheli and Ratz in the 1970s.

---

[18] Ibid. pp. 486–490.
[19] Giora Goldberg, *The Jewish Factor in the Israeli Reaction to the Doctors' Plot in Moscow* in Eliezer Don-Yehiya (ed.), *Israel and Diaspora Jewry: Ideological and Political Perspectives* (Jerusalem 1991) pp. 183–203.
[20] *L'Express* 19–25 June 1967.

Maki's approach was derided by Uri Avneri, the editor of the satirical magazine *Ha'olam Hazeh* and its independent representative in the Knesset. Like Sneh, he had moved towards the Left, but in contrast, he was disdainful of Zionism while embracing a quasi-Canaanite philosophy.

The occupation of the West Bank and Gaza and the commencement of settlements proved to be the catalyst that galvanized and expanded the Israeli peace camp. Siach, the Israeli New Left, was established in Israeli universities when Mapam decided to enter into the Alignment with the Labour party and included many Diaspora Jewish students who had been influenced by the anti-Vietnam war movement in Europe and the United States. In July 1970 the World Union of Jewish Students, meeting in Arad, passed a resolution which stated:

Zionism is the national and also, by virtual of its territorialist aspect, the social liberation and emancipation movement of the Jewish people; it is to be realized in Israel. This goal can only be realized if the national rights of the Palestinian Arabs are considered so that they may be recognized to be a consequence of Zionist ideology.[21]

While there were movements of academics and intellectuals such as the Movement for Peace and Security in the late 1960s – a counterbalance to the Land of Israel Movement – a much broader protest movement only began as a response to the debacle of the Yom Kippur war. Motti Ashkenazi, who had been in command of the only fortified position on the Suez Canal that did not fall, called for Dayan's resignation in 1974 and started a mass petition. While the government established the Agranat Commission to examine the conduct of the military, Ashkenazi and the protesters ensured that the responsibility of the political realm was not bypassed. As a result of public dissension, both Golda Meir and Moshe Dayan tendered their resignations.

The Israeli Labour party had frowned upon any unauthorized contacts with the Arab states. Meir Amit, head of the Mossad (1966), and Nachum Goldman, President of the World Jewish Congress (1970), were invited by the Egyptians to visit Cairo – and both were prohibited by Israeli Prime Ministers. Goldman argued that Nasser would be 'glad to have some agreement, short of formal peace' and he criticized Israeli policy as 'shev ve'al taase' (sit and do nothing).[22] The Foreign Minister, Abba Eban, was willing to allow Goldman to proceed to Cairo, but Golda Meir blocked the visit.

---

[21] *New Outlook* September–October 1970.   [22] *New Outlook* July–August 1970.

Although Matzpen had been in contact with the Democratic Front for the Liberation of Palestine and with the PLO in London, the first real meetings between Israelis and Palestinians took place following the Yom Kippur war. This was, in essence, a practical consequence of the PLO's decision to embark on the road to a two-state solution in 1974. In 1975, a former head of intelligence, Aharon Yariv, and the Mapam veteran Victor Shemtov proposed their formula.

Israel is prepared to conduct negotiations with any Palestinian element that recognizes the State of Israel and United Nations Resolution 242, and disavows actions of terror and sabotage.[23]

In 1976, the Israeli Council for Israel–Palestine Peace was established by Ya'akov Arnon, a former Secretary-General of the Israeli Ministry of Finance. Its representatives, Uri Avneri and Matti Peled, met PLO representatives Said Hammami and Issam Sartawi – both of whom were later assassinated by the Abu Nidal group for their advocacy of a two-state solution. In 1976, Sheli became the first Zionist party to support the formation of a Palestinian state alongside Israel. Figures such as Liova Eliav and Shulamit Aloni who had been pushed out of the Labour party for their dovish views led small, marginalized parliamentary parties. Liova Eliav had once been the Labour party's Secretary-General, yet his attempts to tell Eshkol, Meir and Dayan about the evolution of Palestinian nationalism fell on deaf ears.

Acts of terror against Israeli civilians – Lod airport (May 1972), the Munich Olympics (September 1972), Kiriat Shemonah (April 1974), Ma'alot (May 1974), Tel Aviv (March 1975) – all helped to undermine any initiatives from the peace camp. The United Nations' call for the elimination of Zionism on the basis that it was racist and akin to apartheid strengthened the state of siege mentality in Israel.

Moreover, settling on the West Bank and Gaza was attractive for many Israelis who were unconcerned with politics. A decent quality of life, cheap mortgages and subsidies for potential entrepreneurs were highly seductive and a profound obstacle for Peace Now to overcome. The psychological breakthrough for the minuscule peace movement which allowed it to break out of its confinement on the margins of the Left was Sadat's visit. It challenged conventional attitudes about the Arab world and created political space for different views.

When the peace negotiations began to falter after the Islamiya summit in February 1978, 348 reservists – many of whom had served in elite

---

[23] Bernard Reich. *An Historical Encyclopaedia of the Arab Israel Conflict* (Westport 1996) p. 592.

units – wrote to Begin. They claimed that the Likud government preferred a Greater Israel and a matrix of new settlements on the West Bank and Gaza to peace in the region. The letter struck a note with many Israelis and thousands added their signatures. A few weeks later, 40,000 people turned up for the first demonstration. The reaction was completely unexpected by the organizers who did not even have a name for the group. Yet Peace Now's strength was rooted in the fact that it was non-ideological, unstructured, unfunded and somewhat vague. Its pragmatic use of public relations and its emphasis on remaining within the political consensus tested the government's commitment to peace. Initially, Begin argued with them and refused to accept any petitions from the group. Then he attempted to combat their popularity by establishing his own group, 'Safe Peace'. This collapsed as soon as the government stopped funding it. Golda Meir similarly was distinctly unenthusiastic and Moshe Dayan refused to meet them.[24] The Likud's Ronnie Milo believed that they were funded by the CIA, but still 100,000 demonstrated on the eve of Begin's departure for Camp David.

Such a mass movement had not been seen before in Israel's history. It represented not only a different approach, but an experiment in extra-parliamentary politics – one that was distinctly different from the Ben-Gurion and Begin schools. It reflected the hopes of the new generation of Israelis in the wake of Sadat's visit. The core of Peace Now's adherents came from left-wing youth movements and student activists, but it went well beyond this to include housewives and businessmen, liberal politicians, Sephardi Black Panthers and orthodox rabbis. It based itself on an Athenian mode of activity – open debate and decision-making. Its protests were largely concentrated on settlement activity and on issues such as the annexation of the Golan Heights. In addition, there were developing discussions with West Bank academics such as Sari Nusseibeh through their colleagues in Israel. The Palestinian Communist party also facilitated debate and dialogue.

Yet the stand of the peace camp was undermined in the eyes of the Israeli public by the PLO's refusal to accept a two-state solution. Peace Now formally refused to meet PLO representatives and thereby did not advocate a Palestinian state. To retain the allegiance of those who advocated contacts with the PLO as well as entertaining the Jordanian option of the Labour party, it met only with 'representatives of the Palestinians'. The far

---

[24] Mordechai Bar-On, *In Pursuit of Peace: A History of the Israeli Peace Movement* (Washington 1996) pp. 106–107.

Left in Israel unlike Peace Now distanced itself from any 'Zionist' labelling whereas Peace Now did not disavow Zionism.

Moreover, the far Left was uninterested in embracing the political consensus. It recognized the right of the Palestinians to national self-determination, but did not make this contingent on their recognition of Israel. They argued that the Palestinian issue was the central issue. During the 1980s, peace groups proliferated as did contacts between Israelis and Palestinians. Peace Now became a coordinating agency even for those who were critical of its circumspect approach.

The road to peace is a rather wide freeway with different models going in separate lanes at different speeds. What counts is that they aim in the same direction and that they do not allow themselves to be sidetracked.[25]

TRADITIONAL DIASPORA OPINIONS

The Israeli peace camp exuded a profound attraction for Diaspora Jews who for the most part always found themselves aligned with liberalism and the Left. There was little sympathy for a hard-line Zionism under the Likud. In the United States, Jews, regardless of their socio-economic status, had always voted in great numbers for the Democrats.[26] Despite George W. Bush's almost automatic support for Israeli policy, 78 per cent of US Jews voted for his liberal opponent in 2004. Israeli Jews, by contrast, had different interests. They indicated in opinion polls that given the opportunity they would have voted by the same percentage, 78 per cent, but for Bush.

Although Israel and the Diaspora were profoundly and mutually interconnected, each had an entirely different political agenda and different interests. In Israel, Jews had constructed a Jewish society in the context of a nation state. In the United States, Jews were equal participants in building a multi-cultural society where relationships with non-Jews was a centrepiece of self-definition. While there was a certain disdain for Jews who refused to immigrate to the Jewish state, a beleaguered Israel soon discovered that Diaspora Jews were a vital source of support and by extension a means of enlisting the non-Jewish world. Yet paradoxically non-Jewish

---

[25] Edy Kaufman, 'The Intifada and the Peace Camp', *Journal of Palestine Studies* vol.17 no.4 Summer 1988.
[26] Ben Halpern, 'The Roots of American Jewish Liberalism'; *American Jewish Historical Quarterly* vol.66 1976 pp. 190–214.

opinion was often discounted. Nachum Goldman, the founder of the World Jewish Congress, challenged the founders of the state:

Ben-Gurion taught Israel, and his successors continue this teaching, that it is not important what the non-Jews think but what the Jews themselves do. This is a very nice and impressive phrase, but like many of these formulas, highly exaggerated and fundamentally wrong. We live in a world today where no country, not even the super-powers, can neglect the importance of public opinion.[27]

For Jews the world over, the rise of Israel in 1948 was greeted with deep and profound emotion. The revelations of the Holocaust had been searing and converted Zionism from a minority concern for the Diaspora into an integral part of Jewish identity for a majority. Zionism now transcended ideology and had become a beacon for survivalism. The Holocaust, however, had incinerated the followers of rival answers to the Jewish question. In the shadow of the death camps, the few adherents of such ideologies – communism, Bundism, territorialism as well as the religious ultra-orthodox – who had survived, often moved from an anti-Zionist position to a non-Zionist one. Many were now prepared to put aside the bitter quarrels of the past and to accept the fait accompli of a Jewish state. The Jews of the Diaspora – far from the front line – realized that the fate of the state in 1948 was in the balance and the outcome of the conflict was intricately bound up with the fate and future of the Jewish people. In Athens, a communal leader was called in by the Greek government for discussions about the possibility of large numbers of Palestinian Jews fleeing to Greece in the wake of an Arab military victory.[28] Diaspora Jews understood with great clarity that this was a turning point in Jewish history. The Holocaust was invoked. The Allies had won the war, but the Jews had lost it. 'Never again' was more than a slogan.

New paintings had been hung in the Tel Aviv Museum to accompany Ben-Gurion's declaration of independence. They included Minkowsky's 'Pogroms' and Hirshenberg's 'Exile'. The imagery of wholesale slaughter resonated throughout Diaspora Jewry. The struggle for Israel empowered Jews to act, to redeem themselves. While there were wild demonstrations of public acclamation on 14 May 1948 in New York, hundreds of American Jews quietly volunteered to fight for Israel. Many were the children and grandchildren of immigrants who had left Russia and Central Europe because of official discrimination and populist persecution.

In the USSR, Soviet Jews who had witnessed the decimation of Jewish life under Stalin read about the establishment of the state in *Pravda* and *Izvestia*.

[27] Nachum Goldman *New Outlook* June 1970. [28] Sharef, *Three Days* p. 221.

Soviet foreign policy externally was emphatically pro-Zionist as a means of fragmenting British hegemony in the Middle East. Internally, it continued its traditional policy of banning Hebrew and imprisoning Jews on charges of Zionism whether real or imaginary. Yet the events of 1948 were a watershed. An elderly Kiev Jew confided to his diary that 'the Jews usually sit on benches and chatter about the banalities of everyday life. Now their talk is animated and purposeful. They are prepared to volunteer to fight in this war which they regard as a duty.'[29] The Jewish Anti-Fascist Committee which had been established by Stalin to galvanize Diaspora Jewry's support for the Soviet war effort suddenly became the recipient of appeals for those who wished to fight for Israel. Others took at face value the quasi-Zionist speeches of Gromyko at the United Nations and simply applied to leave. Still others who were under no illusions about Stalin's intentions attempted to leave the Soviet Union illegally given the chaotic conditions prevailing in the post-war period. There were even plans to steal aircraft and fly to Palestine.

The poet David Hofshtein requested the establishment of a chair of Hebrew at the Ukrainian Academy of Sciences[30] despite the banning of Hebrew in the USSR in 1919. The Jewish writers Zvi Praegerson, Meir Baazov, Zvi Plotkin and Aron Krikheli, members of the Marak group,[31] sent a letter to Stalin requesting exit permits.

In the post-war period, a plethora of Zionist groups had sprouted up all over the USSR in the realization of the totality of the Holocaust. Some 1.5 million Jews had served in the Soviet armed forces and over 200,000 had perished. Ironically, those who had been arrested by the NKVD, the Soviet secret police, and deported from the Baltic States on the eve of Hitler's invasion of the USSR discovered that Stalin had not only inadvertently saved their lives, but also facilitated their unexpected role as teachers to the assimilated Jewish masses of Soviet Russia.

In the gulag itself, the news that a Jewish state had been established in Palestine was greeted with bewilderment. In a camp in the remote Komi district in northern Russia, one inmate later recalled:

While I was lying on my wooden bunk I heard the last news from Moscow over the loudspeaker. The announcer reported the official statement that the Jewish state had been proclaimed in Tel Aviv . . . All the exiled non-Jews who were there with me were stunned into silence. Then one by one they rose from their bunks, shook the hands of the Jews and heartily congratulated them. A sweet joy permeated my

---

[29] Baruch Weissman, letter to David Hofshtein, *Yomun Mechteret Ivri* (Tel Aviv 1973) p. 226.
[30] Yehoshua Gilboa, *The Black Years of Soviet Jewry* (Boston 1971) p. 134.
[31] Medubrim rak ivrit – We speak only Hebrew.

entire being, all the sadness and bitterness which had filled my heart disappeared and I suddenly felt reborn. We at once ran to the other camp Jews to tell them the news . . . but this time we spoke Yiddish with great delight. Even those who did not know Yiddish endeavoured to speak a few words in the language which symbolised their membership of the Jewish people.

Each of us produced the little food in our possession and we camp Jews held a feast together. We could not sleep all night long. In our hearts and in our thoughts we were at the front with our brothers and sisters who were engaged in a bitter war, rifle in hand.[32]

The establishment of Israel was thus a profoundly heroic period for Jews the world over. But it raised a number of questions for Diaspora Jews – not least was the question of dual loyalty. In 1950, the President of the American Jewish Committee, Jacob Blaustein, was at pains to point out to Ben-Gurion that US Jews had no political allegiance to Israel. American Jews, he argued, would support the development of Israel 'within the framework of American interests'.

Ben-Gurion repeatedly tied the survival of the Jewish people internationally to the survival of the state.[33] Ben-Gurion and those closest to him, Golda Meir and Moshe Dayan, repeatedly argued that Israel believed that it was acting on behalf of the entire Jewish people. The abduction of Adolf Eichmann in 1960 in Argentina and his transportation to trial and execution in Israel was indicative of this. American Jews especially did not believe themselves to be in exile, but in dispersion – and Ben-Gurion was forced to concede this. Ben-Gurion concluded that the Holocaust had destroyed those Jews who considered themselves to be an ethnic minority including traditional Zionists in Eastern Europe. Moreover, the immigration of Sephardi Jews from Arab countries was one defined more in religious terms than those of the European Enlightenment. The end of mass immigration by the late 1950s suggested that the Zionist imperative of 'the negation of the Diaspora' was flawed. It appeared that Herzl, Jabotinsky, Begin and Ben-Gurion were incorrect in their predictions and those who envisioned a more liberal, open Zionism such as Ahad Ha'am and Moshe Sharett were more perceptive. Moreover, Diaspora leaders such as Nachum Goldman argued that historically the Diaspora was more characteristic of Jewish existence than statehood.[34]

---

[32] Mordechai Palesky, *Die Yiddishe Zeitung* (Buenos Aires) 12 July 1954 in West, *Struggles of a Generation: The Jews under Soviet Rule* p. 42.
[33] David Ben-Gurion, speech to the 24th Zionist Congress, 1956 in Ben-Gurion, *Israel: A Personal History* pp. 486–489.
[34] Goldman, *Memories* p. 313.

Following his first resignation in 1953, Ben-Gurion also left the formal Zionist movement and never returned. After 1948, for Israelis, Zionism seemed to belong to the past, but for Diaspora Jews it continued in the sense of potential future immigration and an identification with the state. In the early 1950s, the Jewish Agency and the World Zionist Organization had been given responsibility for Diaspora affairs as well as the immigration and absorption of Jews. For a majority of Diaspora Jews, Israel became an ongoing component of Jewish identity – not so much Zionism in its traditional interpretation, but more a pro-Israelism.

Ben-Gurion argued that Israel's interests came before those of the Diaspora. This was indicated when Israel voted for sanctions against apartheid South Africa in November 1962 with an inevitable criticism of its Jewish community by Verwoerd. It was argued that such opposition to apartheid was in Israel's interests in terms of strengthening its relationship with Black Africa and the developing world in general. In this case, however, the Israeli Foreign Ministry had debated the issue internally since 1951 and took a strong line against South Africa as a matter of principle regardless of the ramifications for its Jewish community.[35]

Yet Israel was initially reluctant to support the nascent refusenik movement in the USSR after 1967 for fear of undermining contacts with the Kremlin. Despite the capture of Eichmann, there were even hints that Israel had to take into account the damage caused to diplomatic relations with Latin American countries in the hunt for Nazi war criminals such as Josef Mengele. In 1986, Shimon Peres circulated a list of priorities to Israeli embassies around the world – the Diaspora ranked fifth on the list.[36] Yet in tension with this approach, there was Ben-Gurion's dictum that Israel had to take into account the vulnerability of Jewish communities living under totalitarian regimes. Israel refused to abandon Soviet Jewry and South African Jewry when it would have paid politically in the international arena to do so. Despite an American arms embargo and European revulsion against the Argentinian junta in the 1970s, Israel's unsavoury backdoor diplomacy and wheeler-dealing saved the lives of numerous Jewish *desaparecidos* and averted the threat of even more antisemitic attacks.[37]

When it transpired that most Jews were remaining in their countries of domicile, Israel became more than the property of the Zionists, but

---

[35] Interview with Chaim Yahil, Director-General of the Israeli Foreign Ministry 1960–1964 in Michael Brecher, *The Foreign Policy System of Israel* (New Haven 1972) p. 145.

[36] Gabriel Sheffer, 'The Elusive Question: Jews and Jewry in Israeli Foreign Policy', *Jerusalem Quarterly* no.46 1988.

[37] Shlomo Avineri, 'Ideology and Israel's Foreign Policy', *Jerusalem Quarterly* no.37 1986.

belonged to a majority of Jews per se. Ben-Gurion realized that this hinterland of strong support and passionate identification could be transformed into an engine of political advocacy and a selfless resource of funding. Did this mean that Diaspora Jewry also had a right to an opinion and possibly to air opposition to official policy? Meir Grossman, Jabotinsky's former colleague and a long time Revisionist, believed that Diaspora Jews were duty bound to influence Israeli opinion since they were potential citizens of Israel.[38] Significantly, Mapai opposed this suggestion. Ben-Gurion blurred the difference between voicing an opinion and not having the ultimate decision, a vote in an Israeli election. When the question was raised as to who had responsibility for deciding the final destination of funds, Ben-Gurion actually sided with the non-Zionists rather than the Zionists.[39] Yet American Jewish leaders raised their concerns quietly with successive Israeli governments from the killings in Qibya in 1953 onwards. Nachum Goldmann, assertively and openly, and Abba Hillel Silver, more diplomatically, were forthright in their criticisms throughout the 1950s and 1960s.[40]

In addition, Ben-Gurion marginalized non-orthodox Jews in the Diaspora since they were few in number in Israel and in pre-state Eastern Europe. In the United States and Western Europe, however, the adherents of Reform and Masorti/Conservative Judaism possessed powerful movements representing millions of Jews. The indifference of successive Israeli administrations to their concerns increased their sense of resentment and this too had political ramifications.

A NEW ASSERTIVE GENERATION

By the 1980s, a new post-Holocaust generation cared less about accusations of double loyalty, particularly since the advent of multi-culturalism. Nachum Goldmann, as early as 1959, attacked the cul-de-sac of the glorification of the state. He criticized 'the insanity of Hegel's philosophy, making the state the climax of human history and the sacrosanct, supreme value in human development'.[41] While this did not exactly compliment Ben-Gurion's étatism, it certainly struck a chord with Diaspora Jews who did not always agree with the nationalist rhetoric of Israeli politicians while

[38] Charles S. Liebman, *Pressure without Sanctions* (London 1977) pp. 213–214.
[39] Ben-Gurion, *Medinat Yisrael ha-mechudeshet*, pp. 308–309.
[40] Michael Brecher, *The Foreign Policy System of Israel* (New Haven 1972) pp. 137–144.
[41] Nachum Goldman, speech to the Jerusalem Ideological Conference, August 1957 in 'The Vital Partnership', *The Jerusalem Ideological Conference* (New York 1972) p. 131.

Fig. 8.2 Ethiopian immigrants inside an air force C 130 en route to Israel during Operation Solomon, 1991. Reproduced with kind permission from the Israel Government Press Office.

strongly identifying with the state. Goldmann was also a critic of Ben-Gurion's ability to pick and choose which parts of Jewish history fitted his political agenda. This, too, resonated with a Diaspora and an intelligentsia which did not wish to erase unpalatable past events and thereby be selective in their understanding of Zionism.[42]

Although Ben-Gurion denied the Diaspora a voice on the grounds of violation of sovereignty, it was also an implicit recognition that Zionists were both more committed and more knowledgeable than their non-Zionist colleagues who simply accepted that the Israeli government knew what it was doing. Yet the decline of ideology in the Diaspora meant that Jews had no real universalist image of Israel and no will to influence Israel.[43] There was more emphasis on public relations than educating Diaspora Jews about the reality of the country.[44] Ben-Gurion laid the philosophical groundwork that unity and uniformity were one and the same. This consensus shattered during the Lebanon war in 1982.

In part, this was due to the coming of age of a new generation in the Diaspora who, although not living through the Holocaust and the birth of

[42] Ibid. p. 132.   [43] *Liebman, Pressure without Sanctions* p. 234.   [44] *Jewish Chronicle* 12 March 1976.

the state, were also not restricted by the weight of survivalism. The professionals and intellectuals, the better educated and less religious often found a home in Peace Now where the difference between supporting the state while opposing the government was enunciated. The orthodox, fundraisers and the communal leadership tended to support the government without any qualms expressed publicly. During the Lebanon war, Abba Eban referred acidly to such unquestioning views as 'the vulgarity of the philanthropists'.

Diaspora attitudes towards Israeli policies in broad terms seemed to be divided into three parts in the 1980s. One third was untroubled. One third was opposed. The final third tended to support Israel publicly, but was torn between reservations about Israeli policies and the bias against Israel in the media. In 1986, 85 per cent of US Jews identified with Israel.[45] A mean average of 75 per cent was recorded between 1983 and 2001.[46] Yet identification did not mean acceptance of official policies. At the outset of the Intifada in 1987, 45 per cent were indeed troubled by Israel's policies, but they also stated that this did not affect the closeness they felt to Israel.[47]

Following the Lebanon war, there was something of a revolt amongst young Jews who resented being treated as yes-men and the Diaspora as a rotten borough. Many believed that Israel's description as 'a light unto the nations' should be no mere slogan. And they were joined by liberals and rabbis such as Arthur Hertzberg who focused on 'the realm of morality'.[48] Many young American Jews had been sensitized by the Vietnam war and were not as cautious as their parents as to Israel's permanence. As the neo-conservative intellectual Irving Kristol commented during the difficulties of the Yom Kippur war:

I am one of those Jews who has never been able to take good fortune seriously, but rather suspect it as a deception. Only misfortune is real.[49]

Kristol probably spoke for an older generation of liberal Jews who could identify to some extent with his belief that 'a neo-conservative is a liberal who has been mugged by reality'. Such beliefs often led to accusations of antisemitism. Norman Podhoretz published an article entitled 'J'Accuse' in *Commentary*[50] in the aftermath of the Lebanon war and later was engaged

---

[45] Steven M. Cohen, *The 1986 Survey of American Jewish Attitudes towards Israel and Israelis*, American Jewish Committee (New York 1986).
[46] Benjamin Phillips, Eszter Lengyel and Leonard Saxe, *American Attitudes towards Israel*, Center for Modern Jewish Studies, Brandeis University, November 2002.
[47] Cohen, *The 1988 Survey of American Jewish Attitudes towards Israel and Israelis*.
[48] *New York Times* 3 July 1983.   [49] *Wall Street Journal* 18 October 1973.
[50] *Commentary* September 1983.

in a vitriolic exchange with Gore Vidal.[51] Those who criticized Israeli policy during 1982 were more discerning about media coverage – the difference between unpalatable news and biased reporting; the difference between anti-Israeli government and anti-Israel; the difference between ideological anti-Zionism and blatant antisemitism.

The Lebanon war was the tip of the iceberg. The private reservations about the settlements, the prevarications on negotiations with Sadat, the bombings of Beirut in 1980 now came out into the open. Young American Jews who were members of Jewish organizations began to propose highly critical resolutions about the proliferation of settlements at Zionist Congresses as early as March 1983. Yet establishment bodies were also moving in this direction.[52] AIPAC (America Israel Public Affairs Committee) immediately welcomed the Reagan plan in September 1982 whereas Begin was shocked by it. If the PLO gave up acts of terror, 70 per cent of American Jews in 1983 believed that Israel should talk to the organization.[53] By September 1987 – and significantly before the onset of the Intifada – the American Jewish Congress broke ranks with other Jewish organizations to argue for the staging of an international conference. Its statement pointed out that the occupation was corrupting basic Zionist values and that the demographic issue was one that could not be avoided. It condemned the silence of the Diaspora and implied that it too had a responsibility for the safety and security of Israel. A few weeks after the outbreak of the Intifada, the head of the Reform movement in the United States, Rabbi Alexander Schindler, sent a telegram to Israel's President, Chaim Herzog, that 'the indiscriminate beating of Arabs . . . was an offence to the Jewish spirit . . . Israel's present policy was morally wrong.'[54]

A central reason for the often bitter dissension within Jewish communities was the lack of knowledge about Israel. The supply of information was a sensitive matter in Israel since it coloured the views of the recipient. Governments under Golda Meir and Yitzhak Rabin established short-lived Ministries of Information. At the gateway to the electronic age and the emphasis on spin, Israel had to compete with the public relations campaign waged by the Palestinians and the Arab world. However, what was used for

---

[51] *Nation* 22 March 1986; *Washington Post* 8 May 1986.
[52] This had been true in the 1970s with American leaders such as 'the Silvers, Klutznicks or Soloveitchiks', *Ha'aretz* 18 January 1973.
[53] Steven Cohen *Attitudes of American Jews towards Israel and Israelis*, American Jewish Committee (New York 1983).
[54] Edward Bernard Glick, 'America, Israel and American Jews: The Triangular Connection Revisited' in Menachem Mor (ed.), *Eretz Israel, Israel and the Jewish Diaspora: Mutual Relations: Proceedings of the First Klutznick Symposium* (New York 1991) p. 231.

propaganda for non-Jews was simultaneously being distributed to Jews as information. For example, British Jews were repeatedly told that the Israeli Ambassador had been shot by the PLO and not by members of the anti-PLO Abu Nidal group.[55]

When the United States decided to enter into a dialogue with the PLO following Arafat's declaration that 'we totally and absolutely renounce all forms of terrorism including individual, group and state terrorism' in Algiers and Geneva in 1988, the Israeli Foreign Ministry attempted to disrupt it by attributing new acts of cross-border terror to Fatah. The aim was to blur the aims and intentions of different Palestinian groups in the public perception and to lay the blame for any violence at Arafat's doorstep.[56] The chosen instrument of deception was the deputy Foreign Minister, Bibi Netanyahu. Yet many US Jewish organizations resisted his advice and refused to condemn their government and the dialogue. AIPAC and the ADL followed Netanyahu's lead and canvassed support for the Helms amendment which wished to eliminate anyone in the dialogue who had 'directly participated in the planning or execution of a particular terrorist activity which resulted in the death or kidnapping of an American citizen'. It was opposed by the American Jewish Congress and the American Jewish Committee – the amendment fell and the dialogue continued.

The blanket refusal to allow the Diaspora a critical voice was shown to be shallow when the State Comptroller in Israel revealed for the first time in 1988 the sums which named Diaspora philanthropists had given to political parties in the 1988 election.[57] Forty-nine gave at least $30,000 – of which twenty-eight had supported the Labour Alignment. Moreover, the Likud had conducted a fundraising campaign to collect close to $6 million from Diaspora sympathizers. This made a mockery of Ben-Gurion's doctrine of Diaspora non-interference in Israeli internal affairs.

The problem for many Jewish organizations which blindly supported the policies of an Israeli government was that it worked well in the days of Mapai hegemony, but it caused political schizophrenia in a period of alternating Labour and Likud administrations. Many liberal activists had left Jewish organizations on Begin's ascent to power in 1977. This tended to deliver groups such as AIPAC into the hands of the Right and the far Right.

---

[55] *Lebanon: The Facts* BIPAC (London 1982).
[56] Colin Shindler, *Ploughshares into Swords? Israelis and Jews in the Shadow of the Intifada* (London 1991) pp. 140–147.
[57] Shindler, *Israel, Likud and the Zionist Dream* pp. 233–234.

Pro-Israel advocates therefore had tremendous difficulty in adjusting once more to Rabin and his dovish policies in 1992. Rabin furthermore attacked AIPAC for its 'negative confrontational approach'.[58] As AIPAC came back into line, the void was filled by neo-conservatives such as Norman Podhoretz, the editor of *Commentary*, and right-wing activists such as Morton Klein, the head of the Likud-affiliated Zionist Organisation of America (ZOA).

In the 1980s, the Jewish Right in the Diaspora had fiercely condemned those who held dissenting views as 'traitors' or 'self-hating' Jews. In the 1990s, even before the Oslo Accord, those on the Right now reversed their previous stand and were prepared to criticize the policies of an Israeli government.[59] The *New York Times* columnist A. M. Rosenthal now advocated a cut in non-military aid to Israel in order to move the Rabin government further away from 'the musty socialist dogma' that had held back previous administrations.[60] The new leader of the Likud, Bibi Netanyahu, had built up a network of contacts in Congress and in the Republican party – and was close ideologically to the US neo-conservatives. The ZOA bolstered Likud policies and facilitated them through existing networks, becoming a formidable political player and spoiler of Rabin's policies. Through such a parallel lobby, the Likud was able to complicate Clinton's support for the peace process on issues such as aid to the Palestinian Authority and sending US troops as peacemakers to the Golan Heights. The ZOA could not only call upon the bitter dislike of Clinton by the Republicans and the Christian Right, but also on the large ultra-orthodox Jewish communities of New York and Brooklyn.

In Europe and especially in Britain, the split in the Jewish communities was complicated by the rise of the New Left to positions of authority and influence. The substitution of the class struggle by a blanket anti-imperialism meant interpreting all third-world regimes as progressive. The disillusionment of the Left had begun with Israel's collusion with Britain and France over Suez. The appearance of a New Left in the 1960s which was not infatuated with Stalin's Soviet Union embraced the cause of decolonization – and the Palestinian struggle seemed to easily fit in. Unlike the Old Left, it did not struggle with the Jews against fascism, live through the period of the Holocaust or experience the rise of the state of Israel. Its ideological opposition to Zionism appeared before 1967 and before the first settlements on the West Bank. In contrast, those on the Jewish Left in the Diaspora who did identify with Israel and retained a memory and understanding of the Jewish past found themselves at odds with the New Left. There were initially many on the international Left who refused to take the polarized view of Israeli imperialists and Palestinian freedom fighters. Castro refused to break off diplomatic relations with Israel after 1967 – in contrast to the USSR and Eastern Europe – and intervened to prevent the condemnation of Israel on several occasions such as at the International Congress of Intellectuals in April 1968.

Yet many Jewish socialists began to sense a schism with the national Left in their country of domicile. This applied to traditional Zionists as well as non-Zionists who simply accepted Israel's right to exist as a sovereign nation state. Instances such as Noam Chomsky's inability to directly denounce Pol Pot's crimes and his refusal to clarify the use of his name in an introduction to Robert Faurrisson's *Mémoire en Défense* moved the Jewish Left to ask fundamental questions of their non-Jewish comrades. In France, many joined Le Cercle Gaston Crémieux which was affiliated to neither Israel nor the synagogue. It produced strange metamorphoses. Benny Lévy was involved in the events of 1968 and was known in revolutionary circles as 'Pierre Victor'. Lévy founded a Maoist faction, 'La Gauche Prolétarienne', but he became disillusioned with the far Left and became the secretary of Sartre. Influenced by the writings of Emanuel Levinas, he became an ultra-orthodox Jew.[61]

By the 1980s, the views of the New Left featured prominently in the liberal media. Whereas the Jewish Left utilized Peace Now as the vehicle to oppose the war in Lebanon, the liberal press not only criticized Sharon's adventure, but also used the occasion to partly question the wisdom of establishing such a troublesome state. The 1960s had produced a new generation of Jews who embraced other left-wing ideologies outside of Zionism. In addition, many acculturated Jews were embarrassed by the assertiveness of Zionism and the aggressive nature of Sharon's stand. The media utilized their views often disproportionately to emphasize the division within Jewish communities, but not to accurately reflect the nature and proportion of that division.

---

[61] 'From Maoism to the Talmud (with Sartre along the Way): An Interview with Benny Lévy', *Commentary* vol.78 no.6 December 1984.

CHAPTER 9

An insurrection before a handshake

THE MAN FROM LEHI

When Yitzhak Shamir succeeded Menachem Begin as Prime Minister in September 1983, he was perceived both by Herut and the country as a stopgap premier, a lacklustre grey necessity to stop the feared Ariel Sharon and the lightweight David Levy. At the age of sixty-eight, it was believed that Shamir would soon be put out to pasture before he reached the statutory three score and ten. Yet apart from the two-year hiatus of the rotational government, he remained in office until 1992 – only Ben-Gurion had served longer.

He personified neither the drama nor the depression of Begin. He made no memorable speeches and cared little about personal popularity. Unlike Begin, he projected no intellectual pretensions. A Likud election advertisement in 1984 characterized him as almost a grandfather type, yet 'his pleasant smile hides an iron will. Pressures won't bend him.'[1] His world outlook was anchored in the example of the struggle of Lehi – the Stern Gang as the British dubbed it – in the 1940s and a deep ideological belief in a Greater Israel. Like Begin, he had emerged from the radical wing of Betar and joined the Irgun in 1937. In 1940, after some hesitation, he followed Avraham Stern out of the Irgun because the organization had stopped its military campaign against the British in order to cooperate with them in the war against the Nazis. Following Stern's death in a botched attempt by the British to arrest him, Shamir became the chief of military operations of Lehi. Shamir took the *nom de guerre* of 'Mikhael' after Michael Collins, the Irish Republican progenitor of 'modern guerrilla warfare, the first freedom fighter, or urban terrorist'.[2] Like Begin, Shamir had studied the role of national liberation movements such as the Italian Risorgimento and the failure of the numerous Polish revolts. Shamir had been influenced at school through the works of Polish poets such as Mickiewicz and Slowacki.

---

[1] Asher Arian and Michal Shamir (eds.), *The Elections in Israel 1984* (Tel Aviv 1986) p. 217.
[2] Tim Pat Coogan, *Michael Collins: A Biography* (London 1990) p. xxii.

Both Jabotinsky and Begin were entranced by the example of the armies of revolutionary France of 1792 and sought to build a force in their image. Jabotinsky created the Jewish Legion in World War I. Begin viewed the Irgun as an underground army and not as a terrorist group. Shamir was different. He also looked to the French Revolution, but to its Jacobin phase under Robespierre, Danton and St Just.

In the Lehi underground, Shamir studied the Easter Uprising and Irish republican literature. Avraham Stern had already translated sections of P. S. O'Hegarty's *The Victory of Sinn Fein* into Hebrew. Shamir was interested in twentieth-century Communist insurgency – and read Trotsky's *My Life* and admired Mao Ze Dung. Imprisoned in Djibouti in the 1940s, Shamir met followers of Ho Chi Minh and became an admirer of the Vietnamese struggle against the French.[3]

Shamir's parents were originally Bundists, Jewish socialists, who became Zionists after the Balfour Declaration. His father was a follower of Weizmann, yet the son joined Betar after the massacre of Jews in Hebron in 1929. He assiduously read Jabotinsky's articles and was particularly affected by 'Afn Pripitshek' which exhorted young people to 'learn to shoot'. While Jabotinsky placed it within the educational context of defensive military training and the evolution of the new Jew, Shamir understood it as a call to arms. Shamir like Begin was influenced by the Zionist far Right – figures such as Abba Achimeir, Uri Zvi Greenberg and Yonatan Ratosh. Yet whereas Begin reinvented Jabotinsky by selectively quoting his writings and retaining his image as an ideological totem, Shamir adopted a post-Jabotinsky stance and later compared him to the less than admired Ben-Gurion.[4] Begin's attempts to integrate Lehi into the Irgun in 1944 foundered on his insistence that it embrace his interpretation of Jabotinsky. However, Shamir considered the Irgun to be too moderate and unwilling to adopt the concept of 'individual terror'. Shamir had also studied the activities of the Narodnaya Volia, the People's Will, which employed assassination as a political tool – an interest he later discussed privately with Andrei Gromyko at the United Nations as Foreign Minister of Israel. While Lehi was far smaller than both the Irgun and the Haganah, it carried out 71 per cent of all political assassinations between 1940 and 1948 including those of Lord Moyne and Count Bernadotte. Nearly half its victims were Jews – many of whom worked for British intelligence.

---

[3] Interview with Yitzhak Shamir 25 July 2000.
[4] Yitzhak Shamir, *Summing Up* (London 1994) p. 135.

While the Zionist Left made much of Lehi's contacts with representatives of Mussolini's Italy and Nazi Germany, the logic of 'the enemy of my enemy is my friend' prevailed after the war when the organization adopted a pro-Soviet line. On returning to Israel after exile and imprisonment in East Africa, Shamir's economic model for Israel was 'a body which will have extensions in every sphere of life and which with its thousands of eyes and ears will prevent any attempt at sabotage and defection... such an example is the Communist Party in the USSR'.[5] In the mid-1950s, Ben-Gurion allowed former members of Lehi to join the Mossad and Shamir is believed to have been responsible for the letter bomb campaign against German scientists in Nasser's Egypt. In 1970, Shamir finally joined Begin's Herut, was elected to the Knesset and appointed both speaker and then Foreign Minister. Shamir owed his rise to a good deal of luck and a publicly projected lack of personal ambition – and he was the least problematic choice of candidate. This sentiment prevailed in Likud's decision to elect him as Begin's uninspiring successor.

Shamir became Prime Minister when Israeli political affiliations were evenly divided between Left and Right. Within the PLO, there was also a growing polarization between those who wished to continue the armed struggle in the hope of reversing the defeat of 1948 and those who accepted a two-state solution and wished to return to the borders of 1967. While Arafat moved from one side to another to ensure his own position, Shamir was torn between the 'Constraints' Ministers', Sharon and Levy, seemingly to his Right and coveting his job, and those who recognized that there had been an ideological shift amongst sections of the PLO such as Arens, Meridor and Olmert. The Fahd plan of August 1981 and the Fez plan of September 1982 implied that the Arab states were willing to accept a two-state solution with East Jerusalem as the Palestinian capital as well as a less than monolithic interpretation of the right of return. Even Saddam Hussein commented that an independent state for the Palestinians and 'the existence of a secure state for the Israelis are both necessary'.[6]

This movement towards a diplomatic solution of the Israel–Palestine conflict coloured Peres's two years as Prime Minister between 1984 and 1986 under the umbrella of a rotational government. Shamir simply had to grit his teeth in the hope that Peres would neither renege on his promise to

[5] Joseph Heller, 'Avraham (Yair) Stern 1907–1942: Myth and Reality', *Jerusalem Quarterly* 49 Winter 1989.
[6] Response to Congressman Stephen Solarz 2 January 1983 in Yehuda Lukacs (ed.), *The Israeli–Palestinian Conflict: A Documentary Record 1967–1990* (Cambridge 1992) p. 480.

leave office in 1986 without new elections nor secure an agreement to which the Likud was ideologically opposed.

A NEW PATH FOR THE PALESTINIANS

Following his expulsion from Beirut, Arafat conducted a series of meetings on the Reagan plan with King Hussein and agreed to a position which could be integrated into the Fez plan. A joint Jordanian–Palestinian delegation would negotiate with Egypt, Israel and the United States on the question of self-rule. Arafat agreed that the Palestinian representatives would be non-PLO, but would be approved by the PLO. Whereas Peres was becoming less suspicious of the PLO, Shamir recognized this as the first instance of a PLO presence in Israeli–Arab negotiations. Shamir therefore opposed an international conference, a two-state solution and any involvement of the PLO – even behind the scenes.

The opposition within the PLO to indirect negotiations with Israel proved stronger than Arafat anticipated and disrupted his attempt at rapprochement with Jordan. The resolutions of the PNC in Algiers in February 1983 called for the intensification of the armed struggle and the unification of all revolutionary forces into a Palestinian liberation army. It reiterated its rejection of the Reagan plan because it did not endorse the right of return, but supported the Brezhnev plan of September 1980 because it did. Moreover, it argued for closer relations with the USSR and the Soviet bloc. Arafat's authority was further undermined by the pro-Syrian rebellion of forces under Abu Musa in May 1983. Despite this, there were renewed talks between Arafat and Hussein between February 1984 and April 1985.

In November 1984, the PNC opened in Amman in the presence of King Hussein despite Syrian opposition. Hussein precipitously declared that the PLO was now ready to accept UN Resolutions 242 and 338 as the basis for negotiations. By February 1985, the Jordanians had forged the Amman accord with the Palestinians which argued for a confederation and 'land for peace'. Arafat, however, was unable to secure the agreement of the PLO Executive which rejected 'all plans of capitulation' such as the self-rule plan, the Camp David agreement, the Reagan initiative and UN Resolution 242. Despite this, an optimistic Hussein attempted to construct a joint Jordanian–Palestinian delegation and at the end of May 1985 told Reagan that he was now willing to hold direct talks with Israel for the first time. He confidently said that the PLO would recognize Israel in exchange for US recognition of Palestinian national right to self-determination.

Peres, however, still believed in the Jordanian option and called for a summit between Israelis, non-PLO Palestinians and Jordanians within three months. Peres argued against even a partial recognition of the PLO despite the fact that the USA was secretly in contact with the PLO. In July 1985 in an interview with *Der Spiegel*, Arafat implicitly accepted the original UN Resolution 181 which called for partition of Palestine in 1947.

The killing of three Israelis on their yacht in Cyprus and the retaliatory Israeli attack on the PLO headquarters in Tunis further derailed Arafat's diplomacy. The storming of the liner the *Achille Lauro* by the pro-Iraqi Palestine Liberation Front and the killing of the wheelchair-bound US citizen Leon Klinghoffer ensured that the PLO remained off-limits in American eyes. Although Arafat reaffirmed the PLO declaration of 1974 that condemned all operations outside Palestine and 'all forms of terrorism', the PLO Executive and Fatah hardened their stand and he was unable to publicly accept UN Resolutions 242 and 338. By February 1986, the Hussein-Arafat initiative had broken down once more. The PLO Executive formally cancelled the Amman accords on 19 April 1987.

Peres for the first time recognized the Palestinians as a distinct people in April 1986, yet at the same time it was rumoured at the 18th PNC that Fatah was attempting to cooperate with Islamic Jihad and the Abu Nidal group. Abu Abbas who had organized the *Achille Lauro* assault was welcomed onto the PLO Executive. All this delighted Shamir who finally took over the premiership in October 1986. Shamir was clear about his approach to the Palestinians.

The PLO is the body representing all those who do not live in Judea, Samaria and Gaza. Between us and them is an unbridgeable abyss, because they place at the top of their priorities what they call the right of return and the establishment of a Palestinian Arab state in Judea, Samaria and Gaza as a first stage. As for the Arab inhabitants of Jerusalem – and as far as we are concerned, there is no East or West Jerusalem: there is one Jerusalem, the capital of Israel – they cannot be residents of the Israeli capital and at the same time belong to the areas of Judea, Samaria and Gaza in any respect whatsoever.[7]

Shamir never accepted the proposition of 'land for peace',[8] and he worked hard to prevent those who did from implementing it. Shamir's concern therefore was not the Palestinian rejectionists, but those Palestinians who projected a more moderate line. Arafat's inability to

---

[7] Shamir's response to the non-confidence motion, 15 March 1990 in Lukacs (ed.), *The Israeli–Palestinian Conflict: A Documentary Record 1967–1990* p. 265.
[8] *New York Times* 26 February 1988.

stand still ideologically provided ample ammunition for the Likud to discredit him and the PLO. At the same time as glossing over the *Achille Lauro* incident, Arafat advocated enhanced relations with 'Israeli democratic forces'. Shamir also feared that the United States would engage in a meaningful dialogue with the PLO. Arafat, in his speech to the UN General Assembly in 1974, had not lauded Washington, Lincoln and Woodrow Wilson by accident. In Shamir's eyes, the attitude of the Popular Front at that time was much more appropriate – the group left the PLO Executive because it opposed secret contacts with 'America, the enemy of peoples'.[9]

Shamir was vigilant in preventing Peres – now Foreign Minister in the rotational government – from allowing the PLO entry into any negotiations by the back door. He was therefore able to scupper the London agreement – due to a notable lack of US support – reached between Peres and Hussein in April 1987. The demise of the London agreement prefigured the end of the Jordanian option. It also persuaded Peres to move forward without the aid of a US administration during the clandestine Oslo talks a few years later.[10]

Unlike Rabin, Peres was not at first prepared to talk even privately to Israeli peace campaigners who were in dialogue with Palestinian activists. He began to change his view when he became leader of the Labour party and there were quiet contacts through the party's international office. As early as 1980, Peres had told Yossi Beilin privately that they would eventually have to negotiate with the PLO.[11] Although he still pursued the Jordanian option, Peres awaited political developments from the PLO and was a keen observer of the Israeli electorate's readiness to come to terms with Palestinian nationalism.

THE OUTBREAK OF THE INTIFADA

Between Shamir's concerted attempts to block attempts at negotiations and Arafat's fellow-travelling with the Palestinian rejectionists, the Palestinian issue became a secondary matter in the Arab world. At the

---

[9] PFLP statement, Beirut 26 September 1974 in Lukacs (ed.), *The Israeli–Palestinian Conflict: A Documentary Record 1967–1990* p. 316.

[10] Shimon Peres, *Battling for Peace* (New York 1995) p. 352.

[11] Susan Hattis Rolef, 'Israel's Policy toward the PLO: From Rejection to Recognition' in Avraham Sela and Moshe Ma'oz (eds.), *The PLO and Israel: From Armed Conflict to Political Solution 1964–1994* (London 1997) p. 263.

Arab League meeting in Amman in 1987, the Iraq–Iran war was at the top of the agenda. The summit significantly restored Egypt to the Arab world.

In part, this relegation contributed to the outbreak of the Intifada in December 1987. There had been a radical Islamization of Gaza in the 1980s with the construction of many new mosques. The student union in the Islamic University in Gaza was always controlled by the Islamists over Fatah. Significantly, no universities existed before 1967, but under Israeli occupation, six had been opened by 1987.

Moreover, the defeat of the PLO in 1982 and its evacuation from Beirut allowed Iran to fill the vacuum. The Palestinian Islamists were influenced by the struggle of the Shi'ite Hezbollah and its introduction of suicide bombing into Lebanon. Hezbollah proclaimed that it had forced Israel to withdraw from southern Lebanon and this cry was taken up by Palestinian Islamic Jihad which had been inspired by the Iranian Revolution. Acts of terror emboldened Palestinian Islamists and the absence of a national consensus in Israel was taken as an example of weakness.

The Lebanon war had increased the number of incidents in the territories, but the outbreak of the Intifada was predated by increasing violence in 1987 particularly in the Jibalyah refugee camp. This had been mainly stimulated by Islamic Jihad and by the example of the escape of six of its fighters from prison in May 1987. Moreover, an attack by a glider-borne member of the PFLP-GC on Israeli troops at the northern border deeply impressed Palestinians by its derring-do. This could have been prevented. An error by a signals military intelligence unit misreported a key word as *sayara* (car in Arabic) rather than *tayara* (plane in Arabic) and troops prepared for a ground-based attack instead.[12] The Intifada formally started with a traffic accident on 8 December and it was initially run by the United National Leadership of the Uprising who swore allegiance to Fatah, the PFLP, the DFLP and the CP. Moreover, its leaders owed their status to their political activity rather than loyalty to their clan. The Intifada also bore witness to the rise of Islamism and in particular to the birth of Hamas, the Islamic Resistance Movement. As part of the Muslim Brotherhood, they had conducted a campaign against secularism in Gaza in the 1980s. Not only did they liquidate drug dealers, prostitutes and collaborators, but they also fought an ongoing struggle against the Marxists of the Popular Front. This left the PFLP in a considerably weakened position when the Intifada actually broke out.

[12] *Ha'aretz* 18 September 2006.

Arafat's deputy, Abu Jihad, followed the path of armed struggle and disparaged the attempts of his rival, Abu Iyad, and then Arafat himself in embracing diplomatic initiatives based on a two-state solution. Abu Jihad was a pan-Arabist as well as being broadly sympathetic to pan-Islamism. Arafat's relationship with the Iranians had deteriorated and Teheran abruptly cut ties with him, but such contacts continued with Abu Jihad who was also close to Libya. Abu Jihad provided the revolutionary image for Fatah and wanted to export the Intifada to Cairo and Amman. The first communiqué of the Intifada on 8 January 1988 stated that its leaders were under the guidance of the PLO. Significantly, they barred the use of guns and instead used other methods to publicize the Palestinian cause. Intifada activists set fire to crops (particularly in Israel) and woods. The Jewish National Fund indicated that in 1988 four times as many dunams were torched compared with the previous year.[13] There was widespread civil disobedience, the killing of collaborators, the resignation of police from their posts and tax strikes. The Israelis responded by closing schools, colleges and universities as centres of militancy. Ideas which were first pioneered by the American Palestinian Mubarak Awad were tried such as refusing to buy certain Israeli goods such as cigarettes. Yet the Palestinians did not stop working in Israel as the Intifada leadership would have wished. In February 1988, the PLO attempted to repeat the Zionist public relations spectacle of 'Exodus 1947'. The intention was to pack a boat full of Palestinians, claiming 'the right of return' and sail it to the outskirts of Haifa harbour. Before the project could be put into practice, a mine disabled the boat in Limassol and put an end to the idea.

Israeli intelligence failed to predict the Intifada. Initially, most military men including the Minister of Defence, Yitzhak Rabin, dismissed the Intifada as peripheral, yet all sections of Palestinian society took part. While soldiers and settlers were targets, the main focus was on vehicles. The Israeli army believed that the insurrection would be crushed swiftly as in the past.

Almost everything was tried: shooting to kill, shooting to injure, beatings, mass arrests, torture, trials, administrative detention and economic sanctions.[14]

The IDF discovered quickly that it was not a police force and found it difficult to cope when confronted with mass gatherings especially when

---

[13] Aryeh Shalev, *The Intifada: Causes and Effects* (Tel Aviv 1991) p. 79.
[14] Benny Morris, *Righteous Victims: A History of the Zionist–Arab Conflict 1881–2001* (New York 2001) p. 587.

they included a disproportionate number of minors and women. In the first month alone, twenty-six Palestinians were killed.

At the beginning of the Intifada, the IDF was relatively thin on the ground and such small units therefore often found themselves in life-threatening situations. To eliminate the use of guns, Israeli troops were then told to break hands and feet, but not to beat their victims on the head. This policy was enacted against the advice of the IDF's legal advisors whose West Bank representative tendered his resignation.[15] A CBS clip of beatings and bone breaking was broadcast and duly caused an international furore. Tear gas was used and found to be ineffective because it blew away and the Palestinians found a remedy in the use of onions.

As part of its attempt to suppress the Intifada, an Israeli operation assassinated Abu Jihad in Tunis in April 1988. Although the outbreak of the Intifada had also surprised the PLO, Abu Jihad's involvement became increasingly important. Moreover, he wanted to switch from stones to guns in an attempt to spread the Intifada in the Arab world – something both Teheran and Tripoli were interested in. While Abu Jihad had a long history of instigating acts of terror against Israeli civilians, Arab nationalist regimes also had sufficient motivation to eliminate him.[16] Arafat's response to the assassination was to claim that the USA was planning to kill other PLO leaders.[17] By the end of 1988, two divisions of the IDF plus reservists in the West Bank and one division in Gaza had suppressed much of the violence. The combined use of plastic bullets, snipers and undercover units, dressed as Arabs, eventually reduced the death rate.

According to B'Tselem,[18] the Israeli Human Rights group, 1,095 Palestinians were killed in the Intifada by the IDF and 48 by the settlers and others. 197 were under the age of sixteen. In the three years of the Intifada, 30,000 were tried and 66 were deported. Stone throwers were given sentences of between three and six months and a fine where no damage occurred; one to two years where injury had occurred. For children under twelve, parents were requested to guarantee good behaviour or were fined. Administrative detention was for a minimum of six months. 48 Israeli civilians were killed inside Israel and 31 in the West Bank and Gaza. 65 members of IDF, the police and the General Security Services were also killed.

The Intifada further polarized Israeli public opinion. Many Israelis believed that the Intifada had morally corroded the IDF. Others believed

---

[15] Ibid. p. 590.
[16] Pinhas Inbari, *The Palestinians between Terrorism and Statehood* (Brighton 1996) p. 6.
[17] *Washington Post* 11 May 1988.   [18] Morris, *Righteous Victims*, p. 596

that it was naïve to believe in the nobility of war in the first place and that greater force should have been used. The Landau Commission officially sanctioned the use of torture in specific cases in 1987. Significantly, Israeli Arabs identified more closely with the Palestinians.[19] The Israeli construction industry and agriculture which depended on Palestinian Arab labour were severely hit. The Israeli economy lost 1.5 billion shekels in 1988 alone.[20]

AN ISRAELI AWAKENING

Once the smoke had begun to clear, many Israelis started to understand, perhaps for the first time, the plight of the Palestinians and their national aspirations. At the time of the Intifada, 60 per cent of the inhabitants of the territories had been born since 1967 and another 20 per cent were small children in 1967. The Palestinian population was 650,000 in Gaza, 900,000 in the West Bank and 130,000 in East Jerusalem.

During the 1980s, there had been a proliferation of trade unions, research institutes, women's organizations and newspapers. Yet the conditions in the refugee camps had worsened and there was also a sense that the PLO externally had failed them. The Israeli occupation had brought some benefits. Before the Six Day war, there had been mass unemployment in Gaza and less than one in five households had electricity in 1967.[21] Since then, the growth in the Gazan economy had been over 12 per cent and the West Bank exported twice as much to Israel as to Jordan. But there had been a slump in the 1980s in part due to an economic crisis in the Gulf States which reduced the employment possibilities of Palestinians. Moreover, the post-1967 generation tended to compare their standard of living with Israelis' and not with other Palestinians'. They experienced discrimination, lower rates of payment and lack of access to better jobs.[22]

The density of population in Gaza was one of the highest in the world due to overcrowding and a soaring birth rate. 1,600 people were squeezed into a square kilometre. Half the population were refugees, huddled in eight camps. Of these, a sizeable proportion lived in squalor with no running water and open sewage. Others lived in better accommodation built by

[19] B'Tselem Report, *The Interrogation of Palestinians during the Intifada: Ill-Treatment, 'Moderate Physical Pressure' or Torture?* (Jerusalem March 1991).

[20] *Ma'ariv 6* December 1988.

[21] Mark Tessler, *A History of the Israeli–Palestinian Conflict* (Bloomington 1994) pp. 524–525.

[22] Shalev, *The Intifada* pp. 17–18.

Israel.[23] The Jewish settlers in Gaza amounted to 0.4 per cent of the population, but they controlled 28 per cent of state land and used twelve times as much water.[24] Unlike the West Bank where Palestinians possessed Jordanian citizenship, in Gaza most Palestinians were stateless.

Both the Israeli government and the PLO realized that they had to respond seriously to the pent-up rage of the Palestinians. The PLO set out to displace Jordan and to establish itself as the standard bearer of Palestinian aspirations with self-governing institutions. It sought to persuade the superpowers and the UN Security Council to organize an international conference with the PLO in attendance as an independent delegation. It wanted to enter into a dialogue with the USA without any pre-conditions about the recognition of Israel and the cessation of violence.

Within the Israeli cabinet, Rabin, although the central implementer of the Iron Fist policy, advocated in January 1988 that a political solution would have to be found and resisted Likud demands for harsher measures to suppress the Intifada. However, it was the Reagan administration which initiated new moves. At the beginning of March 1988, the US Secretary of State, George Shultz, suggested that bilateral negotiations should start shortly. They would be based on UN Resolutions 242 and 338 to work out the arrangements for a three-year transitional period. This would be preceded by an international conference and final status talks could commence by December 1988. Significantly, the USA did not mention the Camp David agreement or the idea of autonomy which had been their foundational policy in the past. Yet the US approach was still opposed by the PLO. At the end of March 1988, Shultz met with two American Palestinian intellectuals close to the PLO, Edward Said and Ibrahim Abu Lughod. Shultz elucidated his approach shortly afterwards.

Palestinians must renounce terrorism and violence. They must accept the right of Israel to exist in peace and present themselves as a viable negotiating partner. They cannot murder or threaten other Palestinians who maintain contact with the Israeli authorities. For its part, Israel has the responsibility to maintain law and order in the West Bank and Gaza. But Israel must also find a way to respond to expressions of Palestinian grievances. It cannot claim there is no one to talk to while suppressing political expression and arresting or deporting those who speak out – even those who speak in moderate terms.[25]

[23] Ibid. pp. 14–16.   [24] Morris, *Righteous Victims*, p. 565.
[25] George Shultz, address to the Washington Institute for Near East Policy 16 September 1988 in Lukacs (ed.), *The Israeli–Palestinian Conflict: A Documentary Record 1967–1990* p. 109.

Shamir opposed the Shultz initiative because he suspected PLO involvement and a Soviet presence at an international conference would bring demands for a withdrawal to the 1967 borders.

On 31 July 1988, Hussein severed all administrative and legal ties with the West Bank – the Jordanian option had come to an end. Hussein reasoned that Jordan had lost any authority on the West Bank and decided to bolster the East Bank instead. Indeed, Hussein had already begun to argue for an independent PLO presence at any forthcoming international conference on the problem. His decision effectively annulled the Jordanian annexation of the West Bank in 1950. The break meant the cessation of payments to 20,000 civil servants and the loss of Jordanian citizenship for West Bankers. The Jordanian Ministry dealing with the territories was abolished. The number of Palestinian students who were studying in Jordan was reduced and imports from the West Bank fell.

Yet even before Hussein's dramatic announcement, Arafat attempted to utilize the political opening catalyzed by the Intifada, to push for a new Palestinian initiative. Firstly, Arafat declared the Palestinian National Charter to be obsolete. Then in June 1988, his advisor, Bassam Abu Sharif, astonished an Arab summit in Algiers by informing them that the PLO's objective was not in fact the destruction of Israel, but the construction of a Palestinian state. He then proceeded to list common points between Israelis and Palestinians. He remarkably informed his audience that 'no one can understand the Jewish people's century of suffering more than the Palestinians'. Bassam Abu Sharif then proposed direct talks between Israelis and Palestinians, bilateral talks under the aegis of a UN sponsored international conference. Abu Sharif challenged Shamir to arrange a referendum and let Palestinians choose between the PLO and any other group of Palestinians. The PLO, he said, would step aside if the outcome did not go in its favour. Moreover, the PLO would accept UN Resolutions 242 and 338, but not unconditionally. Abu Sharif wanted a state in the occupied territories with a brief transitional period under an international mandate and mooted the possibility of stationing a UN buffer force on the Palestinian side of the Israeli–Palestinian border. Significantly, he ignored the right of return.

This was followed by the publication of Faisal Husseini's plan for a Declaration of Palestinian Independence which meant moving towards a state based on the borders of the two states according to the original 1947 formula of UN Resolution 181. Husseini, a Fatah stalwart and ostensibly the PLO's man in Jerusalem, said that any provisional Palestinian government would include the PFLP's George Habash and the DFLP's Naif

Hawatmeh. Clearly such ground-breaking statements were made with the blessing of Arafat. There was a sense that the PLO was speaking from a position of the higher moral ground and that something fundamentally different was happening. It filled the void left by the collapse of the Jordanian option. While the Israeli Left rapturously embraced such announcements as a new beginning, the Labour party too started to express interest. The Likud and the far Right, on the other hand, denounced it as yet another public relations exercise and a further example of Arafat's duplicity.

On 13 September 1988 Arafat made a speech to the European Parliament saying that he was ready to negotiate with Israel. At the nineteenth PNC in Algiers in November 1988, Arafat publicly accepted UN Resolution 242, albeit with qualifications, and denounced all forms of terrorism. Yet to appease his opponents, Arafat also refused to give up 'the armed struggle against the Zionist entity'. The Palestinian Declaration of Independence was read out. It was stated that UN Resolution 181 which proclaimed the partition of Palestine into two states in 1947 provided 'the conditions of international legitimacy' to the Palestinian people. There was no mention of Israel or a direct recognition of Israel. This required Israeli withdrawal from all territories conquered in 1967 including East Jerusalem. Fifty-five countries including the Eastern bloc and the developing world recognized 'Palestine'.

The Americans were ready to engage the PLO in dialogue, yet Arafat's approach was implicit and indirect. At the beginning of December 1988, Arafat privately gave assurances to US Jewish peace activists in Stockholm, but publicly he was ambiguous about renouncing terrorism and accepting partition. Arafat's address to the UN General Assembly in Geneva on 13 December 1988 recognized an Arab state based on UN Resolution 181 and also UN Resolution 194 which, he argued, provided for 'the Palestinians' right to return to their homeland and property. He spoke about creating peace, 'the peace of the brave'. Arafat refused to say the words which were demanded of him, that 'the existence (of the Palestinians) does not destroy the existence of the Israelis'. Arafat could no longer maintain his lifelong balancing act. He was eventually forced to choose between offending his opponents in the PLO, the advocates of armed struggle, and opening a new chapter in talking to the Americans.

After numerous postponements, he finally renounced all forms of terrorism at a press conference in Geneva. The US–PLO dialogue started straight away. Habash and Hawatmeh duly condemned Arafat's words and stated that his statement did not bind them or the PLO. Shamir, on the other hand, said that it was 'a deceitful PLO act of momentous proportions'.

The young guard of the Labour party, however, called for the dropping of opposition to 'no contacts with the PLO' from the party programme. 54 per cent of Israelis were now willing to enter into talks with the PLO.[26] Yet Arafat was decidedly unenthusiastic about promoting this new approach to the Palestinian public.

THE FALL AND RISE OF IDEOLOGY

The election at the end of 1988 was almost a repeat of 1984 when the vote was split equally between the Left and the Right. In this election, the violence of the Intifada pushed the electorate to the Right with the Likud emerging with forty seats compared to Labour's thirty-nine. There had also been a proliferation of new religious and far Right parties which eroded support for the major parties. In 1984, the combined number of Likud and Labour seats had totalled eighty-four. In 1988, this figure had been reduced to seventy-seven seats. Although Likud promoted a familiar political imagery for public consumption, it seemed that ideology was on the wane. Not one of Herut's first forty candidates actually lived in Judea and Samaria. Its election platform stated:

> Any plan that includes handing over parts of the western Land of Israel to foreign rule, as the Labour Alignment is proposing, undermines our right to the land, leads ineluctably to the establishment of a Palestinian state, compromises the security of the civilian population and ultimately jeopardizes the existence of the state of Israel and thwarts any prospect for peace. There shall be no negotiations with organizations of assassins who seek to destroy the state of Israel. The Arab nation already has self-determination through twenty-one nation states.

Likud's allies on the Right were much more categorical. The National Religious party argued that there was only one state between the Jordan and the Mediterranean and that the demographic problem would be solved by increased Jewish immigration. The Moledet party embraced the idea of population exchange and transfer. Since most of the Jews from Islamic countries had already moved to Israel, it stated that 'we must work to move the Arab population out of Judea, Samaria and Gaza areas to the Arab countries.' Another far Right party, Techiya, stated that no Israeli government had the authority 'to yield up any portion of the Land of Israel whatsoever'. It continued:

---

[26] *Yediot Aharanot* 23 December 1988.

The aim of the Zionist state of Israel is the realization of the fight of the Jewish people to all portions of the Land of Israel under our control; peace is an instrument in the attainment of that aim. The policy of 'peace for land' is a retreat from a Zionist and national approach and dangerous for our existence... The kingdom of Jordan, established by the British in 1922 on seventy-five per cent of historic Palestine and most of whose population and government are 'Palestinian' Arabs, is today the Palestinian state. But if this state initiates a war against Israel, the territories it loses will not be returned.

Yet another far Right party, Tsomet, argued for the annexation of the territories and regarded its Palestinian inhabitants as Jordanian citizens living in the Land of Israel. Yet the leadership of these new far Right parties in the 1980s owed their ideological heritage to the Left. Moledet's Rechavam Ze'evi and Tsomet's Raful Eitan were both members of the Palmach while Yitzhak Tabenkin's sons were founding members of Techiya. The ideological inheritors of the Marxist Achdut Ha'avodah – maximalist exponents of expulsion – were now seen as part of Israel's far Right, closer to the Likud than to Labour.

There was a similar coalescence on the Left. Mapam, the second-largest party in 1949, was now a shadow of its former self. It had shaken off its infatuation with the Soviet Union and still adhered to a dovish policy. It commented that 'the Land of Israel is the common homeland of the Jewish people returning to it and of the Arab-Palestinian people living in it'. Shulamit Aloni and Yossi Sarid, originally dovish Labour dissidents, now led Ratz. They spoke for an expanding peace camp in Israeli politics. 'Our right to self-determination will neither be secure nor complete until the Palestinians are able to exercise the same right. The Intifada cannot be suppressed by force.'

Labour's problem was that Hussein's decision to break ties with the West Bank came before the election and left a gaping hole in Labour's manifesto which wholeheartedly endorsed the Jordanian option. It vaguely stated instead that the party now would be willing to hold talks with those Palestinian figures and elements who recognized Israel's existence, rejected terrorism and accepted UN Resolutions 242 and 338. Yet Labour could only count on a dwindling bloc committed to land for peace. Before 1967, the far Right were under Begin's ideological umbrella and the national religious camp had been almost an appendage of Mapai. In addition to the floating voters, it was the ultra-orthodox and the Sephardim who needed to be courted to establish a bloc of 61 seats in the 120-seat Knesset. The ultra-orthodox were ideologically cool to the settlements on the West Bank and derided the national religious settlers. They were also hesitant about participating in the public life of the country, but were forced to establish political parties in order to fight for funding for their religious institutions.

On one level, they condemned Labour's secularism. On another, they ridiculed the ultra-nationalism of the Likud and the far Right as well as the messianic claims of the religious Zionists. In the hung parliaments of the 1980s, small parties could make outrageous demands on the large ones and succeed beyond their wildest dreams. The Sephardim who had formerly backed Labour and Likud were now fortifying their own ethnic party, Shas, which increased its number of seats at every election. Its spiritual leader, Ovadia Yosef, had broken away from the Ashkenazi-dominated ultra-orthodox institutions and attempted to rejuvenate Sephardi identity. Unlike the Ashkenazim, non-observant Sephardim did not accord secularism the same respect. They always exuded a sense of belonging. In one sense, they were more tolerant and less ideologically rigid than their Ashkenazi counterparts. Moreover, Ovadia Yosef had often expressed dovish sentiments. The Shas manifesto in 1988 stated:

The borders of Israel were stipulated in our holy Bible and the longing of a return to Zion and a Greater Israel has never ceased. It is, however, the duty of Israel's leaders to persist in putting an end to the bloodshed in the region through negotiations for peace.

The Labour party was once again divided. Peres and the doves did not initially want to join a unity government whereas Rabin did. Shamir paradoxically did not wish to form a Likud–far Right coalition even though he was ideologically well disposed towards them. Such a political constellation, he believed, would make him a prisoner of the whims of his opponents within Likud such as Sharon and Levy and the zealots to his Right. On the other hand, a national coalition with Labour would create political pressure from the Left. In addition, a reborn PLO embracing a two-state solution and a new US administration close to the Texas oil industry would push him to produce a new approach to the Israel–Palestine conflict. Shamir concluded that his area of manoeuvre would be least restricted if he allied himself with the pragmatists in Likud, Moshe Arens and Dan Meridor, and Labour's Yitzhak Rabin. Peres agreed to enter government for a limited time in the hope of pushing forward any peace initiatives.

CONSTRAINING THE PRIME MINISTER

In early January 1989, Shamir and Arens put forward a new plan. They argued that the period of autonomy should be reduced from five to three

years, but that Israel would negotiate directly with Palestinians from the
territories. Shamir said that Israel would accept a Jordanian–Palestinian
confederation and a common market of Israel, the Palestinian territories
and Jordan with open access to Israeli ports. Shamir further suggested the
construction of over 40,000 homes for those Palestinians in the territories
who still lived in refugee camps. Rabin augmented such ideas by stating that
Israeli policy could not simply be based on the suppression of the Intifada.
With the end of the Jordanian option, Rabin argued that since Jordan
was now no longer the principal partner in negotiations, Israel would
have to negotiate with the elected representatives from the territories.
Rabin suggested a three- to six-month period of calm in the territories,
then discussion on a transitional period and finally negotiations on a
permanent settlement. The interim settlement would be an expanded
autonomy whereby the elected representatives would implement self-rule
for the territories.

Rabin displayed a readiness to consider a confederation between Jordan
and Palestine. Although this was the first time that a senior Israeli politician
had embraced the idea of Palestinian elections, the PLO was lukewarm to
any such suggestion. Rabin's ideas drew upon the report for 1988 of the head
of military intelligence, Amnon Lipkin-Shahak, which explicitly stated that
the Intifada was being led by the PLO. The implicit suggestion that the
PLO was more than a terrorist organization led to calls for his dismissal by
right-wing Knesset members.

The ideas of Shamir, Arens and Rabin were formally endorsed by the
Israeli cabinet on 14 May 1989. The new Shamir plan was also calculated
to defuse growing opposition on the Israeli Right as well as responding
to the PLO's moderation. Shamir wanted direct negotiations based on the
Camp David Accords and UN Resolutions 242 and 338. There would be no
Palestinian state either in Gaza or on the West Bank and no negotiations
with the PLO. Israel would claim sovereignty during the period of negotiations and there would be no change in the status of Judea, Samaria and
Gaza. The plan called for free elections in the territories where representatives would be chosen to conduct negotiations for a five-year transitional
period of self-rule. Jordan and Egypt would be asked to participate in the
negotiations if they so desired. Later negotiations for a permanent solution
would begin and 'peace between Israel and Jordan will be achieved'.

The Israeli Right was not pleased. The following day, thirty-two members of the Knesset including Netanyahu, constituting the Land of Israel
Front, signed a statement that the Shamir plan would lead to a Palestinian
state and before any negotiations the violence of the Intifada would have to

cease. Jerusalem, they claimed, was a united city under Israeli sovereignty and therefore no East Jerusalem Arab could vote in an election to elect Palestinian representatives.[27] The PLO now hesitantly accepted the idea of elections, but wanted to be represented officially in the election process.

Shamir found himself buffeted on all sides. Moreover, the new Bush administration plunged into the Israel–Palestine imbroglio with a no-nonsense approach. The new Secretary of State, James Baker, addressed an AIPAC conference a week after the publication of the Shamir plan. He called upon the Arab world to end violence and reach out to Israel, close down the economic boycott and repudiate the 'Zionism is racism' resolution. All this had been heard before from previous US governments, but what Baker said next was unprecedented. Israel, he said, should turn away, once and for all, from 'the unrealistic vision of a Greater Israel, forswear annexation, stop settlement activity, allow schools to open and reach out to Palestinians as neighbours who deserve political rights'.[28] This part of Baker's speech was heard in absolute silence. It unsettled an already divided US Jewish community.

Shamir termed the AIPAC speech 'treif' – not kosher – but it further exacerbated tensions within the Likud. Sharon, Levy and Moda'i, the Constraints Ministers, had already voted against Shamir's proposals. Sharon then argued that all violence must stop not only during the election period, but also for as long as negotiations continued. Peres wanted to pull the Labour party out of the government.

Shamir's problem was not only to shore up his polarizing government, but also to ensure that he, himself, was not displaced by his rivals, Sharon and Levy. Ideologically, he was actually close to their position, but his tactical approach was to formally agree to positions and then drag out any negotiations by an eternal diplomatic stonewalling. Sharon brought the issue to a meeting of the Likud central committee where he knew there would be a majority against any sort of ideological compromise. After a rumbustious and humiliating debate, Shamir decided not to risk defeat and refused to put the plan to a vote in the Likud central committee. He argued that it was more important to have unity. He then proceeded to undermine his own plan in order to please the Constraints Ministers. Shamir maintained that there would be no negotiations as long as violence continued, no PLO involvement, no Palestinian state, increased settlement activity

---

[27] *Ma'ariv* 15 May 1989.
[28] Address by US Secretary of State James Baker to the American Israel Public Affairs Committee, 22 May 1989 in Lukacs (ed.), *The Israeli–Palestinian Conflict* pp. 123–129.

and no vote for the Arab inhabitants of East Jerusalem in any Palestinian elections. He further claimed that it was premature to determine whether the plan would become a reality. The Constraints Ministers helped Shamir constrain himself. An exasperated Baker told Shamir to telephone him when he was interested in peace.

Egypt's President Mubarak then put forward his own ten-point plan which focused on Rabin's proposals for elections to include the voters of East Jerusalem as well. It spoke of land for peace and an end to the creation of new settlements. This created a Likud–Labour split in the cabinet and both sides knew that Egypt was acting as an intermediary for the PLO. The Mubarak plan was narrowly rejected.

In October 1989, Baker came up with his own five-point plan. He proposed that there should be an Israeli–Palestinian meeting in Cairo after Israel had approved a list of Palestinians. Both Israelis and Palestinians would come to the negotiating table on the basis of the original Shamir plan. Shamir grudgingly accepted Baker's five points, but the Constraints Ministers wanted assurances. Likud wanted to go to the discussion on the basis of the Camp David agreement alone and to restrict any dialogue to the subject of the elections only. The USA said that it would provide guarantees, but would not amend the Baker plan. Shamir was in no bargaining position since half his party's parliamentary representation opposed the Baker plan without amendments. Likud did not want any Arab inhabitants of East Jerusalem to participate either in the elections or in the Cairo meeting. If there was any connection with the PLO – even in the background – Israel, Shamir stated, would reserve the right to walk out.

The rift between Likud and Labour was growing wider. On 31 December 1989, Shamir dismissed Ezer Weizmann, the Labour Minister for Science and Technology, because he had unofficially contacted the PLO and advised them not to reject participation in the elections. The struggle within the Likud between the pragmatists, Arens, Meridor, Olmert, and the Constraints Ministers became more convoluted. In February 1990, Arens made a last attempt to save the Shamir plan by proposing a series of amendments to the Baker plan. Baker responded by asking a series of questions. Could Jerusalemites who also possessed a residence in the territories be part of the delegation? Could deportees also be a part? Predictably, Arens, Meridor and Olmert were positive in their response, but the Constraints Ministers were implacably opposed. Shamir resorted to his stonewalling tactics and refused to commit himself. The Likud central committee which was under the control of the Constraints Ministers was convened once more to examine the Baker Plan. Sharon resigned, explaining that 'we have a paralysed government'. Labour, too, was divided. Rabin wanted to save the unity government by working with the Likud pragmatists, but Peres wanted to bring down the government. In addition, there was also a personal antagonism between Shamir and Baker. President Bush attacked creating new settlements on the West Bank – and for the first time spoke disparagingly about new settlements in East Jerusalem.

In cabinet, Shamir refused to take a vote on Labour's proposal to approve Baker's proposals and opted to formally dismiss Peres with the objective of forming a narrow government as well as the possibility of early elections. On 15 March 1990, Peres tabled a vote of no confidence in the government – and narrowly won because of the absence of five out of the six Shas members of the Knesset. Peres's speech was designed to woo the vote of the religious camp and he duly berated the secularists for slander and discrimination against the religious. Shas's spiritual mentor, Ovadia Yosef, had already voiced his opinion that Shamir should have responded positively to the Baker plan. Logically, this situation should have been resolved as a narrow Labour government in coalition with the Left, Shas and the ultra-orthodox. However, Eliezer Menachem Schach, the leader of the ultra-orthodox party Degel Ha'Torah, was not convinced and persuaded Shas to return to the Likud. They switched back to once more supporting the Likud. Peres made a second attempt to fill this political void by appealing to another ultra-orthodox party, Agudat Yisrael. This faltered because Schach's theological adversary, Menachem Mendel Schneersohn, the Lubavitcher Rebbe, told his followers not to support Peres. Schneersohn opposed Labour for essentially nationalist reasons, whereas Schach was motivated by anti-nationalist ones. Both men were critical of the modern Zionist movement, yet out of this Byzantine dance, the ultra-nationalist, the defeated and embattled Prime Minister Yitzhak Shamir, was able to forge a new government of the Right and far Right. The Constraints Ministers and their allies were overjoyed. Shamir had openly aligned himself with the ideological approach of the Constraints Ministers and effectively adopted their policies as the new government's guidelines.

The new government continued the Likud's campaign to undermine the US–PLO dialogue. Most Israelis were unaware of the different factions of the PLO and their ideological differences. Some groups such as Fatah agreed to cease all external acts of terror including cross-border raids. Others who disagreed with Arafat's new direction did not. This allowed the Likud government to blur the differences and blame the PLO for each and every problem. Thus, the downing of Pan Am 103 at Lockerbie was immediately laid at the doorstep of the PLO by Shamir, Arens and Netanyahu before any proper investigation had been carried out.[29]

The Israeli government was unusually bereft of assistance from major US Jewish organizations which refused to condemn the White House for pursuing the dialogue. Appeals from Arens and Netanyahu were politely ignored. While the Intifada continued in the West Bank and Gaza, Rabin reported to the Knesset that Fatah had not committed any cross-border raids. The PFLP and other rejectionist groups who were represented on the PLO Executive, however, had indeed staged attacks across Israel's borders. A State Department report in March 1990 suggested that the cross-border attacks were made without the knowledge of Arafat. Shamir attacked this statement and pro-Likud Jewish organizations in the United States attempted to disrupt any attempts at rapprochement. Yet Arafat continued his policy of appealing to both those who wanted to enact the armed struggle and those who followed the path of political negotiations. He would not therefore publicly condemn any cross-border attacks. In May 1990, the Palestine Liberation Front attempted an attack on Israel's popular Nitzanim beach, south of Tel Aviv. Libya provided naval back-up and Iraqi intelligence sponsored the poorly planned operation. Although there were no casualties, US officials met the PLO four times to demand the expulsion of the PLF's Abu Abbas from the PLO executive. And four times Arafat refused. On 20 June 1990 President Bush suspended the dialogue with the PLO.

Ariel Sharon was appointed Minister for Housing in the new Shamir government and immediately embarked on the construction of new settlements and the expansion of old ones in the territories. Unlike Shamir's stonewalling, Sharon's approach to increasing US irritation was blatant, provocative and aggressive. Every time Baker visited Israel, new settlements were established.[30] US leverage, however, was manifested through Israel's growing dependency on American financial support. Since 1987, US aid to Israel had been running annually at $3 billion. In March 1991, the US Congress had given $650 million to Israel to remedy damage caused by the Gulf war.

On coming to power, Gorbachev had loosened the reins on Jewish emigration from the Soviet Union. However, the fall of the Berlin Wall and the collapse of the Eastern bloc had turned this into a flood. Soviet Jews were arriving in Israel in unimaginable numbers. The Palestinians were distinctly unnerved by such a stark realization of the Zionist dream

---

[29] *Jerusalem Post* 30 December 1988.   [30] *Jerusalem Post* 29 April 1991.

and feared that Shamir would further populate the West Bank and Gaza with the new arrivals. The Bush administration was also deeply apprehensive and warned Shamir.

Israel required $45 billion to build houses and create jobs for an expected million Soviet Jews over the next five years. $20 billion could be raised from taxes and investments, but a US loan guarantee was needed to generate further necessary investments. Germany also promised $4 billion, but only once the US went ahead with its loan guarantee. In February 1991, Israel signalled that it wanted to submit a request for $10 billion in loan guarantees to the US Congress. This would mean lower interest rates and a thirty-year repayment period. On hearing Sharon's announcement that he planned to build 13,000 homes on the West Bank over the next two years, Bush seized on the issue of the loan guarantees and twice requested delays in March and September 1991. Although Sharon had qualified his statement by stating that the new homes were not destined for Soviet Jews, Bush linked the loan guarantee to a settlement freeze. The US administration made it clear that it wanted any formal Israeli request to be made only after the Madrid Conference. Bush demanded that Congress delay both discussion and decisions for four months just in case it became an obstacle to peacemaking. Israel, however, still made the application and Congress duly postponed a decision for 120 days. Shamir therefore had to choose between the construction of settlements and the absorption of Soviet Jews. Bush also took the opportunity to attack the mobilizing of pro-Israel advocates to lobby Congressmen. President Bush interestingly depicted himself as 'one lonely little guy' pitted against 'some powerful political forces'.

Sharon, however, was almost oblivious to US displeasure and pressed his ideological agenda. Between July and September 1991, 12,985 dwellings were in an advanced stage of construction. This was five times the number registered both in 1990 and in 1989. Between January and September 1991, there were 6,435 new building starts, a tremendous increase compared with 1990 (1,820) and 1989 (1,410). It was almost twice the number compared with metropolitan Tel Aviv in 1991 (3,700).[31] When Sharon visited the USA in May 1991, the White House showed its anger by instructing the Secretary for Housing and Urban Development not to receive him in an official residence. Instead the meeting took place in the Israeli Embassy.

In the first few months of 1992, before the forthcoming election, there was a further acceleration in initiating new constructions in the territories and there was a proliferation of mobile homes. Peace Now put the cost of

[31] *Ha'aretz* 21 January 1992.

settlement construction in the territories in 1991 at $1.1 billion. The organization argued that the cost was 'a hidden section of the budget, appearing in no budget proposal, with governmental and parliamentary approval neither sought nor given'.[32] US satellite photographs showed that more new buildings were being built in the territories than in Israel itself. In early 1992, the USA adjusted its stand to permitting loan guarantees if the Shamir government just stopped the expansion of settlements. Shamir, Netanyahu and the cabinet rejected this compromise.

FROM KUWAIT TO MADRID

The popular Palestinian approach to the Iraqi invasion of Kuwait and the growing coalition of western and Arab states which resulted in Operation Desert Storm in January 1991 was not to condemn the continuation of Saddam Hussein's bellicosity after a decade-long war with Iran. It reacted instead to the presence of US forces in the Middle East which led in turn to a widespread expression of solidarity with Iraq.

Despite Kuwait's and Saudi Arabia's financial generosity to the Palestinians, their regimes were viewed as Western stooges. Iraq was now seen as the strongman in the Middle East and patron of the Palestinian cause, displacing Egypt and Jordan.

Iraq alone had the land, the people, the resources, and the infrastructure capable of sustaining an indigenous Arab power. As the Arab power most capable of making wars more costly for Israel, it had the greatest likelihood of succeeding where others had failed: that is, to make Israel more amenable to persuasion. Thus, what Palestinians cheered was less Iraq's military prowess than the political implications and consequences of that prowess.[33]

The firing of the inaccurate Scud missiles on Israel therefore delighted many Palestinians. Although Israelis were thankful that Saddam did not fill the warheads of the Scuds with chemical or biological weapons and that virtually no one was killed, several homes were destroyed, mainly in the Tel Aviv area. The Patriot missiles which the USA hurriedly shipped to Israel really could not cope with the Scuds. The Palestinians viewed the conflict in pan-Arabist terms as primarily an Arab–Western conflict. The Kuwait–Iraq discord was demoted to an internal dispute within the Arab world. The PLO central committee met in extraordinary session in

---

[32] *Jerusalem Report* 5 March 1992.
[33] Muhammad Hallaj, 'Taking Sides: Palestinians and the Gulf Crisis', *Journal of Palestine Studies* vol.20 no.3 Spring 1991.

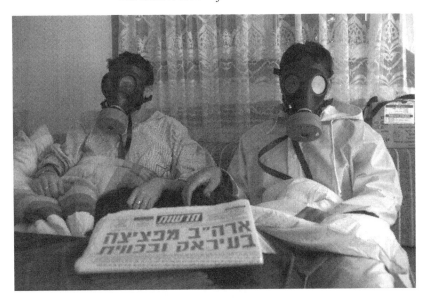

Fig. 9.1. Israeli family wearing gas masks in the sealed room in their home during the first Gulf war, 1991. Reproduced with kind permission from the Israel Government Press Office.

Baghdad to salute 'the valiant Iraqi army under the leadership of the Arab cavalier Saddam Hussein who is defending the Eastern flank of the Arab nation'.[34] The PLO proposed to the Arab League that Iraqi troops withdraw from Kuwait and be replaced by an Arab or international peacekeeping force. Both Saddam and the Palestinians wanted the occupation of Kuwait to be linked to the occupation of the territories and Israel's possession of weapons of mass destruction. Iraq significantly was the only participant in the 1948 war never to sign a permanent armistice agreement with Israel.

Before the Gulf war, about 120,000 Palestinians worked in Israel – over 40 per cent of the labour force of Gaza and one third of the West Bank. During the Gulf war, Israel closed its borders. Soviet immigrants should therefore have filled these opportunities, but since most were highly qualified professionals they, more often than not, refused to take menial jobs. The unemployment rate remained at about 10 per cent. The construction industry – especially with Sharon's housing drive – and agriculture were badly affected by the lay-off of Palestinian labour. The cost of the

[34] Statement by the PLO Central Committee 9 January 1988 in Lukacs (ed.), *The Israeli–Palestinian Conflict*, p. 395.

curfew was estimated to be between $150 and $200 million and the Palestinian economy recovered very slowly. The total stoppage was estimated to have cost $600 million.[35] Moreover, remittances from the Gulf States fell, following Arafat's embrace of Saddam Hussein. By June 1991, there was already fighting between Fatah and Hamas in Nablus over the economic shortages.

While Arafat's apparent alignment with Saddam inculcated despair in the Israeli peace camp, there was still hope that the advances of 1988–1991 could be continued. While Peace Now attacked the European peace camp for opposing the war, there was also dissent from this approach, particularly within Yesh Gvul, which advised soldiers who did not wish to serve in the territories.

The Israeli Right used Palestinian support for Saddam to oppose the Shamir plan and elections for Palestinians. Elections would 'automatically engender an authorized and recognized Arab political entity'. A Palestinian Arab state would ultimately be 'a death sentence' for Israel. Autonomy, Sharon argued, would eventually evolve into a Palestinian state.[36] Yet there were others in the Likud who projected a different attitude. David Levy, the Foreign Minister, pursued a pragmatic rather than an ideological approach. Shlomo Lahat, Mayor of Tel Aviv, and other Likud mayors privately argued in favour of a Palestinian state. Ehud Olmert suggested at an AIPAC conference that all issues were open to negotiation including with the Syrians. Sharon, the standard bearer of the Israeli Right, in response, proposed almost doubling the number of settlers on the West Bank. Although not opposed to Sharon in an ideological sense, Shamir was forced to tactically become a 'centrist' in his cabinet. Sharon and the far Right ministers therefore strongly opposed Shamir's decision to go to an international conference in Madrid, sponsored by Bush and Gorbachev. They threatened to resign from the government, leaving Shamir with only 59 mandates – insufficient to form a blocking majority in the 120-seat Knesset.

The Madrid Conference opened on 30 October 1991. It was modelled on the London agreement of 1987 and based on the premise that a solution could not be imposed. It came about because both Arafat and Shamir found themselves in weakened positions. The United States, following the Gulf war, was in a position of dominance and ascendancy. Its successful

[35] Don Peretz, 'The Impact of the Gulf War on Israeli and Palestinian Political Attitudes', *Journal of Palestine Studies* vol.21 no.1 Autumn 1991.
[36] *Jerusalem Post* 13 April 1991.

coalition included Saudi Arabia and Syria and was backed by the disintegrating Soviet Union and China.

Arafat's backing for the killings in Tiananmen Square, the Soviet coup against Gorbachev and the alignment with Saddam proved too much, not only for the United States, but also for many of his colleagues in the PLO – and there were rumours that he would be displaced. Following the Gulf war, political influence flowed from Tunis to the leaders on the West Bank who were perceived to be more in touch with the reality on the ground. A few days after the end of hostilities in the Gulf in March 1991, Bush called for a new peace initiative in the Middle East which would integrate economic development, arms control and a process of democratization of the Arab world into a solution of the Israel–Palestine conflict. Baker then paid numerous visits to the Middle East.

By June 1991, Baker had approached the Arab states and secured their approval for a conference. Shamir set several conditions for Israel's attendance. For example, he refused to countenance a UN presence even as observers. Even though the European Union attempted to persuade the USA to invite the PLO to attend the conference, Baker assured Shamir that only those Palestinians from the territories – excluding East Jerusalem – who accepted the principle of direct negotiation and accepted peace with Israel would be represented. Shamir had little choice but to accept because of the threat of the withdrawal of the loan guarantees and the fact that all the Arabs states had already responded affirmatively. During the Gulf war, a large majority of Israelis supported Shamir in not retaliating against the Scuds. The army leadership was divided – the Chief of General Staff, Dan Shomron, opposed retaliation, while his deputy Ehud Barak favoured it. In addition to Iraq, Iran and Libya also possessed Scuds which could be directed towards Israel. There was therefore a general feeling in Israel that the missile bombardment had showed how vulnerable Israel was. Public opinion now began to favour diplomacy and problem solving. If Shamir had refused to go to Madrid, there would have been tremendous opposition in Israel, in Washington and amongst US Jews. Israel was assured that the conference would have no power to make decisions and that there would be only direct negotiations.

The Madrid Conference was thus the first time since the Lausanne Conference of 1949–1950 that the parties to the Middle East conflict had seriously faced each other with the exception of the brief Geneva encounter in 1973. This was also the first time that there was a genuine Palestinian representation at an international conference. The Palestinians were clearly under PLO instructions despite being part of a joint Jordanian delegation.

Shamir's intentions at Madrid were to once more stonewall and to draw out negotiations. Unlike Sharon, he went along with the proceedings. He also hoped to attract sufficient right-wing support to keep his coalition together. Thus, shortly before his departure for Madrid, Shamir said that the Green Line did not exist.

Originally the Israeli Foreign Minister, David Levy, was scheduled to attend this conference of foreign ministers with a delegation of professional civil servants and diplomats. Shamir took no chances with the more liberal Levy and decided to go himself. Instead of seasoned diplomats and problem solvers, the Israeli delegation was characterized by its hard-line attitudes and included Netanyahu in charge of public relations – someone whom Levy had wished to exclude. A disillusioned Levy eventually refused to attend the conference. Yossi Ben Aharon and Eliyakim Rubinstein were appointed for face-to-face talks with the Syrians and the Jordanian–Palestinian delegation. One Israeli commentator wrote that Ben Aharon was made of stone.[37] Rubinstein had close familial links with the settler leadership and was a covert advisor to Gush Emunim in the 1970s. Uzi Landau, a strong supporter of Sharon, was also part of the delegation. The Israeli press reported that 91 per cent were in favour of Shamir's attendance at Madrid although 37 per cent thought that nothing would come of it.[38] Madrid for Shamir was therefore a juggling act. He had to be seen to be making progress with the peace process and keeping the USA happy while being sufficiently intransigent to stop his government from collapsing. In another nod to the Right, Shamir telephoned Menachem Begin prior to the conference to obtain his blessing. There were two demonstrations before Shamir departed. One was from the Right to make sure that Shamir did not capitulate. The other was from Peace Now which implored him to secure peace agreements with Israel's Arab neighbours.

There were also rejectionists on the Palestinian side who wished to see the Madrid Conference collapse in acrimony. There were killings of settler families by the PFLP which were designed to provoke the right-wing opposition to Shamir's attendance. Moreover, the leadership of the Intifada was paralyzed by Faisal Husseini's willingness to go to Madrid. The PFLP, DFLP and PCP were all opposed, but Fatah supported it. The rejectionists joined with Hamas to stage a general strike on 23 October 1991 which many ordinary Palestinians complied with. Israel took advantage of this division to arrest many Hamas activists and to sentence its spiritual

---

[37] *Jerusalem Report* 31 October 1991.   [38] *Jerusalem Report* 7 November 1991.

founder, Sheikh Yassin, to life imprisonment for manslaughter, incitement and leading an illegal organization. On the northern border, Hezbollah killed three Israeli soldiers in order to protest against an 'American plot to take control of the region through the peace conference'.[39] Yet 48 per cent of Palestinians supported going to Madrid.[40]

There was a fourteen-member joint delegation of Jordanians and Palestinians with East Jerusalemites excluded. In addition, there was a six-member advisory committee including Faisal Husseini, Hanan Ashrawi and Sari Nusseibeh which effectively comprised the intellectual PLO leadership in the territories. They reported back to Tunis, but also took an independent line. Nabil Sha'ath, the formal PLO representative, was also in Madrid but kept well away from the conference to preserve the appearance of non-involvement.

The Arab states were interested in negotiations with Israel for different reasons. The Jordanians were keen because they had suddenly inherited 270,000 Palestinians pushed out of Kuwait, angry at Arafat's stand during the war, with no jobs and no future. Syria went to Madrid mainly because of the imminent fall of the USSR. After the Gulf war, Bush was now seen as sympathetic towards the Arabs. Yet Syria was far more belligerent than the other Arab delegations. Syrian TV refused to show close-ups of the Israeli delegation. Its Foreign Minister, Faruq al-Shara, refused to take questions at press conferences from Israeli journalists. Yet the Syrian President, Assad, played Madrid both ways. On 19 October, he met Arafat for the first time in eight years, but he also allowed the Palestinian rejectionist leaders, Jibril and Habash, to attend an anti-Madrid conference in Teheran. The Iranians wanted to establish an 'Islamic Front' against Madrid. They had spent 70 per cent of their oil revenue – $12 billion – in 1991 on arms.

The opening conference was followed by five rounds of bilateral talks, beginning in Washington in December. The Jordanian–Palestinian delegation was allowed to divide into sub-committees to discuss specific issues, but there were no formal separate negotiations between Israelis and Palestinians. Israel specified twelve areas of functional authority which it was willing to bequeath to the Palestinians, but there was no offer to evacuate the settlements, withdraw troops or discuss elections. The multilateral talks began in January 1992 in Moscow. There were five working groups – regional and economic cooperation; environment; water resources; arms control; refugees. Syria and Lebanon refused to participate until progress had been made on the bilateral talks.

---

[39] *Jerusalem Report* 31 October 1991.   [40] *Jerusalem Report* 3 December 1992.

The Madrid Conference affected the leadership of both Israel and the PLO adversely in the months that followed. The entire process proved too much for the far Right parties in the Israeli government and they eventually withdrew. Shamir had to bring forward elections from November to June 1992.

Arafat was highly suspicious that Faisal Husseini would emerge as the primary Palestinian leader and attempt to displace him. The external PLO would be replaced by the internal PLO. Indeed, after the conference, Husseini and Ashrawi spoke at many meetings organized by Fatah and formed national committees as well. To Arafat, this sounded like the establishment of an embryonic rival organization. In addition, the Islamists strongly objected to any recognition of Israel and the very idea of negotiating with it. At a debate at the Islamic College in Hebron, Hamas and Fatah members threw chairs at each other. The Islamists also raised the issue of Ashrawi's Christianity. Yet Moshe Arens, the Defence Minister and a supporter of Madrid, effectively allowed PLO gatherings and activities. Speeches at rallies were printed without strict military censorship. Faisal Husseini mounted a public relations campaign to convince the Palestinians that they were on the verge of liberation. Palestinians began to fly the flag and offer bemused Israeli soldiers the olive branch.

The Intifada was effectively over, but it had resurrected the centrality of the Israel–Palestine conflict. The Intifada finally moved the Palestinian leadership away from the notables in the territories towards the leadership of the Intifada. It generated generational conflict and there were arguments about the participation of women. It awakened the Israeli public to the situation of the Palestinians in the territories and it polarized public opinion. The Israeli army which had hitherto prided itself on the doctrine of the purity of arms was now seen to be brutalized through the experience of confronting civilians in revolt. A minority were unable to obey strict army guidelines and committed acts of wanton viciousness. Some were never brought to book while others were given light sentences for their offences by military and civil courts. There were also 200 refuseniks who refused to serve and were imprisoned on average for twenty-eight days. By 1992, there was a widespread feeling that a new political broom was required.

CHAPTER 10

The end of ideology?

THE PROBLEM SOLVER

The election of Yitzhak Rabin in 1992 was not an abandonment of Zionist ideology, but a declaration by the Israeli public that they did not want to be entrapped by it. Many were first-time voters with no clear party loyalty. There was a realization that both Israel and the Palestinians – and indeed the world – had moved on since 1948. Shortly after his election victory, Rabin told the Knesset:

No longer are we necessarily 'a people that dwells alone' and no longer is it true that 'the whole world is against us'. We must overcome the sense of isolation that has held us in its thrall for almost half a century. We must join the international movement towards peace, reconciliation and cooperation that is spreading all over the entire globe these days – lest we be the last to remain, all alone in the station.[1]

Rabin was a disciple of Achdut Ha'avodah's Yigal Allon who had effectively distanced himself from the movement's maximalist ideology when he proposed the Allon Plan after the Six Day war. Rabin similarly followed those who had broken with the rigid ideology of Yitzhak Tabenkin because it no longer accorded with the political reality as he viewed it. Like Allon, he was a territorialist who wished to partition Mandatory Palestine unlike the functionalists of Rafi and the ideologues of the Likud who wished to grant individual autonomy to the Palestinians. While he wished to maintain the security settlements of the Jordan Valley, Rabin said that he would stop the construction of 'political settlements' and that he wanted to bring about Palestinian self-rule within nine months. Moreover, he de-emphasized the violence of the PLO and did not refer to them as a bunch of terrorists.

---

[1] Yitzhak Rabin, speech to the Knesset, 13 July 1992 in David Makovsky, *Making Peace with the PLO: The Rabin Government's Road to the Oslo Accord* (Boulder 1996) pp. 111–112.

Shamir, in contrast, continued to stress the importance of ideology[2] and expressed his admiration for Lenin and Mao.[3] Unlike even some of his colleagues in the Likud, he argued that Gaza was a part of the Land of Israel. Although only a few years older than Rabin, Shamir at seventy-six looked like a man of the past and out of touch with an electorate which wanted a normal life and not a Greater Israel. Shamir had unwisely not made room for Moshe Arens.

The shift to Labour was primarily a result of the Intifada and a perception of PLO flexibility despite the Iraqi war. If the PLO's implied acceptance of a two-state solution in 1988 was not simply window dressing as the Likud suggested, then the fundamental idea in the Palestine National Charter that Palestine within the Mandate borders was 'an indivisible territorial unit' had been revoked. The promotion of partition also meant a relegation of a Palestinian ideological approach.

Given the political volatility of the Israeli electorate, there was no direct attack on ideology itself, but on the effects of the ideology. Labour therefore attacked the notion of disproportionate funds going to settlements and the complications of US–Israel relations, particularly the loan guarantee dispute. Rabin implied a policy of separation between Israelis and Palestinians and that terror would not be tolerated within the Green Line. The implication was that attacks on Jewish settlements on the West Bank and Gaza would be regarded differently. But 57 per cent of Israelis favoured a freeze on the settlements.[4] The demographic outlook suggested that a million new immigrants from the USSR might delay Arab parity with Jews, but it would now occur in 2025.[5]

Voters were distinctly uninterested in building socialism. Rabin also ran a presidential-style campaign – even the party colour was changed from socialist red to patriotic blue. All this appealed to the 260,000 Soviet immigrants who were eligible to vote. They had had enough of the hollow claims of the apparatchiks back in the USSR. Moreover, they were a highly educated and professional group with proportionately more academics and intellectuals compared with the Israeli average. Despite a 6 per cent growth in the economy in 1992, there was also high unemployment. The unemployment rate among Soviet immigrants was far higher than the national figure with between a quarter and a half of the new immigrants unable to locate meaningful work. Academics were cleaning streets and professionals doing menial tasks to make ends meet. Russian orchestras mushroomed

---

[2] *Jerusalem Post* 25 April 1992.   [3] *Jerusalem Post* 17 April 1992.
[4] *Jerusalem Post* 28 September 1991.   [5] *New Outlook* December 1990.

in every town while talented musicians took to busking in the high street.

Each immigrant family was given 30,000 shekels on arrival. This was a very small amount and barely enough to cover living expenses. There were suicides, high stress levels and severe depression amongst the new arrivals. The bureaucracy was overworked and traditionally unsympathetic. The huge immigration was paid for by a 5 per cent rise in income tax and an increase in VAT. The enormous problems with absorption were therefore fertile ground for criticism by Labour. Sharon and Shamir were asked why so much money was now being spent on the settlements instead of within Israel. The Russian Jews, themselves, feared the consequences of a US refusal to provide loan guarantees unless there was a freeze on the settlements. Having had no real opportunity to be full Jews when official Soviet ideology preached assimilation, they were both ignorant of and alienated from Jewish religious traditions. This further distanced them from the Right and the religious. On election day, almost half the Russians voted for Rabin.

While Labour attempted to maintain its natural base of supporters through the Histadrut, it simultaneously moved away from its socialist background. Under the Likud, the government had a stake in 161 companies which accounted for 20 per cent of the country's business activities and employed 75,000 people. It owned Israel Aircraft Industries as well as the Shekem departmental store chain. In March 1992, Israel Chemicals Ltd was sold off. 25 per cent of Bezeq Communications was offered to the public. Although the Histadrut prevaricated, parts of Hevrat Ovdim were sold off and kibbutzim began to sell off companies that they controlled. Ironically although the Likud had espoused Thatcherite doctrine, there was a reluctance to denationalize because certain government-controlled companies were run by party nominees. Privatization meant that ministers lost their fiefdoms and parties lost their influence. Therefore, Sharon opposed the privatization of companies under the aegis of his Housing Ministry.

Rabin personified honesty in politics, as well as realism and pragmatism. 'Politicians to his Right like Netanyahu had the credibility but not the will to make territorial concessions and recognize the PLO; politicians to his Left like Peres had the will but lacked the credibility.'[6] There was a preference for Rabin over Peres who was seen as tainted by 'the old politics'. Both Shamir and Peres had attempted to woo members of the Knesset from the other party by promises of safe seats. Moreover, Labour had instituted primaries whereas Likud still depended

[6] Makovsky, *Making Peace with the PLO* p. 86.

on the wheeler-dealing of its central committee. 108,000 voted in the Labour primaries. Unexpectedly, Rabin polled 40 per cent and Peres 34 per cent which probably reflected public opinion more than the party's hierarchy.

The deterioration of relations with the USA was also a public concern. In January 1992 the USA voted at the UN to condemn Israel for its deportation of Palestinians. A State Department spokesperson initially commented that the Bush White House supported UN Resolution 194 which the PLO had promoted to draw attention to the refugees' right of return.

Labour had benefited from an increase in the electoral threshold for representation in the Knesset from 1 to 1.5 per cent. The number of parties elected thereby decreased by a third compared to the 1988 election. Yet despite the euphoria at Rabin's triumph, Labour gained the same number of seats as in 1984 and even less than in 1981. Moreover, a majority of Israeli Jews actually voted for the Likud and other right-wing parties. In part, it was only the Arab votes which gave Rabin his victory. Rabin could only depend on Meretz, a left-liberal Zionist party which was close to both Peace Now and Labour's doves, for real support. Labour and Meretz could only muster fifty-six seats – some five short of a blocking majority in the Knesset. The Right and national religious could put together forty-nine. Therefore Rabin had to court either the ultra-orthodox Sephardi Shas party or the ultra-orthodox United Torah Judaism party to form a coalition. Rabin negotiated with Shas which had won six seats. The party was ambivalent on the question of Zionism, although many members of Shas served in the army. It was less ideologically fixated on the settlements and its spiritual mentor, Ovadia Yosef, was noted for his dovish political oudook.

There had been a Yemenite list for decades after the first election in 1949. Another ethnic Sephardi party, Tami, was created through a split from the NRP. Shas was in itself a split from Agudat Yisrael. This trend towards ethnicity and representative parties represented the Sephardi dis-illusionment with the Likud and a communal reassertion of its identity. Shas saw itself as more a religious movement than a political one. Degel Ha'Torah's Schach, a leading rabbinical opponent of the chassidim, was originally a much admired spiritual mentor until he made derogatory remarks about Sephardim not being mature enough for political struggle. Many Sephardim who had originally been trained in the Lithuanian school of Torah study deserted him and transferred their allegiance to Shas. The representation of United Torah Judaism was thereby severely reduced in the 1992 election.

There was almost a religious fervour in voting for Shas in 1992. Yeshiva students were encouraged to canvass voters instead of studying Torah. Ovadia Yosef allowed students to sell their tephilin (phylacteries) if they did not have the bus fare to reach the polling station, with the proviso that they had to be prepared to borrow someone else's for prayer.[7] Shas accepted Rabin's invitation to join the government despite the protests of Schach and other ultra-orthodox leaders about the presence of their bête noire, Meretz's Shulamit Aloni, as Minister for Education. Aloni was noted for her devout secularism and her blunt opposition to religious coercion. Unlike her other secular colleagues, she was prepared to be outspoken and, in religious eyes, outrageous. Shas worried about its network of religious schools and saw Aloni's authority as a threat impeding their development. Shas's main political leader was the astute Arieh Deri who once more became the Minister of the Interior. His position while unchallenged within Shas was also politically precarious since he was being investigated for bribery and theft. This allowed Shas to use their leverage on Rabin to periodically press for the dismissal of all charges. Yet Deri had invested heavily in the Arab sector and made numerous appearances in Arab villages. He appealed to them on the basis of religiosity and discrimination, implying Ashkenazi bias against the Sephardim. 13,000 Arabs voted for Shas in the election.[8] The defeated Likud was left with $50 million in debt following its poor showing in the election.[9]

In foreign policy, the new government looked decidedly dovish. Shimon Peres was appointed Foreign Minister while his follower, the leader of Labour's dovish wing, Yossi Beilin, was installed as deputy Foreign Minister. The doves had called for a joint electoral list with Meretz and criticized Peres for sticking to the idea of a confederation and not espousing Palestinian national self-determination. Beilin had developed the technique of 'negotiating' with Palestinians and producing a detailed 'agreement' – to indicate what was possible. He had already signed 'the Notre Dame declaration' with the Palestinian moderate Sari Nusseibeh. Moreover, Beilin encouraged academics to involve themselves in such intellectual exercises with Palestinians. In November 1991, the Labour doves were influential in forcing an inclusion in the party platform that Israel needed to begin a dialogue with the PLO. Rabin, however, remained cautious and was supported by half the cabinet. Yet he revoked the contact law which

7 Aaron P. Willis, 'Shas: The Sephardic Torah Guardians: Religious Movement and Political Power' in Asher Arian and Michal Shamir (eds.), *The Elections in Israel 1992* (New York 1995) p. 137.
8 *Yediot Aharanot* 26 June 1992.   9 *Jerusalem Report* 3 December 1992.

threatened imprisonment for speaking to the PLO. He released 800 prisoners and cancelled 11 deportation orders. He also stated that UN Resolution 242 would now also apply to the Syrian front and said that Israel would make territorial concessions on the Golan Heights. Significantly, Syria stated for the first time that it wanted total peace. Rabin lifted the veto on the participation in the bilateral talks of the Fatah leader, Faisal Husseini, even though he lived in East Jerusalem. Rabin also allowed Palestinians from outside the territories to participate in negotiations.

The election of Bill Clinton strengthened Rabin's hand. He was seen as rational, fair to Israel and not a Republican. For example, he criticized the linkage of loan guarantees to Soviet Jewish immigration. Clinton was also liberal and it was fortuitous that he came to power at the same time as Rabin. By the end of 1992, Meretz was pressing Rabin to open a dialogue with the PLO. Peres was also moving towards such a position and many Labour parliamentarians favoured this as did nearly half the Israeli public.[10]

In July 1993, Peres suggested the establishment of a Palestinian police force in the territories – a suggestion which outraged the settlers. He was also in favour of 'Gaza First'. Rabin wanted to broaden Palestinian representation at the bilateral talks and to project a wider definition of autonomy beyond that stated at Camp David. Although he privately recognized that Israel had already been negotiating with the PLO in the bilateral talks, he did not wish to commit himself to direct talks.

THE OSLO BREAKTHROUGH

The bilateral talks in Washington seemed to be going nowhere mainly because the Palestinians were overtly dependent on PLO approval and led by the dogmatic Haidar 'Abd al-Shafi. By August 1993, Husseini, Ashrawi and Erekat were on the verge of handing in their resignations to Arafat in protest at Tunis's meddling.

Private discussions had always existed between Israelis and Palestinians. The ban on speaking to the PLO in the mid-1980s had led to intermediaries staging suitable events where exchanges were able to take place. The election of Rabin led to a proliferation of backchannels especially after the repeal of the Contact law. The Oslo Accord started life as a discussion under the unlikely auspices of the Norwegian Institute for Applied Sciences (FAFO).

[10] *Yediot Aharanot* 1 January 1993.

There had been a backchannel between Faisal Husseini, Yossi Beilin and Beilin's academic colleague, Yair Hirschfeld, since 1989. FAFO now not only provided the cover, it also funded the process. The Contact law preventing Israeli–PLO discussions was repealed in November 1992 and this allowed the economist Hirschfeld to begin discussions in London with a fellow economist, the PLO's Abu Ala. This dovetailed with Peres's aspirations for a common economic vision in the Middle East. The talks continued in Oslo in January 1993 and were based on the principle of Gaza First. By February, Hirschfeld and another academic, Ron Pundak, had agreed on a Declaration of Principles, based on economic cooperation. Hirschfeld had proposed a UN trusteeship to govern during an Israeli withdrawal over two years. A team was then established in Israel to promote what seemed to be a promising beginning which operated through Hirschfeld and Pundak.

There seemed to be, for the first time in many years, a window of opportunity. Parties looking for solutions were in power in both the United States and Israel. Old age seemed to have mellowed both Peres and Rabin and their rivalry seemed far less important. It was a far cry from 1981 when Peres defeated Rabin for the chairmanship of the party and subsequently demanded his removal from Labour's leadership. The PLO seemed to be in a weakened position and perhaps more amenable to negotiation. Both sides had their rejectionists who could not contemplate compromise. Secrecy therefore prevented both the Likud and its allies on the Right as well as the Islamist Hamas and secular PFLP and DFLP from disrupting the negotiations. Norway, moreover, had a reputation for being neutral.

Peres was originally excluded from the bilateral talks. He was brought back into negotiations following the backlash after Rabin's decision to deport 415 Palestinian Islamists to Lebanon. In January 1993, Peres met Faisal Husseini who was widely acknowledged to be Arafat's representative in the territories. The Oslo channel also provided Peres with the opportunity to insert himself properly into the negotiations, having been marginalized previously. As the talks progressed, both sides began to treat them more seriously. When Rabin deported the Islamists, Arafat significantly did not stop these private talks even though he placed a block on the bilateral public ones. In cabinet, Meretz ironically was pressing Labour to negotiate with the PLO after the deportation of the Islamists – and Rabin and Peres disagreed in order to preserve the secrecy of the Oslo backchannel.

By April 1993, Peres agreed to add Jericho or Jenin to the policy of 'Gaza First', but Israel insisted on controlling the Allenby Bridge to Jordan. Israel also agreed to talk about the status of Jerusalem for the first time.[11] Rabin was sufficiently intrigued to send Uri Savir, the Director-General of the Foreign Ministry, and Joel Singer, a lawyer, to lead the talks. By May 1993, what had started as almost an intellectual exercise by academics assumed an official character.

Savir and Abu Ala agreed that Gaza would be demilitarized and that the Palestinian police would disarm all groups propagating terrorism. Abu Ala asserted that Arafat had 'the capability and will to end terror against Israel'[12] and believed that Arafat's entry into Gaza would turn the population against the Islamists. When Israel sought explicit guarantees from Arafat on how he would deal with any future violence as well as assessing his capability to do so, there was a profound vagueness and imprecision. The IDF would redeploy to outside major population centres on the West Bank which would leave isolated settlements outside the range of effective IDF protection. There would be no immediate evacuation of settlements and it would still leave Israel in control of large parts of the territories. The Palestinians believed that there would be no more expropriations and requisitions of state land for settlements.[13] Israel undertook to transfer education and culture; health; social welfare; direct taxation and tourism to the Palestinians who would hold elections within nine months. The two sides would then commence final status talks within two years when borders, settlements and Jerusalem would be on the agenda. There would be a committee of Israelis, Palestinians, Egyptians and Jordanians to examine the fate of more than 200,000 Palestinians displaced as a result of the 1967 war, but there was no mention of the 1948 refugees.

In Israel, Rabin examined every point raised and refused any proposal from which there was no turning back.[14] Moreover, Rabin did not inform his intelligence officials or Arab experts as well as IDF personnel. Oslo was fashioned as almost an interim deal where there would be an uneasy coexistence between Israelis and Palestinians. The structure of 'peace by stages', however, provided the opportunity for the opponents of the Oslo process to undermine it once it was no longer shrouded from the public gaze. In 1993, there were 120,000 settlers living in the West Bank and Gaza.

In June, Rabin sent a list of questions for the Palestinians to answer. Difficulties were resolved in Israel through discussions between Chaim

[11] Interview with Nabil Sha'ath, *Journal of Palestine Studies* vol.23 no.1 Autumn 1993.
[12] Makovsky, *Making Peace with the PLO* p. 39.
[13] Interview with Nabil Sha'ath, *Journal of Palestine Studies* vol.23 no.1 Autumn 1993.
[14] Avi Shlaim, 'The Oslo Accord', *Journal of Palestine Studies* vol.23 no.3 Spring 1994.

Ramon, the Minister of Health, and Dr Ahmed Tibi who was well known in Israeli Arab circles. Rabin operated through Ramon who dealt with Tibi who acted for Arafat and Abu Mazen. Final differences were resolved when Ramon telephoned Abu Mazen in Tunis. Other backchannels operated simultaneously through the academic Yossi Alpher, who advocated integrating Jordan into the idea of strategic depth such that the West Bank could be demilitarized. Sometimes they became public knowledge such as Ephraim Sneh's meetings in London[15] but the Oslo channel stayed secure.

Arafat, however, was traditionally prone to inject new demands which irritated the Israelis. This also led to a threat by Abu Ala to resign. The breakdown was averted due to Israel's willingness to discuss the issue of mutual recognition in exchange for Palestinian concessions. 'A backchannel within the backchannel' was produced whereby Arafat and Rabin were in effective contact.[16]

The final subterfuge took place when the Norwegian Foreign Minister, Johan Jorgen Hoist, came to Stockholm to meet Peres to ostensibly talk about Israel's alleged theft of heavy water from Norway. The final breakthrough came in Stockholm when Peres and his team together with Holst were negotiating by telephone with Arafat and Abu Ala in Tunis. After an all-night session, an agreement was concluded and Savir and Abu Ala put their signatures to the Declaration of Principles in Oslo.

Rabin only became convinced that Oslo would succeed in mid-August. The negotiations had to be concluded at an accelerating pace because Attorney-General Yosef Harish had called on Shas's Arieh Deri to resign from the cabinet because he faced impending charges. This would probably lead to a coalition crisis and therefore reduce Labour's majority. It placed in jeopardy the Knesset approval for any agreement.

The Israeli cabinet voted overwhelmingly in favour of Oslo with two abstentions. In an exchange of letters, Arafat recognized the right of Israel to exist in peace and security, renounced terrorism and accepted UN Resolutions 242 and 338. Rabin recognized the PLO as the representative of the Palestinian people. On 13 September, the Declaration of Principles was famously initialled by a hesitant, uncomfortable Rabin and a beaming Arafat at a ceremony on the White House lawn.

Ten days later, the Declaration was endorsed by the Knesset by sixty-one to fifty. Labour (forty-four) was only supported by Meretz (twelve) and two Arab parties (five). Rabin's slim majority was bolstered by the refusal of three Likud members to go along with their party's opposition. Shas left

---

[15] *Jerusalem Report* 29 July 1993.   [16] Makovsky, *Making Peace with the PLO* p. 64.

the coalition and abstained. 61 per cent of Israelis immediately supported Rabin following the White House ceremony.[17] Likud, the far Right and the religious proposed five no-confidence motions in the government because it had decided to freeze settlement activity in the territories.

The Chief of Staff, Ehud Barak, had strong reservations on security grounds that Israel would now no longer have responsibility for Gaza and Jericho. There would be a loss of intelligence gathering, a dependency on the Palestinian police and the unfathomable conundrum of how to protect the settlers. The Declaration of Principles stipulated a five-year period of self-rule in Gaza and Jericho. Israel would maintain responsibility for defence and the settlements.

According to the Oslo Index, the peace process was steadily supported for the next six years by the Israeli public at approximately the same level. Between June 1994 and January 2001, there was an overall mean of 49.1 per cent. It only decreased dramatically when acts of terrorism were carried out against Israeli civilians such as a suicide bomb in Jerusalem in July 1997. The Right and the religious polled consistently below this mean, the Left and the secular consistently above it. The imagery of Oslo and support for the peace process were only finally dissipated with the outbreak of the second Intifada in 2000.[18]

THE PLO IN CRISIS

Two thirds of Palestinians supported the Declaration of Principles.[19] It ensured the survival of Arafat and the PLO, but it also created much division in Palestinian ranks. Those involved in the bilateral talks felt that they had been providing a smokescreen while the real work was going on elsewhere.

The leader of the Washington talks, Haidar 'Abd al-Shafi, opposed Oslo on almost ideological grounds. He argued that the Israelis wanted to protect their claim to all of Palestine.[20] There was, after all, no mention in the Declaration that Israel was 'an occupying power'. Hanan Ashrawi was annoyed that the settlements had been left in place whereas the Palestinians at the Washington talks wanted them removed in the first instance. The Washington team had also insisted on Palestinian statehood

---

[17] *Yediot Aharanot* 14 September 1993.
[18] Tamar Hermann and Ephraim Yuchtman-Yaar, *Journal of Peace Research* vol.39 no.5 2002.
[19] *New York Times* 16 October 1993.
[20] Interview with Haidar 'Abd al-Shafi, *Journal of Palestine Studies* vol.23 no.1 Autumn 1993.

and the inclusion of the Arabs of East Jerusalem in all deliberations. Edward Said and the Palestinian diaspora were irrevocably opposed. Nabil Sha'ath diplomatically believed that the agreement with the PLO 'really strikes against Zionist ideology.' In this context, he pointed out that the PLO was characterized more by those Palestinians outside the territories. All its constituent assemblies – the Executive Committee, the PNC – were entirely composed of diaspora Palestinians of the 1948 generation. The PLO Executive Committee met and there were four resignations[21] before Arafat pushed through its affirmation of the Oslo accord.

The sudden promotion of Arafat to centre stage marked a remarkable about-turn in his political fortunes. Arafat had kept his position as head of the PLO because of his considerable political guile and an uncanny ability to play off factions against one another. While Israelis accused him of duplicity, many Palestinians privately simply despaired of his approach.

On 3 September 1991, Arafat made a speech commemorating 1,000 days since the beginning of the Intifada. His words 'we are all in the same trench with the man (Saddam Hussein) fighting imperialism and its allies' and his broad alignment with Iraq displeased the political camp grouped around Abu Iyad.[22] This included Abu Ala, Edward Said, Nabil Sha'ath, Afif Safieh and Abu Mazen. After the mysterious killing of Abu Iyad, Faisal Husseini assumed the role of the main opponent to Arafat's Iraq policy and there were thoughts about replacing him as chairman of the PLO. This was a prospect which appealed to the Americans, the Saudis and even a bemused Rabin who saw half a chance to circumvent the external PLO.

In the eyes of many external observers, Arafat's support for Iraq had delegitimized both the PLO and its role in the peace process. The USSR had disappeared along with its funding to the PLO. Rabin was initially keener on negotiating with West Bank Palestinians since he regarded them as more pragmatic than the external PLO. The accepted wisdom was that the PLO was virtually bankrupt due to Saudi Arabia and the Gulf States cutting off funds following the war with Iraq. However, following the collapse of the London-based Bank of Credit and Commerce International in July 1993, a study by the National Criminal Intelligence Service in the UK determined that the PLO had worldwide assets of between $7 and 10 billion and an annual income of $1.5 to $2 billion through businesses throughout the Middle East and Africa as well as concerns in Europe and the United States. Arafat was believed to control the bank accounts and had the ability to make

[21] Interview with Nabil Sha'ath, *Journal of Palestine Studies.*
[22] Inbari, *The Palestinians between Terrorism and Statehood* pp. 116–117.

expenditures without consulting aides. There was even a story that Arafat maintained an opulent villa for an ex-wife, Najla Yassin.[23] All of this fuelled a feeling of financial mismanagement on the Palestinian street which laid the basis for future accusations of corruption by the Tunis elite.

When Arafat was lost, following a plane crash in the Libyan desert in 1992, Husseini's name often cropped up as a likely successor. Following the Gulf war, Baker wanted to negotiate with Husseini as a means of relegating Arafat to a less central role. Both Clinton and Warren Christopher addressed personal letters to Husseini in 1993 which reaffirmed US assurances. Moreover, following the Madrid Conference, the weight of the negotiations had fallen on his shoulders and that of the internal leadership rather than the external PLO in Tunis. Husseini wanted to establish a police force, an economic institution to accept funding and a parliamentary system – effectively to displace the external PLO. Abu Mazen held similar views.

In view of his weakened position after the Gulf war and the exclusion of the PLO from the Madrid Conference, Arafat was determined to block the emergence of an alternative leadership. Taking advantage of the exclusion of East Jerusalemites and the barring of Husseini, Arafat appointed Haidar 'Abd al-Shafi, who was close to the Communist party, as head of the delegation. Moreover, Husseini wanted the 'West Bank first' option rather than 'Gaza First'. Husseini wanted to recruit 30,000 youths from the territories to form the 'police force', but Arafat wanted the dispersed Palestine Liberation Army which was under his control. The Saudis were prepared to support Husseini as a means of displacing Arafat. They agreed in 1993 to resume payments to the Palestinians of up to $200 million but on the proviso that it was channelled through Husseini.[24] Peres wanted to arrange a meeting between Rabin and Husseini, but Arafat vetoed this because he thought that he alone should meet Rabin.

At one point in 1993, Arafat threatened to convene the PNC to stop the bilateral talks because Husseini was poised to displace him as the USA wanted.[25] Farouk Qaddumi, the PLO's 'Foreign Minister' was in turn worried that Ashrawi would replace him. Arafat also attempted to enlist the support of Hamas against Husseini in a meeting in February 1993, but Saudi Arabia and Iran vetoed this because they were hostile to Arafat.[26] Moreover, the Islamists strongly opposed Husseini's presence at Madrid and accused him of treason and receiving Saudi funds. Even within Fatah, there were those who wished to continue the armed struggle and

[23] *Ha'aretz* 11 December 1994.   [24] *Jerusalem Report* 20 May 1993.
[25] Inbari, *The Palestinians between Terrorism and Statehood* p. 216.   [26] Ibid p. 152.

opposed Husseini. In the summer of 1993, there was fighting between Husseini loyalists and the Fatah tanzim who did not wish to follow a political path. Abu Mazen, significantly, proclaimed an end to revolution and a beginning of state building.

Both Husseini and al-Shafi in Washington were unaware of the Oslo backchannel and Arafat used this ignorance to play one against the other. Indeed, Husseini was asked by Arafat to remonstrate with al-Shafi and to persuade him not to resign following the deportation of the Islamists.[27] Husseini's indecision on moving against Arafat led to both Abu Mazen and Rabin turning away from him.

The clandestine Oslo talks were therefore a convenient vehicle for Arafat to undermine the reputation of the official Palestinian delegation and to prevent his own displacement. Arafat was wary of the followers of Abu Iyad within the PLO and originally wanted the hard line Farouk Qaddumi to go to Washington. After the signing of the Declaration of Principles, several Palestinian moderates were assassinated. Sari Nusseibeh went on a sabbatical and it appeared that Arafat was supporting the armed wing of Fatah to ensure the cohesion of the PLO under his control.

Arafat wanted to ensure that all funding flowed through him. Indeed, the World Bank was astonished to discover that Arafat had established a parallel body in Tunis to the Palestinian Economic Council for Development and Reconstruction (PEDCAR).[28] Clinton had pledged $500 million over five years to the PLO. In December 1993, the USA wanted to channel its funding through PEDCAR rather than the PLO. It also wanted links with Jordan's banking system. Arafat vehemently opposed this. On 1 October 1993, forty-three nations pledged almost $2 billion in aid to the Palestinians together with a grant of $25 million and a loan of $50 million from Israel. Arafat governed through personal appointees and a dependency on his will. The Palestinian Authority (PA) was therefore a very centralized organization. Arafat's approach to funding and financial affairs provided the opponents of Oslo with a potent weapon.

In May 1994 the Cairo agreement was signed, implementing the Declaration of Principles on withdrawal from Gaza and Jericho, the establishment of the PA, security issues and joint Israeli–Palestinian patrols. Arafat returned to Palestinian territory and together with Rabin and Peres received the Nobel Peace Prize. Yet his actions on his return showed that he favoured the Tunis elite over the strugglers of the Intifada. This caused resentment amidst the first claims of corruption, authoritarianism

---

[27] *Jerusalem Report* 20 May 1993.   [28] *Jerusalem Report* 2 June 1994.

and human rights abuse. The PLO closed the pro-Jordanian daily *al-Nahar* temporarily. Another paper, *Akhbar al-Balad*, was closed down permanently. Independently minded journalists were arrested. *Al Quds* practised self-censorship to remain open. Yet Arafat allowed Marwan Bargouti, a leader of the next generation of Fatah leaders, to reform and reconstruct the party.

There were armed units of Fatah all over the Arab world – Badr in Jordan, al-Aqsa in Iraq, Sabra and Shatilla in Yemen, Qadisia in Sudan, al-Quds in Libya and Ajnadein in Algeria. Under the Oslo II agreement in September 1995, there was a recognition that Arafat had virtually doubled the number of police stipulated in the Declaration of Principles. The Israelis armed the police in the hope that they would arrest those preparing acts of terror and would confiscate illegal arms. Significantly, more armoured carriers and machine guns were provided for controlling Gaza where the Islamists were stronger than in the West Bank.

The West Bank itself would be divided into three areas. Area A would contain the main areas of Palestinian population – the 7 main towns which accounted for 2.7 per cent of the West Bank. Here the Palestinians would be accountable for both security and public order. Area B would encompass some 450 towns and villages, accounting for another 24 per cent of territory, where there would be shared authority. Israel was responsible for security until 1997 and the Palestinians for public order. Area C was a mixture of unpopulated areas and the Jewish settlements. This was of strategic importance to Israel and therefore it was responsible for both security and public order.

It was agreed that there would be three redeployments of Israeli troops over an eighteen-month period. All this was due to start on 10 October 1995 when 5,000 prisoners would be released – those without blood on their hands – with the planned pull-out from the major population centres a few weeks later. Elections for the Legislative Council and the head of the Authority were scheduled to take place in January 1996.

The fundamental problem of dealing with the 130,000 settlers remained unsolved. Arafat agreed to the building of a network of new roads to the settlements. Israel was preparing to spend $100 million on a network of twenty bypasses and to improve existing roads to separate settlers from the Palestinians. This was all based on good levels of trust and cooperation between Israelis and Palestinians. Gaza had been effectively divided to allow the 6,000 Jewish settlers to remain. Ironically, the settlements had originally been established to prevent the return of territory. Moreover, the areas under Palestinian control were non-contiguous and isolated in enclaves. Neither were they in control of any of the border crossings on land and sea. Even so, Palestinian support for the peace process at this time reached 71 per cent.[29] In Israel, support for the Oslo process had dropped by a third and the Knesset only approved Oslo II by sixty-one votes to fifty-nine. One experienced commentator pointed out that 'Oslo II represents an inherent contradiction – returning territory, yet retaining the settlements that were established to prevent territory being returned.'[30]

There was an economic agreement about free-trade areas. An economic summit took place in Casablanca in October 1994 with all the Arab states apart from Syria and Lebanon in attendance. Israeli liaison offices were established with Morocco, Oman and Tunisia and it became easier for Israelis to enter Kuwait, Saudi Arabia and the Gulf States. There was an Israeli–Jordanian billion-dollar plan to develop the Jordan rift valley including new roads, railways, desalination and power plants and tourist facilities. There were also ideas for an Egyptian–Israeli pipeline and plans to import gas from Qatar and Oman through a $4 billion pipeline.

Rabin still maintained close contact with Jordan since both countries feared an irredentist Palestinian entity squeezed between them. In correspondence with Rabin, Arafat wrote on notepaper headed 'President of Palestine'. King Hussein had already met Shamir in September 1991. Following the Declaration of Principles, an agreement with the Israelis was swiftly processed and diplomatic relations established. Hussein feared any Palestinian backlash within Jordan and especially from the Islamists. Yet in the Jordanian election in November 1993, the Islamists were roundly defeated. The agreement between Jordan and Israel was concluded with a signing by Rabin, Hussein and Clinton in July 1994. Syria and Lebanon now had no option but to join the peace process.

Syria's ruling Alawites were neither Sunni nor Shi'ite, and therefore President Assad needed an external enemy to unite Syrians around the regime when 70 per cent population were Sunni. Assad's objection to Oslo was essentially a pan-Arabist approach in that the Arabs had not operated as a united bloc. He also criticized Jordan for signing a separate peace with Israel. He had long argued that Syria would not make a separate peace before a solution of the Palestinian question. Even the reclaiming of the Golan Heights, conquered in the Six Day war, was depicted as 'originally occupied in a battle waged for Palestine'.[31] Moreover, Assad was also

---

[29] Khalil Shikaki 'The Peace Process, National Reconstruction and the Transition to Democracy in Palestine', *Journal of Palestine Studies* vol.25 no.2 Winter 1996.

[30] Joseph Alpher, *Jerusalem Report* 2 November 1995.   [31] *FBIS* 8 May 1990.

Minister of Defence when the Golan was lost in 1967. 100,000 left the area
and it was claimed that there was now a considerable constituency within
Syria for action on the Golan issue.[32] Assad also feared that Syria would
lose its prominent position and Lebanon would also come within Israel's
sphere of influence. There was also fear of the emergence of a Middle
Eastern common market which Israel would dominate. Moreover, Syria
continued to point out that Israel was also not culturally part of the Arab
world. Although Rabin exuded a certain respect for Assad, in Israel, there
was little trust for the ruler of Syria, given his unremitting hostility and his
ruthlessness, and given his crushing of the Muslim Brotherhood at Hama.
Rabin said in 1994 that any agreement with Syria would be ratified by a
national referendum.

Rabin deliberately did not institute simultaneous negotiations with
Israel's neighbours. He believed that this would necessitate that they follow the lead of Syria as the most radical and strongest of all the frontline
states. This also fortified the idea of negotiating with Syria alone since any
agreement with such a centralized, authoritarian state would bring the rest
in its wake.

In early 1993, before the evolution of the Oslo backchannel, Rabin was
keen to pursue the Syrian track as the rapprochement with the United
States had not materialized following the cooperation of Damascus in the
Gulf war. He was aware of the growing danger of Teheran's backing for
Islamism in the region and was keen to detach Syria from its alignment
with the ayatollahs. In early August 1994, Rabin proposed a full withdrawal
from the Golan Heights over a five-year period to Assad via the Americans
in exchange for normalization and agreed security arrangements.[33] Assad
responded positively and indicated that he was prepared to proceed alone
with the Lebanese – and to leave the Palestinians to their own devices.[34]
In the summer of 1994, there was a first meeting between the Israeli and
Syrian Ambassadors to the United States.[35] This was followed by a meeting
of the two Chiefs of Staff a few months later.

This had been stimulated by the USA acting as an intermediary. In
January 1994, there was a meeting between Assad and Clinton to restart
the Syrian–Israeli track. Yet there was profound disagreement as to the

---

[32] Raymond A. Hinnebusch, 'Does Syria Want Peace? Syrian Policy in the Syrian–Israeli Peace Negotiations', *Journal of Palestine Studies* vol.26 no.1 Autumn 1996.

[33] Dennis Ross, *The Missing Peace: The Inside Story of the Fight for Middle East Peace* (New York 2004)
p. 111.

[34] Ibid. p. 112.

[35] Itamar Rabinovich, *Waging Peace: Israel and the Arabs 1948–2003* (Princeton 2004) pp. 61–62.

understanding of 'human rights' and 'acts of terror'. It was also unclear what Assad meant by 'normal relations in the area'. There was little meeting of minds.[36] Rabin seemed to be amenable to returning at least part of the Golan Heights. Syria wanted a return to the borders before 1967 which allowed Syria access to the Sea of Galilee. Israel argued that this did not concur with the international borders agreed during the Mandate period. Israel proposed a three-stage withdrawal from the Golan over five years with Syria in parallel establishing diplomatic relations. Assad didn't want diplomatic relations before withdrawal. Israel wanted a dismantling of Syria's chemical weapons and a reduction in its armed forces. Syria accepted demilitarization of the Golan with forces stationed on either side. Israel wanted an early-warning station on Mount Hermon which Syria rejected.

[36] *Washington Post* 17 January 1994.

CHAPTER II

The killing of a Prime Minister

THE RETURN OF THE REJECTIONISTS

At the core of the initial opposition to the Oslo Accord and the ongoing peace process was a refusal to ditch ideological 'truths' and compromise. In Israel, the rejectionists comprised the national religious, led by the settlers, and the security-conscious members of the Right. Amongst the Palestinians, the Islamists reiterated their belief that the Jews did not have a right to national self-determination and therefore they could never accept a two-state solution. Their opposition to Oslo was supported by the secular nationalists of the PFLP, the DFLP, Fatah's Tanzim and other groups who wished to reverse the outcome of the 1948 war by continuing the armed struggle. On the northern border Iran, freed from the decade-long war with Iraq, encouraged Hezbollah to implement cross-border attacks to kill and abduct Israeli soldiers as a means of disrupting the evolving peace process.

The Oslo Accord and the decision to participate in negotiations and diplomacy left an ideological vacuum which Hamas and Islamic Jihad willingly filled. The abandonment of the revolutionary road of armed struggle was a dramatic and indeed abrupt change for many Palestinians. Most of the organizations on the PLO Executive refused to join the Palestine Authority.

The PLO's entry into Jericho and Gaza witnessed a drop in the living standards of 30 to 40 per cent during the first year of the peace process. Moreover, the PLO was in financial straits after the Gulf war. In November 1994, the official unemployment rate was at 30 per cent, but unofficially at 60 per cent. 'The garbage is still uncollected, the sewage overflowing, the streets, unpaved.'[1] The campaign of suicide bombing by the Islamists forced a closure of the territories to ensure a measure of protection. Yet this

---

[1] *Jerusalem Report* 3 November 1994.

meant that 120,000 day labourers were unable to cross into Israel for work. This dealt a severe blow to the Palestinian economy, but it also persuaded Israelis to decrease their dependency on Palestinian labour. In 1995, only 10,000 Palestinians worked in the Israeli construction industry compared to 80,000 in 1993. Over 70,000 foreign workers had arrived to take their place. The deteriorating economic situation for the ordinary Palestinian also worked to the Islamists' advantage.

Hamas, Islamic Jihad and Hezbollah all arose at a time of religious intensity in the Islamic world. It was encouraged by the success of the Iranian Revolution and the growing disillusionment with Arab nationalism. In Gaza, the gruelling poverty and the loss of hope especially amongst the refugees turned many towards the comfort of religion. There was also a stronger traditionalism in Gaza compared to the West Bank. Between 1967 and 1987, the number of mosques on the West Bank almost doubled from 400 to 750. In Gaza, it tripled from 200 to 600.[2]

In the 1950s, Nasser had brutally suppressed and outlawed the Muslim Brotherhood. It had already assassinated the Egyptian Prime Minister in December 1948. Such ideological differences translated in the 1990s into support either for Fatah or for Hamas.

Shortly after the White House signing of the Oslo Accord, the Center for Palestine Research and Studies indicated that 74 per cent supported a democratic system similar to that of Israel. Yet the West Bankers were far more open about embracing democracy and the rights of opposition than their compatriots in Gaza.

The Islamists were also less liberal in their approach to women. In May 1995, 78 per cent of Fatah supporters said that they would vote for a woman, compared to 48 per cent of Hamas supporters.[3] Palestinian support for the Islamists dropped when progress seemed to be made. Moreover, the educated and the youth showed a greater support for the opponents to Oslo.

Hamas emphasized turning Palestine into an Islamic society before the liberation of all of Palestine including the uprooting of Israel. They therefore invested a lot of effort in education and social welfare in order to bring up 'an Islamic generation'. In 1973, the spiritual leader of Hamas, Sheikh Ahmed Yassin, founded al-Mujamma' al-Islami (the Islamic Centre). In the 1990s, 60 per cent of Gaza's population of 800,000 were

[2] Ziad Abu-Amr, 'Hamas: A Historical and Political Background', *Journal of Palestine Studies* vol.22 no.4 Summer 1993.
[3] Khalil Shikaki 'The Peace Process, National Reconstruction and the Transition to Democracy in Palestine', *Journal of Palestine Studies* vol.25 no.2 Winter 1996.

under nineteen. There were Islamist welfare associations which provided schoolbooks and clothes for orphans; food parcels for poor families during Ramadan; low fees for medical services; loans to students at universities. Funds were often raised abroad and funnelled to Islamist social projects. By early 1995, 40 per cent of Gaza's mosques were said to be under Hamas influence.[4] Youth leaders taught Hamas ideology and the teachings of Ahmed Yassin. 150 kindergartens were run by Hamas charities. Until the Intifada, the Islamists shied away from using armed resistance to the Israeli occupation. The Israelis therefore did not focus on them as a serious opponent. They were seen as a rival to the PLO – a rival which could be manipulated to cause problems for the central enemy, Palestinian Arab nationalism.

Hamas owed its ideological pedigree to the Muslim Brotherhood and its mentors were naturally Hasan al-Banna, 'Izz al-din al-Qassam and Sayyid Qutb. The Brotherhood had established its first branch in Jerusalem in 1945 and within two years there were twenty-five branches in Palestine. Through its front organization, the Islamic Association, the Brotherhood soon began to control more of the waqf (an Islamic trust) which itself controlled 10 per cent of all Gaza's real estate – housing blocks, shops, public buildings. It owned land and employed many people.[5]

Palestine in its entirety was understood as a waqf – even though there was no basis for this in sharia law – of which no part could be given away under any circumstances. This distinguished the Islamists from the nationalists. The struggle against Zionism was existentially a religious struggle which should involve Muslims as well as Palestinians and Arabs. The nationalists, like the Zionists, traced its ideological genealogy to the French Revolution, European nationalism and the dictates of rationalism. Unlike Hamas, Fatah could make a considered decision to agree to a political compromise and partition the land. Significantly, when the PLO was founded in 1964 it made no mention of God.

According to article 13 of the Hamas Charter, the ceding of western Palestine to Israel was therefore an irreligious act especially as Israel was an illegitimate entity. All peace initiatives and international conferences were therefore an irrelevance. Hence Hamas condemned the PLO's recognition of Israel and its acceptance of UN Resolutions 242 and 338. The PLO always distinguished between Jews and Zionists; the Islamists made no such distinction.

---

[4] *Jerusalem Report* 26 January 1995.
[5] Ze'ev Schiff and Ehud Ya'ari, *Intifada: The Palestinian Uprising* (New York 1989) p. 224.

Unlike the PLO, Hamas was adept at absorbing nineteenth-century European stereotypes of Jews and extrapolating them. Article 22 of the Hamas Charter stated:

For a long time, the enemies have been planning, skillfully and with precision, for the achievement of what they have attained. They took into consideration the causes affecting the current of events. They strived to amass great and substantive material wealth which they devoted to the realization of their dream. With their money, they took control of the world media, news agencies, the press, publishing houses, broadcasting stations, and others. With their money they stirred revolutions in various parts of the world with the purpose of achieving their interests and reaping the fruit therein. They were behind the French Revolution, the Communist revolution and most of the revolutions we heard and hear about, here and there. With their money they formed secret societies, such as Freemasons, Rotary Clubs, the Lions and others in different parts of the world for the purpose of sabotaging societies and achieving Zionist interests. With their money they were able to control imperialistic countries and instigate them to colonize many countries in order to enable them to exploit their resources and spread corruption there.

You may speak as much as you want about regional and world wars. They were behind World War I, when they were able to destroy the Islamic Caliphate, making financial gains and controlling resources. They obtained the Balfour Declaration, formed the League of Nations through which they could rule the world. They were behind World War II, through which they made huge financial gains by trading in armaments, and paved the way for the establishment of their state. It was they who instigated the replacement of the League of Nations with the United Nations and the Security Council to enable them to rule the world through them. There is no war going on anywhere, without having their finger in it.

Zionist ideology was perceived as emerging from Judaism rather than from European nationalism – an evolution from Judaism more than a rebellion against it. The conflict was depicted within a religious framework between Judaism and Islam rather than between Israel and Palestine. Zionism was considered to be 'a racist entity responsible for translating the aggressive Jewish idea into a belligerent reality'.[6]

Zionism was seen as the virus which carried secularism and modernity into Islamic societies, the agent of 'westoxification'. 'Destroying values, corrupting consciences, deteriorating character and annihilating Islam. It is behind the drug trade and alcoholism in all its kinds so as to facilitate its control and expansion.' Yet the Koran spoke of the Jews as a people with an important book. Indeed, Islam had traditionally been kinder towards Jews compared with Christianity, but on the basis that Jews played a secondary

6 Meir Litvak, 'The Islamization of the Palestinian–Israeli Conflict: The Case of Hamas', *Middle Eastern Studies* vol.34 no.1 (London 1998).

and submissive role. Assertive Jews were therefore an affront to Islamist sensibilities.

Under the wing of Islam, it is possible for the followers of the three religions – Islam, Christianity and Judaism – to coexist in peace and quiet with each other. Peace and quiet would not be possible except under the wing of Islam. Past and present history are the best witness to that.

Hamas viewed the plans of the Zionists as expansionism without limits.

Today it is Palestine, tomorrow it will be one country or another. The Zionist plan is limitless. After Palestine, the Zionists aspire to expand from the Nile to the Euphrates. When they will have digested the region they overtook, they will aspire to further expansion, and so on. Their plan is embodied in the 'Protocols of the Elders of Zion', and their present conduct is the best proof of what we are saying.

The Charter also carried many secular–national ideas albeit in Islamist guise.[7] Although the Hamas Foreign Minister, Mahmoud Zahar, vowed in 2006 never to change a word of the Charter, some observers believed that it was of lesser importance and was actually surpassed by later declarations.[8] Even so, such a well-publicized tirade unnerved even the most dovish of Israeli doves. Whereas traditionally Islam had been more benevolent towards Jews in contrast to deicidal Christianity, Islamism evoked the idea of 'the eternal Jew'. There was therefore no difference between the Jewish enemies of the Prophet in seventh-century Arabia and those in the late twentieth century. Importing from European antisemitism notions such as the depiction of Jews as the enemies of God and the existence of a world Jewish conspiracy assisted in cementing the idea of 'the eternal Jew'. The fear of Jewish domination of the Middle East and of Islam became a dominant theme in the Arab media.

The Hamas Charter was a synthesis of Koranic imagery, historical distortion and undiluted antisemitism – as evidenced by the mention of the tsarist antisemitic forgery, the Protocols of the Elders of Zion. The growth of Hamas and Islamism led to a sigh of despair from the Israeli peace camp, not because the Islamists were opponents of Zionism, but because there was no possibility of a dialogue and no desire for peace. Hamas's smaller rival, Islamic Jihad, was even more revolutionary and believed in jihad primarily and therefore placed the immediate liberation of Palestine before the construction of an Islamic society in Gaza and the

---

[7] Shaul Mishal and Avraham Sela, *The Palestinian Hamas: Vision, Violence and Coexistence* (New York 2000) pp. 50–53.
[8] Khaled Hroub, *Hamas: A Beginner's Guide* (London 2006).

Fig. 11.1. Hamas greeting card to mark the end of Ramadan. The Israeli is depicted as a Jew with horns, an old European stereotype. Reproduced with kind permission from the Israel Government Press Office.

West Bank. The Iranian Revolution in 1979 was instrumental in the establishment of Islamic Jihad. The Muslim Brotherhood, however, was critical of Khomeini and the Iranian Revolution especially after the outbreak of the war with Iraq. Islamic Jihad had been founded by Fathi Shikaki and 'Abd al-'Aziz Auda, refugees from 1948 who had grown up in the camps in Gaza. They were influenced by militant offshoots of the Muslim Brotherhood in Egypt such as Tandhim al-Jihad (the Jihad Organization). Islamic Jihad therefore shared a common goal with Fatah in the 1980s – the armed struggle and the liberation of Palestine. There were also contacts with Fatah's Abu Jihad who opposed Arafat's diplomacy and it participated in occasional military operations with Fatah. Islamic Jihad also objected to the Muslim Brotherhood's fraternization with Arab regimes such as Saudi Arabia and Egypt.

The opposition of the Muslim Brotherhood to armed resistance changed with the advent of the Intifada. In addition to Sheikh Yassin, the founding members of Hamas were professionals – a doctor, a pharmacist, and many involved in education. The Brotherhood was forced to act since the Intifada was being led by the PLO and the younger generation of Islamists – in the face of the Brotherhood's inactivity – was beginning to follow Islamic Jihad. Yet the Brotherhood wanted to press on with its intention of Islamizing Palestinian society and did not wish to jeopardize what it had achieved so far by openly embracing the armed struggle. It therefore established a separate front organization which it could influence, but with which it did not wish to be associated in case of the Intifada's failure.[9] The establishment of Hamas paralleled the establishment of the United National Leadership of the Intifada which looked to the PLO.

Hamas began abducting and killing Israeli soldiers in February 1989. Sheikh Yassin was arrested in May 1989 and sentenced to fifteen years. There were mass arrests of Hamas members in October 1990.

Hamas saw itself as part of the resurgence of Islamism in the Middle East and therefore rejoiced in the victory of the Islamic Salvation Front in Algeria in 1991. Unlike Islamic Jihad, it was lukewarm towards the Islamic revolution in Iran and critical of Khomeini for theological reasons. Unlike Islamic Jihad, it did not blur the Sunni–Shi'ite division. Like Fatah, it supported Iraq against Iran, but was quiet about its position on the Iraqi invasion of Kuwait which was popular with the Palestinian populace. This was due to the fact that it received funding from both Saudi Arabia and Kuwait. Unlike Arafat and the PLO, it did not receive the opprobrium of the funders who transferred their financial largesse to the Islamists in place of the nationalists.

Rabin was concerned about Iran after the Iran–Iraq war and the growth of Islamism. Hamas was filling the political void in Gaza and he believed that Israel was in the front line facing the advance of Islamism. Two thirds of Palestinians supported the Oslo Declaration of Principles, but the day after the signing there was a suicide bomb attempt on a police post outside a Gaza refugee camp. Suicide bombing was an outcome of the philosophy and practice of the Iranian Revolution and was transmitted initially to Hezbollah who then transmitted it to Palestinian Islamic Jihad. In turn, this was emulated by Hamas. The end of the conflict with Iraq had allowed Iran to turn to the export of its revolution to other parts of the Islamic world. The Madrid Conference and the general peace process was the common ground that brought together Shi'ite Iran and Sunni Hamas. It also aligned Hamas with the rejectionist front of ten Palestinian organizations, domiciled in Damascus. A Hamas representative, 'Imad al-Alami, was installed in Teheran and the organization attended a conference in the Iranian capital in October 1991 to protest against the Madrid Conference.

---

[9] Ziad Abu Amr, *Islamic Fundamentalism in the West Bank and Gaza: Muslim Brotherhood and Islamic Jihad* (Bloomington 1994) p. 67.

By 1992, there was cooperation between Hezbollah and Hamas and 3,000 Hamas operatives were being trained in Lebanon by the Iranian al-Quds unit.[10]

Hezbollah was a minority amongst the Lebanese shia. Yet its followers had a fearsome reputation as fighters and pioneers of suicide bombings in the Middle East. In the early 1980s, it had killed 241 Americans in Beirut and 30 Israelis in Tyre in separate attacks. It was patronized by both Iran and Syria – an odd couple who had cooperated against Saddam during the war in the 1980s. This relationship had been cemented by the Iraqi invasion of Kuwait and Moscow's refusal to advance credit to Syria for arms purchases in 1987.

Hezbollah's self-appointed task was to wear down the Israeli presence in southern Lebanon and to facilitate the collapse of the South Lebanese Army. The Iranians were training Hezbollah both in the Bekaa Valley and in the Shi'ite neighbourhoods of South Beirut and supplying the organization with anti-tank missiles. The Iranians were also training Islamists from a number of countries at Arussa outside Khartoum. Iran had financed Sudan's purchase of military equipment from China for $300 million and Sudan's new military government had opened its doors.[11] Hezbollah's objective at this time was not simply to recover Lebanese territory occupied by the Israelis, but also to undermine the peace process initiated by the Madrid Conference. Hezbollah had been the only militia which had not disarmed following the Taif Accord in 1989 which brought an end to the Lebanese civil war. For Israel, an ongoing war of attrition on the Lebanese border was marked by continuing troop movements, disruption of everyday life for those who lived near the border and an increasing financial expenditure.

Following the killing of Hezbollah's Secretary-General, Abbas Mussawi, in an Israeli air attack, the group retaliated beyond Lebanese borders. The Neve Shalom synagogue in Istanbul was attacked and an Israeli diplomat was killed in Ankara. In December 1992, the growing connection between Hezbollah and Hamas was implicitly recognized when Rabin deported 415 Palestinian Islamists to southern Lebanon. They were left in no-man's land, but under American pressure he was forced to allow them to return.

Rabin saw Iran's increasing involvement as a potent threat to any peace accord with the Palestinians. In part, he pursued the Syrian track of negotiations as a means of prising Syria away from Iran. Although national interests were displacing ideology as a yardstick of government in Teheran,

---

[10] *Jerusalem Report* 21 December 1992.   [11] *Jerusalem Report* 23 January 1992.

undiluted hatred of Israel seemed a fundamental tenet of faith in Khomeini's legacy. Teheran's opposition to the growing peace process was an opportunity to fill a political vacuum and to spread its influence in the Arab world by identifying with the Palestinians and defending Islamic values. Moreover, Iran saw Israel as a challenge to its own aspirations in the region. The creation of Israel was understood as original sin. Partition and compromise were not an answer; only a liquidation of the state and evicting the Jews from Palestine provided a solution. While many of Iran's secular intelligentsia began to align themselves with the Palestinians in the 1960s since they perceived it as an anti-colonialist struggle, Khomeini built on this in the Islamic Republic. The Islamists projected resistance to Israel as a sacred duty and as 'a struggle between a pristine Islamic civilization and a blasphemous Zionist creed'.[12] While Khomeini's views were in part a reaction to the Shah's close relationship with Israel, his writings sometimes verged on anti-Jewish invective, suggesting that the Jews were distorters of the Koran and opposed to 'the foundations of Islam'.[13] The tsarist forgery 'The Protocols of the Elders of Zion' was openly published in Iran. The Holocaust was relegated to a secondary status where fewer victims had perished, according to the Iranians, and later projected as a questionable event.

Yet Iran had accepted arms from 'the Zionist entity' in the 1980s when Iraqi forces, generously supplied with arms by both the USA and the USSR, were at the gates of Teheran.[14] Israel feared that a victorious Saddam would be hailed as a conquering hero in the Arab world and then turn his powerful army on both Israel and other countries in the Middle East. Saddam's store of chemical weapons and his propensity to develop weapons of mass destruction was a deep concern as witnessed by Israel's attack on the Osirak nuclear reactor. Israel's transfer of arms continued even after Iran helped in the establishment of Hezbollah in Lebanon and thereby provided military expertise which would later be utilized to attack Israel.

In July 1993, Rabin launched Operation Accountability and attacked Hezbollah in southern Lebanon. 300,000 Lebanese fled and 100 katuyshas were fired which led to the evacuation of many northern Israeli towns. The Chief of Staff, Ehud Barak, implemented aerial bombardment, long-range artillery and naval firings on the Lebanese coast.

---

[12] Ray Takeyh, *Hidden Iran: Paradox and Power in the Islamic Republic* (New York 2006) p. 197.
[13] Ibid. p. 193.
[14] Sohrab Sobhani, *The Pragmatic Entente: Israeli–Iranian Relations 1948–1988* (London 1989) pp. 145–147.

Hezbollah, however, was well prepared with arms caches and bunkers. The Lebanese Prime Minister, Rafik Hariri, appealed to Damascus and it in turn called upon the USA to help instigate a ceasefire. Following Syria's intervention, Hezbollah agreed not to fire missiles on northern Israel if Israel stopped its air strikes. Moreover, Syria also stopped arms supplies to Hezbollah. Some fighters were disarmed by the Lebanese army. The Sunni Arab world quietly applauded as the western media condemned the action.

The Declaration of Principles brought an intensification of Islamist actions in order to disrupt any rapprochement between Israel and the Palestinians. On 25 February 1994, Baruch Goldstein, a West Bank settler, killed twenty-nine Muslims at prayer in the Ibrahimi mosque in Hebron. Goldstein's killings were designed to avenge previous Islamist attacks. This initiated a Hamas decision to attack Israeli civilians within the Green Line. A few weeks later, suicide bombers blew themselves up in the Israeli towns of Afula and Hadera. Palestinian professionals who largely supported the peace process and held permits to enter Jerusalem to work were now barred for security reasons. By the end of 1994, there was a downward spiral into suicide bombings, killings and abductions. A bus bombing took place in the centre of Tel Aviv; a bicycle bomber blew himself up at an army roadblock; two gunmen ran down a Jerusalem mall firing at shoppers. In January 1995, twenty-one Israelis were killed at Beit Lid and another bus bombing took place a few months later in Ramat Gan. To coincide with Oslo II, Hezbollah killed fourteen soldiers – an event of this magnitude had not happened since the Lebanon war of 1982. Moreover, Hezbollah was willing to implement cross-border attacks.

Between May 1994 and February 1995, 59 Israelis were killed – this was twice the rate before Oslo. During the six years of the Intifada over 140 Israelis were killed. Between 1993 and 1996, nearly 300 were killed. In the eyes of most Israelis, Oslo had therefore not brought peace and security, but death and destruction. Each time a suicide bombing took place, Rabin's standing in the polls plummeted and with each subsequent attack his political recovery was slower. The bombings of the Islamists within Israel not only lowered Rabin's standing in the eyes of the public, it also sabotaged his separation policy of confining Palestinian violence to the West Bank and Gaza.

The Likud wanted stronger measures against Hamas and demanded a cessation of talks with the Palestinians while there were attacks on Israeli civilians. Unlike Egyptian and Jordanian intelligence, the Israelis found it much more difficult to infiltrate Islamist cells. Collaborators were now less willing to work with Israeli intelligence because the IDF was pulling out of the West Bank and Gaza. Unlike the PLO in the past, Hamas operations were decentralized. Israelis were perplexed. A peace agreement had actually brought an increase in violence. Israelis now saw the Palestinians as not fulfilling their part of the Oslo Accord. Any belief in Arafat now dissipated. He was seen as duplicitous and unworthy. The bombings were viewed as merely an extension of his negotiating method. One leading Israeli commentator wrote about the Palestinian leader:

Sometimes the PLO leader sent his men without the authority for serious bargaining, sometimes he reneged on agreements, already put in writing, sometimes he simply didn't send the right people to the negotiations. Sometimes he was pragmatic and to the point with Israeli delegations which came to see him in Tunis; sometimes he pounded on the table, swept away with complaints and threats.[15]

Significantly, Rabin had commented that 'peace will not be possible until Arafat has his own *Altalena*.'[16] The sinking of the *Altalena*, an Irgun arms boat, in 1948 by Ben-Gurion's new model army had almost provoked a civil war. Begin, who had been present, prevailed upon his followers to follow the path of politics, but it was never forgotten that Rabin had been in charge of the forces that had fired on the *Altalena* and put an end to the Irgun's desire for military separatism. In contrast, Arafat would seek to co-opt or to create division amongst his opponents, but not to confront them militarily. In late 1991, Hamas was asked to join the PLO, but it demanded 40 per cent of the seats in the PNC as a precondition.

Moreover, there was a mutual understanding that no matter the depth of the differences between Hamas and Fatah, they would not attack each other. It was accepted that the intense rivalry between nationalists and Islamists had always been a feature of Palestinian political life. By the 1990s, the introduction of Hamas into the equation had deepened the chasm between the two sides and there were more frequent instances of conflict.

Al-Ittihad hospital, north of Jerusalem, had to be closed in August 1991 because of Fatah–Hamas feuding. Shawkat Zeid al-Kiliani, the President of Al Najah university, fled the country after being threatened by Hamas activists. There were Fatah associated gangs such as the Black Tigers which attacked groups of Hamas supporters. There were even Israeli intelligence reports on an assassination plan to kill Fatah's Faisal Husseini. The Islamists disparagingly labelled those Palestinians who wanted a two-state solution as 'the servants of the Jews'. But Hamas's political fortunes were now on the rise. There were several instances of Hamas triumphing over

[15] Ehud Ya'ari, 'Upping the Ante', *Jerusalem Report* 5 May 1994.
[16] Ross, *The Missing Peace: The Inside Story of the Fight for Middle East Peace* p. 94.

Fatah such as in the elections to the accountants and physicians' unions. The student unions were also becoming radicalized. The Islamic University of Gaza was a stronghold of Hamas while al-Azhar University in Gaza followed Fatah. The Palestinian national struggle gradually became coloured by Islamic symbolism such as an increased use of quotations from the Koran by Fatah – and even by the Marxist PFLP.

Arafat was perceived to be losing authority and growing progressively weaker. He was unable to either control the Islamists or to prevent Israeli reprisals. The Islamists were seen to obey only their own authorities and to possess greater group discipline. The PLO feared that when veteran Fatah fighters from outside the territories finally marched into Gaza, they would not be welcomed as a victorious army, but as an occupying force. In March 1994, Hamas had already liquidated Abd al-Lafi, a commander of the Democratic Front's Red Star militia. Arafat carefully watched his Islamists rivals. His last-minute public refusal in front of the world's press to sign maps on Jericho at the meeting in Cairo in May 1994 was more theatre for the benefit of the Palestinian street than diplomacy on behalf of the Palestinian people. In a mosque in South Africa, he compared the Gaza–Jericho accord to the Prophet's agreement with the Jews of Qurayish in 628 – a measure of temporary expediency to be overturned ten years later.[17] Yet what appeased the Islamists angered the Israelis.

In November 1994, all this came to a head. Palestinian police clashed with Hamas supporters outside a mosque in Gaza. 16 were killed and 200 injured. Islamic Jihad passed a death sentence on Nasser Yusuf, the head of the security forces in Gaza and Jericho.

In February 1995, Arafat attempted to crack down on the Islamists. Many Hamas Friday preachers were interrogated by Palestinian intelligence and Arafat announced that the Palestinian police had prevented ten suicide attacks. Military tribunals were instituted and sentences were handed down based on the detested Emergency Regulations of 1945. *Istiqlal*, the newspaper of Islamic Jihad, was closed down. Several hundred Islamists were arrested, placed in prison and their beards shaved off. In June 1995, Arafat came to an informal agreement with them to stop their attacks.

THE RIGHT'S BACKLASH

There had been occasional voices in the Labour movement who argued that any Israeli leader who signed an agreement with the Palestinians would

---

[17] *Ha'aretz* 23 May 1994.

place his life in danger and end up like Anwar Sadat.[18] Rabin and most of the political elite ridiculed such thoughts. They had been conditioned by the dictates of Jewish history to believe that evil would strike them from without, not from within.

Yet Rabin expected the response to Oslo to be 'ugly'.[19] Even so, the reaction transcended the characteristics of a normal political struggle. It ended in his assassination, the election of Bibi Netanyahu and a lingering death for the Israeli–Palestinian peace process. The killing was 'an ideological–religious assassination',[20] a blow against moving away from a chosen pathway.

Netanyahu held a high profile both in the Likud and in Israel generally. He was well known for his advocacy work as 'the Abba Eban of the CNN era' through his ability to argue coherently in the media and his fluent command of English. Netanyahu easily became Likud leader in March 1993 in succession to Shamir through a well-funded campaign which was backed by right-wing American Jews. They knew him as a master of the soundbite from his time in the Israeli Embassy in Washington and as Israeli representative to the United Nations. Both Sharon and the 'Princes' – the children of Irgun fighters – such as Dan Meridor and Ehud Olmert took no part in the election because it was understood that Netanyahu's lead amongst the Likud voters could not be overtaken. Yet there were internal divisions with the party. David Levy felt humiliated once more by his defeat and discriminated against as a Sephardi. Despite the fact that Netanyahu's father was a well-known academic and writer on Revisionist Zionism, Arik Sharon and the Princes believed that Netanyahu was an inexperienced interloper.

While the Left had united as Meretz, the Right was increasingly fragmented both on ideological and personal grounds. Netanyahu initially attempted to reform his party and to provide it with a constitution. He also attempted to unite the right-wing and religious parties around the Likud. Tsomet and Moledet alone had ten seats in this Knesset. These parties, together with the National Religious Party, met every Monday morning, under Netanyahu's chairmanship, in order to coordinate parliamentary work and street protests against the Rabin government.[21] Indeed, the Right came close to winning in the 1992 election. If they had been united, it was argued, perhaps they could have secured victory. Netanyahu projected a presidential style, but his ideological approach initially was no more than

---

[18] *Davar* 29 May 1992.   [19] Ross, *The Missing Peace* p. 90.
[20] Ehud Sprinzak *Ha 'aretz* 5 May 2000.   [21] *Jerusalem Report* 29 July 1993.

a modernized version of Begin's approach. He favoured a Greater Israel and didn't accept the demographic argument.[22] Israeli sovereignty would prevail over the territories, but there would be four urban areas where 80 per cent of the Palestinians would exercise local autonomy. He delegitimized the PLO, supported the settlement drive and condemned the Intifada as solely a display of terrorism. His economic policy was based on the prevailing wisdom of Thatcherism and Reaganomics and he described himself as 'a market oriented capitalist'.

Netanyahu's approach of both fraternizing with the far Right and distancing himself from it was repeated in the United States. Having lived in the USA for some considerable time, he argued that US government policy on the Israel–Palestine question should now not be influenced solely by the official stand of the Israeli government. Up until then, opposition parties of whatever political stripe did not openly act against the policies of an elected Israeli government in the United States. In addition, the Likud had strongly demanded that Diaspora Jewish organizations should not take positions which rejected Israeli government positions. Supporters of the Likud vehemently berated groups such as Peace Now for opposing the Begin and Shamir governments.

Even before the Oslo talks were revealed to the world, AIPAC supporters were confused about the new Israeli government's approach and divided about Rabin's ascendancy to power. The polarized approach of Begin and Shamir and the demonization of the Palestinians were easy to absorb. Now, everything they had argued during the previous decade no longer had the same ring of truth. At the AIPAC conference in March 1993, the executive director was berated for not mentioning the PLO in a speech on Israel's security. The Israeli Ambassador was criticized for suggesting willingness to consider territorial concessions on the Golan Heights.

The Oslo Accord accelerated such dissension. The Likud and its supporters in the USA abruptly changed their approach on legitimate Diaspora dissent. Now, they argued, it was permissible to criticize since Israel's very survival was at risk due to the folly of the Left. There had been a labelling of Middle East professionals in the Bush administration such as Dan Kurtzer and Aaron Miller – American Jews who were critical of the settlement drive – as 'self-hating Jews' by Likud's advocates in the USA. Another American Jew, Richard Haass, was a specialist on the National

---

[22] Ilan Peleg, 'The Likud under Rabin II: Between Ideological Purity and Pragmatic Readjustment' in Robert O. Freedman (ed.), *Israel under Rabin* (Boulder 1995) pp. 151–152.

Security Council and had helped formulate Bush's strategy on linking the issue of the loan guarantees with a settlement freeze.

Netanyahu sought to neutralize such people whose liberal views were closer to those of the Israeli Labour party. He had built up a broad network of right-wing ideological adherents, religious supporters of the settlements in the territories, sympathizers in the Republican party, Christian evangelicals and neo-conservative Jewish intellectuals during his tenure in the United States. After Oslo, Clinton suspended anti-PLO legislation and granted aid to the PA via the Middle East Peace Facilitation Act. On becoming party leader, Netanyahu reactivated this coalition – and some of its constituents wished to bring down Clinton. A trio of former Shamir government employees and advisors, Yossi Ben-Aharon, Yigal Carmon and Yoram Ettinger, were involved in unofficially lobbying Congress to prevent the stationing of US troops in the event of an Israeli withdrawal from the Golan Heights. They had originally been part of a Netanyahu-affiliated group which raised funds for Israel advocacy in the USA.[23] They also encouraged Congressional monitoring of PLO compliance and linking any funding of the Palestinians towards ends such as the cancellation of the PLO Charter. A Washington public relations firm was hired to discredit the PLO.

Moreover, following the Republicans' landslide in November 1994, the GOP was now in control of both the House and the Senate for the first time in forty years. Even though 70 per cent of US Jews adhered to a liberal outlook and always voted for the Democrats – a figure only exceeded by American blacks – the unofficial Likud lobbying took on a greater significance. In the early days of the Oslo Accord, such activities did not bother Israeli diplomats, particularly as Clinton firmly aligned himself with Rabin's policies. However, when the peace process began to run into difficulties together with Republican dominance in the legislature, Netanyahu's front men then began to exert more influence. By mid-1995, Israeli diplomats began to label them 'a disinformation team'.

While trying to unite the broad Right, Netanyahu also attempted to marginalize his rivals such as Levy and Sharon in the Likud. Yet he was unable to silence them and it was estimated that a majority of Likud's thirty-two parliamentary representatives did not support him. On the one hand, he was projected as a telegenic celebrity with a gift for the golden phrase; on the other, he appeared to be an inexperienced manager of colleagues and an ineffectual politician. Above all, he feared being accused

[23] *Jerusalem Post* 13 July 1995.

of ideological apostasy by his enemies as he attempted to modernize the Likud. He ensured that the Likud central committee had to have a 75 per cent majority before new primaries could be held to elect a new leader. He also attempted to demonstrate his radical credentials by introducing proposals such as limiting the Supreme Court's jurisdiction over the territories and the death penalty for terrorists.

The Declaration of Principles posed an ideological and psychological challenge to both Netanyahu and the Likud. He attacked the Oslo Accord as tantamount to a new Munich agreement with Rabin playing the part of Chamberlain. But Oslo also had internal repercussions. It effectively split the Likud between those who were unable to renounce the approach of Menachem Begin and those who believed that a political adjustment had to be made to accommodate the new reality of Palestinian nationalism. Even before Oslo, there had been calls for a new direction. Meir Shitreet, a Likud development town mayor, had commented that 'the Land of Israel is not a religion'. Moshe Arens, who left politics after Likud's failure, argued that the Israeli public did not relate to notions of a Greater Israel as a response to the violence in the territories. Even Ehud Olmert asked whether Gaza must be 'an integral part of the state of Israel forever'.[24]

Netanyahu had to straddle the two camps within the Likud. His sympathy initially was with the ideologues due to the challenge of Oslo. This was not an opportune time for a debate, he reasoned, on such a fundamental subject and therefore he counteracted any challenge to the belief system constructed around Jabotinsky and Begin. A radical opposition to Oslo therefore allowed him to define his leadership, cement his coordination with the far Right and control Sharon. But he had to take note that there was a growing group of younger Likud members who wished to reflect the desire of many voters for a pragmatic solution to the conflict with the Palestinians.

Significantly, three Likud members of the Knesset abstained in the vote on the Declaration of Principles, including Roni Milo who was running as the party's candidate for mayor of Tel Aviv. In addition, another fifteen Likud mayors including those representing towns such as Netanya and Herzliya declared their support for the Oslo Accord. To some extent, this represented a revolt by the middle classes against the inflexibility of ideology – a revolt which the Likud could not ignore. Moreover, the Likud was not synonymous with Begin's Herut, but comprised other groups with different ideological pedigrees. Thus, the Liberals' Yitzhak

[24] *Jerusalem Report* 16 July 1992.

Berman and the State List's Zalman Shoval argued for an innovative approach which was not limited by ideology.

Initially, Netanyahu appeased such a growing tendency by stating that he would honour past agreements,[25] but he then distanced himself from this approach as the rapprochement with the Palestinians stagnated and disillusionment set in. Netanyahu declared himself against street violence,[26] but at the same time bound himself more tightly to the far Right and their protests against Oslo. As the Islamist campaign of attacks began, Netanyahu concentrated on advocating better anti-terror measures, greater security and opposing any withdrawal from the Golan Heights. Netanyahu promoted the image of a strong leader with military experience and recalled his five-year service in the crack military unit, the Sayeret Matkal. It marked the first steps in a transition from concentrating on ideology to emphasizing security.

Many of the early protests against Rabin were organized by the religious right and Netanyahu was happy to integrate them into his broad campaign of opposition to the Oslo Accord. It also betrayed his weak position in the Likud. Since the far Right could provide him with a platform and this provided an opportunity for greater media coverage, he therefore appeared at mass demonstrations and visited settlements.

Yet the disadvantage of flirting with the far Right often meant being tarnished by association with outlandish policies. Moledet's Ze'evi called upon the military to defy the government. Others embraced Oslo in order to interpret it legalistically and thereby undermine it. Groups such as Peace Watch were established, which modelled itself on Helsinki Watch which monitored compliance with the Helsinki Accords on European Security and Human Rights.

The ultra-nationalism of the Right dovetailed with the religiosity of the settlers in the employment of inflammatory language to attack Rabin and his government. On the eve of the signing of the Declaration of Principles, demonstrators accused Rabin and Peres of treason. Fringe groups such as Kach and Kahane Chai raged against the peace process and were prepared to attack Rabin at every public function that he attended. Other groups such as 'Women in Green' declared that 'this junta is raping the Jewish people'.[27] Zo Artzeinu, led by mainly US Jewish activists, directed its activities through organized roadblocks to bring transportation to a standstill. Its leader proclaimed that the government should be held

---

[25] *Jerusalem Report* 16 December 1993.   [26] *Yediot Aharanot* 29 September 1993.
[27] *Jerusalem Report* 30 November 1995.

responsible for its crime against Judaism. The settler magazine *Nekuda* called it 'a government of blood' while Tsomet's Raful Eitan called the ministers 'a bunch of judenrat quislings'.[28]

While Netanyahu and other Likud leaders distanced themselves from such accentuated rhetoric by formally opposing the labelling of Rabin and Peres as 'murderers' and 'traitors', they too jumped on the bandwagon of using incendiary language. Netanyahu accused Rabin of 'direct responsibility for stirring up Arab terror and for the horror of this massacre in Tel Aviv. You are guilty. This blood is on your head.'[29]

At a demonstration against Oslo II, a few weeks before Rabin's assassination, journalists noted that Netanyahu and his colleagues used the following amongst other terms of critical abuse:

'wicked', 'insane', 'diseased', 'treacherous', 'reckless', 'obsequious', 'mentally deranged', 'assimilated', 'destroying the dream of the Jewish people', 'possessed with making concessions', 'disconnected from Jewish values and tradition', 'a two time collaborator – once with a terrorist organization and once against Jews', 'leading Israel to suicide', 'shrinking Israel into Auschwitz borders'.[30]

The crowd at the demonstration chanted 'Rabin is a traitor' and the Kahanists depicted him dressed in a Nazi uniform.

In July 1994, Arafat visited the territories for the first time since 1967. Ehud Olmert as the new mayor of Jerusalem said that he would bring 500,000 protestors to block the roads so that he could not pray on the Temple Mount. Olmert argued that Arafat would bring tens of thousands of worshippers and proclaim a Palestinian state there and wouldn't leave.

Outside the Rabins' home Yitzhak's wife, Leah, was compared to Clara Petacci, Mussolini's mistress. The demonstrators said that the Rabins would share the same fate. On another variation of the 'fascist' theme, Rabin was compared to Marshal Petain who, although legally elected, capitulated and collaborated with the Nazis. Part of this was a deliberate policy to 'break' Rabin and to lower his self-confidence – indeed the Yesha (Judea, Samaria and Gaza) Council of settlers invited psychologists to their early meetings.[31]

Death threats proliferated. Rabin reacted stubbornly to all these provocations and was openly disparaging towards his opponents. He, in turn,

---

[28] Yoram Peri (ed.), *The Assassination of Yitzhak Rabin* (Stanford 2000) pp. 4–5.

[29] Amos Elon, 'Israel's Demons', *New York Review of Books* 21 December 1995.

[30] *Ha'aretz* 6 October 1995 in Yaacov Bar Siman-Tov, 'Peace Making with the Palestinians: Change and Legitimacy' in Efraim Karsh (ed.), *From Rabin to Netanyahu: Israel's Troubled Agenda* (London 1997) pp. 176–177.

[31] *Ha'aretz* 22 October 1999.

called the Likud 'allies of Hamas' and other opponents 'degenerates'. Moreover, he refused to take precautions such as wearing a bullet-proof vest.
Instead, the Labour party now began to attack the Likud as being both
passive and proactive in the campaign against Rabin. Netanyahu responded
by accusing them of 'organized incitement'.[32] Other members of the Likud
accused Labour of 'Bolshevik tactics'[33] and of instituting 'a blood libel'
against the Right. Yet Netanyahu had remained silent as the far Right
worked itself up into a paroxysm of hate. He attempted to be both the
respectable leader of the opposition as well as the man who stood in solidarity with the most vociferous opponents of Rabin's policies. There was no
condemnation of their vilification and demonization. At Rabin's funeral,
Leah Rabin categorically refused to shake Netanyahu's hand or to accept
his condolences. The Left pointed out that recent violence in Israel had
come from the Right. The writer Amos Elon, invoking the direction of
Hebrew writing, cynically commented that 'the bullets in Israel are always
shot from right to left'.

RABBIS AND AYATOLLAHS

The Hamas campaign of attacks and killings against the settlers straight
after the signing of the Declaration of Principles radicalized the settlers and
they criticized the government and the IDF for not protecting them. No
distinction, however, was made between the PLO and the Islamists. There
was considerable anger at Rabin who hitherto was known as 'Mr Security'
and the government's decision to supply the Palestinian police force with
weapons. The situation also created new groups in a spirit of vigilantism.
The settlers were worried about an IDF pull-out and being left under the
protection of the Palestinian police. Goldstein's killing spree in a Hebron
mosque was a reaction to this growing fear.

His action radicalized more Palestinian Arabs and persuaded Hamas
to extend its campaign into Israel proper and to utilize suicide bombers
beyond the Green Line. Yet Goldstein's action further radicalized some
Jews with his example of self-sacrifice and retaliation. The settlers' anger
was turned towards the Oslo agreement which they argued had made the
outbreak of Hamas violence possible. The settlers' radio station, Arutz
Sheva, began to broadcast vitriolic contributions.

---

[32] *Yediot Aharanot* 13 October 1995.
[33] Akiva Nof, 'Thoughts Following the Murder', broadcast on Arutz Sheva, 17 November 1995.

After the Goldstein killings, Rabin and his cabinet agreed to the removal of seven families in Tel Rumeida in central Hebron. Four prominent rabbis from the national religious camp including former Chief Rabbi Goren issued halachic rulings (according to Jewish religious law) against the evacuation.

We must give our life in the struggle against this vicious plan of the government of Israel which relies on the Arabs for its majority and be prepared to die rather than allow the destruction of Hebron.[34]

Endorsed by other settler rabbis and opposed by more moderate ones, such a ruling was unprecedented. Yet despite many calls to remove the Hebron settlers, Rabin did not want to further antagonize his opponents and backed down. However, Rabin did not mince his words; he labelled those rabbis who opposed him as 'ayatollahs'. Rabin's stubbornness and his political policies challenged deeply held ideological beliefs, both nationalist and religious. It was truly a crisis of faith for the national religious Zionist movement. Amos Oz perceptively commented that 'a man who changes is often a traitor in the eyes of those who can never change'.[35]

There was a tremendous gulf of bitterness between the pragmatic, secular Rabin and the settlers. It was not only political, but also deeply personal. It impinged on understanding Jewish identity and defining 'Jewishness'. Orthodox Judaism had had great difficulty in coming to terms with Zionism. Judaism throughout the centuries had developed its own understanding of government and law. In modern-day Israel, these coexisted. For the youthful demonstrators, the rabbis' ruling was often held in higher esteem than the elected legislators' pronouncement. Although Israel was indeed a democratic oasis in the Middle East, some of its citizens came from countries where democracy had either been suppressed or was highly selective. There was a dependency on the rabbis for leadership and political guidance. This empowered them beyond their natural authority based on scholarship and learning.

Following the bombings of the Islamists, the Yesha Council of Rabbis discussed placing the government on trial on the basis of *din rodef* (a law permitting the killing of an assailant who was about to strike) and *din moser* (the law concerning a Jew who has informed on and betrayed another Jew to non-Jewish authorities).[36] Both rulings had been codified in the third century by rabbis acting under fundamentally different conditions. It was

---

[34] *Ha'aretz* 7 March 1994 in Sprinzak, *Brother against Brother* p. 248.
[35] Amos Oz, *Times* 7 November 1995.   [36] Sprinzak, *Brother against Brother* pp. 253–258.

known that this issue was a matter of discussion amongst rabbis in both Israel and the United States. One writer termed it 'a halachic character assassination'.[37] Yet it was becoming common knowledge amongst an increasing number of people that such private discussions between rabbis had taken place. The very existence of such private debate began to influence some of their youthful followers. The rabbis did little to dissipate and inhibit such sentiments amongst the radical fringe.

Although he acted alone and was not given rabbinical authorization, Yigal Amir mentioned the *din rodef* repeatedly to his friends beforehand. After the murder, he said that he acted according to a *din rodef* issued by a few rabbis. During his interrogation, he argued that 'once something is a ruling, there is no longer a moral issue.'[38] Amir was inspired by the Biblical example of Pinchas ben Eleazar who killed Zimri ben Salu who had been consorting with a Midianite woman. God's wrath for the Jewish people was averted because Pinchas displayed 'amongst them his passion for me'.[39] This was understood as a source of zealotry and by some, a justification for it. Amir saw Rabin as an outsider. He told interrogators straight after the killing that Rabin was not 'his Prime Minister'. The Goldstein killings and its celebration by the radical fringe had fortified the belief in such circles that murdering non-Jews – and by extension outsiders – was permissible in Judaism. In addition to *The Day of the Jackal* on Amir's bookshelf,[40] investigators also found *Baruch HaGever* (blessed is the man) – an edited series of writings to honour the memory of Baruch Goldstein.[41]

Rabin was killed by bullets fired from a Beretta, following a Peace Now rally designed to bolster support for the government and to encourage the Prime Minister in his political path. While there was a lot of soul-searching in the national religious camp, the first question asked by Israelis was who was really responsible?

An analysis was often placed in abeyance by religious Jews due to the blanket criticism from angry secular and perplexed liberal Jews. Bar-Ilan University was accused of propagating death and discrimination under the guise of academic discourse. Religious Jews responded by rationalizing that a defence of Judaism took priority amidst a growing denial that the campaign against Oslo had little to do with Amir's action. The modern orthodox writer and educator Rabbi David Hartmann, however, believed

---

[37] Ehud Sprinzak, 'Israel's Radical Right and the Countdown to the Rabin Assassination', in Peri (ed.), *The Assassination of Yitzhak Rabin* p. 110.

[38] Ibid. p. 124.   [39] Numbers 25:10–14.   [40] *Independent* 6 November 1995.

[41] Sprinzak, *Brother against Brother* pp. 258–266.

that Amir was no aberration, but a victim of 'the culmination of a long process of indoctrination and so-called learning'. He commented:

The halachah (Jewish law) is, of course, not as simple-minded as the killer thought. There are sufficient other resources in the tradition – humane and pacifist ones – to counterbalance the dogmatism. The tragedy is that a group of fanatical and politicized rabbis has in recent years become dominant over all other voices in Israel. They continue to block out opposing views.[42]

The British Talmudic scholar Rabbi Louis Jacobs further attacked this mode of interpretation of the Torah, arguing that it is actually contrary to halachah.

Leaving aside the distortion of Judaism that results from treating the halachah in isolation from other Jewish values – pan-halachism as Heschel calls it – this is not, in fact, the halachah. The harm is done by people treating a halachic view they favour – chiefly on political grounds – and then invoking the concept of halachah as the direct word of God to be obeyed unquestioningly even when this involves the sacrifice of the most cherished moral convictions.[43]

Amid contorted explanations and conspiracy theories, the revered US Rabbi Aharon Soloveitchik argued that denial was not acceptable conduct:

I also failed in not sufficiently protesting those who sought license for murder. [Therefore] we cannot say that 'our hands did not shed the blood'.[44]

It was pointed out that Amir had recently broken up with a long-time girlfriend whom he had hoped to marry and was depressed. It was also revealed that the leader of a radicalized far Right group, Eyal, whom Amir was close to, turned out to be an informer for the intelligence services.

Amir was branded with 'madness' and 'delusion' after the killing, but he was regarded as just another right-wing activist – neither deranged nor unstable – before the killing. He was not even on a list of 'dangerous' right-wing students that the Bar-Ilan University administration was monitoring.

The official inquiry, the Shamgar Commission, investigated the assassination, but glossed over the incitement which was deemed not to be within its remit. A secret appendix revealed that the Shin Bet informer had been involved in attacks on Arabs, Communist parliamentarians and the Druze chairman of the students' union at Tel Aviv University. It castigated the Shin Bet, the internal security services, for not acting according to

---

[42] Amos Elon, 'Israel's Demons', *New York Review of Books* 21 December 1995.
[43] Louis Jacobs, 'The Rabin Assassination', *Judaism Today* no.4 Spring 1996.
[44] Aviezer Ravitsky '"Let Us Search Our Path": Religious Zionism after the Assassination' in Peri (ed.), *The Assassination of Yitzhak Rabin* p. 150.

procedure in the open car park where the murder took place. The head of the Shin Bet was held most responsible for all the slip-ups.

The death of Rabin remained a painful and traumatic memory for years to come for the secular Left. Above all, they remembered the incitement.

Although the assassin was apprehended and sent to prison, because he was the one who fired the three bullets, those who drew a bulls-eye on Rabin's back and told him that the Prime Minister was a permissible target have never been forced – perish the thought – to account for their actions.[45]

It was not just Israeli Jews who were shell shocked from this tragic episode in their history. Both the PLO and the Israeli Arab community were devastated by the removal of Rabin from the political scene in such a manner. Only the Islamists were pleased; they looked upon the assassination as an act of God in revenge for the killing of Fathi Shikaki, the founder of Islamic Jihad a few weeks before.

[45] Yossi Sarid, *Ha'aretz* 1 November 2006.

CHAPTER 12

The magician and the bulldozer

THE VIRTUAL AND THE REAL LIKUD

The narrow election victory of Bibi Netanyahu in 1996 was unexpected and dismayed a wide coalition stretching from the refugee camps of Gaza to the White House. Despite Peres's unconvincing attempt to act as if he was Rabin's natural successor, a series of suicide bombings convinced the Israeli public that the Oslo process had brought neither peace nor security. The peace process, it was reasoned, needed to be slowed down, but not extinguished.

Netanyahu's victory by default did little to earn him the public's trust. He was instead dubbed 'the magician' because of the unexpected result. Israeli journalists showed little love for Netanyahu. In one sense, they projected the election as almost a referendum on the Rabin assassination in the expectation that Peres's victory would have been 'a minimal moral compensation' for the killing of the Prime Minister.[1]

There was also a deep resentment within the Likud within weeks of winning power. Netanyahu initially attempted to marginalize his colleagues in the Likud by not consulting them either during coalition negotiations or in appointing government ministers.

Moreover, Netanyahu desperately wished to keep Sharon at arm's length and to keep him out of the inner cabinet. Indeed, he was unable to present his government because of the dispute over a portfolio for Sharon. On a personal level, there was no love lost between the two. In the past, Sharon had ridiculed Netanyahu, referring to his public explanation of extra-marital affairs, when he commented that 'there are leaders who solve problems and others who get caught with their pants down'.[2] Netanyahu, in frustration, spoke of Sharon's incessant and tireless subversion. When the pressure from the Right proved too great, he simply expanded the cabinet and created the Ministry of National Infrastructure for Sharon.

---

[1] Nachum Barnea, *Ha'aretz* 30 April 1999. [2] *Jerusalem Report* 24 February 1994.

From the outset, Netanyahu attempted to behave in presidential fashion since this was the first occasion that Prime Ministers could be elected directly. He preferred technocrats in his government rather than politicians. He wanted to place before the Knesset the 'Norwegian law' which would require all new ministers to resign their parliamentary seats on entering government. The exceptions would be the Prime Minister and four deputy Prime Ministers.

Netanyahu wanted to revamp the Prime Minister's Office on the model of the White House. He planned a Council of Economic Advisors, an Office of Budget Management and a National Security Council. He also promised privatization, an end to dependency on the USA and cuts in the national budget.

Netanyahu also unveiled 4.9 billion shekels in cuts without consultations. There were price rises in the cost of health care, hospital fees and education. Cuts in child allowance and in benefits for the elderly did not impress the Likud's working-class constituency. Public transport fares would increase by 13 per cent but members of Knesset saw their salaries increase by up to 40 per cent.

Few of these innovations and proposals came to fruition as he provoked a backlash that he was unable to contain. Netanyahu soon became a disappointment to his mentors Arens and Shamir. The Likud's Silvan Shalom illuminated the sense of contradiction which he and many others felt. 'Bibi is in government and the Likud is in opposition.'[3]

Once again, David Levy was nominally appointed Foreign Minister, but Netanyahu, like Shamir, ensured that he was bypassed in the negotiations with the Palestinians. He excluded Levy from both private and public meetings with the Americans. Professional diplomats were similarly excluded by Netanyahu's coterie of advisors. The diplomats became mere figureheads whose purpose was solely to explain policy.

Moreover, the new policy of reciprocity led to a profound cooling of relations with the Palestinians. The ambiguity of the Declaration of Principles allowed both sides to build trust in the spirit of the accord. Netanyahu now insisted that the letter of the agreement should be adhered to and quickly found Palestinian violations. In turn, the Palestinians discovered violations of Israeli adherence to agreements. This descent into diplomatic frigidity soon spread to the Arab world. Qatar and Tunisia said that they would not open ties with Israel despite previous promises. Morocco's King Hassan refused to see Netanyahu.

---

[3] *Jerusalem Post* 3 September 1996.

Yet both Netanyahu and Sharon understood that the game had changed. The Palestinians were no longer 'terrorists' or a partner that did not exist. The Palestinians had returned to history – and more specifically to Israeli history – and their presence could not be ignored.

As Minister of National Infrastructure, Sharon carried out a hectic programme of road building both within Israel and in the territories. Under Rabin there had been a suspension of such activities. Sharon, true to his Mapai origins, was keen to construct a network of roads, tunnels and bridges which would connect Jewish settlements on the West Bank to Israel. In September 1996, he was present at the opening of a four-kilometre tunnel road which connected Gush Etzion with Jerusalem. Only Israelis could use this road. Palestinians had to go via Bethlehem and Beit Jala. Rabin had supported this project which had been initiated in 1986, but he also cancelled some ten others to construct roads in the territories.

Sharon was also in charge of the ministerial committee that dealt with Bedouin affairs. He announced that he wanted to move 50,000 Bedouin from the Negev who were living illegally on state land and resettle them in five or six new towns. This would take ten to fifteen years. In parallel, Sharon wanted to move more Jews into the Negev and into the northern Galilee regions, two areas with large Arab populations.[4]

On 2 August 1996, Netanyahu's cabinet ended a four-year effective go-slow on settlement construction. The cabinet would now only be invited to vote when new settlements were proposed. Significantly, Netanyahu refused to allow the setting up of a ministerial panel on settlement expansion, in order to keep Sharon at bay.

Even so, his government started to act on some 300 plans for new settlements which had been in the bureaucratic pipeline for years. Avigdor Lieberman, the new Director-General of the Prime Minister's Office, compiled a report which wanted to reinstate special benefits for settlers on a par with those living in development towns in Israel. Such subsidies had been nullified when Rabin came into office.

In 1990, Sharon had proposed up to twenty settlements straddling the Green Line, but less than half were actually built. Moreover, Rabin's government pointedly failed to support these settlements. In August 1996, Deputy Housing Minister Meir Porush announced the building of 5,000 homes for 70,000 people as a resurrection of the Sharon plan. A Housing Ministry spokesman commented that 'this government sees the Green Line as being purely theoretical'.[5] Sharon instructed the Israel Lands

---

[4] *Jerusalem Post* 27 November 1996.   [5] *Jerusalem Post* 20 August 1996.

Administration to draw up plans for three settlements on the Golan encompassing 900 new homes. This would bring the total of homes on the Golan to 2,500 by the year 2000.[6]

In 1997, Israel began to withhold part of the taxes that it collected on behalf of the PA. This represented 35 to 40 per cent of the PA's budget. The Netanyahu government announced that it had carried out this move because the PA refused to restrain the Palestinian Islamists.

The plummeting lack of confidence in Netanyahu boosted Sharon's standing in the party. He attempted to exemplify traditional Likud values through his building initiatives whereas Netanyahu was depicting himself as less ideological and more pragmatic. Yet partition had become a fact[7] and was increasingly expounded by many of the younger generation within the Likud. Sharon now regarded the post-Oslo arrangements for the Palestinians as tantamount to a state. In an age when ideology counted for less and security was the central concern, both Netanyahu and Sharon competed to propose doctrines of limited sovereignty for the Palestinians. Each time that Netanyahu made a proposal, such as an 'Allon plus' plan, Sharon would seemingly outflank him from the Right. Sharon's voracious appetite for authority and recognition gradually began to overwhelm Netanyahu. Sharon opposed the Hebron agreement in January 1997, but unlike Benny Begin, he did not resign from the government. He argued against the release of twenty-three female Palestinian prisoners. In February 1997, Sharon supported the construction of Har Homa near Bethlehem. Despite three appeals from Clinton not to proceed, in March 1997 Netanyahu responded by offering 2,600 housing units for Har Homa and 3,500 units for Arabs in the Jerusalem area.

Sharon next opposed any yielding of Area C – the part of the West Bank controlled entirely by the Israelis – to the Palestinians despite the fact that it seemed to contradict the terms of Oslo II. Instead, he proposed giving up parts of Area B to the Palestinian area – land which both sides controlled. Sharon spoke of making 'certain modifications to Oslo' and of developing 'security zones' in the West Bank. He also advocated a greater Jerusalem stretching down to the Dead Sea and the retention of the trans-Samaria highway in the event of war.[8]

Despite his oppositional views, Sharon was grudgingly given a say in Israeli policy towards the Palestinians. By late 1997, it was clear that he was not being regarded as a pariah by either the Americans or the Jordanians.

---

[6] *Jerusalem Post* 24 November 1996.   [7] *Jerusalem Post* 20 December 1996.
[8] *Jerusalem Post* 4 March 1997.

In part, this was a reaction to Netanyahu. In part, it was a recognition that Sharon, 'the bulldozer', was authoritative and often innovative. US diplomats and envoys such as Dennis Ross and Martin Indyk now began to regularly consult Sharon. They noted that it was Sharon who had brought about the dismantling of Yamit in 1982. The acts of aggressive behaviour and outright hostility towards US representatives during the Lebanon war were forgotten. Gone was talk of 'Jordan is Palestine' and there were even suggestions that Sharon's position and that of the Beilin–Abu Mazen plan were not poles apart.[9] Indeed, Sharon told the Jordanians that he would be willing to make major concessions on the West Bank.[10]

Yet part of the old Sharon remained and he was convinced that he had been right in his conduct during the Lebanon war. Indeed he brought a libel suit against an *Ha'aretz* journalist who had written that he had lied to Begin about advancing on Beirut in 1982 – even though Begin's son testified that his father did not know of Sharon's intentions beforehand. In 1998, Sharon opposed the US demand to agree to a second redeployment involving a transfer of 13 per cent of territory while Netanyahu vacillated.

In January 1998, David Levy finally resigned as Foreign Minister. Although Netanyahu took responsibility for the work of the Foreign Ministry, the first overtures to Sharon to take over were made in the spring of 1998. Four months of secret negotiations followed, culminating in a signed agreement which detailed Sharon's sphere of influence. Although Sharon continued to publicly deny that he wanted the position, his opposition to the second redeployment became increasingly muted. When talks between Netanyahu and the new Labour leader, Ehud Barak, on forming a unity government broke down, Sharon finally accepted the position of Foreign Minister. Like Begin in 1981, Netanyahu was prepared to appoint Sharon to an influential position in the Israeli cabinet. For Sharon, it was rehabilitation. For Netanyahu, it was a public confirmation of his weak standing.

It was a remarkable comeback for Sharon who was hitherto a pariah in Israel and detested in the Arab world. Indeed, the State Comptroller's report in 1992 had described Sharon's tenure at the Ministry of Housing as being defined by mismanagement, nepotism, suspected illegalities, favouritism, overspending and corruption. At the age of seventy, he became the third general, after Allon and Dayan, to serve as Foreign Minister.

Within a couple of days, he left to join the negotiations with the Palestinians at the Wye Plantation. Clinton arranged a dinner that brought

---

[9] *Ha'aretz* 9 November 1998. [10] *Ha'aretz* 26 November 1998.

Arafat and Sharon together for the first time. Sharon passed a note to Arafat's aide which informed the Palestinian leader that he had publicly said that he would not shake his hand. Instead, Sharon nodded in Arafat's direction and over dinner they talked about farming.

Sharon helped to formulate the Wye memorandum whereby 13 per cent would be transferred from Area C and 14.2 per cent from Area B. It represented a sixfold increase of the area under the full control of the Palestinian security forces. At the end of a twelve-week period, the territory under Israeli control would decrease from 73 to 60 per cent of the West Bank while that under full or partial Palestinian control would increase from 27 to 40 per cent. Yet only part of the agreement was implemented due to the fragmentation of the government. Sharon instigated a transfer of 2 per cent from Area C to Area B and 7 per cent from Area B to Area A. The agreement was marked by a detailed reciprocity and a stepwise approval of stages by the Israeli cabinet which was dependent on Palestinian action.

Sharon was in transition. He had to demonstrate a new political expediency in having to balance his domestic constituency and the demands of his new position. On the one hand, he was urging the settlers to grab more land. On the other, he was agreeing to returning territory to the Palestinians. Before Wye, he vehemently objected to Netanyahu's agreement with Clinton to discuss the creation of a seaport in Gaza. He argued instead that Israel should wait until they saw what had happened with Dahaniyeh airport. Yet around the negotiating table at Wye, he was highly receptive to the Palestinians' request for a seaport to the extent that the cabinet secretary, Danny Naveh, threatened to resign. On returning to Israel, Sharon argued that the proposal wasn't binding and reverted to his original position.[11]

Although the Palestinians opened Dahaniyeh airport in Gaza, the Israeli government approved the construction of eleven bypass roads and issued the first tender for the construction of 1,025 apartments at Har Homa. In cabinet, the Likud was significantly divided. Four ministers voted for the Wye agreement, five abstained. This was the first time that a Likud government had ceded territory to the Palestinians. This did not reflect the Knesset vote where seventy-five voted in favour and only nineteen against. Even so, the Wye memorandum divided the Likud into pragmatists and ideologues. In the 1980s, Sharon and the Constraints Ministers had monitored Shamir with an ideological magnifying glass. In 1998, ironically only Shamir and a diminishing circle remained loyal to the 'not an inch' ideology of the Likud. As one journalist

---

[11] *Ha'aretz* 25 June 1999.

commented: 'They have become the representatives of a slowly vanishing political world, addressing a virtual Likud.'[12] In contrast, Yossi Beilin had signed an agreement with the Likud's Michael Eitan which reflected a political convergence between sections of the two main parties. Likud effectively accepted the principle that most of the West Bank would have to be under Palestinian sovereignty. Labour, however, recognized that the settlers would not be thrown out of their homes and settlements would not be evacuated.[13]

While a strict adherence to ideology was now a divisive factor, the positions of both Netanyahu and Sharon were in addition conditioned by their rivalry and desire for power. Both learned that ideological positions were easier to hold when in opposition, but hard choices had to be made in government.

The Wye memorandum also initiated the first fragmentation between the Likud and the NRP which Begin had first cemented with his over-tures to Gush Emunim in the 1970s. The common denominator of the nationalist demand and the religious desire for a Greater Israel no longer held. While both Sharon and Netanyahu drowned out party dissidents with nationalist rhetoric, documents such as a letter to the Lubavitcher Chassidim which both had signed in 1996, promising an end to the trans-fer of territory to the Palestinians, could not be wished away.[14]

The Wye agreement split the government such that Netanyahu was forced to call for early elections. The electorate was tired of the stagnation that had taken place during Netanyahu's tenure. There was a discernible lack of confidence in Netanyahu as a leader and many viewed his lack of experience as reinforcing Arafat's insincerity in producing a cocktail of confusion. Although Netanyahu had attempted to move the Likud away from its traditional ideological positions, the transition was proving traumatic. The liberal wing of the Likud, however, defected to a new centre party. Israel under Netanyahu dragged its feet in undertaking a second redeployment and did not actually transfer any territory to the Palestinians.

Netanyahu had opposed the exchange of 1,150 Palestinian prisoners for 3 Israelis in 1985. Therefore it was not surprising that there was a delay in releasing Palestinian prisoners and transferring funds to the PA. The building of the airport and seaport in Gaza was repeatedly postponed.

---

[12] *Ha'aretz* 30 October 1998.
[13] Yossi Beilin, *The Path to Geneva: The Quest for a Permanent Agreement 1996–2004* (New York 2004) pp. 94–97.
[14] *Ha'aretz* 26 October 1998.

The plan for the safe route which would connect the West Bank to Gaza was never carried out. The public therefore welcomed Ehud Barak to the premiership in 1999 after the resounding electoral defeat of Netanyahu. Barak was viewed as someone who would remove the logjams and advance the peace process.

Barak had been Chief of Staff under Rabin. He was responsible for Operation Accountability (1993) and Operation Grapes of Wrath in Lebanon (1996) and was known for his readiness to resort to the use of force. He had also been Deputy Commander of the Israeli force that invaded Lebanon in 1982. Under Rabin, he had been Minister of the Interior and under Peres, Foreign Minister until June 1996.

Although he defeated Netanyahu in the premiership by a margin of 12 per cent, the party race was much less clear. Labour, now called 'One Israel' for the purposes of the election, had decreased from thirty-four to twenty-six seats while the Likud plummeted from thirty-two to nineteen. It was also rumoured that Barak wanted to form a government of national unity with the Likud. Indeed, Barak and Sharon shared a common military history and he had a well-grounded respect for the new leader of the Likud.

Instead, Barak formed an administration which included right-wing parties such as the NRP, Shas and the Russian immigrant party of Natan Sharansky, Yisrael B'Aliyah, to achieve a blocking majority of sixty-one. The NRP was given the Housing portfolio and the settler population grew at an unprecedented rate. To those on the Israeli Left, this was the beginning of their disappointment with Barak. According to one observer, he had formed 'an eccentric government which defied any diplomatic logic'.[15] Although Israelis and Palestinians met at Sharm el Sheikh in September 1999 and effectively restored the Wye agreement, the presence of this right-wing bloc in government could be not ignored.

Indeed, the NRP and Sharansky voted against the Sharm el Sheikh arrangements while Shas absented itself. Barak thereby began to make sympathetic noises in their direction. Only a few weeks after the election, he announced that Israel would remain in the West Bank settlements of Ofra and Beit El 'forever'.[16] He also refused to freeze the construction of new settlements and did not act when hilltop outposts were erected.

Moreover, while Barak was said to be in possession of a brilliant mind and a belief that even impossible tasks were indeed possible, he was less adept at managing his colleagues, rivals and opponents. His inability to draw 'red lines' ideologically or to have meaningful discussions with those

[15] Baruch Kimmerling, *Ha'aretz* 4 October 2000.   [16] *Jerusalem Post* 4 June 1999.

close to him alienated many. There was a sense that he suspected his Israeli colleagues as much as his Palestinian enemies. The messages that he sent out to friend and foe were decidedly mixed. Perhaps most importantly his negotiating positions were unclear.

Although emotionally sympathetic to Gush Emunim, the settlers' movement, and mentally conditioned by his thirty five years in the military, Barak was rationally 'left-wing'. On all matters relating to permanent status, he positioned himself to the left of many leaders of the peace camp. He understood that the occupation corrupts Israel, and he understood the Palestinian desire for a state. He even admitted on television, that if he were Palestinian he would almost certainly have become a freedom fighter in one of the terrorist organizations. However, this ambivalence – the contradiction between his emotions and his rationality – created a dissonance that amplified his natural inability to market any policy.[17]

When Barak became Chief of the General Staff in 1991, he inaugurated a slimming down of the army to produce a smaller, more functional force.[18] He exempted large numbers of young people from compulsory service and dismissed thousands of career army personnel and civilians. On forming his government in 1999, he excluded the Labour party leadership from the negotiating process. He attempted to keep Peres out of government and appointed Yossi Beilin, Shlomo Ben-Ami and Chaim Ramon to inappropriate posts. The architects of Oslo were marginalized. Moreover, he did not handle strikes or the grievances of Israeli Arabs in an acceptable manner. All this was reflected in increasingly gloomy opinion polls about the prospect of peace.[19]

A RETURN TO CAMP DAVID

Barak's approach was to deal with Syria rather than with the Palestinians in the hope of striking an agreement. He had made an election pledge to get Israeli troops out of Lebanon within a year. Assad ruled his country with a rod of iron and any agreement was likely to stick. Bringing Syria in from the cold would strain Assad's relationship with the Iranian ayatollahs which had been forged in the 1980s as a common front against Saddam Hussein. In addition, success on the Syrian front would strengthen Israel's negotiating position with the Palestinians. Through intermediaries such as Patrick Seale and Lord Michael Levy, it seemed that Assad was ready to resume

---

[17] Ron Pundak, 'From Oslo to Taba: What Went Wrong? *Survival* vol.43 no.3 Autumn 2001, pp. 31–45.
[18] *Ma'ariv* 10 April 1991.
[19] Tamar Hermann and Ephraim Yuchtman-Yaar, 'Divided yet United: Israeli–Jewish Attitudes towards the Oslo Peace Process', *Journal of Peace Research* vol.39 no.5 September 2002 p. 604.

serious discussions with Israel.[20] History had recorded that under Rabin, there had been intensive negotiations which had come to nothing. Yet Assad continued to show his interest in peace. Following the Madrid Conference in 1991, 4,000 Syrian Jews, concentrated in Damascus, Aleppo and Al Qamishli, were quietly allowed to join relatives in Brooklyn, New York. 1,600 of them subsequently emigrated to Israel.

Moreover, Netanyahu's friend, the US businessman and diplomat Ronald Lauder, forged secret contacts and met President Assad on numerous occasions in 1998. Lauder submitted two plans to Assad on Netanyahu's behalf, offering first a withdrawal to the 1923 border and then to an agreed line based on the 1967 border.[21] There would be a withdrawal of both sides from the Golan with the positioning of early-warning stations in between. When Sharon was appointed Foreign Minister, he told Lauder to break off all contacts with Syria.[22] Barak, however, revived them, but moved slowly. Barak believed that a final withdrawal from southern Lebanon could be part of the Syrian deal. There were even preparations for a 1 May 2000 referendum on a Syrian–Israeli peace treaty.[23] Barak's government had also prepared a request to the Americans for an aid package of $17 billion to compensate for the loss of the Golan Heights.[24]

There were intensive discussions between Barak and the Syrian Foreign Minister, Faruq al-Shara, at Blair House, Washington and in Shepherdstown, West Virginia which led to the clarification of the differences between the two sides, but not to a resolution. In part, the process was drawn out because Barak was not prepared at that time to confirm that Israel would withdraw to the 4 June 1967 border – an agreement which Rabin, Peres and even Netanyahu had been willing to accept. Moreover, Syrian reticence and publicly unfriendly behaviour towards Israel did not endear the Israeli public to returning the Golan Heights to Assad. In addition, the activities of a highly active Golan lobby made Barak even more cautious in his discussions.

Al-Shara's serious illness delayed matters further, but Clinton was prepared to engage Assad in public discussion to attain a breakthrough which seemed perfectly possible after Barak's belated acceptance of Israeli withdrawal to the 1967 border. The Lebanese, in particular, were keen that an agreement be reached since it would counteract Hezbollah's claims that it was responsible for Israel's departure from southern Lebanon. An ailing Assad, however, prevaricated and stonewalled in his meeting with Clinton

[20] Ross, *The Missing Peace* p. 520.   [21] *Ha'aretz* 17 January 2000.   [22] *Ha'aretz* 20 January 2000.
[23] *Ha'aretz* 19 January 2000.   [24] *Ha'aretz* 4 January 2000.

in Geneva in March 2000, contrary to the US President's expectations. A few weeks later Assad was dead.

Assad would have been prepared for an agreement in late 1999, but by March it became clear to him that his days were numbered and that he had to ensure the succession for his son, Bashar. There was already internal criticism in Syria at the prospect of such an agreement with the Israelis.[25] A major decision such as peace with Israel would have to wait. It became secondary in Assad's calculations.[26] Moreover, disillusionment with Barak began to gather apace and it affected the Palestinians far more intensely than the Israelis.

The Israelis had assumed that the spirit of Oslo would transform Gaza into 'the new Singapore' and that Arafat and the Arab states would combat home-grown Islamists and the influence of the Iranian Revolution.[27] Even Rabin implied that an authoritarian Arafat would control local dissent because he would not allow appeals to the judiciary and prevent civil rights organizations from raising problems.[28]

There was intense Israeli public suspicion of Arafat. Did he really believe in Oslo? Or was it merely a tactical manoeuvre? Unlike Sadat and Hussein, there was no genuine Palestinian attempt to win over the Israeli public. The output of the Palestinian media and the guidelines of the educational system seemed to suggest that Oslo had never taken place. While Arafat had declared himself publicly for a non-violent path, his supporters in Fatah did not disown their commitment to the armed struggle. Arafat's studied reluctance to act against those who would use violence led many Israelis to ask if a two-state solution was really the Palestinian goal. Was the political Right correct after all, in stating that this was merely the first step towards a Greater Palestine?

Although the Israeli economy grew during the Rabin years, the Palestinians had actually become impoverished because of Oslo. Between the Declaration of Principles and the defeat of Peres in 1996, there were 342 days of total closure of Gaza. Unemployment increased in parallel with a general economic decline.

The central issue for the Palestinians was that Oslo had brought no end to settlers and settlements in the West Bank and Gaza. There had been an additional 100,000 settlers since 1993 and 30 new settlements. Under Rabin and Peres, between 1992 and 1996, the Jewish population increased by

[25] Rabinovich, *Waging Peace: Israel and the Arabs* pp. 135–138.
[26] Ross, *The Missing Peace* pp. 588–589.   [27] Uzi Landau, *Jerusalem Report* 28 September 1998.
[28] *Yediot Aharanot* 7 September 1993.

48 per cent in the West Bank and by 62 per cent in Gaza.[29] The Oslo
agreement had said nothing about settlements and 'natural growth' was
interpreted liberally. This was supposed to be dealt with at a later stage.
Arafat and supporters in Tunis went along with this. The local Palestinian
leadership, however, exhibited a scepticism initially and an anger later that
Arafat should have permitted this. Rabin's intention may have been to
ultimately eliminate many of the settlements, but he did not wish to hand
over the political mainstream of Israeli politics to a belligerent Right. The
suicide attacks of the Islamists and the election of Netanyahu put paid to
any meaningful consideration of evacuating the settlements.

Oslo enabled the dissection of the West Bank into enclaves through
the accelerated construction of different transportation systems for Israelis
and Palestinians so that a separation ideology would be enacted. The
paving of 250 miles of roads effectively destroyed territorial contiguity.[30]
The Oslo II agreement moreover gave a formal legal seal of approval to
the confiscation of Palestinian land for the building of bypass roads. In
Gaza, the settlements and the roads grew to approximately a third of the
area, with Arab Gaza cut into enclaves. By the summer of 2000, Area
C which was under Israeli control comprised 60 per cent of the West
Bank. The expansion of settlements, the development of outposts and the
construction of transportation bypasses meant a growing Israeli presence
in the West Bank instead of the gradual transfer of land to the Palestinian
Authority. In the absence of any agreement, the Palestinians came to believe
that Oslo had given carte blanche to settlement expansion rather than the
establishment of their own state alongside Israel.

Although this might have been expected under a Likud government,
both Rabin and Barak permitted this state of affairs as a means of keeping
the Right at bay and their coalitions in power. Barak began the construction of 1,943 housing units in the West Bank in 2000. In the last quarter of
2000, there were plans to construct 954 units compared to 368 in the last
quarter of 1999. The Housing Ministry also issued a tender for development work in Kochav Ya'akov, south of Ramallah, doubling the settlement's
population.[31] The construction of settlements inherited from Likud governments proceeded apace. The Palestinians perceived a power imbalance
and this distorted negotiations. Moreover, they seemed no nearer to the
proclamation of a Palestinian state. Even Peres was often ambivalent on

[29] Shlomo Ben-Ami, *Scars of War: Wounds of Peace: The Israeli–Arab Tragedy* (London 2006) p. 216.
[30] Sara Roy, 'Why Peace Failed: An Oslo Autopsy', *Current History*, vol.101 no.651 January 2002.
[31] *Ha'aretz* 27 February 2001.

the need for a state and the evacuation of settlements. Instead he projected a variation of the Jordanian option through 'a Benelux arrangement'.

Barak's secrecy before the Camp David summit in July 2000 led to antagonism and suspicion within Labour and the resignation of several right-wing parties from his government. The existence of the backchannel in Stockholm and secret talks between Shlomo Ben-Ami and Abu Ala a few months earlier had been exposed through a leak in the press, probably by Abu Mazen and his supporters. Arafat, too, was in a weakened position. The five-year interim period expired in May 1999 and the lack of results from the Oslo process was now bringing the first hints of a reversion to the armed struggle from the Islamists and by younger rivals such as Marwan Bargouti. Barak's failure to deliver Abu Dis and other villages near Jerusalem, as well as the non-implementation of the third redeployment, strengthened their resolve.

The evacuation of settlements and the lack of territorial contiguity were becoming central issues for the Palestinians. They wanted a state with East Jerusalem as their capital. UN Resolution 194 and 'the right of return' became a more prominent feature of Palestinian demands. The Israelis could never accept the absolutist interpretation of the Palestinian right of return since this would mean the demographic implosion of their state. They wanted Arafat to suppress Islamist and rejectionist groups which had been carrying out acts of terror against Israeli civilians.

The Camp David summit was indeed a 'tragedy of errors',[32] coloured by a lack of preparedness on the part of the Palestinians and an indifference on the part of Arafat. As far back as September 1999, Barak had told the Knesset that he would embark on negotiations for a final status agreement, implicitly bypassing the Oslo pathway. By the summer of 2000, he was ready to move in this direction instead of discussing a third redeployment. Yet he projected mixed messages. His negotiating technique was less than understood and his bottom line obscurantist. He insisted that no written records were kept and that no Israeli maps were placed on the negotiating table. There was also no personal chemistry between Arafat and Barak. Arafat was perceived as unwilling to place counter-proposals on the negotiating table. Barak believed that Arafat saw truth as relative.[33]

From his standpoint, Arafat felt bludgeoned into attending the summit. He preferred a gradualist approach rather than a total resolution within one meeting. This mindset led to inconsistency and a plethora of different

---

[32] Hussein Agha and Robert Malley, 'Camp David: The Tragedy of Errors', *New York Review of Books* 9 August 2001.
[33] Benny Morris, interview with Ehud Barak *New York Review of Books* 13 June 2002.

approaches from subordinates. Although Arafat wished any discussion of the issue of Jerusalem to be deferred to another time, Barak indicated that he was willing to divide the city, much to the consternation of the Right and religious parties in Israel.

The Israeli negotiators, Shlomo Ben-Ami and Gilad Sher, suggested the annexation of the central blocs of settlements close to the Green Line – some 10.5 per cent of the West Bank. The Palestinians would have most of the border with Jordan. In Jerusalem, the northern Arab neighbourhoods would be under Palestinian sovereignty. The inner neighbourhoods would be under Israeli sovereignty but serviced by the Palestinian capital, al-Quds.[34]

Unlike the Abu Mazen–Beilin agreement in 1995, Barak was reluctant to offer Israeli territory in compensation – and when he did, some 1 per cent, it did not match Palestinian demands for an equal land swap. Yet the Halutz dunes near Gaza – some 200 square kilometres in area – were available for exchange. The Palestinian negotiators were dissatisfied with the Israeli proposal since it did not offer territorial contiguity. Palestinian rhetoric centred on the fact that they now resided in 22 per cent of Mandatory Palestine and they were unable to decrease that figure.

Yet according to Ben-Ami, Arafat seemingly accepted 8 to 10 per cent of the West Bank without any insistence on equal swaps of territory. In easily passing over this essential point, discussion concentrated on Jerusalem and the right of return which produced deadlock and the failure of the summit. Arafat later reversed his position.[35]

Nabil Shaath said that he expected Israel to allow 10 to 20 per cent of the refugees to return – some 400,000–800,000 people.[36] At the end of failed negotiations, Israel reverted to proposing interim arrangements instead of the lofty heights of a final status agreement. Arafat rejected Clinton's proposal to divide 'the holy basin' into equal parts as well as Palestinian 'sovereign custodianship' of the Haram[37] while the Israelis exerted full sovereignty. Arafat argued that he could not defy international Muslim opinion on this. Significantly, no Arab leader was willing to intercede to persuade him to the contrary. The Palestinian leader instead demanded three quarters of the Old City including the Armenian quarter.[38]

The situation after the failure of a confused summit was therefore ripe for violence. Over decades, Arafat had perfected a method of manipulating difficult situations to ensure his own survival and to gain political

[34] Ross, *The Missing Peace* p. 674.   [35] Ben-Ami, *Scars of War* pp. 248–249.
[36] Ibid. p. 249.   [37] Ibid. pp. 256–257.   [38] *Al Hayat* 5 October 2002 in *Memri* no.428.

advantage. As early as May 1999, Arafat had warned that the PLO was quite capable of igniting another intifada. The escape route was to ride the tiger of political pressure and not to shrink from the use of violence if necessary. This had tided him over disastrous decisions such as the alignment with Saddam Hussein in 1990 or the war against Syria in the 1970s.

A LONG WALK TO DISASTER

Ariel Sharon, now the leader of the Likud in place of the defeated Netanyahu, was perceived as a caretaker chairman. Far behind in the opinion polls, his chances of winning an election were believed to be extremely slim.

The political situation in the summer of 2000 now provided him with a real opportunity to seize the crown. Barak had failed in negotiations with both the Palestinians and the Syrians. His government had disintegrated and his standing had plummeted in the opinion polls. In his absence, there had been a huge demonstration of over 150,000 against the Camp David talks. Barak had unprecedently offered to divide Jerusalem – something which not even the dovish Yossi Beilin had done in his clandestine negotiations with Abu Mazen in 1995. There were hints that he wanted Sharon's Likud to shore up the government coalition. Moreover, Palestinian resentment was palpable and it seemed that it was only a matter of time before there would be an outbreak of violence. This would automatically generate a move to the Right. Moreover, Arafat, if true to form, would not act against it, but implicitly guide it through his inaction.

Sharon's traditional mode of operation would be to exacerbate a situation which would pander to public fear and anxiety. He would then reveal himself as the saviour of that situation. His walk on the Temple Mount, accompanied by supporters and a phalanx of policemen, at the end of September 2000 was in character. It was designed in part to indicate that the Likud would never agree to the division of Jerusalem or to giving custodianship of the Temple Mount to the Palestinians. It proved, however, to be the catalyst which ignited the Intifada.

The Temple Mount for the Jews or the Haram as Sharif for the Muslims was the location where nationalism and religion met. Throughout 1929, there had been an officially inspired Arab campaign to interfere with Jewish worship at the Western Wall. In August 1929, against the advice of their elders and the police, there was an orderly silent march of 300 Jewish youths to the Western Wall which was matched by a Muslim demonstration the following day. The Mufti of Jerusalem, in response to the Jewish demonstration, called upon all Muslims to come to Jerusalem to defend the holy sites. Rumour had it that the Wall had been given to the Jews by the British who had also armed them. The British were standing by, it was said, and permitting the wholesale murder of innocent Muslims. It was even put around that a bomb had killed hundreds of Muslims on the Haram.

Such an incitement led to the killings of fifty-nine Jews in Hebron and Safed. In his testimony in camera to the Shaw Commission, Major Alan Saunders, the head of the Palestine Police, said that after the two demonstrations, he believed that the Arabs were only interested in driving out the Jews.

The whole Arab population wanted to make it clear to the world that they were not going to tolerate the Jews, the old or new ones. If a man was a Jew, it was good enough for him to be killed and stamped out.[39]

The Commission of Enquiry under Sir Walter Shaw sat at the end of 1929 and defined the Jewish demonstration 'as having been more than any other single incident an immediate cause of the outbreak'.[40]

Shortly after the Six Day war, Ben-Gurion had protested about the actions of Chief Rabbi Shlomo Goren who insisted on praying on the Temple Mount. In a letter to Abba Eban, Ben-Gurion complained that no one in government seemed to be aware of 'the grave danger that we can expect from this wild behaviour'.[41]

In more recent times, there had been a clash on the Temple Mount in September 1996 about the opening of an ancient Hasmonean tunnel – at the urgings of Netanyahu and the Likud mayor of Jerusalem, Ehud Olmert – despite warnings from Israeli intelligence.[42] In this incident, sixteen Israelis and eighty Palestinians were killed.

Although Sharon, when a government minister, had prevented the Temple Mount Faithful group of religious zealots from entering the area, now he insisted on his national right as a Jew to visit the Temple Mount. This tinderbox was a location which united nationalist and Islamist, Palestinian and Israeli Arab. Moreover, there was resentment that unless Muslims from Gaza worked in Israel, they were denied travel permission and therefore were unable to worship in the al-Aqsa mosque. Sharon's very presence, given his history, would be seen by the Palestinians as a provocation and a challenge.

[39] Testimony of Major Alan Saunders, Commission of Enquiry on the Disturbances of August 1929. Evidence taken in camera. PRO CO 967/91.
[40] Report on the Palestine Disturbances of August 1929, Command Paper 3530 p. 155.
[41] David Ben-Gurion, letter to Abba Eban 16 August 1967 in Ha'aretz 12 December 2002.
[42] Ha'aretz 25 September 1996.

Fatah's Tanzim had participated in Nakba day for the first time in the spring of 2000 and there had been three days of clashes. Sharon's walk on the Temple Mount was skating, as one writer commented, on 'the thinnest ice of the Arab–Israeli conflict'.[43] The potential for an outbreak of violence was very real. Sharon also understood that this was a sensitive time politically since the post–Camp David discussions about the future of the Temple Mount were ongoing. There was also Palestinian frustration that Arafat's intention to declare a state on 13 September had come and gone.

Conversely, there seemed to be little Palestinian awareness and sensitivity both in 2000 and previously to any Jewish emotional attachment to the Temple Mount. Arafat, Yasser Abed Rabbo and other Palestinians disputed the very existence of Herod's Temple on the site.[44] It was easier to perceive the issue as yet another Zionist incursion into the Palestinian domain. Yet Shlomo Ben-Ami, the Minister of Internal Security, was told by Israeli intelligence that there was no concerted risk of violence. This was implicitly confirmed by Jibril Rajoub, the Palestinian head of Preventive Security on the West Bank, who told Ben-Ami that Sharon could visit the Haram, but not enter a mosque on security grounds.[45]

Following Sharon's walk, there were violent attacks by Palestinians on Israelis in the vicinity of the Haram. The Israeli police switched to using live ammunition after the Chief of the Jerusalem police had been knocked unconscious. The killings of Palestinians led to the belief that the Israelis had carried out a premeditated massacre on the Haram. This, in turn, led to the use of live ammunition by Palestinians on the West Bank. The al-Aqsa Intifada had commenced.

In a letter to the US Secretary of State, Madeleine Albright, on 2 October 2000, Sharon criticized her for having insinuated that his visit to the Temple Mount 'caused tension' and that it ignited further disturbances. He argued that all this was part of a premeditated campaign initiated by the PA and pointed to an attack in Gaza some ten days previously.[46]

In reality, although there was deep Palestinian frustration, there had been little overt violence immediately before Sharon's walk. Sharon's visit further stirred an already volatile brew, erupting in an outburst of Palestinian anger. In turn, Arafat could claim that he bore no responsibility for later events and blamed them solely on Sharon's visit.[47] It therefore appeared initially that Sharon had played into Arafat's hands, but that

[43] Yoram Meital, *Peace in Tatters: Israel, Palestine and the Middle East* (London 2005) p. 96.
[44] *Le Monde* 25 September 2000.   [45] Ross, *The Missing Peace* p. 674.
[46] www.Freeman.org.   [47] *Ha'aretz* 24 June 2001.

assumption was predicated on the belief that Arafat could control the violence. However, Arafat did not have any strategy for the Intifada. It was clear to both Israelis and Palestinians that Arafat's attempt to exploit the Intifada could have terrible consequences. The Palestinian academic Yezid Sayigh wrote:

Whatever the material contribution of successive Israeli governments to the collapse of the Oslo framework or Israel's moral and legal responsibility for its own behaviour since autumn 2000, Arafat is guilty of strategic misjudgement, with consequences for the Palestinians of potentially historic proportions.[48]

Arafat was unconcerned when Fatah took up arms and instead left for minor events abroad.

THE DESCENT INTO THE ABYSS

After the failure of Camp David, Barak nullified any proposals made and instead brought back Peres and Beilin into the peacemaking process. Barak attempted to return to the legacy of Oslo. In one sense, it was already too late. Barak authorized the use of firearms against the Palestinians at the start of the Intifada and Shaul Mofaz, the Israeli Chief of Staff, responded to the violence with overwhelming force which effectively poured oil on the fire. Two iconic images inflamed the situation: the killing of twelve-year-old Mohammed al-Durrah, crouching with his father and caught in the crossfire, and the lynching and mutilation of two Israeli reservists in a police station in Ramallah. The Palestinians believed that the Israeli government and public did not want peace. The Israelis believed that the Palestinians wanted the destruction of Israel.

There was also considerable unrest amongst Israeli Arabs. The politics of identity had persuaded many Israeli Arabs to turn towards their own parties in the 1990s. In 1992, over half the Arab vote went to non-Arab parties. By the end of the decade, this had fallen to below 30 per cent. The Israeli Arabs consisted of approximately 20 per cent of Israel's population – the remnant who had neither fled nor been expelled in 1948. Arab academics in Israel considered them as 'an indigenous minority' which viewed 'the ethnic state that was founded on its homeland as a forcible dictate'.[49] They were an invisible part of the Israeli population and no major political party

---

[48] Yezid Sayigh, 'Arafat and the Anatomy of a Revolt', *Survival* vol.43, 2001, pp. 47–60.
[49] Nadim Rouhana, Nabil Saleh and Nimer Sultany, 'Voting without a Voice: About the Vote of the Palestinian Minority in the 16th Knesset Elections' in Asher Arian and Michal Shamir (eds.), *The Elections in Israel, 2003* (New Brunswick 2005) p. 218.

wished to admit them to government. They had many names: 'the generation of 1948', 'the Arab minority in 1948' and more recently 'Israeli Palestinians'. Sharon's walk ignited their frustrations as well.

A decision to investigate Hadash MK Mohammed Barakeh, who was accused of inciting Israeli Arabs to attack policemen, provoked a severe reaction by a meeting of Arab leadership in Kafr Manda. They threatened to attack police if they came to demolish Arab houses. There was also a strike in Nazareth to protest the police's incompetence in handing violence and crime.

In reaction to Sharon's walk and the killings on the Temple Mount, there were violent demonstrations in Umm al Fahm, Tamra, Nazareth, Fureidis and other villages on 1 October 2000. Israeli Arabs were killed and unrest spread to mixed Arab–Jewish towns such as Acre, Haifa and Tiberias. Buses were set alight, molotov cocktails were thrown and forest fires started.

In Wadi Nisnas, the Arab area of Haifa, Amram Mitzna, the Jewish mayor, and Arab members of the council attempted to calm the situation. In some mixed towns, attacks on individual Jews provoked Jewish youths to attack Arabs, ending in gangs of youths throwing stones at each other. In Jerusalem, ultra-orthodox youth attacked Palestinians working on building sites. In the Hatikva neighbourhood of Tel Aviv, demonstrators forced Arab employees of the Avazi restaurant to flee and then set it on fire. The Or Commission, which was established to investigate the outbreak, criticized the Israeli police for lack of preparedness and possibly using excessive force to disperse the mobs. It suggested that the police should actively promote the notion that Israeli Arabs were not enemies of the state. The violence claimed the lives of twelve Israeli Arabs, one Jew and one Palestinian citizen. The Or Commission recommended that Shlomo Ben-Ami, the minister responsible, should not hold that post again.

Frantic attempts were made by the international community to save the negotiating process from dissolving in chaos, but to no avail. Shlomo Ben-Ami attempted to break the cycle of violence by withdrawing troops from around Joseph's tomb in Nablus. There was also a lower police profile on the Temple Mount and in the Old City.

Moreover, time was running out. Barak had called a new election and would have to stand against Sharon – the man who refused to negotiate during an outbreak of violence. Clinton, who had done more than any other US President to bring the two sides together, was about to leave office. At the end of December 2000, a final meeting in the USA produced the Clinton Parameters.[50] These outlined the framework for negotiations

---

[50] Ross, *The Missing Peace* pp. 801–805.

and posited an end-of-conflict agreement and an end to all claims. It proposed giving 94 to 96 per cent of the West Bank to the Palestinians with a land swap of 1 to 3 per cent. It also considered the possibility of swapping leased land.

The settlements along the Green Line which contained 80 per cent of the settlers in blocs would be annexed by Israel with the least number of Palestinians affected. There would be territorial contiguity and an Israeli withdrawal over three years as an international force was gradually introduced. A small Israeli force would remain in the Jordan Valley for another three years. There would be Palestinian sovereignty over their airspace and a strong security force, but it would be 'a non-militarized state'. On Jerusalem, the Clinton Parameters stated that 'what is Arab is Palestinian, what is Jewish is Israeli.' There would be de facto Palestinian control of the Haram and Israeli sovereignty over the Western Wall. Clinton commented further that ' I believe Israel is prepared to acknowledge the moral and material suffering caused to the Palestinian people as a result of the 1948 war.'

In order to be consistent with the two-state approach, there would be 'no specific right of return to Israel'. There would be a return to historic Palestine and a right to a homeland. The return could be to five different locations:
1. a state of Palestine
2. the areas transferred to Palestine in a swap
3. rehabilitation in a host country
4. resettlement in a third country
5. admission to Israel
Clinton further argued that this should be the interpretation of UN Resolution 194.

The Clinton Parameters implied the evacuation of all Jewish settlements in Gaza and the establishment of a multi-billion-dollar fund. Clinton stipulated that negotiations could only take place within the Parameters, but that there could not be debate on the Parameters themselves.

Both the strength and weakness of the Clinton Parameters was that they were vague. For example, the Parameters did not preclude the Palestinians from forging military agreements and the concept of 'demilitarization' was not clearly defined. Although Barak clearly had reservations about agreeing to Palestinian sovereignty over the Temple Mount, the Israeli government accepted Clinton's approach on 28 December 2000 – only for Barak to formally backtrack ahead of the forthcoming election. Shaul Mofaz, the outspoken head of the IDF, openly criticized Barak's acceptance of the Clinton Parameters – 'an existential threat to Israel'.

Similarly Arafat initially refused to respond and then prevaricated to the point of rejection in a meeting with Clinton. Moreover he did not respond to advice from international leaders – and especially from within the Arab world.

Although the Parameters were flexible and not detailed on issues such as Jerusalem, borders, refugees and settlements, there was concerted Palestinian opposition. Yasser Abed Rabbo, the head the negotiating team, said that the Clinton proposals were one of 'the greatest ruses in history and belong in the same class as the Sykes–Picot agreement (of 1916)'.[51] Marwan Bargouti and Fatah wanted Arafat to take a more aggressive stand.

The Islamists warned Arafat that acceptance of the Clinton Parameters would mean a more violent and intense Intifada. Arafat's concern was reflected in the release of one of the senior Hamas leaders, Abdel Aziz al Rantisi, from prison. Abu Ala, who had negotiated the Declaration of Principles in Oslo, said that they did not meet the minimal requirements of the Palestinian people. The Parameters were also opposed by the Communists, the independents of the Democratic Alliance, the youth and students, the Tanzim and the leaders of the refugee camps. The Mufti of Jerusalem rejected the idea of any Palestinian concessions over the Temple Mount. Some Palestinian spokesmen even suggested that there would be a referendum.

All this reflected Palestinian public opinion in January 2001. During the previous couple of months, the Israeli onslaught, targeted assassinations and general collective punishment hardened Palestinian opinion against even the most reasonable of offers. Palestinian newspapers refused to take advertisements for Israeli products before the festival of Id al Fitr.[52]

While mindful of entrenched domestic opinion, Arafat also believed that he could lever further concessions from Barak and seemed oblivious – until it was too late – of the looming shadow of Sharon waiting to take Israel in a different direction. After a considerable delay, Arafat produced a standard answer to Clinton's ideas at a White House meeting in early January 2001. He embraced them with a plethora of reservations. Ben-Ami commented wryly: 'He never formally said no, but his yes was a no.'

A last throw of the dice came days before the election at Taba. Barak was prepared for an 8 per cent annexation of the West Bank and an equal swap of land.[53] The Palestinians rejected this and dismissed the possibility of dismantling over 100 settlements and the handing them over to Palestinian refugees. The settlement blocs were considered as outposts of Israel rather than as settlements in their own right.

---

[51] *Ha'aretz* 1 January 2001.   [52] *Ha'aretz* 28 December 2000.   [53] Ben-Ami, *Scars of War* p. 274.

Arafat may have astutely waited for Bush rather than respond to the Clinton Parameters. He initially hoped that the new Republican administration would be more sympathetic to the Palestinian cause, given the approach of the first President Bush. Ben-Ami commented:

One would have had to be blind not to understand that these were also the last days of the Israeli Left in power, maybe for many years. An Israeli team consisting of Yossi Sarid, Yossi Beilin, Amnon Shahak and myself as its head cannot be repeated in years to come. In other words if an agreement was not to be reached then, there would be no agreement at all, and both Israelis and Palestinians would be thrown into a wilderness of blood, despair and economic decline. Nevertheless, I discerned no sense of urgency or missed opportunity among my Palestinian friends.[54]

Was this 'a moment of truth' for Arafat who could not accept partition and an end to the armed struggle? Yet he had embarked on the diplomatic search for a two-state solution after 1974. He had agreed to the Oslo formulations in 1993 despite widespread Palestinian opposition. Were the Palestinians simply unable psychologically to give up the absolutist interpretation of the right of return of an estimated four million refugees and their descendants? As Ben-Ami bitterly remarked: 'The Palestinians looked for justice rather than for a solution.'[55]

Yossi Beilin further noted an implicit weariness of Arafat's stand by the Palestinian negotiators at Taba.[56] Although progress appeared to have been made, Taba marked the last diplomatic gasp of Barak's 'peace cabinet' which had coalesced around him in the dying weeks of his administration. Arafat heralded in a new era when he accused Israel of using depleted uranium at the Davos summit with his fellow Nobel Peace Prize winner, Shimon Peres, on the same platform.[57] Barak broke off talks with the Palestinians. A few days later he lost the election to Sharon by a margin of nearly 25 per cent on a very low turnout and an Israeli Arab boycott. The Palestinian rejectionists had elected the Israeli rejectionists.

---

[54] Ibid. p. 277.   [55] Ibid. p. 279.
[56] Beilin, *The Path to Geneva* p. 230.   [57] *Ha'aretz* 29 January 2001.

CHAPTER 13

'He does not stop at the red light'

2001: A SHARON ODYSSEY

Arik Sharon achieved his life's ambition when he decisively beat Barak in 2001 in the direct election for the premiership with 36.39 per cent of the eligible vote. Because of Barak's indifference to Israeli Arab concerns and the riots in October, there was a mass abstention of the Arab vote. Ironically, Sharon had made disparaging remarks about Israeli Arabs over the years including that 'it was not the place for Israeli Arabs to determine who would be Prime Minister'.[1] Yet in not voting for Barak, they did partially determine that Sharon was elected by a huge majority.

The Palestinian reservations about the Camp David proposals and the Clinton Parameters and the minor progress at Taba were seen by the Israeli public as rejectionism which deliberately dovetailed with the outbreak of violence. A comparison with 1936, the outbreak of the Arab Revolt, was in the air. A few urged havlagah (self-restraint), but an increasing majority believed in retaliation. Sharon was widely seen in Ben-Gurion's clothes at this moment in history: someone who would be politically and militarily decisive – and protect the Jews from the suicide bombers.

Sharon indicated that his past thinking had not changed. He had told a right-wing rally in November 2000 that 'the Oslo agreement no longer existed'.[2] In a visit to a high school in mid-January 2001 during the election campaign, he said that he regarded the Lebanon war of 1982 as one of the most justified of Israel's wars – and subsequently as 'a war of salvation'.[3] In a press conference in April 2001, he declared that 'the war of independence has not ended'. The title of Uzi Benziman's 1985 book *He Does Not Stop at the Red Light* therefore seemed to be entirely appropriate for the Sharon of 2001: an unstoppable political entrepreneur who knew no boundaries.

[1] *Ma'ariv* 27 December 1989. [2] *Ha'aretz* 23 November 2000.
[3] *Jerusalem Post* 26 September 2002.

His initial approach therefore seemed to be merely a continuation of the past and there was no hint of any disengagement from any part of the West Bank and Gaza. He did not believe that any agreement based on mutual trust would last and that only a deterrence based on Israel's military prowess could maintain a state of non-war. Sharon did not believe that there would be 'a permanent status agreement' in the short term. It was more a question of managing the conflict than of resolving it. His thinking was based on the belief that Israel's lack of legitimacy in the Arab world was the essential cause for the longevity of the conflict. Only when there had been real reform and change within the Arab world, when terrorism and incitement ceased, he argued, could a genuine peace agreement be arrived at.

A situation must not develop in which Israel retreats and is chased by terror. Once you accept that, it will never end. Terror will keep chasing us.[4]

It also opened the way to unilateral action and ignoring Mahmoud Abbas. Sharon's bleak depiction of the future with no grand vision of an end to the conflict coincided with the evaporation of the idealism that had fuelled the Israeli peace camp. The failure of Barak, the rise of suicide bombing and Islamism generally and the machinations of Arafat had burst the bubble. The Clinton Parameters and the Taba talks were airbrushed out of existence by the new political orders in both Tel Aviv and Washington. When Arafat telephoned Sharon a couple of days after the election and suggested a resumption of negotiations, Sharon bluntly responded that there first had to be 'a complete cessation of violence'. In one sense, Arafat's refusal and probable inability to confront the Islamists as well as his desire to ride the Intifada to extract political advantage had played straight into Sharon's hands.

Sharon's ideological approach of never negotiating under 'threats of terror' and his projection of himself as the guardian of Israel's security had been constant throughout his political odyssey and guided his approach now as Prime Minister. In an address at a memorial ceremony on the anniversary of the Yom Kippur war in 2001, he argued that if Israel had responded forcefully to Egyptian missile movements in August 1970, the war might not have broken out at all. Similarly, if there had been a prompt response to Palestinian violations of the Oslo Accords, then the Intifada itself might have been averted.[5] In this fashion, Sharon promoted himself

[4] Ari Shavit, 'The General', *New Yorker* 23 and 30 January 2006.
[5] *Ha'aretz* 18 September 2002.

as the voice of the harsh reality. It was the very opposite of Peres's 'New Middle East'.

Moreover, Sharon never accepted the concept of a two-state solution in the sense of Israel and Palestine, side by side, as two territorially contiguous entities. The Palestinians would remain encased in 'truncated enclaves of humiliatingly circumscribed independence', amounting to 42 per cent of the territories.[6] New outposts and the expansion of settlements therefore continued apace on the West Bank. The term 'natural growth' was introduced to cover not only the natural increase of the settler population, but also the influx of new settlers from Israel proper.

The US State Department also announced with Sharon's election that the Clinton Parameters were no longer a US or Presidential proposal. George W. Bush was initially as uninvolved as Bill Clinton had been integrated in the vagaries of Middle East peacemaking.

Sharon's first move had been an attempt to draw the defeated Labour party into government and to appoint Barak as Minister of Defence. Although Barak declined, this offer signalled that there would be no change and indeed an intensification of Barak's approach to the Intifada. Barak had initiated the policy of targeted killings of those Palestinians planning or enacting acts of terror against Israeli civilians. On 9 November 2000, a helicopter gunship killed Hussein Abayat, a senior Fatah activist whom the IDF accused of masterminding attacks in the Bethlehem area and in southern Jerusalem. It coincided with Arafat's meeting with Clinton and provoked a response from Marwan Barghouti that 'Fatah would respond by continuing and expanding the Intifada'.[7]

In the past, Israel had occasionally embarked on targeted killings of leaders of militant groups which had carried out acts of terror against Israeli civilians. Zuheir Mohssein of al-Saiqa had been killed in 1979 on the French Riviera, and in 1995, Islamic Jihad's founder, Fathi Shikaki, had met a similar fate. Israeli helicopter gunships eliminated Abbas Mussawi, the Secretary-General of Hezbollah, in 1992, when a convoy of cars in which he was travelling was hit. The targeted killing of Yehiya Ayash, the Hamas bomb maker, in January 1996 had generated a wave of bus bombings in the urban centres of Israel and been a major factor in the defeat of Peres at the polls a few months later. This opened an ongoing debate both within the Defence establishment and within the public at large. The killing of Mussawi, Ayash and Shikaki clearly had not paralyzed their organizations and others had quickly replaced them.

---

[6] *Ha'aretz* 13 April 2001.   [7] *Ha'aretz* 10 November 2000.

The other side of the argument was that such operations disrupted the plans of suicide bombers and acted as a deterrent. By 2001, the IDF was concerned about the Lebanonization of the Intifada where Palestinian Islamists would emulate the example of Hezbollah. Other commentators argued that the policy of targeted killings derived from domestic considerations.

The hits were meant to placate an angry and frustrated public, drum up public opinion in support of the government and its decisions, and raise national morale. In practice, the liquidations only broaden the cycle of violence and create a superfluous balance of revenge.[8]

An additional problem was that the use of Apache helicopters firing anti-tank missiles at the instigators of suicide bombings also killed innocent bystanders. When Abayat was killed, a fifty-two-year-old mother of seven was also killed and many others wounded. A small number of pilots refused to carry out such missions because they disagreed with the morality of such a policy. Neither did it make any difference whether a target had previously supported the peace process. When Thabet Thabet, the Secretary-General of Fatah in Tulkarm, was killed, it was pointed out by many left-wing Israelis that he had been a supporter of the Oslo Accords and had participated in activities with Peace Now to promote coexistence. The Likud's Dan Meridor, who was chairman of the Knesset Foreign Affairs and Defence Committee, expressed opposition to the assassination policy. He argued that Israeli law did not allow people to be harmed without trial unless they were preparing or in the process of carrying out an act of terror. The election of Sharon and a plethora of Islamist-inspired suicide bombings swept away such legal niceties.

Sharon fine-tuned the conflict and escalated it when he deemed it necessary. Following a suicide bombing in Netanya in May 2001, F-16 fighters were employed for the first time to attack Palestinian security headquarters in Nablus and Ramallah. This led to the recall of the Egyptian Ambassador to Israel. Yet Sharon kept open the lines of communication with Arafat as his son, Omri, met the Palestinian leader on several occasions in April 2001. After the bombing of a Tel Aviv night club, the Dolphinarium, when many teenagers were killed, Arafat for the first time condemned such violence and promised to rein in Fatah. Such a comment did not please those – within both Fatah and the Islamists – who wished to continue the armed struggle in the belief that they could

[8] Yossi Melman, 'Wiping out the Liquidation Policy', *Ha'aretz* 12 November 2000.

thwart the military determination of the Israelis to crush them. Any Israeli reverse was lauded and magnified. Even the space shuttle *Columbia*, whose crew included an Israeli astronaut, was deemed to be on an espionage mission against the Arab and Muslim nations. One Islamic preacher saw its explosion and the destruction of its crew as God's punishment and a demonstration of 'divine omnipotence'.[9]

A report of the Palestinian security service analyzed the timing of the bombings.[10] It concluded that Hamas and Islamic Jihad were provided with information by sympathizers within the PA and planned the bombings with political as well as purely military objectives. Thus the attack on the Sbarro restaurant in August 2001 was designed to disrupt an initiative to send international observers to Bethlehem and Rafah to implement the Mitchell Report. The attack on a Jerusalem bus in June 2002 was designed to undermine the authority of a new Palestinian Interior Minister who had been foisted on Arafat.

The Intifada took on a culture of nihilism, coloured by suicide bombings directed at Israeli civilians and targeted killings which also killed Palestinian civilian bystanders. In March 2001, a ten-month-old Israeli, Shalhavet Pass, was killed in her father's arms. In May 2001, a four-month-old Palestinian, Iman Hijjo, became the youngest victim of the conflict. Two days before the Twin Towers were attacked, a fifty-five-year-old Galilee villager became the first Israeli Arab suicide bomber when he detonated his load on the platform of Nahariya railway station. Moreover, suicide bombings did not recognize any difference between Israeli doves and hawks. The Moment café, a favourite meeting spot for Jerusalem's liberals, was blown up, killing Peace Now activists who had just come from a demonstration outside the Prime Minister's residence. Protesters against the occupation had been killed by a protester against the occupation.

In 2001, the cost of a suicide bombing was estimated at $142.[11] Suicide bombers were not the simple-minded and the impoverished. Neither were they all male and adults. Some were those who had dishonoured their families and this was a path towards erasing their shame. Others were not. Hanadi Jaradet, a young lawyer by profession, mourned the deaths of her brother and cousin at the hands of the Israelis. She blew up Maxim's restaurant, an Arab–Jewish joint enterprise in Haifa, wiping out entire families. For the Palestinians – even for those who opposed the Islamists and disagreed with suicide bombing – these people were heroic martyrs who

[9] *Jerusalem Post* 3 February 2003.   [10] *Ha'aretz* 8 January 2004.
[11] *Sunday Telegraph* 9 December 2001.

had sacrificed themselves for the cause of a free Palestine. For the Israelis, they were inhuman terrorists who murdered indiscriminately and illogically. Ceasefires came and went – and the suffering continued.

The new Bush administration had initially distanced itself from the Israel–Palestine conflict as a reaction to the apparent failure of the Clinton initiatives. Iraq was now a priority on the new US political agenda, and there was an ongoing wrangle between Powell and the State Department and neo-conservative ideologues such as Cheney, Rumsfeld and Wolfowitz over the direction of foreign policy. The publication of the Mitchell Report in May 2001 called for a cessation of violence and a return to the negotiating table. In the heat of escalating violence, however, such recommendations were easily glossed over, and instead the USA concentrated on 'confidence building measures'. With the Americans immobilized and the Europeans unwilling to criticize Arafat too harshly, Sharon stepped up his retaliatory policy and intensified the policy of targeted killings. State Department pronouncements bemoaned Palestinian suicide bombings and Israeli targeted killings in the same breath, but Cheney by August 2001 had already begun to voice 'understanding' for Israeli military policy.

The catastrophe of 9/11 was the pivotal event that tipped US policy towards the conflict in the direction of the neo-conservatives. On 17 September 2001, Sharon gave a number of interviews indicating that he would not change his policy on negotiating while there was still violence. The Bush administration, however, wanted a period of calm in the Middle East while it tried to build a coalition of states in the Arab world to align them with 'the war against terror'. Sharon, however, was adamant that Israel would not carry out a policy of self-restraint. It would not pay a necessary price to please Bush. There would be no concessions, Sharon argued, while violence continued. Instead, under the cover of world attention directed towards New York, there was an intensification of retaliatory attacks on the Palestinians and Sharon refused to allow Peres to meet Arafat.

Sharon as Prime Minister had attempted to curb his predilection for bombast and provocation. Yet he occasionally slipped back into his old ways when he likened American attempts to build a consensus in the Arab world at the expense of Israel as undiluted appeasement and Munich all over again. The White House was aghast and Sharon eventually apologized.

Bush had accepted a two-state solution and Powell began working on plans for 'a viable Palestinian state' without any consultation with the Israelis. Sharon responded by working with his Foreign Minister, Labour's Shimon Peres, to develop a 'Gaza First' option, based on 'separation by agreement'. Peres had advocated the dismantling of the Gaza settlements since this would permit a measure of contiguity for an emerging Palestinian state and the development of a Benelux economic arrangement of Israel, Palestine and Jordan. Sharon expressed extreme reservations about any settlement evacuation since he had been permitting the construction of outposts. Yet he had seemingly re-evaluated his view of Palestinian nationalism. His view that 'Jordan is Palestine', he believed, was now somewhat redundant because of the reality of the Palestinian Authority.[12] This was a far cry from his 1974 call for the overthrow of King Hussein and transforming the Hashemite kingdom into a Palestinian state.[13] Peres's proposal also met resistance from the Left. Yossi Beilin argued that this represented a dilution of the Oslo spirit and the Clinton Parameters. Sharon's opponents in the Likud soon forced Sharon to backtrack, explaining that this was merely a means to soften Bush's new approach.

At the same time, Sharon responded militarily to the assassination of Minister for Tourism Rechavam Ze'evi by the PFLP. Ze'evi, who was a vociferous proponent of voluntary transfer, was from Sharon's Mapai generation and had fought in 1948. Sharon also broadened the IDF's area of operation into Area A, the Palestinian area of control as proposed by Oslo II in 1995. Arafat's avoidance policy came under assault not only militarily by the Israelis, but also internally by figures such as Mohammed Dahlan.

Washington continued to project a two-handed approach. Yet Bush was clearly tiring of Arafat's static approach to attacks on Israeli civilians. In a speech to the UN in November 2001, he commented that there was 'no such thing as a good terrorist'. In addition, the USA put Hamas and Islamic Jihad on its list of terrorist organizations. Powell sent General Anthony Zinni to the region to facilitate the initiation of negotiations. Yet Zinni's visit was marred by suicide bombings in Afula, Hadera and Jerusalem. Bush was highly irritated by this attempt by the Islamists to wreck any movement towards resuming negotiations and became more critical of Arafat's approach. Bush's comments about action rather than words produced further suicide bombings and new attacks on Palestinian targets in response. However, this time, the US response was far more muted and less condemnatory. Sharon's government noted this change and announced that Arafat through his inaction had become irrelevant. Sharon sent tanks to surround his headquarters in Ramallah.

Although Arafat had placed the spiritual mentor of Hamas, Sheikh Yassin, under house arrest, the situation began to deteriorate in 2002.

---

[12] *Ha'aretz* 13 April 2001.   [13] *Ma'ariv* 29 November 1974.

Airstrikes against Palestinian police positions were resumed. In January, the Israelis stopped an arms boat, the *Karine A*, containing fifty tons of war materiel and documentation which tied it to the Palestinian Authority. Sharon confided to the daily *Ma'ariv* that he wished that he could have eliminated Arafat twenty years previously in Beirut.[14] Transient ceasefires were broken by Islamist bombings and Israeli reprisals. The Saudis floated a new peace plan which provoked interest, and the US supported UN Security Council Resolution 1397 based on the Mitchell plan. Yet within the Likud, a hardening of the line was taking place. A Likud central committee meeting voted to reject a Palestinian state 'west of the River Jordan' despite Sharon's pleas that it would aggravate relations with Washington. It also allowed Netanyahu to relaunch himself as the standard bearer of the Right and demand a stronger approach from Sharon.

Once again, US moves to end the bloodshed were wrecked by the bombing of the Park Hotel in Netanya, just as the Passover service was commencing. This was followed by further suicide bombings in Jerusalem, Tel Aviv and Haifa. This tipped the balance in the cabinet against any dialogue with Arafat and isolated advocates such as Peres. Sharon responded with Operation Defensive Shield whereby the major Palestinian cities were once more occupied and searched for militants and armaments. By advancing into Area A, this move effectively reversed the Oslo II agreement. In March and April 2002 alone, 479 Palestinians and 78 Israelis died. Even though over 300 Palestinian public figures in a statement condemned the policy of suicide bombing,[15] a beleaguered and embattled Arafat in his compound became more and more a target for US criticism.

On 24 June 2002, Bush gave a speech which effectively redefined US policy on the Israel–Palestine conflict. Its emphasis was essentially on regime change in the Palestinian Authority – the replacement of Arafat – and the democratization of government. This was a victory for the neoconservatives in the Bush administration and a conceptual reappraisal in approaches to a solution. The Palestinians were asked to elect new leaders 'not compromised by terror' and to build 'a practicing democracy, based on tolerance and liberty'. A free-market economic system, a new constitution and the establishment of a judicial system were seen as vital components. Only then would the USA support 'the creation of a Palestinian state whose borders and certain aspects of its sovereignty will be provisional until resolved as part of a final settlement'. The majority of Bush's speech laid the

---

[14] *Ma'ariv* 1 February 2002.   [15] *Al-Quds* 19 June 2002.

blame at the feet of Arafat and 'an unaccountable few'. It was a remarkable demolition of Arafat – without naming him and the regime that he had established. Arafat had survived nine Israeli Prime Ministers and seven US Presidents, but he was now confronted by both Bush and Sharon. The Bush speech symbolically relegated both the Oslo Accords and Arafat, the 1994 Nobel Peace Prize winner, to history. It also stood in stark contrast to the approaches of both Peres and Powell, who believed that only Arafat could negotiate on behalf of the Palestinians – and deliver. One Israeli writer commented:

The Rose Garden speech is a fairly profound Jeffersonian understanding – an understanding that draws a clear moral boundary between those who are committed to democracy and stability and those who are not so committed, between those who want life here and those who sow death here. . . . For more than a generation, the Palestinians have made sophisticated use of liberal–democratic terminology in order to attack Israel, without seeing this terminology as seriously obligating themselves as well.[16]

For Sharon and the Likud, this represented a tremendous victory in delegitimizing Arafat and neutralizing his involvement. Yet the issue of reform and democracy was one that divided the Likud. Natan Sharansky, a former refusenik and a product of the Soviet dissident movement, and Bibi Netanyahu, an Americanized Israeli close to the neo-conservatives, were true believers. Sharon and others probably perceived such talk of democracy to be mere wishful thinking on the part of the unworldly Americans. Neither the right of return of the refugees nor Jerusalem was mentioned. Israel was asked to do very little immediately; the onus was on the Palestinians to reform.

The Bush speech was undoubtedly a prelude to the approach taken in Iraq after the invasion in 2003. But it also demanded an Israeli withdrawal to the pre-Intifada borders and a cessation of settlement activity as detailed in the Mitchell Report. The framework of a provisional state would probably be established in Areas A and B – some 42 per cent of the West Bank and most of Gaza. This posed a challenge to the Israeli Right and to the settlers. It suited Sharon as he did not wish to develop any meaningful political initiatives before a general election in 2003. His energies were directed towards military action to reduce the number of attacks on Israeli civilians and to dislodge Arafat from his position of power.

---

[16] Ari Shavit, 'A Democratic Palestine, with No Discounts', *Ha'aretz* 27 June 2002.

THE PALESTINIAN STRUGGLE WITHIN

After the capture of Saddam Hussein, the Israeli military permitted the publication of details about an attempt to assassinate the Iraqi leader in November 1992. The Sayeret Matkal, an elite special operations force, would have landed commandos in Iraq and fired sophisticated missiles at him during a funeral. The attempt was cancelled, after an accident at the Tze'elim training base in the southern Negev which resulted in the deaths of five soldiers. Although the plan was never put before the cabinet, Rabin's initiative to proceed with the attempt illustrated the Israeli fear that Saddam, given his history of bellicosity, would attack Israel with biological or chemical weapons.[17]

Before the invasion of Iraq in 2003, the Israeli Health Ministry was ready to initiate a massive inoculation campaign against smallpox for an estimated 2.0–2.8 million people. In August 2002, the security cabinet had proceeded with the inoculation of 15,000 frontline rescue workers and military personnel, ambulance services, hospital and health maintenance organization employees, firemen, policemen, soldiers, Environment Ministry officials – and members of the charitable organization Zaka, which collected body parts, in the event of suicide bombings.[18] The Tel Aviv University Peace Index for the end of December 2002 indicated that 58.1 per cent of Israelis supported retaliation if Iraq attacked Israel with conventional weapons. This figure rose to 81.4 per cent if Saddam used non-conventional weapons. Although the United States strenuously opposed Israeli involvement in the war, Sharon reserved his right to respond, especially if Israel suffered casualties or was hit with biological and chemical weapons.[19] American Patriot batteries were posted around Israel's population centres, and the US administration offered to cover expenses resulting from preparations made prior to the war.

When the invasion took place, Hamas organized a protest of 30,000 in Gaza after Friday prayers where there were calls for Saddam to bomb Tel Aviv. *Al-Quds*, the largest Palestinian daily, described the collapse of Baghdad as a nakba (catastrophe). Leading neo-conservatives in the US administration such as Paul Wolfowitz were confident, however, that a pacified Iraq would allow them to proceed with 'pushing for a Palestinian state' and 'dealing with the settlements'.[20]

The pending invasion of Iraq and the easy election victory of Sharon over Labour's Amram Mitzna plus the deepening spiral of Palestinian despair

[17] *Ha'aretz* 16 December 2003. [18] *Ha'aretz* 23 December 2002.
[19] *Jerusalem Post* 26 September 2002. [20] *Washington Post* 17 January 2003.

and nihilism persuaded the Egyptians to convene a meeting of twelve Palestinian factions in Cairo in the hope of facilitating a ceasefire and a return to normal politics. However, they were unable to reach an agreement because of the opposition of the Islamists. Such moves were actually initiated by Palestinians close to Mahmoud Abbas, the PLO Executive Committee secretary, and European diplomats who had met in Doha, Qatar, in August 2002. Hamas offered to consider a halt to attacks on Israeli civilians within Israel itself, but not across the Green Line, if the Israeli government ceased all its attacks on Palestinian civilians. Hamas was in a weakened position and facing a financial crisis through a curtailing of Saudi funding after 9/11. Sharon's response was brutally reductionist – all Palestinian organizations, with no exceptions, must clearly commit to an end to terror and acts of violence. Only then would Israel agree to halt its military activities inside the Palestinian areas.

In November 2002, Mahmoud Abbas spoke to the leaders of the popular committees of the refugee camps in Gaza. He depicted the armed struggle as a deviation from the natural course of the Intifada. It was 'a military battle, not a popular uprising expressing popular rage'. He ridiculed those who had initially argued that the Intifada would bring down the Sharon government and said that what had really taken place was 'the complete destruction of everything we built under Oslo'. He further commented:

As a result of Oslo, we returned to our cities and obtained some of our homeland and here we are, in it. The phenomenon of the lost Palestinian at the airport and border control is over, and now he can return to his homeland if he wishes. Between 250,000 and 300,000 people returned to the homeland. The refugee problem still exists, but at least the phenomenon of displacement has been ended by negotiations and peace. It was impossible to end it by war.[21]

Many Palestinian fighters, however, believed that Israeli society was on the point of disintegration, its morale undermined by suicide bombings and continuous attacks. Mahmoud Abbas's criticisms were dismissed. In February 2003, he proposed 'a one year demilitarization of the Intifada' which was immediately rejected by both the Islamists and the PFLP. They pointed instead to the declaration by the al-Aqsa Martyrs' Brigades, the military wing of the Fatah Movement, that it would resume bombings deep into Israel. The Islamists claimed that this was proof that Mahmoud Abbas and those who adopted his stand represented a small minority not only among the Palestinian people, but also within Fatah itself.

---

[21] *Al Hayat* 26 November 2002 in Dispatch 449, MEMRI 15 December 2002.

Mahmoud Abbas attempted to prevent Hamas and Islamic Jihad from establishing themselves as a substitute for the PLO and instead tried to persuade the Islamists to join the PLO. Hamas reasoned, on the other hand, that it would gain recruits from Fatah and boost its standing in the Palestinian street by maintaining its independence and its reputation for probity. At the Cairo conference, Hamas's Ismail Haniyeh proposed a comprehensive reform process within the PLO's departments and institutions. Such ideas resonated with the public sense of disappointment with the PLO's Tunis elite.[22] The British, unlike the Americans, were very keen to cultivate the Islamists and to co-opt them into a process of demilitarization. The US view was that Hamas remained a terrorist organization and should be disempowered.

In May 2002, following concerted international pressure on Arafat, a former International Monetary Fund official, Salam Fayyad, who had been appointed Finance Minister, began to introduce modern financial practices. Fayyad, later appointed as Palestinian Prime Minister in June 2007, commissioned a study by Standard & Poor and the Democracy Council, a non-profit organization, as part of an effort to track down the Palestinian Authority's assets.

The PLO, however, had found it difficult to make the transition to a governing body and was engaged in dozens of commercial enterprises. The Palestinian Authority possessed a 23 per cent stake in the Oasis Hotel Casino Resort in Jericho, which was valued at $28.5 million. In addition, Arafat ensured that he was the paymaster of a plethora of individuals and institutions, especially military groups, in order to exert a centralized political control. An official report compiled by the IMF therefore indicated that some 8 per cent of the Palestinian Authority's budget was managed by Arafat. The IMF analysis, based on data provided by the PA, indicated that between its establishment in 1995 and the onset of the Intifada in 2000, some $900 million in revenues was simply unaccounted for. According to the report, the 2003 budget for Arafat's office totalled $74 million, of which a sum of $34 million was listed as 'transfers'.

The IMF report also published, for the first time, the official number of security personnel registered as receiving wages from the PA – 56,128, almost 20,000 more than the number stipulated by the Oslo Accords. Many security personnel thereby received their wages in cash via the heads of the various security organizations.[23]

---

[22] *Al-Sharq al-Awsat* 23 February 2003.   [23] *Ha'aretz* 11 November 2003.

Moreover, American pressure forced the release of customs duties totalling $100 million that Israel should have transferred to the Palestinians. During the Intifada, Israel had argued that Arafat would utilize it for his own schemes and for financing acts of terror. With Fayyad acting competently, the PA began to pay off unpaid bills for essentials such as electricity, water and fuel. Rumours abounded, however, of Arafat's secret bank accounts in Switzerland and monthly transfers of $100,000 to his wife and child in Paris. Yet even after the publication of the IMF report, Arafat's office still administered 10 per cent of the total expenditure in September 2003.[24]

The Islamist response to Israeli military actions was the firing of Qassam rockets into Israel and particularly at the town of Sderot, just inside the Israeli border. The PA seemed both unable and unwilling to prevent the use of these primitive missiles. Hamas wanted to develop these homemade rockets so as to achieve a kind of mutual deterrence with Israel. Hezbollah was the model to emulate since they had responded to any Israeli incursion into southern Lebanon by firing a barrage of Katyusha rockets at civilian dwellings in northern Israel. Hamas's political office in Damascus remained in contact with Hezbollah in Lebanon and was fortified by Iranian and Syrian support.

Hezbollah periodically attempted to encourage the Palestinian Islamists to achieve a military stand-off in Gaza similar to the one which prevailed along Israel's northern border. Hezbollah therefore attempted to infiltrate agents into the Palestinian territories. There were several cases of Islamists who had received military training and attended classes in chemistry and physics in Iran and Sudan. Ibrahim Mohammed Ja'bari, who attempted to enter Gaza in March 1999, admitted that he had been trained by the al-Quds military academy in Teheran and his scientific study included the use of radiological substances.[25]

In January 2001, Israeli security officials arrested Hezbollah agent Jihad Shuman, who had a British passport in the name of Gerard Shuman. In October 2002, security officials arrested Fawzi Ayoub, a senior Hezbollah official, who had entered Israel on a forged US passport. In May 2003, Israel's navy seized a fishing boat carrying a Hezbollah activist, Hamad Muslam Moussa Abu Amra, an expert in bomb-making. The boat carried thirty-six CDs with instructions on how to assemble bomb belts for suicide bombers. Israel also discovered twenty-five detonators for rockets and a radio-activation system for remote-control bombs.

---

[24] *Jerusalem Post* November 18, 2003.   [25] *Yediot Aharanot* 8 August 1999.

In the past, Iran, Hezbollah and Ahmed Jibril's Popular Front for the Liberation of Palestine–General Command were all involved in smuggling weapons to the territories. The Israeli navy intercepted two seaborne attempts when it apprehended the *San Torini* in May 2001 and the *Karine A* in January 2002. The latter contained Katyushas, Saggar anti-tank missiles, Kalashnikovs, mines, mortars – and over 3,000 pounds of C4 explosive for the arming of suicide bombers. Even Arafat entertained the possibility that the *Karine A* was a Hezbollah operation.[26]

Hamas's refusal to call for a ceasefire persuaded Sharon to continue the armed campaign against the Islamists, overriding European pleas for restraint. Many Israelis were sceptical about a hudna – a ceasefire of limited duration – was it merely an opportunity to rearm and regroup? The first hudna had been negotiated with the Quraysh tribe by the Prophet in Mecca in 628 and then abrogated several years later. To what extent was any ceasefire merely tactical? Arafat's speech in South Africa in May 1994 seemed to reflect his understanding that the Oslo Accords were of a transient nature.[27] This was not exactly a comment out of the blue as Arafat's early background in the Muslim Brotherhood had given rise to similar utterances during his career.[28]

Moreover, Hamas was ideologically unable to recognize Israel. It was often unable to mention it by name, preferring 'the Zionist entity' or 'the occupation government'. Palestine was regarded as part of Dar al-Islam (the domain of Islam), whose sovereignty could never be transferred to non-Muslims. The Hamas charter stated that there could be no concession of principle in 'granting recognition to murderers and usurpers as rights which are not theirs over land in which they had not been born'. Hamas perceived the struggle with the Jews in almost existential terms as one which could last centuries. Therefore recognizing Israel through the giving up of land would be a betrayal of future generations. Peace initiatives were seen as illusory. Indeed, the Hamas charter envisaged a Palestinian state won through jihad (holy war) and not through negotiation. Its founder, Ahmed Yassin, argued that terror attacks were religiously legitimate. In September 2003, he reiterated his belief that the only method of securing the release of Palestinian prisoners was to kidnap and exchange Israeli soldiers. In December 2003, in an interview in *Der Spiegel*, Yassin rejected the continued existence of Israel beside an independent Palestinian state and suggested that a Jewish state could be established in

[26] *Ha'aretz* 23 June 2002.   [27] *Ha'aretz* 23 May 1994.
[28] Shlomo Ben-Ami, *Scars of War: Wounds of Peace: The Israeli–Arab Tragedy* (London 2006) p. 214.

Fig. 13.1. Sheikh Ahmed Yassin, the mentor of Hamas, on trial in Gaza, 1991. Reproduced with kind permission from the Israel Government Press Office.

Europe instead. Yassin spoke about 'interim solutions' and a one-state solution.[29]

In 1993, Yassin had made a distinction between a suhl (peace) and a hudna (a limited ceasefire). The immediate goal of Hamas was a state in the West Bank and Gaza, based on the 1967 borders. Yet it also continued to promote its long-term ideological aspiration of an Islamic state in the whole of Palestine including Israel. This repeated offer of a hudna gave the impression that Hamas accepted the notion of a two-state solution and that it would eventually recognize Israel. By distinguishing between its long-term plan and its short-term goal, Hamas exuded a deceptive sense of flexibility while not compromising on its core convictions.

Arafat feared the growing power of the Islamists especially as international pressure to reform his administration publicly revealed incompetence, corruption and the aggrandizement of power. In March 2003, Arafat cancelled elections for the workers' union at Al-Azhar University in Gaza City for a second time since Hamas and Islamic Jihad would in all likelihood score a major victory.[30] Arafat was able to shield himself from public scrutiny through the genuine appreciation of the Palestinian people for his

[29] *Ha'aretz* 6 December 2003.   [30] *Jerusalem Post* March 17, 2003.

arduous odyssey on their behalf. As the perceived father of the Palestinian people, all flaws and faults were secondary. When the United States refused to have any dealings with him, the Palestinians considered it as an attack upon themselves. When members of the Israeli cabinet considered his assassination, Arafat's approval ratings in the polls increased tremendously. When he was threatened with deportation and exile, it evoked memories of the disaster of 1948.

Yet the issue of killing Arafat was raised by Likud cabinet members on several occasions in the belief that he was ultimately responsible for the actions of the Islamists. His removal, it was argued, would create a totally different political environment. Such comments often occurred after attacks on Israeli civilians, particularly after the Park Hotel bombing during Passover 2002 and after the wave of suicide bombings in September 2002 that led Israel to renew its siege on the Muqata, Arafat's Ramallah headquarters.

A determined assault on Jenin, 'the martyrs' capital', from which many suicide bombers had emanated, earned Israel a great deal of criticism. In an attempt to resurrect memories of Beirut in 1982 and the killing of Palestinians in Sabra and Shatilla, Palestinian commentators claimed that more than 500 civilians had been massacred and buried in mass graves. Other claims suggested that there had been blanket bombing and that the refugee camp in Jenin had been completely levelled. Sharon was compared to Milosovic.

This attempt to halt Operation Defensive Shield attracted the sympathy of the UN and the Europeans. However, groups such as Human Rights Watch indicated that much of the factual evidence indicated that the Palestinian spokesmen had been economical with the truth. The Israelis responded by arguing that it had been a pitched battle between armed Islamist groups and Fatah and that only fifty-two to fifty-six people had been killed. The Palestinian fighters, they argued, had extensively wired buildings with explosives with the intention of embarking on a struggle. Some twenty-three Israeli soldiers had been killed in the fighting.[31]

Yet for sections of the PLO gathered around the figure of Mahmoud Abbas, one of the architects of Oslo, it was clear that Arafat had become a liability in the task of nation building. They gratefully seized on US and Israeli demands that a Prime Minister be appointed in the hope that Arafat's grip on power would be loosened. While Arafat eventually consented to the appointment of Mahmoud Abbas as Prime Minister, this

[31] Yehuda Kraut, *Camera* 1 August 2002.

did not mean that he wanted to relinquish any control over the numerous armed groups that he financed. Mahmoud Abbas wanted to appoint Mohammed Dahlan as the head of the new government's security services, but Arafat insisted that all such decisions required his approval. The Americans wanted the Palestinian security services combined into three divisions which reported directly to the PA Minister of the Interior. Instead Dahlan was only given authority over counter-intelligence apparatus and the uniformed police. Arafat remained in charge of five different security organizations – General Intelligence, the National Security Forces, Force 17, Military Intelligence and the naval forces. Arafat then established the National Security Council, to oversee these organizations, and appointed his close associate Hanni al-Hassan in a central role. At the same time, Arafat started to make many new appointments to the Ministry of the Interior. In contrast, Mahmoud Abbas spoke about the futility of the Intifada and wished to dismantle Fatah's al-Aqsa Brigades before moving towards confronting the Islamists. Mahmoud Abbas tried to replace Arafat's men with those closer to his own approach. Thus he and Foreign Minister Nabil Sha'ath tried to remove Nasser al-Kidwa, the PLO observer at the United Nations, who strongly supported his uncle, Yasser Arafat.

On taking office, Mahmoud Abbas stated that the Palestinians would not accept anything less than 'the establishment of our independent state with Jerusalem as its capital; a genuine, contiguous state without any (Jewish) settlements, on all of the territories occupied in 1967 in conformity with international law'. This espousal of a two-state solution may have found an echo in the Israeli peace camp, but the Sharon government was not going to give any meaningful leeway to Mahmoud Abbas (Abu Mazen). On the day when Mahmoud Abbas declared his opposition to terrorism, an Apache helicopter gunship fired four missiles at a car in Khan Yunis, killing two leaders of the PFLP.

Mahmoud Abbas's pleas to the Islamists to disarm fell on deaf ears. Hamas and Islamic Jihad instead carried out a spate of suicide bombings including that of a Jerusalem bus, full of passengers. Despite his pledge to contain the situation, five suicide attacks killed twelve Israelis in forty-eight hours. It soon became clear to the Israelis that despite his views on the Intifada, Mahmoud Abbas would not confront the Islamists militarily but instead aimed at persuading them through diplomacy. Yet all Hamas would offer was a hudna to cease the killing of civilians in Israel, but not within the territories. From the outset, Mahmoud Abbas's policies were rejected by the Islamists and undermined by Arafat. This, in turn, weakened him in the eyes of the Sharon government, who expected him to use force against those who effectively did not recognize the central authority of the government.

The situation of the Palestinians was worsening. The UN Relief and Works Agency for Palestine Refugees in the Near East (UNRWA) stated on 30 April 2003 that 12,737 Palestinians had seen their homes demolished in Gaza and the West Bank, with the average monthly rate more than doubling over the past three months. By the spring of 2003, nearly 2,000 Palestinians – combatants and non-combatants – had been killed. An IDF analysis suggested that 22 per cent were members of Hamas and Islamic Jihad while 17 per cent were Fatah and Tanzim activists.[32] Among a growing number of Palestinians, the Islamists were seen as the bastion of resistance to the Israeli military.

It was only after Sharon's election victory and Mahmoud Abbas's installation as Prime Minister designate that the Road Map was formally published at the end of April 2003. It reiterated the essential points of Bush's Rose Garden speech with its emphasis on democracy and reform. It envisaged a three-stage process which would lead to a Palestinian state. The first stage called for an end to Palestinian violence and a policy 'to arrest, disrupt and restrain individuals and groups' planning and carrying out attacks. Israel had to withdraw from Palestinian territory progressively as the violence subsided. The Road Map demanded a freeze of all settlement activity including the natural growth of settlements.

The published Road Map, however, was not a direct reflection of Bush's speech because the intervening year had allowed for modification. Moreover, when the Road Map was initially announced, the White House did not emphatically endorse it even though Colin Powell and the State Department had been involved. In addition, the Europeans, the UN and Russia had no wish to marginalize Arafat. France did not wish to cut off European Union funding to Palestinian institutions or to label Hamas a terrorist organization. Sharon, who was mindful of not alienating his supporters prior to the election, did not wish to make any meaningful decisions. He also demanded US supervision alone rather than supervision by the collective Quartet of the United Nations, the European Union, Russia and the United States.[33] Yet the Peace Index for December 2002 showed that 57 per cent of Israelis were in favour of two states for two peoples.

Sharon attempted to ameliorate public opinion by publicly embracing for the first time the idea of a Palestinian state. It was not, however, the

[32] *Ha'aretz* Thursday, 13 March 2003.   [33] *Ha'aretz* 23 October 2002.

traditional idea of two territorially contiguous states, side by side, but one where Palestinian sovereignty was relegated to enclaves. This distinction was often blurred in the public mind. Sharon listed fourteen reservations about the Road Map; moreover, it was unclear which version he had actually accepted.[34]

On the Palestinian side, Mahmoud Abbas was condemned by the Islamists for his willingness to proceed along a diplomatic path and for not wholeheartedly supporting the Intifada. At the Aqaba summit with Bush and Sharon in 2003, he had called for a demilitarization of the Intifada and the implementation of peaceful means to end the Israeli occupation. He denounced terrorism as 'inconsistent with our religious and moral traditions and . . . a dangerous obstacle to the achievement of an independent, sovereign state'. The CIA was enlisted to provide two-week training courses in Jericho to Palestinian security personnel in counter-insurgency techniques.

ISLAMISM ASCENDING

Following Mahmoud Abbas's investiture, the popular Tel Aviv music club Mike's Place was bombed by two British Muslims, Asif Mohammed Hanif and Omar Khan Sharif, who had entered Israel from the Gaza Strip. The two suicide bombers studied in Syria and were probably recruited by Hamas in Damascus. In Gaza, they posed as left-wing activists and attended events sponsored by the International Solidarity Movement as a means of deflecting attention away from their goal. Unlike in the West Bank, a security fence surrounded Gaza. This was the first time a suicide bombing attack had been carried out from there during the thirty-one months of the Intifada.

Moreover, some of the Palestinian security forces refused to act against Hamas's Qassam rocket units which were operating from the southern Gaza Strip. For the first time, Arafat issued personal deployment orders to Palestinian forces in Gaza to enforce a ceasefire.[35]

But Mahmoud Abbas's support for the Road Map and his pronouncements at Aqaba persuaded Hamas to break off all discussions with him. Moreover, Arafat also criticized his comments at Aqaba. It was clear that Mahmoud Abbas's authority was limited and that most armed groups did not wish to give up their struggle against Israel. Palestinian collaborators,

---

34 Baruch Kimmerling, 'From Barak to the Road Map', *New Left Review* no.23, September–October 2003.

35 *Ha'aretz* 20 June 2003.

real and imaginary, were killed and the Governor of Jenin was beaten and kidnapped by members of the al-Aqsa Martyrs' Brigades. Abdel Aziz al Rantisi, a senior figure in Hamas, commented that the group 'will not renounce the principle that Palestine is Islamic. We will not renounce any inch of Palestine, the right of return, and Jerusalem, and we will not abandon our detainees.'[36] Yet for all such bravado, Hamas and Islamic Jihad declared a unilateral ceasefire on 29 June 2003 and Sharon responded with withdrawals from Bethlehem and part of Gaza.

The decisions in the Aqaba summit also caused problems for Sharon and highlighted the growing split within the Likud. In order to smooth the path for Mahmoud Abbas, before the meeting Israel released 100 prisoners including Ahmed Jubarah, the oldest and longest-held Palestinian prisoner. He had been convicted for his part in a 1975 bomb attack when a refrigerator packed with explosives in Jerusalem had killed thirteen people. Arafat made him a special advisor on prisoners. Relatives of the Israelis killed condemned his release.

In his speech at Aqaba, Sharon spoke about the importance of territorial contiguity in the West Bank for a viable Palestinian state. The Council of Jewish Settlements in Judea, Samaria and the Gaza District (Yesha Council) described it as 'a surrender to Palestinian terror'. Shlomo Aviner, the head of the Ateret Kohanim yeshiva and the rabbi of Bet El Alef settlement, wrote that

it is prohibited to cede parts of our land to a foreign people, and any move in this direction is meaningless and has no halachic or legal validity. The government was elected to fulfill the historic mission of building the Jewish state in its country and has no mandate to destroy it. The nation is not bound by any move to this effect.[37]

Jewish settlers responded by setting up new outposts in the West Bank as the government formally began to dismantle others, erected after March 2001, under the terms of the Road Map plan. Violent clashes erupted between settlers and security forces when Israeli troops attempted to dismantle the first outpost, Mitzpeh Yitzhar, adjacent to the West Bank settlement of Yitzhar, south of Nablus. Hundreds of settlers barred the way and set fire to Palestinian-owned wheat fields and olive groves in an attempt to disrupt

---

[36] Al-Jazeerah Television 6 June 2003.
[37] Shlomo Aviner, 'Our Great People, Burn the Road Map', *B'Ahavah ube'Emunah* quoted on Kol Israel Reshet Bet 13 June 2003.

the operation.[38] According to Peace Now, there were 102 outposts, of which 62 had been established after March 2001.[39]

The Road Map was opposed by powerful groups on both sides of the divide. Straight after the Aqaba summit, a joint unit of members of Hamas, Islamic Jihad and the al-Aqsa Martyrs' Brigades, dressed in Israeli Army uniforms, penetrated an army outpost and killed four soldiers. In Jerusalem's Zion Square, tens of thousands of Israeli demonstrators protested against the Road Map and the Aqaba meeting earlier that day. Knesset members and ministers from the Likud, National Union, National Religious party, Shas and United Torah Judaism all spoke at the demonstration. Yet a poll conducted by Tel Aviv University's Jaffee Institute for Strategic Studies showed that 59 per cent of the Israeli public was willing to remove all settlements located outside major settlement blocs.

The ceasefire of Hamas held for six weeks until a bombing killed twenty-one Israelis in Jerusalem in August 2003. The continuation of this violence and his political impotence to stop it also brought about the resignation of Mahmoud Abbas and his replacement by Abu Ala. Bush's promise to establish a backchannel and go straight to final status talks fell by the wayside.[40] Both the United States and Israel would not entertain going back to the status quo ante – however deeply disguised. Arafat remained in control, but clearly his power and his credibility were on the wane.

Hamas, it appeared, was not ready to give up the armed struggle, even temporarily, and Sharon was certainly not ready to give up reprisals and retaliation. Israel had attempted to eliminate the Hamas leadership in September 2003 by dropping a 250-kilogram bomb on a building where Sheikh Yassin was meeting the organization's leadership. In January 2004, Israeli ministers were openly announcing that Yassin was 'marked for death'.[41] It was reported that US officials had had clandestine talks with Hamas in Qatar whereby an American proposal for a cessation of suicide bombings, matched by an Israeli cessation of targeted killings, was rejected by Yassin and Rantisi. The formal Hamas position was to offer a ten-year ceasefire in exchange for an Israeli withdrawal to the 1967 borders. Rantisi pointed out that this did not mean an acceptance of a two-state solution, but 'a phased liberation' of all of Palestine.

Yassin praised a twenty-two-year-old mother of two, Reem Salih Al-Reyashi, who blew herself up at the Erez Crossing into Gaza. Al-Reyashi's story illustrated another aspect of the Islamist agenda. She was from a

[38] *Ha'aretz* 19 June 2003.   [39] *Jerusalem Post* 18 June 2003.
[40] *Newsweek* 21 June 2004.   [41] *Ha'aretz* 16 January 2004.

well-known and well-to-do Gaza family, but she had the misfortune of being discovered having a love affair. Yet her suicide video proclaimed the official Hamas line that she had always aspired to become a martyr. She stated that she had always told herself, 'Be filled with every possible grudge for the Jews, the enemies of your religion and make sure your blood is a road leading to paradise.'[42] Her exit through a suicide bombing provided a way of redeeming family honour. Four Israelis died in the incident.[43] This was the first time that Hamas had deliberately used a woman as a suicide bomber. 'Jihad', said Yassin, 'was the duty of men and women'.[44]

Following an exchange of prisoners between Hezbollah and Israel, Yassin argued that Hamas would kidnap Israeli soldiers in order to secure the release of Palestinians in Israeli prisons. The IDF was further concerned that Hamas would emulate Hezbollah in building up a deterrence capacity to resist the military might of the Israelis. Suicide bombings, the firing of Qassam missiles at Israeli border towns and the smuggling of war materiel through tunnels under the Egyptian border were all directed towards that end.

Muhammad Deif, the commander of Hamas's military wing, 'Izz al-din al-Qassam Brigades, had been involved in suicide bombing since 1996. In a rare interview, he illustrated Hamas's approach:

However, with the help of Allah, those human bombs made some balance with the Israeli fortified tank and warplanes. We would like to confirm to our people that the engineers and technicians in the 'Izz al-din al-Qassam Brigades are working day and night so as to develop our capabilities to strike our enemy. And, the total destruction of a huge Israeli Merkava tank with less than 35 kilograms of explosives in the northern Gaza Strip is concrete evidence of these strenuous efforts.[45]

Hamas had indeed improved its missile capability. The new Nasser 3 ensured that it detonated on impact. Manufactured in the Gaza Strip, it was encased in a 110-120 millimetre-diameter steel water pipe and contained some 20 kilograms of improvised solid propellant. This was obtained from available chemicals such as potassium nitrate fertilizer and powdered sugar.[46] Although the IDF had developed artillery-locating radar to detect and attack Qassam teams, it recognized that only a presence at all launching grounds would actually totally suppress the launching of such missiles.

[42] Benny Morris, review of Matthew Levitt's *Hamas: Politics, Charity and Terrorism in the Service of Jihad* (New Haven 2006) in *New Republic* Online 10 July 2006.
[43] *Yediot Aharanot* 18 January 2004.   [44] *Jane's Defence Weekly* 14 July 2004.
[45] *Jerusalem Post* 15 January 2004.   [46] *Jerusalem Post* 25 March 2004.

There had been a plethora of suicide bombings during the first few months of 2004. It was a double suicide bombing in Ashdod, hitherto not targeted, which persuaded the Israeli security cabinet to order the killing of Yassin. In parallel, an emergency meeting took place in Arafat's Muqata compound in Ramallah. The Interior Minister, Hakem Balawi, and the commander of the National Security forces, Haj Ismail Jabbar, both called upon Arafat to act against Hamas and Fatah's military wing, the al-Aqsa Martyrs' Brigades. Other ministers added their voices, but Arafat refused to move.[47]

The founder of Hamas met his death when a helicopter gunship fired three missiles at him as he left a Gaza mosque. Although this happened at a time when Israel was perceived as moving the peace process forward and Hamas as retarding it, the killing of Hamas's spiritual leader caused consternation in many European capitals. The British Foreign Secretary, Jack Straw, commented that 'the killing of an elderly man in a wheelchair was unjustified'. The IDF pointed out that Hamas had carried out fifty-two suicide attacks, killing 288 Israelis and injuring 1,646. The killing of Yassin provoked demonstrations all over the Arab world including one in Nazareth by thousands of Israeli Arabs.

Abdel Aziz Rantissi was named as Yassin's successor in Gaza. Yet he too suffered a similar fate only a few weeks later, probably because of his desire to forge closer links to Iran and Hezbollah. This was followed by the assassination of a senior Hamas operative, Izz al-Din al-Sheikh Khalil, in Damascus; the capture of the head of the Hamas military wing in Hebron, Imad Kawasmeh; and the killing of Adnan Al-Ghoul, the organization's chief explosives engineer. Such losses by the brazen actions of the Israelis psychologically debilitated the Palestinians, who felt both humiliated and powerless.

Mahmoud Zahar succeeded Rantisi, but Hamas had lost some crucial figures. It also understood that the political situation had changed. The killings of Yassin and Rantisi persuaded Hamas to follow a political road. Although Zahar pledged to continue armed resistance, the proposed withdrawal from Gaza convinced Hamas that it should seek a power-sharing arrangement with Fatah. Ismail Haniyeh, a Hamas leader in Gaza, advocated that 'partners in blood should be partners in the decision making'.[48] The Palestinian public was weary of the rigours of the Intifada and experiencing financial ruin. The Arab states were also tiring of Hamas's intransigence and the Arab League passed a resolution condemning violence against all civilians without distinction. Hamas attacked this as 'implicitly denouncing the operations of the Palestinian resistance against Israeli

---

[47] *Ha'aretz* 16 March 2004. [48] *Jerusalem Times* 8 April 2004.

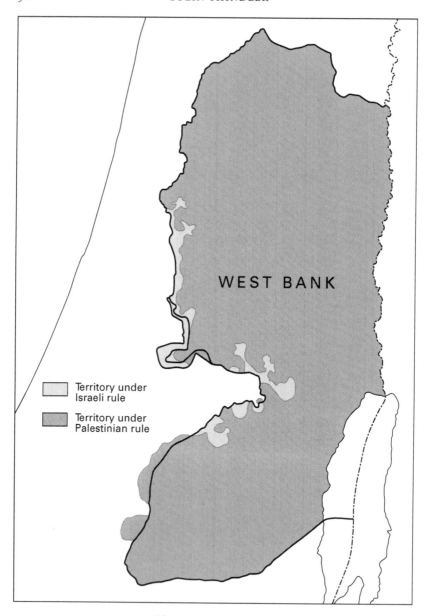

WEST BANK

Territory under
Israeli rule

Territory under
Palestinian rule

5. The Geneva Initiative, 2003.

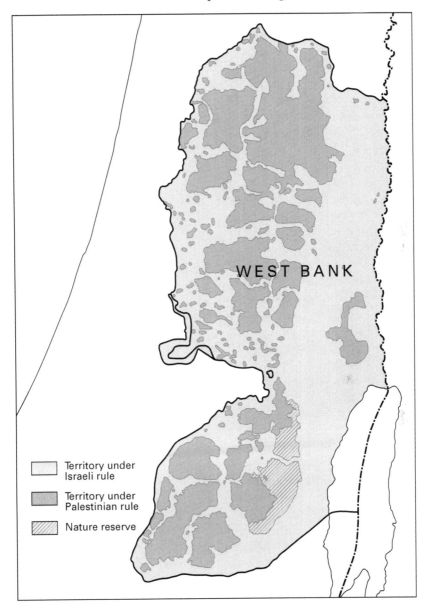

WEST BANK

Territory under
Israeli rule

Territory under
Palestinian rule

Nature reserve

6. The Disengagement plan, 2003.

occupation'.[49] The new leadership also wanted to distance Hamas from being included as adversaries in 'the war on terror'. Indeed, previously Hamas had occasionally sent operatives for training in al-Qaeda camps in Pakistan and Afghanistan. The removal of Yassin and Rantisi caused a polarization to occur within Hamas. Three foci were developing, the hard-line political bureau under Khalid Meshal in Damascus; the military wing, 'Izz al-din al-Qassam Brigades; and an evolving political leadership, dealing with the reality on the ground led by Ismail Haniyeh.

DISENGAGEMENT FROM GAZA

Sharon's announcement to disengage from Gaza came as a tremendous shock to his critics both on the Left and on the Right. A year previously, he had commented that the fate of the most far-flung settlements in Gaza, Netzarim and Kfar Darom, was to be regarded in the same light as that of Tel Aviv.[50] The formal announcement to evacuate seventeen Gaza settlements and another four in the West Bank in February 2004 represented the first reversal for the settler movement since 1968. It inevitably divided his party. It was strongly supported by Trade and Industry Minister Ehud Olmert and Tzipi Livni, the Minister for Immigration and Absorption, but Foreign Minister Silvan Shalom and Finance Minister Benjamin Netanyahu equally strongly condemned it. It was also uncertain whether this was simply the beginning of further evacuations.

Sharon vaguely and tantalizingly hinted that 'painful choices' would have to be made and that the Palestinians did not have 'unlimited time at their disposal'.[51] He even used the hitherto taboo term 'occupation' in an altercation with angry Likud members of the Knesset.[52] He told them, 'controlling 3.5 million Palestinians cannot go on forever. You want to remain in Jenin, Nablus, Ramallah and Bethlehem?'

In a remarkable interview in *Yediot Aharanot*, Olmert softened the political ground beforehand by stating that the choices were effectively withdrawal to the 1967 Green Line or unilateral withdrawal where Israel would define its own borders. Olmert raised the demographic question as the central issue and ridiculed suggestions that this could be counterbalanced by increased immigration or giving the vote to émigré Israelis and Diaspora Jews. If Palestinians in a Greater Israel demanded the vote, Olmert

---

[49] *Jerusalem Times* 27 May 2004.   [50] *Ma'ariv* 11 December 2002.
[51] *New York Times* 27 November 2003.   [52] *Ha'aretz* 27 May 2003.

Fig. 13.2. Sharon and Olmert discuss the Disengagement plan during a Knesset session.
Reproduced with kind permission from the Israel Government Press Office.

argued that it would irreparably damage the democratic nature of the state.
'On that day, we lose everything... the thought that the struggle against
us would be headed by liberal Jewish organizations who shouldered the
burden of the struggle against apartheid in South Africa scares me.' Olmert
also hinted at a Palestinian presence in Jerusalem – via the villages of al-
Ayzaria and Abu Dis. Olmert prophesied that there might indeed be an
outbreak of considerable violence initially from the Palestinians, but this
would then diminish significantly.

Whereas Sharon was an old Mapainik and admirer of Ben-Gurion's
pragmatism, Olmert's family had imbibed the ideological approach of
Jabotinsky. Even so, Olmert pointed to the error of extrapolating from the
past into the future. 'No one knows how Jabotinsky, Begin and Shamir
would have reacted today', he commented. He also pointed out that Begin
made realistic decisions once he had attained power. 'He did not impose
our sovereignty on the entire land. He was wise, responsible and a democrat'. Finally, Olmert recognized that such views would not only initiate
a government crisis, but also severely threaten the internal stability of the

Likud. An editorial in the same edition of *Yediot Aharanot* commented that 'when "not-one-inch" Olmert recommends unilateral withdrawal, that is a genuine ideological turnaround'.[53]

Sharon's opponents in the Likud immediately viewed the disengagement from Gaza as the first stage in further evacuations. Yet Sharon vowed to retain the Jordan Valley as a security zone, to preserve a link to the Hebron settlements and to control the Temple Mount. He had been deliberately vague about peace initiatives during the 2003 election. Sharon had condemned his opponent, the new Labour leader Amram Mitzna, for his proposals for an immediate withdrawal from Gaza and a unilateral evacuation from the West Bank if no agreement had been reached after a year's negotiations with the Palestinians. Unlike Sharon's Disengagement plan, Mitzna said that no Jewish settlement would remain outside the new border. Mitzna planned to remove 35,000 settlers from their homes and 55,000 Palestinians would come under Israeli rule. The Labour party said that it would also redirect $3 billion in funding for Jewish settlements to poor communities in Israel. A year later, Sharon and Olmert adopted much of Mitzna's plan as their own.

In a revealing interview,[54] Dov Weisglass, a senior advisor to Sharon, explained that the Disengagement plan was a means of freezing the diplomatic process to prevent the establishment of a Palestinian state and any discussion on borders, refugees and Jerusalem. It made it possible 'to park conveniently in an interim situation that distances us as far as possible from political pressure . . . and forces the Palestinians to prove their seriousness'. Sharon, he commented, believed that the Palestinians had to undergo 'a deep and extended sociopolitical change' and that even a long-term interim agreement was now not possible. Out of 240,000 settlers, 190,000 would not be moved. Weisglass's bluntness provoked international criticism and a demand for clarification from the US State Department. Such an analysis was also designed to calm the fears of the Right as well as attracting the centre.

The far Right National Union and the National Religious party, however, threatened to bring down the government while the Likud itself was split down the middle. Even the IDF Chief of Staff Moshe Ya'alon publicly expressed reservations about the Disengagement plan. Labour and Meretz, on the other hand, concentrated on the unilateral nature of the proposal and the fact that the PA had been ignored. When the Knesset voted on Sharon's statement on the plan, only forty-six voted in support, while

---

[53] *Yediot Aharanot* 5 December 2003.   [54] *Ha'aretz* 8 October 2004.

forty-five voted against it. Sharon threatened to implement his plan if the Palestinians did not initiate any moves to comply with the Road Map. Hamas denounced the proposal as worthless while Islamic Jihad argued that it was only the terror ignited by the Intifada that had forced the Israelis to consider disengagement.

Moreover, Israel had already completed the first stage of a security barrier of trenches, guard towers, fences, walls and barbed wire. When the Disengagement plan was first announced, the 145-kilometre northern section of the barrier had already been completed and a recently approved 370-kilometre southern section was being constructed. The Palestinians denounced the barrier – the Apartheid Wall – as a land grab, a move which had been carried out without any consultation. Many Palestinians viewed this as yet another mark of humiliation and an obstacle to their free movement. Thousands of Palestinians would now find themselves encased and separated from the West Bank. The encirclement of Palestinian cities would lead to enclaves and thereby destroy the very contiguity of territory under the control of the PA.

This also alarmed the White House since it undermined the very idea of a two-state solution. The settlers, too, resented the presence of the barrier since it placed many of them on the wrong side and cut them off from Israel. Most Israelis, including many on the Left according to opinion polls, approved of its construction since it kept out suicide bombers. Gaza's fence, it was argued, had prevented the import of suicide bombers into Israel. The Palestinians, however, also saw the barrier as the evolving borders of Israel.

There were also economic implications. The Intifada had decreased Israel's dependence on Palestinian labour. Tens of thousands of foreign workers from countries such as Thailand and the Philippines had come to work in Israel and displaced Palestinian labour. Sharon wished to keep the Palestinians within Palestine and to participate in the building of a strong economy. At a Donors' Conference in Rome in December 2003, the Foreign Minister, Silvan Shalom, presented a plan to boost economic conditions and employment in the West Bank and Gaza that envisaged the construction of industrial parks along the seam line.

The US was concerned that the Disengagement plan would effectively be a substitute for the Road Map. It initially opposed the annexation of West Bank territory and the construction of an eastern fence between West Bank Palestinian cities and the Jordan Valley. It also opposed moving settlers from the Gaza Strip to the West Bank. Sharon's motivations in announcing the Disengagement plan were numerous. In his statement to the Knesset in March 2004, he commented that the plan would prevent a diplomatic vacuum that would expose Israel to diplomatic initiatives from foreign countries. There was also a momentum of rising protest within Israel – refuseniks who refused to serve in the territories, fighter pilots who refused to bomb Gaza and the condemnatory press conference of the four former heads of the General Security Service.

Above all, it was clear that Sharon feared the Geneva Initiative of Yossi Beilin and Yasser Abed Rabbo. This plan, which built on the Beilin–Mahmoud Abbas plan and the Clinton Parameters, envisaged two contiguous states, an Israeli annexation of some settlements close to the Green Line and, in return, land in the Negev ceded by Israel to the Palestinians. There would be a division of the Old City of Jerusalem, the Western Wall under Israeli sovereignty, the Temple Mount under Palestinian sovereignty. There would be a curbing of attacks on Israeli civilians and the return of refugees to five possible different locations – but not a wholesale 'right of return' to Israel. Not only was this condemned by the Israeli Right, but there were mass demonstrations against it by the Islamists in Gaza and a call for Yasser Abed Rabbo to be punished.[55] Fatah condemned it because it compromised the right of return. But crucially for Sharon, the Americans warmed to the Geneva proposals. Bush said that it was 'a productive contribution',[56] and Powell met its authors. The Quartet also signalled its intention to discuss its ideas.

However, Sharon, like Hamas, wished to lay the spirit of Oslo to rest. He did not want to negotiate with an enfeebled Palestinian Authority that could not deliver. He insisted that he would not negotiate while there was conflict; the Islamists additionally ensured that he could argue that there was no one to talk to. Beilin and indeed Peres were willing to talk as the violence continued.

Sharon's announcement on disengagement was made shortly after Beilin announced his initiative, which indicated a glimpse of a different future. Clearly, Sharon had no intention of being outflanked on the Left, but he was worried that the White House might take up the Geneva Initiative or a similar plan called 'the People's Voice' – a mass petition which tens of thousands of Israelis and Palestinians had signed.

An opinion poll found that 31 per cent of Israelis supported the Geneva Initiative, 38 per cent opposed it and 20 per cent had not yet formed an opinion. Even 13 per cent of Likud voters supported the Initiative, which

---

[55] *Ha'aretz* November 21, 2003.   [56] *Washington Post* 5 December 2003.

was negotiated without the consent of the government.[57] Former President Jimmy Carter was present at the launch and the Initiative was endorsed by Blair, Chirac and Nelson Mandela. Representatives of Egypt and Morocco also spoke warmly in support of the agreement. Yasser Arafat, however, kept his distance. The US Secretary of State Colin Powell's decision to meet Beilin and Abed Rabbo provoked an outraged response from the Sharon government.

Sharon had spoken about the principles of disengagement to the Americans at a meeting in Rome in November 2003. In his Knesset speech, Sharon argued that there were several choices for Israel. The first was to destroy the PA and de facto annex the West Bank and Gaza. The second was to follow the Geneva Initiative, which would be a security disaster for Israel and be impossible to implement. The third choice would be to do nothing, which would open the way to imposed solutions.

They believe we should first withdraw from all the territories, and then, simply by force of a written agreement, the Palestinians will stop the terror. These people, who garner a wide range of support around the world, primarily in Europe, will not stop pressuring Israel to abandon its demand that the Palestinians fight terror. Since the Palestinians are doing nothing, the pressure is focused on us. It is easier to pressure a westernized democratic country like Israel. . . . Our activities are not a pleasant sight. Every day around the world, pictures are transmitted of people standing at Israeli roadblocks, of Israeli soldiers in the streets of Palestinian towns and there are horror stories of alleged Israeli abuse of Palestinians.[58]

He later claimed that he had told Shamir in 1988 that a separation of territory was required if Israel was not to be forced back to the 1967 borders.

Sharon then argued that disengagement would prevent a political collapse, reduce friction between Israelis and Palestinians and contribute to 'the stabilization of security and reduction in terror'. The Disengagement plan, he argued, was anchored in the US proposals and would ensure 'the political and security interests of Israel for many years to come'.

There would be territorial contiguity between Gaza and the northern West Bank. Israeli troops would withdraw from these areas and dismantle their military installations but would maintain a presence along the Philadelphi Route, the border between Gaza and Egypt. There would be a movement towards reducing the number of checkpoints in the West Bank, and the Gaza settlements would be transferred to the Palestinians

---

[57] *Ha'aretz* 1 December 2003.
[58] Ariel Sharon's speech at Israel's Annual Hi-Tech Conference 31 March 2004. www.pmo.gov.il.

in the hope of promoting economic activity in the region. According to the World Bank, private investment in the territories had fallen from $1.25 billion in 1999 to $50 million in 2002 because of the security situation.

After some hesitation, the Israeli Left in general welcomed Sharon's plan as a first step in leaving the territories, a first step along the road to the Geneva Initiative. Yet there was still amazement at Sharon's ideological volte-face. In the Knesset debate, the Meretz leader Yossi Sarid had reminded Sharon that he once commented that he viewed the Gaza settlement of Netzarim as no less important than Tel Aviv. In a similar vein, Sharon had previously described the settlement of Kfar Darom as a strategic asset since it had held up the Egyptian army for a vital few days during their advance in 1948. Sharon also marginalized the ideological Right. The far Right's Avigdor Lieberman argued for a redrawing of the borders such that contiguous Arab populated areas in Israel would now be part of the new state of Palestine in exchange for the Jewish settlement blocs on the West Bank and in Gaza. This idea probably pushed even more Israelis into Sharon's camp and earned opprobrium from Israeli Arabs.

Changing the political habits of a lifetime was no doubt spurred on by the events of 11 September 2001 and the spate of suicide bombing. The reoccupation of large parts of the West Bank in the spring of 2002 and the political and physical decline of Arafat were also factors. However, the death of his wife and the growing influence of his sons in a tightly knit group of advisors probably pushed him in a new direction. Even so, Sharon's approach to Palestinian nationalism still rested on the belief that there could be no peace until there was a genuine change in the way the Arab world perceived Israel.

CHAPTER 14

An unlikely grandfather

IDEOLOGY AND EVACUATION

Sharon's ideological heritage originated in Mapai even though he had actually founded the Likud in 1973. His ideological mentors were David Ben-Gurion and Moshe Dayan rather than Jabotinsky and Begin. He believed therefore that only a policy of military strength would win respect from the Palestinians and the Arab world in a hostile neighbourhood. Like Ben-Gurion, he argued that a display of national resilience would indicate that the country could not be brought to its knees through acts of violence. His political opponents, however, echoed Sharett's reservations. In a lecture in 1957, given shortly after his resignation, Sharett commented:

Without diminishing the importance of day-to-day security, we must always bring the question of peace into our overall calculations. We have to curb our reactions. And the question remains: has it really been proven that reprisals establish the security for which they were planned? . . . Do people consider that when military reactions outstrip in their severity the events that cause them, grave processes are set in motion which widen the gulf and thrust our neighbours into the extremist camp? How can this deterioration be halted?[1]

The arguments, fifty years later, had still not been resolved.

Sharon was a maximalist on the basis that settlements improved security – and not for nationalist or religious reasons. He had argued in the 1970s that 'there had to be an upper Jenin, an upper Nablus and an upper Ramallah just as there is an upper Nazareth'.[2] As a minister in Begin's first government, he expounded his reasoning for colonizing the West Bank in September 1977:

If we want a strong independent state, we must give up settling just on the coastal strip and move elsewhere. Otherwise Israel would consist of a mass of concrete

---

[1] *Jerusalem Post* 18 October 1966.   [2] *Jerusalem Post* 18 July 1973.

from Ashkelon to Nahariya, all within the range of Arab guns and having to rely on friendly powers for protection.[3]

The Disengagement plan seemed to fly in the face of decades of advocacy on behalf of the settlers. In a speech to the Knesset in October 2004, he quoted from a well-known essay by Moshe Beilinson, a leader of Mapai, in favour of retaliation against Arab attacks during the Arab revolt of 1936.[4] Significantly, Beilinson, unlike Ben-Gurion, did not acknowledge the existence of an Arab national movement in Palestine in 1936 and preferred to remain true to his Achdut Ha'avodah roots of class solidarity between Jews and Arabs. In the same speech Sharon repeated Menachem Begin's comment that the religious settlers possessed 'a messianic complex'.

Sharon tried to find precedents that would justify his ideological about-turn. When a journalist asked him whether he felt any guilt towards the settlers, he responded by quoting from an article which Jabotinsky had written in 1915. In the article, Jabotinsky challenged the indispensability of the settlements:

We have never seen a settlement as an end in and of itself. We have seen it as one of the most powerful means of state-oriented Zionism for achieving our sovereignty over the land of Israel. To us, a settlement has been precious as one of our finest cards in the statesmanship game of the future. But should this settlement suddenly become an impediment in the crucial statesmanship game – to this we shall not agree. A settlement is a means and no more than that. The fact that we love its green orchards, its golden fields and its proud labourers is irrelevant. For us, they are the political avant-garde. It happens that for the sake of a common interest the avant-garde suffers severe losses. We send them our blessings and continue on our way.[5]

His Disengagement plan from Gaza in 2004 was based on the notion that some settlements now decreased security for Israel. In later speeches, he put forward the demographic problem as a reason for the withdrawal. While the Israeli Left looked at Sharon in a new light, the Palestinians condemned the plan, demanding bilateralism and not unilateralism as the approach.

During the first few months of 2004, Sharon pursued two goals. The first was to indicate to both the Palestinians and the Israeli public that disengagement did not mean military weakness. The second was to persuade the White House to agree to the Disengagement plan and to modify the Road Map.

---

[3] *Jerusalem Post* 4 September 1977.   [4] *Ha'aretz* 25 October 2004.
[5] Vladimir Jabotinsky, 'Activism', *Di Tribune* 15 October 1915 quoted in Ari Shavit, 'The General', *New Yorker* 23 and 30 January 2006.

Under increasing Israeli pressure, the Palestinian Authority, led by an ailing Arafat, was descending into greater chaos. Civil law and order were breaking down. Arafat's inability to delegate authority or to decentralize his administration assisted Sharon in tightening the military screw. The UN Office for the Coordination of Humanitarian Affairs pointed out that the majority of the checkpoints in the West Bank did not actually separate the West Bank and Israel but instead blocked passage between Palestinian villages and cities. As the Israeli organization Machson Watch – mainly middle-aged women who berated soldiers young enough to be their sons – monitored such roadblocks, Palestinian hardship deepened. While Hamas was hit particularly hard through the assassinations of Yassin, Rantisi and others in leadership positions, Arafat was integrated into Sharon's 'war against terror' as a potential target.

Hezbollah was particularly active in guiding the al-Aqsa Brigades and maintaining contact by telephone. Arafat had actually started to cut their funding. Hezbollah, however, stepped in to fill the financial vacuum. In an attempt to regain control for Fatah, Mahmoud Abbas began to pay militants not to carry out attacks against Israeli civilians. On 25 February 2004, the IDF raided a Ramallah bank and returned with $6.7 million allegedly sent by Hezbollah, Iran and Syria in order to finance military operations. Hezbollah funding had previously contributed to the double suicide bombing on 5 January 2003 which killed twenty-three people, the Jerusalem bus bombings of 29 January and 22 February 2004 and the Ashdod bombing of 14 March.

The IDF's Intelligence Corps research and assessment branch claimed that the funds were taken from accounts recently unfrozen by Arafat in November, thereby overturning Mahmoud Abbas's decision to freeze them.[6] Although many suicide bombing attempts were thwarted, others were successful. One plan was to hijack two buses and to take them and their passengers to the Church of the Nativity in Bethlehem as a means of securing the release of Palestinian prisoners in Israeli prisons. Sharon's approach was to prevent such an escalation in Gaza and a Lebanonization of the Palestinian conflict in general. The withdrawal from southern Lebanon in 2000 had been hailed as a victory by Hezbollah. Hamas absorbed that belief and concluded that it could emulate Hezbollah's example. Other Israelis argued that Sharon's raison d'être was to provoke the Islamists overtly, to cantonize the West Bank and Gaza and to make the idea of

---

[6] *Jerusalem Post* 3 March 2004.

a Palestinian state a political fiction – essentially to destroy Palestinian national aspirations.

Not only was Arafat marginalized, but so were Mahmoud Abbas and other members of Fatah who regarded the Intifada as both futile and counter-productive. Sharon and the Islamists reinforced each other's absolutism. After Yassin's killing, an appeal by many Palestinian public figures for a return to 'a widespread, popular and peaceful Intifada' was quickly ignored by the Islamists and the al-Aqsa Brigades.[7] In recognition of the increasing authority of the Islamists, Arafat was intent on forming a broad coalition between the PLO and Hamas. This soon ran aground when Hamas demanded the restoration of the cancelled articles of the PLO's National Charter which referred to the establishment of a Palestinian state on all of the land of historic Palestine – the non-recognition of a two-state solution and the elimination of Israel.[8]

The settler population had increased by 16 per cent since Sharon became Prime Minister – three times the rate of growth in the Negev and Galilee regions. In the Gaza settlement of Kfar Darom, which was scheduled for evacuation under the terms of the Disengagement plan, the population had increased by 52 per cent. There was a 35 per cent increase in the number of new building projects started in the settlements in 2003 alone, according to the Israeli Central Bureau of Statistics. In contrast there was also growing public resentment at the funds spent on the settlements. An Israeli Treasury report indicated that between 1990 and 2003, 846 million Israeli shekels were given in mortgages to settlers and 301 million shekels were still owed in back payments. Members of the Knesset Finance Committee claimed that the government rewarded settlers who did not pay back their mortgages by spreading out the remaining debts over twenty-five years at a subsidized interest rate of 4 per cent a year.[9]

Sharon's visit to Washington in April 2004 paid unprecedented dividends. A letter written by Bush to Sharon modified the Road Map to incorporate disengagement. It defended Israel's right to take action 'against terrorist organizations' and maintained that the right of return should be limited to a Palestinian state only. But Bush, for the first time, accepted Israel's right to retain the major settlement blocs close to the Green Line and not to return to the 1967 borders.

In light of new realities on the ground, including already existing major Israeli population centres, it is unrealistic to expect that the outcomes of final status negotiations will be a full and complete return to the armistice lines of 1949, and all previous efforts to negotiate a two-state solution have reached the same

---

[7] *Al Ayyam* 25 March 2004.   [8] *Jerusalem Times* 10 April 2004.   [9] *Ma'ariv* 2 April 2004.

conclusion. It is realistic to expect that any final status agreement will only be achieved on the basis of mutually agreed changes that reflect these realities.

Bush effectively confirmed what had been a central point of negotiation between Israelis and Palestinians during the dying days of the Clinton administration. Yet the Palestinians regarded this as 'a second Balfour Declaration' because for the first time an American President had formally recognized settlements that had been established on territory conquered in 1967. The Palestinians perceived that there had been a shift away from the Road Map in that there should be a total settlement freeze and the question of the refugees left until final status negotiations between the two sides. Arafat's reaction was to signify that this was the death knell of the Oslo process. In a speech studded with religious quotations and references to Palestinian martyrs Arafat was unambiguous about the 1967 borders and the right of return.

Yet in an interview in June 2002, Arafat said that he was ready for a plan based on the Clinton Parameters which would involve adjustments to the 1967 borders.[10] Bush's letter was resented because the fate of the Palestinians was being decided without them. Arafat and the PLO were demonstrably portrayed as bit actors in the Palestinian drama.

The same approach was taken to the construction of the separation barrier or security fence, as the Israelis termed it, or the Apartheid Wall, as the Palestinians called it. The central idea was to create an obstacle impermeable to suicide bombers attempting to penetrate Israel itself. An automatic consequence was to separate Israel from the West Bank. While both sides agreed that it was a monstrosity, the Palestinian objection was not so much against its existence as against its path. As in all likelihood such a barrier would mutate into a political border, the Palestinians were keen that it should only be built along the Green Line in concurrence with their demand for an Israeli withdrawal to the pre-1967 border. Although the Palestinian leadership had accepted the reality of border modifications during the Clinton years, the bitterness engendered by the Intifada and the rise of Islamism propelled them to denounce both the barrier and the Bush letter.

SEPARATING FROM THE PALESTINIANS

The origins of the barrier lay in Yitzhak Rabin's preference for a separation between Israel and the Palestinians. During the 1992 election campaign, after the killing of an Israeli girl, Rabin spoke about taking 'Gaza out of

---

[10] *Ha'aretz* 23 June 2002.

Tel Aviv'.[11] Following the Dizengoff bombing in the heart of Tel Aviv in October 1994 by Hamas, Israel closed the Gaza border and sealed off the West Bank. Rabin gave a press conference in which he argued that there had to be a separation, not just 'a technical closure'.

We have to decide on separation as a philosophy. There has to be a clear border. Without a border demarcating the lines, whoever wants to swallow 1.8 million Arabs will just ring greater support for Hamas.[12]

The actual construction of an obstacle to bring about separation emerged in 1994 after the first Islamist suicide bombings in Hadera and Afula in Israel. Under pressure from the heads of the Emek Hefer and the South Sharon regional councils, Rabin ordered the construction of two concrete walls, 2.5 metres high and 1,800 metres long, to separate the Israeli villages of Bat Hefer and Matan from their Palestinian counterparts Kafr Shueika and Kafr Habla.[13] Separated by a distance of 200 metres, Israeli residents had complained of being fired upon by their neighbours. Rabin asked his Minister of Public Security, Moshe Shahal, to prepare a plan to construct 'a separation fence'. The idea was not new. During the Mandate, the British had enlisted the service of a police officer, Charles Tegart, to construct a fence along the northern border to prevent incursions from Lebanon and Syria. Tegart also instigated a system of roadblocks which became known as 'Montgomery's teeth' after their use against Rommel in the Western Desert. Moreover, the idea of a barrier was not unknown in the Arab world. In 2004, Saudi Arabia began construction on an agreed separation barrier between itself and Yemen. In October 2006, Saudi Arabia and Iraq agreed to build a fence between the two countries.

In his last Knesset speech in October 1995 before his assassination, Rabin argued for a modification of the Green Line including the addition of Gush Etzion, Efrat, and Beitar and the annexation of Ma'ale Adumim and Givat Ze'ev to Jerusalem. Settlements would continue to be established on the West Bank and he compared them with the example of the Gaza settlements. All this was the first step in the election campaign that Rabin expected to fight against Netanyahu. His standing in the polls had been severely damaged by the Hamas suicide bombing campaign and he attempted to reposition himself to appeal to both Left and Right. His consolidation of settlements along the Green Line and the existence of the Shahal Commission suggested that Rabin was moving towards a position

[11] Neill Lochery, *The Israeli Labour Party: In the Shadow of the Likud* (London 1997) pp. 212–213.
[12] David Makovsky, "How to Build a Fence," *Foreign Affairs* vol.83 no.2 March–April 2004.
[13] *Ha'aretz* 19 December 2001.

of separation from the Palestinians. It could also be argued that this was designed purely to entice support for the 1996 election. While only the outline had been drawn – and this could be changed in the event of an election victory – Clinton significantly did not raise any objections.

Rabin's espousal of separation differed from Peres's vision of a 'New Middle East', based on economic cooperation. It also spelled the end of a policy which had been inaugurated by Moshe Dayan in 1977.[14] Dayan, like Peres, believed that economic well-being would mollify nationalist passions. The rise of Islamism and Israel's defence against suicide bombings put an end to this belief. The long closures and increasing unemployment meant a gradual economic separation. The Palestinian workforce which earned its daily bread through employment in Israel was gradually reduced and replaced by Jews from the former Soviet Union and foreign labourers.

After Rabin's death, Netanyahu made certain to keep the barrier off the government's agenda since it posed problems for the Likud at a point of ideological transition. For the Right, the barrier meant partition and the end to a Greater Israel. Yet the idea of physical separation was never far below the surface. When Sharon opposed the Hebron agreement in January 1997 on security grounds, he wrote to Netanyahu suggesting that walls should be built around the Jewish enclave in the city.

When Netanyahu was defeated by Ehud Barak in 1999, the idea of a separation barrier was resurrected. Barak argued that it should be built along the border decided in the final settlement agreed with the Palestinians.[15] He commented that 'the intention isn't to create a bubbling pressure cooker, but good neighbourhood relations'.[16] By October 1999, he was privately proposing that there should be no Jewish settlements on the Palestinian side of the barrier.[17]

The outbreak of the al-Aqsa Intifada persuaded ten different regional councils in 2001 to institute their own barriers as security measures. The Emek Hefer local authority built more walls and an electric fence. The Gilboa regional council began the digging of a deep trench. The Sharon government refused to contemplate a barrier because it would imply a unilateral withdrawal. One commentator pointed out that the emergence of a barrier represented the reversal of the spirit of Oslo, but also of policies that had hitherto operated in the territories.

[14] Neill Lochery, *The View from the Fence: The Arab–Israeli Conflict from the Present to Its Roots* (London 2005) p. 5.
[15] *Yediot Aharanot* 27 October 2000.   [16] *Ha'aretz* 22 October 1999.
[17] Yossi Beilin, *The Path to Geneva: The Quest for a Permanent Agreement 1996–2004* (New York 2004) p. 114.

Instead of a slow process of peace and conciliation, only at the end of which the border and the barrier will be decided, it would be better to start with the border fence now and only afterwards to deal, for good or for ill, with every neighbour who will take his place behind it. The dovish slogans may therefore have to be updated – instead of 'Peace Now, border later', let it be 'Border Now, peace later'.[18]

At the end of his term of office, Barak asked Uzi Dayan, the head of the National Security Council, to develop a detailed plan for a barrier. In 2001, Sharon was advised by both the security services and President Katzav to build a barrier.[19] By the beginning of 2002, there were many proposals for a barrier, which cut across party lines. Many on the Right opposed it because it would leave numerous settlements outside on Palestinian territory. In 2007, 65,440 settlers resided in seventy-four settlements, east of the fence route. Many on the Israeli Left also found themselves in a moral and political dilemma. A barrier such as the existing one surrounding Gaza had clearly prevented suicide bombers from entering Israel. All such acts of terror moved Israelis further to the Right and undermined the peace camp. Similarly, for those Palestinians who espoused a two-state solution, it prevented Islamists from presenting themselves as 'the resistance to the occupation'. Yet the barrier trapped tens of thousands of Palestinians in the seam between it and the Green Line. Others were separated from their fields, still others from their places of work and their schools.

When Sharon finally agreed to build the barrier in June 2002, following the Passover bombing in Netanya, opinion polls suggested that not only did it find favour amongst the overwhelming majority of Israelis, but a sizeable proportion of the Left also supported its construction. In August 2003, the Peace Index registered 63 per cent of Meretz voters in favour of the barrier and indicated that 55.5 per cent of Israelis overall wanted to leave settlements outside.[20] Yet a physical barrier also prevented dialogue between Israelis and Palestinians. Such discussions now took place in Europe. It also cut off Israelis from the Palestinian reality. As one political observer noted:

Fences and concrete walls may bring about 'good' neighbours, but only because they prevent any contact with them. The neighbours are neither 'good' nor 'bad'; they simply become invisible.[21]

The energies of the Left and the Right were instead directed towards determining the actual path of the barrier. The Right wished to push it

---

[18] Doron Rosenblum, *Ha'aretz* 7 December 2001.   [19] *Yediot Aharanot* 26 April 2002.
[20] *Ha'aretz* 7 August 2003.
[21] David Newman, 'Barriers or Bridges? On Borders, Fences and Walls', *Tikkun* vol.18 no.6 November–December 2003.

eastwards to encompass as many settlements and water sources, natural springs and wells as possible. The Left wished to move to as close to the Green Line as possible. The Association for Civil Rights in Israel petitioned the country's Supreme Court in December 2003 to permit Palestinians to move freely through the gates of the security barrier. The Supreme Court was approached on other occasions; often as a result the barrier was moved closer to the Green Line. In June 2006, it ordered the state to dismantle the fence which encircled the settlement of Tzufin. The government was forced to admit that the real reason for its erection had not been to ensure security, but to advance plans to create an industrial zone in Tzufin.[22]

Approximately a quarter of the West Bank settler population was scheduled to be left outside the barrier. At a cost of almost $2 million per kilometre, it would accomplish a de facto annexation of between 8 and 10 per cent of the West Bank, leaving 20,000–30,000 Palestinians on the Israeli side. Moreover, as a result of the stagnation of transferring land to the Palestinians under the terms of Oslo II, Area C, some 60 per cent of the West Bank, was still under Israeli control. Palestinians were forbidden to build there and two-thirds of this territory through expansion remained under the jurisdiction of the settlers.

While such settlement consolidation west of the barrier was taking place, the development of bypasses to those outside continued. This compartmentalization of the West Bank diminished Palestinian territorial contiguity. Whereas Bush had spoken of a Palestinian state 'that is viable, contiguous, sovereign and independent' in his letter, the actual Disengagement plan mentioned Palestinian territorial contiguity as applying only to the northern West Bank where the evacuation of four settlements was planned. In the whole of the West Bank, 'Palestinian transportation contiguity' was substituted. This meant a series of roads and bypasses, aimed at total separation between Israelis and Palestinians. Although Sharon had accepted the idea of a Palestinian state, it was one which was highly fragmented in enclaves and non–territorially contiguous. It was radically different from the Clinton Parameters and the Geneva Initiative.

Moreover, the Israelis had tried to reassure the Americans in a letter to the US National Security Advisor, Condoleeza Rice, that the barrier would not be there forever; it would be

a security rather than a political barrier . . . temporary rather than permanent and therefore should not prejudice any final status issues including final borders.[23]

---

[22] *Ha'aretz* 15 June 2006.
[23] Letter from Dov Weisglass to Condoleeza Rice, *Jerusalem Post* 19 April 2004.

American pressure tried to ensure that the barrier approach as close to the Green Line as possible and coerced the Israelis initially not to include Ariel and Kedumim, which jutted out into the West Bank. The US State Department proposed a cut in loan guarantees to Israel which would match their expenditure on constructing the barrier and bypass roads in the West Bank. This persuaded the Israelis to consult the Americans on the path of the second stage of the barrier. In order to assuage American objections, they pointed to the fact that thefts were 40 per cent lower in the area cut off by the barrier and that in two separate infiltrations by Nablus suicide bombers, the bombers had to make their way to south of the fence in order to get into Israel.

While the Americans accepted that the barrier would make an indentation into the West Bank in order to protect Ben-Gurion airport against missile attacks, they opposed any penetration northeast of the Green Line toward Ramallah. To circumvent American objections, Ariel, Modi'in, Gush Etzion and the south Hebron settlement blocs were all placed under the wing of the fence, but not enclosed within it. The army proposed to create a 400-metre security zone around each settlement outside the barrier. The Americans were concerned that the barrier around Jerusalem would further truncate a Palestinian state. Ironically Sharon, who vowed that Jerusalem would never be divided, allowed the barrier to segment the city. In March 2006, the Americans objected to Israeli plans to build a new neighbourhood in the E-1 zone between Jerusalem and Ma'ale Adumim.

The United States had softened its stand on the barrier when Mahmoud Abbas resigned as Prime Minister of the PA and Arafat once more reasserted his centralized control. The United States vetoed a UN Security Council resolution condemning the barrier and was in a minority of 4 when 144 members of the UN General Assembly passed a similar resolution. The Palestinians made the barrier a cause célèbre and ensured that the UN took the issue to the International Court of Justice at the Hague. The Court duly gave its non-binding decision that the structure was illegal and should be dismantled. Attempted suicide bombings continued in areas where the barrier had not been erected. This allowed Sharon to refute the Court's decision in the name of Israeli security.

BETWEEN PRAGMATISM AND IDEOLOGY

Sharon's strongest supporter within the Likud in advocating disengagement was Ehud Olmert. Sharon had saved Olmert from parliamentary oblivion when he was placed thirty-third on the list of potential party candidates for the 2003 elections. Sharon put Olmert in charge of the election campaign instead. Ehud Olmert hit out on two fronts – against the Geneva Initiative from the Left and opposition to disengagement from within his own party, led by Netanyahu and Shalom. Yet even Likud veterans such as Moshe Arens came out against the Disengagement plan. He argued that any disengagement should be linked to an ability to take action against militant Palestinian organizations. Since neither Arafat nor Mahmoud Abbas was willing to take the necessary action, then the Jordanians, he suggested, should once more be approached.[24]

Sharon had already faced a raucous reception at a Likud conference in January 2004 when he announced that some Jewish settlements would have to be relinquished. On his return from Washington in April, Sharon warned that if the Likud did not approve the Disengagement plan, then the hard-won pledges in Bush's letter would become null and void. When the Likud held a party referendum in which a little more than half the members voted, it came as no surprise that almost 60 per cent voted against Sharon's Disengagement plan.

Despite Bush's pledges, they also noted that a settlement freeze was called for as well as the uprooting of settlement outposts. Despite the fact that Netanyahu controlled the Likud central committee, it did not represent the views of the ordinary Likud voter. The Peace Index for May 2004 indicated 59 per cent of Likud voters supported the Disengagement plan, reflecting a majority support in the country.[25] The results of the Likud referendum embarrassed Bush, who had to respond to both Arab and European protests about his letter to Sharon. Indeed, in Britain, fifty-two ambassadors and heads of mission – mainly to the Arab world – took the unprecedented step of publishing their opposition to the letter.[26] Yet the Likud referendum result provoked the first public discussion about the formation of a new party to support the Disengagement plan.

Successive Israeli governments were always reluctant to disclose how much was being spent on the settlement drive. There had been a study by the economist Dror Tsaban for Peace Now in 2002 and the Adva Center monitored investment in the territories, but information from politicians, treasury officials and economic leaders was often incomplete and misleading. No government report had ever been published on this sensitive subject. In 2003, *Ha'aretz* carried out a detailed investigation and analysis of the non-military cost of the settlements on the West Bank and Gaza and concluded that it amounted to approximately 50 billion shekels – 'a

[24] *Ha'aretz* 6 January 2004. [25] *Ha'aretz* 12 May 2004. [26] *Independent* 27 April 2004.

conservative figure and . . . the real figure is possibly higher'.[27] The investigation also believed that between 1.5 and 2.5 billion shekels from the annual defence budget went on direct and indirect expenditure on the settlements.

Sharon had pledged to uproot all illegal outposts on the West Bank in accordance with the Road Map and went about it in a half-hearted manner initially to placate both the settlers and the Likud. The Sasson Report in 2005, commissioned by the Prime Minister's Office, demonstrated that at least 70 million shekels had been spent by the Ministry of Housing on eighty-one illegal outposts during the tenures of Netanyahu and Sharon.

Although Oslo had effectively frozen new settlements, the Sasson Report also indicated that five outposts had been established during Rabin's premiership at a cost of 10 million shekels. Many were located on private or partially private land. Whereas outpost construction decreased under the Rabin government as the peace process moved forward, the coming to power of Netanyahu reversed this approach and the construction of new outposts and the thickening of old ones seemingly did not require government approval.

Sasson took as her basis the Begin Government resolution that, following a Supreme Court ruling on the settlement of Elon Moreh in 1979, no settlement should be established on anything but state land. Yet, according to the report, twenty-four illegal outposts had been established since Sharon's election victory in 2001. Moreover, operating indirectly through regional councils, the Ministry of Construction and Housing had

created a special budgetary clause, named 'general development miscellaneous' and used it for financing unauthorized outposts. In 2001, the amount in this section was 17 million shekels. In 2002, it was 34 million shekels. No criteria were set for the usage of this money. There is no public transparency concerning the goals and exploitation of this budget.

This damning report concluded:

Any government policy must obey the law. All officials and politicians are governed by law. The actions described are not a matter of political views. It is a matter of law enforcement, a question of the rule of law.

Clearly, many a West Bank settler believed that 'a Zionist deed' transcended such an argument. Moreover, a Netanyahu government resolution of 2 August 1996 argued that only the Minister of Defence had the authority to authorize outposts. While this appeared to place an obstacle in the

---

[27] *Ha'aretz* 2 October 2003.

construction of any future settlement, Netanyahu also stated in the cabinet meeting that 'the previous government (of Rabin) placed chains and bonds upon the natural development of the Jewish communities in Judea, Samaria and Gaza'[28] and this policy would be reversed.

This led to the obfuscation of the definition of 'the area of jurisdiction of a settlement'. It meant in practice that a new settlement could be constructed as a 'neighbourhood' of an old one. Kfar Adumim spawned Nofei Prat and Shchunat Alon. Nofei Prat then begat Nofei Prat West. A decade later a Settlement Watch report claimed that 90 per cent of all West Bank settlements deviated from their areas of jurisdiction – and that most which did so were outside the security barrier.[29]

The cabinet vote on the Disengagement plan was a close call. Sharon dismissed two far Right Ministers a couple of days before the vote and secured the support of Netanyahu and Shalom by excluding any mention of the exchange of letters between Bush and Sharon which clearly stated that settlements would ultimately be evacuated. Seventeen out of the forty Likud members of Knesset refused to support the bill, designed to fund the evacuation and resettlement of the Jewish settlers of Gaza, in November 2004. The division was clearly a further demonstration that the party was split on such a fundamental issue. This was underlined when the Likud Central Committee gave Sharon a wafer-thin majority for a proposal to reschedule the party primaries. On this occasion, 91 per cent turned out to vote to choose in reality between Sharon's more pragmatic approach regarding the evacuation of settlements and Netanyahu's more ideological one.

Although there had been a vocal and emotional campaign by the Gaza settlers – a central slogan was 'Jews do not expel Jews' – the actual evacuation of the Gaza settlements in September 2005 went off without any undue violence. Unlike both Rabin and Barak, Sharon confronted the settlers. Despite receiving compensation, the unhappy settlers staged demonstrations and protests, wrote petitions and went on hunger strikes. In some cases, they vented their frustration on Palestinians and there was a spate of olive tree uprootings. The IDF and the police, however, were determined and underwent intensive training so as not to react to provocations. In most cases, settlers left with a quiet dignity. Others left in a rage at the enforced and humiliating end of a quarter of a century of hard work. In Kfar Darom, there was civil disobedience and the settlers and their supporters

---

[28] Government Communiqué on Settlement Activities, 2 August 1996.
[29] Peace Now Settlement Watch report, June 2007.

were removed by force. By December 2005, the first crops leaving former settler greenhouses – now run by the Palestine Economic Development Company – reached the Israeli market.[30]

Yet although nearly 9,000 Jewish settlers had been evacuated from Gaza in 2005, the Central Bureau of Statistics revealed that 12,000 new settlers had actually moved to the West Bank. The total Jewish population at the end of 2006, according to the Interior Ministry, was 268,379. The average growth of the Jewish population in the West Bank was 5.8 per cent in 2006 compared to a 1.4 per cent growth for the population in Israel itself.[31]

Disengagement and the evacuation of settlements represented an ideological challenge to the proponents of redemptionist Zionism – the variant of religious Zionism that had been dominant since 1967. Disengagement actually brought to the surface other debates within the world of religious Zionism such as cooperation with the secularists and the value of bodies of non-religious knowledge. The rabbis were split on what advice to proffer to religious soldiers who were carrying out the evacuation. Some accepted that this action represented the democratic will of the people. Others left it as a matter of individual conscience and refused to endorse a call for mass disobedience. Former Chief Rabbi Avraham Shapira did ask soldiers to disobey orders, yet only sixty-three actually did so.

Some, such as Rabbi Dov Lior, understood territorial compromise to be a transgression of the Torah, and therefore obeying orders to evacuate was tantamount to a desecration of the Sabbath. He gave dispensation to his supporters to use their telephones on the Jewish Sabbath if they noted the approach of IDF troops with the specific aim of removing settler outposts.[32] Disengagement, it was argued, was actually part of a broader assault by the secular state on religious Zionism, of which an example was the recent dismantling of the Ministry of Religious Affairs. On the other hand, Aharon Lichtenstein opposed insubordination as it fragmented the moral fabric of Israeli society. Rabbi Shlomo Aviner, a follower of Avraham Yitzhak Kook, argued that a ruling over all areas of the Land of Israel must be supported by the majority.

If the majority decides to relinquish their hold on parts of the Land of Israel, they may be committing a sin, but their decision changes the halachic reality. The individual has no obligation to control all parts of Israel. His responsibility is limited to settling somewhere in the Land of Israel. Only the majority is commanded to rule over all parts of the Land of Israel. That's why Lebanon is not considered part of the Land of Israel, King David conquered it without the support of the people.[33]

[30] *Ha'aretz* 11 December 2005.   [31] *Ha'aretz* 9 January 2007.   [32] *Jerusalem Post* 14 July 2009.
[33] *Jerusalem Post* 30 September 2005.

The disengagement set in motion a fragmentation of religious Zionism into redemptionist, Kookist and Mizrachi camps – representing the evolution of their movement. The historical positioning of the religious Zionists between the ultra-orthodox and the secularists led some to deepen their religiosity while still maintaining their Zionism. Others argued that disengagement from Gaza did not mean disengagement from the state of Israel.

Throughout 2005, Sharon and his supporters were dependent on Peres and Labour party support for disengagement in both government and the Knesset. Isaac Herzog, the Labour Minister of Construction and Housing, halted building in fifty West Bank settlements and issued new regulations for the distribution of caravans to settlers in a bid to halt the establishment of hilltop outposts.

By November 2005, months of bitter in-fighting in the Likud and in government came to a close when the newly elected leader of the Labour party, Amir Peretz, pulled his ministers out of the government coalition. New elections became inevitable and the split in the Likud could no longer be papered over. Despite the fact that centrist parties were electorally unsuccessful, Sharon announced his intention to run as the leader of a new party, Kadima. The first opinion polls indicated that it had garnered wide support amongst the Israeli public. Some 62 per cent of Likud voters and 42 per cent of Labour's now favoured Kadima.[34] Despite the traditional failure of centrist parties, this seemed to be a genuine realignment of political forces.

OLMERT'S ARRIVAL AND HAMAS'S ASCENT

In Sharon's government, there were in reality six Kadima ministers and six Likud ministers. Even the party 'princes' – those whose background was in the Irgun 'fighting family' – begged to differ. Uzi Landau remained with the Likud while Tzipi Livni moved to Kadima. Moreover, the schism in the Likud represented an ideological unravelling of the party which Begin and Sharon had established in 1973. Former Mapai adherents who had left the party with Ben-Gurion and effectively moved to the Right now left the Likud to join Kadima. Similarly, Shimon Peres, who had followed Ben-Gurion out of Mapai but returned to the Labour party, also joined Kadima.

The new party attracted those who did not need ideology as a political container but thought independently. Ehud Olmert had fallen out with Menachem Begin in 1966 and left Herut. He joined the Free Centre, which eventually became a constituent of the Likud. Kadima, in one sense, was a party influenced by both Ben-Gurion and Jabotinsky whereas the

[34] *Ha'aretz* 9 December 2005.

Likud still looked to Menachem Begin. Likud was left with a rump of true believers who soon returned Netanyahu to its helm. Above all, Kadima was the party of Arik Sharon, whose military prowess and political astuteness were now held in awe by the Israeli public in the aftermath of the Intifada. He was now depicted as the wise grandfather of the nation – a dramatic change in public imagery from past perceptions.

Yet within a few weeks of the emergence of Kadima, Sharon suffered a mild stroke. He recovered quickly and his public relations people made light of it, but the writing was on the wall. Even after Sharon's second stroke, his incapacitation and removal from the political equation, Kadima prospered under Ehud Olmert in the election of 2006 – even though 25 per cent of its original supporters ultimately changed their minds and voted for other parties. Kadima's victory was helped by the scuppering of the law which provided for the direct election of the Prime Minister, which had produced political instability throughout the 1990s. Once more, Israelis voted solely for the party. The fragmentation of the large parties was also prevented by raising the minimum threshold for Knesset representation to 2 per cent of the vote. Surplus vote transfer laws were in the process of being abandoned.

Israelis also voted for Kadima because despite the Intifada the economy had picked up in 2004 with a lessening of tension. Foreign investment stood at $5.3 billion compared with $537 million in 1993. The GDP increased by 2.4 per cent in 2004 and was accompanied by a rise in employment. Exports of goods and services increased by 14 per cent in 2004.

Olmert's convergence plan of withdrawing from parts of the West Bank remained the hope of the Bush administration, the Quartet and the G-8 group of nations – all of whom endorsed it without formally ditching the Road Map. Olmert's government was led by Kadima and Labour – Amir Peretz became Minister of Defence. It was a coalition of those who supported separation from the Palestinians. Kadima believed a unilateral withdrawal would help to manage relations with the Palestinians while Labour still clung to the hope of a permanent status agreement with Mahmoud Abbas.

There had also been a dramatic change on the Palestinian political scene. While Sharon's Disengagement plan had the support of 64 per cent of Israelis, it was also endorsed by 73 per cent of Palestinians.[35] But any real political change was stifled while Arafat remained at the helm. Arafat's death in November 2004 cleared a political and psychological space for both the Israeli and Palestinian administrations.

[35] *Jerusalem Times* 8 April 2004.

Moreover, Mahmoud Abbas's only political rival was effectively removed when a Tel Aviv district court found Marwan Barghouti, the Fatah prince-in-waiting, guilty of murder for authorizing attacks that killed a Greek Orthodox monk in the West Bank in 2001, an Israeli at the Jewish settlement of Givat Ze'ev in 2002 and three people at a Tel Aviv restaurant in 2002. Significantly, Mahmoud Abbas was appointed chairman of the Executive Committee of the PLO within hours of Arafat's demise. He had lasted only a few months in 2003 as the first Prime Minister of the Palestinian Authority and failed to wrench any power away from Arafat. His relations with Arafat were tense and often antagonistic.

Israeli hopes – both in Sharon's government and in the peace camp – were high because Mahmoud Abbas had always been critical about the rationale behind the Intifada. He soon spoke about an end to the armed struggle and embarking instead on 'the democratic road to liberation'.[36] Yet like Arafat, Mahmoud Abbas did not believe in using armed force against the Islamists and their allies. Afraid of provoking a civil war and having none of Arafat's commanding authority, he was unable to stop the firing of Qassam rockets from Gaza into Israel. A few days after the election, six Israelis were killed at the Karni Crossing into Gaza.

The Islamists had called for a sixty-day moratorium on military action before the January 2005 Palestinian presidential election. In addition, Mahmoud Abbas deployed 2,000 police officers in northern Gaza in an attempt to prevent the firing of Qassams and mortar shells. This was part of a broader exercise in reversing Arafat's policies and generally reforming the PA. He dismissed a large number of Arafat's military and civilian advisors as well as the 1,000 staff employed by his predecessor's Ramallah office. He apologized to Kuwait for the PLO stand during the first Gulf war and he described the efficacy of the Qassams as 'completely useless'.[37] Sharon and Mahmoud Abbas agreed to a formal cessation of hostilities in February 2005 and the following month thirteen Palestinian factions agreed to 'a period of calm' until the end of the year.

Mahmoud Abbas had persuaded Hamas to agree to this because he had promised to integrate them into the PA if they participated in the elections for the Legislative Council and stopped the armed struggle for a limited period. Hamas recognized that Mahmoud Abbas was not Arafat and that policies of pragmatism and reform were now being followed. Hamas in turn believed that if it fared well in the elections, it would be able to inhibit any rapprochement with Israel. Already in December 2004, Hamas had won 9 constituencies out of 26 in municipal elections.

[36] *Daily Star* 9 December 2004. [37] *Jerusalem Post* 4 January 2005.

This was far different from the elections of 1996, when Hamas had advocated a boycott – and the Palestinians turned out in unprecedented numbers to vote for Arafat. At that time Fatah secured 68 out of 88 seats.

In 2005, in local elections, it swept Nablus, a Fatah stronghold, with 73 per cent of the vote. The swing to Hamas was largely a reaction to Fatah's stagnation, corruption and indolence. The Legislative Council election which took place in January 2006 registered a massive swing to Hamas, unexpectedly taking 76 seats out of 132 in the Legislative Council. Half the vote was based on constituencies; the other half was by proportional representation. Even though Abbas had promised to call a general conference of Fatah – the first since 1989 – its vote was badly affected by dissension and division, with too many standing as independents. Indeed a week before the elections, there were 120 independent Fatah candidates against 130 official ones.[38]

Moreover, the old guard in Fatah feared the rise of the younger generation. This resulted in Hamas's garnering 44 per cent of the vote compared to Fatah's 41 per cent. Effectively Palestine was now divided between the nationalists and the Islamists.

In bypassing the PA, Sharon's unilateralism had further weakened Abbas and now Hamas reaped the electoral harvest. Hamas now controlled one wing of the Palestinian government, but not the right to negotiate with the Israelis. This remained the prerogative of Mahmoud Abbas and the PLO.

Abbas duly appointed Hamas's Ismail Haniyeh as Prime Minister, but he asked Hamas to accept all UN resolutions and Arab League decisions including the Saudi peace initiative as well as all PLO agreements with the Israelis since 1993. This was the price of joining Fatah in negotiations with Israel.

In addition, Abbas quickly transferred responsibility for the security forces, information and finance to the office of the President. He further created the post of Secretary-General, who would be in charge of personnel and salaries. The outgoing parliament in which Fatah possessed a majority allowed Abbas the right to appoint a nine-judge constitutional court which had the right to resolve any dispute between the presidency and parliament. This included the right to place laws in abeyance. Hamas, needless to say, began to overturn all these measures as soon as it attained power.

Israel, on the other hand, declared that it would not recognize any Palestinian government that included Hamas unless it ended the armed

---

[38] Graham Usher, 'The Democratic Resistance: Hamas, Fatah and the Palestinian Elections', *Journal of Palestine Studies* vol.35 no.3 Spring 2006.

struggle and decommissioned its weapons. Like Abbas, Olmert stated that Hamas had to accept all previous agreements and called upon it to amend its charter to recognize Israel's right to exist as 'a Jewish state'.

All of this was anathema to Hamas, which could not extend any sort of recognition. As Khaled Meshal pointed out, 'Oslo is not only dead, it has rotted'.[39]

When it became apparent that Israel was implicitly recognized in the Prisoners' Document, which its representative formulated with Fatah, Hamas withdrew its signature.

Hamas's broad response was that that it would adhere to existing Israel–PLO agreements as long as they did not conflict with 'fundamental Palestinian national principles'. It argued that it would not renounce the armed struggle while Israel occupied Palestinian land. How far the occupation stretched was unclear. Its stand appeared to be a state in the West Bank and Gaza with sovereignty in Jerusalem, but this was not a permanent solution.

Israel's conditions were endorsed by most of the Quartet – the US, the UN and the EU – but not its fourth member, Russia, which invited Hamas to Moscow. Turkey and South Africa also asked Hamas representatives to visit them. Olmert further stated that Israel would suspend the monthly transfer of tax rebates amounting to $50 million per month. Moreover Abbas was dependent on the US and the EU to pay the wages of 135,000 public sector employees with nearly a million dependents.

In June 2006, Israeli forces arrested sixty government ministers, parliamentarians and activists including the deputy Prime Minister, Nasser al-Shaer.

Hamas vehemently opposed the sanctions of the international community. Khaled Meshal therefore visited Egypt, Turkey, Saudi Arabia and Iran. The Muslim Brotherhood, operating in eighty-six countries, initiated a worldwide fundraising campaign. Iran reportedly offered to increase its financial aid to Hamas substantially.

Both Hamas and Islamic Jihad continued to fire Qassam rockets from Gaza into Israel and made attempts to establish a rocket base on the West Bank as well – this continued after the Gaza settlements had been evacuated. Islamic Jihad – perhaps marking the tense theological difference with its rival, Hamas – refused to participate in any election.[40]

Yet Hamas was not a product of the spirit of the European Enlightenment as perhaps Fatah and other national liberation movements could claim to be. While exhibiting national characteristics and opposed to colonialism

[39] *al-Jazeera.net* 26 January 2006. [40] *Ha'aretz* 15 December 2004.

and occupation, it owed more to the Iranian Revolution and the example of Hezbollah in Lebanon. It seemingly could not recognize Israel or embrace a two-state solution although early Islam accepted Dar al-'Ahd (the Land of the Covenant), where non-Muslim rule over territory outside Dar al-Islam was permitted. Instead it spoke only of tahadiyah (a period of calm) or a hudna (a short-term truce). It projected itself as both a governing authority and a resistance movement. Its policy during the election was based on Sheikh Yassin's pronouncements that Hamas would accept an interim agreement of a Palestinian state within the areas conquered by Israel in 1967. There would be a complete evacuation to the pre-1967 borders, the removal of all settlements, the absolutist interpretation of the right of return, no demilitarization of the Palestinian state and a retaining of the Mandate borders of Palestine.

While there was no mention of eradicating Israel in its election manifesto, there was no acceptance of it either. Hamas neither recognized Israel nor accepted it as a permanent fixture. There was no unambiguous statement of an Israeli state alongside a Palestinian state. Its absolutism was predicated on the fear of being sucked into a process of stages and the suggestion of packages.

This road constitutes an attempt to weaken the Palestinian position, to lure the Palestinians into lowering the ceiling of their demands and to use the time factor and pressure which will not work with us.[41]

Indeed, Khalid Meshal was clear about the goals of Hamas only a few weeks after its victory in the polls. In a mosque in Damascus, he stated:

Palestine means Palestine in its entirety – from the Mediterranean to the Jordan, from Ras al-Naqura to Rafah. We cannot give up a single inch of it. Therefore we will not recognise the Israeli enemy's right to a single inch.[42]

Its defeat of Fatah in the polls had been a surprise to Hamas. It had hoped to emerge as a powerful opposition rather than as a government. It was therefore psychologically as well as politically not prepared to make fundamental decisions about the conflict. All this sharpened the ideological differences with Fatah.

Only the far Left in Israel advocated negotiations with Hamas – albeit with uncertainty. The mainstream Left resigned itself to accepting that Hamas's refusal to recognize Israel was based on an ideological delegitimization. The idea that Hamas wanted not only to repair Palestinian

---

[41] Reuters interview with Khaled Meshal, *Ha'aretz* 10 January 2007.
[42] MEMRI special dispatch 1083 1 February 2006.

society, but to prepare it for the next round in the hope of reversing the war of 1948, was a belief that could not be dispelled. The main hope of the Israeli Left lay therefore in bolstering Mahmoud Abbas and condemning the Olmert government for effectively abandoning him.

THE RISE OF HEZBOLLAH

The eyes of the Israeli government had been focused since 2000 on the West Bank and Gaza and on suppressing the Intifada. In May 2000, the Israelis had withdrawn overnight from southern Lebanon and left a political and military vacuum, which was not filled by the Lebanese government. Instead, Hezbollah claimed a victory in forcing the Israelis out. This built on Hezbollah's claim to be the military protector of Lebanon. Even Arab nationalists, opposed to the Islamists, believed that this was the first time that an Arab group had liberated land from Israel. There were many Palestinians who perceived Hezbollah's 'victory' as a model which should be emulated. Indeed, the Hezbollah Secretary-General, Hassan Nasrullah, made a victory speech in Bint Jbail shortly after the withdrawal, pointing to the clear difference between the failure to deliver the Oslo Accords and the success of the armed struggle.

The Shi'ite community of southern Lebanon had actually been friendly to the early Zionist settlers and many Palestinian Jews holidayed there in the 1920s. When fighting took place, they were given temporary refuge in Shi'ite villages. Members of the Shi'ite village of Kila worked on Jewish farms in the Metulla area.[43] The Lebanese civil war in the 1970s and the presence of Palestinian armed groups in the area catalyzed a trend towards a militant resurgence of the Shi'ites. The Shi'ite revolution in Iran in 1979 was seen as a beacon of hope by an impoverished community. The Israeli incursion in 1978, Operation Litani and the invasion of 1982 to confront the PLO presence in Lebanon resulted in the mobilization and radicalization of the Shi'ites.

After the PLO departure from Beirut, Amal, the Shi'ite militia joined the National Salvation Front. The Islamists strongly objected and broke away to form Hezbollah. Suicide bombing, which had been employed in the war against Saddam's Iraq, was imported from Iran. Hezbollah activity in support of Palestinian Islamists was confined to the Middle East although they were held responsible for the bombing of the Israeli embassy in Buenos Aires in 1992 and the city's Jewish Cultural Centre

---

[43] *Ha'aretz* 9 August 2006.

two years later. Hezbollah's opposition to Israel was uncompromising: 'Even if hundreds of years pass by, Israel's existence will continue to be an illegal existence'[44] on the philosophical basis that 'a falsehood cannot be transformed into a righteousness over time'. Zionism was deemed to have emerged from Judaism – 'a Torah and Talmudic ideology' – rather than from nineteenth-century European nationalism. The Jews were perceived to be an untrustworthy people. Even the Holocaust was often depicted as a Jewish conspiracy. Hezbollah regarded Zionism as the central enemy of Islamic civilization. The organization recalled that the Prophet Mohammed had defeated the Jews at the battle of Khayber. Hezbollah's long-range missiles were named after this. The mobilizing slogan directed against Israel was 'Khayber, Khayber, O Jews, the army of Mohammed will return'.

An early manifesto in 1985 illustrated Hezbollah's approach towards its southern neighbour.

Our primary assumption in our fight against Israel states that the Zionist entity is aggressive from its inception, and built on lands wrested from their owners, at the expense of the rights of the Muslim people. Therefore our struggle will end only when this entity is obliterated. We recognize no treaty with it, no ceasefire and no peace agreements, whether separate or consolidated.[45]

In the 1980s, Hezbollah opposed the Camp David agreement, the Fahd, Reagan and Brezhnev plans – any scheme which implied recognition.

A recurring phrase of Sheikh Mohammed Fadlallah, the spiritual mentor of Hezbollah, was that 'there were no innocent Jews in Palestine'. All this was very different from the PLO, which was just beginning to engage the Israeli peace camp in discussion. Following the conclusion of the Iran–Iraq war and apparent rapprochement between the PLO and 'the Zionist entity', Teheran began to support the alternative Palestinian agenda through the strengthening of Hezbollah's ties with Hamas. In part this meant the delivery of arms and the training of personnel. In May 2006, Nasrallah said that the organization had accumulated more than 12,000 missiles since 1992.[46] Newer weapons arrived in 2005 including advanced Russian anti-tank missiles. Iranian personnel had been stationed in Lebanon since 2002 to train Hezbollah fighters in their use. Moreover, Syria passed on information to Hezbollah. This was based on agreements with both Moscow and Teheran to share intelligence. There was a new listening post on the Syrian side

[44] As Safir 24 August 1998 in Amal Saad-Ghorayeb, *Hizbu'llah: Politics and Religion* (London 2002) p. 135.
[45] As Safir 16 February 1985 in *the Jerusalem Quarterly* no. 48 Autumn 1988.   [46] Memri no.1176.

of the Golan Heights, operated jointly with Iran, and this, itself, emerged out of a broader strategic accord between the two countries in November 2005.[47]

According to Israeli intelligence, Hezbollah received on average $50 million per year from Iran in addition to arms and ammunition from both Iran and Syria. Hezbollah's social network was based on its ability to build through its construction company, Jihad al-Bina, and the organization's partnership with government corporations such as the airport authority. Above all, it built its support on its ability to respond to the needs of ordinary people. In July 2006, it was believed to be providing services to about 10 per cent of Lebanon's citizens.[48] It also received funds from cultivating hashish fields in southern Lebanon and the Bekaa Valley – money-making concerns to which the Lebanese government objected.

Under Hezbollah, southern Lebanon experienced a remarkable recovery in the 1990s with the construction of hospitals, schools and community centres, but there were also bunkers and military bases. Hezbollah also embarked on transforming itself from being purely an armed militia into a political party. In the 2003 municipal elections, Hezbollah won 40 per cent of the Shi'ite vote; the rest went to Amal. In the general election in 2005, it won 12 out of the 27 seats allocated to the Shi'ites in the 128-seat National Assembly.

In October 2000, a few months after the Israeli withdrawal from Lebanon, three Israeli soldiers were killed in a botched kidnap attempt by Hezbollah on the northern border. Barak did not respond. He did not want to fight on two fronts as he was preoccupied with the outbreak of the Intifada. Starting with a kidnap attempt at the border village of Ghajar on 21 November 2005, there were five more attempts to abduct Israeli soldiers in the coming months. For the first time since October 2000, Hezbollah was actually successful in July 2006. A couple of months before this, Israel had warned Hezbollah through US and French diplomats that there would be a large-scale response if this continued. Even so, it came as a surprise when Israel responded vehemently. Hezbollah, however, stood its ground and a thirty-four-day war ensued.

Hezbollah was not a national movement opposing an occupation, in the sense that Hamas was. It was not a war against settlements. This, its Islamist colouring and refusal to countenance any dialogue with even dovish Israelis led to a broad backing for government action by the Israeli public. There was no fragmentation of the national consensus of the

[47] *Ha'aretz* 3 October 2006. [48] *Ha'aretz* 26 July 2006.

kind that had prevailed in 1982. There was a dearth of protests against the war. Israelis differentiated between Hezbollah and the Palestinian question.

Hezbollah's excuse for ongoing attempts to kidnap soldiers from within Israel was the Israeli occupation of eighteen Shabaa farms, occupying twenty-five square kilometres, on the edge of Mount Hermon. In the 1970s, the Palestinians began to fire rockets into the Hula Valley in northern Israel, leading to the gradual Israeli presence. In addition, Israeli control of the farms meant that water from the melting snow of Mount Hermon could be directed to irrigate northern Israel.

The Shabaa farms had been in Syrian territory since the border was drawn by the British and the French in 1923. There was a verbal agreement between Syria and Lebanon in 1946 to divide the Shabaa lands between the two countries. Maps presented by the Lebanese government to the UN in the 1960s indicated that the territory was still part of Syria. There were, however, Lebanese citizens who held land deeds for the Shabaa farms under Syrian control. The farm owners paid taxes to Beirut and registered births and deaths in Lebanon. The Syrians permitted farmers to cross the border into Syria to feed the sheep. The maps of the UN force supervising the disengagement agreements between Israel and Syria also showed that the farms were in Syria. Syria recognized the farms as Lebanese territory but did not supply any legal documentation for fear of prejudicing its broader territorial claims to Lebanon. Indeed, in many Syrian textbooks, Lebanon appears as part of a Greater Syria.

Before the 1982 war, Syrian forces were deployed in this area. Israel therefore regarded the Shabaa farms as belonging to Syria.[49] There was also a growing belief amongst Israelis that returning the Shabaa farms would not appease Hezbollah. In June 2005, Nasrallah had given a speech in Dahiyeh in which he argued that Lebanon would not be complete without the Shabaa farms or 'the seven villages in northern occupied Palestine'.[50] This referred to the seven Metawali Shi'ite villages on the Israeli side of the border when it was delineated in 1923. Their inhabitants left for the safety of other Metawali villages on the Lebanese side of the border in May 1948 when Safed fell.

Perhaps the central reason for kidnapping soldiers was to trade them or their bodies for captured Arab fighters. The bodies of the 3 soldiers who were killed in 2000 were swapped for 59 Lebanese killed in fighting

[49] *Ha'aretz* 1 December 2000.   [50] *An Nahar* 15 September 2006.

and 435 Arab prisoners via German interlocutors. In addition, Hezbollah repeatedly called for the return of Samir al-Kuntar, who was sentenced in Israel in 1979 to 542 years' imprisonment. Going ashore at Nahariya in northern Israel, he shot dead a father and his four-year-old daughter. The mother, in hiding, smothered her baby to stop her from crying.

Sharon was urged in 2005 by his National Security Advisor, Giora Eiland, to launch a diplomatic initiative to settle the Lebanese–Israeli issues but did not do so because of his preoccupation with the Palestinians and disengagement. In May 2006, Olmert convened a preparatory discussion about Lebanon with the defence establishment and the Foreign Ministry. Giora Eiland once more presented a plan for an agreement, which included withdrawal from the Shabaa farms, the release of Arab prisoners and no more sorties beyond the Israel–Lebanon border. The Israeli military opposed this because they argued that Syria would not respect a deal over the Shabaa farms since it was a point of dispute between Syria and Lebanon. Olmert's compromise was withdrawal, but only in the context of a wider agreement including the disarming of Hezbollah and the redeployment of the Lebanese army.

In July 2006, Hezbollah fired missiles at an Israeli patrol on its side of the border, killing three soldiers and kidnapping two. Israel implemented airstrikes and the shelling of targets in southern Lebanon. Hezbollah's response to the Israeli attack was to put into practice its military preparations through the use of Katyushas, short-range missiles, fired into northern Israel and the threat of long-range missiles against major Israeli cities. Israel had kept medium- and long-range missiles under surveillance and destroyed them on the first night of the conflict; the short-range missiles, however, were ignored. During the summer of 2006, more than 4,000 missiles, mainly short-range Katyushas, were fired into northern Israel, leading to a concerted depopulation of the area. The Israeli military was unable to stop this.

Hezbollah's relative success in the war was due to an extensive series of fortified bunkers and a twenty-five kilometre reinforced tunnel system, buried deep underground, along the border with Israel. This was used to store and transport short-range missiles, weapons and men with great efficiency. Firing positions were protected such that the Israelis were unable to detect any heat emission. These were built after 2003 under the supervision of North Koreans, who had built up considerable expertise in tunnel construction since the Korean war. North Korea also transmitted to Hezbollah its expertise in defensive warfare, which it had been refining in the expectation of an American-led invasion ever since the 1950s.[51]

North Korea had built up a close relationship with Khomeini's Iran in the 1980s in supplying training and weaponry in the war with Saddam Hussein. This lucrative trade was further accentuated by North Korea's economic woes and the mass famines of the 1990s. An extension of this was the supply of war materiel to Hezbollah, whose leadership visited Pyongyang. Israel's intelligence failure to note the construction of the tunnels occurred in the wake of Barak's decision to leave southern Lebanon suddenly in 2000. The vacuum had been filled by Iran's deepening involvement in the region and the subsequent call upon North Korea's expertise.

During this conflict, the Israeli political and military echelon appeared to be indecisive and seemed to be changing tactics on almost a daily basis. Olmert was deeply concerned about repeating the errors of 1982, which had fragmented the national consensus. The Israeli military on the northern border, however, had been allocated meagre resources and fewer troops. Because of the IDF's preoccupation with the territories, there was a general laxity in supervision on the part of the General Staff. Moreover, Israeli troops, both in the regular army and amongst the reservists, were insufficiently trained. There were outdated maps and faulty equipment. The Intifada had led to cutbacks in the training budget and their exercises were directed towards the Palestinian territories and not towards Lebanon. The IDF therefore employed tactics which were suited to the ramshackle and uncoordinated Palestinian forces, but not to the well-trained Hezbollah. The navy, for example, did not expect Hezbollah to possess Iranian ground-to-sea missiles.

On the basis of US emphasis on air power, Dan Halutz, the IDF Chief of the General Staff, persisted in its use even though a ground operation was necessary, only giving the go-ahead in the final stage of the war. Moreover, the General Staff did not prepare for a ground incursion in time. Halutz only asked the government to call up reservists at a late stage. The political leadership, Olmert and Peretz, did not possess military expertise and relied solely on the military. The political echelon clearly knew little about the real state of affairs within the IDF.

The use of air power was paramount in attempting to stop the transportation of missiles from Syria and other parts of Lebanon. At first, the Israeli air force bombed transportation routes. This tactic, however,

---

[51] Testimony to the US District Court for the District of Columbia, 'Kaplan et al. vs Hezbollah et al.' Proposed Findings of Facts and Conclusions of Law, 2011.

gave way to creating a mass flight of civilians to create pressure on both Hezbollah and the Lebanese government to stop the firing of Katyushas on northern Israel. The bombed roads and the bridges, however, were impassable. Those fleeing the fighting were often unable to move. This tactic had been used before by the Israelis in Operation Accountability (1993) and in Operation Grapes of Wrath (1996). At that time, the Lebanese government made successful appeals to Syria and Iran which led to the imposition of a fragile ceasefire.

On this occasion, Syria did not intervene with Hezbollah and was therefore deliberately sidelined by the United States. In 2006, UN Security Council Resolution 1701 to redeploy the Lebanese army in the south and massively increase the UNIFIL force of 2,000 was carried out without Syrian involvement.

Hezbollah's missiles such as the Fajr-5 could hit Haifa and the Zelsal-1 would put Tel Aviv at risk. Many of these were either not used or put out of action by the Israeli military. Finally, ground troops moved in, often ill equipped and certainly unfamiliar with the terrain. In 1982, the Israeli invasion forces had swept past the border villages. Moreover, their withdrawal in 2000 and the liquidation of their ally, the South Lebanese Army, had left the Israelis bereft of good intelligence. This was most prevalent in the area south of the Litani River, from which most of the Katyushas were fired.

The gain for Israel was the deployment of the Lebanese army for the first time in forty years, and many more foreign troops were now stationed in southern Lebanon. Although Hezbollah tightly controlled press coverage and did not offer information that could produce negative coverage, between 500 and 800 Hezbollah fighters were believed to have been killed.

Hezbollah was severely criticized by one of the leaders of the Lebanese Shi'ites. The Mufti of Tyre in an interview in *al-Nahar* reminded Hezbollah that it only spoke for a minority of Shi'ites in Lebanon. No one in the Shi'ite community, he pointed out, had authorized Hezbollah to drag it into a war.[52]

Hezbollah, however, did not desert its posts when faced by the Israeli military and impressed both Israelis and the Arab world. According to Tel Aviv University's Peace Index, 74 per cent of Israelis thought that they were good fighters.[53] This short war cost the lives of 1,200 Lebanese and 157 Israelis. The financial cost of the war was estimated at $3–4 billion.[54]

[52] *An Nahar* 22 August 2006.   [53] Peace Index; 31 July–1 August, 2006.   [54] *Ha'aretz* 13 August 2006.

Israel did not produce a knock-out blow to Hezbollah, and the vulnerability of the northern border was exposed. Its bombing campaign was seen as less than successful. Even though many Israelis viewed it as a war of deterrence, the sight of fleeing villagers produced harsh international condemnation of Israeli actions. In addition, Hezbollah often placed its missiles in civilian areas and the Israeli response consequently killed innocent Lebanese bystanders.

Many Israeli Arabs who lived close to the border were also victims of Katyusha rocket attacks. Not all the Arab villages in the north of Israel had bomb shelters. Only after 1991 did the Israeli government legislate that all private contractors automatically had to build bomb shelters as well. In Lebanon, despite the millions of dollars expended by Syria and Iran, nothing was spent on equipping ordinary Lebanese civilians with air raid shelters.

Moreover, Israel fired some 1,800 missiles, which contained 1.2 million cluster bombs. These seem to have been fired during the last ten days of the conflict. There were also reports that phosphorus shells had been fired. Both types of armament were not banned by international law, but they were considered to be indiscriminate weapons and were condemned by groups such as the International Red Cross for their use against civilians in built-up areas.[55] Yet Hezbollah capitalized on the inertia and inefficiency of the Israeli military. As one commentator observed, 'Hezbollah won the moment they didn't lose – and governments lose the moment they don't win.'[56]

Hezbollah's ability to stand firm united Sunnis and Shi'ites, Islamists and nationalists – at least temporarily. The use of anti-tank missiles and short-range missiles was also an inspiration to many Palestinians, who wished to emulate Hezbollah in Gaza. A survey of over 1,200 Palestinians conducted by the Palestinian Center for Policy and Survey Research in Ramallah towards the end of the conflict in Lebanon suggested that 63 per cent of the respondents wanted to adopt Hezbollah's tactics of attacking Israeli towns with missiles. Only 38 per cent opposed this course of action. Indeed, it was reported at the end of 2006 by the Israeli military that a large number of Hamas supporters had left Gaza for advanced training in Iran.[57] As President Mahmoud Ahmadinejad later pointed out, 'Iran and Lebanon are two parts of the same body.'[58]

---

[55] *Ha'aretz* 13 September 2006.
[56] James Dobbin, member of the RAND Corporation, at a discussion of the US Institute of Peace in August 2006, *Ha'aretz* 18 August 2006.
[57] *Ha'aretz* 18 December 2006.   [58] *Ha'aretz* 17 February 2007.

The second Lebanon war led to the resignation of Dan Halutz and to at least forty inquiries into Israeli failures during the conflict. While there was virtually no fragmentation of the public consensus during the clash with Hezbollah, public attacks were now directed – for the first time in many years – against the leadership of the IDF. The public had been lulled into a false sense of security after incursions such as Operation Defensive Shield into the Palestinian territories.

The war against Hezbollah, however, indicated Israel's vulnerability and the state of unpreparedness of the IDF. Public anger extended to the politicians, and both Olmert and Peretz were condemned for their lack of competence. Olmert did not establish a coordinating group to manage the conflict. The military leadership exploited this weakness. Kadima dropped dramatically in the polls. Netanyahu and the Likud made an unexpected political comeback. In essence, the debacle in Lebanon undermined 'the third way' of the political centre. The backlash against both politicians and the military resulted in the termination of the Right's control of the IDF, but its resurrection in the political arena. The previous heads of the IDF, Mofaz, Ya'alon and Halutz, all identified politically with the Right. The more liberal Gabi Ashkenazi had been passed over by Sharon and Mofaz in succession to Ya'alon. Shortly after the appointment of Halutz, Ashkenazi tendered his resignation. It was no accident therefore that Ashkenazi was brought out of retirement to take over as Chief of the General Staff in January 2007 with a mandate to return the IDF to its former efficiency.[59]

---

[59] *Ha'aretz* 23 January 2007.

CHAPTER 15

A brotherly conflict

THE AFTERMATH OF THE LEBANON WAR

The Israeli failure in the second Lebanon war in July 2006 to win a decisive victory against Hezbollah shattered public belief in both the government and the military. The effect of a war on two fronts and the missile barrage in the north of the country induced a sense of vulnerability in the public mind. The political ramifications were the undermining of the centre parties and a shift to the Right and far Right.

The initial findings of the Winograd Report in April 2007 were particularly scathing and placed responsibility at the government's doorstep:

A leader who sends his army into an extensive military operation has an obligation to the country, the fighters of the Israel Defense Forces who risk their lives, and the citizens both of Israel and Lebanon. These obligations include an in-depth analysis of the necessity for a military move, its timing and its nature, and of the chances of its success given the area. We saw that the rash decisions to go to war made by the government headed by Olmert did not meet these conditions.[1]

The forthrightness of the report even brought forth expressions of respect for the Winograd Commission's deliberations from Hezbollah's Nasrallah, but within Israel it ignited a plethora of calls for Olmert's resignation from across the political spectrum. Within Kadima there were moves afoot to replace Olmert with Tsipi Livni, who had hardly been criticized in the report. The head of the IDF, Dan Halutz, had resigned in January 2007 and it was widely expected that Olmert would follow him.

The full Winograd Report was finally released on 30 January 2008; it attributed no personal responsibility to Olmert. Moreover, the debate in the Knesset went in Olmert's favour by a sliver of votes, by 59:53. Netanyahu was ahead in the opinion polls and this concentrated the minds of Olmert's internal adversaries. The hopes of both Livni and Barak of displacing

---

[1] *Ha'aretz* 1 May 2007.

Olmert were therefore temporarily dashed. However, the report listed all the shortcomings of this ill-planned military campaign. There was no exit strategy and no clearly defined war aim. Was it to have been a short and sharp incursion by selected forces or a full-scale assault? The political and military leadership dithered about sending in ground forces, and when it actually did so, it was too little too late. But most crucially it was unable to prevent the firing of missiles and gave a boost to Iranian ambitions in the region. Olmert was fatally weakened.

Moreover, a report by Mubadarah, an Israeli Arab group, suggested that many Arab villages in northern Israel did not have access to safe rooms and bomb shelters or possess emergency sirens.

In the aftermath of the Lebanon war, there existed an ongoing possibility of a confrontation in Gaza. The threat had persuaded EU monitors at the Rafah Crossing, led by Italian Major General Pietro Pistolese, to make preparations to leave Gaza. For the first time since the ceasefire of 26 November 2006, the al-Qassam Brigades of Hamas claimed responsibility for a volley of rockets and mortar shells. This was in response to the killing of nine Palestinians by the IDF. This escalation prompted an exodus of inhabitants from Sderot, which had borne the brunt of the bombardment, and a threat by the al-Quds Brigades, affiliated to Islamic Jihad, to send in a wave of female suicide bombers to blow themselves up in front of advancing Israeli troops. Only a few months before, Mervat Mas'ood, an al-Quds operative, had killed herself in Beit Hanoun and Fatima Najjar had blown herself up near the Jabalia refugee camp. On 20 May 2007, two young mothers were arrested at the Erez checkpoint en route to Ramallah. The Israeli security services believed that once in the West Bank, they were to have been fitted with explosives belts, which they planned to detonate in Tel Aviv and Netanya.[2]

This rise in tension between Hamas and the Israelis was paralleled by internal Palestinian conflicts. Fatah and Hamas militants had been waging a low-level conflict, which had raged since the victory of Hamas in the legislative council elections at the beginning of 2006. Despite the repeated efforts of their leaders to paper over the cracks and maintain a prolonged ceasefire, such decisions were not heeded on the Palestinian street. Fatah torched Islamic University buildings while Hamas did the same to the al-Quds Open University. Gunmen still maintained their roadblocks and refused to return abducted members of the other side. Indeed the firing of missiles into Israel was largely left to Islamic Jihad and other groups. Even

[2] *Ha'aretz* 13 June 2007.

within Hamas, division was rife. There were tensions between its political leaders and its military wing. In April 2007, a group of 200 protested in Gaza against the unity government and stated that they would only follow the orders of Mahmoud Zahar, the former Foreign Minister, and Said Sayyam, the Minister of the Interior. The Israelis suspected Hamas of transferring Qassam rockets to Islamic Jihad, which, unlike Hamas, did not adhere to any ceasefire. In February 2007, an Islamic Jihad operative, twenty-five-year-old Omar Ahmed Abu al-Rob of Jilabun, had pressed the 'on' switch five times in an attempt to blow up a bus, full of passengers, bound for Rishon L'Zion. The batteries in his explosives belt had been inserted incorrectly.

There were also deep ideological differences between Hamas and more radical Salafist organizations such as Jaysh al-Islam and Fath al-Islam. The leader of Jund Ansar Allah provoked an armed clash with Hamas by proclaiming an Islamic Emirate in Gaza. Such differences were often acted out by actions towards the small number of Christians in Gaza. The Protestant Holy Bible Society premises were attacked and at least forty Internet cafes and video stores were sacked. Armed men opened fire on a celebration at an UNWRA school which was considered 'un-Islamic' by the Salafists. The Italian activist Vittorio Arrigoni, who worked with the International Solidarity Movement, was kidnapped and killed by Tawhid wa al-Jihad in April 2011. The BBC correspondent Alan Johnston was kidnapped by Jaish al-Islam and disappeared without any claim of responsibility. Such a lack of central authority led the IDF to enact a harder line. After a failed attempt to infiltrate a car bomb into Tel Aviv, the Israeli military rebuilt roadblocks in the Qalkilya area, which had previously been dismantled.

Although more than 150 missiles had fallen in and around Sderot during the second week of May 2007, Olmert resisted any escalation of retaliatory measures and rejected a plea to renew targeted assassinations from the Israeli military. There was, however, profound suspicion in Gaza that an incursion would be carried out to offset the effect of the Winograd Commission findings. The prospect of an imminent Israeli attack led Fatah, Hamas, Islamic Jihad, the PFLP and the DFLP to implement a conditional hudna. Yet the al-Qassam Brigades also warned that they were now capable of extending the range of their missiles beyond Ashkelon, following a rare raid into Khan Younis by the Israelis.[3]

---

[3] Ezzedeen Al-Qassam Brigades (Hamas) www.alqassam.ps 23 May 2007.

Yet any unilateral cessation in hostilities by Hamas was not always recognized by other Palestinian factions, in particular, the al-Aqsa Martyrs' Brigade, which although nominally affiliated to Fatah depended strongly on Hezbollah for financial support. Any hudna or ceasefire proclaimed could therefore be broken on advice from Hezbollah in Beirut. Similarly Islamic Jihad depended on other Arab states and in particularly Syria. The financial connections occasionally surfaced. The US State Department accused the Central Bank of Iran of channelling $50 million between 2001 and 2006 via a subsidiary bank in London to Hezbollah in Beirut. Hezbollah was then said in turn to have passed on funds to Hamas.[4] Iran's Bank Saderat denied its involvement in such transactions.

The Prisoners' Document of Fatah's Marwan Barghouti of Fatah and Abdul Khaleq al-Natshe of Hamas was the basis for healing the rift between nationalists and Islamists. Yet many in Hamas were not happy with it, and there was no proper discussion with Fatah about its proposals. Even so, the Mecca Agreement of March 2007 emerged out of this – more because of external Arab pressure than of factional compromise. The ambiguity, however, in the wording of the Mecca Agreement between Fatah and Hamas to work together to form a unity government led to different interpretations. In an interview on the al-Qassam Web site, Mahmoud Zahar stated that Hamas did not recognize the Oslo Accords or the Geneva Initiative. Yet Hamas agreed that the PLO had the authority to negotiate on behalf of the Palestinian people. Significantly Hamas maintained that 'respecting' agreements signed by the PLO did not mean 'accepting' them. Hamas was willing to establish a state in the West Bank on the basis of the 1967 borders, but this did not mean that it would forgo ambitions to reclaim the rest of Palestine. Indeed, Zahar argued for the right of the Palestinian refugees to return to the 1948 borders and not the 1967 ones. Liberated Palestine would be an Islamic state which would join a union of Arab states. Moreover, it was argued that Israel could not be recognized because recognition would contradict the teachings of the Quran. Zahar referred to verse 7 of al-Israa, the seventeenth chapter of the Quran, which recalled the destruction of the Temple in Jerusalem.

While Islamic Jihad welcomed the agreement, albeit with reservations, the Bush administration unequivocally stated that the US would not recognize the new Hamas–Fatah administration if it did not explicitly recognize Israel.

---

[4] International Narcotics Control Strategy Report 2009, United States Department of State Bureau for International Narcotics and Law Enforcement Affairs, March 2009, p. 284.

Further attempts to stop the violence such as the Sanaa Declaration, signed by Musa Abu Marzuk of Hamas and Azzam al-Ahmad of Fatah in March 2008, similarly became redundant the moment the ink dried on the page.

THE TAKING OF GAZA

The Palestinians were clearly divided. A poll of the Palestinian Center for Public Opinion in January 2007 indicated that 35 per cent supported Abbas for President whereas Haniyeh mustered a creditable 26 per cent.[5]

As early as February 2007, several UN agencies warned that the fighting prevented the delivery of humanitarian aid. UNRWA temporarily suspended food deliveries and shut down schools which accommodated 35,000 children. The Secretary-General of the Palestinian Popular Resistance Committees (PRC) warned of the possibility of civil war.

As militants from both sides ignored hudnas and agreements by their leaderships, there was an arms race to bolster their efforts. Mohammed Dahlan, an inveterate enemy of Hamas, was appointed National Security Advisor by Abbas in March 2007, and Hamas responded by strengthening the al-Qassam Brigades and establishing the Executive Forces. Hamas and its allies depended on Iranian and Syrian arms and ammunition while Fatah and the PA were actively assisted by Israel and the United States. In the first few months of 2007, thousands of American assault rifles were delivered to the PA – weapon deliveries which Hamas repeatedly attempted to hijack. In April 2007, the US Congress approved a $59 million aid package to restructure Fatah's armed groups such as Force 17.

In November 1994 and January 1996, Arafat had turned his forces on Hamas and prevailed easily. In the summer of 2005, his successor, Mahmoud Abbas, had sent his forces into the Hamas stronghold of Zaytoun and encountered stiff resistance. By 2007 Hamas's military forces were no ragged makeshift army and no pushover. The al-Qassam Brigades consisted of 15,000 members and its Executive Force another 6,000. It could also count on support from Fatah's al-Aqsa Martyrs' Brigade, the Popular Resistance Committees, Islamic Jihad and a plethora of smaller groups.

While Hamas had established a powerful military force in Gaza, the same was not true in the West Bank. There were therefore numerous attempts to infiltrate the PA's security forces and police. As part of this military rivalry, there was an attempt by a Hamas unit from the West Bank town of

---

[5] Palestinian Center for Public Opinion poll 160 22 January 2007.

Qalqilyah to detonate a car bomb in Tel Aviv during the Passover holiday. The Egyptians also apprehended a suicide bomber before he was able to enter Israel.[6]

By June 2007, the street fighting in Gaza had reached such a pitch that there was open warfare between the two groups – and it was abundantly clear that Fatah was losing the struggle for military dominance. More than 150 Gazans were believed to have been killed and another 100 in the months afterwards. Hamas imprisoned several hundred Fatah loyalists. In the West Bank, where Fatah and its allies were considerably stronger, it was a different story. Hamas's work here was focussed mainly on political and charitable activities rather than on military ones. The Israelis had rounded up the majority of Hamas leaders and imprisoned them in Israel. The PA arrested more than 30 Hamas leaders within days of losing power in Gaza. The Hamas-controlled al-Aqsa television station in Ramallah and its counterpart Sana TV in Nablus were attacked. In Jenin, the al-Quds Centre for Photography, the An Nur press centre and the al-Isra' press house were all torched.

In Gaza Christian institutions such as the Latin Church and the Rosary Sisters school were once more attacked. Crosses were destroyed and copies of the Bible were burned. A Christian academic, Professor Sana al-Sayegh, was kidnapped and forced to undergo a conversion to Islam against her will. Rami Ayyad, the proprietor of the Holy Bible Association, was killed after death threats and his association's building was torched. He had been targeted after the Danish cartoons controversy of 2005. Moreover, Haniyeh refused to meet leaders of Gaza's 3,000 Christians.[7] The YMCA library in Gaza city was destroyed. Many of these actions had been committed by Salafist elements both inside and outside Hamas. They believed in a return to the values of the first generation of Muslims and its interpretation of the Quran and the Hadith. Asma Jahangir, the UN Special Rapporteur on Freedom of Religion and Belief, commented that women were especially vulnerable in Gaza. A ban had been declared on women riding motorbikes. The distribution and sale of several West Bank dailies, *al-Quds*, *al-Ayyam* and *al-Hayat-al-Jadida*, in Gaza was stopped. An anthology of forty-five Palestinian folk tales was removed from bookshelves for perceived sexual references. Dance and music groups were gradually suppressed.[8] There had been honour killings in Gaza and many women now felt obliged to cover their heads. As Hamas appointed judges to implement sharia law, the PA

---

[6] *Ha'aretz* 10 April 2007. [7] *Jerusalem Post* 6 August 2007.
[8] Beverley Milton-Edwards and Stephen Farrell, *Hamas* (London 2010) pp. 171–172.

stopped funding the judiciary in Gaza. The friction between nationalist and Islamist Palestinians serving sentences in Ketziot and Ofer prisons in Israel became so intense that they were separated.

Following the debacle in Gaza, Mahmoud Abbas suspended basic Palestinian laws to allow the installation of an emergency government without parliamentary approval. Fatah leaders in Gaza fled for their lives via Egypt or into Israel. The homes of Muhammed Dahlan, Fatah's military leader in Gaza, and Intisar al-Wazir, the widow of Abu Jihad, were ransacked. Abbas appointed the Finance Minister in the unity government, Salam Fayyad, as Prime Minister. He had received a university education in Beirut and Texas and worked for the World Bank for sixteen years. He had represented the IMF in the West Bank and Gaza between 1996 and 2001 before being appointed Minister of Finance by Arafat. Fayyad favoured the building of institutions rather than the often frustrating and tortuous peace negotiations. He argued for an international airport in the Jordan Valley and an oil refinery.

The taking of Gaza by Hamas now made it easier for the US and the EU to deal directly with Mahmoud Abbas's PA rather than the proposed unity government of Hamas and Fatah. Both swiftly lifted their political and economic embargo, which had been imposed in March 2006. Israel recognized the Fayyad government and transferred the hitherto frozen Palestinian taxes to it. In addition Abbas and Fayyad had quietly dismantled Hamas's financial network on the West Bank, banning nearly 100 charity committees. Israel also released 250 Palestinian prisoners. Prominent ones such as Marwan Barghouti remained in prison.

There was also an empowerment of the forces which were loyal to Mahmoud Abbas on the West Bank. US-trained PA forces took over the policing of Nablus (November 2007) and Jenin (May 2008). The Americans continued to run training courses for the Palestinian police in Jordan and for the presidential guard in Jericho.

At the Annapolis conference in November 2007, the Bush administration brought together Olmert and Abbas in an attempt to find a solution based on a modification of the 1967 borders. The Palestinians significantly followed the Clinton Parameters much more closely on the future of Jerusalem than did the Israelis. These, however, were difficult times for the realization of any agreement, given the ongoing tension with Hamas's consolidation of its control over Gaza.

Hamas gradually placed the tunnels from Egypt into Gaza under its control and away from the individual clans. This allowed Hamas to expand its arms smuggling operations. Grad Katyushas were smuggled in and fired into Israel. This Katyusha had a range which was double that of the homemade Qassam. Hamas's focus on smuggling and developing its stock of missiles was complemented by its attempt to observe the hudna. This was reflected in a decrease in the number of missiles fired – from 110 Qassams in August 2007 to 85 the following month.

The northern front had been quiet since the Lebanon war. There had even been an exchange of dead combatants between Israel and Hezbollah. Samir al-Kuntar, originally sentenced to 542 years for multiple killings in 1980, was also released as a means of gaining further information about Ron Arad, an air force navigator, missing in action since 1986. Yet despite such mediation through the Germans, the lesson of the Katyusha bombardment of northern Israel by Hezbollah in the summer of 2006 was not forgotten by either Israeli politicians or the military. Between $250 million and $400 million was being spent on the fortification of educational and public institutions in the Negev region. The fear of the evolving missile, fired from Gaza, carrying new types of warhead and reaching farther into Israel, had already resulted in an 8 per cent drop in the number of students in educational institutions in Sderot on the Israeli border with Gaza.

The fragility of the situation had previously been exemplified in the inability of Palestinian students to leave for studies abroad. In August 2007, a bus shuttle service to take students to the Egyptian border and then into Egypt itself was instituted. Within a few weeks it was suspended because the IDF deemed the crossing too susceptible to mortar fire. Even so, this led to an appeal by an Israeli NGO to the Supreme Court to allow a Palestinian student and his wife to return to their studies at the University of Bradford in England.

Since Hamas's ascent to power, the IDF had effectively laid siege to Gaza – finely attuning what was allowed in to the political exigencies of the moment. Indeed, household incomes fell by 20 per cent and unemployment increased dramatically. Members of the Israeli cabinet now held meetings to discuss the supply of fuel, electricity and water to Gaza. The Ministry of Defence resolved to restrict the power supply to Gaza in the hope of inhibiting the manufacture and firing of missiles. A Hamas spokesman had publicised the fact that Qassam missiles were being adapted to carry new warheads which could carry a multitude of weapons such as tear gas, cluster munitions and thermite to melt through armoured vehicles.[9]

[9] Interview with Abu Obaida about the al-Qassam Brigades 5 December 2007.

The Israeli fuel company Dor Alon, which had supplied the PA since 1994, cut off fuel and gas supplies to Gaza shortly after Hamas's takeover, but it pledged to continue supplies to Gaza's power plant. The Palestinian officials who normally oversaw the fuel transfers at the Karni Crossing had simply disappeared. A third of Gaza's population had been cut off from the electric grid during the fighting between Hamas and Fatah. Yet the Attorney-General, Menachem Mazuz, ruled against any disruption to the power supply in Gaza. The resurrected Ehud Barak, now Minister of Defence in Olmert's government, bristled at such a decision and refused to accept the ban. Instead he promised to institute 'some power restriction'.

Yet the ongoing Peace Index survey of Tel Aviv University which was conducted at the end of October 2007 indicated that a majority – some 71 per cent of Israelis – were in favour of measures that would affect the Palestinian population in Gaza such as cutting off electricity and restricting the supply of fuel. The 12 per cent who condemned this approach were opposed for humanitarian reasons. A majority of the Left Zionist Meretz party were against this policy. Yet other findings did not indicate any significant change in the Israeli public's attitudes from the height of the peace process in the 1990s. A majority still believed that 'most Palestinians have not accepted the existence of Israel and would destroy it if they could'. Some 54 per cent believed that it was preferable to sign a peace agreement with the Palestinians rather than aspire to the vision of inhabiting a Greater Israel. Indeed some 48 per cent advocated preserving the democratic nature of the state over its Jewish character. On these basic questions, it was clear that the al-Aqsa Intifada, the rise of Palestinian Islamism and the suicide bombings had not persuaded the average Israel to change his or her mind.

In one sense, Prime Minister Olmert reflected this widespread view, but he went further in stating that it was actually in Israel's interest to secure an agreement with the Palestinians and not to place the onus on its opponents. He repeated his opinion that if a Palestinian state was not created, 'the alternative was a South Africa style apartheid struggle'. In an interview in *Ha'aretz* on the sixtieth anniversary of the UN decision to partition historic Palestine into two states, he elucidated the demographic argument that Israel could not remain both Jewish and democratic if it colonized both the West Bank and Gaza. He argued that the first to condemn the evolution of Israel into such a state would be 'our power base in America', the Jewish organizations.

By the beginning of 2008, the public mood was not prepared to listen to Olmert, whose days as Prime Minister were perceived to be numbered. Outside the dwindling peace camp, the halcyon days of the Oslo Accords were increasingly seen as a time of naiveté. 'Nowism' had had its day. Although violence appeared to be on the decrease – there was a drop of 45 per cent in the number of Palestinians killed in 2007 in clashes with Israel compared to the previous year – vigilance intensified. Even the tourism industry began to recover. In February 2008 the number of tourists who visited Israel was up by 46 per cent from the same month in 2007.

Even so, during the first five weeks of 2008, 330 rockets were fired from Gaza – one-third of the 2007 total. The IDF budget had been increased from $9.7 billion (2006) to $13.6 billion (2008) – a 40.2 per cent increase since the second Lebanon war. Suicide bombing still occurred – in Eilat (January 2007) and in Dimona (February 2008). Such incidents were, of course, nothing on the scale of the recent past, and Hamas continued to argue that it was un-Islamic to target civilians, but since Israel was 'a militarised society', this could be justified.[10] Several tons of potassium nitrate were also discovered in sacks of sugar in an aid shipment in a truck bound for Gaza. Israeli military strategy was thus directed towards thwarting Hamas's intention to expand and develop its missile arsenal and to prepare for the inevitable next round.

A SYRIAN BOMB?

Another plank in Israel's conflict with Hamas was to prevent the passage of missile components to Gaza from Hezbollah in Lebanon. The chain of delivery, however, connected Damascus, Teheran and Pyongyang. There had been unofficial discussions between individual Israelis and Syrians with links to their respective governments between September 2004 and July 2006 via the Swiss Foreign Ministry. Coherent understandings such as the basis for a peace agreement had been formulated. The Syrians had hoped to come in from the cold, improve their relations with the West and thereby lift the US embargo on their country. President Assad feared that the loss of oil revenues would lead to an economic downturn, which in turn would cause problems for the longevity of the regime. Such discussions stagnated with the second Lebanon war in the summer of 2006. The military pendulum in Syria then swung in the opposite direction with an emphasis on developing non-conventional weapons. Syria had been in possession of between 60 and 120 Scud C missiles, which had been purchased from North Korea in the early 1990s. It was believed in the West that Syria was now experimenting with fitting different warheads onto

---

[10] Interview with Abu Obaida, "Ezzedeen Al-Qassam Brigades" www.alqassam.ps 5 December 2007.

the Scuds – arming them with chemical, biological and possibly nuclear weapons. The testing came to a halt with a mysterious explosion of one of these missiles on 23 July 2007 at a military complex near Aleppo, when 'dozens of Iranian engineers and Syrian officers' were reported to have been killed.[11] One report suggested that there had been an escape of the nerve gas sarin.[12]

The North Korean dimension of the desire to bolster both Hezbollah and Hamas had been highlighted during the second Lebanon war. North Koreans were believed to have played a decisive role in the construction of underground tunnels on the Lebanese side of the border which permitted the swift transfer of Hezbollah militants from one place to another and provided shelter from Israeli attacks. The head of the research division of Israeli Military Intelligence said that the tunnels had been constructed with 'an elaborate system of elevators' which allowed missile launchers and mortars to be raised to the surface and fired by remote control from below.[13] Similar tunnels had been located by the South Koreans in the Demilitarized Zone between the two Koreas. In addition, North Korean scientists were believed to have been killed in the Aleppo explosion. Operating through a series of fronts, North Koreans were thought to be supplying arms, training and technology to Hezbollah and to the Syrians. This was coupled with several masking techniques such as the mislabelling of goods and false descriptions. On the ship the *Grigorio 1*, en route from North Korea to Syria, the Cypriot authorities discovered an arms consignment labelled 'weather observation equipment' in September 2006.

In June 2007, Israel launched a satellite, the *Ofek-7*, which was soon diverted from observing Iran to monitoring Syria, where it took high resolution photographs of military installations. On 14 August, the North Korean Minister for Foreign Trade signed an agreement in Damascus to cooperate in 'trade, science and technology'. A team of Israeli special forces was covertly sent into Syria to collect samples of earth around an installation deep in the Syrian desert. A private Israeli investigator who searched the Internet for information on companies informed the Israeli press that a ship, the *al-Hamad*, flying the North Korean flag, had docked at the Syrian port of Tartous on 3 September, ostensibly carrying a consignment of cement.[14] The Israeli military, however, believed that it was in fact nuclear material, deposited at what was purported to be an agricultural college, at Dayr as-Zwar, close to the Iraqi border.

[11] *Jane's Defence Weekly* 17 September 2007. [12] *Der Spiegel* 18 June 2008.
[13] *Ha'aretz* 18 June 2008. [14] *Ha'aretz* 16 September 2007.

North Korea had originally agreed to denuclearize gradually and to accept inspections by experts in exchange for economic aid. The suspicion was that North Korea was now disposing of its spare nuclear material and extensive expertise in other ways in return for hard cash. The Syrian reactor was said to resemble North Korea's plutonium facility at Yongbyon. The nuclear path from Pyongyang to Damascus was eased by both Teheran and A.C. Khan's nuclear network. Iran was believed to have invested heavily in the project and to view it as a potential replacement for its own nuclear facilities. The transfer of nuclear material was an instrument of leverage on the West and President Bush had warned the North Koreans in 2006 not to outsource their nuclear programmes.

On 6 September the Israelis, on the ground and in the air, destroyed the complex.

Through a variety of indirect sources, from the US Department of Defence to the British *Sunday Times*, information was gradually leaked about an Israeli attack on the Syrian nuclear installation. In a coordinated attack, a Shaldag commando team on the ground with a squadron of F15s and F16s in the air had combined a bombing raid with collection of the nuclear material.[15]

Israeli technology circumvented Syrian radar systems and the aircraft passed unmarked into Syrian air space. At the same time, Lebanon mysteriously suffered severe communications disruptions which only returned to normal a few days after the raid. Israel subsequently divulged its information to an outraged Turkey, concerned that Syria would indulge in nuclear proliferation on its doorstep.[16]

This was the first of further setbacks for the Assad regime. On 12 February 2008, Imad Mughniyeh, a co-founder of Hezbollah, chief of external operations and its Deputy Secretary-General, was killed by a car bomb in Damascus. He was believed to have been responsible for the bombing of the Israeli Embassy (1992) and the Jewish Community Centre (1994) in Buenos Aires. In August 2008, Brigadier General Mohammed Suleiman, who was in charge of weapons research and development, arms procurement and transfers to Hezbollah, was mysteriously killed at his holiday home – ostensibly by a shot from a passing speedboat. Suleiman was believed to have transferred Syrian SA-8 anti-aircraft missiles to Hezbollah. In 2009, a vessel, the *Monchegorsk*, which was purported to be carrying Iranian arms ultimately destined for Gaza, was intercepted by the Cypriots en route to Latakia in Syria.

---

[15] *Sunday Times* 23 September 2007. [16] *New York Times* 10 October 2007.

TEHERAN AND THE MISSILE WAR

The rise of Iran and its developing missile capability not only worried the Israelis, but also caused great concern in several Sunni Arab regimes nearby. As early as 2001, the Jordanians had foiled at least seventeen Iranian-sponsored attempts to fire rockets and mortars at targets in Israel from its territory.[17] In Lebanon, it was sponsoring training camps in the Beka'a Valley. Hezbollah's Imad Mughniyeh had purchased the *Karine A* in 2001 at the behest of Teheran and filled it with arms for Gaza. Hezbollah together with the PFLP-GC – with close ties to Iran – were involved with other arms ships such as the *Santorini* and the *Calipso-2*.

In 2006 Teheran had warned the Gulf Cooperation Council that it would retaliate against them if the Gulf Arabs allowed the US to use bases on their soil. As early as January 2007, a delegation from the Conference of Presidents of Major American Jewish Organizations visited Dubai and Abu Dhabi to discuss the matter. It had the blessing of both the Israeli and American governments. The United Arab Emirates still adhered to a trade boycott against Israel, yet its government considered indirect discussions with Israel important.

Although therefore part of a wider conflict, Israel conducted an ongoing campaign to prevent Iranian missile parts from entering the tunnels of Gaza. The Iranians tried different entry points. They were prevented by the Turkish authorities but received a more welcoming reception from the Sudan, where members of the al-Qassam Brigades had been trained by the Iranians in 1999. In March 2009, the Iranian Defence Minister visited Sudan and signed a series of military cooperation agreements. In any event, the Sudanese regime was unable to control large areas of the country, and this proved convenient for both the Iranians and Hezbollah.[18]

Unmanned drones attacked a convoy of trucks outside Port Sudan in late January and in early February 2009. A suspected arms ship was reported to have been sunk in the Red Sea.[19] The Israelis believed the trucks were carrying Iranian Fajr 3 missiles which were destined for Gaza and ultimately to be fired on Tel Aviv. In this long-range attack, 1,400 kilometres from Israel's borders, some fifty smugglers and their Iranian handlers from the Revolutionary Guards were killed.[20]

At the same time, Egyptian security forces discovered a large cache of rockets, mines and mortar shells as well as three anti-aircraft missiles near

[17] Matthew Levitt, *Hamas: Politics, Charity and Terrorism in the Service of Jihad* (New Haven 2006) p. 175.
[18] *Ha'aretz* 27 March 2009.   [19] ABC Television 27 March 2009.   [20] *Sunday Times* 29 March 2009.

the Gaza border. Early in 2009 it was reported that Egypt had arrested four members of Iran's Revolutionary Guard who had entered Egypt on fake Iraqi passports.[21]

Up until 2006, Israel did not develop adequate defences against short-range missiles such as the Qassam. Although research was ongoing, it was not considered central enough to Israel's security needs to divert resources to it. The State Comptroller's report in May 2007 remarked that it was only three years after the appearance of the Qassam that the then-head of the IDF, Moshe Ya'alon, decided to appoint his deputy to look into the problem.

The 4,000 Katyushas fired by Hezbollah during the second Lebanon war with the ensuing partial depopulation of northern Israel was a dramatic wake-up call. If the first Qassams possessed a range of seven to eight kilometres in 2001, their progeny in 2007 were able to reach Ashkelon, more than twenty kilometres away. The addition of the chemical compound ammonium perchlorate doubled the range. Moreover, it was not only Hamas that began to acquire a missile arsenal. The Popular Resistance Committees manufactured the al-Nasser-4 while Islamic Jihad had the al-Quds-3. Iran invested considerable sums in both those who carried out research and those who fired missiles from Gaza.[22]

The Israeli fear increased as Ashdod and Beer Sheva came within range. Both the IDF and the PA made strenuous efforts to ensure that the West Bank would not become a launching pad for missiles directed at the heartland of civilian areas of Israel. In October 2009, the IDF discovered an explosives laboratory in Abu Dis, just outside Jerusalem, where rockets and pipe bombs were being manufactured.

Israel military planners developed a multi-tiered system to cope with missiles – from the short-range Katyushas and Qassams to long-range Iranian missiles such as Zelzal and the Shihab. Some like the Scuds were based on North Korean technology and were notoriously inaccurate. In April 2009, the Israeli Police's National Bomb Disposal Laboratory identified at least three types of Chinese-made missiles being fired from Gaza.[23] In December 2009, a Russian-made S-5K rocket landed near Kibbutz Alumim near Gaza.[24]

In November 2009, the head of Israeli Military Intelligence told a Knesset committee that Hamas had successfully launched a Fajr-type missile with a 60-kilometre range into the Mediterranean.[25] A few days later, the head

[21] *Ha'aretz* 15 May 2009.   [22] *Jerusalem Post* 28 February 2008.   [23] *Jerusalem Post* 1 April 2009.
[24] *Jerusalem Post* 6 December 2009.   [25] *Jerusalem Post* 3 November 2009.

of the IDF, Gabi Ashkenazi, reported to the same Knesset committee that Hezbollah was in possession of missiles with a range of over 300 kilometres.[26] It was estimated that Hezbollah's arsenal comprised some 40,000 missiles including the Syrian-made M600 with a payload of 500 kilograms and a greatly improved navigation system. Yet Israel's experience in 2006 in the north and the ongoing situation in the Negev region in the south indicated that there was an urgent need to counteract short-range missiles.

The Iron Dome system was therefore given the go-ahead on 1 February 2007 at a cost of $250 million so as to neutralize incoming missiles from Gaza. It was developed by Rafael Advanced Defence Systems in Israel, whose workers were given rabbinic dispensation to work on the Jewish Sabbath to ensure that it would become operational as quickly as possible. It operated through a radar system in conjunction with Tamir missile interceptors. Its drawback was that it could only be effective against missiles fired from more than 4 kilometres away. The distance from the outskirts of Beit Hanoun in Gaza to the periphery of Sderot in Israel was 1.8 kilometres; it would therefore take nine seconds to hit its target. The Iron Dome required at least fifteen seconds preparation time and fifteen seconds flight time.[27] The first Iron Dome battery was deployed outside Beer Sheva in March 2011 during an intensive period of the firing of missiles by Islamic Jihad and then redeployed to Ashdod the following August. In all, some thirteen batteries would be produced in the areas affected by missile attack. In addition Prime Minister Netanyahu argued in June 2011 that the battery would eventually be used along the border of any future Palestinian state to prevent a missile assault on Israeli cities.[28] The Ministry of Defence stated that it would invest nearly $1 billion in its development and manufacture in the coming years.[29] Despite the prohibitive cost of using the system, several European countries expressed an interest in purchasing it.

Another system considered by the Israelis was the US Nautilus system, which used a cheaper chemically based laser beam with much shorter preparation and reaction times. This laser beam worked by heating the missile, causing it to explode. Another possibility considered was the Phalanx anti-aircraft system, which could intercept missiles up to 1.5 kilometres away. Shooting 6,000 shells per minute, it operated at twice the speed of a Qassam and used radar to track the incoming missile.[30] Unlike Israeli systems, it was highly effective against mortar shells. Ehud Barak pointed out that such a multi-tiered strategy would prevent 90 per cent of all missiles from seeking

---

[26] *Ha'aretz* 14 November 2009.   [27] *Ha'aretz* 22 February 2008.   [28] *Jerusalem Post* 30 June 2011.
[29] *Ha'aretz* 9 May 2011.   [30] *Ha'aretz* 14 February 2008.

their target – it did not, however, account for the crucial remaining 10 per cent.[31] Israeli military personnel confirmed that the Iron Dome could not provide 'hermetic protection' for every part of Israel.[32] Moreover, a profound question was debated within the defence establishment – 'In a time of war, which demanded protection, military bases or cities?'

The near-inevitability of a new missile war forged an even closer technological relationship between Israel and the US, who were already long-term partners in the development of the Arrow missile system, which was designed to eliminate high-flying long-range Iranian missiles. Indeed between 1989 and 2005, a sum of $2.4 billion had been spent by both countries in developing the Arrow programme. Ground crews in Israel operated two radar systems – the Israeli Green Pines and the American X-Band. 'David's Sling', scheduled for deployment in 2013, was designed to intercept medium-range missiles such as the Iranian Fajr 5 and Zelzal 2 as well as some of the more sophisticated Scuds. This involved cooperation between Rafael and Raytheon, the US military contractor.

There were also reports that the Israelis were cooperating with the Germans to develop a system that would differentiate between decoy missiles and those carrying a nuclear warhead.

This multi-tiered protective shield against a range of missiles of varying sophistication, range and origin was perhaps the opening episode in an evolving missile confrontation. The electronic umbrella erected by Israel similarly began to evolve as a result of its opponents' detection of its flaws and faults. No system offered 100 per cent protection. The Wikileaks documents disclosed that a Mossad official claimed in November 2009 that many Hezbollah missiles would strike Tel Aviv in the event of a confrontation.[33]

All this complemented the utilization of the enlarged military budget to revamp the IDF, following the stalemate in the conflict with Hezbollah in 2006. This involved the purchase of a squadron of F-35s, fifth-generation stealth aircraft which would be delivered in 2014. The development of UAVs (unmanned aerial vehicles), the protection of tanks and combat ships and the enhanced training of soldiers were initiated when Gabi Ashkenazi became IDF chief in 2007.

New satellites were launched, but new technological advances brought new problems. The high-resolution *TecSar* satellite, however, was not totally successful since it suffered two weeks of darkness every two months.

---

[31] *Missile Monitor* 19 October 2007. [32] *Jerusalem Post* 27 March 2011.
[33] *Jerusalem Post* 3 January 2011.

The spectre of Ahmadinejad with his proverbial finger on the button unnerved Israel. While there was a lot of tub-thumping by Israeli politicians about Iran, ordinary citizens were acutely aware that many had similarly ridiculed Hitler in his early days in power.

The Natanz fuel enrichment plant was 8 metres underground and surrounded by a 2.5-metre wall. The Iranians were believed to be working towards the production of 500 kilograms of weapons grade uranium annually. When Iranian centrifuges at the Natanz nuclear facility went spinning wildly out of control in 2010 and its computers seemed to have taken on a life of their own, analysts eventually discovered that the malfunctioning was due to the remarkable agility of a virus called Stuxnet. It did not steal data but was able to manipulate a control system against the will of its masters. Although little could be ascertained, it was believed that only Israel – most likely Unit 8200 in military intelligence – or the National Security Agency of the United States had the technological ability and the imagination to conduct such a sophisticated attack. It was believed that, on taking office, President Obama had built on the Bush administration's initial efforts and expanded the development of cyberweapons in collaboration with the Israelis. Natanz was attacked on three occasions and the virus bookmarked its actions with the number 19790509. Some interpreted this as 9 May 1979 – the day a Jewish businessman, Habib Elghanian, was executed by the Khomeini regime on charges of spying for Israel.[34] Other codes were interpreted as referring to the Jewish Queen Esther of ancient Persia and another to the day when President Ahmadinejad spoke at Columbia University when he addressed the occurrence of the Holocaust. The possibility of a counter-attack in cyberspace was given added significance by the creation of a National Cybernetic Task Force in Israel in July 2011. A few weeks later, the IDF announced the formation of a cyberdefence division. The Israelis feared that their national institutions would be compromised and initiated electronic protection for the Tel Aviv Stock Exchange and the national rail network. In April 2012, the W.32 Flame virus attacked Iran's oil industry and caused severe disruption.

Another development in the preparations for any future conflict with Iran was the introduction of a fleet of Heron TP drones in February 2010. Unlike previous pilotless aircraft, this drone was capable of remaining in the air for at least twenty hours and could fly at an altitude of 40,000 feet. It could reach the Persian Gulf, jam Iranian communications and provide surveillance intelligence. At the end of August 2011, Israel Aerospace

[34] *Guardian* 31 May 2011.

Industries unveiled an unmanned miniature aircraft, weighing all of four kilograms, called 'Ghost'. This device, which could hover while maintaining its altitude, was able to provide 'intelligence imagery in real time to soldiers in urban areas'.[35]

In addition, there were numerous unexplained incidents within Iran itself. There were mysterious explosions which took the lives of many Revolutionary Guards at Khoramabad in October 2010 and at the Amir al-Momenin munitions depot in November 2011. The latter base was believed to house the Shahab-3 ballistic missile, and amongst those killed was Major General Hassan Moghaddam, allegedly a central architect of Iran's missile programme. This added to the mystery of the killings of several Iranian scientists and an attempt to assassinate Fereydoun Abbasi-Davani, a senior official in the nuclear programme. In January 2012, a magnetic car bomb killed the deputy director of commercial affairs at the Natanz plant on his way to work – an incident Hillary Clinton, the US Secretary of State, strongly condemned. All of this could not have been facilitated by outsiders operating in isolation. It seemed highly likely that opponents of the regime were involved. Numerous observers believed that the perpetrator of such events and coordinator of such actions was the Mossad.

Iran, operating through its Revolutionary Guards corps and Hezbollah operatives, responded and conducted a campaign against Israeli and Jewish institutions throughout 2012. Attempts to kill Israelis were mostly unsuccessful and were uncovered by local authorities in at least eight countries beforehand. However, in July 2012, a busload of Israeli tourists was blown up by a suicide bomber in the Bulgarian resort of Burgas which resulted in the deaths of six people.

[35] *Ha'aretz* 21 August 2011.

CHAPTER 16

Bialik's bequest?

THE CALM BEFORE THE STORM

Hamas had made great strides in revamping its image in the West. Shortly after its election in 2006, it had started to employ public relations experts.[1] Its officials had taken to wearing suits and implied that Hamas now accepted a two-state solution. The siege of Gaza, supported by Bush and Blair, was depicted in absolute terms and as verging on a humanitarian crisis. It also attempted to play down the anti-Jewish elements in its charter and any mention of Christendom's assault on Islam during the crusades. In 2008 Mahmoud Zahar would never have repeated his May 1995 criticism of Hanan Ashrawi, one of the post-Oslo Palestinian negotiators, that 'she is a woman, she is a Christian and she smokes'.[2] Suicide bombing was no longer considered an appropriate weapon. Comments that Israel's conduct towards the Palestinians was actually revenge for the Prophet's treatment of the Jewish tribes in Medina nearly fourteen centuries previously were no longer heard.[3]

In the late 1990s, its Political Bureau under Khaled Meshal had prepared a memorandum of explanation for western diplomats which advocated a battle of 'total liberation of Palestine from the sea to the river', putting an end to 'the Zionist project and establishing an Arab Islamic state in the whole of Palestine'. It rejected the many agreements signed at Oslo, Wye River and Sharm al-Sheikh because they bestowed legitimacy upon Israel and opened the way to normalization with Arab and Muslim countries.[4] These basic ideas remained and were fundamental in preventing any agreement with Fatah.

---

[1] *Guardian* 20 January 2006.
[2] Beverley Milton-Edwards and Stephen Farrell, *Hamas* (London 2010) p. 66.
[3] *Jerusalem Post* 24 December 1993.
[4] Azzam Tamimi, *Hamas: Unwritten Chapters* (London 2009) pp. 278–281.

The idea of Palestine as a waqf, a religious endowment, first promulgated by the Muslim conquest of the land in 638, was a tenet of Hamas's core belief – a belief which did not brook any compromise. This ruled out any peace negotiations with the Israelis. While Hamas made great overtures to western governments, it made no move to the Israeli one. While Hamas officials repeatedly spoke of 'a Palestinian state within the 1967 borders', it never added 'alongside the state of Israel and in agreement with it'.

In an interview with *al-Jazeera* at the end of April 2008, Khaled Meshal had defined a tahadiyeh – a period of calm – as 'a tactic in conflict management'.[5] In part, Hamas wished to rejuvenate itself militarily. In part, it wanted to present itself as the responsible voice of the Palestinian resistance prior to the presidential election in December 2008. Hamas believed that it had a unique opportunity to take over the other arm of government, the presidency.

On 19 June 2008, Hamas agreed with the Egyptians to declare a 'tactical tahadiyeh' for a period of six months. Israel's acceptance of the truce was an indirect recognition that Hamas held the political and military cards in Gaza. The announcement of a period of calm was accompanied by a barrage of forty Qassams and ten mortars. The IDF Chief of Staff, Gabi Ashkenazi, was highly sceptical about any truce, which he believed would not hold for any length of time. His fundamental belief was that the IDF and Hamas were inevitably set on a collision course.

The political leadership of Hamas struggled to maintain control of both its armed wing as well as other factions in order to preserve the tahadiyeh. Two Qassams were unleashed by the al-Aqsa Martyrs' Brigade a week after the agreed cessation of firing of missiles. Israel responded by closing the border crossings into Gaza and thereby fortifying the blockade – the very opposite of Hamas's raison d'etre for ending the hostilities. The attack had been provoked by the killing of a seventeen-year-old militant in a village near Hebron. The Hamas Prime Minister, Ismail Haniyeh, resolved to break the cycle of violence by appealing to all Palestinian factions to honour the truce. It was followed up by the arrest by Abu Qusai, the al-Aqsa Brigades spokesman, by Hamas forces.

Hamas took advantage of the truce to fortify its defences by planting mines in different parts of Gaza and to eliminate any internal threat to its authority. It clashed with the Jaish al-Islam, reputed to have been inspired by al-Qaeda. Even though it had occasionally appeared at the same events

5 *al-Jazeera* 26 April 2008.

such as the Popular Arab and Islamic Congress in Sudan in 1995, Hamas had kept its distance from al-Qaeda and confined its struggle to Palestine. Yet Hamas had also provided seed funding to Nabil Awqil to build a cell of activists on his return from a training camp in Afghanistan. His family played host to Richard Reid, the British 'shoe bomber', when he visited Gaza.[6]

The remnants of Fatah in Gaza were held responsible for an explosion on Gaza's beach which killed five leading Hamas militants. Hamas responded by arresting 160 Fatah loyalists and closing some forty institutions. Dozens of Fatah activists fled to Israel in the hope of reaching the West Bank. Yet both the Israeli Ministry of Defence and the Palestinian Authority refused to allow them to travel. Mahmoud Abbas insisted that Fatah had to maintain a presence in Gaza. In Israel, the Association of Civil Rights petitioned the High Court of Justice to halt the deportation back to Gaza.

The fighting in Gaza proved to be the bloodiest clash since the Hamas takeover. Even at Birzeit University on the West Bank there were fights between students allied to both groups.

Although the number of missile attacks had dramatically decreased, six weeks before the expiry of the six-month truce, the Israeli Air Force staged its first strikes since hostilities formally ceased. Israeli special forces entered Gaza near Deir el-Balah to destroy a tunnel which commenced in a house owned by the Abu Hamam family. The IDF claimed that this was a 'ticking tunnel' which was to be used to abduct Israeli soldiers. The Israeli incursion catalyzed the firing, mainly by Islamic Jihad militants, of more than twenty missiles. Islamic Jihad and the leadership of Hamas's al-Qassam Brigades were in favour of ending the truce. The political leadership of Hamas was not so sure.

The increase in violence led Israel to halt cash transfers from the West Bank to their Gaza branches. This meant that the PA was unable to pay the monthly salary of 77,000 civil servants who were loyal to Mahmoud Abbas. Hamas, however, was able to continue paying their civil servants because of funds smuggled from Egypt. This led to a joint appeal to Olmert from the President of the World Bank, the IMF's Dominique Strauss-Kahn and the Quartet's representative, Tony Blair.

Hamas's central aim was to lift the blockade of Gaza. The tahadiyeh had not brought this about. The holding of the abducted soldier, Gilad

---

[6] Matthew Levitt, *Hamas: Politics, Charity and Terrorism in the Service of Jihad* (Washington 2006) p. 37.

Shalit, had not produced a resolution of the situation. Although there were undoubtedly deprivation, shortages and accelerating unemployment, a campaign to depict Gaza as a starvation zone had proved unsuccessful. It was estimated that almost a thousand tunnels were in operation by the end of 2008. Some were equipped with electricity and telephone lines. When Israel limited the volume of fuel allowed into Gaza, engineers laid underground pipelines into Gaza such that the cost of a litre of petrol fell dramatically. Labourers who were formerly employed in Israel now found work in excavating and maintaining the tunnels. Many of the conventional institutions of everyday life were circumvented by this new mode of delivery of goods. Businessmen began to purchase their own tunnels as part of their property portfolio. A wide variety of goods from live sheep to Viagra tablets to state-of-the-art electrical appliances traversed the tunnels. These passages ingeniously mitigated the effect of Israel's leverage on what could be transferred at the border crossings. The Israelis seemingly accepted this new mode of economic innovation, but the passage of arms and war materiel through the tunnels remained a matter of major concern.

By mid-November 2008, nearly 150 missiles had been fired into Israel. One had landed in Ashkelon's industrial zone. Both sides soon began to speak about ending the tahadiyeh. The Salafist elements of Hamas's al-Qassam Brigades began to oppose the reticence of the movement's political leadership in calling for the abandonment of the truce. A few days before its official end, Hamas formally announced the termination of the tahadiyeh. The Gaza leadership, however, appeared unwilling to commit itself to the finality of the decision, which stood in stark contrast to the stand of the political bureau, which was ensconced in Damascus.

In the approach to Christmas 2008, Islamic Jihad's al-Quds Brigade, Fatah's al-Aqsa Martyrs' Brigade and the Popular Resistance Committees' An Nasser Salah Addin Brigades fired scores of missiles, hitting a kibbutz youth clubhouse, a home in Sderot and public places in Ashkelon. All this generated threats of retaliation from the Israelis. The leadership of Hamas in Gaza went underground for fear of being targeted for assassination. Its institutions and security installations were evacuated. On the Israeli side of the border, officials worked to connect towns within a thirty- to forty-kilometre radius of Gaza such as Ofakim, Netivot and Ashdod to an early warning system. The Minister of Defence, Ehud Barak, and the IDF deceptively played down calls for a ground operation. Yet the public mood in Israel was a call for action to stop the developing problem of attacks by bigger and better missiles from the Islamists. Even Meretz, the party of the Israeli peace camp, called for military action against Hamas.[7]

Although the tahadiyeh had been the longest since the outbreak of the al-Aqsa Intifada in 2001, Israel, too, had numerous reasons for initiating a confrontation with Hamas. The Gaza blockade had not led to a total collapse of the Islamist regime. Neither had it taken on the mantle of responsibility as had Arafat and the PLO after 1993. Instead it continued to advocate the armed struggle through missile warfare. It had not evolved a realistic political programme with which to negotiate with Israel and was seemingly only partially able to control other factions in Gaza. The Egyptians had proved ineffective in halting the inflow of arms through the tunnels. Moreover President-elect Obama was due to take office on 20 January – and it was highly unlikely that he would be as accommodating as his predecessor. With the Likud riding high in the opinion polls and an election not far off, demonstrating resolution and strength was a factor colouring the stand of Netanyahu's opponents, Labour's Ehud Barak and Kadima's Tsipi Livni – both of whom hoped to succeed Olmert.

OPERATION CAST LEAD

Operation Cast Lead occurred during the Jewish festival of Chanukah, which commemorated the victory of the Hasmoneans over the forces of Hellenism 2,000 years previously. It was named after a children's poem, 'In Honour of Chanukah', by Chaim Nachman Bialik, the Hebrew national poet. The poem contained the verse

> My teacher brought me a spinning top
> Made of the finest cast lead
> Do you know in whose honour?
> To honour Chanukah!

Israel had banned the entry of the foreign press into Gaza in mid-November 2008 ostensibly on security grounds and after the renewal of rocket fire. In Gaza, Hamas had moved swiftly to exert control over the local press shortly after its takeover. It temporarily banned Fatah newspapers such as *al-Ayyam* and closed a pro-Fatah radio station. The newspaper was banned once more in February 2008 after it published a cartoon of Haniyeh. Hamas began to issue government press cards to journalists of whom they approved. The Palestinian Journalists Syndicate protested that it stopped them from

---

[7] *Ha'aretz* 25 December 2008.

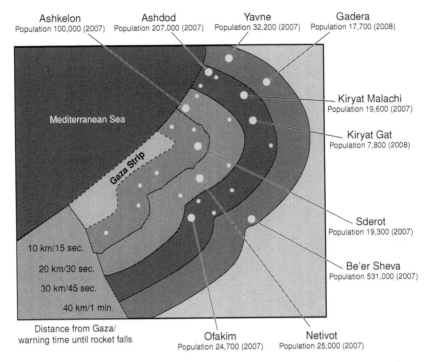

Fig. 16.1. The range of missiles fired from Gaza. Reproduced with kind permission from the IDF Spokesperson Unit.

doing their job, and they were supported by their colleagues in the Foreign Press Association. When Operation Cast Lead commenced, therefore, no foreign journalists were present in Gaza, and Palestinian journalists were under close scrutiny from Hamas.

The IDF had formulated a blueprint for an attack at the very inception of the tahadiyeh in June 2008. It paralleled the build-up of arms and military preparation which Hamas was making. An intensive intelligence operation was initiated which brought back information about missile silos, training camps, the headquarters of different groups and the location of the homes of senior militants. The plan was activated after the increase in the number of missiles fired in November 2008.

There was a deep fear that a ground operation would result in widespread Israeli casualties. Should such a military operation be a limited one? Should air power be used in a location where there was a concentration of civilians? The IDF Southern Command pushed Barak and Ashkenazi to initiate the operation, but there was a profound desire to avoid any entanglement with Hamas's forces. Barak and Ashkenazi opposed any attack on Rafah. This militated against any consideration of regime change and delivering a death blow to Hamas.

It was also accompanied by a disinformation campaign which was designed to keep Hamas and its allies on the back foot. Whilst the cabinet discussion was publicized as one dealing with 'global jihad', there was instead a five-hour detailed discussion about the minutiae of the proposed operation, particularly in the light of the lessons learned from the Lebanon war of 2006. Israel further announced that it would open the crossings to Gaza within a few days, and there would be further deliberations before any military action was contemplated. Ehud Barak declared Gaza to be 'a special military zone', one notch below a formal proclamation of war against an enemy state. In the light of all this, Hamas's decision to evacuate its personnel from its buildings was consequently reversed.

There were two initial waves of jet fighters and attack helicopters which struck at over 170 targets such as the Hamas training camp at Tel Zata and the headquarters of the al-Qassam Brigades in northern Gaza. The Israelis employed a new bomb, the GBU-39, purchased from the United States, which could pierce steel-reinforced concrete. It was utilized to attack underground Qassam launchers and bomb tunnels. The initial loss of life was extensive. Nearly 230 Palestinians were killed on the first day and almost 800 injured. Hamas lost its chief of police and Gaza's central district governor. Of those killed 80 were police cadets who were present at a passing out parade. Palestinian civilians reported that they had received recorded messages telling them to leave their homes since they were adjacent to Hamas buildings and were likely to be hit. Radio broadcasts were broken into, texts sent to mobile telephones and leaflets dropped. Yet the death toll of civilians increased dramatically.

In the days that followed, Israel bombed the Islamic University and government buildings. It also gave the green light for a limited call-up of soldiers in case a ground operation was required.

On the West Bank, PA officials quickly stated that they would be ready to assume authority once Hamas had been vanquished. However, whether Israel was actually striving for regime change in Gaza was an open question. Hamas and other Gaza based groups responded with a barrage of missiles including a Chinese-made katyusha with a forty-kilometre range which reached Beer Sheva. All schools within this range were closed. One missile hit a bus shelter in Ashdod, killing a woman. Another landed on a construction site in the centre of Ashkelon, killing an inhabitant from the Bedouin town of Aroer and injuring other Arab workers from Rahat.

Hezbollah in Lebanon was watched closely as the opening up of a second front in the north seemed highly likely. Hezbollah had been restocked with more sophisticated missiles in greater numbers by both Iran and Syria. The IDF Home Command also feared that Hamas was in possession of even longer-range missiles and that the 333,000 inhabitants of Rishon L'Zion and Rehovot would be targeted next. These municipalities were instructed to prepare their bomb shelters for their citizens. Many thousands of Bedouin who were living in unrecognized villages, however, lacked shelters and were not given any early warning of a missile attack.

While few Jews protested and the Israeli peace camp was divided in its view of the assault on Gaza, the Arabs of Israel staged demonstrations and closed shops and schools. It was more a call for unity between Palestinians against Israeli action than an overt identification with Hamas. This built on an increasing estrangement from Israeli Jews. According to a survey conducted by the University of Haifa, an overwhelming majority of Israeli Arabs considered the Israeli bombing of Lebanon during the conflict in 2006 to be a war crime. While some 48 per cent justified the use of missiles by Hezbollah, an Israeli Arab rights group, Mubadarah, indicated that 70 per cent of Israeli Arab villages in northern Israel did not yet have access to safe rooms or bomb shelters. To cap this, it was recorded that some 28 per cent of Israeli Arabs believed that the Holocaust had never taken place.[8] With the death of Rabin in 1995 and the outbreak of the al-Aqsa Intifada, the mutual alienation between Jews and Arabs in Israel had deepened. *The Future Vision of the Palestinian Arabs in Israel*, issued by Israeli Arab academics and intellectuals in December 2006, called for a consociational system/binational state which would replace the existing 'liberal system'. This was the first time that a representative body of Israeli Arabs had enunciated their current situation and projected a vision of the future. While this undoubtedly echoed the views of a majority of Israel Arabs, it evoked 'a sense of threat' and was condemned by even liberal Israelis. With the drift to the right, there was a sense of political impotence. When Rabin had been elected in 1992, the Arab parties together with the Left could account for sixty-one seats. In the 2009 voting which ultimately elected Likud's Netanyahu this bloc could account for only twenty-seven seats.

Demonstrations took place at the outset of the conflict in Nazareth, Umm el-Fahm, Taiba and Ibillin. In the second week of the war, 10,000 Israeli Arabs attended a demonstration at Sakhnin in which Arab members of the Knesset called for Olmert, Livni and Ashkenazi to be tried for

---

[8] *Jerusalem Post* 18 March 2007.

'war crimes' at an international tribunal. In contrast, the far Right called upon the government to act against Israeli Arabs who held this view – 'No citizenship without loyalty!' The head of Yisrael Beitenu, Avigdor Lieberman, suggested that the Sakhnin demonstrators were loyal only to Hamas.

In comparison, the West Bank was quiet. A daily demonstration, starting from Ramallah's Manara Square, attracted few adherents – and even fewer as time went on. This was due in part to Mahmoud Abbas's desire to crack down on any display of support for Hamas while professing solidarity with the Palestinians of Gaza. Partly it was due to the enhanced prosperity of the West Bank under Salam Fayyad's stewardship. But most of all, the West Bank was a bastion of support for Fatah, which had been first routed then oppressed by Hamas in Gaza. This had been accentuated by the fact that Hamas operatives had taken advantage of Operation Cast Lead to settle scores with Fatah members who were still in Gaza. Hamas classified them as 'collaborators' and executed some Fatah opponents in a caravan on the site of the former Jewish settlement of Rafiah Yam.[9] The Palestinian Ministry of Prisoners' Affairs published the names and locations of 181 Palestinians who had been executed or kneecapped or suffered broken legs.[10] Haidar Ghanem, a former worker for B'Tselem, the Israeli human rights group, was executed. In February 2009, Amnesty International issued a report about Hamas's actions towards 'collaborators' and called upon the organization to establish 'an independent, impartial and non-partisan national commission of experts' to investigate any abuses committed by its forces during Operation Cast Lead.

Syria immediately broke off the indirect negotiations with Israel which had been mediated by Turkey. The Turkish Prime Minister, Recep Tayyip Erdogan, the head of an Islamic party, reacted strongly and publicly froze any contact with Olmert. He argued that the attack on Gaza during talks with Syria was 'a show of disrespect towards Turkey'. During these unofficial exchanges, Syria was asked to ensure Hezbollah would confine itself to being purely a political party while Hamas's Khaled Meshal would be expelled from Damascus. Syria's representative at the talks, who was also an American citizen, even visited Jerusalem to stress Syria's desire for a peace agreement with Israel. It was even argued that Syria considered itself part of the Sunni world and wished to distance itself from Iran.[11]

The Supreme Leader of Iran, Ayatollah Khamenei, called upon all believers in the Islamic world to help the Palestinians of Gaza. The student section

---

[9] *Ha'aretz* 8 January 2009.   [10] *Ma'an* 2 February 2009.   [11] *Ha'aretz* 16 January 2007.

of the Basij established the Quds-Esteshhad units, designed to attract those who wished to participate in martyrdom operations. The Basij students demonstrated outside the home of the Nobel Peace Prize laureate, Shrin Ebadi, and accused her of sympathy for Israel. This took place shortly after the closure of her human rights centre and a raid on her law firm's offices.

For Latin American countries such as Venezuela and Bolivia, the Israel–Palestine conflict suddenly became a pertinent issue. Both wished to remain independent of the United States and therefore gratefully accepted the embrace of Teheran. Iran had developed ties with Ecuador, Paraguay and Uruguay and granted Cuba some $270 million in credits.[12] Bolivia was said to be exporting uranium ore to Iran.[13] Indeed in a determined drive to establish a presence in America's backyard, Iran had established cultural centres in sixteen Latin American countries. Both Venezuela and Bolivia broke off diplomatic relations with Israel amidst Hugo Chavez's assertion that 'a holocaust' was taking place in Gaza.

Israel targeted the leadership of Hamas as well as other groups. Nizar Rayyan, a renowned authority on the Hadith, who was regarded as the spiritual mentor of the movement after Sheikh Yassin's assassination, did not go underground like the other leaders of Hamas and was subsequently killed in his four-story home in the early days of Operation Cast Lead. He was believed to be more influential in Gaza than the political leaders of Hamas. He was avowedly hostile to Fatah and was believed to have been responsible for the killing of many of its members during the 2007 takeover of Gaza. In 2001, he sent one of his sons on a suicide bombing to the Gaza settlement of Alei Sinai.

The Israelis in particular targeted those involved with advancing rocket technology in Gaza. Mohammed Madhoun's home was hit because the building was used as both a laboratory and a factory to produce missiles. As had been the case during the Iraq war, Salafist mosques were used to store weaponry. A mosque in the Jabaliya camp was similarly hit as it was used as a storage facility for Grad missiles and Qassam rockets. A series of secondary explosions due to the detonating weaponry took place.

The vexed problem of armed opponents operating from civilian premises created all sorts of political, military and moral dilemmas. At the end of the first week of the conflict, the IDF hit and demolished the prestigious American School in Beit Lahiya in Gaza. The school taught an American curriculum in English. The IDF argued that the school's main building was a legitimate target since its campus had been used to fire missiles.

---

[12] *Washington Post* 20 November 2007.   [13] *Ha'aretz* 25 May 2009.

The legal advisor to the Ministry of Defence, Ahaz Benari, had set out a legal opinion on 7 December 2008 on firing at populated areas. He argued that such shelling was only permissible in open areas. In urban areas, shelling was likely to miss the missile launchers but would instead kill a large number of civilians. Any retaliatory fire, Benari argued, should be aimed at military targets and should be able to distinguish between military targets and civilians and their property. If there were civilian casualties and damage was done to property, then the IDF had to be certain that 'the damage is not much greater than the expected military benefit' – an exercise in proportionality. Benari argued that carpet bombing would result in the destruction of lives and property. He reminded the IDF that international law allowed them to inform residents of an area intended for shelling and to permit them to prepare for a short-term evacuation.[14]

However, in a real conflict, such legal qualifications were often marginalized. An IDF spokesperson bluntly announced on 3 January:

Those who use civilians, the elderly, women and children as 'human shields' are responsible for any and all injury to the civilian population. Anyone who hides a terrorist or weapons in his house is considered a terrorist.[15]

The Israeli cabinet decided to launch a ground incursion, one week into conflict, despite past trepidation about taking this direction. All of the units which were deployed in Gaza had undergone training at the IDF's Ground Forces Command Urban Training Centre near Tze'elim. They became familiarized with the periphery of Gaza, the labyrinthine Kasbah and the densely populated refugee camps. Soldiers from the Givati and Golani brigades swiftly divided Gaza into two. A call-up of tens of thousands of reservists was then issued. The Hamas central intelligence headquarters in Shati was severely damaged. Israel employed ships off the coast of Gaza as well as aircraft.

Yet this assault inevitably produced a rising number of civilian dead – a number disputed by each side. The Israeli refusal to allow foreign journalists into Gaza, even if embedded with the military, caused an uproar. It also meant that Hamas ruled the airwaves in Gaza, and few Palestinian stringers were prepared to contradict the official version of events. Both Hamas and Israel ironically concurred that it would be international pressure that would bring hostilities to a close. The EU had requested a forty-eight-hour ceasefire, which Olmert rejected. The UN Security Council voted 14–0 with the US abstaining in calling for 'an immediate and durable ceasefire'.

---

[14] Ha'aretz 17 December 2008.
[15] Israeli Ministry of Foreign Affairs Web site. See http://www.mfa.gov.il/MFA/Government/ Communiques/2009/Second_stage_Operation_Cast_Lead_begins_3-Jan-2009.htm.

Khaled Meshal told *al-Jazeera* that Hamas would not even consider a ceasefire until the Israelis withdrew from Gaza and opened the border crossings. It was believed that both Tsipi Livni and Ehud Barak wanted an end to hostilities, but that Olmert and the security cabinet wanted the very opposite – an expansion of the operation. The fighting therefore continued. President Sarkozy was already visiting the region while the Obama inauguration was looming.

On the nineteenth day of the conflict, Hamas accepted an Egyptian proposal for a ceasefire while Israel declared a unilateral one. Israeli political parties quickly reverted to their traditional stands. The left-wing Meretz welcomed the 'overdue' ceasefire while the far Right Yisrael Beitenu regarded it as 'a deathtrap'. Talab el-Sana, a member of the United Arab List-Ta'al, believed it to be 'a publicity stunt meant to reduce international pressure'. Hours after the ceasefire took effect, eight Qassams and three mortar shells were fired into Israel. A chicken coop in the Shafir Regional Council was hit.

The central features of Israel's war aims were the weakening of the Hamas administration and the destruction of its missile capability. In contrast, Hamas feared that it was about to be toppled and replaced by Mahmoud Abbas and the PA. It was therefore in Hamas's interests to emphasize the humanitarian costs of Operation Cast Lead, to depict the conflict as one of helpless civilians at the hands of a ruthless military machine, to turn the Israelis into latter-day Prussians and the Palestinians into the heirs of past Jewish suffering. The Vatican's Justice and Peace Minister, Cardinal Renato Martino, agreed and told an Italian daily that Gaza more and more resembled a concentration camp.[16] Gaza was projected as a twentieth-first-century Warsaw ghetto, which deserved the support of all decent people. The longer the conflict continued, the more photographs of disfigured and dismembered women and children were distributed to the world's press. And this depiction of events did indeed receive the support of an increasing percentage of liberal opinion. Many Diaspora Jews similarly began to ask for explanations. By the third week of the conflict, Israel had effectively lost the battle for international public opinion. In Europe, in particular, there had initially been a nuanced indifference. By the war's end, the tide had turned decisively against Israel.

The Arab world was enraged by the killing of over thirty at a UN-run school where thirteen hundred people, according to UNRWA, had sought refuge as a respite from the bombing. The Israelis explained that they had

[16] *Jerusalem Post* 8 January 2009.

returned fire into the school grounds when mortar shells were directed at them from that location. The IDF released a video from 2007 which showed militants releasing missiles from just outside the school walls. The IDF's Gaza Coordination and Liaison Administration claimed in February 2009 that in fact only twelve people had been killed – nine members of Hamas and three non-combatants. The IDF argued that it had noted that very few stretchers had actually been taken in to evacuate the dead and wounded. Yet the incident recalled the Qana killings in April 1996 when over a hundred civilians were killed in a makeshift shelter.

GOLDSTONE IN THE QUAGMIRE

The conflict therefore staggered to an unresolved halt, mired between accusation and counter-accusation. Gaza had been battered, and a large number of people had been killed – the number of non-combatants was disputed. Hamas remained in control of Gaza and the supply of missile parts continued. Yet Hamas had also been severely weakened and was essentially forced towards a truce. The number of rockets passing over Gaza's borders decreased dramatically as storage facilities were repaired, ready for new consignments of missile components. Hamas subsequently was willing to induce other Islamist groups such as Islamic Jihad to stop firing missiles and to observe a Hamas initiated ceasefire.[17] Israel had achieved a prime objective at a cost of considerable damage to its international reputation.

Israel's Attorney-General, Menachem Mazuz, gave an early warning that a wave of international lawsuits would be filed against soldiers who had participated in Operation Cast Lead. Indeed, after the shelling of the UN school, the UN Commissioner for Human Rights told a meeting of the UN Human Rights Council that the incident appeared to have all 'the elements of war crimes'. Human Rights Watch further accused the IDF of using white phosphorus shells, which in densely populated areas could burn civilians and ignite homes. In Spain, a judge ordered an investigation for war crimes by seven former security officials, including the then–Minister of Defence, the chief of the General Staff and the head of the Air Force, into the killing of Salah Shehadeh, a leader of the al-Qassam Brigades, in 2002 together with his wife and all his children plus several other Palestinian civilians. He had been a longtime central figure in Palestinian Islamist military circles and the founder of al-Mujahidoun al-Filastinoun, a precursor of the al-Qassam Brigades, in the 1980s. Spain's national court

---

[17] *Jerusalem Post* 25 March 2011.

ruled decisively against the judge a few months later, but it did reflect the growing use of universal jurisdiction and international law in general to confront Israel in the court of public opinion rather than on the battlefield.

In an age of legal action and the use of the electronic media in the megaphone war, the IDF had established a unit to train combat soldiers in each company in filming conflict situations.

The Israelis had learned the lesson during the second Lebanon war, in which Hezbollah was very adept in releasing selective information to the media. The most sensitive statistic was that of the loss of life during a conflict – and its separation into combatants and non-combatants. Each side had its vested interests in ensuring a favourable ratio. The IDF therefore established a Coordination and Liaison Administration unit to compile all factual information and photographic evidence.

The number of combatants killed during Operation Cast Lead therefore became an issue of intense debate. The Palestinian Center for Human Rights listed 223 combatants who had been killed. Hamas recognized 158 in its statements. Ehud Barak told Israel's Channel 10 television that more than 700 had been killed. A few weeks after the end of hostilities, the IDF's Gaza Coordination and Liaison Administration stated that 580 were combatants.[18] One point of dispute was the large number of police who were killed during a graduation ceremony on the first day of the conflict. As civil policemen under a Hamas regime, were they policemen or Hamas members? In its own report, B'Tselem, the Israeli human rights organization, listed 348 combatants and 248 policemen as separate categories.

Hamas projected its survival as an Israeli failure. It had not, it insisted, caved in to military pressure but had arrived at the decision to initiate a ceasefire independently. It remarked that it maintained the ability to fire missiles into Israel. The initial military communiqué from its al-Qassam Brigades was to claim that more 'Zionist soldiers' had been killed than its own fighters. Four helicopters were disabled, 'a reconnaissance aircraft' was brought down and forty-seven tanks, bulldozers and troop-carriers were destroyed whole and in part. Two Israeli soldiers were abducted but subsequently killed along with their captors in an F-16 airstrike.[19] While many of these claims were contradicted by both Israeli and Palestinian sources, they did reflect a concerted push to claim a victory of sorts.

The conflict had been initiated by the IDF as a deterrent to Hamas and its allies. However, such deterrence had had a heavy toll in human life in

---

[18] *Jerusalem Post* 15 February 2009.
[19] Military Communiqué, "Ezzedeen Al-Qassam Brigades" Information Office, 19 January 2009.

densely populated Gaza. The Arab world was determined to establish an international investigation into the nineteen days of an assault on Gaza. The UN Fact Finding Mission on the Gaza Conflict, established by the president of the UN Human Rights Council (UNHRC) and chaired by Richard Goldstone, a South African judge, reported at the end of 2009. Initially the brief had been to omit any consideration of the activities of the Palestinian organizations in Gaza. The conduct of Hamas was included by Goldstone, but not officially mandated. The UNHRC, itself, had already spoken about 'the current military aggression in Gaza' in a resolution adopted on 12 January 2009. A similar sentiment was echoed by one of the commission's British members in a letter to the *Times*.[20] To many Israelis, this seemed as if the die had already been cast in that there had been an unofficial policy to target civilians. At the end of 2006, Kofi Annan, then UN Secretary-General, had strongly criticized the UNHRC for its fixation on Israel and sense of selective outrage. Up until the advent of the Arab Spring in 2011, Gaddafi's Libya, Assad's Syria and Mugabe's Zimbabwe had never been the focus of a single resolution by the UNHRC. Neither had there been any investigations into the conflicts in Chechnya or Sri Lanka to ascertain whether or not war crimes had been committed.

Israel under Netanyahu's centre Right–far Right coalition refused to cooperate, citing the chequered record of the UNHRC. Goldstone and his team were therefore not allowed into Israel and not permitted to examine the effects of the missile barrage on southern Israel. However, the Netanyahu government's refusal to initiate an immediate investigation and to appoint 'an independent, autonomous commission' deprived the Israeli population of the possibility of considering what sort of military options were available to the IDF and how it conducted itself. Part of the rationale for not doing so was the widespread conviction within Israel that the Goldstone Commission was part of a larger campaign to turn Israel into a pariah state and to delegitimize the right of its military forces to take appropriate action rather than a genuine effort to determine the rights and wrongs of the Gaza conflict. Any objective critique at home would be deemed criticism abroad. Yet there were some Israelis who argued that the pendulum had swung too far in the opposite direction. Significantly, it was evidence produced through Israeli investigations which led Goldstone later to change his mind publicly on the issue of whether civilians were deliberately targeted.[21]

[20] *Times* 11 January 2009.   [21] *Washington Post* 1 April 2011.

The other members of the commission publicly confirmed their original views. Yet Goldstone's retraction of the central charge of intentionality against Israel caused a degree of backtracking by NGOs that had previously been adamant in their charges. The focus now moved towards 'indiscriminate warfare' rather than deliberate killing.

As a Jew, Goldstone came in for much personal opprobrium from Jewish communal leaderships around the world. Although Mandela had appointed Goldstone to a post-apartheid Constitutional Court, his record as a judge under apartheid was called into question despite a historic ruling which struck at the heart of the Group Areas Act. An Israeli daily newspaper ran an accusatory story about Goldstone's legal rulings under apartheid.[22] This too was utilized to challenge the findings of the report which bore his name.[23]

Each side in the conflict suspected the other's version of events of being partial, predetermined and seriously flawed. Internationally and within legal circles, there were differences of opinion. The US House of Representatives termed the Goldstone report 'irredeemingly biased' while the European Parliament endorsed it. In Israel, a broad section of the population was similarly hostile to the UNHRC's deliberations. Regardless of their attitude to Operation Cast Lead, there was a feeling that everything had already been cast in stone. The belief that the commission had an ideological agenda led to a blanket refusal of many Israelis, especially in Sderot, to cooperate with any number of inquiries – a refusal to answer questions or to give opinions. In turn, Goldstone's report noted that many Palestinians in Gaza were reluctant to talk about their experiences and surmised that their hesitation may have stemmed from 'a fear of reprisals'. Almost by definition, there was limited access to the facts and a dilution of the complexity of the situation. Goldstone, however, repeatedly argued that it was a fact-finding mission rather than a judicial investigation. In the minds of most Israelis, it was difficult to separate the two.

Moreover in both Israel and Gaza, the ideological opponents of the Oslo Accords were now in power. The previous decade of violence had been the polar opposite of the hopes engendered by the peace process in the 1990s. The resulting political polarization and intense bitterness reached their zenith in attitudes towards the Goldstone report; in the absence of a proper judicial inquiry within Israel, the findings of the report were dismissed in their entirety. Should a mosque be bombed if it was a storage facility

---

[22] *Yediot Aharanot* 7 May 2010.   [23] *Forward* 12 May 2010.

for missiles? Goldstone argued that it was valid to do so when congregants were not present. Should white phosphorus be used in warfare even though there were no legal prohibitions against its use? Goldstone argued that to utilize it in built-up areas was 'systematically reckless'. Such vexed questions were never considered by an Israeli judicial inquiry unconnected with either government or military.

Moreover, since international law did not recognize context such as provocation, Operation Cast Lead was, in one sense, considered in a vacuum. The writer Leonard Fein commented, 'Those laws do not ask whether a war is justified: they ask only how a war is conducted'.[24] For both Israelis and Palestinians, this was highly unsatisfactory, for it negated the history and grievances of the conflict. Although there were debates about whether or not the Goldstone report had undermined international humanitarian law, numerous Israelis believed that it had certainly set its stamp of approval on lawfare[25] – 'the strategy of using or misusing law as a substitute for traditional military means to achieve military objectives'.[26] In 2004, the International Court of Justice found that the separation barrier did not accord with international law and ruled that Israel could not justify its construction through 'a right of self-defence or on a state of necessity'. Yet Israel continued to build the 500-mile structure since, it argued, the barrier had prevented suicide bombers from entering Israel. A majority of Israelis concurred with that view.

The debate about what had actually happened during this brief conflict was soon transposed to the arena of the megaphone war, eliminating a striving for objectivity and rendering any judgement suspect.

Goldstone's commission was challenged on numerous points of interpretation. Goldstone argued that the police killed on the first day were not automatically members of the al-Qassam Brigades as the Israelis claimed. Yet some were said to have been armed with anti-tank weapons. If they were a uniform part of the Hamas military infrastructure, as the IDF claimed, what was the nature of such an attachment?

It was, however, the question of the intentionality of the IDF to kill Palestinian civilians which drew the strongest Israeli response. Did deterrence mean deliberately causing a large number of civilian deaths? Undoubtedly there was also a real effort to avoid risking soldiers' lives, given the casualty

---

[24] *Ha'aretz* 11 October 2009.
[25] Laurie R. Blank, 'Finding Facts but Missing the Law: The Goldstone Report, Gaza and Lawfare', *Case Western Reserve Journal of International Law* vol.43 March 2011.
[26] Kelly D. Wheaton, 'Strategic Layering: Realising the Potential of Military Lawyers at the Strategic Lawyers at the Strategic Level', *Army Law* vol.1 no.6 2006.

rate in the second Lebanon war. How this interacted with the imperative not to imperil civilians was more easily contemplated in the planning room than on the ground. What the General Staff instructed and what commanders on the ground implemented in the heat of the battle may not have been one and the same. Some Israeli critics claimed that previously accepted rules of engagement had been supplanted by a 'zero risk' approach. Moreover, the reaction of the Israeli public to the large number of casualties during the second Lebanon war effectively weakened and then terminated the Olmert government. It was in the Netanyahu government's interest to have learned that lesson.

A central charge against the Goldstone Commission was that it had treated each side as if it was a straightforward clash between armies and not an asymmetrical war whereby one side dressed as civilians and there was no discernible front line. The Goldstone report glossed over the fact that Hamas had attempted to blur the distinction between combatant and non-combatant. It was argued that this new kind of conflict put in question the status of the police cadets killed on the first day. Without an institutionalized army, were such police cadets just another way of 'putting combatants on the payroll of the state while assigning them clear military roles'? Israel had demonstrated in 2002 that it had refrained from an aerial attack on Jenin because there would have been high civilian casualties. The retreat of the Palestinian Islamists into a civilian heartland meant that decision-making had devolved to a much greater extent to the soldier on the ground – whether to pull the trigger or not. To what extent had ordinary soldiers internalized the rules of warfare in such very different circumstances? There seemed to be little recognition that the IDF had attempted to separate its military opponents from the civilian population. One drafter of the Israeli army's code of ethics pointed out that according to statistics provided by B'Tselem, for every 1 Palestinian combatant killed, 3 non-combatants died. If the killing of the police cadets was included, the ratio was 2 combatants killed for every 3 non-combatants. Yet Hamas and its allies numbered at least 15,000, if not more. The ratio therefore in Gaza before the conflict was 1 combatant to every 100 non-combatants, given that the population of Gaza was 1.5 million. Therefore if the IDF had the deliberate intention of killing civilians, how did it reduce the figure from 1:100 to 1:3? Could such a ratio therefore be construed as an instance of 'reckless shooting and targeting'?[27]

---

[27] Moshe Halbertal, 'The Goldstone Illusion', *New Republic* 6 November 2009.

In contrast, Goldstone argued that the sheer large number of civilian fatalities could not have been unintended. The doctrine of deterrence had led to 'the application of disproportionate force and the causing of great damage and destruction to civilian property and infrastructure and suffering to civilian populations'. 'Deliberate guidance' had been issued to soldiers so as to blur the dividing line between combatants and non-combatants. For many Israelis and Diaspora Jews, this accusation was a red flag to a bull, coloured by historical stereotypes. Many Israeli commentators argued that to have followed such a course would have been politically irrational.

Goldstone also relied heavily on facts and statistics from NGOs – many of whom had defined Israel's action as aggression at the inception of the conflict. This too aroused the ire of many Israelis as such organizations often had a track record of removing the context for IDF actions and under-researching the military operations of Palestinian Islamists. Indeed the Goldstone report was accused of pulling its punches when considering the question of Hamas and the use of human shields during Operation Cast Lead.

The underplaying of the role of Palestinian Islamism and the restrained mild language used in the report were evidence, the Israelis claimed, of a preordained verdict. Musa Abu Marzuq of Hamas's political bureau regarded the findings of the Goldstone Commission as nothing less than an acquittal of its actions.[28] Even Israeli organizations such as B'tselem and 'Breaking the Silence', which had been critical of Operation Cast Lead and had cooperated with Goldstone, protested against the selective use of evidence and testimony.

Yet such organizations were pleased by other aspects of the report. Goldstone did not retract the charge that the IDF had targeted part of the civilian infrastructure in Gaza, for example, the shelling of a major water and sewage disposal installation at al-Sheikh Ejlin.[29]

The flaws in the entire UNHRC initiative had actually swamped and thereby prevented any arguments for an independent judicial inquiry in Israel – something both government and military wished to avoid. It was therefore left to groups such as 'Breaking the Silence' to collect soldiers' testimonies and to raise difficult issues. By placing them in the court of Israeli public opinion at a time of international condemnation, peppered

[28] *Jerusalem Post* 16 October 2009.   [29] *New York Review of Books* 14 July 2011.

by flawed explanations and incorrect analyses, such groups encountered the full opprobrium of the Netanyahu government. The forces of populism such as radio talk show hosts Irit Linor and Kobi Arielli, who urged the beating up of such testifiers, were indicative of a growing mood in Israel.[30]

[30] *Jerusalem Post* 28 July 2009.

CHAPTER 17

Stagnation and isolationism

BLOCKADES AND FLOTILLAS

One legacy from the Gaza war was the imposition of an Israeli naval blockade of Gaza on 3 January 2009. A World Bank report in October 2011 noted that unemployment in Gaza in 2009 had reached 41 per cent and that 71 per cent of its citizens drew 'at least one form of social assistance'. Gaza's isolation had meant that the pool of labourers – some 27,000 in 1998 – who had originally worked in Israel now no longer had employment. Moreover Israel had formerly accounted for over 90 per cent of Gaza's exports. By the end of 2008, the per capita consumption in Gaza was 40 per cent below its 1999 level. The International Monetary Fund reported that in 2009 the annual growth rate in Gaza was 1 per cent while the West Bank boasted an increase of 8.5 per cent due to the resumption of funding by the international community.

The Karni Crossing under Israeli military control was the only official method of transferring goods and accessing general passage into Israel. While 89 per cent of all critically ill patients were allowed to travel into Israel for treatment at the beginning of 2007, this figure had dropped to 64 per cent by the year's end, following the Hamas takeover. Similarly a report in 2010 from the UN's Food and Agriculture Organization noted that 46 per cent of all agricultural land had become inaccessible in the aftermath of Operation Cast Lead. There had also been a dramatic drop in deep sea fishing due to the imposition of a limit around Gaza.

Yet Netanyahu had promised the Quartet's special envoy, Tony Blair, in February 2011 to allow sufficient building material into Gaza to construct new electricity, sewage treatment and water plants. Netanyahu also promised Blair to promote Gaza exports and specifically textiles and agricultural produce. There was also an agreement to reopen negotiations to develop two natural gas fields, one owned by the Israelis, the other by the Palestinians. A second shopping mall in Gaza was due to open in 2012.

In contrast, the Hamas Ministry of National Economy in Gaza placed a ban on importing clothing which had been manufactured in Israel and announced a new set of restrictions on other Israeli goods.

While the GDP in Gaza began to catch up in 2011, following its severe decline after the Hamas takeover, the unemployment rate was still over 30 per cent and, according to the Palestinian Central Bureau of Statistics, 38 per cent lived below the poverty level. The Israeli determination to regulate the economy, jobs and standard of living by remote control reflected a profound suspicion that the Islamists in Gaza had no intention of seeking a political compromise with Israel and would never renounce the armed struggle. Israel's actions in tightening its grip were catalyzed by the fact that Hamas and other Islamist groups would attempt to replenish their missile stockpiles by sea. There was also the fear that groups armed with missiles would sail from Gaza to attack Israeli cities farther up the coast.

The idea of a flotilla to reach Gaza was not new. In 1988, a PLO boat en route for Haifa was damaged in unexplained circumstances by a mine in Limassol harbour. In August 2008, two vessels, sponsored by the Free Gaza movement, set sail from Cyprus on the twenty-four-hour journey to Gaza. They carried hearing aids and balloons for the inhabitants. The ships intended to traverse the international waters boundary, the 1996 Oslo Accords boundary (twenty nautical miles from the Gaza coast), the 2002 Bertini agreement boundary (twelve nautical miles from the Gaza coast) and a 'fishing limit' imposed by the Israeli navy since October 2006. Olmert and Barak did not regard the boats as a security threat, and they were allowed to dock in Gaza, where their passengers were offered Palestinian citizenship and passports by Prime Minister Ismail Haniyeh.

The Free Gaza movement had been formed in 2006 and attracted pro-Palestinian activists, the far Left and concerned humanitarians from Europe and the US. It sponsored another boat in October 2008, which carried an Irish Nobel Peace Prize winner and an Israeli Arab member of the Knesset. This, too, was allowed to reach Gaza. Other boats followed, but the line was drawn when a Libyan boat, the *al-Marwa*, was turned back by Israel. It was deemed 'an act of piracy' by Libya's ambassador at the UN. The approach by the Israeli navy seemed to allow those boats sponsored by the Free Gaza movement through but to restrict those sent by Libya, Qatar, Lebanon and Iran since they involved a perceived security risk. Not all were welcomed by Hamas either. Hezbollah banned the Lebanese singer and model Haifa Wehbe from boarding an all-woman vessel, the *Mariam*, on the grounds that her 'nudity' and immodest dress would degrade the other women participants. On another trip, Bahrani diplomats quietly

Fig 17.1. The *Mavi Marmara*. Courtesy of the Free Gaza Movement.

visited Israel to secure the release of five of their citizens. Another ship, the *Amalthea*, was funded by Saif al-Islam Gaddahi's International Charity and Development Foundation. The Greek Cypriots soon imposed a ban on all Gaza-bound vessels.

The implementation of a formal blockade during Operation Cast Lead provided a focus for further activity which was designed to draw attention to the siege of Gaza. A vessel was rammed by Israeli ships in early February 2009 and towed to Ashkelon. In June 2009 another boat was taken to Ashdod. On 31 May 2010, a six-ship flotilla attempted to break the blockade, Israeli naval commandos boarded, violence broke out and nine Turkish Islamists were killed. This placed yet another nail in the coffin of the changing relationship between Israel and the Turkish government of Recep Tayyip Erdogan. Turkey had already withdrawn its ambassador and banned joint military exercises in the wake of Operation Cast Lead. It now stopped military flights over its territory. In the midst of a furious row between the two countries, which had established their own judicial inquiries, the UN instigated the Palmer Commission. This reported in August 2011 and concluded that for the purposes of international law, 'an international armed conflict' existed between Israel and Hamas. Israel therefore satisfied the requirements of international law in imposing a blockade. The Palmer report differed from the conclusions of the Turkish inquiry and that of the UN Human Rights Council on several crucial points. The Turkish inquiry argued that the blockade formed 'an indivisible part of Israel's land restriction policy' and was therefore illegal. Palmer disputed the claim that the blockade was an instance of collective punishment, as both the Turkish and UNHRC inquiries believed. The Palmer Commission also queried the motivation of the organizers of the six-boat flotilla. If it was purely a humanitarian mission to the people of Gaza, why were 700 people in total on board 'and for what purpose'? Why did only three of six boats carry humanitarian assistance, which was of questionable value and quality? No Gaza port could accommodate such a large boat as the *Mavi Marmara*, where the killings had taken place, yet the flotilla's organizers rejected the possibility of docking in al-Arish in Egypt or at Ashdod in Israel – and then transporting all the goods into Gaza by road. The report concluded that the organizers did anticipate an altercation with Israeli forces.

The Palmer report criticized Israel for acting disproportionately and stated that the loss of life and injuries were 'unacceptable'. It also attacked Israel's perception of the aims of the flotilla and stated that boarding 'without warning or consent and the use of such substantial force treated the flotilla as if it represented an immediate military threat to Israel'. Yet the Palmer Commission was unable to distinguish between the Turkish and Israeli versions of events. Was there live fire from the Israeli speedboats and helicopters before or during the commando assault? It concluded that the Israelis were unlikely to have fired as they descended onto the boat. It did note that some of the passengers were well prepared for a fracas. They carried gas masks, bulletproof vests, slingshots and chains. Pre-agreed positions were stationed in the event of an attack. Doctors and medical personnel had discussed the possibility of casualties beforehand.

The flotilla consisted of several groups from Europe which were determined to end the siege on Gaza including the Turkish IHH, which had purchased the *Mavi Marmara* for more than $1 million. The Israeli judicial inquiry described IHH as 'a humanitarian organisation with a radical Islamic orientation'. The Palmer report noted that a hard core of IHH activists was allowed to board in Istanbul without any real supervision. Erdogan's government viewed such Islamist groups in a more benevolent light.

The IDF investigation found flaws in the planning of the Israeli operation and stated that its preparation was based on a distinct lack of intelligence information. It concluded that efforts, first begun by the Defence

Ministry in 2008, to develop technology that could stop large ships at sea should be accelerated.

The fallout from the incident was dire for Israel. Although Turkish Islamists had been at the centre of the violent events, it was the uninvolved western activists who provided the explanations to their home countries. This included less than friendly treatment, after disembarkation, by the Israelis. This too was strongly criticized in the Palmer report. South Africa and Ecuador recalled their ambassadors while Nicaragua suspended diplomatic relations with Israel.

Yet all of this was also connected to a distancing from United States policy generally and the fruit of Iranian influence. The US was itself also highly critical. The State Department had advised 'caution and restraint' while Hilary Clinton called Israel's policy towards Gaza 'unsustainable'. The British reviewed defence exports to Israel and cancelled five licenses, relating to the Sa'ar 4.5 gunships.

The *Mavi Marmara* incident enhanced the desire to breach the Israeli siege of Gaza by sea. The boarding of a ship, the *Victoria*, in international waters in February 2011 by Israeli commandos led to the discovery of six C-704 anti-ship missiles in four sealed containers with instruction manuals in Farsi. The ship, which contained some fifty tons of weaponry, had been loaded in Latakia, Syria. It was due to unload its cargo in Alexandria en route to Gaza.

Netanyahu probably echoed popular opinion as well as the Right in Israel when he called such international criticism 'hypocrisy' and labelled Gaza 'a terror state funded by the Iranians'. Public opinion recalled the lynching of two Israelis who had taken the wrong turn during the al-Aqsa Intifada and strongly identified with its soldiers. All this compounded Israel's growing isolation and marked up another foreign policy failure for the Netanyahu government. In an attempt to repair his poor relations with the White House, Netanyahu flew to the US to meet President Obama in 2010 and to discuss a security cabinet decision to ease the blockade. Netanyahu had prepared a list of material and equipment that would not be allowed in: a range of chemicals used in the manufacture of explosives, hunting knives and machetes, lasers and night-vision goggles, missile related computer technologies and much more. It was feared that construction material which was urgently needed to repair the damage caused in Operation Cast Lead would be confiscated to build bunkers and strengthen tunnels. It was further proposed that material would be allowed under PA authorization and international supervision.

SETTLERS AND SETTLEMENTS

The election of Benjamin Netanyahu as the head of a centre Right–far Right coalition at the beginning of 2009 produced a range of policies designed to accelerate and fortify the settlement drive on the West Bank. Indeed the new Foreign Minister, Avigdor Lieberman, had lived in the settlement of Nokdim for the past twenty years. Although opinion polls continued to suggest that a majority of Israelis opposed the settlements, the fear of an outbreak of violence and Islamist suicide bombers had persuaded them to vote for the centre Right and the far Right to defend them and provide an enhanced sense of security. However, voting for the Right also entailed support – political and financial – for the settlers. For the Israeli voter, security at home came before opposition to the settlements.

The demographic problem due to the higher Arab birthrate remained. Rabbi Shlomo Aviner, head of the Ateret Cohanim yeshiva in Jerusalem, had proposed offering West Bank Arabs between $50,000 and $100,000 if they would agree to emigrate.[1]

By the end of 2012, the number of settlers on the West Bank was expected to be more than 350,000 and, if East Jerusalem was included, a population in the region of more than half a million. The state budget for 2011–2012 suggested that over 2 billion shekels had been allocated to the settlements. Yet the population growth on the West Bank was more than double that of Israel itself. In part this was due to a continuous migration from Israel to the territories and an increase in the number of haredi settlers in towns such as Betar Illit and Kiriat Sefer. Indeed although the settlements amounted to less than 5 per cent in terms of area, the control which they exerted, according to the municipal lines drawn, covered more than 40 per cent of the West Bank.

The Palestinians had long indicated that the settlements were a central cause of discontent and a fundamental stumbling block placed before an equitable peace agreement. The al-Aqsa Intifada had caused a concerted shift to the Right and the election of a series of governments which either had accelerated settlement or were reluctant to initiate an evacuation. Moreover, the withdrawal from Gaza had not stopped the Qassams and more Israeli towns were now in range. As one commentator remarked, 'The lesson of the Gaza withdrawal indicated that land for peace proved to be land for missiles'. Sharon had been able to garner support within Israel for the withdrawal because of his reputation as the strongman of the Right.

[1] *Jerusalem Post* 21 January 2007.

His successors inherited neither his reputation nor the situation. In the eyes of the Israeli public, the evacuation of 2005 had actually decreased security. Moreover, Hamas had squandered the opportunity to develop the evacuated settlements.

In September 2008, the cabinet discussed a potential $700 million evacuation-compensation bill, which would provide 18 per cent of settlers with over 1 million shekels (over $300,000) if they relocated from the West Bank. If they moved to the under-populated Negev, the compensation would be even higher. The bill was promoted within Kadima by Haim Ramon, formerly of Labour, who wished to secure the return of settlers who lived east of the security barrier. It was opposed by former Likudniks within Kadima such as Tsipi Livni and Shaul Mofaz. Nearly half the members of the Knesset stated their intention to oppose it either on ideological grounds or because 'it was the wrong time'.

In a widely publicized speech at Bar-Ilan University in 2009, Netanyahu argued that 'we have no intention to build new settlements or set aside land for new settlements'. This comment, early on in Netanyahu's premiership, was not matched by subsequent developments. The Netanyahu government was far more ideologically committed to the settlements than the previous Kadima administrations, which had accepted the principle of evacuation and withdrawal.

Netanyahu spoke differently to his domestic audience at the inception of a ten-month settlement freeze. In a speech at the settlement of Kfar Etzion in January 2010, he argued that the settlement blocs would remain part of Israel forever – and that this was accepted by a majority of Israelis and was gradually being 'instilled in international consciousness'.

Despite the move to the Right, there was still occasional opposition to the integration of the settlements into the mainstream of Israeli society. Thus although the Ministry of Education recognized Ariel University College, an application to the Council for Higher Education was rejected on the basis that it could not operate beyond the Green Line. Yet the 2011–2012 state budget allocated 900 million shekels to support Ariel University College, Orot College in Elkana and Herzog College in Alon Shvut – all in the territories. The conflict between academia and the far Right intensified in July 2012 when the Council of Higher Education of Judea and Samaria recognized Ariel University College as a fully fledged university with the backing of the Minister of Education, Gideon Sa'ar, and other government ministers. This was strongly opposed by the National Academy of Sciences, the Council of Higher Education and the heads of the existing seven universities in Israel.

The far Right in the Israeli cabinet moved against Ehud Barak, the Minister of Defence, a former Labour party leader and opponent of the settlements. In June 2011, the cabinet voted to strip Barak's right to veto construction on the West Bank by the World Zionist Organization's Settlement Division.

Although few Palestinian complaints against the settlers received legal redress, at a session of the Jerusalem District Court, a settler from the outpost of Esh Kodesh was sentenced to eighteen months' imprisonment for abducting and assaulting a fifteen-year-old Palestinian in 2007. He was ordered to pay the victim 50,000 shekels in compensation.

Arafat had accepted the Oslo II agreement with Rabin, just before the latter's assassination. This effectively initiated the acceptance of a future Palestinian state as a series of enclaves within a host of Jewish settlements linked by bypass roads and tunnels. The al-Aqsa Intifada simultaneously distracted public attention from the settlements and hardened opinion. By 2012, there were now third-generation settlers on the West Bank. Within a few years, it would be half a century since the first settlements on the West Bank had been established. Moreover, unlike the withdrawal from the Gaza settlements, there was no guarantee that there would not be violence if an Israeli government attempted to evacuate settlers from the West Bank.

East Jerusalem also proved to be a contentious area of settlement construction. Although Barak had offered to divide Jerusalem in 2000, succeeding Kadima and Likud governments rushed to encircle Arab boroughs with new Jewish neighbourhoods. This had been accentuated by a desire to migrate from the city to the suburbs. US pressure had prevented a neighbourhood, provisionally called Mevaseret Adumim, from connecting Jerusalem territorially to the nearby settlement of Ma'ale Adumim. Instead the E 1 road was built to link the two locations and more generally to the Gush Etzion bloc. This policy served to fragment the contiguity of these Arab areas. In the 2011–2012 budget 180 million shekels were allocated to building a road which would connect Jerusalem's Pisgat Ze'ev neighbourhood to the main highway linking Modi'in and Tel Aviv. Since 1967, the Arab population of East Jerusalem had quadrupled, yet few building permits were granted and there was a resulting housing shortage. This in turn led to the erection of buildings without permission – and to their subsequent demolition by the Israeli authorities. Arab locations in Jerusalem such as Silwan, Ras-il-Amoud and Sheikh Jarrah all resonated with Jewish history and therefore were targeted for settlement and purchase. The new Nof Tsion neighbourhood, supported by right-wing groups such as Elad and Ateret Cohanim, grew. This led to renewed confrontation at weekly demonstrations between the often-secular peace camp and the adherents of religious Zionism.

While no new settlements were commenced, the idea of 'natural growth' was much promoted. This was related to the area of jurisdiction of each settlement – an item of information which the Civil Administration was highly reluctant to reveal. The Bar-On industrial zone, which was used by the Kedumim local council, was actually outside any area of jurisdiction.

Since there were no restrictions on migration from Israel to the territories, a need for further expansion was therefore automatic. The construction of the neighbourhood of Matityahu East, in Modi'in Illit, entailed the building of 1,500 new apartments. Part of this project was situated on private land, belonging to the Palestinian residents of the village of Bil'in. The National Fraud Squad discovered that the neighbourhood was being built by two companies which were registered in Canada. Despite appeals to the Supreme Court and against its ruling calling for a halt to the construction, the work continued apace, regardless of the illegalities involved. Such lawsuits were not uncommon but seemed to make little difference to settlement construction.

The settlement of Migron emerged as a cause célèbre. It had been initiated as a consequence of the Oslo process whereby the construction of a Ramallah bypass road was mooted. Its building rendered a nearby height a strategic point. During the al-Aqsa Intifada, it therefore was designated as the location to build a circular antenna since it overlooked Highway 60. Within less than two years, this morphed into a plan to build 500 housing units, which was supervised and funded by the Ministry of Housing and Construction without authorization. Even Sharon stated that he was committed to its evacuation, but there was no public action.

Migron was built on land which according to the land registry was privately owned by Palestinians. A lawsuit for 1.5 million shekels was filed by five Palestinians from the villages of Burka and Dir Dibwan in October 2008. The settlers in contrast believed that they had purchased the land. Mobile homes soon followed and these housed some forty-six families. The state agreed to implement the judgement of the Supreme Court to evacuate and move the embryonic settlement to nearby Geva Binyamin. The settlers' spokesman pointed out that the attachment of the Jews to the Land of Israel predated any decision by the Supreme Court by several thousand years. By July 2011 the Supreme Court noted that the evacuation of Migron had still not taken place and its inhabitants had not made any statement either recognizing the court ruling or formulating plans for the future. A few months later the Supreme Court rejected a compromise between the government and the Migron settlers to be allowed to remain until November 2015. The Court ordered the demolition of the outpost by 1 August 2012. Netanyahu stated that he respected the ruling, However a few months later he accepted a proposal from the far Right to legally bestow retroactive approval on such buildings constructed on private Palestinian land. Migron was finally evacuated September 2012.

In another clash between the Supreme Court and the government, Netanyahu was unable to prevent the evacuation of settlers from the Ulpana neighbourhood of Beit El in the West Bank in the summer of 2012. Once again several of Ulpana's buildings were constructed on private Palestinian land. Despite this, Netanyahu pledged to add 300 new homes to Beit El itself and another 500 to West Bank settlements.

In September 2011, following the dismantlement of three buildings by the army, a mosque in the village of Qusra, south of Nablus, was set on fire. In addition, IDF equipment was vandalized at a base in the Binyamin region. Observers asked whether this was part of a retaliation policy. Indeed Ehud Barak, the Defence Minister, attempted to implement a tougher approach against settler violence and especially against illegal outposts, erected by 'the hilltop youth'. Major-General Avi Mizrachi called for the yeshiva in the settlement of Yizhar to be closed down and implied that it was a source of 'Jewish terror' in instigating attacks on West Bank Palestinians.[2] In November 2011, the Ministry of Education closed down the high school which was attached to the yeshiva. This in turn induced a rise in attacks against IDF personnel and against Palestinians. The far Right acquiesced in this campaign against the military. One member of the Knesset labelled the outgoing military commander of the West Bank, Brigadier-General Nitzan Alon, 'a post-Zionist'.[3]

Other sites such as Maskiot and Sansana which had been authorized long before were now open to inhabitants in 2008, thereby effectively creating two new settlements.

The Europeans began to take action against settlements and asked for settlement produce to be distinguished from that produced in Israel. The EU no longer recognized settlement produce as emanating from Israel under the terms of its free trade agreement. Even so, the Netanyahu government compensated the settlers in the 2011–2012 budget to the tune of 22 million shekels for loss of earnings. Mul-T-Lock, part of the Swedish company Assa Abloy AB, moved its production from the West Bank to Israel – as did the Barkan wine company, which transferred its operation to

[2] *Ha'aretz* 17 July 2011. [3] *Ha'aretz* 25 October 2011.

Kibbutz Hulda. Israeli companies reportedly had severed their connection with building work on West Bank settlements in return for being awarded contracts to build the new Palestinian city of Rawabi.

The Netanyahu government, given its ideological complexion, had embarked on a vigorous settlement expansion programme. Netanyahu in his first premiership and Shamir before him had been beset by a strong campaign on behalf of the settlers by parties and politicians to the Right. If previously Sharon had been the defender of the settlers, he was now replaced by Avigdor Lieberman of Yisrael Beiteinu. Lieberman had called on Mahmoud Abbas to resign, labelling him as 'the greatest obstacle' to peace in the region, and opposed any political gestures towards the PA. His party had grown dramatically, and not only was the far Right dominant in the Knesset, but its views were held by a majority of the forum of seven senior cabinet ministers. Labour's Ehud Barak and Likud's Dan Meridor were now in a distinct minority. This reflected the shift in Israeli politics to the Right in the aftermath of the al-Aqsa Intifada and the ongoing conflict with Palestinian Islamism. The fate of the twenty-three hilltop communities which the Sharon government had defined as 'illegal' and which successive administrations had previously pledged to dismantle was now a subject of legitimate discussion within the cabinet.

Although the electorate voted for Kadima as the largest party in the 2009 election, Tsipi Livni had been unable to form a government since the smaller parties in any future coalition ideologically favoured Netanyahu. The traditional Left, the parties of the Oslo Accords, was severely reduced in size. Labour was a shadow of its former self while Kadima, a centre-Right party, was now seen as the best bet to inhibit the far Right. Netanyahu, as in his previous premiership, was unable to make any pragmatic decisions without destabilizing his government. This affected Israel's relations with its traditional ally, the United States, now led by Barack Obama.

Since Operation Cast Lead, there had been little meaningful dialogue with the PA. Mahmoud Abbas insisted on a cessation of all building projects on the West Bank and in East Jerusalem. Given the ideological outlook of the Netanyahu government, this request was continually rejected. Instead Netanyahu argued that the PA should recognize Israel as a Jewish state – an idea which neither Begin had invoked in the peace treaty with Egypt in 1979 nor Rabin with King Hussein in 1994 in the peace agreement with Jordan. In fact Netanyahu himself had never raised this during his first tenure in office in the 1990s. The former Israeli Ambassador to the United Nations, Gabriella Shalev, regarded the demand as superfluous and argued that 'there were no preconditions for talks with the Palestinians'.

The US invested much time in 2009 and attempted to secure a path which would enable direct talks and negotiations to take place. There were even hints of withholding US credit guarantees from Israel – as had been the case with President Bush in 1991. Eventually American pressure worked and in November 2009, Netanyahu proclaimed a ten-month moratorium on settlement construction.

Yet there was no moratorium on settlement planning or the takeover of Palestinian farmland by settlers. A week after the moratorium was initiated, a plan for a new neighbourhood of 360 housing units in the settlement of Talmon was approved. The plans to construct 3,171 housing units passed through various stages of approval between January and March 2010. At least twenty-eight settlements continued to build in defiance of the government. Observers noted that work was proceeding in settlements such as Ariel, Elkana North, Peduel and Kfar Tapuah.[4]

The Defence Ministry then sent in troops to destroy the foundations of structures, dismantle temporary dwellings and confiscate heavy machinery. Yet whereas 30 million shekels had been put aside by the Finance Ministry to compensate the settlers for the moratorium, Barak's request to transfer 12 million shekels from security to reinforcing the IDF's activities on the West Bank was rejected by a Knesset committee.

The ongoing drive by the far Right to reclaim areas in East Jerusalem was exemplified by the struggle over the Sheikh Jarrah neighbourhood in Jerusalem. In 1892, Muhammed and Ibrahim Mao had leased the land for ninety years to a Jew, Yosef Meyuhas, who divided it into sixty plots. In 1948, the Jewish inhabitants fled to Israel during the war and Palestinian refugees took their places. In 1967 Sheikh Jarrah as part of Jerusalem reverted once more to the Israelis as the result of the victory in the Six Day war. In 1970 the Knesset passed a law which gave Israelis the right to regain property in East Jerusalem. Clearly Israeli courts struggled with the question as to who had the greater right. In 1997 and 2006, the Jerusalem District Court found in favour of the Jewish claimants. A subsequent appeal to the Supreme Court was rejected in 2010 and opened the way to the forcible evacuation of its Arab inhabitants. This became a cause célèbre for the Israeli Left with weekly demonstrations by a solidarity committee.

In March 2011, the Netanyahu government approved a plan to build hundreds of new apartments within existing settlements such as Ma'ale Adumim and Ariel in response to the killing of five members of the Fogel family in the settlement of Itamar. It similarly responded to the PA's

---

[4] *Ha'aretz* 2 January 2010.

successful application to join UNESCO in October 2011 by approving building plans in Efrat and Ma'ale Adumim. A plan to build 1,100 apartments in Gilo, just over the Green Line, in November 2011 antagonized Angela Merkel, who had actually led the campaign to block the PA's efforts to attain membership through the UN Security Council. Germany had been among the 14 countries to vote against the PA's admittance into UNESCO – 107 voted for and another 52 countries abstained. The move to build in Gilo further undermined the Netanyahu government's credibility in international circles. In response, Germany threatened not to proceed with the construction of a Dolphin submarine which had been commissioned by the Israeli military.

In July 2011, the Civil Administration, acting on government instructions, declared private land belonging to the Palestinian village of Karyut to be state land, thereby retrospectively legalizing the building of homes. This had originally been a temporary outpost of the settlement of Eli.

As Israeli lawyers remarked, before the construction moratorium, the courts had always left it to the government to choose when exactly to enact instructions to demolish a structure. After the moratorium, the government argued that instead a survey of property rights should be implemented so that a retroactive legalization of hitherto illegal structures could be considered. In addition to the case of the village of Karyut, another three outposts were considered for legalization.[5]

DITHERING IN THE WHITE HOUSE?

As early as May 2009, Vice President Joe Biden had called upon Netanyahu to support a two-state solution rather than Palestinian autonomy. A few weeks later, Netanyahu responded by adopting the principle of 'a demilitarized Palestinian state alongside a Jewish Israeli state' in a speech at Bar-Ilan University. Unlike the Bush administration, the Obama White House was quick to condemn demolition of Palestinian homes in East Jerusalem, the construction of houses between Ma'ale Adumim and Jerusalem and the prevarication in moving Migron to another location. Obama's first trip to the Middle East had been to Cairo in June 2009, not Tel Aviv, in an attempt to heal the rift with the Muslim world in the aftermath of the Bush administration. Indeed Hamas's Khalid Meshal praised Obama's new rhetoric – while calling for the dismissal of General Keith Dayton who had trained the PA forces. Perhaps for the first time, US voices were suggesting

[5] Michael Sfard, 'The Lesser Known Settlement Freeze', foreignpolicy.com 10 May 2010.

that Israel was being transformed from an asset into a liability as far as US interests in the Middle East were concerned. The United States was committed to withdrawal from Iraq and Afghanistan over a period of time and the Israel–Palestine conflict came to be seen as a source of instability in the region. General Petraeus argued that such a diplomatic impasse threatened the safety of US forces in the region. In a testimony to the Senate Armed Services Committee in March 2010, he remarked that anger over the Palestinian question in the Middle East 'limits the strength and depth of US partnerships with governments and peoples . . . and weakens the legitimacy of moderate regimes in the Arab world'.[6]

The lack of chemistry between Netanyahu and Obama, particularly over the settlement issue, caused the Israeli Ambassador to the US to admit that the relationship between the two countries was at its lowest ebb for thirty-five years.[7] Although there had been periods of tension between Washington and Tel Aviv in the past, there was a sense that a turning point had been reached. Significantly, the 2010 Annual Survey of American Jewish Opinion indicated that most US Jews viewed Obama and his approach to Israel in a positive light. Israeli polls, on the other hand, suggested that Obama was supported by less than 10 per cent of the Israeli public.[8] Obama had originally embarked on a policy of decisive conduct which would resolve the Israel–Palestinian imbroglio. Although the aspirations of his administration in terms of an end result were probably not greatly different from previous ones, Obama demanded a total settlement freeze and seemed to bypass decisions reached with the Bush White House. It gradually began to dawn on the Obama White House that given the reality of the ideological complexion of the Netanyahu government, the call for a total freeze would have to be watered down to achieve even a modicum of movement. The vexed question of building in Jerusalem had always been left on the back burner by previous administrations. Therefore even during the moratorium, building in East Jerusalem continued to be authorized by Netanyahu's government. The Housing Ministry put out a tender to bid for the construction of 198 housing units in Pisgat Ze'ev and 377 homes in Neve Ya'akov. This authorization of new construction immediately prior to the visit of Vice President Joe Biden to Israel in March 2010 proved to be incendiary. The construction of a further 112 new apartments in Betar Illit and 1,600 homes in East Jerusalem's Ramat Shlomo brought forth a furious denunciation of such plans by Biden. Ironically Biden was regarded as a

---

[6] Statement of General Petraeus to the US Senate Armed Service Committee 16 March 2010.
[7] *Ha'aretz* 15 March 2010.   [8] *New York Times* 1 November 2009.

friend of Israel and his visit was designed to thaw out the frosty relations between the two administrations and to elevate them to a more congenial level.

The Palestinian Authority had demanded a cessation to all settlement construction before real negotiations. Significantly US Secretary of State Hillary Clinton supported Netanyahu's conviction that ongoing settlement construction had not prevented and should not prevent the two sides from sitting down together. Amidst Netanyahu's apologies to the Americans that it was an administrative error, he reaffirmed that the Gan Hamelech park would proceed in Silwan in Jerusalem, as would the construction of Ramat Shlomo in the future.

A summit held shortly afterwards between the two leaders produced no joint statement, no photo opportunity and no dinner between Obama and Netanyahu. Obama was reported to have walked out, leaving a White House telephone for Netanyahu to consult his colleagues. Eventually the Israeli Prime Minister retreated to his embassy. The disastrous nature of the encounter recalled those of previous impotent Likud Prime Ministers who were similarly constrained by powerful right-wing cabinet colleagues from taking an initiative. Yet there was no large-scale revolt by the settlers or even the far Right during the period of the moratorium. In addition, numerous observers remarked that Netanyahu had made no concerted effort to ditch Lieberman in favour of Tsipi Livni in order to move his coalition towards the political centre.

Obama reputedly offered to initiate American pressure on Mahmoud Abbas to hold direct talks if Netanyahu would institute a four-month moratorium on building in East Jerusalem. Opinion polls suggested that 49 per cent of US citizens believed that Israel should stop building settlements as it hindered any possibility of a rapprochement between the two protagonists.[9] In addition there were American calls to stop the demolition of Palestinian homes and the eviction of their inhabitants.

Britain's Prime Minister, Gordon Brown, had gone further in 2008 and called upon British citizens not to purchase either land or homes in the settlements. The British further attempted to link a settlement freeze with an upgrading of relations between the EU and Israel.[10]

Although building in Jerusalem slowed down considerably in the aftermath of the Biden visit, Netanyahu attempted to refurbish relations with the Obama White House. One idea was the establishment of a Palestinian state within temporary borders while delaying any discussion on Jerusalem.

---

[9] *Rasmussen Report* 17 March 2010, rasmussenreports.com.   [10] *Ha'aretz* 18 December 2008.

Yet this had been mooted in the second stage of the Road Map of 2003 and was opposed then by the Palestinians because it maintained the Israeli presence on the West Bank. Moreover, even temporary borders and a Palestinian state would require Israeli withdrawal and evacuation of settlements – something other ministers in the Netanyahu government would not tolerate. On the issue of East Jerusalem, Netanyahu argued that he did not regard it as a settlement, and any withdrawal from Arab neighbourhoods would allow 'Iran' to enter.

A week after Netanyahu's more successful meeting with Obama in July 2010, approval was given to build 250 apartment units in Pisgat Ze'ev in East Jerusalem. In general there was no movement towards formulating a credible basis for opening direct talks. Yet the cycle of futile argument concluded with a refusal by the Netanyahu government to extend the freeze on settlements. A 'Washington process', designed to avert a political relapse, was started a few weeks before the end of the moratorium, yet it collapsed virtually at its inception. Even a US promise of twenty F-35 advanced stealth fighters did not entice members of the Israeli cabinet to renew the moratorium.

In November 2010, the announcement of plans to advance the construction of 1,345 housing units in East Jerusalem brought forth another strong rebuke from the White House. The Israeli argument was that the government had built in every part of the city during a period when agreements had been signed by Egypt and Jordan. Since 1993 there had been direct negotiations with the Palestinians.

There was therefore a rising frustration in Washington and beyond that no initiative would unblock the impasse. Land seemingly had become more important than peace. The ripples from the Goldstone report and the flotilla incident were still felt. Netanyahu was compared by the noted journalist Tom Friedman to a man who jumps off the top of an eighty-floor building and for seventy-nine floors believes that he is flying. 'It's the sudden stop at the end that tells you you're not'.[11]

Following Hamas's continuation of the firing of missiles after the withdrawal from Gaza, Israeli public attitudes towards abandoning West Bank settlements had clearly hardened.

The Obama White House therefore had little progress to show by 2012. The growth of the West Bank settlements seemed unstoppable. The Macro Center for Political Economics calculated that the settlements were worth $18.8 billion in May 2011. This would be part of the cost of evacuating

[11] Thomas L. Friedman, 'I Believe That I Can Fly', *New York Times* 13 November 2010.

the settlers – a prospect which seemed unlikely in the midst of the severe global economic crisis of the early twenty-first century.

According to opinion polls, the vast majority of US Jews continued to support Obama's general endeavours as traditional voters for the Democrats. In stark contrast, a majority of Israeli voters who were solely concerned with attitudes towards Israel continued to oppose him. US Republicans sensed an opportunity to woo Jewish Democratic voters away from their traditional voting pattern. Obama often had had to face defamatory comments that he was un-American and a secret Muslim. Many sensed that the less than perfect relationship with Netanyahu's government could become yet another weapon in a future election campaign. The House Speaker, John A. Boehner, invited Netanyahu to address Congress in May 2011. Marginal constituencies with heavy Jewish populations were seen as Republican targets in the elections. While there appeared to be a coalescing of interests and a strengthening of ties between the American Right and the Israeli Right, a survey by the Public Religion Research Institute in April 2012 indicated that 67 per cent of Jewish voters held 'mostly' or 'very' unfavourable opinions of the Republican presidential candidate, Mitt Romney. In contrast, Romney received a red carpet treatment during his visit to Israel in July 2012. In a controversial speech, Romney's approach was synchronized to dovetail with that of the Netanyahu government. There was no mention of its settlement policy in the West Bank.

CHAPTER 18

An Arab Spring and an Israeli winter?

A DOWNWARD SPIRAL?

From the 1980s onwards, any outbreak of violence had resulted in a move to the Right in Israel. The rise of Islamism in the Arab world and particularly in the West Bank and Gaza in the first decade of the twenty-first century resulted in a move to the far Right. The perception of the Israeli electorate was that strong leaders and a determined government were required to defend them. However, both the Right and the far Right had other items on their governing agenda.

Netanyahu was sometimes seen as the prisoner of his coalition of the centre Right and the far Right. Avigdor Lieberman had replaced Ariel Sharon as his critic within. Pleas to ally the Likud instead with Kadima fell on deaf ears. The pattern of Netanyahu's tenure was to come out in support of an issue when there was a public outcry, only to backtrack partly when it had died down. In a pre-election year, he was acutely aware of the necessity not to leave the centre ground to Kadima or newly emerging politicians such as Yair Lapid. Sometimes the differences between the centre Right and the far Right surfaced, as in Lieberman's harsh condemnation of Netanyahu for his opposition to the establishment of a Knesset committee to investigate the funding of Israeli human rights organizations.

The far Right and the Right within the Likud itself proposed a raft of legislation during 2011 which its opponents claimed was a blatant attempt to row back from the vision of Israel as an open and liberal society. Coming in the aftermath of the Goldstone Report, this was viewed by many as an attempt to rein in Israeli dissenters.

In particular, there were proposals for vetting Supreme Court judges by the Knesset. The attempt to politicize the Supreme Court was manifested in an attempt to pave the way for a right-wing candidate who would eventually succeed the present incumbent, Dorit Beinisch. There was also a move to limit the number of Bar Association representatives on the committee that appoints judges in favour of an increased role by the Minister of Justice.

There were also attempts to amend the libel laws and thereby persuade the media to adopt a more servile disposition for fear of incurring large fines in court cases.

The vote of the Knesset of 47–38 in passing a law which made it a civil offence to call for boycotts of people or institutions 'which may cause economic, cultural or academic damage' was another case in point. This was passed despite the opinion of the Knesset's legal advisor that it constituted 'a severe violation of freedom of expression'. One Israeli commentator estimated that approximately 10 out of 5,000 Israeli professors had actually articulated such views.[1] Indeed many regarded the real motivation behind this move as a means of shutting down liberal voices in Israeli academia. The original bill proposed a fine of 30,000 shekels on anyone convicted and a ban on entering the country for those who were neither citizens nor residents of Israel.

Such decisions by the politicians earned the condemnation of many serving diplomats and civil servants as an infringement upon freedom of speech.

Although there was rising irritation with such boycotts from abroad, this move, stimulated by the far Right, was in response to an informal boycott of Israeli institutions on the West Bank. Thus although Ehud Barak recognized a five-year-old decision to turn the Ariel University Center of Samaria into a full-fledged university, more than 150 Israeli academics, unusually including many scientists, signed a petition to boycott the institution. Actors and playwrights similarly boycotted the new auditorium in Ariel.

Ironically Hamas was similarly irritated by NGOs and raided the offices of the al-Mezan Center for Human Rights, Bonat al-Mustaqbal and others in Gaza in April 2010. Al-Mezan called upon the Hamas government to ensure respect for the law and allow such organizations to operate freely.

The Jewish Diaspora felt very uneasy with this drip-drip curtailment of civil liberties in Israel. The perception of anti-democratic and illiberal behaviour was enhanced by what appeared to be a political move to dilute the right of opponents to express their opposition. Israeli Arabs were perceived to be the target of Yisrael Beitanu's Citizenship Law, which enabled courts to revoke the citizenship of people convicted of treason. This, in itself, was a watered-down version of the party's demand for a loyalty oath

---

[1] Carlo Strenger, *Ha'aretz* 31 May 2011.

to a 'Jewish and democratic state'. Moreover, the law was opposed by the Shin Bet, which felt that existing legislation was quite adequate.

The far Right colouring of such laws significantly clashed with the liberal inclinations of Diaspora Jews – many of whom continued to be involved in local struggles for civil rights. Indeed such condemnation was not limited to those on the Left. Both the right-wing Zionist Organization of America and the loyalist Anti-Defamation League voiced their displeasure publicly.

Two bills were proposed to limit donations to Israeli NGOs from foreign states. One proposed a ceiling of 20,000 shekels while the other suggested a 45 per cent tax. Opponents of such measures pointed out that the government would prove to be the final arbiter as to which non-profit associations would be permitted to receive funds from abroad. While governments and foreign organizations would be subjected to scrutiny, no such appraisal would be directed at individual foreign donors. Therefore, donations from Jewish donors in the Diaspora to the political party of their choice would still be permitted. In 2002, Israel had signed a trade agreement with the EU which forged a greater cooperation. Article 2 stipulated that the agreement would be based on 'respect for human rights and democratic principles'.

There were also rumblings within Israel's centre Right such as the public attack of the veteran Likud leader Moshe Arens on far Right politicians who wished to remove Arabic as one of the official languages of Israel.[2] There was also a division within the Likud itself. Opponents of such legislation such as Dan Meridor and Benny Begin, who were the heirs of the Irgun's Fighting Family legacy and adherents of Jabotinsky's liberal conservatism, found themselves labelled as 'leftist collaborators' within the Likud.

A National Referendum Law, however, was also passed which would require the approval of eighty Knesset members – two-thirds of all members – to ratify any agreement to cede territory. If a decision to give up land was accepted by a majority which was less than eighty, then the issue would go to a referendum.

Occasionally Netanyahu distanced himself from this trend such as in the bill proposed by his own party that permitted the Knesset's Constitution, Law and Justice Committee to veto the appointment of Supreme Court judges. But on the whole he took no action to inhibit such an erosion of previously accepted rights. In November 2011, under pressure from US and European governments as well as Diaspora organizations, Netanyahu suspended the parliamentary process to enact bills which were directed against

---

[2] *Ha'aretz* 15 November 2011.

the funding of foreign governments of many Israeli NGOs concerned with human rights. All this further distanced the Netanyahu administration from the US's first black president, who was also a lawyer.

Netanyahu's reluctance to act had, in part, been based on his fear that he would be outflanked by his rival on the Right, Avigdor Lieberman. Indeed an opinion poll in March 2011 of almost 72,000 Likud members suggested that some 83 per cent of respondents opposed the very creation of a Palestinian state.[3] Several months previously, Lieberman had presented his own plan about transferring territory of Arab population concentration from Israel to the PA.

The Saudi peace initiative of 2002 was marginalized by successive Israeli governments, and the Netanyahu administration followed in this tradition. While there were undoubted caveats and qualifications, Crown Prince Abdullah had told an Arab summit in Beirut in March 2002 that if the government of Israel abandoned force and embraced true peace, 'we will not hesitate to accept the right of the Israeli people to live in security with the people of the region'. While this was an advance on previous Arab League formulations such as the Khartoum declaration of 1967, it was not utilized as a basis for any public negotiations. The inability of the Netanyahu government to put forward any alternative revived Palestinian plans to seek recognition as a state by the United Nations.

On the other hand, for the duration of the ten-month moratorium, the PA had not engaged in any meaningful dialogue with the Netanyahu government, which it seemingly believed to be a futile exercise. Indeed Netanyahu repeated his willingness to freeze settlement construction on government land if Mahmoud Abbas resumed talks. However, most settlement construction was carried out by the private sector on private land – and in this area, Netanyahu would not agree to a freeze. The political stagnation leading to a complete impasse between Israelis and Palestinians did not lead to a new Intifada, but to a turning away towards unilateralism, towards seeking UN recognition for a state in the West Bank, Gaza and East Jerusalem. This resonated with some commentators in Israel who argued that 'peace' could be separated from 'statehood'. Others believed that negotiations between states might actually prove more fruitful. International support for a Palestinian state was mounting. At the end of November 2010, President Lula da Silva recognized Palestine on behalf of Brazil. The US vetoed a UN resolution which condemned Israeli settlement activity – yet the resolution boasted almost 120 sponsors. Arafat's

---

[3] *Jerusalem Post* 11 March 2011.

declaration of independence in Algiers in 1988 similarly attracted the recognition of 100 states – a recognition which proved to be an illusion. Netanyahu argued that a real Palestinian state would only emerge out of a negotiated peace agreement.

In 2011, the Israeli government embarked on a seemingly futile attempt to persuade governments not to vote for recognition of a Palestinian state. Europe, in particular, was targeted; there Germany and the East Europeans seemed disposed not to support the Palestinians' initiative. The West Europeans in contrast were much more sympathetic to Palestinian aspirations even if this did not materialize in a 'yes' vote. An opinion poll in Britain, whose government had refrained from openly supporting a Palestinian state, indicated a majority in favour of its doing so. There was also division within Israel itself with many academics and intellectuals arguing that Israel should actually embrace such an initiative and work with the PA to enter into realistic negotiations. 'A creative and courageous approach to leveraging the Palestinian initiative will not end the conflict. But it could make it far more manageable'.[4]

The Israeli government had little to show for its limited attempts at negotiation in most areas. Gilad Shalit remained in a Hamas prison despite mediation by the Egyptian government and by German negotiators for a prisoner exchange. Moreover, many Israelis were hesitant about trading prisoners who had been involved in the killing of civilians. Hamas demanded the release of, amongst others, Hassan Salama, who had orchestrated a wave of suicide bombings in the 1990s. He was held responsible for the killing of sixty-seven Israeli citizens and sentenced to several dozen consecutive life terms.

Outside of events which Israel could neither predict nor control, the country's isolation was due to the cumulative effect of the fallout from the attack on Gaza, the flotilla affair and the Netanyahu government's apparent indifference to international condemnation of its policies on settlement expansion. The discovery that the Mossad had used forged passports to kill a Hamas arms dealer, Mahmoud al-Mabhouh, in a Dubai hotel at the beginning of January 2010 added to this. In an age of electronic surveillance, Mossad operations were now traceable. Britain was particularly angry since this episode was not a new occurrence. In 1979, a British charity worker, 'Erika Chambers', who claimed to be a graduate of the University of Southampton, was implicated in the assassination of Ali Hassan Salameh, one of the chief architects behind the Munich massacre of Israeli athletes.

[4] *New York Times* 24 June 2011.

In 1986, a lost bag full of forged British passports was discovered – and Mrs Thatcher reputedly reduced the Mossad operation in Britain.[5]

In July 2012, the Israeli State Comptroller added to the government's woes and produced a damning report about Netanyahu's handling of the raid on the *Mavi Marmara*. The 150-page report argued that Netanyahu's leadership at the time was flawed and studded with 'substantive and significant shortcomings'. The National Security Council was not instructed to report on the situation. Some Ministers were left completely in the dark. The IDF chief, Gabi Ashkenazi, had warned about the probability of a violent confrontation, but was seemingly passed over. The State Comptroller inferred that all the safeguards that had been put in place by the Winograd Committee after the second Lebanon war in 2006 had been ignored.

ISRAEL AND THE ARAB SPRING

The sense of isolation was heightened by the advent of the Arab Spring. In Egypt the hegemony of military rule, in place since 1952, appeared to be coming to an end with the overthrow of Hosni Mubarak. It evoked a comparison with the fresh spirit of the Free Officers' Revolt of Neguib and Nasser half a century previously. The drive towards democracy in theory was applauded, but most Israelis wondered what the final outcome would be. Would it truly be an Arab Spring or a winter of discontent? Would Egyptian nationalism be replaced by Egyptian Islamism? In October 2011, US Embassy and National Security officials were already in dialogue with the Muslim Brotherhood's Freedom and Justice party. The Egyptian journalist Mamdouh El-Waly became the first post-revolution chairman of the Egyptian Journalists' Syndicate after winning in free elections with a large turnout.[6] Yet he only secured his victory with the backing of the Muslim Brotherhood – was this a harbinger of the shape of things to come?

The suspicion that the hopes for a new dawn in Egypt were dangerously misplaced was roused when the results of the first rounds of parliamentary elections were declared. The Muslim Brotherhood and the Salafist al-Nour party attracted some 65 per cent of the electorate's support. In contrast, support for the liberals and reformers attracted only a quarter of this figure. While the intellectuals had courageously protested in Tahrir Square, some 25 million citizens chose a different path and voted for the Islamists. As one prominent Israeli journalist commented in hindsight:

[5] *Sunday Times* 16 March 1987. [6] *Al-Ahram* Online 27 October 2011.

We should have known from the start that Hosni Mubarak would be replaced not by the Google youth, but by the Muslim Brotherhood.[7]

The Salafists probably garnered 20–25 per cent of the votes. Al-Nour denounced the democratic ideal but accepted the machinery of democracy such as the staging of elections and a majority verdict. While women were included in al-Nour's election list of candidates, a women's rally in support of the party included only male speakers.

Although a delegation from the Egyptian Brothers visited Ismail Haniyeh in Gaza in October 2011, the Muslim Brotherhood seemed to be factionalizing into ideological and pragmatic wings. Issues such as the representation of women in positions of authority were bitterly contested. While the Palestinian Authority publicly welcomed the Arab Spring, the emergence of a powerful Islamist government in Egypt led by the Brotherhood was deeply worrying. The actor and film maker Juliano Mer-Khamis had been shot dead in a refugee camp in Jenin in April 2011. Mer-Khamis had been active in establishing the Freedom Theatre in the city and many believed that this had stoked the ire of the Islamists.

For all his authoritarianism at home, Mubarak had maintained the peace with Israel for over thirty years. Although his temporary successors proclaimed the continuation of the Camp David Accords, signed by Begin and Sadat, there were increasing signs that even a cold peace might be problematic in a post-Mubarak Egypt. As the pace of change in Egypt slowed, the anger of the Tahrir protesters began to focus on Israel. The killing of several Egyptian soldiers, following the killing of Israelis in southern Israel, probably by the Popular Resistance Committees, resulted in a declaration of apology, but no amelioration of the situation. Indeed it highlighted the increasingly porous nature of Gaza's border with Egypt such that Palestinian Islamists now had an easier route to pass into Israel. It was even argued that a factor in securing the release of Gilad Shalit in October 2011 from a Hamas prison cell after more than five years' captivity in Gaza was pessimistic Israeli predictions about the future course of the Arab Spring – especially in Egypt.

When protesters broke into the Israeli embassy in Cairo in September 2011, the swift action of Egyptian commandos allowed the staff to escape without suffering any personal violence. The Israelis had called upon President Obama to intervene. His quiet handling of the situation resolved it without bloodshed, but the incident also signified the increasingly

---

7 Ari Shavit *Ha'aretz* 29 December 2011.

difficult relationship between Israel and Egypt and the need for American intermediaries.

The final outcome of the prolonged Egyptian electoral process was a narrow victory for the Islamists in 2012 and the election of Mohammed Morsi, the candidate of the Muslim Brotherhood, as the new president. Morsi had previously opposed any normalization of relations with Israel, yet maintained a silence on abrogating the 1979 Camp David agreement. In July 2012, Morsi met both Mahmoud Abbas and Khaled Meshal, but spent considerably more time with the latter. Moreover Hamas steadfastly had refused to support its long-term ally, Bashar Assad, in the Syrian civil war. In part, it was because the Muslim Brotherhood in Syria was fighting to overthrow the Assad regime. In part, it was because the Egyptian wing of the Brotherhood had come to power. The Sunnis of Cairo had replaced the Shi'ites of Teheran in the political affection of Hamas.

Yet it was Turkey under Recep Tayyip Erdogan which effectively led the charge in isolating Israel. Effectively excluded from EU membership, it had begun instead to repair its relations with Iraq, Iran and Russia and this paralleled a process of distancing itself from Israel. Turkey grew close to Iran economically and the two countries aimed to triple their bilateral trade to $30 billion by 2016. It was also emerging as a strong economic power. Its economy grew by 8.2 per cent in the third quarter of 2011. Like the Iranians, the Turks intended to build several nuclear reactors. By 2011, Erdogan had won his third term of office. This, in part, was due to the changing nature of the Turkish electorate. Many voters had migrated from rural areas into the cities and participated for the first time in public discourse. The influence of the secularized elite and the military was clearly waning. Public opinion on Israel was hardening regardless of Netanyahu's policies.

Erdogan facilitated the provision of cheap accommodation and fuel for the less well-off in Turkish society and opened up the educational system. He also liberalized the clampdown on the Kurdish language, allowing a television channel in the language and Kurdish literature departments in Turkish universities. There was also more stringent enforcement of an Islamic code of behaviour – restrictions on alcoholic drink and a barring of some Internet sites.

Amidst talk of neo-Ottomanism, with its newly found economic might, Turkey hoped to revive its political influence in the region and reintegrate itself into the Middle East as a power broker. Operation Cast Lead and the flotilla killings of Turkish citizens provided a genuine issue with which to stoke nationalist fires at home and indeed to further its foreign policy aims abroad.

Erdogan had actually been honoured with the 'Courage to Care Award' by the Anti-Defamation League, a flagship organization of US Jews, in June 2005. During the award ceremony, he stressed his country's close ties to Israel. His increasingly acerbic rhetoric towards Israel certainly marked a break with the past. This manifested itself through a repeated emphasis on human rights violations in the Israel–Palestine conflict in a concerted attempt to isolate Israel. Yet he often voiced a selective outrage elsewhere and was happy to congratulate Ahmadinejad on his victory in the controversial Iranian election in 2009. He also expressed doubts about whether genocide had been committed in Darfur. In the absence of an acceptable form of apology from the Netanyahu government and the Israeli refusal to pay compensation for the killing of Turkish civilians, the Erdogan government angrily rejected the Palmer Commission's findings. It was unable to accept its conclusion that Israel's blockade of Gaza was legal and in accordance with international law. Instead Ankara stated that it would take its case against the blockade to the International Court of Justice. Although the Palmer report was highly critical of Israeli action, Erdogan drastically downgraded diplomatic relations with Israel. He sought instead to build new alliances with the victors of the 2011 Arab Spring such as post-Mubarak Egypt. Erdogan visited Egypt in September 2011 amidst talk of sending Turkish warships to accompany future flotillas to Gaza. Yet he significantly refrained from his proclaimed intention of visiting Gaza, probably because of Egyptian pressure. Egypt in part viewed Turkey as a rival for leadership in the Middle East. Erdogan extended his trip to incorporate visits to Libya and Tunisia, both of which had changed regimes.

Despite the admonitions of many Israeli officials, Netanyahu felt that an apology to the Turks would be regarded as weakness by the Arabs. Lieberman believed that it would open up the way to lawsuits against IDF personnel. In response, Netanyahu started to forge better relations with Greece and several Balkan states which had historically been ruled by the Ottoman Turks – and therefore possessed long memories. Lieberman, for good measure, had been advised by aides to consider helping the Kurdish PKK.[8] Although this was subsequently denied by Lieberman, the Kurdish organization responded by stating that Israel should first apologize for aiding in the capture of its leader Abdullah Öcalan by the Turks in 1999.

Erdogan's visit to Egypt occurred a few days after the sacking of the embassy and this incident seemed symbolically to catalyze the emergence of a new alignment of forces against Israel. It also symbolized the great

[8] *Yediot Aharanot* 9 September 2011.

expansion of trade with the Arab world under Erdogan. When he argued before the Arab League that 'the barrier to peace in the region is the mentality of the Israeli government', he made a point of carefully distinguishing the people of Israel from their elected representatives. Similarly Turkey had differentiated between hostility towards Israel and a civilized relationship with the United States. Moreover the White House desperately needed Turkish goodwill in the Middle East and was prepared to tolerate the increasingly acerbic criticism of Israel. Turkey thereby agreed to host an early warning radar system as part of NATO's missile defence strategy. All this and an ongoing criticism of Assad's crackdown on protesters in Syria did not ingratiate Ankara to Teheran despite improved political and economic ties.

Yet despite the plummeting relationship of Israel and Turkey, the volume of bilateral trade was $2.7 billion during 2010–2011, which allowed Turkey to sell $1.5 billion in goods to Israel.

The flash points between Turkey and Israel began to proliferate by the autumn of 2011. Following a visit to Jerusalem by the Cypriot Foreign Minister, an agreement was entered into by Greek Cyprus and Israel to explore any possible maritime gas sources. Ankara vehemently objected as it argued that Turkish northern Cyprus had a right to all natural resources.

In December 2011, Israel significantly refused to renew the export license for Elbit Systems and Israel Aerospace Industries so that they could proceed with a $140 million deal signed with Turkey in 2009. The cancellation of the sale of an advanced camera system which could be installed in fighter aircraft was designed to prevent any transfer to hostile countries by Turkey.

The deterioration of relations with Turkey conversely spawned a blossoming of contacts with Greece, which desperately needed friends as the country rapidly sank into the whirlpool of economic catastrophe. President Karlos Papoulias visited Israel in July 2011 and Israeli tourists began to visit Greece instead of Turkey. The Greeks obligingly blocked ships bound for Gaza from leaving their shores, thereby preventing another flotilla incident.

The Israelis objected to the use of the GöK Türk satellite, scheduled to be launched by Ankara in 2013, to fly over Israel and possibly survey security installations. The satellite had been constructed with French assistance in cooperation with an Italian company. Turkey argued that Israel had been photographing Turkish territory for many years.

Although the Arab Spring had played out differently in different countries, it did seem to be spawning a new alignment of formerly friendly states against Israel in the absence of any new initiative from the Netanyahu government.

Israel remained relatively silent as this drama of regime change in the Arab world was being played out – although some such as the former head of the Mossad, Danny Yatom, complained that the rapid US abandonment of Mubarak sent the message that Washington's allies in the Middle East could not rely on America.

The uprising in Syria was of particular concern to Israel. What would happen to the store of biological and chemical weapons if Assad fell? Would the Alawite heavy hand of Bashar Assad be replaced by a Sunni Islamist one? On the other hand, such a successor regime might distance itself from Iran. Ironically on one occasion, Syria sent tanks over its border with Lebanon – and not a word was said by Beirut.

Syria's ongoing search to acquire nuclear power still worried Israel. UN investigators discovered a building in the town of al-Hasakah which was uncannily similar to the design of a uranium enrichment plant which had been supplied to Gaddafi when Libya had embarked on a nuclear programme. The Assad regime did not respond to an International Atomic Energy Agency (IAEA) request to visit the complex.

In late November 2011, *Die Welt*, citing 'western security services', reported that North Korea had been involved in supplying 'maraging steel' to a Syrian complex near Homs.[9] The transfer of such material by North Korea had been prohibited by UN Resolutions 1718 (2006) and 1874 (2009). This would have enabled Iran to modify its centrifuges to produce an enriched uranium for nuclear purposes as well as upgrading missile warheads.

Islamism was no doubt attractive to many in Arab countries: 'Islamism provides an answer to people who feel that they have been prevented from being themselves'.[10] If Islamism did emerge – even as the power behind the throne – what sort of Islamism would triumph? Would it be Salafist or closer to the Erdogan model?

Anwar Sadat always regarded Egypt as the solitary Arab state – all the rest, he surmised, were merely a collection of tribes. Israel was keenly aware that Egypt led the Arab world and that the attitude of its largest neighbour could change overnight. Indeed members of the Muslim Brotherhood attended the meeting in Cairo in which President Obama had promised better relations with the United States. Any sign of a retreat from past agreements was monitored, dissected and analyzed. There were also worries that Egypt would switch off the supply of natural gas to Israel, and the pipeline running

---

9 *Die Welt* 24 November 2011.
10 Hussein Agha and Robert Malley, 'The Arab Counter-Revolution', *New York Review of Books* 29 September 2011.

through Sinai had been repeatedly vandalized. The military coalition that governed Egypt in the interim period reassured their international partners that the Camp David Accords of 1979 with Israel would continue. Yet other voices wished to renegotiate them.

For the Palestinians, the advent of Arab Spring held out new hope of possibilities to highlight their case. At the beginning of the Egyptian protests, Mahmoud Abbas allowed both pro- and anti-Mubarak demonstrations. During the upheaval, several Palestinian prisoners escaped from their Egyptian jailors and made their way back to Gaza.

There were ongoing protests in Bil'in, Ni'lin, Nebi Salah, Wallaja, Silwan and Sheikh Jarrah. Such protests signified the lack of success of the military option which Hamas had embraced. In Nazareth, the Balad party staged a march whereby demonstrators carried Egyptian and Tunisian flags.

Many prominent Israeli figures began to voice their belief that simply battening down the hatches was no substitute for meaningful proposals. The outgoing Mossad chief, Meir Dagan, complained that Israel had failed to put forward a peace initiative and had ignored the Saudi proposal. Mahmoud Abbas told Israel Television that he believed that the Arab world had made a mistake in rejecting UN Resolution 181 in 1947, which called for a two-state solution. In drawing unspoken comparisons with the Netanyahu administration, he stated that he had been very close to concluding an agreement with Ehud Olmert, who had agreed to an Israeli withdrawal from 93.5 per cent of the West Bank.

This political vacuum allowed the PA to push for UN recognition of Palestinian statehood. Indeed Mahmoud Abbas during his UN speech in September 2011 spoke about 'the Palestinian Spring'. While the US promised to veto any proposal for nationhood in the UN Security Council, the General Assembly was heavily in favour of according recognition to the Palestinians. The Palestinians proposed to opt for a Vatican-type status of less than full membership.

Although the May 2011 Peace Index of Tel Aviv University suggested that a majority of Israelis feared that a declaration of a Palestinian state would lead to a third Intifada, there were many Israelis, particularly on the Left, who welcomed the declaration of a state

In June 2011, Israelis staged a demonstration in Tel Aviv in support of a Palestinian state as the 194th member of the United Nations. Many intellectuals and academics in Israel such as the Nobel Prize winner Daniel Kahneman, the philosopher Avishai Margalit and the novelist Ronit Matalon supported the idea of UN recognition of a Palestinian state. Seventeen Israel

Prize winners endorsed a petition calling for Palestinian independence outside the Tel Aviv hall where Ben-Gurion had proclaimed independence in 1948. In the *New York Times*, eighteen retired generals, twenty-seven Israel Prize winners, five former diplomats and five current or former university presidents signed a full-page advertisement. President Shimon Peres labelled Abbas as 'the best leader Israel will work with'.

In contrast, the Netanyahu Foreign Ministry had bowed to the inevitable at an early stage. It initiated a diplomatic drive to create 'a moral minority' amongst the divided Europeans. Yet there was undoubtedly a consensus in Israel that 'a Palestinian state' was meaningless in the absence of meaningful negotiations: more public relations than public reality.

The centre Right–far Right coalition was in danger of fragmenting if a pragmatic proposal was put forward. Indeed Avigdor Lieberman walked out when Mahmoud Abbas began to address the United Nations. Therefore, stasis was the central option despite the PA's refusal to negotiate even during the settlement freeze.

AN UNKNOWN FUTURE

At the beginning of 2012, Israel's population stood at 7,836,000, of whom 75.3 per cent were Jews and 20.5 per cent were Arabs.

Yet there were severe disparities in the standard of living. The gap between the rich and the poor was widening. Even so, on one level, Netanyahu could happily point to a growing GDP, low unemployment and low inflation – a situation which was profoundly different from the conditions in Europe. The advent of tent cities and waves of protest during the summer of 2011, however, pointed to a different, darker reality.

A tent was pitched in Tel Aviv's Rothschild Boulevard on 14 July. By August 2011, it had proliferated to create ninety tent cities. An estimated 300,000 protesters came onto the streets to make their voice heard. There were also tent camps in several Arab villages. The government was disparaging at first, labelling the first Tel Aviv demonstrators as 'sushi eaters' – spoilt middle-class youngsters. Yet all over Israel, it was clear that such social protests knew neither class nor political boundaries.

The gradual elimination of government responsibility for basic social services through 'outsourcing' had resulted in the diversion of funds to reduce high income taxes. This was balanced by higher indirect taxes (such as on petrol and cigarettes) which affected the lifestyle of the poor. For the Israeli protesters of 2011, the reality of neo-liberal economic policies amounted to a transferring of resources from the poor to the rich. Indeed, by 2011, the UN Development Programme listed Israel as the fourth most unequal society in the world.

The protesters wanted a fundamental change in the economic system not merely a cosmetic reform, as had been the case in the past. They advocated higher taxes for the well-to-do and changes in both inheritance tax and capital gains tax. Warren Buffett was frequently quoted. Netanyahu, however, was a free marketeer – an admirer of Margaret Thatcher, Friedrich Hayek and Milton Friedman. Symbolically electricity prices were raised 10 per cent during the protests.

Netanyahu appointed a committee of experts, headed by Manuel Trajtenberg. It concluded that the rash of protests had been stimulated by 'a deep sense of injustice' and that the public wealth was unfairly distributed. It unexpectedly called for a cut in the $13 billion defence budget, which was 7 per cent of GDP. It recommended beginning education earlier, at three years old; a longer school day; increased taxes for the well-off and private corporations and housing reforms. All this struck at Netanyahu's preference for the free market and privatization. Several months later, there were signals in the Israeli press that Netanyahu intended to backtrack on his promises on education and defence cuts.

By 2012 Netanyahu's administration was under attack both domestically and internationally. Tsipi Livni's resignation as leader of Kadima and the party's subsequent entry into government as part of a wall-to-wall coalition of ninety-four seats was viewed as balancing the far Right. Yet as suddenly as Shaul Mofaz had marched the party into government, he about-turned and led it out again. Most observers viewed this as the death throes of a centrist party which had originally showed so much promise.

Lieberman was emerging as a possible rival for the leadership of the Israeli Right and as a future contender for Prime Minister. Yet there were bumps in the road ahead. He had informed Vladimir Putin that the 2011 Russian elections were free and fair – much to the astonishment of many former Soviet Jews in Israel. His party had proposed an Armenian genocide memorial day to antagonize the Turks further. An election beckoned, but would it enhance the move to the right? Or would it repeat 1992, when the Israeli electorate perceived Shamir's rift with President Bush as a bridge too far? Yet there was no discernible Rabin-type figure on the political horizon who could reverse the decline of the Left.

For all the controversy surrounding Operation Cast Lead, the number of rockets fired in 2010–2011 was 1,100 – one-sixth of the number fired in the years before the operation.[11] In contrast, the Israeli defence establishment began to note the improvement in the quality of anti-aircraft missiles in Gaza, amidst the knowledge that gangs of smugglers had raided military storage facilities in Libya during the struggle against Gaddafi. These stolen weapons including missile components had subsequently been sold to Islamist groups in Gaza. The IDF believed that there had been an increase of 15–20 per cent in weaponry in 2011 including the Russian manufactured Kornet anti-tank missile. Moreover, the Iron Dome had only been 75 per cent successful in 2011 in stopping missiles which had been fired from Gaza. In October 2011, the Israeli cabinet discussed the possibility of purchasing anti-missile systems to protect civilian aircraft landing at the tourist resort of Eilat. With an increase in the number, sophistication and range of the missiles targeted at them, many Israelis wondered what the future would hold.

[11] *Ha'aretz* 1 January 2012.

Bibliography

Adelman, Jonathan, *The Rise of Israel: A History of a Revolutionary State* (London 2008).

Alden, Chris and Aran, Amnon, *Foreign Policy Analysis: New Approaches* (London 2011).

Amr, Ziad Abu, *Islamic Fundamentalism in the West Bank and Gaza: Muslim Brotherhood and Islamic Jihad* (Bloomington 1994).

Arian, Asher (Alan), *The Elections in Israel: 1969* (Jerusalem 1972).

The Second Republic: Politics in Israel (Chatham 1998).

Arian, Asher (Alan), and Shamir, Michal, *The Elections in Israel 1984* (Tel Aviv 1986).

The Elections in Israel 1992 (New York 1995).

Avner, Yehuda, *The Prime Ministers: An Intimate Narrative of Israeli Leadership* (London 2010).

Banks, Lynne Reid, *Torn Country* (New York 1982).

Bar-On, Mordechai, *Shalom Achshav: Li-dioknah shel tenuah* (Tel Aviv 1986).

The Gates of Gaza: Israel's Road to Suez and Back 1955–1957 (London 1994).

In Pursuit of Peace: A History of the Israeli Peace Movement (Washington, DC 1996).

Moshe Dayan: Israel's Controversial Hero (London 2012).

Begin, Menachem, *The Revolt* (London 1979).

Beilin, Yossi, *Mechirav shel Ichud: Mifleget Ha'avodah ud milchemet yom kippur* (Tel Aviv 1985).

The Path to Geneva: The Quest for a Permanent Agreement 1996–2004 (New York 2004).

Ben-Ami, Shlomo, *Scars of War: Wounds of Peace: The Israeli–Arab Tragedy* (London 2006).

Ben-Gurion, David, *Anakhnu veshkheneynu* (Tel Aviv 1931).

'Mission and Dedication', *Israel Government Yearbook 5711* (Tel Aviv 1950).

'Israel among the Nations', *Israel Government Yearbook 1952* (Jerusalem 1952).

'Jewish Survival', *Israel Government Yearbook 1953/4* (Tel Aviv 1954).

Mi-ma'amad le-am (Tel Aviv 1955).

Rebirth and Destiny of Israel (London 1959).

Medinat Yisrael Ha-mechudeshet (Tel Aviv 1969).

Israel: A Personal History (London 1971).

Yoman ha-milhamah: milhemet ha-'atsmaut (Tel Aviv 1982).

Ben-Zvi, Abraham, *John F. Kennedy and the Politics of Arms Sales to Israel* (London 2002).

Lyndon B. Johnson and the Politics of Arms Sales to Israel (London 2004).

Bialer, Uri, *Between East and West: Israel's Foreign Policy Orientation 1948–1956* (Cambridge 1990).

Bilski Ben-Hur, Raphaella, *Every Individual a King* (Washington, DC 1993).

Caplan, Neil, *The Israel–Palestine Conflict: Contested Histories* (London 2009).

Carter, Jimmy, *Keeping Faith* (London 1982).

Clinton, Bill, *My Life* (New York 2004).

Cohen, Amichai and Cohen, Stuart, *Israel's National Security Law: Political Dynamics and Historical Development* (London 2011).

Cohen, Avner, *Israel and the Bomb* (New York 1998).

Cohen, Stuart, *Israel and Its Army: From Cohesion to Confusion* (London 2008).

Coogan, Tim Pat, *Michael Collins: A Biography* (London 1990).

Cordesman, Anthony H., *Israel and Syria: The Military Balance and the Prospects for War* (London 2008).

Crossman, Richard, *Palestine Mission: A Personal Record* (London 1947).

A Nation Reborn (London 1960).

Dalsheim, Joyce, *Unsettling Gaza: Secular Liberalism, Radical Religion, and the Israeli Settlement Project* (Oxford 2011).

Dalton, Hugh, *High Tide and After: Memoirs 1945–1960* (London 1962).

Dayan, Moshe, *Story of My Life* (New York 1976).

Don-Yehiya, Eliezer (ed.), *Israel and Diaspora Jewry: Ideological and Political Perspectives* (Jerusalem 1991).

Dowty, Alan, *Israel/Palestine* (Cambridge 2008).

Eban, Abba, *Abba Eban: An Autobiography* (New York 1977).

Elpeleg, Zvi, *The Grand Mufti: Haj Amin al-Hussaini, Founder of the Palestinian National Movement* (London 1993).

Evron, Boaz, *Jewish State or Israeli Nation* (Bloomington 1995).

Evron, Yair, *Israel's Nuclear Dilemma* (New York 1994).

Filc, Dani, *The Political Right in Israel: Different Faces of Jewish Populism* (London 2010).

Fishman, Judah L., *The History of the Mizrachi Movement* (New York 1928).

Flapan, Simcha, *Zionism and the Palestinian Arabs* (London 1979).

Freedman, Robert O., *Israel under Rabin* (Boulder 1995).

Fund, Yosef, *Perud O hishtatfut: Agudat Yisrael mul ha 'Tsiyonut u Medinat Yisrael* (Jerusalem 1999).

Gelber, Yoav, *Palestine 1948: War, Escape and the Emergence of the Palestinian Refugee Problem* (Brighton 2001).

Gilboa, Yehoshua, *The Black Years of Soviet Jewry* (Boston 1971).

Gilmour, David, *Dispossessed: The Ordeal of the Palestinians 1917–1980* (London 1980).

Golan, Galia, *Israel and Palestine: Peace Plans and Proposals from Oslo to Disengagement* (Princeton 2008).

Goldman, Nachum, *Memories* (London 1970).

Gorney, Joseph, *The British Labour Movement and Zionism* (London 1983).

Grosbard, Ofer, *Menachem Begin: Portrait of a Leader* (Tel Aviv 2006).

Haklai, Oded, *Palestinian Ethnonationalism in Israel* (Philadelphia 2011).

Herzl, Theodor, *The Jewish State* (London 1936).

Altneuland (New York 1960).

Hroub, Khaled, *Hamas: A Beginner's Guide* (London 2006).

Inbari, Pinhas, *The Palestinians between Terrorism and Statehood* (Brighton 1996).

Jabotinsky, Vladimir, *Neumim 1905–1926* (Tel Aviv 1957–1958).

Neumim 1927–1940 (Tel Aviv 1957–1958).

Karsh, Efraim (ed.), *From Rabin to Netanyahu: Israel's Troubled Agenda* (London 1997).

Palestine Betrayed (London 2010).

Klein, Menachem, *A Possible Peace between Israel and Palestine: An Insider's Account of the Geneva Initiative* (New York 2007).

Laqueur, Walter and Rubin, Barry, *The Israel–Arab Reader: A Documentary History of the Middle East Conflict* (London 1984).

Levenberg, Shneur, *The Board and Zion* (Hull 1985).

Levitt, Matthew, *Hamas: Politics, Charity and Terrorism in the Service of Jihad* (New Haven 2006).

Liebeskind (Rakovsky), Aviva, Davis, Moshe and Hovav, Meir (eds.), *The Living Testify* (Jerusalem 1994).

Liebman, Charles S., *Pressure without Sanctions* (London 1977).

Litvin, Baruch and Hoenig, Sidney B. (eds.), *Jewish Identity: Modern Responsa and Opinions on the Recognition of Mixed Marriages* (New York 1965).

Lochery, Neill, *The Israeli Labour Party: In the Shadow of the Likud* (London 1997).

The View from the Fence: The Arab–Israeli Conflict from the Present to Its Roots (London 2005).

Loebl, Eugene, *Sentenced and Tried: The Stalinist Purges in Czechoslovakia* (London 1969).

London, Artur, *On Trial* (London 1968).

Lorch, Netanel (ed.), *Major Knesset Debates* (London 1993).

Lukacs, Yehuda (ed.), *The Israeli–Palestinian Conflict: A Documentary Record 1967–1990* (Cambridge 1992).

Luz, Ehud, *Parallels Meet* (New York 1988).

Makovsky, David, *Making Peace with the PLO: The Rabin Government's Road to the Oslo Accord* (Boulder 1996).

Mandel, Neville J., *The Arabs and Zionism before World War I* (London 1976).

Maoz, Moshe, *The PLO and Israel: From Armed Struggle to Political Solution 1964–1994* (London 1997).

McDonald, James G., *The Time for Discussion Is Past in Palestine: A Jewish Commonwealth in Our Time* (Washington, DC 1943).

Meir, Golda, *My Life* (New York 1975).

Meital, Yoram, *Peace in Tatters: Israel, Palestine and the Middle East* (London 2005).

Menashri, David, *Post-Revolutionary Politics in Iran: Religion, Society and Power* (London 2001).

Mendes-Flohr, Paul and Reinharz, Jehuda (eds.), *The Jew in the Modern World: A Documentary History* (Oxford 1980).

Merhav, Peretz, *The Israeli Left* (London 1980).

Michener, James A., *First Fruits: A Harvest of 25 Years of Israeli Writing* (Philadelphia 1973).

Miller, Rory, *Inglorious Disarray: Europe, Israel and the Palestinians since 1967* (Columbia 2011).

Milton-Edwards, Beverley and Farrell, Stephen, *Hamas* (London 2010).

Mor, Menachem, *Eretz Israel, Israel and the Jewish Diaspora: Mutual Relations: Proceedings of the First Klutznick Symposium* (New York 1991).

Morris, Benny, *The Birth of the Palestinian Refugee Problem* (Cambridge 1988).
Israel's Border Wars 1949–1956 (Oxford 1997).
Righteous Victims: A History of the Zionist–Arab Conflict 1881–2001 (New York 2001).
The Road to Jerusalem: Glubb Pasha, Palestine and the Jews (London 2003).
The Birth of the Palestinian Refugee Problem Revisited (Cambridge 2004).
One State, Two States: Resolving the Israel/Palestine Conflict (London 2009).

Namir, Mordechai, *Shlichut b'Moskva* (Tel Aviv 1971).

Nasser, Gamal Abdul, *The Philosophy of the Revolution* (Washington, DC 1955).

O'Hegerty, P. S., *The Victory of Sinn Fein* (Dublin 1924).

Oren, Michael B., *The Origins of the Second Arab–Israeli War: Egypt, Israel and the Great Powers 1952–56* (London 1992).

Pardo, Sharon and Peters, Joel, *Uneasy Neighbours: Israel and the European Union* (New York 2010).

Parfitt, Tudor, *The Road to Redemption: The Jews of the Yemen 1900–1950* (Leiden 1996).

Parker, Richard B. (ed.), *The Six Day War: A Retrospective* (Gainesville 1996).

Pedahzur, Ami, *Jewish Terrorism in Israel* (New York 2011).

Peleg, Ilan and Waxman, Dov, *Israel's Palestinians: The Conflict Within* (Cambridge 2011).

Penslar, Derek J., *Israel in History: The Jewish State in Comparative Perspective* (London 2007).

Peres, Shimon, *Battling for Peace* (New York 1995).

Peri, Yoram (ed.), *The Assassination of Yitzhak Rabin* (Stanford 2000).
Generals in the Cabinet Room: How the Military Shapes Israeli Policy (Washington, DC 2006).

Quandt, William B., *Camp David: Peacemaking and Politics* (Washington, DC 1986).
Peace Process (New York 1993).

Rabinovich, Itamar, *Waging Peace: Israel and the Arabs 1948–2003* (Princeton 2004).

Ram, Uri, *The Globalization of Israel: McWorld in Tel Aviv, Jihad in Jerusalem* (London 2007).

Raphaeli-Tsentiper, Arieh, *B'ma'avak l'geulah* (Tel Aviv 1956).

Ravitsky, Aviezer, *Messianism, Zionism, and Jewish Religious Radicalism* (Chicago 1996).

Reinharz, Jehuda and Shapira, Anita (eds.), *Essential Papers on Zionism* (New York 1995).

Roe, Nicholas (ed.), *Voice of Hezbollah: The Statements of Sayed Hassan Nasrallah* (London 2007).

Rosenblatt, Samuel, *The History of the Mizrachi Movement* (New York 1951).

Ross, Dennis, *The Missing Peace: The Inside Story of the Fight for Middle East Peace* (New York 2004).

Russell, Bertrand, *Zionism and the Peace Settlement in Palestine: A Jewish Commonwealth in Our Time* (Washington, DC 1943).

Saad-Ghorayeb, Amal, *Hizbu'llah: Politics and Religion* (London 2002).

Sachar, Howard, *A History of Israel: From the Rise of Zionism to Our Time* (New York 2007).

Sadat, Anwar, *Revolt on the Nile* (London 1957).

Sayigh, Yezid, *Armed Struggle and the Search for State: The Palestinian National Movement 1949–1993* (Oxford 1997).

Schectman, Joseph B., *The Jabotinsky Story: Rebel and Statesman 1880–1923* (New York 1956).

Schiff, Ze'ev and Ya'ari, Ehud, *Israel's Lebanon War* (London 1985).
  Intifada: The Palestinian Uprising (New York 1989).

Segev, Tom, *The First Israelis* (London 1986).

Sela, Avraham and Ma'oz, Moshe, *The PLO and Israel: From Armed Conflict to Political Solution 1964–1994* (London 1997).

Shalev, Aryeh, *The Intifada: Causes and Effects* (Tel Aviv 1991).

Shalom, Zaki, *Ben-Gurion's Political Struggles 1963–1967: A Lion in Winter* (London 2006).

Shamir, Yitzhak, *Summing Up* (London 1994).

Sharef, Ze'ev, *Three Days* (London 1962).

Sharett, Moshe, *Yoman Ishi* (Tel Aviv 1978).

Sharfman, Daphna, *Living without a Constitution: Civil Rights in Israel* (New York 1993).

Sheffer, Gabriel, *Moshe Sharett: Biography of a Moderate* (Oxford 1996).

Sher, Gilead, *The Israeli–Palestinian Peace Negotiations 1999–2001* (New York 2006).

Shimoni, Gideon, *Jews and Zionism: The South African Experience 1910–1967* (Cape Town 1980).

Shindler, Colin, *Ploughshares into Swords? Israelis and Jews in the Shadow of the Intifada* (London 1991).
  Israel, Likud and the Zionist Dream: Power, Politics and the Zionist Dream from Begin to Netanyahu (London 1995).
  The Land beyond Promise: Israel, Likud and the Zionist Dream (London 2002).
  The Triumph of Military Zionism: Nationalism and the Origins of the Israeli Right (London 2006).

Israel and the European Left: Between Solidarity and Delegitimization (London 2012).

Shuckburgh, Evelyn, *Descent to Suez: Diaries 1951–1956* (London 1986).

al-Shuqayri, Ahmed, *Forty Years in Arab and International Life* (Beirut 1969).

Sobhani, Sohrab, *The Pragmatic Entente: Israeli–Iranian Relations 1948–1988* (London 1989).

Sofer, Sasson, *Begin: An Anatomy of Leadership* (Oxford 1988).

Sprinzak, Ehud, *Brother against Brother: Violence and Extremism in Israeli Politics from the Altalena to the Rabin Assassination* (New York 1999).

Stauber, Roni, *Holocaust and Heroism in Israel's Public Discourse in the 1950s: Memory and Ideology* (London 2006).

Stein, Leslie, *The Making of Modern Israel 1948–1967* (Cambridge 2009).

Stock, Ernest, *Chosen Instrument: The Jewish Agency in the First Decade of the State of Israel* (New York 1988).

Tabenkin, Yitzhak, *Neumim* (Tel Aviv 1976).

Takeyh, Ray, *Hidden Iran: Paradox and Power in the Islamic Republic* (New York 2006).

Tamimi, Azzam, *Hamas: Unwritten Chapters* (London 2009).

Tessler, Mark, *A History of the Israeli–Palestinian Conflict* (Bloomington 1994).

   Public Opinion in the Middle East: Survey Research and the Political Orientations of Ordinary Citizens (Bloomington 2011).

Teveth, Shabtai, *Ben-Gurion and the Palestinian Arabs* (Oxford 1985).

   Ben-Gurion: The Burning Ground 1886–1948 (Boston 1987).

Tirosh, Yosef, *The Essence of Religious Zionism: An Anthology* (Jerusalem 1975).

Unna, Moshe, *Separate Ways: In the Religious Parties' Confrontation of Renascent Israel* (Jerusalem 1987).

van Crefeld, Martin, *Moshe Dayan* (London 2004).

Warhaftig, Zorach, *Refugee and Survivor* (Jerusalem 1988).

Weissman, Baruch, *Yomun Mechteret Ivri* (Tel Aviv 1973).

Weizmann, Chaim, *Trial and Error* (London 1949).

West, Benjamin, *Struggles of a Generation: The Jews under Soviet Rule* (Tel Aviv 1959).

Wistrich, Robert S., *Terms of Survival: The Jewish World since 1945* (London 1995).

Zohar, David M., *Political Parties in Israel: The Evolution of Israeli Democracy* (New York 1974).

Index

Bold page numbers refer to illustrations.